# THE MIDDLE AGES

Edward Peters, General Editor

*The First Crusade: The Chronicle of Fulcher of Chartres and Other Source Materials.* Edited by Edward Peters

*Christian Society and the Crusades, 1198–1229.* Sources in Translation, including The Capture of Damietta by Oliver of Paderborn. Edited by Edward Peters

*The Burgundian Code: The Book of Constitutions or Law of Gundobad and Additional Enactments.* Translated by Katherine Fischer Drew

*The Lombard Laws.* Translated, with an Introduction, by Katherine Fischer Drew

*Ulrich Zwingli (1484–1531), Selected Works.* Edited by Samuel Macauley Jackson. Introduction by Edward Peters

*From St. Francis to Dante: Translations from the Chronicle of the Franciscan Salimbene (1221–1288).* G. G. Coulton. Introduction by Edward Peters

*The Duel and the Oath.* Parts I and II of Superstition and Force, Henry Charles Lea. Introduction by Edward Peters

*The Ordeal.* Part III of Superstition and Force, Henry Charles Lea. Introduction by Edward Peters

*Torture.* Part IV of Superstition and Force, Henry Charles Lea. Introduction by Edward Peters

*Witchcraft in Europe, 1110–1700: A Documentary History.* Edited by Alan C. Kors and Edward Peters

*The Scientific Achievement of the Middle Ages.* Richard C. Dales. Introduction by Edward Peters

*History of the Lombards.* Paul the Deacon. Translated by William Dudley Foulke. Introduction by Edward Peters

*Monks, Bishops, and Pagans: Christian Culture in Gaul and Italy, 500–700.* Edited, with an Introduction, by Edward Peters

*The World of Piers Plowman.* Edited and translated by Jeanne Krochalis and Edward Peters

*Women in Medieval Society.* Edited by Susan Mosher Stuard

*Felony and Misdemeanor*

*Julius Goebel, Jr.*

# Felony and Misdemeanor
## A Study in the History of Criminal Law

*With an Introduction by Edward Peters*

University of Pennsylvania Press/1976

# CONTENTS

# "*Ex parte Clio*"

"To the grave and learned writers of Histories," Edward Coke once remarked, "my advice is that they meddle not with the Laws of this Realm, before they confer with some Learned in that Profession."[1] The tack of Julius Goebel, Jr.'s *Felony and Misdemeanor* is precisely the opposite one. Vast generalizations built upon the minutely detailed scholarship of nineteenth-century German legal historians and "the lawyer's ritual of historical investigation which has become a mechanical gesture, bereft of all piety" were the twin targets of Goebel's brilliant book, which was published in 1937 and has remained a classic—sometimes an underground classic—in legal history ever since. Driven by his conviction of the need for "enlightened historical research . . . inquiry animated by a lively appreciation of the law as a cultural phenomenon, conducted with critical detachment and tolerant of sources other than the docket and the opinion book," Goebel planned a three-volume study of the development of English criminal procedure, of which Volume I, the present *Felony and Misdemeanor*, was the only volume ever to appear. In spite of the unsuitability of the title for a volume that deals with the character of early European criminal procedure, its development on the Continent, and its impact upon the conquered kingdom of Anglo-Saxon England in the years following the Norman Conquest, *Felony and Misdemeanor* is a great book, a mine of well-digested and generously provided erudi-

[1] There is a fine discussion of Coke's phrase and of the historical outlook of sixteenth- and seventeenth-century English lawyers generally in Donald Kelley, "History, English Law and the Renaissance," *Past and Present* 65 (1974), 24–51.

tion on the earliest criminal laws of Europe, and in many ways the greatest product of one of the most learned, professional, and wide-ranging legal historians of his generation.

Julius Goebel, Jr., was born in Menlo Park, California, in 1892 and grew up in the Midwest, receiving his B.A. and M.A. degrees in Political Science at the University of Illinois in 1912 and 1913. Goebel received his Ph.D. in Political Science from Columbia in 1915. His doctoral dissertation, *The Recognition Policy of the United States,* was published in 1915 and reprinted in 1968. Goebel was admitted to the District of Columbia bar in 1918 and practiced law in Washington until 1921, when he returned to Columbia as a lecturer in the Faculty of Political Science. He received his LL.B. degree from the Columbia Law School in 1923 and joined its faculty in 1925. In 1930 Goebel was named director of the Foundation for Research in Legal History, whose first publication was his own *Felony and Misdemeanor* in 1937. In 1938 he became George Welwood Murray Professor of Legal History, and he held the Murray chair until his retirement in 1961, when he became Murray Professor Emeritus. Goebel died in New York City in 1973.[2]

The range of Goebel's teaching and scholarship was enormously wide. He developed and taught, from 1928 until 1961, the most sophisticated course in legal history in any American law school, The Development of Legal

[2] On Goebel's career and life the best account is that of Joseph H. Smith, "Julius Goebel, Jr.—A Tribute," *Columbia Law Review* 73 (1973), 1372–82. Vol. 73 of the *Columbia Law Review* is dedicated to Goebel's memory, and it contains several other memoirs of Goebel besides Smith's. A complete bibliography to 1961 may be found in William C. Warren, "Julius Goebel, Jr.— An Appreciation," *Columbia Law Review* 61 (1961), 1195–1200.

Institutions, and he subsequently taught Civil Procedure and Family Law, and published several influential casebooks in these fields. His writings cover, if possible, an even wider range than his teaching. From his earliest works, a 1923 monograph on *The Equality of States* and his 1927 study of the problem of sovereignty over the Falkland Islands, to the last major works of his retirement, *The Law Practice of Alexander Hamilton* and *The History of the Supreme Court of the United States: Antecedents and Beginnings to 1801*, Goebel wrote professionally across a spectrum of learning as broad as any in American scholarship.[3] In his 1938 review of *Felony and Misdemeanor*, T. F. T. Plucknett remarked perceptively that Goebel "has written a book of great distinction which carries on the high American tradition of Bigelow, Thayer, Ames, and Wigmore." In the same year Heinrich Mitteis, perhaps then the dean of living medieval legal historians, said: "The still youthful science of medieval legal history in the United States has won for itself with this work an enduring and honorable place."[4] Other reviews of the book upon publication were written by many of the best legal historians of the period and were uniformly favorable. The book has since been regarded as the best and most complete treatment in English of early European criminal procedure. It has proven to be as

[3] *The Law Practice of Alexander Hamilton*, 2 vols. (New York, 1964, 1969). A third volume is forthcoming. Goebel was selected to write the first volume of *The History of the Supreme Court of the United States*, commissioned under the Oliver Wendell Holmes Devise, and his contribution was published in 1971.

[4] Plucknett, in *Law Quarterly Review* 54 (1938), 298; Mitteis' remark concluded a long and important review of *Felony and Misdemeanor* that was reprinted in Mitteis' *Die Rechtsidee in der Geschichte: Gesammelte Abhandlungen und Vorträge* (Vienna, 1957), pp. 318–38.

valuable to historians as to lawyers, and in its recognition
of "the law as a cultural phenomenon," *Felony and Misdemeanor* signaled an important change in the nature of
legal history and historical studies, generally, that took
place in the first half of the twentieth century.

The origins of legal history as a formal discipline are
obscured in the ideological, confessional, and constitutional conflicts of the period between the eleventh and the
seventeenth centuries in which they occurred.[5] The particular triumphs of the sixteenth, seventeenth, and eighteenth centuries, however, consisted chiefly in the areas
of archival preservation, textual criticism, and the increasing perception on the part of scholars that the study of
the history of law required a different kind of mental
activity and a different kind of discourse from those developed by other historians, and legal history was eagerly
seized upon by Enlightenment political theorists, such as
Montesquieu, and Enlightenment reformers, such as Bec-
caria, to play a part in the larger movements for intellectual and social reform that eighteenth-century thinkers
proposed. The modern age of legal history, however, began in nineteenth-century Germany, when such scholars
as Savigny and Grimm introduced both new critical principles and a new sophistication in interpretation to its
study, and others produced superb critical editions of
essential documents and many minutely detailed studies
of technical problems. More, indeed, than the fashionable
fields of political, constitutional, diplomatic, and military

---

[5] Some of its beginnings are traced by Donald Kelley, "Clio and
the Lawyers: Forms of Historical Consciousness in Medieval Jurisprudence," *Medievalia et Humanistica,* n. s. 5 (1974), 25–49, and
Kelley, *Foundations of Modern Historical Scholarship* (New York,
1970).

history, legal history profited earliest from the revolution in historical methodology that took place between the seventeenth and nineteenth centuries. Even for all of its modernity, however, nineteenth-century German legal history labored under several important disadvantages as well. Since legal materials are one of the largest single kinds of evidence for the early history of Europe, it is essential that they be studied in the context of cultural history, with help from anthropology and social history. Although nineteenth-century legal history was a sophisticated discipline internally, neither cultural studies nor anthropology had reached a parallel degree of sophistication, nor did they until the twentieth century. Thus, the large generalizations that legal historians were prone to make, given the high quality of their textual and scholarly studies, had little support from areas outside the law itself. A second disadvantage was the preponderance in many fields of intellectual endeavor of the model of historical development that placed the nation-state as the goal of all societies and the concept of the undifferentiated *Volk*, out of which the nation-state grew, as the common seedbed of all societies. Thus, even the most meticulous legal historians were often tempted in generalizing to impose a nineteenth-century standard of historical and anthropological change upon the old and new inhabitants of Europe between the fourth and twelfth centuries. A third disadvantage was the extraordinarily sharp cleavage that both ancient and modern historians placed between the end of the Roman world and the beginnings of Germanic Europe, a cleavage that allowed little room for what has been one of the most fruitful fields of historical investigation of the twentieth century, that of sub-Roman culture, in which the reciprocal influences between Roman and

Germanic peoples have been revealed as remarkably complex and far-reaching. Closely related to this notion of cleavage between Roman and Germanic Europe was the growing nostalgia, itself a product of the Romantic movement, for the purity of the primitive *Volk* and its lack of "contamination" by influences Roman or other. A final disadvantage was the authority of the legal profession itself, which tended either to surround legal history with the arcana of professional discourse or to satisfy itself with a perfunctory "historical introduction" to internal principles of contemporary law wholly without reference to changing contexts of historical interpretation.

Thus the history of law, shrouded by some of its earliest and most influential practitioners by the double veil of minutely detailed scholarship and often unsupported generalizations, has traditionally been the most difficult of all fields to integrate with other kinds of historical knowledge. As Hermann Kantorowicz once put it:

> . . . in the overwhelming and universal success of German historical science, in Law as well as in every other field, during the nineteenth century there was an unsound and almost uncanny feature. It is this feature that explains the success of that magnetic power and is at the same time a warning against it. It is, as I would put it, the combination of extreme methodological exactness and completeness in the *collecting* and *stating* of facts with a dangerous, though less extreme, fancifulness and arbitrariness in the *interpretation* and *systematization* of these facts. One could probably discover a corresponding feature in other manifestations of the modern German spirit, but in legal history it is quite obvious.[6]

[6] Review of *Felony and Misdemeanor* in *Cambridge Law Journal* 6 (1936–38), 447.

The conclusions of a precocious, professional, but unsupported tradition of Germanic legal history and the
effusions of modern lawyers' perfunctory "historical introductions" to technical problems became Goebel's twin
targets in *Felony and Misdemeanor*, and indeed in many
other writings and addresses throughout his career.[7]

Julius Goebel wrote at a time when many historians
were challenging the traditions of historical methodology
and the fashionable domination of legal, constitutional,
political, and diplomatic history. In France a decade
earlier the so-called *Annales* school of historians, led by
Marc Bloch and Lucien Febvre, had urged a new kind of
history that explored more deeply the social, economic,
and cultural bonds of past societies, not only the nation-
states, but families, towns, and regions as well. One of the
greatest triumphs of this school was the appearance of
Bloch's own *La société féodale* in 1940. Bloch, Febvre, and
others also argued for a closer relationship between history and the social sciences, and in 1937, the year of the
publication of *Felony and Misdemeanor*, the anthropolo-
gist E. E. Evans-Pritchard published his *Witchcraft, Ora-
cles and Magic among the Azande*, one of the seminal
works in modern anthropology and a key link in the
subsequent association of anthropology and historical
study. Goebel's *Felony and Misdemeanor*, then, was part
of a larger historical revolution that had as its goals increased interdisciplinary study, a broadened definition of
culture, a new interest in social and economic history, and
a reluctance to extrapolate from one field of research to

---

[7] Particularly in Goebel's "Learning and Style in the Law—An
Historian's Lament," *Columbia Law Review* 61 (1961), 1393–
1400.

another without considerable circumspection and professional caution.

Since Goebel wrote, and in part because of his influence, the legal history of early Europe has done much
toward becoming integrated with other kinds of history.
Perhaps the most immediately impressive area in which
links have been forged has been, certainly not surpris-
ingly, in the area of political culture and the exercise of
power, especially in our perception of the relative inter-
relationships among Roman, canon, and common laws.
Other recent studies of other areas of legal history have
continued the level of fine technical scholarship of the
best of earlier German legal history but have also opened
themselves to the social and cultural contexts in which
legal history occurs. In certain areas, however, neither
interest nor integration has been high. The history of
criminal law has remained one of these, and it is in the
interests of those who would like to see further integration of the lower reaches of legal and social history that
this book is being reprinted. For in it, Goebel focuses not
on the high road of legal theory, but on the practice, procedure, and enforcement and coercive powers of those
who held courts and controlled so large a share of what
later came to be called public order. Among the many
virtues of *Felony and Misdemeanor* is its consistent
eschewing of traditional concepts of the communities of
early Europe, grounded as they were in the unsophisti-
cated political assumptions of nineteenth-century historians, and its focusing instead upon the actual operation of
the law and the courts.

The very nature of Goebel's view of the historical
process accounts for much of the polemical tone of his
introduction and other parts of *Felony and Misdemeanor*.

The reader who begins the book perplexed at the polemic will, however, soon get past it into Goebel's history, and very high quality history it is. The following brief summary of the argument hardly does justice to the wealth of materials, not only in the text itself, but in the footnotes, where there are frequently and succinctly buried what in another historian's hands would become small monographs in themselves. Nor is Goebel solely concerned with secular courts. *Felony and Misdemeanor* is one of the first modern works of legal history to take into account the spiritual values and spiritual politics of early European history. Goebel's pages on infamy, the Peace and Truce of God, and the coercive power of the Church, particularly in the matters of excommunication and interdict, reveal an extensive knowledge of Church history and a felicitous understanding of the social consequences of the spiritual dimensions of early European culture.

*Felony and Misdemeanor,* which deals with the formation of criminal procedure among the Germanic kingdoms of the fifth and sixth centuries and ends with criminal procedure in the England of Henry I, is the first volume of an uncompleted three-volume study. Later volumes might have described the legal reforms of Henry II and, in spite of these, the "long and tedious road before the crown: the ambuscades of franchise rights must be frustrated, the system of private accusation must be integrated with and finally made to serve public justice, and public justice itself must be made remorseless and inevitable. It was in the process of accomplishing these objectives that criminal procedure assumed the contours which it still in general possesses." This volume, however, deals with periods far earlier than the twelfth century of Henry II,

and it focuses upon "the jurisdictional significance of early and crude attempts to classify crime, for jurisdiction is the first reason for making distinctions. . . . It is only later," Goebel continues, "when criminal law is the subject of the stiff metaphysics of the king's judges, that the attempt to inject substantive content into felony begins." Goebel is thus in agreement with Maitland's famous *dictum* that the substantive law is secreted among the interstices of procedure in early Europen history, and procedure and jurisdiction occupy most of Goebel's concern.

Chapter I, "The Foundations of Early Law Enforcement," begins with a discussion of the need to understand early Norman and earlier Frankish law in order to understand the development of English criminal law after the Norman conquest, when the Frankish-Norman tradition was grafted on to native Anglo-Saxon traditions. Goebel then goes back to the beginning, the vexing question of the nature of public order in the Germanic kingdoms that succeeded to the western Roman Empire after the fifth century in Europe. He deals first with the famous theory of the institutionalized folk peace, the violation of which is the earliest European crime and leads to outlawry and the beginning of feud. Successfully attacking the excessively romantic picture of the folk peace, Goebel goes on to consider the character of feud and composition procedure and the theory of the king's peace and the role of royal authority in elaborating an idea of public order. In these last sections, Goebel reiterates the practical character of these early institutions, the give-and-take in establishing composition, the right of judgement, and, most important, the ways by which judgement could be enforced. A fine modern study that might serve as supple-

mentary reading to this chapter is J. M. Wallace-Hadrill's
essay on "The Bloodfeud of the Franks."[8]

Goebel's second chapter deals less with the undifferentiated social violence of the early period of Germanic history
than with the changing character of public violence and
the recognition on the part of kings of this new kind of
danger. Earlier law and custom regarding feud and composition presumed, Goebel suggests, a known offender,
against whom feud and confiscation can be waged and
with whom (or with whose kindred) composition can be
arranged. The new law responded to the appearance of
the professional unknown malefactor. The failure of private redress opened the way for royal intervention, and
the stimulating discussion on pages 66–76 of the sixth-
century *Pactus pro tenore pacis* suggests the complex
mental and institutional response to the new social phenomenon of the unknown criminal. "The procedure of
the *Pactus* for dealing with theft had the effect of marking
out as a matter of law a class of persons, already existing
as a result of economic change, who did not fit into the
traditional system of remedies." Goebel goes on to demonstrate the growth of the concept of *infamia* and the increased latitude of the powers of royal judges as a result.
The growing use of the inquest also expanded crown
authority (or rather king's authority). The chapter concludes with a description of the royal development of
afflictive and economic sanctions and increasing royal
willingness to regard crime essentially as a breach of the
faith, *fidelitas*, owed by all subjects to the king: "the

[8] In *The Long-Haired Kings and Other Studies in Frankish
History* (New York, 1962).

Carolingians sought to create a paramount notion of order based upon a direct obligation to the crown."

Chapter III, "The Dispersal of Jurisdiction and Norman Reception of Frankish Law," deals with a phenomenon that has engaged many scholars, none of whom has posed his questions as graphically as Goebel:

> . . . the sources [for the history of the ninth and tenth centuries] tell us of dissolution, of perversions of power, of the reorientation that invasion and starvation make necessary in the orderly pattern of administration, of spasmodic instead of measured governmental action. From these conflicting tales we must draw conclusions as to how the complex system of dealing with wrongdoing fared; what happened to the feud, the composition plea, the inquisition, the public punishment; where was initiative lodged if, indeed, there were those who were disposed to take it? For all the familiar forms are still to be found. The feud persists, but it is something different than the internecine brawls of an earlier day. In the course of the tenth century it becomes the conflict between two lords with men at arms. The professional bad man is only too evident, but he is no longer a man without substance who skulks in the woods, but like as not a *baro* with an adulterine castle for a retreat. Inquisitions there are, but they are taken by others than the king's judges.

It is precisely the process of the decay of jurisdictional unity, seen by Goebel in the transformation of the old Frankish immunity and in the circumstances that allowed certain older aspects of the law to survive:

> Those portions [of the Carolingian system of suppressing and prosecuting wrongdoing] . . . that depended chiefly upon local organization or ingrained custom, like the

feud or handhaving procedures, appear to have had hardy roots. They are the progeny of violence, and violence is the chief preoccupation of men both great and mean in the tenth century.

By the tenth century, Goebel argues, the objective of criminal prosecution was no longer peace and order, but the creation of fiscal prerogatives for whoever held jurisdiction.

Out of the disintegration and fractionalization of Carolingian institutions, Goebel traces in Chapter IV, "Criminal Procedure and Feudal Government," that process by which the control over jurisdiction is considered (and bitterly fought over) as primarily a source of income for courtholders, the result of "the deadly pressure of social change upon the outmoded structure of rights and remedies." Goebel's grim catalogue of the violent inventiveness of new kinds of punishments and the violent rapacity that considers only the courtholder's and enforcer's rights to income reminds us that indeed the law survived, but exclusively as an economic instrument in the hands of blind and remorseless warlords.

Chapter V, "God's Peace and Duke's Peace," develops the brilliant insight that the ecclesiastical invention of the Peace and Truce of God gave the Dukes of Normandy, hitherto unable to overcome the particularization of jurisdictions, an effective tool—in their right to carry out ecclesiastical sanctions—to overcome much of that particularization. In this chapter, Goebel's mastery of ecclesiastical sources and his willingness to use them makes his discussion of the peace movements especially enlightening.

The final chapter returns to the point at which Goebel

had originally intended to start out, that of "Anglo-Saxon Institutions and Norman Justice." Here Goebel steps onto an old and dangerous battlefield. *Felony and Misdemeanor* has received most of its criticism for this chapter, particularly for Goebel's treatment of Anglo-Saxon institutions. From the days of Freeman and Round to those of Richardson and Sayles, the respective extent, weight, profundity, duration, and nature of the Saxon and Norman contributions to English life after 1066 have been matters of universal discord and little agreement. No one who enters upon the field of this question leaves it unchallenged, if not unscathed, and Goebel has received his share of criticism, just as everyone else has, although *Felony and Misdemeanor* is not as widely known to English historians as it should be. This chapter, almost a quarter of the book, deals with the questions of private jurisdiction in Anglo-Saxon England, royal prerogative and fiscal rights, and the growth of a franchise theory, crown rights, and the king's peace under the Norman kings.[9]

*Felony and Misdemeanor,* as it stands, is really the preface to a larger work that was never written. Thus, there is little specifically about felony and misdemeanor in it. There is, however, much essential information concerning the background and history of the mental (and, more important, jurisdictional) distinctions that are an important part of early European intellectual as well

[9] See the review by H. M. Cam, *American Historical Review* 43 (1937–38), 583–87, and Cam, "The Evolution of the Medieval English Franchise," *Speculum* 32 (1957), 427–42, rpt. in H. M. Cam, *Law-Finders and Law-Makers in Medieval England* (London, 1962), pp. 22–43.

as legal history. In his brief remarks on page 250, Goebel shows himself well aware of the significance of the early etymological history of *felonia*, particularly the strong overtones of breach of faith and trust that remained firmly attached to the term and the concept until well into the thirteenth century.[10] Not the least attractive and useful feature of the book, in fact, is Goebel's skill as an etymologist and his sensitivity to the semantic universes of the terms he studies.

"No matter how supple the rule," Goebel observes in his Introduction, "the rush of life is always swifter." Throughout the book he never loses sight of the tension between the rule of law and the rush of life, and it is his awareness of that tension and his perception of the cultural and social causes of it that give *Felony and Misdemeanor* its essential character.

Edward Peters
*Philadelphia, 1975*

[10] There are further notations on the history of *felonia* in Stefan A. Riesenfeld's review of *Felony and Misdemeanor* in the *California Law Review* 26 (1937–38), 405–10 at 409-10. See also Adalbert Dessau, "The Idea of Treason in the Middle Ages," trans. in Fredric L. Cheyette, ed., *Lordship and Community in Medieval Europe* (New York, 1968), pp. 192–97. The most recent survey of the legal source materials for Goebel's period is Rudolf Buchner, *Die Rechtsquellen, Beiheft* to Wattenbach-Levison, *Deutschlands Geschichtsquellen im Mittelalter. Vorzeit und Karolinger* (Weimar, 1953). A recent study of the legal side of medieval culture is Gerhard Köbler, *Das Recht im frühen Mittelalter* (Vienna, 1971), with an extensive bibliography. The phrase *"Ex parte Clio"* in the title of this Introduction is, needless to say, also a coinage of Goebel's, from a 1954 review article in the *Columbia Law Review*.

On the Peace and Truce of God, see Hartmut Hoffman, *Gottesfriede und Treuga Dei* (Stuttgart, 1964), and H. E. J. Cowdrey, "The Peace and Truce of God in the Eleventh Century," *Past and Present* 46 (1970), 42–67.

The editor wishes to thank the staff of the Yale Law Library for their assistance.

THE Foundation for Research in Legal History of the Columbia University School of Law was established in 1930 as a result of a generous gift by Mr. George Welwood Murray together with subventions by the Legal Research Committee of the Commonwealth Fund and by the Trustees of Columbia University. The first study to be undertaken by the Foundation dealt with the distinction between felony and misdemeanor, but it soon became apparent that a far-reaching inquiry into the history of English criminal procedure would be necessary. The present volume is the first fruit of this study and carries the story to the year 1135. The second volume, which is in process of completion, is being written by me in conjunction with Mr. Irwin Langbein. It will resume with the reign of Henry II and carry the development of criminal procedure into the Yearbook period.

Having been charged with the direction of the Foundation's investigations it is appropriate that I should acknowledge the obligations I am under to those who have sponsored this project as well as my debt to those who have aided me immediately in the preparation of the present volume. Dean Young B. Smith, who first conceived the notion of a permanent establishment for furthering legal-historical research as an indispensable part of the Columbia program for a university law school, has been a steadfast supporter in developing the work of the Foundation. In this, too, the officers and the Legal Research Committee of the Commonwealth Fund have manifested a generous enthusiasm. The President and Trustees of Columbia University likewise have facilitated my task both with funds and otherwise.

The extent to which I have trespassed upon the time and patience of my friends and colleagues in completing this book is very great. I am in particular under obligations to Mr. Irwin Langbein who was associated with me for four years and who, because of his own researches in late twelfth and thirteenth-century English materials, contributed much towards sustaining the proper focus of my work in continental and early Anglo-Norman sources. Professor Karl Llewellyn has labored over my manuscript for many hours and has enabled me to clarify many doubtful points. Professor A. Arthur Schiller has given me constant aid on the several problems of Roman law. My assistant, Mr. Donald Tilton, has been indefatigable in relieving me of tedious tasks connected with the research on this volume. The manuscript was read for the Commonwealth Fund by Professor Max Radin of the University of California and I desire to express my gratitude for his kindness and forbearance. Mr. Roger Howson, Librarian of Columbia University, has put at my disposal all the resources of the library and has from time to time waived regulations, which scholars find irksome, with a tolerance that has not been unappreciated.

Finally I desire to acknowledge the interest of Mr. George Welwood Murray. He has not only read and criticized the various recensions of each chapter but has displayed an indulgence for their shortcomings that has been an unceasing comfort. To him I may speak in the words of Richard Fitz Neal: "I have followed, indeed, myself as the worst of masters. Nevertheless, thou compelling me, I have, without guide or pattern, done what I could."

J. G., Jr.

*New York, December 3, 1936*

# TABLE OF ABBREVIATIONS

THE form of citation used in this volume is in general that employed in American law reports and law reviews: the volume number precedes the author's name or the title, and the page number follows immediately after the title reference or the edition number. Wherever this method cannot conveniently be followed, the conventional lay form of citation is used. The *Corpus Juris Canonici* is cited in the American manner. In the case of the Anglo-Saxon dooms, the liber number precedes the name of the book and the chapter number follows.

*A.H.R.—American Historical Review*
*A.K.K.R.—Archiv für Katholisches Kirchenrecht*
v. Amira, *Grundriss d.G.R.*—v. Amira, *Grundriss des Germanischen Rechts* (3 ed., 1913)
*Arch. Anj.—Archives d'Anjou* (Marchegay Ed., 1843–54)

*B.E.C.—Bibliothèque de l'Ecole des Chartes*
BSB—*Sitzungsberichte der Preussischen Akademie der Wissenschaften* (Berliner Akademie)
Bethmann-Hollweg, *Civilprozess*—Bethmann-Hollweg, *Der Civilprozess des Gemeinen Rechts* (1864–73)
Beyerle, *Rechtsgang*—Beyerle, *Das Entwickelungsproblem im Germanischen Rechtsgang* (*Deutschrechtliche Beiträge,* vol. 10, no. 2, 1915)
Birch—Birch, *Cartularium Saxonicum* (1885–93)
Böhmer-Mühlbacher, *Regesten*—Böhmer-Mühlbacher, *Die Regesten des Kaiserreichs unter den Karolingern* (2 ed., 1899)
Brunner, *D.R.G.*—Brunner, *Deutsche Rechtsgeschichte,* vol. 1, 2 ed., 1906; vol. 2, 2 ed., 1928 (v. Schwerin Ed.)
Brunner, *Forschungen*—Brunner, *Forschungen zur Geschichte des Deutschen und Französischen Rechts* (1894)

*C.—Codex Justinianus*
*C.D.I.—Collection des documents inédits sur l'histoire de France*
*C.L.R.—Columbia Law Review*
*C.R.R.—Curia Regis Rolls*
*Cap.—Capitularia Regum Francorum, Monumenta Germaniae Historica, Legum,* Sec. 2 (Boretius-Krause Eds., 1883–93)
*Cod. Theod.—Codex Theodosianus* (Mommsen Ed., 1905)

*D.—Digesta Justiniani*

*D.B.—Domesday Book* (Record Commission, 1834)

*D.R.G.—Deutsche Rechtsgeschichte*

Davis, *Regesta*—Davis, *Regesta Regum Anglo-Normannorum* (1913), vol. 1

Declareuil, *H.D.F.*—Declareuil, *Histoire générale du droit français* (1925)

*Decr.—Decretum* of Gratian, unless otherwise indicated

*E.H.R.—English Historical Review*

Flach, *Origines*—Flach, *Les origines de l'ancienne France* (1886–1904)

*Form.—Formulae Merowingici et Karolini Aevi, M.G.H., Leg.,* Sec. 5 (Zeumer Ed., 1886)

> *Form. And.—Formulae Andecavenses*
>
> *Form. Aug.—Formulae Augienses*
>
> *Form. Extrav.—Formulae Extravagantes*
>
> *Form. Imp.—Formulae Imperiales*
>
> *Form. Marculfi—Formulae Marculfi [I or II]*
>
> *Form. S. Emm.—Formulae St. Emmerami*
>
> *Form. Sal. Bign.—Formulae Salicae Bignonianae*
>
> *Form. Sal. Merk.—Formulae Salicae Merkelianae*
>
> *Form. Sal. Lindbrg.—Formulae Salicae Lindenbrogianae*
>
> *Form. Sen.—Formulae Senonenses*
>
> *Form. Sen. Rec.—Formulae Senonenses Recentiores*
>
> *Form. Tur.—Formulae Turonenses*

Grimm, *D.R.A.*—Grimm, *Deutsche Rechtsaltertümer* (4 ed., 1899)

*H.D.F.—Histoire du droit français*

*H.E.L.—History of English Law*

*H.F.—Recueil des historiens des Gaules et de la France* (Bouquet-Delisle)

*H.L.R.—Harvard Law Review*

*HSB—Sitzungsberichte der Heidelberger Akademie der Wissenschaften*

Hessels—Hessels and Kern, *Lex Salica* (1880)

Hinschius, *K.R.*—Hinschius, *Das Kirchenrecht der Katholiken und Protestanten im Deutschland* (1869–97)

*Inst.—Institutiones Justiniani*

K.R.—*Kirchenrecht*

Kemble—Kemble, *Codex Diplomaticus Aevi Saxonici* (1839–48)

Liebermann, *Gesetze*—Liebermann, *Die Gesetze der Angelsachsen,* vol. I (1903)

Liebermann, *Wörterbuch*—Liebermann, *Die Gesetze der Angelsachsen,* vol. II, pt. 1 (1906)

Liebermann, *Glossar*—Liebermann, *Die Gesetze der Angelsachsen,* vol. II, pt. 2 (1912)

Liebermann, *Erklärungen*—Liebermann, *Die Gesetze der Angelsachsen,* vol. III (1916)

The following abbreviations are used to cite the dooms:

*Af.*—*Aelfred*

*As.*—*Aethelstan*

*Atr.*—*Aethelred*

*A. Gu.*—*Aelfred-Guthrum*

*Cons. Cn.*—*Consiliatio Cnuti*

*Eg.*—*Eadgar*

*E. Gu.*—*Eadward-Guthrum*

*Em.*—*Eadmund*

*Ew.*—*Eadward*

*Grið*—Special Protection

*IIn.*—*Leges Henrici*

*Hn. Com.*—*Henrici I Comitatus*

*Hn. Cor.*—*Charta Henrici I Coronati*

*Hn. Lond.*—*Henrici Charta London.*

*Hu.*—*Hundredgemot* (I Eg.)

*Inst. Cn.*—*Instituta Cnuti*

*Lad*—*Willelmes Lad*

*Leg. Edw. Conf.*—*Leges Edwardi Confessoris*

*Leis Wil.*—*Leis Willelme*

*Northu.*—*Northumbrian Priests' Law*

*Q.*—*Quadripartitus*

*Wer.*—Wergeld Payment

*Wl. Art.*—*Willelmi Articuli X*

Loening, *K.R.*—Loening, *Geschichte des Deutschen Kirchenrechts* (1878)

*M.G.H.* or *Mon. Ger. Hist.—Monumenta Germaniae Historica*
  Except for the *Lex Salica* (Behrend Ed., 1897) the continental folklaws
are all cited from editions in the *Monumenta* as follows:
  *Lex Alamannorum* (Lehmann Ed., 1888)
  *Lex Baiuwariorum* (Merkel Ed., 1865)
  *Leges Burgundionum* (de Salis Ed., 1892)
  *Lex Frisionum* (Richthofen Ed., 1863)
  *Leges Lombardorum* (Blume-Boretius Ed., 1868)
  *Lex Ribuaria* (Sohm Ed., 1889)
  *Lex Saxonum* (Richthofen Ed., 1887)
  *Leges Visigothorum* (Zeumer Ed., 1902)
*M.I.Ö.G.—Mitteilung des Instituts für Österreichische Geschichtsfor-
  schung. EB.—Ergänzungsband*
Mansi, *Concilia—*Mansi, *Sacrorum Conciliorum Nova et Amplissima Col-
  lectio* (1759–98)
Mayer, *D.F.V.G.—*Mayer, *Deutsche und Französische Verfassungsge-
  schichte* (1899)
*Mem. Ant. Norm.—Mémoires de la Société des Antiquaires de Normandie*
Migne, *Patrologia—Cursus Completus Patrologiae, Series Latina* (Migne
  Ed., 1857–79)
Mitteis, *Lehnrecht—*Mitteis, *Lehnrecht und Staatsgewalt* (1933)
*Monasticon—*Dugdale, *Monasticon Anglicanum* (1817–30)

*N.R.H.—Revue historique de droit français et étranger; Nouvelle revue
  historique de droit français et étranger*
*Neues Archiv—Neues Archiv der Gesellschaft für ältere Deutsche
  Geschichtskunde*

Orderic—Orderic Vitalis, *Historia Ecclesiastica* (Le Prévost Ed., 1838–
  55)

*P.J.—Pièces justicatives*
*P.R.—Pipe Rolls*
Pollock and Maitland, *H.E.L.—*Pollock and Maitland, *History of English
  Law* (2 ed., 1899)

R.C.—Record Commission
R.S.—Rolls Series
Round, *Calendar—*Round, *Calendar of Documents Preserved in France*
  (1899)

*S.L.N.—Summa de Legibus Normannie* (Tardif Ed., 1896)

S.S.—Selden Society

Schröder, *D.R.G.—*Schröder, *Lehrbuch der Deutschen Rechtsgeschichte* (6 ed., v. Künssberg Ed., 1922)

Sohm, *F.R.G.V.—*Sohm, *Die Fränkische Reichs und Gerichtsverfassung* (1871)

Stapleton, *Rot. Scacc. Norm.—*Stapleton, *Magni Rotuli Scaccarii Normanniae* (1840)


*T.A.C.—Très ancien coutumier* (Tardif Ed., 1881)

*Tait Essays—Essays in Honour of James Tait* (Edwards, Galbraith and Jacobs Eds., 1933)

Tardif, *Mon. Hist.—*J. Tardif, *Monuments historiques* (1866)


*Untersuchungen—Untersuchungen zur Deutschen Staats- und Rechtsgeschichte*


*WSB—Sitzungsberichte der Wiener Akademie*

Waitz, *D.V.G.—*Waitz, *Deutsche Verfassungsgeschichte,* vol. 1, 3 ed., 1880; vol. 2, 3 ed., 1882; vol. 3, 2 ed., 1883; vol. 4, 2 ed., 1884; vols. 5–8, 1874–78


*Z.R.G.[2]—Zeitschrift der Savigny-Stiflung für Rechtsgeschichte. Germanistische Abteilung* unless otherwise specified, as *Kan. Abt.—Kanonistische Abteilung*

---

*ags.—*Anglo-Saxon

*Cap.—Capitula,* chapter; *Capitulare,* capitulary

*Cart.—Cartularium; cartulaire;* cartulary

*Chron.—Chronicon;* chronicle

*Conc.—Concilia; concilium;* council

*Const.—Constitutiones*

*Dipl.—Diplomata*

*Leg.—Leges*

*ofris.—*Old Frisian

*ohg.—*Old High German

*on.—*Old Norse

*os.*—Old Saxon
*SS.*—*Scriptores*
*Script.*—*Scriptores*
sol.—*solidus*
*T.R.E.*—*tempore regis Edwardi*

# INTRODUCTION

TO a profession which for some seven centuries has made a
cult of its historical method, apology for a study of the
growth of criminal procedure should be superfluous. There is,
however, in this volume much that will seem schismatical to
those accustomed to the lawyers' ritual of historical investigation. In America, at least, this ritual has become a matter of
mechanical gesture, bereft of all piety, pervaded with pettifog-
gery. For here this method to which jurists point with pride has
been used for but mean tasks. It is the small and immediate issues of instant litigation which drive the practitioner to the past
in a myopic search for ruling cases and precedents. What does it
profit him to contemplate the devotions of a Maitland or a
Holmes? History is his drudge: the lay brother who may serve,
but never teach.

The intellectual study of our law has been so closely associated
with the needs of the bar, that even circles which should rise
above the standards of practice are dominated by an office utili-
tarianism. From this bondage has sprung a type of academic
historiography which is but a mere didactic elaboration of the
briefmaker's art. For every Melville Bigelow[1] or J. B. Moore[2]
there are a score of "historical introductions" to text and case-
book. Designed to lend a weight of learning, they are none the
less a mere *décor* too often inept and amateurish. Untouched by
any sense of historical values, they treat the growth of doctrine
as something projected on a horizontal plane of rational manipulation unmindful of its perpendicular support in time or
circumstance. In expositions of the doctrine of consideration,
the judgments of his majesty's judges in the seventeenth century rub shoulders with those from the American backwoods
two hundred years later. To legitimate the control of business,

---

[1] Bigelow, *History of Procedure in England* (1880); *Placita Anglo-
Normannica* (1879).

[2] Moore, *International Adjudications,* 5 vols. (1929–33).

Tudor sumptuary statutes are forcibly wedded to the legislative indiscretions of the seventy-third Congress. Standing commonly in no perceptible organic relation to the subjects which they profess to introduce, these confections, if happily they are not forgotten, inevitably lead the novice to emulation.

That so fantastic a conception of history should prevail as a convention in the bulk of our legal literature is attributable in some degree to the intellectual tyranny which the judicial opinion exerts. It is a truism that to know the common law its history must be known. Our courts, however, seek enlightenment on the past chiefly in the judgments of their predecessors. These judgments are rarely treated as single but complex assessable facts, for the mass of relevant data of which they are merely parts is usually ignored. In consequence, the antecedent judicial opinion is elevated to a status of preposterous importance as a source. Worse than this, the pronouncement of the bench employing this nucleolar theory, since it possesses validity as law, becomes authoritative as history. While it is no doubt traversable it is undemurrable, for its primary use is as law and not as history. So the *communis error* passes as coin among the lawyers. The fine gilding of rationalization conceals the inherent flaws, but it can never avert the peril that bad history may in turn make bad law.

It is impossible to treat the inaccurate historical finding as a vagary the effect of which is spent in the opinion embodying it. Whether it serves immediately to found a rule of law or is a mere premise of judicial reasoning, as a part of the precedent it possesses a malignant vitality. For however skilfully the conclusions of a case so grounded are isolated and manipulated as abstractions, they are conceived in error and they carry the seed of their tainted inheritance. Examine any of the progeny of Bonham's case,[3] that repository of misstatement, or of Hale's

[3] Cases assembled in Plucknett, *Bonham's Case and Judicial Review*, 40 *H.L.R.*, 30.

blundering exegesis on Magna Carta[4] and the strength of the lines sprung from the miscegenation of bad history and facile reasoning becomes apparent.

The extirpation of such faulty strains is a task beyond the powers of a lawyer historian employing only journeyman methods. Still less may one look for aid from the systematic jurists; for whatever the school tie which they affect, their business is not with the pedigree of their premises but with what can be done with them. Oblivious of the fact that the fruit of a transcendental history may be a revealed jurisprudence, they are embarrassed only by what cannot be disciplined into their systems. The schoolmen's "reasons of practicality and convenience" which shelter such mavericks may preserve the elegance of their structure, yet the very words of the formula suggest an appeal for enlightened historical research. By this we understand inquiry animated by a lively appreciation of the law as a cultural phenomenon, conducted with critical detachment and tolerant of sources other than those in docket or opinion book. There are in our literature sufficient examples of such investigations to leave the question of proper approach and method in no doubt. They are, however, so few in number and stand in such isolation with respect to professional literature at large that their influence upon both manner and matter of brief or judicial opinion has been negligible. This is a defeat which if too long sustained will leave the profession forever lodged in the grooves made comfortable by Coke. It will assure scientific history a detachment from the ways of practice as complete as that of biblical criticism from the sermons of a country parson.

It is conceivable that by the mere increase of scholarly production the time will come when courts will prefer delicate historical surgery to the rude custom of impaling counsel with a crossbow bolt taken at random from the arsenal of medieval

---

[4] For example, *Thompson* v. *Utah*, 170 *U.S.*, 341.

precedent.[5] We have, however, no great confidence even in the force of overwhelming example unless at the same time means are found of convincing lawyers that such products can be useful and that their own technique can be improved. This must, of course, be taken in a qualified sense; for few at the bar could eke out an existence should they embrace the exacting standards of science. None the less, even a slight widening of the scope of "practical" inquiry would tend to break down the barriers which now separate history from precedent hunting.

Since the time of Bracton, lawyers have found in the objective of certainty justification for recurring to the past. By this they have meant certainty in respect to particular rules of law although the implications of this word have not been constant. The medieval jurists read into it all their authoritarian philosophy;[6] the Stuart lawyers were obsessed by a blind veneration for what stood in the books;[7] and today it is usual to rationalize this ordinary psychological trait by asserting that expectancies are based upon judicial pronouncements of record, that only by cleaving to what has been determined can prophecy be made as to the future action of judicial bodies. Despite shifts in the rationale of certainty, the methods used to attain this end have not perceptibly varied. The historical approach, as we have indicated, has been centered upon the statement of the rule. It has commonly failed to embrace an inquiry into the circumstances conditioning the statement, still less into its effect upon a subsequent society. The tendency is to treat rules as distillates of human experience possessing an inherent specificity which makes unnecessary more than a fugitive scrutiny of circumstance.

This seems to us a most unstable foundation for accurate prediction. Judicial repetition may lend a formal air of historical continuity; it may even convince that the changes in life are

[5] So the revival of the Statute of Winton (13 Edw. I) in *Babington* v. *Yellow Taxi Corp.*, 250 *N.Y.*, 14. Contrast *Hynes* v. *N. Y. C. Ry. Co.*, 231 *N.Y.* 229.

[6] Bracton, *De Legibus*, 1, 1b; *Y.B.* 32 *Edw. I*, 32 (R.S.).

[7] Coke, *Second Institute* (1809 ed.), Proeme.

merely on the surface. But if a judgment is honestly striving for a socially desirable result, how can there be certainty regarding the effects of employing an old rule unless we are privy to its reaction upon society both at and from the time it was first stated? There is no steady and synchronized onward march of judge-made rule in step with human activity, for litigation is fortuitous. A century may separate a first and second statement. No matter how supple the rule, the rush of life is always swifter. By inference, by analogy, and by novel reasoning, the disembodied spirits of the books may be reanimated to captain new circumstances. Predictability, however, ceases the instant recourse is had to this process of making the old respond to the new.

The ultimate utility of an approach which serves to widen the base of predictability by bringing the legal rule into proper relation with circumstance will not be lightly preferred by those habituated to the illusory certainty of precedent finding. On the other hand, there may be more reason to hope that those who occupy themselves with legal reform will perceive that a thorough understanding of the historical antecedents of their problems can be of substantial aid in determining what should be rooted out and what should be preserved. Where such problems concern matter so ancient as our scheme of criminal procedure, command over the details of past experience seems particularly desirable. For the structure of this procedure has undergone but little material change since the end of the thirteenth century. The great age of most of its component parts makes it peculiarly vulnerable to charges of obsolescence, especially when some specific device is singled out with no reference to the structure as a whole or to the manner of its growth. Only when one considers in full detail the struggle to perfect what we now possess, indifferent though that be, does the fact become apparent that experience has left us only a narrow choice in the formalities of dealing with the perennial sameness of crime. One tends to lose faith in some panaceas if one knows that they have been tried and have failed. One acquires new hope for others when one realizes that they are substantially identical with devices once used successfully but for one reason or another abandoned.

As the story of our criminal procedure now stands, there is no possibility of coming to an intelligent and informed decision as to whether and in what detail it can be defended in its present form. Our histories of criminal procedure commonly begin at the point when the great medieval experiments in law enforcement had come to an end and when the system was operative in England substantially as it exists today. What they record from the close of the thirteenth century onward is chiefly the mechanics of form, the elaborations of dogma, the occasional subtractions from or additions to the machine constructed by the Norman, Angevin and Plantagenet kings. It is for the most part history narrowly conceived—minutiae on the certainty of indictments, antiquarianism on the *peine forte et dure,* brevities on the writ of error, hapless dodging of difficult points like the rise of informations or the growth of misdemeanor. It is history usually accurate in detail but unreliable in generalization and unintegrated with the social and political life of the period. It is history that takes for settled and for granted the results of those great battles over law enforcement waged by the generations preceding Edward I (1272–1307): the struggle for state initiative in major crimes, the growth of sanctions, the shift in approach from tort to crime, the fights of crown and immunists—in fact, every fundamental postulate of the king's courts in respect of causes criminal from the fourteenth century to the present day.

We conceive that it was these postulates which gave to English criminal law its whole direction and that the legal developments of the high middle ages cannot be understood without an account of what went before. One hesitates to regard the jury as the buckler of the oppressed, once one realizes how long it served as a sword for the oppressor. The pettifogging over indictment spelling seems less absurd, when one knows that it reflects habit ingrained by four centuries and more of judicial haggling over the verbal faults in private oral accusation. The truly archaic character of our whole machinery for dealing with malefactors becomes apparent when one realizes that only a part of it is upstart, post-conquest English and that our jurisdiction, forms of trial, process and punishment were pre-determined in alien lands by alien peoples.

All of this must be our justification for carrying back the tale of English criminal procedure to what some lawyers may view as a dim and incredible genesis. But once the series of begettings is attacked, the complexities of lineage will obviously need explanation. The bearings of our procedure are roughly both Norman and Anglo-Saxon; yet, when one scrutinizes them closely, there are strange quarterings—Frankish, Visigothic, Roman and Danish. Of these the strongest and most vigorous is the Frankish.

It has long been known that the Normans when they settled in Neustria received much of the legal heritage of the people they had conquered, but no consistent attempt has been made to measure the extent of this reception. For the preliminaries of this task are themselves not without complexity. Frankish law possesses two well-defined strains: that of the folklaw, the ultimate antiquity of which we may never accurately know, and that of king's law, the monuments of which commence with the conqueror Chlodwig (†511) and run, now in fragments and then in bulk, down to the tenth century. Both folklaw and king's law are part of the great Salic tradition in Neustria and, in the surviving monuments of both strains, the problems of wrongdoing and how it was to be dealt with are predominant. In the folklaw bloodfeud and composition, bargain procedure and individual prosecution are predominating motives. In the king's law the ideal of a legal order, a procedure controlled by officials, and sanctions exacted by authority are active. In both there is a definite infusion of barbarized Roman law. The Franks no more than the Normans were able to insulate themselves against the insidious power of a riper culture.

Into these basic constituents of later Norman jurisprudence inquiry will here be made, and in a great deal more detail than would be necessary if this literature were available to English-reading scholars. There have, indeed, been occasional excursions into these sources by the historians of English law but, largely because these were haphazard, the results have not always been happy. Most baleful of them all has been the transplantation of the notions of folkpeace and king's peace into early English law as the basic point of departure in our criminal procedure. At the time this transplantation took place, these theories were in great repute among continental scholars; but as we shall show these ideas of peace were not a part of early Germanic law and were never of the importance usually ascribed to them.

Besides these more general problems, we shall have to consider the structure of folklaw procedure, its methods of process and its types of sanction. We shall have to do this because the sphere of royal intervention in law enforcement was initially narrow and, even up to the end of Carolingian supremacy, existed largely by way of supplement to the ordinary system of settling wrongs. The king's law, too, will have to receive close attention, for to it fell the task of coping with professional malefactors and, in the course of stopping other gaps in the ancient scheme of remedies, it evolved new forms of process and more telling methods of inflicting penalties. On the modern mind most of this will strike with outlandish effect. But it was a strange society, where bloodfeud raged along the banks of the placid Cher, where saints were banished, where kings were foresworn, where generations of nameless ruffians lurked in the forests and preyed upon the Frankish beeves. A strange society, but one which forged a rustless sword for justice.

The Franks were endowed with something of the Roman

capacity for devising well-wearing legal institutions. Yet, even so, it is doubtful whether many of their more artful procedures would have survived the shock of Norman invasion and the subsequent century of guerrilla wars, had their administration not been well localized. Initially this had occurred through design, by granting to great magnates, both temporal and spiritual, power of government and justiciation in their estates, and then by protecting the grantees through making them "immune" from certain interferences of public officers. Later, as the West Frankish Kingdom crumbled under the onslaughts of the Northmen, these immunities absorbed powers not granted, and arrogated to themselves privileges hitherto specifically reserved to the crown. The autonomic growth of the great feudatories— the counties, duchies, bishoprics and abbeys—begins at this point. In this wise, moreover, is Frankish law preserved to a greater or less degree. This phase of administration deserves close scrutiny, for we believe it to be demonstrable that the immunity was the unit where Frankish law found asylum and consequent reception in Normandy.

A study of the manner in which Frankish forms were preserved does not, however, account for the peculiarities of Norman usage on the eve of the English conquest. Society in northern France had undergone such radical changes in the course of the tenth and early eleventh centuries, changes which these forms were in many cases made to fit, that some account will have to be taken of the impact of feudalism upon criminal law. Here we shall have to consider above all the decay of the institution of composition, the enhanced authority of the courtkeeper, the effect upon the form of trial of diverting judicial profits into his hands, and above all the development of the two great medieval sanctions, forfeiture and escheat.

Against this background of a folklaw and an imperial law, both diverted to the uses of petty prelates and rapacious barons, must then be viewed the great movement for the institution of the truce or peace of God, through which a people weary of bloodshed strove to restore some semblance of a long-forgotten public order. Despite the impression which the movement leaves of a deep change in men's hearts, it was at first without marked results. Because it was procedurally insignificant, the peace of God creeps but slowly into secular law. It is in Normandy, first of all, that a sagacious prince appreciates how this otherwise feeble ecclesiastical gesture toward law and order can be capitalized. By slowly assuming the responsibility for the enforcement of the sworn peace, the Norman dukes succeed in establishing a prerogative over certain causes criminal that gives them an authority more far-reaching than they had theretofore exercised as lords paramount. This they are not slow to convert into the "peace of the duke," the order enforced by the duke's officers against all. It is just before these first steps are taken that the kingdom of the Anglo-Saxons is conquered.

At this point begins the amalgamation of the two systems of law, the Frank-Norman and the Anglo-Saxon. We shall consider those phases of English law and administration to which the Conqueror fell heir and for which he with sovereign instinct found use. It was a meeting, strange even in history, of a mature law with the image of its own childhood. For the English law of the Confessor's time resembled the ancient Frankish folklaw as it existed before its Norman reception and before it had undergone metamorphosis at the hands of the French feudatories. The continental law fell with crushing force upon certain institutions, others it tolerated for a space, and still others were preserved as they stood or were refashioned to conform to Norman standards. This process will be considered at length, for the subsequent predominance of the crown in matters criminal was due to the formulation and execution of a franchise theory in respect of blood justice, and to the maintenance of an almost monopolistic control over certain procedural devices. In criminal law the crown plea becomes a royal prerogative in connection with particular offenses through the fact that adjective rights in general were first asserted and maintained.

Once the principle is established that certain procedures for certain cases are a matter of royal prerogative, the corollary that the crown may alter procedural forms or make substitutions is inevitable. Even though political circumstances were then favorable, Henry II's introduction of the presentment jury for crime (1166) was successful to a great degree because his ancestors had settled the crown's authority in procedural matters; only reasons of form justify the common view that English criminal procedure begins with this measure. Despite the revolutionary character of Henry's innovation, there was in practice a long and tedious road before the crown: the ambuscades of franchise rights must be frustrated, the system of private accusation must be integrated with, and finally made to serve, public justice, and public justice itself must be made remorseless and inevitable. It was in the process of accomplishing these objectives that criminal procedure assumed the contours which it still in general possesses.

Since it is not until the thirteenth century that distinctions between major and petty crime begin to have any great significance in the procedure of the English royal courts, the focus of attention, where it is not upon the undifferentiated wrongs, will here be chiefly upon the serious offense—what now comes to be called felony. We shall be concerned chiefly with the jurisdictional significance of early and crude attempts to classify crime, for jurisdiction is the first reason for making distinctions. It is only later, when criminal law is the subject of the stiff metaphysics of the king's judges, that the attempt to inject substantive content into felony begins.

This marks the commencement of a profound change in the attitude toward problems of wrongdoing. Theretofore lawyers had thought about crime concretely in terms of an arson, a rape or a homicide—not generally in terms of felony. Their approach to specific offenses was in terms of procedures, a fact which may account for the volatility of criminal law up to the close of the thirteenth century. The mad patchwork of law enforcing devices was, however, as provoking as an offer to deraign to the medieval passion for system. The challenge was not to go unanswered. The result was a concentration upon substance, an inelastic array of clichés.

Once the major offenses had been ticketed as felony it was inevitable that every procedural incident should become associated with the generalization—so the forms of trial, so process, so the final sanctions, so the nebula of ancillary doctrine like the learning on benefit of clergy, the rules about homicide in the commission of felonies, the complete reduction of final judgment to a formula. Until Tudor times practically everything[8] outside this large and almost watertight compartment was trespass, very little of which came before the central courts by indictment. This, of course, tended to circumscribe all judicial thinking about crime. For example, it led, in the case of statutes restricting recourse to the Holy See, to the *praemunire* doctrine— a sort of diluted felony concept. It is only after the Star Chamber with its large equitable powers commenced to play with a riot theory and after the misdemeanor concept began to take form in the sixteenth century that new matter is given lodging elsewhere than in the Procrustean bed of felony. This new law had, however, to grow in stature before it produced any effect whatever upon the bailiwick of which felony had so long been seised. There was no rescue for him who fell within its reaches except by the tricks already perfected to cheat it: the purchase of a pardon for homicide by misadventure, the race to the sanctuary, the mumbling of a psalm where the Book fell open. Regarded from the angle of honest enforcement, nothing could have been more indecent than the structure of evasions which the rigid felony

---

[8] Even the Statute of Treason (25 Edw. III, st. 5, c. 2) handles treason as a species of felony.

doctrine made inevitable. Nothing could have been more out-rageous than the necessity under which judges were placed when these tricks were unavailing to proceed under their formulae. "Burn him gently," said the King's Bench (1672), directing the branding of a man convicted of killing his wife's lover caught in *flagrante delicto*, "for there can be no greater provocation than this."

The eventual piecemeal dismemberment of the felony con-cept by the gradual abolition of some of its medieval incidents did not end the domination it exercised over procedure. In America, for example, it remains now a test for jury trial, again a test of jurisdiction. In this same way other classifications of the medieval lawyer still stand, apparently as irrefragable as ever, stumbling blocks to lucid thought, blocks to which our procedural forms are chained. Indeed, it is a singular commen-tary upon the philosophic endowments of our bar that these most shallow and most mischievous products of medieval Eng-lish justice should remain enshrined in statute, in law reports and, one suspects, in the judicial breast. Reason is of no avail to combat the stultifying effects of these classifications; they can be discredited only by the relentless unrolling of procedural rec-ord, back to a time before they were conceived. This is why we have ventured so far into the past. This is why we have dwelt so uncompassionately upon detail. For if the components of our scheme of enforcement can be seen in correct historical perspec-tive, if means and one-time ends are brought into proper bal-ance, our legal heritage may be viewed with certain detachment and accorded such respect as experience may show it has de-served.

# CHAPTER I

## THE FOUNDATIONS OF EARLY LAW
## ENFORCEMENT

THE vitality of procedure as an historical phenomenon lies less in its relative stability of form than in its responsiveness to change in respect of function. Its most significant problems are consequently not the tracing of the outward history of particular devices, the cumulating of dated technical detail, but the explanation of functional mutations in relation to social or political changes, which induce new uses in despite of ancient "certainty." A chronicle of the candid form is essential to the tale of the artful use; indeed the two are not properly separable. Even though it is sometimes convenient to treat them as distinct phases, a proper balance of emphasis must be maintained if conclusions regarding procedural purpose are to have any validity. But attention to form, because it is easier to trace, must never outweigh considerations of use. Neither must the two be allowed to fall out of step in point of time. Otherwise the history of procedure becomes a meaningless record of events and its connection with life indecipherable.

An approach to English criminal procedure from this angle requires the reconsideration of much that has become so orthodox that questioning verges on legal heresy. Its history has been recounted chiefly from insular sources. It has been built not only in terms of form, but on the theory that by proceeding from more recent known facts, the remoter unknown is discoverable. This last theory, an elaboration of the lawyers' method of precedent, is valuable in dealing with technical matter. But it is otherwise inadequate, because concentration upon result so flattens the whole perspective of function that changes in the purpose of procedure drop from view. Thus in the picture of our criminal law, the assumption by the state of wide responsibilities for re-

pressing and punishing crime, because it has modern significance, has been made the central event, and the whole sweep of
legal detail has been made to sustain the dominance of this conception. Whatever has disturbed the symmetry of the composition has been omitted or brushed in dingy chiaroscuro. It is not
for mere reasons of taste that one must find fault with this presentation. It is because the formula after which it is drawn is too
rigid to capture the restless movement of procedural development. Granting the overshadowing significance for modern procedure of the substitution of a public process for private revenge,
the eventual results throw little light on the mechanics of the
substitution whereby extant devices were being stripped of ancient implications to accommodate them to new ends. The very
substitution itself was a slow shift in the major premise of law
enforcement and one comprehensible, therefore, only in terms
of a long series of shifts in minor premises, extending over generations of courtkeepers and of malefactors.

The more thorough exploration of the remote past necessary
to avoid an over-foreshortened view of English procedural history means, of course, that a study of island sources alone cannot
suffice. This was demonstrated by Brunner when he demolished
old fables about the jury and established the Frankish pedigree
of English law.[1] Not only details of trial procedure, but jurisdiction, process, sanctions, indeed the whole theory of law enforcement imported by the Norman conquerors into England, had
roots in regions far from the green shires perambulated by the
judges of these kings. Yet few scholars have ventured to explore
across the channel. For when Brunner wrote, the Victorian cult
of Anglo-Saxonism was at its height; nor has it to this day entirely waned.[2] Pre-conquest Norman law remains a matter of

[1] Brunner, *Entstehung der Schwurgerichte* (1872), *passim,* esp. 127–31,
145. See also v. Amira, *Zweck und Mittel der Germanischen Rechtsgeschichte* (1873), 42.
[2] 2 Holdsworth, *H.E.L.* (1923), 146. "England probably had little to
learn from Normandy itself, from Norman institutions and Norman law."

shadowy contours.[3] But it deserves rescue from the oblivion of over-generalization. It must be pursued through the vicissitudes of its early development wherever this hunt may lead.

An acceptance of Brunner's basic view that English legal history is at various points inextricably bound to the history of continental law[4] does not mean that the problems mentioned can be solved by the particular methods which he used. His work was carried on in the tradition of that group of scholars who treated all Germanic peoples as forming a cultural unity and who consequently approached early medieval law as something less affected by national influences or even local peculiarities than by a sort of all-pervading undifferentiated Germanic *Volksgeist*.[5] So, for the earliest period, between the *Germania* of Tacitus and the first monuments of Frankish law, an artful but artificial reconstruction was achieved by making the sources of central Europe speak as of a time quite other than their own,

[3] So in 1 Pollock and Maitland, *H.E.L.* (2 ed. 1905), 64 *et seq.*

[4] *Cf.* Brunner's review of Bigelow, *Placita Anglo-Normannica* (1879), and *History of Procedure* (1880) in 2 *Z.R.G.*[2], 202, 214. "Worthy as is Bigelow's exposition of Anglo-Norman procedure in matter of detail, yet on the whole it offers proof that in the present state of science it is somewhat dangerous to write the history of the older English law without exact knowledge of Norman, Frankish and old French legal history."

[5] This cultural nexus had been indicated as early as 1828 by Grimm, *Deutsche Rechtsaltertümer* (4 ed. 1899). It was systematically developed as a method for the study of criminal law by Wilda, *Das Strafrecht der Germanen* (1842; vol. 1 of his *Geschichte des Deutschen Strafrechts*). In his introduction, *ibid.*, 2 *et seq.*, Wilda says, "On the criminal law of the Germans there are no definite limits to be set either in space or time. We have to deal not with the exposition of the law of a state and country but of a people (*Volk*). . . .

"We have to deal here, not with an account of events which may only be arrayed on the thread of chronological continuity, in order that their world historical interrelation may be understood. The subject of our task is the development of conditions which have this essential foundation in the common folkways (*Volkstümlichkeit*) of the Germanic peoples, the exposition of ideas which have put their impress upon legal institutions and have given them their form, or rather, which as spirit have created their living body." It is unnecessary to repeat in detail all the arguments by which the use of Scandinavian sources is justified by Wilda.

and then by drawing heavily upon the much later Scandinavian materials because these were conceived as representing an ancient culture level, unspoiled by contact with the Roman world. Conclusions of philologians regarding word affinities have played a great role in the application of this method, as also have the researches of ethnologists on the family trees of the barbarian peoples.[6] That chronology hindered the jurists of this method but little is apparent, yet since they purported to be dealing with an institutional development, this lack has glared less than if they had been writing of the lives and successions of kings.[7] Circumstances of place were similarly as little embarrassing to them as if the literary historians had never hatched out a milieu theory. Bare spots in Frankish law were simply filled out by use of Anglo-Saxon or Lombard or Visigothic materials. A systematic structure of great seeming perfection resulted. But it is one that trembles at the least questioning of the foundations on which it is erected.

The functional mutations of so precise a matter as procedure cannot properly be studied if one remains under the spell of a conception of culture as indiscriminately broad as this, with so slight a respect for time, so faint a regard for local circumstance. It is true that a reconstruction of function must be made largely from the materials of social and cultural history, since mere forms of procedure do not always mirror functional change. But an abandonment of the skin and bones tradition of the common lawyer does not mean that the flabby standards of "sociology" nor yet the fancies of nineteenth-century romanticism must be embraced. Form and function can be synchronized. They can be followed in proper succession if a due regard is had for time and place and circumstances.

[6] I Brunner, *D.R.G.* (2 ed., 1906), 33 *et seq.* deals in detail with the various tribal relations on the basis of comparative philology.

[7] That the philosophical views of the writers had much to do with the manner in which the theories developed was seen as early as 1876 by Löning, *Der Vertragsbruch im Deutschen Recht* (1876), 50, n. 19.

In the case of English criminal procedure these strictures are forced upon one by the very nature of its first and most baffling problem. This arises out of the impact of the Norman upon Anglo-Saxon institutions, the first a composite of variegated cultural elements, the second essentially an indigenous and homogeneous growth. In the conflict between these two the issues of fact cannot be formulated unless each is treated as a distinct cultural identity, and unless the individual lines of growth are held separate. This premise can only be maintained by refusing to employ Anglo-Saxon materials to supplement Frankish sources of Norman law where these are silent. It is essential again to handle these Anglo-Saxon materials of and for themselves, without the prejudicing inferences commonly drawn from the same continental law whose impact one hopes to study. Moreover, as to each body of law there must be the least possible telescoping of time; otherwise we shall have on our hands an only slightly different sort of "system" than the one we are endeavoring to escape.

Since the problem here to be studied is in no sense the depiction of a "background" of English criminal procedure, but the difficult business of tracing certain of its aspects through the ramifications of two distinct lines of development, observing the eventual contact of the two, and following the resultant process of integration, it is well to begin with its most harassing phase, and the one least understood—to wit, the development of Norman procedural institutions. These have a past of considerable complexity. For they are "Norman" only by reason of adoption, and their history before they were received and then subjected to the hammerings of a feudal society, runs back, through the ordinances of Carolingian and Merovingian kings, to the primitive code of the Salic Franks and beyond that to a time of which little can ever be known. A reasonably satisfactory chain of title may be constructed for them on the basis of Frankish materials alone. This method will here be followed, for by the tests already posited the northern sources are not to be regarded as apposite (save as suggestions), and the legal monuments of tribes inhabiting regions remote from the Frankish lands have value likewise chiefly for purposes of comparison.

The difficulties which the Frankish sources themselves present (sixth–tenth centuries), due to the obscurity of the texts, the uncertainty of dating, the gaps and the forgeries, have led to the formulation of certain theories regarding the postulates of Germanic law at large for the purpose of bringing the materials into a rational order. These theories have been current for so long that they are now traditional "knowledge." Indeed the theories have been so thoroughly worked into the presentation of the materials which they seek to explain that only a total reinvestigation makes it possible to challenge them. And challenge inevitably results from the method here followed.

These theories proceed from the assumption that the existence of any sort of procedure having to do with wrongs depends upon some prevailing conceptions of public order. With this assumption there can be no quarrel providing the expression "public order" is used accurately and is used with caution when speaking of primitive forms. For "public" does not necessarily imply the existence of organized authority, and "order" does not have to mean an utter absence of violence from processes of law. No one would deny that movement in procedural history during the dark ages was to a great extent conditioned by modifications in the conception of public order, which in turn were partly the result of changes in the order itself, i.e., in the social and political structure, and to a less degree in the social ethics of the community. Indeed our first duty will be to observe how far the alterations in this basic conception involved changes in the immediate ends for which existing procedural forms were used. Agreement upon this assumption, however, does not signify accord with any specific doctrines which have been grounded upon it, nor with the dogmatic manner in which "proofs" of these doctrines have been assembled and the insistence upon their pervasiveness in the face of evidence to the contrary. We propose to meet the orthodox theorists upon their own ground. We propose to observe the mutations of public order in relation to procedure during the so-called Germanic and Frankish periods and to see how far the record will either support their hypothesis or require revision.

### THE "PEACE" THEORY

Most basic to the orthodox discussions of wrongdoing in early medieval times, is a theory so long entrenched that it has acquired the quality of a credo. This is the theory, a familiar also of English criminal law, of a *Peace*—whether this be a folk, a king's or a public Peace.[8] This Peace is said to have been the

---

[8] Brunner, *Grundzüge der Deutschen Rechtsgeschichte* (Heymann Ed. 1925), 18 *et seq.* summarizes in convenient form the "peace" doctrine and is in substantial accord with the more extensive accounts of 1 Brunner, *Deutsche Rechtsgeschichte* (2 ed. 1906), and of v. Schwerin, in 2 Hoops, *Realenzyklopädie des Deutschen Altertums, s.v. Frieden*. For the reader's convenience it has been translated.

"The Germanic criminal law is based on the idea that he who breaks the peace puts himself without the peace. The breach of the peace is either one which exposes the actor to the enmity of the injured party and his sib, or one which makes him the enemy of the whole group. In the former case it is a matter for the injured party, or his sib, to secure satisfaction. The whole group did not protect the misdoer from the sib as to whom he had forfeited the peace, but he was by law at the mercy of the feud or revenge of his opponents if the latter did not prefer to demand wergeld or amends. The right of feud and revenge to which the blood-friends of the misdoer were exposed, existed in cases involving blood and honor. A homicide accomplished in the course of permitted revenge, had to be publicly announced, or be made generally obvious as such, or it would be treated as a wrongful killing. In petty cases the right to revenge was forbidden and only a judicial claim to emendation (*compositio*) was established. A wergeld atoned for the homicide; otherwise most of the acknowledged wrongs were estimated in penalties which either arose through a division of the wergeld or are to be attributed to a certain basic amount which varied in the several laws. If amends or wergeld was sued for judicially, the offender had to pay to the public authority or the community a certain sum—among certain tribes a quota of the whole *compositio*, among others a fixed amount, called the peace money (*fredus*). This was the price for the inter-

equivalent of law;[9] it is supposed to have prevailed among the Germanic peoples at large even in those almost legendary centuries before the Franks swept over Gaul. The sib[10] as well as the earliest groups that had political characteristics, the *civitates* of the Teutons,[11] are spoken of as peace associations, i.e., fraternities that had as an object the protection of members against wrongdoing either from within or without. This idea was cast into an extraordinarily theoretical form by Waitz when he wrote:[12] "The peace is the relation in which all stand while and in so far as all remain in the union and in the law on which the community rests. Whoever acts against this commits a breach of the peace. The breach of the peace is a wrong, the violation of the law is a breach of the peace. Whoever breaks the peace even if only as to an individual injures the whole group, for he injures that holy order in which all stand and through which alone their union has significance."

ference of authority or community in restoring the peace. In the event of serious misdeed the offender incurred outlawry (*Acht oder Friedlosigkeit*). The outlaw is not only excluded from the peace or legal community, but may and should be killed *bootlessly* as an enemy of the people by anyone. Outlawry in very ancient times did not have the merely negative content, as we still often hear, that the outlaw is exposed to unexpiable killing but he *must* be dealt with by the whole group as their enemy. Outlawry demands an execution of outlawry. The pursuit of the outlaw is a public duty of all members of the people; he is free as a wolf, *wargus: 'gerit caput lupinum.'* He ceases to exist in the law as kinsman, husband or father. Neither his sib nor his near family can protect him or harbor him. His property is exposed to waste or forfeiture. His house is destroyed by breach or firebrand, the work of his hands is annihilated. His possessions are forfeited, i.e. taken over by public authority to which they lapse in so far as the injured party is not satisfied out of them. Outlawry appears sometimes in strict and sometimes in mild form. The former, the older and original form, was deemed inexpiable, the latter gave the outlaw a claim to buy himself back into the peace by a fixed money payment." On "sib" *cf. infra,* note 10.

[9] Wilda, *op. cit.,* 225.

[10] On the derivation of the word and the meaning it also has of peace, *cf.* Grimm, *D.R.A.,* 467. We are using the word sib, in the sense of the group based upon kinship.

[11] Schröder, *Lehrbuch der Deutschen Rechtsgeschichte* (6 ed. 1922), 15, 21.

[12] 1 Waitz, *Deutsche Verfassungsgeschichte* (3 ed., 1880), 421.

It will be observed that the fact basis posited for this conception is a group that has been formed on the basis of kinship, and that any breach of peace or law is a matter for group action. The individual acquires legal importance only by virtue of his association and continued membership in the group. This capacity of the individual has been described as *mannhelgi* (man-holiness),[13] a term derived from the Scandinavian sources. It has been taken by many writers as valid for the tribes that inhabited central Europe.

Since the adherents of the peace = law theory see the individual's capacities as a result of his membership in a group, in the event of a breach of the "peace" the reaction is not merely that of an unattached individual but of the whole association. At the same time, since the individual committing the breach likewise has these capacities (either because he is of the group or of another group which has a like "peace") it is necessary that he be deprived of these capacities before he can be dealt with. It is theoretically not enough that he be simply expelled as a matter of fact from the association; he must have his "peace" taken away—in other words be deprived of his legal protection. It is in this manner that outlawry is conceived. The imposition of outlawry is the condition *sine qua non* of any group action toward the wrongdoer.[14]

[13] V. Amira, *Das Altnorwegische Volkstreckungsverfahren* (1874), 2. Kaufmann, in 2 *Deutsche Altertumskunde* (1923), 215, n. 3 states that *mannhelgi* is the word for a man's honor.

[14] A detailed examination of the peace theory as proclaimed by its major prophet, Wilda, discloses that peace is to him not merely the *"de facto* state of undisturbed repose, the opposite, in particular, of enmities which kindle hatred and bloody persecution (feud); peace in its more technical significance is . . . the order and assured state of affairs under the hegemony of the laws." "Peace or manholiness was the aim and accomplishment of the community, whose existence was itself conditioned upon the peace. . . . Manholiness, however, is the inviolability of the person as well as his goods that by virtue of the peace appertains to every member of the peace association. As manholiness and peace are synonymous, so are peace and law. . . ." Wilda goes on to say that an injury of the right of the individual was a breach of the peace of all, for in one peace and one

The process of definition and classification does not cease at this point. In addition to the general "peace" the existence of a

friendship were all those who belonged to a community or sacrificial fraternity which in turn were organized on the basis of kinship.

As to the proof for all this, Wilda relies almost exclusively upon Scandinavian sources. He does mention the prologue of the *Lex Salica* where the Franks are described as "fortis in arma; profunda in consilio; firma in pacis foedere" and refers to the prologue of the *Emendata* "Placuit atque convenit inter Francos et eorum proceres ut propter servandum inter se pacis studium, omnia incrementa rixarum inter se resecare deberent, et qui ceteris gentibus juxta se positis fortitudinis bracchio preeminebant ita etiam legum auctoritate praecellerunt." (*Cf.* texts in Hessels, *Lex Salica* [1880], 422–3.) This seems to have reference only to a state of peace in a very general sense, i.e. as the advantages of international peace are today considerable in respect of domestic order.

When he comes to speak of breaches of the peace, Wilda says that every true wrong was a breach of the peace. "The expression, breach of the peace, *is not universally current in the sources which are the object of our investigation,* [our italics] since it has also a narrower meaning, so that e.g., it is more frequently found in relation to the breach of a particular (plighted) or a higher peace like the king's peace. This does not, however, detract from the general character of this conception and where the substantive term is lacking there is frequently a circumlocution, i.e., 'he has broken the peace.' "

Wilda further relies on the existence of the *fredus* or as he calls it "peace money" (*supra* n. 8) as evidence of the concept breach of the peace. The *fredus* is the share of composition taken by public authority. Much has been argued about the theory on which it is exacted. *Cf.* generally Grimm, *Deutsche Rechtsaltertümer,* 656. Grimm says it is payment to the king for breach of the peace, but he admits that it can exist when there is no composition, citing *Lex Rib.,* 23 "quod si servus servum percusserit, nihil est, sed tamen *propter pacis studium* 4 den. comp." Inasmuch as slaves were not by the orthodox theory "in the peace," the phrase obviously has reference simply to a general use of the word peace as in the passage from the *Lex Salica* cited above. On this matter note also 1 Brunner, *D.R.G.,* 230, *et seq.,* who says *fredus* is paid for the intervention of public authority in settling the dispute. Brunner takes his philology from van Helten, *Zu den Malbergischen Glossen,* etc. in 25 *Beiträge zur Geschichte der deutschen Sprache und Literatur,* §§182* and 141. Brunner states that where a wrong is settled out of court no *fredus* is paid. This seems to exclude the idea that peace is bought back, and weakens *pro tanto* Wilda's argument.

In a more recent examination of the word *fredus* by Kralik in 38 *Neues Archiv der Gesellschaft für ältere Deutsche Geschichtskunde* (1913), 32, the latter says, "The meaning of *'peace money'* which was due the king or the people, hence the fiscus for the broken peace (Grimm, *D.R.A.,* 656) cannot be proved for *os., frid; ohg., fridu; ags., frid;* and *on., friðr.* Only in

"higher peace"[15] had been postulated as to various places, persons or times. This "higher peace" has been deduced from the existence of particular sanctions as to wrongs committed in respect of these objects, sanctions that were applied not as the result of private initiative but rather proceeded from the community as a whole or were set in motion by authority. The evidence, though all late, bears some indication of great antiquity and is most simply described as tending to show that a special protection was sought. To refer to this protection as a "higher peace" is misleading in that the expression suggests a peace of the same nature as the writers' general peace but of a higher degree.[16] To speak of all the special protections as aspects of a "higher peace" implies further the existence of one theory com-

*ofris.* is *frethio* usual in the sense of amends for breach of the peace." Note further that what Tacitus calls *pars mulcta* is probably *fredus*. On this *cf.* Baumstark's queries in his *Ausführliche Erläuterung . . . der Germania des Tacitus* (1875), 493; and his *Urdeutsche Staatsalterthümer* (1873), 470 *et seq.,* especially his very critical remarks on 470, n. 2, re the "peace" doctrine.

It should be observed further, that no writer has satisfactorily explained how the "peace" of the sib becomes the peace of the larger group, probably because no one knows how the larger tribal groups were formed out of collections of sibs. The transition from sib-peace to folk peace (*Volksfrieden*) is as mysterious as the later transition of folk peace to king's peace. The account on which most writers rely is in 1 Gierke, *Das Deutsche Genossenschaftsrecht* (1868), 35 *et seq.,* a fabric of pure conjecture.

For an attack upon the philological soundness of assuming a substantial identity of peace and law, *cf.* Huberti, *Friede und Recht,* in 5 *Deutsche Zeitschrift für Geschichtswissenschaft* (1891), 1 *et seq.* Huberti perceived in the *Landfrieden* of the later middle age the first real steps by which public order and punishment displaced the private or quasi-private system of dealing with wrongs. He attempts therefore to restrict the older "peace" concept to a descriptive term of a mere state of fact. To the same point see Lehmann, *Der Königsfriede der Nordgermanen* (1886), 2, n. 1. Lehmann employing northern sources asserts that peace and law are not there used synonymously.

[15] Wilda, *op. cit.,* 233. *Cf.* also Schröder, *D.R.G.,* 79.

[16] Wilda's explanation, *op. cit.,* 232, is by no means clear. Nor does the term appear in his citations from the laws. His, *Strafrecht der Friesen im Mittelalter* (1901), 129, n. 5, gives the terms, *thi hagiste; di allerhagiste ferd,* but these are of comparatively late date and appear to refer to special protections.

mon to all. Neither of these conclusions is maintainable. There is no demonstrable single motive for the establishment of all these special protections, let alone for any single underlying juristic concept. One may suppose that church and moot are to be held inviolable because of the nature of the business there transacted. But the particular protection extended to a man's home may well rest largely upon nothing more pretentious than expediency, and the so-called army peace may be no more than a primitive form of the essential discipline which has come to be embraced in modern articles of war.

It is true that in the first three instances the sanction comes into play in a manner that leads one to surmise a common origin. The so-called church peace (which probably existed even in pagan times as to temples or places of sacrifice) arises out of the belief that the place is under the guardianship of the gods and the special punishments of offenses committed in relation to holy places are laws in aid of the gods.[17] The moot peace[18] bears some relation to the church peace because the meeting place is supposed originally to have been a place of sacrifice as the place of sacrifice has also become a place of meeting.[19] But

[17] Wilda, *op. cit.*, 231 *et seq.*

[18] The existence of a moot peace among the Frankish tribes is open to question. Wilda admits that of the "real German" folklaws only the *Lex Salica,* and this in the glossed editions, mentions a moot peace. *Cod. Fuldensis,* XVI, 4: "Si quis hominem qui alicubi migrare disponit et dirigere habet praeceptum regis et si aliunde ierit in mallum publicum [to court] extra ordinationem restare eum facit aut adsalire praesumpserit 200 sol. culp. jud." Compare, however, texts in Hessels, *Lex Salica,* and Behrend, *Lex Salica* (2 ed. 1897), c. XIV, §4. The latter (to which we hereafter refer) gives the following text: "Si quis hominem qui migrare voluerit et de rege habuerit praeceptum et abbundivit in malum publico (produces it in public court) et aliquis contra ordinationem regis testare praesumpserit. . . ." Behrend interprets this as an impeachment of the royal precept. If this version is preferred, Wilda's theory of a support for moot peace falls to the ground. Sohm, *F.R.G.V.* (1871), 106, states that according to the folklaws it is the privilege of free men to come armed to the court, a fact which speaks against and not for a moot peace. Brunner, 2 *D.R.G.,* 759, asserts there is a moot peace in Frankish times, relying on Wilda.

[19] Grimm, *D.R.A.,* 793; *cf.* also 1 Brunner, *D.R.G.,* 196; Burchard, *Die Hegung der Deutschen Gerichte* (1893), 4 *et seq.*

the sanction here is imposed primarily for a breach of the actual enclosure[20] within which the moot is held, for the mere cutting of the thread encircling the meeting place is treated with particular severity. This fact relates church protection with moot protection because it is demonstrable that ancient magic inheres in the notion of enclosure.[21] In other words there is an underlying sacral purpose in the protection. In the safeguarding of the house,[22] it is conceivable that a similar sacral motive may be involved. Not only is house breach itself severely punished, but during bloodfeud the house under certain circumstances is treated as an inviolate place of refuge. Here again, what draws down the sanction seems to be a breach of enclosure. The Germanic house is palisaded,[23] a fact which at once suggests an analogy to the enclosure of the court-place.[24] Moreover, the existence in the *Lex Salica* of a particular offense of close breaking at a period when breaking into the house itself has become

[20] Grimm, *D.R.A.*, 809, 851; Brunner, 1 *D.R.G.*, 197, says that peace reigns because of the judicial order (ban) that is pronounced at the time of enclosure. On the persistence of the idea of moot enclosure, *cf.* the poem *Muspilli* (circa 880), line 77, in Braune, *Althochdeutsches Lesebuch* (3 ed. 1888) 80; and Usener, *Vorträge und Aufsätze* (1907), *Das Amecht in Luxemburg,* 149, at 151.

[21] On the sacral-superstitious origin with examples from Greek and Italian antiquities, Usener, *op. cit., Über Vergleichende Sitten und Rechtsgeschichte,* 113 *et seq.* The mythological aspects of the matter are discussed in Simrock, *Handbuch der Deutschen Mythologie* (3 ed. 1869), 490 *et seq.*

[22] Perhaps not achieved until a relatively late date: Planitz, *Die Vermögensvollstreckung im Deutschen Mittelalterlichen Recht* (1912), 52, n. 20. Beyerle, *Das Entwickelungsproblem im Germanischen Rechtsgang,* (*Deutschrechtliche Beiträge,* vol. 10, no. 2 [1915]), 130, n. 35 (hereafter cited *Rechtsgang*), indicates his leaning to this view; *contra,* 2 Brunner, *D.R.G.,* 758, n. 15.

[23] Heyne, *Fünf Bücher Deutscher Hausaltertümer* (1899), 13 *et seq.;* 98 *et seq.;* 2 Kauffmann, *Deutsche Altertumskunde,* 550, 564.

[24] The analogy is strengthened by reference to the sacral symbolism of enclosure discussed in Usener, *op. cit.,* 113 *et seq.* in relation to town walls. He emphasizes the fact that into the late middle ages scaling walls etc. is treated as a sacrilege. See also *Chronicle of Lanercost* (Maxwell Ed. 1913) 201 for a late English example. Roman theories, in *Inst.* 2, 1, 10. Against the view here advanced *Pactus Alamannorum V,* 3: 6 sol. amends

more severely tariffed suggests that it was originally the enclosure which was protected.[25]

The three instances discussed present the strongest case for a
peace theory in so far as a state of quiet may be said to exist in
a place which is protected against disturbance.[26] But there is
nothing to show that a violation of the protection is looked on as
made against the insured quietude, or that in this primitive society the state of quiet has been transmuted into a legal concept.
The special protection, moreover, is something which stands
outside the customs and laws for dealing with ordinary wrongdoing, slowly impinging upon them, but until well into the middle ages it remains something exceptional.

The ingenious manner in which are combined any facts that
might serve as the support for the structure of inference and
conjecture regarding the "peace" of Germanic peoples at large
is nowhere better illustrated than when the advocates of this
theory come to their reconstruction of its negative side—peacelessness. We have seen that peacelessness or outlawry is supposed
to have been the repercussion of a wrongful act, its first and most
essential legal consequence which puts the wrongdoer in the
situation of a hunted animal. The existence of this first step
whereby the primitive sanctions against crime were set in motion has been inferred chiefly from the vernacular expressions[27]
—none of them antedating the earliest legal sources—used to
describe the situation of an offender in some way involved in
the process of retribution. The oldest words, the Old High Ger-

for entries *in curte* and 12 sol. in the house. *Cf. Lex Alamannorum* 9, 10;
*Lex Baiuwariorum* XI, 1, 2.

[25] So *Lex Salica,* 11; 16; 27, 22. Other examples, Wilda, *op. cit.,* 605.
Brunner suggests rather artfully (2 *D.R.G.,* 732) that attempted robbery
may be here indicated.

[26] Grimm, *Deutsches Wörterbuch, s.v. Hag* II and *befrieden* gives examples of how there is a transference of ideas in the use of the ambiguous
*befrieden:* from the fact of protection accorded by an enclosure the state of
peace so produced describes the process of enclosing.

[27] V. Amira, *Grundriss des Germanischen Rechts* (3 ed. 1913), 237;
Schröder, *D.R.G.,* 83.

man *âhta,* and the earlier Anglo-Saxon *flyma,* mean literally and respectively *pursuit* and *flight.* But when they are arrayed with the Scandinavian *friþlös*—peaceless, and *utlaeger*—outlawry, or the later Anglo-Saxon *utlagh* which comes in with the Danes,[28] they are seen as expressing something more artful—the idea of being out of the peace or out of the law. By tearing these words from the culture in which they grew, by ignoring any consideration of chronology, all are made to express a universal basic conception—the notion of peacelessness, a conception which is supposed to underlie not only the whole scheme of process in the early folklaws but the sanctions taken against body and goods as punishment.

While it would be idle to deny that under some circumstances the Germanic peoples resorted to outright proscription, because this may be deduced from the report of Tacitus regarding the treatment of traitors,[29] there is reason to doubt that any such measures were used in regard to offenses at large. Certainly the words like *âhta* and *flyma* can in themselves be taken as merely descriptive, saying no more than that the wrongdoer will be pursued and that being in flight he incurs the risks of anything which skulks from cover to cover. The malefactor is certainly peaceless in the factual sense that he will not be let alone; any legal sense of being without the law, or of having been ejected from a "peace" is not demonstrated. Indeed the little we do know about Germanic customs before the great migrations is itself an implicit denial of any notion of outlawry, either as a necessary process of law, or as an inevitable and automatic result of a criminal act. The primary consequence of a homicide or robbery was that the offender would be subjected to the revenge of the group or individual he had injured—bloodfeud.[30] In prehistoric times this must be taken to have been a mere state

[28] Liebermann, *Die Friedlosigkeit bei den Angelsachsen (Festschrift für Brunner,* 1915), 18.
[29] *Germania,* c. 12.
[30] Beyerle, *Rechtsgang,* 22.

of fact, neither permitted nor forbidden; it can be spoken of as an institution only in the sense that it was a more or less inevitable expectancy. There is no historical propriety in dressing up the wrong as a breaking of the peace, or the reaction of revenge as an expulsion of the malefactor from "the" peace and his subjection to the fate of the wolf.

It is important to observe at this point that the advocates of the peace theory have by no means sought to deny that revenge in the form of feud is the focal point of the early law about wrongs. But they have stubbornly insisted upon institutionalizing revenge by forcing it into their scheme of peace and peacelessness, and so have made of it a process of law. Since every misdeed results automatically in some form of outlawry consequent upon the violation of public peace, no man (it is supposed) could proceed to feud unless the misdoer were in this unhappy state of peacelessness. The formula fashioned by von Maurer states the most extreme position: "without a breach of the peace, no outlawry, without outlawry no selfhelp."[31] Even Brunner, who eventually conceived of outlawry as possessing a negative content, in the sense that the wrongdoer had forfeited his legal protection, rather than that he was in all cases subject to destruction at the hands of his fellow men, believed that peacelessness was a condition *sine qua non,* before the injured could proceed to feud, since in the feud is seen the very negation of all order.[32] This peacelessness of the man involved in feud has been described as a "relative outlawry," that is, an outlawry not as to the community at large but as to the kin of the injured party. He can be dealt with summarily by them only if he is out of the "peace."[33]

[31] In 16 *Kritische Vierteljahrschrift,* 92.

[32] 2 Brunner, *D.R.G.,* 612, 762–3, 769.

[33] The precise expression "relative outlawry" is not used by Wilda, but he states (*op. cit.,* 269) that "the injured party could act toward a misdoer as against an outlaw"; *cf.* 274 and 307. Schröder, *D.R.G.,* 81, remarks that "in ordinary breaches of the peace" the wrongdoer becomes the enemy of the injured and his sib, and in the event of a serious breach, of the people,

It is not necessary to expatiate upon the dogmatism which loads upon the emotional reaction of anger and hate such a complicated conceptual apparatus. The little we know about pre-migration Germanic society permits us to infer no more than that the individual was protected if he was strong and his sib was powerful.[34] Out of the fact of group protection comes the fact of group war, of feud. And this war is not contingent upon any precedent outlawry, but is a sanction immediate upon the misdeed, complete when a saturation point in revenge and counter-revenge is reached.

It is hardly to be denied that a romantic view of the ancient Teutons as somehow a profoundly law-abiding people, coupled with a very modern reluctance to admit that violence can be lawful has had a great deal to do with all these jurists' theories about peace and outlawry. But this hypersensitivity toward a violent assertion of a sense of wrong or claim of right is of little avail in estimating with any accuracy the institutions of a people whose first and most frequent contacts with the classical world were on the field of battle and in whose occupations the employment of arms was usual. It is true that the feud was eventually to a certain degree institutionalized, in short, what was once *de facto* becomes *de jure,* and when we say *de jure* we use the expression in a very loose sense.[35] But this process does not begin until there had developed an organization more extensive than

the gods, and the king. Brunner, 1 *D.R.G.,* 223, moves with caution. He remarks: "The misdeed as such sets a man out of the peace, and establishes the lawful enmity of the injured"; and at 232, "Just as the feud signifies the enmity of a sib whose revenge is justified, so outlawry (*Friedlosigkeit*) signifies the enmity of all the people." Brunner's statement seems equivocal. Gierke, *Schuld und Haftung,* (*Untersuchungen,* no. 100) 14, uses the expression *relative outlawry. Cf.* also v. Amira, *Das Altnorwegische Vollstreckungsverfahren,* 45; *Grundriss des Germanischen Rechts,* 238 *et seq.*

[34] Beyerle, *Rechtsgang,* 25.

[35] A point of some difficulty in this connection is the question of whether or not the state of feud as it is dealt with in the folklaws, is conceived of as a lawful state of affairs. Those writers who adhere to the fiction of relative peacelessness are in the dilemma of not being able to deny

the sib, with wider powers of a rudimentary governmental sort. In central Europe the documents all indicate that this regulation and restriction of feud is the first phase in the growth of public control over wrongs.[36] But at no point do the documents disclose even a suspicion of relative peacelessness or that an "outlawry" as to kin was metamorphosed into an outlawry as to the whole people. The feud is treated essentially as a troublesome state of fact. Regarded in this light, therefore, *"the relative peacelessness" of the writers is nothing but the feud itself,* for the situation in which the wrongdoer finds himself as to the injured individual and his sib, is factually the equivalent of peacelessness.[37] Outside of the kindred no man is concerned—the great group as a whole are neutrals in the warfare.[38]

If we can dispense with the idea of "relative peacelessness" in the sense of the wrongdoer being ejected from the peace before the feud can set in, either by his act itself, or as the result of some public pronouncement of which there is no evidence,[39] then it becomes obvious that the process of feud or of extra-judicial

that feud is lawful. Brunner, 1 *D.R.G.,* 223, indicates it is lawful. The matter is discussed in the text *infra.*

[36] Beyerle, *Rechtsgang,* 32, 70. On the influence of the Church, Schröder, *D.R.G.,* 370; on the efforts to reduce feud, *ibid.,* 372 *et seq.;* Dahn, *Fehdegang und Rechtsgang der Germanen* in 2 *Bausteine,* 90. It should be further pointed out that the special procedure whereby the offender was cast out of the sib and handed over to the injured party is coeval with the procedure discussed in the text, and tended likewise to reduce feud. *Cf.* Beyerle, *loc. cit.,* where Brunner's assertion that this procedure was a split-off or mitigation of outlawry is challenged. Brunner's conclusions were first stated in his article, *Abspaltungen der Friedlosigkeit* reprinted in *Forschungen zur Geschichte des Deutschen und Französischen Rechts* (1894), 444, 469.

[37] This is indicated by His, *Strafrecht der Friesen,* 166 where, speaking of "restricted" outlawry, he says this is the feud. To this view, 1 Brunner, *D.R.G.,* 219 seems to adhere.

[38] 1 Brunner, *D.R.G.,* 224; Beyerle, *op. cit.,* 25.

[39] The weakness of the conventional theories about relative peacelessness is illustrated by the fact that nowhere is there any proof presented that anything more than the wrongful act was needed to make a man "peaceless" for his misdeeds. 1 Brunner, *D.R.G.,* 224, states "A notification of cessation of peace and a declaration of feud was not necessary. The

settlement of the war is narrow in scope and does not require participation of the group beyond the immediate kindred.[40] Indeed, the methods of dealing with wrongs being what they were, there is reason to doubt whether there is originally involved at any point any conception of "public" order (excepting the few cases, like treason or desertion) either in the sense of a state guaranteed by law or at least in the sense that such a guarantee was the aim of primitive regulation. If there is any concept of public order it is very vague and has its limits in social rather than legal implications. In the folklaws the almost complete identification of the list of wrongs with the list of matters for which feud can be waged[41] seems to be a confirmation of this view, for the reaction to any of the acts that are wrongs is one that lies in the hands of the individual or his kindred and not in any external authority.[42] Indeed, even in this period re-

wrong as such changed peace into enmity." Schröder, *D.R.G.,* 84, to the same effect. Both these writers agree that the *faidosus* (i.e. the man against whom feud is waged) did not lose either his goods or his family ties, and no one, as in their general outlawry, was hindered in aiding him. The fact that a house peace protected him (*Lex Alamannorum,* 44 [45], *Lex Frisionum* Add., 1, 1; *Lex Saxonum,* 27) is further a denial of the peaceless position of the wrongdoer. V. Amira, *Grundriss d.G.R.,* 239, indicates that a secondary stage of development was the proclamation of outlawry as an indispensable condition before proceeding. 1 Siegel, *Geschichte des Deutschen Gerichtsverfahrens* (1857), 17, thinks there are circumstances, such as when the killer is not found with a body, where there has to be a declaration of feud, but his view is not prevalent.

[40] We except, of course, the case of quasi-public intervention such as the church arbitration mentioned by Gregory of Tours, *Historia Francorum (M.G.H., Script.),* VII, 47.

[41] These are all listed at length by Beyerle, *Rechtsgang,* 50 *et seq.* They include homicide, wounds and bodily injury, imprisonments, injuries to honor, false accusations, violations of *mundium,* abduction, seduction, rape, robbery, theft, malicious destruction of property, arson, breaking into home (in the sense of the *ags. hamsocn*), sorcery and perjury. Beyerle (at 65), points out that with the exception of desertion from the army (*Lex Alamannorum,* 90) the so-called "public wrongs" in the folklaws are never a matter of private emendation.

[42] The unanimity of the folklaws on the matter of what constitutes a wrong is of course no index of its "public" as against "private" character. To avoid any erroneous procedural implications it is safer to treat the

sort to feud, while recognized as a means of dealing with wrong-doing, is never spoken of as a right.[43] In other words, although

ordinary crime or wrong simply as an act which involves an interference with the body or with things, inducing revenge or a willingness to be cooled by payment. The classification of Tacitus (c. 12)—*scelera* and *flagitia*—and the later *ohg. firina* and *missitat* are classifications not between "public" and "private" wrongs, although the believers in a general outlawry see such implications. They are an ethical division between the very bad and the bad. We cannot hope to penetrate very far into the basic concepts of right and wrong. And the tariffs of the folklaws, since they are the evaluations of "private" injuries based on man values in the case of bodily harm or chattel values in the case of theft, are of no help in discovering the germs of a "public" offense.

[43] Beyerle, *Rechtsgang*, 43 *et seq.* Note further, Sohm, *F.R.G.V.*, 104 states that feud is not a "delict" in the folklaws, which is far from admitting it is a right. He cites (n. 5) a passage from Gregory of Tours, *Vitae Patr.*, VIII, 7, that illustrates the 6th century view. 1 Brunner, *D.R.G.*, 221, describes *faida* or feud as the enmity subsisting between hostile parties citing the Lombard *Edictus Rothari*, 74 (*cf.* also 45, 162, 326) *Faida quod est inimicitia*. Brunner goes on to say that this state of hostility is recognized by the law in that an act of revenge is not treated as a misdeed but as an act which is not to be emended. In 2 *ibid.*, 692, n. 1, and 693, n. 4, Schwerin, his editor, is hard put to deny Beyerle's position, and he lamely concludes that we can at least use the expression "right of feud" in the sense that from the standpoint of the group as a whole it is not a wrong (*Unrecht*). Schröder, *D.R.G.*, 86, refers to feud as "permitted revenge or self-help." Beyerle's position is based in part on what he regards as evidence that the acts of revenge are not necessarily to be composed. He admits where wergeld stands against wergeld, the act of revenge is not to be amended if it does not involve others than the immediate parties in interest. But the evidence that in the calculation of composition a system of set-off was used where all injuries that occurred in the course of hostilities are estimated appears to him as persuasive that an act of revenge was not necessarily free of legal consequences. He suggests that Brunner's evidence that the act of revenge was not a case for amends relates entirely to the case of handhaving offenses.

Beyerle's position that there is no "right" of feud, does not adequately explain the manner in which the institution of feud was regarded. Certain passages in the *Lex Salica* seem to confirm what was said in the text that the state of feud was at least not unlawful. Thus *Lex Salica*, 41 Add. 2 provides that where a man's head had been impaled, the method of signifying a killing in the course of justified homicide (1 Brunner, *D.R.G.*, 226), it is not to be removed without the consent of the revenger. Similarly, *Lex Salica*, 41, 8, dealing with killing of a person found at a cross roads with hands and feet cut off by his enemies, which Behrend (81) in his note treats as clear proof for the existence of a right of feud. *Cf.* on the

it is not unlawful to resort to revenge, nevertheless, this resort is not had as of right, in the sense of a right recognized or confirmed by the laws themselves. The whole tendency and purpose in the folklaws of the Frankish empire is rather toward restricting bloodfeud, and furthering the process of emendation. But the feud continues, incompatible though it may be with the ends of the rudimentary state.

If revenge and feud represent one lowest stratum of organized action against wrongdoing, a second stage is the growth of composition which, gaining ground, eventually becomes the normal anticipation of the man injured.[44] As early as the time of Tacitus emendation was in existence,[45] but nothing is known as to how the substitution of a pecuniary sanction in place of feud was effected. One may conjecture that the machinery for settling the injury by payment had much to do with this, and that the earliest phase was a mere private arbitration arranged between the kindred groups, a process eventually succeeded by regular recourse to governmental agencies—at which point procedural devices may be said to come into being.[46] This is a reasonable conjecture because even in developed Frankish procedure private arbitration exists side by side with regular judicial proceeding and back of both is the latent threat of feud.

matter, Mayer-Homberg, *Die Fränkischen Volksrechte,* 163 *et seq.,* especially what he has to say regarding the tendency of the late *Lex Ribuaria.* Mayer-Homberg believes that apparent denial of a right of feud in the latter is due to the influence of legislation of Childebert II.

The parallel between feud and modern war is worth noting. War is a "legal condition of things in which rights may be prosecuted by force" (7 Moore, *Digest of International Law,* 153). This does not mean that all acts committed in the course of war are lawful. So the feud can be described as a lawful state in which some acts are not lawful.

[44] The notion of composition is familiar to students of English law and it is consequently not discussed in the text. On the concept in early "Germanic" times, *cf.* 1 Brunner, *D.R.G.,* 226 *et seq.*

[45] *Germania,* c. 12.

[46] Schröder, *D.R.G.,* 86 *et seq.,* and Brunner, *loc. cit.,* both indicate the choice between a judicial or private settlement. *Cf.* Brunner, *Sippe und Wergeld,* in 3 Z.R.G.², 1; 2 Grimm, *Deutsche Rechtsaltertümer,* 645.

The notion of amends for injury may be regarded as a considerable advance in the direction of a non-violent settlement of wrongs, but it would be pretentious to suppose that any of the measures aimed at a discouragement of the feud were the fruit of a new and extensive social objective intended to substitute for kinsmen's revenge. They do not give birth to any theory of peace, because they are mere surrogates for war[47]—war which is not excluded from the procedural picture even at the moment of final settlement. The agencies of government, such as they were, are employed without any perceptible alteration of the existing framework of remedies or of the anticipation of the parties. Continual resort to courts or private arbitrors and the concomitant development of procedural devices might eventually *create* a concept of public order but this was at best a by-product rather than a consciously predetermined objective. That it was a very feeble by-product stands out in Gregory of Tours' story of the feud of Sicharius and Chramnisind,[48] for as late as the Merovingian days the claims of outraged kinship out-

[47] Amends are paid to buy off war. So Brunner, 1 *D.R.G.*, 120 speaking of the division of money among the kinsmen says "It does not depend upon the heirs alone but upon the whole group whether revenge shall be wreaked or whether it shall be bought off." Compare also v. Amira, *Grundriss des G.R.*, 243 *et seq.* Schröder, *D.R.G.*, 88, says the wrongdoer by payment buys his way into the peace. He does not indicate whether or not he means this is a collateral result. This fits his theoretical structure but it wants proof. It should be noted also that the notion of damages is not absent as witness the scaling of amounts according to the nature of the injuries. Apart also from the relation of the act and the amends is the element of economic advantage. "I will not carry my dead son in my pouch," says a father scorning wergeld, Grimm, *D.R.A.*, 647, note. Further in Gregory of Tours, *Historia Francorum* (*M.G.H., Script.*) IX, 19, Sicharius taunts Chramnisind that he has gotten rich from wergeld of his slain relatives. Compare also the Anglo-Saxon proverb cited by Grimm, in 1 *Zeitschrift für Geschichtliche Rechtswissenschaft*, 326 "bugge spere of side oðe bere"—buy the spear from the side [of the injured] or bear it, i.e., fight with it. On the relation of the composition to the older sacral penalties, *cf.* the summary in Beyerle, *Rechtsgang*, 31 *et seq.*, and his criticism of the ruling views.

[48] Gregory of Tours, *Hist. Franc.*, VII, 47; Sicharius is celebrating Christmas with his friends. A priest sends a servant to invite some guests.

weighed in the eyes even of the king the procedure designed by law to check the violence of blood feud.

There are many reasons why the participation of primitive authority in emendation proceedings offered small foothold for the creation and extension of ideas of public order. Recourse to it was not obligatory; even where men invoked the "state" in lieu of settlement *inter partes,* it applied no sanctions for the offense. The share it had in the pecuniary settlement, the so-called *fredus,*[49] was solely a payment for its intervention and was not a penalty for the offense. In the case of the isolated un-emendable offenses it did possess sanctions, but these were not initially extensible to the ordinary run of wrongs because it cannot be shown, even when records first begin, that so keen and so general a sense of injury existed as to a homicide or an arson that penalty was bound to displace compensation. Moreover, any such action would have involved the prior forging of some cen-

One of the latter kills the servant. Sicharius hearing this goes with his guests to protect the priest. Austrigisil then brings his friends and a fight ensues. Sicharius flees aided by the clerics. Austrigisil breaks into the house of the priest and takes Sicharius' silver and gold (which had evidently been brought along), and kills four servants. Sicharius complains before the count's court in Tours. Austrigisil, it is decided, shall pay the lawful amends for the killing of the servants and taking the property. The judgment is not executed forthwith, and Sicharius hearing his property has been deposited in the house of Auno, kinsman of his enemy, allies himself with Audinus, and *"postposito placito"* breaks into the house where his enemies are sleeping, kills Austrigisil and others. The clerics then intervene with the authorities and summon both parties to an assembly. The former offer to pay whatever the guilty party may owe, but Chramnisind, the surviving kinsman of Austrigisil, refuses to listen to composition. Sicharius retires to Poitiers where he is struck down by a servant. Chramnisind hears a report that Sicharius is dead, so he gathers his kinsmen, plunders Sicharius' house, burns it, kills various servants and takes all the property. The count then summons the parties, and the judge decides that Chramnisind for his act shall forfeit half the composition that previously had been due him (which Gregory says is against the law but was done to insure pacification) and that Sicharius shall pay the other half. The church supplies funds for Sicharius and the case closes with an oath by both parties to remain friends. The later outbreak of the feud is recounted in Book IX, 19.

[49] *Supra,* note 14.

tral semi-unified law backed by sufficient political strength to erase the differences implicit in the prevailing principle that tribal laws had a personal and not a territorial application.[50] On the other hand, the evolution of procedure for pacific settlement offered opportunities for the piling up of minute interferences with the parties' freedom of action that in the end would add up to a substantial measure of control in the interest of public order without destroying the idea that a misdeed was essentially the concern of the kinsmen on the two sides. This is where one must look for the evolution of a principle competitive with the institution of war, and not in the supposed formulation or encouragement of an idea of general peace, let alone in such improbable notions as manipulations of outlawry either in the guise of a whole people declaring a feud justified[51] and making common

---

[50] 1 Brunner, *D.R.G.*, 382 *et seq.*, has the best account of this in Frankish times. The various tribal laws are the laws for the members, and have no territorial applicability. He cites from Agobard of Lyon, *Adversus legem Gundobadi,* (*M.G.H., Leges,* III, 504) to the effect that often five men would meet none of whom would "have a law in common with the other." Individuals living out of the immediate circle of their tribe would be dealt with on the basis of the law in which they were born. Brunner states this was not an "old German" principle, and is first developed in the *Lex Ribuaria* (31, 3; 61, 2); the *Lex Salica,* he thinks, has no trace of a principle of personality. Nevertheless, it was the spread of the Salic Frank hegemony over widely separated territories that caused the development of the rule.

[51] Suggested by Dahn, *Fehdegang und Rechtsgang, 2 Bausteine* 115. Of course the prevalence of the notion that outlawry is involved as a consequence of all wrongs necessarily has obfuscated the issue—what does the group as a whole do? On this there is little basis for inference before the sixth century. Nevertheless imagination has here run riot. Consider for example how writers have interpreted c. 5 of the *Decretio* of Childebert II of 596 (1 *Cap.* 16) c. 5; "De homicidiis vero ita iussimus observare, ut quicumque ausu temerario alium sine causa occiderit vitae periculum feriatur: nam non de precio redemptionis se redimat aut componat. Forsitan convenit ut ad solutionem quisque discendat nullus de parentibus aut amicis ei quicquam adiuvet; nisi qui praesumpserit ei aliquid adiuvare, suum weregildum omnino componat quia iustum est ut qui novit occidere discat morire." This is an attempt to lay down a rule of general application on wanton homicide, which Wilda, *op. cit.,* 393, believes to be the equivalent of modern murder. The injured kin apparently have the right of refusing to compose, the wrongdoer cannot offer wergeld, and if the hostile

cause with the injured kindred or as a punishment[52] or as a general device for dealing with contempts.[53]

## COMPOSITION PROCEDURE AND COMPOSITION THEORY

Adherence to the meager record of legal institutions among the Germanic peoples of central Europe reduces measurably the postulates commonly thought to underlie the whole scheme of law enforcement during the so-called Frankish period. In-

kinsmen will compose, the wrongdoer's kindred are relieved of collateral liability. The *vitae periculum feriatur,* Brunner—anxious for support for his outlawry theory—thinks is not intended as an indication of public punishment, but merely that the misdoer is to be killed as an outlaw (2 *D.R.G.,* 696, n. 19). Mayer-Homberg, *Die Fränkischen Volksrechte,* 165, asserts since this edict purports to do away with feud in certain cases, its provisions are treated as extending outlawry. Actually the provision is most probably an introduction of a death penalty for a situation previously emendable.

[52] Even in the *Lex Salica* the one presumable reference to folklaw outlawry (55, 2) where the violator of a grave is declared *wargus,* i.e., *expellis* (14, Add. 5, 3a) is not cast in terms of punishment. It provides an expulsion from the district, as a later source, the *Emendata,* explains. The duration of the expulsion is contingent upon composition with the kinsmen and represents thus a form of distraint rather than a punishment. It is characteristic of the early capitulary extension of the death penalty not to exclude the possibility of *redemption* as in *Decr. Child.,* c. 5 cited above, so that even the new sanction of afflictive punishment hangs as a threat of final process rather than inevitable punishment. Compare also *Decr. Child.,* c. 5 on abduction of women (on which offense, Wilda, *op. cit.,* 848) where the penalty is put in absolute form but subsequent formulae indicate the practice of composition: *Form. Marculfi II,* 16; *Form. Tur.* 16; *Form. Sal. Lindbrg.* 16 (cited from Zeumer, *Formulae,* in *M.G.H., Leg.,* Sec. 5).

[53] This contempt proceeding is *royal* not *folk,* and operates within narrow limits, *infra,* p. 52. Mitteis, *Studien zur Geschichte des Versaümnisurteils,* in 42 *Z.R.G.²,* 143 points out if we exclude the obvious additions from royal sources (1 Brunner, *D.R.G.,* 431), the folklaws show nothing regarding a folk contempt proceeding, because the nature of the early procedure was such (viz., summons by bargain) that a contempt proceeding was not essential. Since the judicial summons, as Beyerle points out, is a later development (*cf.* 1 Brunner, *D.R.G.,* 432, n. 21) and proceedings were instituted by an agreement to have a day (Beyerle, *Rechtsgang,* 79 *et seq.*) there is no room for a contempt of court or a judgment *in contumacia.* The most that exists is the sanction for breach of the agreement.

stead of a nicely rounded conceptual system suspended on the twin supports of peace and peacelessness one must begin with a few facts not easily correlated as a matter of modern legal theory: the employment of some afflictive sanctions for unemendable wrongs; the feud; the existence of composition and a core of procedure relating thereto. These matters are determinative of the direction in which organized authority will be active in *developing* a notion of public order. They are determinative because the kinship group and its reaction to injuries remains a dominant social phenomenon throughout even the period of Carolingian hegemony. There is no effort to destroy this; the effort is merely to curb it. Simultaneously certain new tendencies develop out of the use of administrative devices, created as the state becomes strong enough to handle lawlessness where no occasion for private action existed. Nearly everything accomplished by the Frankish rulers toward developing a reign of law and a notion of public order can be accounted for in terms of controlling feud and of filling the gaps where no man was ready to unsheath his sword. These policies will be here considered chiefly in terms of procedure. We shall commence by considering the composition procedure and what was done with it.

Here, of course, main bearings must be taken from the *Lex Salica,* presumably our earliest source.[54] But we must move with caution, for the text of even the oldest surviving manuscript is no mere statement of folkcustom or the rules of folkjudging but is dotted with scraps of king's law.[55] It shows consequently a con-

[54] 1 Brunner, *D.R.G.,* 427 *et seq.,* for the orthodox learning regarding this code. Later literature is cited in the notes *passim*.

[55] The distinction between *Volksrecht* (folklaw) and *Amtsrecht* (official law or king's law) in the early codes was made by Sohm, *Fränkische Reichs und Gerichtsverfassung,* 102 *et seq.,* with some reference to the analogy of the Roman distinction between the *ius civile* and the *ius honorarium*. The folklaw is the customary law of the tribe. The capitularies he describes as norms for the exercise of royal power and not norms of general application (*Rechtsnormen*). As to such a compilation as the

trol of amends procedure advanced to such degree that details of the composition process in its more primitive state are already blurred.

The accretions of king's law in the *Lex Salica* do not, however, obscure the underlying function of the amends procedure. On the contrary, every detail of the process indicates that since wrongful acts produce feud, the process itself exists to dissolve this threatened or actual state of war; there is no sign that it is designed to effect a dissolution of an antecedent outlawry.[56] This procedure, moreover, since it is an implicit denial of the desirability of feud, takes account of the almost ineradicable social-

---

*Lex Salica* the distinction of Sohm is particularly important in the case of provisions like c. 1. In relation to the problems under discussion there is no reason to be involved in the issue whether the folklaw is customary since we are concerned only with the distinctions between law that takes its origin from the people and with whose administration they are directly connected, and the law that emanates from the king, his officials or his court. Both "laws" as 1 Brunner, *D.R.G.,* 407 has shown were in part customary and in part ordained. For the control of procedure what is involved is the coexistence of two powers in law administration. This is indicated by the way in which, on the one hand, royal authority penetrated into the folk procedure at various points either to complement it, to expand it, or to twist it in some new direction. On the other hand the early rise to power of the king and the existence of a king's court among the Franks made possible a legislative development more or less independent of the people at large or their local judicial representatives, the doomsmen. The exercise of this power by the crown differed in respect to the various peoples or tribes (1 Brunner, *D.R.G.,* 408, for examples). The most important particular in which royal activity manifested itself in its law by fiat (*infra,* c. II) will be the growth of a principle of territorial as against personal law. Interesting in this connection are the remarks of Mayer-Homberg, *Die Fränkischen Volksrechte,* 398 *et seq.,* with reference to the role of the *Lex Salica.*

[56] With the magnificently systematic picture drawn by Brunner, *Abspaltungen der Friedlosigkeit (Forschungen,* 444 *et seq.*), we are necessarily in disagreement. Brunner assumes that the phenomenon of outlawry or peacelessness, as it appears in the northern and especially the Scandinavian laws, is one which was likewise indigenous in central Europe. He further is committed to the anachronism of regarding all wrongs as being on the same footing in respect to the reaction which they caused. This viewpoint rests upon an assumed classification already disposed of in the text.

ethical urge for revenge,[57] by embracing certain forms whereby the procedure once instituted, some assurance of its continuance would be guaranteed, and whereby, once it was ended, some assurance would be given that the cause of action would not be revived by violence. This was essential, further, because judgment in a local court during most of the Frankish period, did not itself conclude the parties and did not (to use our own phrase) constitute *res iudicata*.[58]

In the early Frankish sources, there were well-defined vestiges of the pristine characteristics of amends procedure. Despite the

[57] So, Gregory of Tours, *Historia Francorum*, IX, 19: after Sicharius and Chramnisind had sworn to end their feud, the former taunted the latter for having accepted composition. Chramnisind said to himself (*in corde*), "If I do not revenge the death of my kinsmen, then I deserve no longer to be called a man, but to be called a cowardly woman."

[58] Gál, *Die Prozessbeilegung nach den Fränkischen Urkunden VII–X Jahrhunderts, Untersuchungen zur Deutschen Staats und Rechtsgeschichte,* no. 102 (1910), 4, points out that the constant appearance of agreements and judicial orders regarding a repetition of suits would be inexplicable if the Frankish courts had rendered judgments with the force of law, and that in this it differed from the Roman law of the Frank kingdom and the Lombard law. Compare for later Frank-Norman law the statement in *Leges Henrici*, c. 54, 4 (1 Liebermann, *Gesetze der Angelsachsen* [1906] 574): "Item si iusto iudicio inter eos actum sit, nullatenus fieri debet, ut quod iudicio finitum est velud infectum repetatur." The still later development in England is indicated in Bracton, *De Legibus et Cons. Angliae* (Rolls Series), f. 435, where the final concord is put on the same footing as the *exceptio rei iudicatae*.

Gál refers to the fact that the earliest records show a Frankish judgment for the plaintiff contained simply the determination of a contractual duty to perform. Compare also Siegel, *Geschichte der Deutschen Gerichtsverfassung* (1857), 148, who describes the judgment of the doomsmen as not declaratory but constitutive, in the sense of stating what is to be done. *Cf.* Brunner, *Zeugen und Inquisitionsbeweis (Forschungen,* 90, n. 2). In other words, it is nearer to a chancery decree than a judgment on the merits at common law. Gál concludes there was no fundamental obstacle to a renewal of suits. It should be added that there is some controversy as to whether or not a judgment in the king's court was conclusive. *Cf.* Schröder, *D.R.G.,* 416, who says it was not. His proof is Carolingian, viz. the *Capitulare Legibus Additum* of 803, c. 10 (1 *Cap.* 114) which threatened with fine or corporal punishment the revival of actions in the ordinary courts; the *Capitulare Saxonicum* of 797, c. 4 (1 *ibid.,* 71) permitted a revival. *Contra,* 2 Brunner, *D.R.G.,* 687. *Infra,* Chapter II, note 106.

changes wrought by king's law it is obvious that this procedure was originally dominated by the will of the litigants; in short, like modern arbitration between sovereign states, it was utter bargain procedure. Each step toward settlement depended upon consensual agreement—so the summons, the suspension of hostilities, the contract to observe the judgment, the final concord. Since there was only the alternative of actual hostilities if proceedings broke down at any point, various procedural forms had the immediate purpose both of keeping the plea moving and holding the belligerent sibs at bay. Thus, once there had been agreement to litigate, an armistice *pendente lite* was a next necessary step. For this no Frankish formula like the Icelandic[59] or other Scandinavian rituals has been preserved, but it is clear enough from passages in early chronicles that a bargained suspension of hostilities was an integral part of Merovingian amends procedure.[60] This arrangement enabled the cause to get under way, but was a merely temporary forestalling of warfare.

[59] 1 *Grágás*, 114, reproduced with a German translation by Beyerle, *Rechtsgang*, 114–116. For other Scandinavian rituals v. Amira, 2 *Nordgermanisches Obligationenrecht* (1895), 296. In the Anglo-Saxon laws a similar practice is indicated by II *Eadward*, 7 (Liebermann, *Gesetze*, 189–191).

[60] The evidence is collected by Beyerle, *Rechtsgang*, 117 *et seq.* Directly in point is the chronicle of Fredegar (*M.G.H.*, 2 *Scrip. Rer. Merw.*), II, 58. But see the objections of v. Schwerin in 36 *Z.R.G.*[2], 513. More convincing is Fredegar, *Continuatio.*, 2; 3; 4; and Gregory of Tours, *Historia Francorum*, III, 8; VII, 2. The only reference in the folklaws that bears immediately on the matter is Lombard, *Liutprand* 42 (of 732) "Si quis iudex . . . inter homines qui aliquam discordiam habent trewas tulerit, etc.," which points to official intervention probably short of a judicial order. Beyerle treats as probative, evidence regarding the post-Carolingian *treuga* (His, *Gelobter und Gebotner Friede*, 33 *Z.R.G.*[2], 139 *et seq.*). Cf. also his reference to Frensdorf, *Beiträge zur Geschichte und Erklärung der Deutschen Rechtsbücher*, in *Göttinger Nachrichten* (1894), 52 who describes the distinction taken by Bernard of Pavia in his *Summa Decretalium* between *treuga* and *pax*: *treuga* is the security extended as to persons and things where a dispute is unsettled, *pax* is the termination of a dispute. Bernard makes reference to an entirely different set of circumstances growing out of the disordered period that preceded the *Landfrieden* of the German Emperors. There is undoubtedly an historical con-

A further agreement, looking toward final pacification, was therefore necessary—an agreement to observe the judgment[61] whereby the parties bound themselves to make proof or settle as the doomsmen might determine. This carried the plea to the point of judgment. But as the judgment once reached did not bind *ipso vigore,* a final concord (*Ger. Urfehde; ags. unfaeðe*)[62] was requisite. This was the culminating point in the proceeding, for while the final concord was not directly essential to the actual

nection between pre-Carolingian procedure and the *treugas* of the eleventh and twelfth centuries, but this later evidence is not directly probative for early Frankish law.

[61] Beyerle, *Rechtsgang,* 139. The conclusion of an agreement to observe judgment was a necessary consequence of the nature of judgments in Frankish folkcourts. They derive, of course, from the methods of extrajudicial composition, the precursor of judicial settlement. Where liability was admitted, the judgment runs to the amount of amends. Since execution may involve payment in cash or a credit transaction through a contract with adequate pledges, or by gage, symbolizing the amount due (Brunner, *Sippe und Wergeld,* 3 Z.R.G.², 8 *et seq.*), a bargain had to be struck. Where the liability was not admitted the judgment was directed to proof or payment of composition. The proof by oath or ordeal was conceived as alternative satisfaction to the opposing party, and hence in very early times was rendered to the party and not the arbiter. A contract of fulfillment was requisite. The document (*anno* 876) cited in 2 Brunner, *D.R.G.,* 482, n. 60 indicates the dual character of the judgment "repromiserunt quo ita facerent (proof by witness) quod si non fecerint, D (the pledge), suam legem componat et inantea ipse episcopus et eius advocatus faciant quod lex est." The judgment-finder stands originally in a quasi-contractual relation to the parties who demand a judgment as of right, but gradually with the development of a greater governmental control the count (*comes-iudex*) is interposed between parties and judgment-finders and it is he who addresses the question "quod lex est" to the latter.

2 Brunner, *D.R.G.,* 483, has pointed out that the executory judgment can be directed to the making of a contract of fulfillment; if it is final judgment, a contract to make composition (*M.G.H.,* 1 *Dipl.,* no. 66 [693], "sic ei fuit iudecatum, ut in exfaido et fredio solidos quindece pro ac causa fidem facere debirit"). He further indicates that in Merovingian times the tendency is already manifest to point the judgment not toward an engagement but toward execution, and that this tendency became effective with the development of a method of execution against contempts.

[62] 1 Brunner, *D.R.G.,* 226; Grimm, *D.R.A.,* 907, and *cf.* the Frisian formulae in *ibid.,* 53; Wilda, *op. cit.,* 229. Wilda's suggestion that the Anglo-Saxon laws required an oath to observe the king's peace as a part of the final concord is answered *infra,* Chapter VI, pp. 375, 426.

adjudication of the plea, it was vital both for the maintenance and execution of the matter adjudged and to the future peaceful relations of the litigants. It settled the immediate matter in dispute, and more broadly purported to establish a brotherhood[63] between the enemy sibs,[64] and to fix a party peace protected against breach by special sanctions.[65]

[63] The formation of artificial brotherhoods is a well-known phenomenon in early medieval times. There is a discussion of these by Pappenheim, *Über Künstliche Verwandtschaft im Germanischen Rechte*, 29 Z.R.G.[2], 304 *et seq*. Compare also His, *Todschlagsühne und Mannschaft, Festgabe für Güterbock* (1910), 347, where most of the references are for later medieval law. There may be a continuous history here. *Cf.* the *homagium de pace servanda* of the Norman law, *Summa de Legibus* (Tardif Ed.) XXVII, 5. We have indications of the same thing in English law in the *osculum pacis* where a concord is effected; *cf. Select Pleas of the Crown* (Sel. Soc.), 82.

[64] Löning, *op. cit.*, 550, suggests that the person receiving composition assumes a certain suretyship to protect the payer. *Cf. Form. Marculfi II*, 18; *Form. Sal. Lindbrg.*, 19.

[65] Schröder, *D.R.G.*, 86, n. 42 states generally that the breach of the final concord is an unemendable act (*Meintat*). Wilda says (*op. cit.*, 231) that among the Scandinavians it was regarded as a shameful and dire act which could not be composed, but that in the "German" laws it is less severely dealt with. These views are misleading. The problem is at first essentially one of sanctions for the observance of a bargain.

The final concord viewed as a contract contemplates two things: 1) the execution of the judgment which is comprehended in the concord, as the formulae of the late Merovingian period show; 2) the performance of the agreement to remain at peace, the content of which as Gál (*op. cit.*, 5) has pointed out is negative. The duty upon the parties is in either case contractual, so that any action taken against a recalcitrant would have its starting point in the sanction for a broken bargain. At first the initiative lies with the parties for until an independent judicial power is developed the execution of the judgment depends on their good will in performing the contract. Löning, *Der Vertragsbruch im Deutschen Recht*, 50, n. 19 referring to Sohm (*Process der Lex Salica*, 199–219) suggests that the situation changed after the Edict of Chilperich (561–84), c. 7 (8), which he thinks was directed at the forced payment of the composition without necessity of bargain and so reduced party agreement to a mere procedural form. But *cf.* Beyerle, *Rechtsgang*, 150, n. 42. Once the agreement to observe judgment is made, the *fides facta* (i.e., plighting of faith) proceedings indicated in *Lex Salica* 50, 1, 2, 3, will give a right of distraint, by the creditor himself or through the agency of the count; on which compare Löning, *op. cit.*, 50, and 2 Brunner, *D.R.G.*, 594 *et seq*. Brunner treats distraint as an exercise of judicial power derived from a limited outlawry of

The final concord, since it was directed at a complex objective, was an elaborate affair. In the earliest sources, the ending of the dispute required an act of renunciation by the loser and an agreement not to renew the argument by force or by plea.[66] The renunciation was effected by the loser tossing down a staff (*festuca*) as a symbol of defeat,[67] this being followed by an oath of

property and suggests (n. 10) that *Lex Salica* 50, 1, 2, gives a choice of extra-judicial distraint and that 50, 3, is a later addition which allows the creditor to turn to the royal count.

Of course the growth of an autonomous judicial authority and the growth of power to deal with contempt (*infra*, p. 52) involved a fortification of the contract sanctions. In the *Lex Salica*, however, the contempt rules are in their infancy and the point of departure is still that failure to fulfil procedural bargains is not contempt, but is a breach of *fides facta*. On this whole problem *cf.* further, Gierke, *Schuld und Haftung*, 144 *et seq.*; Mayer-Homberg, *Die Fränkischen Volksrechte*, 261 *et seq.*, especially 266 regarding the Ribuarian law.

As to the peace sworn in the final concord, if Schröder correctly surmises concord breach to have been so wicked as to be unemendable, it is strange that clauses of security were embodied in the *securitates* (*infra*, note 71). Thus a concord for homicide, *Form. Sen.*, 11, "ut nullunquam tempore de iam dicta morte nec de ipsa leude (wergeld) nec ego ipse nec ullus de heredibus meis nec quislibet ullas calumnias nec repeditionis agere nec repedire non debeamus. Quod quia adtemptaverimus, nullum obteneat effectum et insuper inferamus tibi una cum sotio fisco auri untias tantas esse multando, et presens securitas omni tempore firma permaneat." Compare also *Form. Sen.* 51; *Form. Marculfi II*, 18 (a double penalty); *Form. Sal. Bign.*, 9; *Form. Extrav.*, I, 8. Gregory of Tours, *Historia Francorum* IX, c. 20 gives the purport of the treaty ending feud between King Guntram and Childebert II (587) "hoc etiam huic addi placuit pactione, ut si qua pars praesantia statuta sub quamcunque callidate . . . transcenderet, omnia beneficia . . . amittat. . . ." While it is possible to regard these provisions as directed only at a renewal of the suit, nevertheless, the nature of feuds was such that any new act of hostility would be regarded as a revival of the old feud, as, for instance, in the Sicharius-Chramnisind feud already mentioned. However, these penal clauses are usual in other types of settlements as e.g., disputes over land. *Cf.* on this Gál, *Prozessbeilegung, 47 et seq.* and generally Löning, *op. cit.*, 132 *et seq.*

[66] Fredegar, *Chron.*, III, 71; Gregory of Tours, *Historia Francorum*, IX, 20.

[67] On this procedure, *cf.* Gál, *op. cit.*, 25 *et seq.*, who indicates that by the tossing of the *festuca* the dispute is symbolically ended and not to be renewed. Brunner (2 *D.R.G.*, 489–490) supposes a concomitant oral declaration. The question naturally arises whether the written concord

pacification.[68] When the payment of composition is on a credit basis[69] the ceremonies for hardening the bargain increase. The marks of the earlier phases through which the final concord passed linger even after the concord is absorbed into regular judicial proceedings.[70] We observe this in the late Merovingian as well as the Carolingian formulae. What is ceremony at first is transmuted eventually into the pallid phrases of a document, the so-called *securitas*,[71] the ancestor of the concords that we later find in English law.

Such in brief are the characteristics of the early Frankish composition procedure. Within this framework judicial authority[72]

(*securitas*) when it becomes usual serves on delivery the symbolic function of the staff; discussed in Gál, *op. cit.;* Beyerle, *op. cit.,* 161 (n. 27). Probably the written concord bears a relation to the actual proceeding itself similar to that of the English indentures which are cast in the form of a remembrance. The Cluny documents recited in Gál (*op. cit.,* 33), all of the 10th or 11th centuries, indicate simply that concern with the dispute is thrown up when the stick is thrown in. (Compare also, for later phraseology two 12th century cases, Bigelow, *Placita Anglo-Normannica,* 264, *History of Procedure,* 371.) If the *festuca* is taken as the gage of the amount in question, the exfestucation in these composition cases has a much narrower significance. Some documents cited by Gál indicate this.

[68] Beyerle, *Rechtsgang,* 162–3. In the exposition of the *Liber Papiensis, Edict. Rothari,* 143 (*M.G.H.,* 4 *Leges,* 313) is given the form of assurances exacted by the judge from the litigants. This, of course, is Lombard. Gál, *op. cit.,* 42, states that there was no legal duty to make a final concord in Merovingian times, but that in the Carolingian period it could be ordered by the court. Furthermore he denies (p. 44) that the court participated in the formulation of the accord in the earlier period. Not until the end of the 8th century is there evidence of such judicial participation. The early formulae show mere mediation.

[69] Brunner, *Sippe und Wergeld,* 3 *Z.R.G.*[2], 8.

[70] Gál, *op. cit.,* 18 indicates that even when the agreement to observe the judgment is supplanted by the court's order, the concord itself remains an essential part of the procedure. Note, however, that the concord itself persists. The judicial process was, of course, not an exclusive method of settlement.

[71] Discussed, Gál, *op. cit.,* 16 *et seq.* Gál (p. 19) states that the *carta composicionis* is the counterpart of the *securitas.* As the former document (*Form. Marculfi II,* 16; *Form. Tur.,* 16; *Form. Sal. Lindbrg.,* 16; *Form. Sal. Merkel.,* 19) is a formula for dowry in case of *raptus,* it may be surmised that this is a special form of concord used only for this contingency.

[72] On the constitution of Frankish courts, Sohm, *F.R.G.V.,* 57 *et seq.,*

asserts itself either to act autonomically, as in the case of process,[73] or to collaborate in the striking party agreements. Even in the oldest texts of the *Lex Salica* there are signs of this expanding power of the courts. Yet it is a gradual expansion for the bargain motive is predominant. Throughout the Merovingian period the courts are largely cast upon party volition and their function is essentially directive until the reforms of Charlemagne.

The interplay of litigant will and judicial authority and the limits within which each is active in the procedural scheme is clearly shown at those points where the procedure cuts closest to the underlying purpose for which it exists—the prevention of feud. Specifically, in the preliminary suspension of hostilities and in the formulation of the final concord, one may observe this process at work.

We have already noticed the fact that party bargains to suspend fighting were used during the Merovingian period.

150 *et seq.;* other references collected in Schröder, *D.R.G.,* §25. We use the expression local court or folkcourt to describe the court held by the count, whether *mallus publicus* or a special court summoned *ad hoc.* The hundred court to which all freemen owe suit is the ordinary court of the Salic Franks. It is at first presided over by the elected *thunginus.* The regular session held at stated intervals is the *mallus publicus.* The court can also be specially summoned to hear pleas. A group of the most experienced and worthy men (constituting at least seven), the "rachinburgs," act as judgment finders. The count is initially merely the executory officer. During the course of the sixth century the presidency of the court falls into the count's hands. He rides circuit for the hundreds in his district, there being no special county court. The system was reformed by Charlemagne who restricted the duty of suit to three *placita generalia* a year. The question is unsettled whether these *placita* were county or hundred courts. Charlemagne further instituted a bench of standing assessors (*scabini*) who functioned as judgment finders in the general courts (subject to vote of the whole body of suitors), and at the specially summoned court (*minus placitum*). After 811, the count also holds *communia placita* in the district of a *missus* for criminal and other business during the months when the *missus* is not functioning. On the *missi dominici, infra,* Chapter III, pp. 166 *et seq.* On the king's court, 2 Brunner, *D.R.G.,* 181.

[73] So in the development of a judicial in place of a party summons, Beyerle, *Rechtsgang,* 91, 96.

There is some evidence that the presiding judicial officer, the *iudex* or the count, actually intervened to arrange the armistice, but it is not until the reign of Charlemagne that he was vested with authority to command the maintenance of peace.[74] Even then the sanctions at the disposal of local officials were not sufficiently potent to make this power completely effective.[75] This may be inferred not only from rather late rules directing that the *faidosus* (i.e., the man against whom feud is waged)[76] be protected when he goes to court, but also from capitularies forbidding the carriage of arms in court.[77] The reappearance of the bargained armistice after the collapse of the Carolingian dynasty suggests, moreover, that this procedural form never was completely supplanted by the judicial peace order.

On the other hand, the procedure with reference to final concord is considerably more illuminating on the growth of judicial power. It is possible here to mark three distinct stages of development. Initially the court appears to have exercised little more than a mediatorial function.[78] But it has certain responsibilities

[74] The German writers use the word *Friedegebot* (*pax decreta*). This is a bidden, ordered or commanded peace. We come across a similar idea in 13th century England in the court orders: *"pacem tenere,"* and *"ut X firmam pacem habeat."*

[75] In the case of the king's court, orders are enforceable by virtue of the king's ban (*infra*, note 107), violation of which costs sixty shillings. The local officers have a power to order in Charlemagne's time (*Cap. Miss.* [802] c. 57 [1 *Cap.* 104]) but penalties for violation are small. The count does not have an *ex officio* power to wield the king's ban, 2 Brunner, *D.R.G.*, 225.

[76] Thus, Beyerle, *Rechtsgang,* 132, suggests that the provisions of the *Lex Frisionum,* Add. 1, 1, which gives a protection in court, church, etc., of the *homo faidosus* are connected with the development of temporary pacification, and are collateral reinforcements of the suspension of hostilities during the course of composition.

[77] *Capitula per Missos cognita Facienda* (803–813) c. 1 (1 *Cap.*, 156). *Capitulare Missorum in Theodonis Villa II,* (805) c. 5 (*ibid.*, 122, 123); for the Italian dominions of Lothar, *Memoria Olonnae* (822–3) c. 5 (*ibid.*, 317, 318).

[78] In contrast to the Visigothic and Burgundian laws the Frankish show only a slight tendency to restrict party initiative in making concord. (Gál, *op. cit.,* 39 *et seq.*) In the *Pactus pro tenore pacis* of Childebert and

in respect to the fiscal interest, viz., the *fredus,* and hence a direct concern in the conclusion of the bargain. The manner in which the rights of the fisc are covered in certain concord formulae suggest that the court participates in the bargain as a party in interest, a fact which at once establishes and yet limits its discretion. The second stage of judicial activity is reached when, without dispensing with formal concord, doomsmen and presiding officer enjoin upon the parties the observance of peaceful relations. The third stage occurs as a result of the judicial reforms of Charlemagne providing a sharp increase in judicial power: peace may be ordered by the court;[79] the parties can be compelled under special penalty to observe their agreements.[80]

Chlothar, c. 3 (1 *Cap.* 5) provision was made against composition of theft (*furtum*), but this was directed only against secret agreements. The question how far fiscal motives predominated, as against the possibility of punishment, is difficult to answer, although one may well believe that the notion of public punishment was scarcely advanced to a point where it would be a determinative factor. We have an interesting analogy much later in England, where the license for concording appeals must come from the king, and where the competing motives are fiscal against the crown's interest in public order. *Cf.* for example: R. C., *Excerpta e Rotulis Finium, 1216–1272,* 214 (1231); 264 (1234); 293 (1235); 303 (1236). Compare also *Summa de Legibus* (Tardif Ed.) LXXV, 3.

[79] Löning, *op. cit.,* 134, relates the Carolingian capitularies, against the feud, *Cap. Haristallense,* (779) c. 22, (1 *Cap.,* 46); *Cap. Saxonicum,* (797) c. 9 (1 *Cap.,* 72); *Cap. Missorum Generale* (802) c. 32 (1 *Cap.,* 97) and *Cap. Originis Incertae* (813) c. 2 (1 *Cap.,* 175) to the *Cap. de partibus Saxoniae* (779–790) c. 31 (1 *Cap.,* 68) and the *Cap. de Legibus Addenda* (818–819) c. 13 (1 *Cap.,* 284) both of which he interprets as intended to coerce pacification. Of the last two the latter agrees with his view but the former only by a stretch of the imagination. More to the point is the *Cap. in Theodonis Villa II* (805) c. 5 (1 *Cap.,* 123) cited in Löning's text, which indicates pacification is to be compelled, with a risk of recalcitrants being hailed before the king. If anyone kills after pacification he is to make composition, lose his perjuring hand, and be put in ban. As Löning very truly points out the sanctions are now increased; a new killing would be homicide, contempt of court and breach of the *fides facta.*

[80] It has been suggested that the final order to observe peace was a form which traveled from the king's court to local courts. Beyerle, *Rechtsgang,* 163. *Form. Aug.,* Coll. B, 40, is an example of a document issued by a count in a folkcourt. *Cf.* also Gál, *op. cit.,* 83. It should be noted that in the

The significance of this legislation lay chiefly in the circumstance that new sanctions were brought to bear. The concord as a part of the composition procedure was not displaced, but the position of the court itself *vis à vis* the parties is enhanced. The element of consensus is not quite expunged, because it is necessary to the execution of the pecuniary settlement. Judicial power concentrates upon the pacification. When this power ceases to speak with authority the bargained concord again becomes the sole and not too effective means of concluding disputes.

We have described the peace-making aspects of the composition procedure, not merely to establish the course of evolution from party bargains to a judicial control more nearly related to our own conceptions of the latter, but to indicate how dependent in the scheme of the folklaws was the preservation of order upon the will of the disputants. The "general peace" as the equivalent of legal order could not have had any great significance when, in the first place, feud could be sustained without flavor of wrong, and when, secondly, even after a judicial proceeding, violence could be resorted to for the same cause of action unless there had been a binding final concord.[81] Quite apart from the important role the latter played in the matter of the conclusiveness of a judgment, it is obvious from its very prevalence that it served a broader social purpose. We do not mean to suggest that the contractual pacification was the only basis of public order up to the time when, in certain cases, an official prosecution of wrongs became usual; back of concords there certainly dwelt a notion that a peaceful state of affairs was desir-

---

late *Cap. Legg. Add.*, c. 13, cited above, the instructions are that pacification is to be *per sacramentum*. This indicates a mere order is not enough, an oath must be taken. There is possibly a distinction to be made between king's court and local practice.

[81] Löning, *op. cit.*, 133, sees the final concord entirely as a part of the composition procedure, and hence (note 1) challenges the position of Wilda, *op. cit.*, 229 *et seq.*, that in this institution there is a "higher" peace. We go further and assert that if there was a "general" peace these concords have nothing whatever to do with it.

able.[82] At the very most, however, the final concord was a device that dealt only with the sorest spots in a turbulent age, and even if one could imagine such a multiplication of such agreements that a legal condition of "general" public order resulted, it is impossible to suppose that such agreements would be observed or enforced on any such scale in the absence of a central authority that possessed a vast and mobile police power.

The truth is that the immediate purpose of composition procedure was too narrow to permit of any wide extension by this device of the state's authority over wrongdoing at large. The process depended too much upon individual or small group initiative. It remained essentially an alternative rather than a successor to settlement by violence. Public prosecution and public punishment could consequently find here little foothold. The exploitable possibilities of this type of public or state control over the feud-composition procedure as a practical matter were exhausted in the most advanced stage of judicial control over pleas when a judicial summons and a judicial injunction to observe the peace had come to crowd out party bargains. It is true that enhancement of the state's role in composition pleas and the legislation eventually directed toward the restriction of feud together had the effect of strengthening such notions of order as were implicit in the composition process itself, making them somewhat more palpable as a postulate for further action by the state. But these concepts could acquire reality only if state intervention were not a fortuitous but a regulated and standardized

---

[82] And from the angle of fiscal profit, the state benefits by the *fredus*—the money that is paid for intervention of judicial authority. The provisions of the *Pactus pro tenore pacis* against secret composition of thefts can be regarded as the expression of the state's desire to preserve its fiscal interest. Beyerle, *Rechtsgang,* 166 appositely describes the public authority as co-creditor in the composition, for this is indicated by such expressions as *inter tibi et fisco* in the formulae. He points out, however, that the judicial order to observe the peace gradually pushes the earlier bargains out of the picture, but that the latter had much to do in opening the way for royal penalties for breach of the order to keep peace.

affair, in other words, when public authority displaced individual whim.

Since a scrutiny of the function of composition procedure at large fails to yield a defined conception of public order in the sense harped on by the dogmatists, it is scarcely to be expected that proofs can be supplied by a study of single procedural forms used in the course of composition.[83] This may be observed from what has been said about the *securitas* which came to end disputes. It is less obvious in the forms of complaint, for these suggest more explicitly the idea of an order transgressed by acts of violence.

Most of the formulae of complaints relate to land actions, but there are some which recite acts of violence to persons or personalty. In these cases there is an allegation by the pleader that the defendant has acted *in malo ordine*,[84] that is to say that he has done something in bad order, or against good order.[85] This

[83] Certainly not in explicit terms of "peace" for *pax* is a technical word. In the *securitas* it means pacification much as in a modern treaty. *Cf.* the title to *Form. Marculfi II*, 18, "Securitas pro homicidio facto si se pacificaverint." *Form. Marculfi II*, 13 is an adoption where *pax* is used in the sense of good relations, and similarly in *Form. Marculfi II*, 14, an agreement regarding inheritance. *Cf.* also *Form. Salicae Merkel.*, 20.

[84] Thus Zeumer in the index of his edition of the *Formulae* gives *ordo = modus*. Note, however, that Gengler, *Germanische Rechtsdenkmäler* (1875), in his glossary *s.v.*, *ordo* gives the meaning of *malo ordine* as equivalent to *iniuste* or against the legal order. Compare also Grimm, *D.R.A.*, 4, who seeking for a German rendering suggests *weise = modus*. The opposite of *malo ordine* is sometimes indicated as *legitime ordine* (*M.G.H.*, 1 *Dipl.*, 34, n. 37 [659]), sometimes *quieto ordine*, a favorite use in some charters. *Ordo* is used in a case (*M.G.H.*, 1 *Dipl.*, 58 n. 66 [693]) in the sense of right or authority. In this same case *malo ordine* is the equivalent of *per forcia* (i.e., like the English *vi et armis*). This expression occurs in some formulae.

[85] This phrase is most often found in connection with claims to property. In the *Formulae* the following may be consulted: *Form. Tur.*, 30, where, although robbery is involved, the statement is *malo ordine adsallivit; Form. Tur.*, 32 where there has been *raptum,* with the woman's consent "in coniugio sibi malo ordine contra legem et iustitiam sociasset," one may quaere whether the property value of the woman is involved; *Form. Tur.*, 33, where there has been assault and robbery the *malo ordine* modi-

meaning is arrived at by eliminating various possibilities. The phrase, according to late Lombard commentators, has no connection with the *mala fides* of the Roman law when used in land actions.[86] Arguing from analogy, it has no connotation of malice in criminal law,[87] particularly since the formulae date from a time when proof of the wrongful act itself convicts,[88] and since such expressions as "at the instigation of the devil and in the commission of sin"[89] describe, albeit naïvely, the offender's state of mind. The *malo ordine* is added to express the idea that the act was against the law, that it was wrongful. This has

fies the *adsallisset*. The *Tours* formulae date from Merovingian times. The *securitas Form. Sen.*, 11, dates from the first years of Charlemagne's reign, and speaks of a killing *malo ordine*. Similarly the *Form. Sal. Lindbrg.*, 19, which dates from the end of the 8th century. Compare also the late *Form. Extrav.*, I, 8.

The most frequent appearances of the *malo ordine* phrase are in cases relating to realty, but land records are preserved when all else is destroyed. In the *Lex Ribuaria*, 57, the term appears in connection with manumission *per denario*. Here the man freed, if his freedom is challenged *inlicite ordine* may defend himself by battle. (*Cf.* Brunner, *Freilassung durch Schatzwurf* in *Historische Aufsätze . . . an Georg Waitz* [1886] 55.) In connection with sales, *malo ordine* appears in *Lex Rib.*, 59, 8. See also the use of *inlicito ordine* in *Lex Rib.*, 72, 1. *Cf.* finally *Lex Alamannorum*, I, 2. On the *Lex Baiuwariorum, infra*, note 91.

[86] In the *Expositio, Liutprand*, 90, §2 (*M.G.H.*, 4 *Leges*): "Lex ista decens 'malo ordine possederit' quibusdam videtur de eo solo, qui sciens res alienas possideat, dicere eo quod in Institutionum lege quadam lege que est 'Super est de officio iudicis' [*Inst.* IV, 17, 2] credens esse suam bona fidei possessor, sciens vero esse alienam male fidei possessor esse asseritur. Sed veraciter arbitratum est, sive a sciente sive a nesciente res aliena (possessa esset) malo ordine dixisse eam esse possessam."

[87] The curiously objective manner in which the secrecy of murder is stated in *Lex Salica* 41, 2, 4, and *Lex Ribuaria* 15 by describing methods of concealment, and the absence of any conceptualized expression like our "malice" seems to bear us out. Murder is deduced from circumstances like hiding the corpse in water or covering it with branches. Compare also Halban, *Das Römische Rechte in den Germanischen Volkstaaten* III (*Untersuchungen*, 89 [1907]), 268, n. 3. 2 Brunner, *D.R.G.*, 715, lists the words such as *per malum ingenium, per invidiam, in inamicitiam* that are used to express our "malice."

[88] Brunner, *Über Absichtslose Missetat im Altdeutschen Strafrecht* in *Forschungen*, 487 *et seq.*

[89] *Form. Sal. Lindbrg.*, 19.

been established for the land actions[90] and it is hardly to be denied that where distinctly delictual matter is at issue the meaning is the same. But it is prudent not to impute too much substantive content to this phrase, since its presence in the formulae must undoubtedly be accounted for on grounds of immediate procedural function.

In formulary procedure, barring cases of mere tautology, the presence of words and phrases has ordinarily a procedural purpose. The form once set is grimly static; still, additions do occur in response to contemporary need. The most rigid type of such procedure is supposed to have consisted of a complaint in form certain with which the answer must concur in every detail,[91] the plaintiff's purpose being presumably to force admission or denial, at which juncture a judgment occurs which will either be final or advance the cause to the stage of proof. In the formulae

[90] Hübner, *Immobiliarprozess,* 34. He emphasizes the point that all pleas in German law are originally delictual (*Deliktsklagen*) and those for land retain these characteristics. This characteristic he thinks is expressed by the allegation *malo ordine* (*ibid.,* 44). Hübner indicates that the allegation is intended to convey the idea of an act by the defendant contrary to law ("ein rechtswidriges Verhalten des Beklagten").

[91] Thus *Lex Baiuwariorum* 17, 1, speaks of an entry upon (*invaserit*) the fields or garden of another *contra legem malo ordine,* and 17, 2, the man who enters thus, swears: "non invasi contra legem." The normal expectancy in a period of strict formulary procedure is that the form used in the action would conform to the statute. We must assume that 17, 1, since it makes the entry a matter of composition, contemplates a complaint which corresponds with the terms of the law, i.e., an allegation that the act was *contra legem malo ordine.* In these circumstances the defense that entry was not *contra legem* would include an answer to the allegation *malo ordine,* and we could say the two were equivalent. Against this argument compare Grimm, *D.R.A.,* 33, who states that to the allegations of the plaintiff the defendant answers "de torto me adpellasti," a sort of blanket retort. All of Grimm's examples are from the later Lombard law, and are not probative for the early period, particularly as a blanket defense is characteristic of a much later stage of procedural development. The formulary procedure required a word for word reply. *Cf.* Brunner, *Wort und Form im Altfranzösischen Prozess (Forschungen,* 260). What Hübner has to say about the way the *malo ordine* is met, supports the position in this note; *cf.* his *Der Immobiliarprozess der Frankischen Zeit (Untersuchungen,* no. 42) 95, *et seq.*

where *malo ordine* is employed the acts complained of are circumstantially described.[92] There are no words directly alleging peace breach—which one would expect if the concept of peace existed. In later Germanic and English law when a peace concept does come to exist, we have a peace breach formula. The question, nevertheless, arises whether or not these words of *malo ordine* can be regarded as an equivalent. Clearly, however, in a system of law and procedure where certain kinds of killing, burning and dispossession are countenanced, viz., in feud, a reference to "order" is qualified. It by no means embraces a conception that all violent acts are infractions of a peace. It goes no further than an allegation that the act *in malo ordine* falls into the category of violence not lawful or, at least, of which the person injured can complain without risk of the penalties for a false complaint. The situation is such that the plaintiff will wish to allege that his case falls in the category of acts for which liability is already fixed so that the defendant should answer as an aggressor. At the same time, by asserting the wrongfulness of the act he attempts to foreclose an answer which might put him to proof and not the defendant.[93] But the doomsmen give a judgment of

[92] For example, *Form. Tur.*, 30; 32; 33; *Form. Sal. Bign.*, 9.

[93] The anticipation of the Salic law is that the defendant will make proof (2 Brunner, *D.R.G.*, 502), but there are cases where the law specifically stipulates proof by one or the other party. Beyerle's view is that in its earliest phases the composition plea supposes purgation by the defendant as a matter of duty. When proof is made to the judge and not the other litigant, both sides can offer to prove, and direct proof comes to be preferred over mere compurgation (*Rechtsgang*, c. 3). It should be observed that as the judgment lies midway between the initial pleadings and the making of proof, and as the judgment declares both what is the law and who is to prove and how, or the law and the sentence (*Form. Tur.*, 32), the complaint must be formulated so as to produce 1) a favorable ruling on the law, and 2) a ruling on proof favorable to the plaintiff. We believe *the question of the law judgment was one where proof could be required*, not in the ancient formal sense but rational proof. The power of the presiding judge to inquire through witnesses has been traced to the Visigothic *Codex Euricianus* through *Lex Baiuwariorum*, 9, 18, and *Lex Alamannorum*, 42, where a proceeding of rational proof to foreclose compurgation is stipulated. The issue, "was the conduct wrongful?" is clearly formu-

law as well as a direction as to proof or liability. This judgment must take into account the fact that there is considerable range of permitted violence. Consequently, for all the plaintiff's care to meet this situation, his allegation that the acts complained of are in "bad order" may nevertheless have the effect of permitting the defendant to avoid an answer of denial by excepting to the charge,[94] i.e., he can show that he killed in feud, that he acted in self-defense, that he took under color of right.[95] These facts show clearly enough that we are not dealing here with an allegation of a general peace, but with a much narrower conception of order, to which the procedure is adapted.

The use of *malo ordine* in a great diversity of cases, particularly those which are not delictual, leads one to suppose that the scope of judicial action was probably increased through the power which the courts clearly had of inquiring into the wrongfulness of the acts complained of,[96] and thereby slowly extend-

lated by the *malo ordine*. In a number of early Frankish cases we see the court interrogating the defendant, *infra*, note 96. If the defendant does not deny but confesses (*Form. Tur.*, 32) there will be immediate sentence. If he excepts (*infra*, note 94) the judgment is found in terms to meet the issue so raised (*M.G.H.*, 1 *Dipl.*, 45, n. 49; *Form. And.*, no. 28). The plaintiff can offer testimony when he complains (*M.G.H.*, 1 *Dipl.*, 103, n. 16) and here is judgment forthwith. The rule *Lex Rib.*, 67, 5, where plaintiff makes a positive case by foreoath is a development of this. The rule *Lex Rib.*, 59, 8, is the formalized result of the exception practice, i.e., if the defendant can produce charters he does not answer the *malo ordine* of the complaint.

[94] The view once held that in Frankish procedure no exceptions were possible is now abandoned: Beyerle, *Rechtsgang*, 240 *et seq.;* van Kuyk, *Historische Beschouwingen over het Antwoord* (1908), 46 *et seq.* Certainly the defense in such cases as, e.g., *M.G.H.*, 1 *Dipl.*, 62, no. 70; p. 45, no. 49, is to be treated as by way of exception.

[95] *Form. Sal. Bign.*, 9, "quod faciente inimicum ipsum hominem occidisset." *Form. Tur.*, 30, is apparently an official complaint not set forth but defendant denies that he killed *malo ordine*, but *necessitate conpulsus*. On the color of right *cf.* in the earliest formulae, *Form. And.*, 47.

[96] This followed from the defendant's exception and is indicated by early cases. 13 *Neues Archiv* 157 (648); *M.G.H.*, 1 *Dipl.*, 53, n. 59; p. 62, no. 70; and the curious case after a default, *ibid.*, p. 58, no. 66. The later formulae are clear from *Form. Sen. Rec.*, 7; *Form. Aug.* (B), 40; *Form. S. Emm.*, 1 and 2; *Form. Sal. Merk.*, 27 and 28.

ing the limits of forbidden conduct. Except, however, where out-right legislation added to the courts' powers, this process was a mere cumulation of cases where amends were payable. There was here no shift in the basic standards of order, such as they were, which underlay the system of procedure.

The complaint and the final concord are the two procedural forms where, if anywhere, one would expect to discover support for the conception of a general peace. We have shown that this expectation is vain, when one considers these forms in terms of the persistence of folklaw. It remains to be seen whether, in view of the intrusion of king's law into even the earliest sources, a different interpretation may be maintained. The validity of such an approach is questionable as long as the development of royal authority in the composition process is seen for what it was, a strengthening of administration,[97] and not a reconstruction of the whole social scheme on which the expectancy of litigants rested. But such a view, based though it be on what has been said about the scope and function of composition, meets obstruction in the premise which the adherents of a general peace have formulated for the Frankish period, namely, that the folkpeace becomes the king's peace.[98] Every folklaw provision, every writ, every capitulary law has been expounded on the basis of this as-sumption, so that whatever is identifiable as king's law is inevi-tably treated as a manifestation of this process. This theory rests on evidence not yet discussed. It must be here examined, for it is critical not only as to the matter already discussed but likewise as to the growth of law-enforcing devices outside the feud-com-position scheme that are as yet to be examined.

### THE THEORY OF THE KING'S PEACE

The growth of a king's peace is supposed to proceed in two ways: the crown extends a personal "peace"; the crown also, by

---

[97] Sickel, *Beiträge zur Deutschen Verfassungsgeschichte, M.I.Ö.G.,* 3 EB., 455.
[98] 2 Brunner, *D.R.G.,* 55.

assuming charge of law enforcement generally, becomes the guardian of the old folkpeace. The second part of this theory depends largely upon inferences drawn from the presumable establishment of a personal king's peace. This peace is one of those "higher peaces" already mentioned. As usually depicted it consists of a special protection which the law accords the king's person, and of certain prerogatives which the crown exercises by reason of its unique legal and political status.

The evidence regarding the special protection for the king in early Frankish law is conflicting. In the *Lex Salica* interferences with his personalty are amended with a higher rate of composition than in other cases,[99] but unlike the Lombard[100] or Anglo-Saxon law[101] there is no sign of a personal inviolability in the use of any special sanctions for violence committed in his castle or in the vicinity of his person.[102] On the other hand, the history of Gregory of Tours indicates that the Roman idea of *laesae maiestatis* had gained a foothold in the law,[103] for the killing of a king is punished with death[104] and lesser offenses to royalty were

[99] The ratio between the king and an ordinary man is roughly as 3 to 1; *cf. Lex Salica*, 25, 4; 38, 2, Add. 2.

[100] *Rothari*, 36.

[101] Liebermann, *Glossar, s.v., Königsfrieden*. For the Scandinavian practice, Lehmann, *Der Königsfriede der Nordgermanen*, 215; Wilda, *op. cit.*, 259–260. The rules in *Lex Alamannorum*, 29, 2; 31; *Lex Baiuwariorum*, c. 2; *Lex Frisionum*, 17, 2, regarding the protection of the local duke, are probably the reflection of royal legislation.

[102] 2 Waitz, *D.V.G.*, pt. 1, 196: "There is no question among the Franks of a wergeld for the king." Brunner, 2 *D.R.G.*, 60, states that a capitulary of Pippin of 768 assumes a local king's peace (in the sense of the Anglo-Saxon laws) because of the triple amends for theft in the king's court. But this document deals only with property violation in respect of which Frank kings had a recognized right to a higher tariff and has nothing to do with fighting or shedding blood in the king's court as in the case of Anglo-Saxon or Lombard laws.

[103] So Waitz, 2 *D.V.G.*, pt. 1, 195, and compare the list of passages cited from Gregory's *Historia*, at 196, n. 3. See also Roth, *Geschichte des Beneficialwesens* (1850), 130–131. Roth thinks the death penalty attached to a killing of the king and hence no wergeld. For an indication that there are traces of an idea of *laesae maiestatis* in the Salic law, *cf. Lex Salica*, 14, 4.

[104] *Historia Francorum*, II, 42.

strictly dealt with. The significance of this evidence as a statement of law and not merely of policy is however somewhat diminished by the account of King Gunthram pleading with an
assembled multitude not to kill him as they had his brother.[105]
One may suppose a certain popular resistance to Roman theories
that would explain the painful concentration of the Merovingian kings upon fabricating a direct bond of fidelity to the
crown. It will later be shown that until the ninth century the
fidelity notion was without general implications for criminal
law, and the net result of the Merovingians' efforts to place
themselves beyond plot and assassinations goes no further than
the provision of the late *Lex Ribuaria* inflicting death penalty
for infidelity.[106]

Although there is no reason to assume a mystic personal peace
safeguarding the Frankish king and his environs, it is not to be
denied that he possessed prerogatives arising out of his political
preeminence enabling him to make exceptions to the ordinary
course of the law. The most vital of these prerogatives was the
so-called ban power—the power to make orders and to have for
disobedience a mulct of 60 shillings,[107] an amount collectible in

---

[105] *Historia Francorum,* VII, 8: "adjuro vos, o viri cum mulieribus
qui adestis, ut mihi fidem inviolatam servare dignimini, nec me, ut fratres
meus nuper fecistis, interematis."

[106] *Lex Ribuaria,* 69, 1. Compare also *Form. Marculfi I,* 32, where the
death of the king is included in instances of rebellion.

[107] The variety of meanings attached to the word *bannus* makes it necessary for us constantly to specify in what sense it is being used. *Cf.* Grimm,
*Deutsches Wörterbuch, s.v., Bann.* Schröder, *D.R.G.,* 121 calls the right of
ban the authority to issue administrative penal ordinances. Waitz, 2
*D.V.G.,* pt. 1, 210 *et seq.* apparently regards it as the general royal ordinance power. Brunner, 1 *D.R.G.,* 200 *et seq.;* 2 *ibid.,* 46 *et seq.,* distinguishes between Peace-ban, Administrative-ban and Ordinance-ban. Some
remarks about the history are in Sickel, *Zur Geschichte des Bannes* (1883),
3. The earliest reference in terms: Gregory, *Historia Francorum,* V, 26,
and compare VIII, 30, for the army ban. Most of what is written about the
ban is derived from its use by the Carolingians. The evidence in Merovingian times is feeble. Sohm, *F.R.G.V.,* 103 *et seq.,* sees in the ban no legal
restriction but the manifestation of sovereign power. The 60 shillings

certain cases by a purely administrative procedure.[108] The first explicit mention of the king's ban is made in connection with royal authority over the army, and this may well be where the ban originates. In any event it carries over to other phases of royal authority, becoming eventually, as Sohm[109] described it, the *imperium* of German institutions.

This power of the crown to do something exceptional manifests itself at the very dawn of Frankish supremacy in the extension to individuals of particular royal protection.[110] The notion of special protection has been discussed in relation to specific places. Its application to individuals or classes of persons appears to have had an origin quite independent of causes which gave rise to place protection. Personal protection of course is implicit in the sib's concern with injuries to its members and more narrowly in the *mundium* or guardianship exercised by the head of a family over its members, including the half-free and the slaves.[111] These relationships found expression in the law in certain responsibilities, such as the liability of the sib for its mem-

mulct for violation he sees as a penalty and not related to the compensatory tariffs of the folklaws. He (169 *et seq.*) holds separate from the king's ban all other manifestations of official ordinance power to which money penalty is attached. Brunner, 1 *D.R.G.*, 200, attempts to correlate all these powers to order and fine for disobedience, and appears to find some connection with the judge's command that "peace" be observed in the court with an inherent ban power. This cannot be proved from early sources. On the contrary the judicial mulcts of the *Lex Salica* of 15 sol. (1, 1, 2; 48, 1 Add. 2; 49, 2, 3) are not based on a contempt, nor are they multiples of king's ban, but are the folklaw tariff for bargain breach, *Lex Salica* 50; *cf.* Beyerle, *Rechtsgang,* 105.

[108] 2 Brunner, *D.R.G.*, 54 states that where there was simultaneously a "breach of the peace" and a violation of the ban, the ban penalty was collectible only after a judgment, if the misdeed was denied and not handhaving. He cites one case of the year 802. In mere administrative matters the fisc used an administrative distraint.

[109] Sohm, *F.R.G.V.*, 103.

[110] So the letter of Chlodwig to the bishops (507-11) 1 *Cap.* 1-2.

[111] 1 Gierke, *Das Deutsche Genossenschaftsrecht,* 21 *et seq.*; 1 Brunner, *D.R.G.*, 93 *et seq.*; in 2 Graff, *Althochdeutscher Sprachschatz* (1834–1846) 813 the Latin *protector* = *munt.*

bers,[112] or the head of the house for acts of the slave.[113] They constitute the usual or normal type of protective associations, but the protection of the king is abnormal because it put the individual outside the ordinary operation of the law. For this reason it is difficult to account for king's protection as some have done, as a guardianship substituting for the sib as the latter declined.[114] And the explanation that it is evolved out of the *tuitio* of the Roman law does not account for all its peculiarities.[115] These suggestions are apposite in explaining the later phases when whole classes of persons are taken under the royal wing— women, infants, clerics, Jews and merchants,[116] as the ban power

[112] This is of course a much broader protection relationship than that involved in the narrower guardianship functions of the sib over women and infants where there was no father, on which *cf.* 1 Brunner, *D.R.G.,* 124 *et seq.* The notion discussed in the text is explained by Brunner and others as the "peace-association" (*Friedensverband*) of the sib, *ibid.,* 119.

[113] 1 Brunner, *D.R.G.,* 92; 2 *ibid.,* 723 *et seq.*; G. Meyer, *Die Gerichtsbarkeit über Unfreie und Hintersassen,* 2 *Z.R.G.²,* 90 *et seq.*

[114] Schröder, *D.R.G.,* 355, 121, where the *verbum regis* (royal protection) is treated as a phase of ban power. Brunner in 2 *D.R.G.,* 63, indicates that passages in the *Lex Salica* which give the king a right to the wergeld of a sibless man are logical deductions of a general royal protection. His instance of the fisc's claims to the heritage and wergeld of the *cartularii* (persons freed by charter) seems to be attributable to Carolingian legislation, since in *Lex Alamannorum* 16, the church was entitled.

[115] Tamassia, *"Verbum Regis" Franco e "Auxilii Latio" Romana,* in 88 *Archivio Giuridico* (1922) 3 *et seq.* Tamassia's argument is very ingenious. He traces the relation of the Frankish use of *sermo* (i.e. protection) to the terminology in the Byzantine law as the equivalent of λόγος, used in the sense of security, important in connection with charters of immunity to the church. He cites also two cases of an imperial *verbum* (protection) as a safe conduct from letters of Pope Gregory the Great. Tamassia thinks that the *verbum regis* assumes the meaning of protection by logical deduction from the fact of having promised to defend. He believes moreover that the expression originally has nothing to do with the ban. Relating the *verbum regis* to the *auxilii latio* of the tribune of the plebs, he indicates the power of the latter passing to the emperor was acquired by the German kings as proconsuls of Gaul. His chain of title includes evidence of a similar institution among the Ostrogoths and its adaptation by the church.

[116] 2 Brunner, *D.R.G.,* 72–73. Consult also the *Cap. Missi Gen.* (802)

of the king expands.[117] But in its earliest phases the protection was probably no more than the king capitalizing his political position and particularly the control of his own court for the benefit of favorites.

The special term by which the royal protection is known is the *verbum regis*, an expression occurring at least once in the *Lex Salica* in this sense.[118] Some idea of its scope can be gathered

c. 5 (1 *Cap.* 93) where churches, widows, orphans and pilgrims are named, and frauds, robberies and injuries generally are forbidden.

[117] The ban power is already evidenced, according to Brunner, in the penalty for *raptus* of a girl in *verbo regis* mentioned in the *Lex Salica*, 13, 6. This needs some explanation. The word *bannus* means, originally, *order*, and by derivation is applied also to the penalty for violation of the order; Schröder, *D.R.G.*, 122. The mulct of 60 sol. is consistently maintained as a basic ban penalty even during the Carolingian period; Sickel, *Zur Geschichte des Bannes*, 4. It is important to note in this connection that the *bannus* differs essentially in theory from the *fredus*. The latter, it will be recalled, is the money which, as a part of the final composition, goes to the state for its intervention in the settlement of a wrong. It was not primarily conceived of as penal and hence differs from the basic theory of the 60 sol. penalty. The idea of exacting a payment as a pure penalty represents a development outside the theory of the law of composition. Waitz, in 2 *D.V.G.*, pt. 2, 292, indicates Roman influence. Schröder, *D.R.G.*, 370 suggests also ecclesiastical influence. The fact that the ban is first mentioned in connection with the failure to perform military service is a sufficient explanation of the necessity of a penal provision. Military duty stands outside the ordinary range of kinship relations, and its violation is a different sort of wrong than those for which feud can be waged. On the use of the ban here Sickel, *Zur Geschichte des Bannes*, 3 *et seq.* Of course, as Waitz points out, the use of the ban as penalty in connection with the judicial power is closely related to the army ban, as are likewise the confiscation provisions of the laws. For detailed references see 2 Waitz, *D.V.G.*, pt. 1, 210; pt. 2, 286, 360. See also 2 Brunner, *D.R.G.*, 50.

[118] *Lex Salica*, 13, 6. The title concerns the *raptum* of free women: "Si vero puella qui trahitur in verbum regis fuerit fritus exinde MMD dinarios qui faciunt solidos LXIII est." In some texts the word *furban* appears in place of *fritus* (*fredus*) which leads Sohm, *Fränkische Reichs und Gerichtsverfassung*, 109, to assert that here the king's ban stands in place of the old *fredus*.

Reference should be made to *Lex Sal.*, Cap. I, 6 (Hessels, 72), regarding the remarriage of a widow and the king's claim in the absence of heirs to a share in her original *dos* effectuated by putting her "in verbo regis." *Cf.* Schröder, *D.R.G.*, 333; and Brunner, *Die Fränkisch-Romanische Dos*,

from two stories in Gregory's history. In one case[119] is told the
tale of a girl who kills her would-be ravisher while he is sleeping, and who then flees to the king. The latter "in his mercy
then not merely gave her her life but even ordered there be issued
a precept that she be placed in his protection (*in verbo suo po-
sita*)" so that she should never suffer violence at the hands of the
deceased's kindred. In the other instance,[120] a killing after final
concord, the perpetrator would have escaped retribution had not
his victim been in the protection of the Queen Brunichild,
wherefore he was obliged to flee and his property was then confiscated.

In the first of these instances are two facts worthy of consideration. The king issues a precept by which the protection is
granted, and he is able to forestall the consequences of feud.
Now we know that even in the *Lex Salica* is attested the notion
that the crown would punish contempt of a royal precept.[121]
The documented *verbum regis,* therefore, gave the advantage
that a breach of the protection was an offense against the king.
In addition to the rather negative benefit of having his ad-
versary subject to a severe money penalty if he flouted the precept, the chief advantages of the position in which a person in
*verbo regis* stood, lay in the fact that he had a triple wergeld,
that he was eventually protected against civil claims of relatives,
that he was privileged to have pleas tried in the king's court, and
that he could appear by representative.[122] The number of formu-

*Sitzungsberichte der Berliner Akad.* (Hist.-Phil. Klasse, 1894), 545; see
also *Lex Sal.,* Cap. I, §7. Compare *Lex Ribuaria,* 35, 3.

[119] *Historia Francorum,* IX, 27.

[120] *Ibid.,* IX, 19. Compare also the letter of Radegundis in *ibid.,* IX, 42.

[121] *Lex Sal.,* 56. Compare the king's speech in Gregory, *Hist. Franc.,*
VIII, 30. See also *Lex Sal.* 14, 4.

[122] *Lex Salica,* Cap. I, 7. There is here a cumulation of privileges. On
wergeld, Sickel, *Beiträge zur Diplomatik* III, 74 *Sitzungsberichte der
Wiener Akad.* (1864) 265 *et seq.;* Brunner, *Zeugen und Inquisitionsbeweis*
(*Forschungen,* 88) 134–5. The protection against civil claims, *Lex Sal.,*
Cap. I, 7 (Hessels, 71). On judicial privileges, Brunner, *Mithio und Sper-
antes,* in *Festgabe für Beseler* (1885), 4 *et seq.* In general on the effect of

lae[123] dealing with these *verba* are some indication of the consequence of this institution in the development of a law that moved outside the normal composition procedure.

Standing alone, this special protection suggests nothing of a general king's peace; indeed its employment throws doubt on the very existence of this idea or at least of its legal sufficiency. Certain bold spirits, however, have sought to relate the special protection to the spread of their king's peace by correlating all the references to *verba regis* with certain passages in the laws which use the expression *"extra sermonem regis."* Out of this correlation has been constructed a system of protection with two sides, the special protection to individuals and a general protection that covers the population at large.[124]

The phrase *extra sermonem regis,* from which a general protection has been deduced, occurs in the *Lex Salica*[125] in connec-

the *sermo regis, cf.* also Halban, *Königsschutz und Fehde* in 17 *Z.R.G.*², 63 *et seq.,* who does not differ with Brunner and Sickel on the two phases of protection; Frensdorff, *Recht und Rede,* 477, has well-founded doubts regarding the existence of this double protection. The discussion in 2 Brunner, *D.R.G.,* 62 *et seq.,* treats the whole matter under the rubric "King's Protection" as distinguished from the preceding section on "King's Peace."

[123] Sickel, 3 *Beiträge zur Diplomatik,* 182, points out that of the twelve formulae, only three can be placed before the year 800. *Form. Marculfi I,* 24, goes back to the seventh century, and note the expression "sub sermonem tuicionis nostre." The other formulae are discussed by Sickel and also by Halban, *Königsschutz und Fehde,* 69 *et seq.,* who emphasizes that in relation to general law the king's protection remains true to the principle that the general law is departed from only when unavoidable.

[124] 2 Brunner, *D.R.G.,* 55, 63. Sickel, 3 *Beiträge zur Diplomatik,* 47 *Sitzungsberichte der Wiener Akad.* (1864) 241, speaking of the king's protection, says there have been two distinguished types: "That which arose out of the one-time folkpeace, the king's peace which appertains to the whole people, and a special king's peace for spiritual institutions, for certain classes of helpless persons or for individuals on the basis of a special grant." He mentions also Roth's theory of an ancient protection for the *trustis dominica* and Maurer's notion of a protection emanating from the king's ownership of land.

[125] *Lex Salica,* 56; Cap. II, 8 (Hessels, 106); and compare also the Edict of Chilperich, c. 10 (1 *Cap.* 10).

tions which have been described as outlawry—an outlawry in the sense that the individual is set out of the king's peace and consequently, as a peaceless man, may be killed, cannot be harbored and suffers forfeiture of his goods.[126] There can be no doubt that one of the chief reasons for thinking that by *extra sermonem regis* is indicated an expulsion from the king's protection is the fact that such an idea complements the *in sermonem tuitionis nostris* employed in certain formulae for the king's special protection. This logic assumes that *sermo* is a word of single meaning, and that the *extra sermonem* of the *Lex Salica* is necessarily the opposite of the *in sermone tuitionis* of the formulae. This cannot be maintained if the several passages in early sources where the expression or variance occurs—*Lex Salica,* 56 and 106, Edict of Chilperich, c. 10—are viewed in terms of procedural function instead of being combined to produce juristic ideas *in vacuo.* In the *Lex Salica* itself, where the expression *extra sermonem* occurs it is a part of the final process against a defendant who refuses attendance at the king's court. In the Edict of Chilperich it is a punishment against professional malefactors.

*Lex Salica* 56 supplies the want of a folkcourt procedure for dealing with contumacy[127] by giving the plaintiff the right of

---

[126] 1 Brunner, *D.R.G.,* 201, n. 29; 2 *ibid.,* 55; Sohm, *Sermo Regis, Berichte der Sächsischen Gesellschaft der Wissenschaften* (1901), 1, thinks the *sermo regis* is synonymous with the king's ban; it is the "word" of the king as the representative of the people; the word of the king creates the peace; a man out of the king's word is out of the peace. He further suggests the relation of *sermo* to the assembly about the king and for this has a similar syllogism. Böhtlingk, *Sermo Regis,* in *ibid.,* 45, takes the full passage in *Lex Salica,* 56, "tunc rex ad quem mannitus est [summoned] extra sermonem suum ponat eum. Tunc ipse culpabilis et omnes res suas erunt." He thinks the first sentence is the basis for the second. If the "extra sermonem" meant outlawry, the "tunc ipse culpabilis" would be a senseless redundancy. Consequently he offers the suggestion that the king will not be bothered with the contumacious one any more. He is then condemned without a sentence in judgment for the matter about which complaint has been made.

[127] *Supra,* note 53.

recourse to the king's court. This remedy, a matter of king's law, lies not after a mere contempt of summons in the folkcourt but at a later stage: after the bargain to observe the judgment has been made,[128] and the defendant fails to appear. The royal summons then ensues and if the defendant fails upon successive summons to appear, the king puts him out of his *sermo;* then a judgment and confiscation of goods. Harboring of the contumax entails a 15 sol. mulct. The same procedure is stipulated in *Lex Salica* 106 for the case of proceedings between two *antrustiones* (king's guardsmen), the provisions here apparently taken bodily from the earlier passages.[129] In both the cases the defendant *extra sermonem* remains in this state until he settles his legal obligations.

In contrast with these rules Chilperich's Edict uses the *extra sermonem* not as mesne process but as a punishment. It is so used against only the judgment-proof professional malefactor who lurks in the woods. The edict contemplates a complaint before neighbors carried to the doomsmen (*rachymburgi*) with proof by the complainant in the form of a foreoath. This has the effect of making certain the fact that the defendant is a bad man who does wicked acts in the district, has no substance and is in hiding. The count and the accuser then go to the king who puts the malefactor *extra sermonem;* he may be killed by anyone without risk of feud.[130]

---

[128] So Mitteis, *Studien zur . . . Versaümnisurteils,* 42 Z.R.G.², 148.

[129] So Sohm, *Process der Lex Salica,* 187, n. 10.

[130] Edict of Chilperich (561–84) c. 10 (1 *Cap.* 10). That the *extra sermonem* is here something extraordinary, and not intended to apply to persons at large who are contumacious but capable of settling their obligations is even more obvious if one reads the passage in connection with the immediately preceding chapters. In c. 8 the Edict has revised the old law about distraints. (*Cf.* 4 Bethmann-Hollweg, *Civilprozess,* 521 *et seq.;* Planitz, *Vermögensvollstreckung,* 48 *et seq.*) It goes on to deal with the *malus homo* who commits evil deeds and has no property to make composition. This man is to be taken by the count and offered at successive sessions of the court to his kin for redemption. At the fourth court if he is not redeemed he is then turned over to his accusers to be dealt with as

It is clear from the nature of the proceedings described in the *Lex Salica* 56 from which alone a general rule as to ordinary persons is to be deduced, that there is no justification in assuming as did Brunner and others, that the defendant ever was *in sermone,* i.e., protected. Quite apart from the illogic of the assumption it would have to be *in sermone regis* to match the *extra sermonem regis* of the text. This would point to a royal protection—a *verbum regis,* always a special thing, yet the passage itself lays down a remedy in no way contingent upon any special rights of the defendant. This dilemma Brunner (and others) sought to avoid by postulating a lower level of protection, i.e., a king's peace extant as to all subjects, and he based his premise on his interpretation of *extra sermonem* as a general outlawry, because of the confiscation of the defendant's property and the prohibition on harboring.

This seems very fanciful. The rule of *Lex Salica* 56 is a rule of

they see fit. (On this proceeding, *infra,* Chapter II, p. 87.) C. 10 makes provision for the *malus homo* who is described as doing wrong in the district, without substance and lurking in the woods, in other words the professional judgment-proof criminal. He is condemned by the crown if the description of *malus homo* is established *certe,* i.e. if the plaintiff has complained to his neighbors and the foreoath has been taken before the doomsmen (*rachymburgiis*) on which *cf.* Beyerle, *Rechtsgang,* 251. On the basis of this certainty (implying a judgment) then (tunc) the count and the plaintiff accuse before the crown and the king "mittemus foras nostro sermone ut quicumque eum invenerit quomodo sic ante pavido interfitiat." In this last sentence some words are probably missing; it is exceedingly obscure. Brunner, 2 *D.R.G.,* 607, n. 12, says the *malus homo* is killed as an outlaw. Other interpretations collected in Goldmann, *Beiträge . . . zur Kapitularien* in 36 *M.I.Ö.G.,* 588. The case is clearly a special form of *extra sermonem,* fixed for the professional malefactor and giving a right to kill him. The attempt to treat the words *sic ante* as a reference to earlier practice (i.e. Sohm, *Process der Lex Salica,* 188; Kern's note in Hessels' *Lex Salica*) suggests a practice of killing as to any person *extra sermonem* under *Lex Salica,* 56. We believe the *sic ante* = *ut supra* and refers to the earlier paragraph regarding the *malus homo* turned over to his accusers for execution, i.e. it is a reference to the execution, the remedy here being given to anyone. It can hardly be a rule as to the *extra sermonem* of *Lex Salica,* 56 because: 1) this proceeding is limited to persons who have failed to observe the bargain for judgment, 2) the law there specifically contemplates a chance for the defendant to satisfy claims, 3)

the king's court made to solve the problem of contumacy there. It is obviously based not on a theory of protection or peace but on contempt of royal process. The word *sermo* has here no implications of king's protection as in the formulae of the *verbum regis* (which use the expression *in sermone tuitionis*), but stands for some other idea. There have been many suggestions by philologians as to what is here intended, based on the notion that *sermo* is a Latin rendition of a Frankish word.[131] At the very

the evidence cited *infra* note 133 shows that exile and not killing was the substance of the ordinary sentence.

[131] The suggestions about *sermo* are based on the alleged relationship of *Lex Sal.* 56, the later *Lex Sal.,* Cap. II, c. 8 (Hessels, 106), *Lex Sal.,* Cap. I, c. 5 (Hessels, 70), and the *Edict of Chilperich,* c. 19. Frensdorff, *Recht und Rede,* 458, works backward from the use of *verzellen, verrufen,* and *verfesten* used in the sources of the middle ages. He points out (481) that the assumption has been that the local courts once had the power of outlawry, but that by Merovingian times it had become a royal prerogative. (*Cf.* Sohm, *F.R.G.V.,* 98, 162.) This view he thinks does not jibe with the one piece of evidence that the folklaws had only local and provisional expulsion (*Lex Salica* 14, Add. 5; 55, 2). The *extra sermonem regis ponere* = the *ohg. fartellan* = *dijudicare.* The several forms of outlawry vary extensively (in the sense of the size of the district over which a court has jurisdiction) and intensively (as to the consequences). In this connection should be noted also the *Lex Salica,* Cap. I, c. 5 (Hessels, 70) dealing with the free woman who marries a slave. All her goods go to the fisc "et illa aspellis faciat (fa.)." Frensdorff denies that the *aspellis* is a corrupted form of *expellis.* He shows, further, that *spillon* in *ohg.* means to announce, to tell, that *spill* = *sermo, narratio* (so, the English *gospel*). Consequently he relates this passage to the *extra sermonem* of *Lex Salica,* 56, and suggests a reading "illa aspellem fiat."

Van Helten, *Zu den Malbergischen Glossen* (25 *Beiträge zur Geschichte der Deutschen Sprache* [1900] 225) §161 on *Lex Salica* 56, states merely that the king's protection has been withdrawn. In dealing with the *Lex Sal.,* Cap. I, c. 5 Van Helten (§170) agrees with Brunner. *Aspellis,* he says, is an adjective derived from *āspilli* or *āspelli,* compounded of "ā" (= ar) and "spell." The latter he relates to *owfries. eedspil* = court district, *mnd. dingxpil* and so decides it means jurisdiction. The *faciat* he renders *faciatur.* Kern, in Hessels, *Lex Salica,* §269, translates the word "given to perdition" or given up, relating the *aspellis* to *on. spilla,* to spoil; *ohg. spildi* = *effusio.* The *faciat* (fa. in cod. 11) he reads *fiat.*

While a mere lawyer naturally hesitates to tilt against the subtleties of philologians it is necessary to point out that they have not exhausted the range of possibilities. The *Lex Salica* refers to legal proceedings in terms of discussion or dialogue, e.g., *Lex Sal.,* 57 (*discutere*); so too *Edict. Chil-*

least it implies that the defendant is barred from the king's court in a sense less than peacelessness for when he is put *extra sermonem* it is *then* (*tunc*) that judgment passes against him and his property is confiscated; certainly if by *extra sermonem* he

*perich* c. 8 (1 *Cap.* 9). The *ohg. sprâhha* = speech, = court (Braune, *Althochdeutsches Lesebuch, Glossar. Cf.* also Grimm, *D.R.A.,* 826 and for the later usage, Hartung, *Die Deutschen Altertümer des Nibelungenliedes* [1894], 106–7). *Sprâhha* is also the *ohg.* gloss for *sermo* or *colloquium.* Isidore of Seville in his *Etymologiae* (Oxford ed.) vi, 8, 3 defines *verba* as words generally addressed, and *sermo* as a dialogue or *conlatio.* The *sermo* of *Lex Salica* 56 and 106 we believe may be a rendition of a Frankish form of the *ohg. sprâhha* = court. Compare also Tacitus, *Germania,* c. 6, regarding the exclusion from the *concilium* of persons who lose their shields; *cf. Lex Rom. Burg.,* 11, 3: "ut infamis de iudicio expellatur et in exilio deportandus." *Decr. Child.,* c. 2 (1 *Cap.* 15) "de palatio nostro sit omnino extraneus. . . ."

On the range and importance of the idea of exclusion from the *colloquium,* there is some late evidence in the old Saxon Genesis (c. 830). Text in Behaghel, *Heliand und Genesis* (1903); translated in Koegel, *Geschichte der Deutschen Literatur, EB.* 1 (1893). Cain has killed Abel. He believes it is an unemendable offense and that he can be killed by anyone. God then says: "Here you shall still live in this land for a long while, although you have made yourself so hated, encompassed in crime; yet will I make peace for you (i.e., a protection). I will set on you such a sign that you will truly remain in the world, although you are not worthy; but you shall live from now on in flight and homeless, so long as you behold this light and clean men shall curse you, and *never again shall you come to speech* with your Lord and pass words with him."

The interpretation of *extra sermonem* here suggested is, however, limited to *Lex Salica* 56 and 106 and *Ed. Chilp.* c. 10. We do not believe *Lex Sal.,* Cap. I, c. 5 (Hessels, 70) refers to *extra sermonem regis.* Brunner, 1 *D.R.G.* 241, n. 47 and 2 *ibid.,* 615 n. 17, says the woman is outlawed and is killed as an outlaw. The passage provides that if the kinsmen kill the woman there will be no emendation required. Death penalty is not mandatory. The public is only forbidden to harbor the woman. Actually what the law offers is an alternative: the woman may be executed by her kin, *or* she is *aspellis* and cannot be harbored by anyone. The slave goes to the wheel. The offense is conceived as an act of unchastity and a violation of status, matters regulated by *Lex Sal.* 13, 8 and 25, 6 (*cf.* Beyerle, *Über Normtypen . . . der Lex Salica* 44 *Z.R.G.*[2] 249).

The policy of non-Frankish folklaw in the same situation is to inflict death or beating and servitude (*Lex Vis.,* III, 2, 3; *Lex Burg.,* 35, 2, 3; though in the later *Lex Rib.* 58, 18 the woman herself is to decide whether the slave dies or she goes into servitude). The privilege given by *Lex Salica* 19 to the kinsmen to kill the woman consequently is in accord with neighboring laws. The alternative of outlawry is nowhere attested. This

were put out of the law there would be need for no further judgment. It is proper to describe it as an outlawry only in the sense of a process outlawry—i.e., a suspension of procedural rights.

That the *extra sermonem* is something less than the ferocious peacelessness of the writers is clear from contemporary chronicle and hagiography, which mark at the same time the probable maximum of the defendant's sentence.[132] These sources show nothing of wolf's head and peril of life. They indicate that what happens to the defendant is the imposition of an exile in the technical sense of the late Roman law, which involved loss of

can befall the free man but is not a penalty on women. We believe, therefore, that despite the provision regarding confiscation the *aspellis* has reference to something else. This is indicated by the thoroughly indurated European custom of stripping and beating unchaste women. So Tacitus, *Germania*, c. 19, tells of the unchaste woman stripped and beaten out of the village. Boniface in a letter 746-7 (*M.G.H., Ep.,* 342) recounts the Saxon custom of driving the woman out of the district, tearing her clothes from her girdle and beating her from village to village. See also for later times Grimm, *D.R.A.,* 711 *et seq.;* Ducange, *Glossarium, s.v., trocina.* The universality of cutting the shift at the girdle as a derisory punishment is indicated in *Leges Wallicae,* II, C. 1, 42 (Wotton Ed.); Biblical precedent possibly apposite here is in II Samuel 10, 14; I Chron. 19, 4. The possibility that this punishment of stripping and beating is intended by *Lex Sal.* 70 is pointed by the fact that in the *ohg., arspelle, aspelle, arspellis,* etc., are glossed to the Latin *nates* (3 Steinmeyer-Sievers, *Die Althochdeutschen Glossen,* 19, 73, 43; 3 Graff, *op. cit.,* 94). The word persists today in German dialects, Müller, *Rheinisches Wörterbuch* (1928) *s.v.;* 1 Kehrein, *Volksbrauch und Volksitte in Nassau* (1872), 48. In the Suabian dialect *arschböller* means blows on the buttocks (1 Schmid, *Schwäbisches Wörterbuch,* 28). Compare finally on the matter also *Lex Salica* 2, 3, "si quis scroba in *asso* subaterit," a passage which philologians' delicacy has left unexplained, but which is on its face obvious enough. We believe consequently that a punishment of beating plus confiscation is inflicted, and that while the effect of being hounded out of the vicinage may be equivalent to the old Salic regional expulsion, it is not the procedural exile of *Lex Sal.* 56.

[132] Jonas, *S. Columbani Vita,* c. 34, c. 41 (87 Migne, *Patrologia,* 1031, 1033), indicates clearly that the saint was *extra sermonem regis.* No one dares sell him food but it is brought secretly, for the people fear the wrath of the king. See also the *S. Leodegarii . . . vita altera, ab auct. anon.,* c. 6, 7 (96 Migne, *Patrologia,* 352-353). Compare also Gregory, *Hist. Franc.,* V, 49: Leudastes wants to flee to Paris, but the king has ordered that no one shall take him in. He hides and his wife is taken and exiled. Leudastes subsequently (VI, 32) gets a king's precept that he can live in

status, internment, banishment and confiscation.[133] These accounts taken in connection with incontrovertible proof that Ro-

Tours. A similar interdict on food while a man was in sanctuary, *ibid.*, IV, 18.

It should further be observed that Gregory gives numerous instances where *exilium* is used as a punishment: e.g., V, 26; VIII, 31; IX, 10; X, 19. Indeed, this punishment is used as a major sanction by the crown even for serious offenses (for example, *Hist. Franc.*, VIII, 31; V, 21; V, 25; Fredegar, *Chron.*, IV, 54; *Vita Amandi*, c. 15 in 2 Mabillon, *Acta Sanctorum*, 684; *Vita Ausberti*, c. 31 in 2 *ibid.*, 1012; *Vita Lupi*, c. 12 in 1 Bolland, *Acta Sanctorum* [1 Sept.], 259; and *M.G.H.*, 1 *Dipl.* 44, n. 48). It seems absurd, consequently, to suppose that a man *extra sermonem regis*, as a matter of mesne process, could be killed by anyone.

[133] In the early Roman law *exilium* was a voluntary departure of a Roman citizen, and ensued when an individual desired to avoid trial. It was also used after apprehension in capital cases (i.e., where a man's *caput* was at stake) when a magistrate allowed self-exile. The trial continued after departure and culminated in property confiscation. Then followed a popular decree, an administrative measure, denying the accused shelter, water and fire. The doctrine of self-exile disappeared during the principate. Banishment originated from the so-called relegation, the limitation of free choice of residence either by command to leave a place or to reside in a special locality. The *relegatio* was introduced by Sulla and used by the early emperors. In the time of the principate it was combined with the idea of voluntary exile. *Relegatio* was a power inherent in *imperium* and hence if abused was not in violation of statutes. It was utilized only against free persons and took four forms: 1) *Relegatio* without changing status, loss of *caput*, or internment; 2) *Relegatio* without change of status or loss of *caput* but with internment (*relegatio in insulam*); 3) *Relegatio* without internment, but with loss of *caput* (after Tiberius, with loss of citizenship and confiscation); 4) *Relegatio* with internment, loss of *caput*, loss of citizenship (after Tiberius, confiscation). The term *exilium* is used in this later period for *relegatio*.

In the case of a provincial expulsion it was the province to which the exile could not return. Internment could be house, city, or district confinement. In this respect the Frankish practice resembles the Roman. In the time of Tiberius this penalty becomes independent and is known as *deportatio*. It entailed all penalties although some property might be left for provisioning a deportee. Exile for life involved a partial confiscation. *Contra* if for a limited time. The *Sententia* of Paul (222–235 A.D.) give a picture of the punishment, the crimes for which it was inflicted, and the variations according to status. In the Digest, consult D. 48, 22; D. 48, 8, 3, 5; D. 48, 10, 1, 13; D. 48, 13, 3; D. 38, 2, 14, 3; D. 32, 1, 1, 3; D. 48, 13, 7; D. 49, 16, 13, 6; in the Code 5, 5, 3, 1; C. 2, 15, 2, 1; C. 9, 47, 8; C. 1, 2, 5; C. 9, 38, 1. *Cf.* on the whole matter Mommsen, *Römisches Strafrecht*, 68 *et seq.*, 1045 *et seq.*; Costa, *Crimi e Pene* (1921), 44, 93 *et seq.*, 199 *et seq.*

man fiscal practices were adopted by the Franks[134] constitute not merely an indirect traverse of the view that *Lex Salica* 56 and 106 are utterly in the alleged Germanic tradition, but they are directly probative of a reception of Roman ideas. Indeed, the parallel between the *extra sermonem* and the penalty provided in the Burgundian Roman law for calumniators (*ut infamis de iudicio expellatur in exilio deportandus*)[135] is so close as to be nearly conclusive. It is consequently not too reckless to suggest that the source of the contempt theory which underlies these passages is Roman and not Germanic, particularly since the use of confiscation as process against a contumacious defendant in causes criminal was a well-defined Roman doctrine.[136]

[134] *Infra,* Chapter II, note 129.

[135] *Lex Burg. Rom.,* 11, 3. Compare here *Cod. Iust.* II, 58, 2, 5; *Cod. Iust.* VII, 50, 3 = *Cod. Th.* 4, 16, 1 = *App. Leg. Vis.* 20, 1.

[136] The state of knowledge about this is unsatisfactory. Best accounts in Mommsen, *Römisches Strafrecht,* 326; Wlassak, *Anklage und Streitbefestigung im Kriminalrecht der Römer* (1917), 55 *et seq.;* Geib, *Geschichte des Römischen Kriminalprocesses* (1842), 593 *et seq.* The absent defendant could apparently be condemned in cases less than capital and punishments up to relegation imposed, *D.* 48, 19, 5. The property was sequestered for a year, after which confiscation took place if the defendant did not appear, exactly as under the later Frankish *forisbannitio.* Thereafter the defendant could clear himself but the property remained to the fisc, *C. Th.* 9, 1, 2. *Cf.* also *D.* 48, 17, 1; 2; 5.

Since the later Frankish crown procedure of *forisbannitio* and *missio in bannum* (*infra* Ch. II) resembles the Roman law more closely than the earlier rules discussed above, the suggestion in the text would be more plausible if the connection between this procedure and that of the *Lex Salica* had been worked out. The *forisbannitio,* however, is ordinarily treated as a distinctly Carolingian development, its origin conveniently described as a split-off of outlawry. (2 Brunner, *D.R.G.* 609; Planitz, *op. cit.,* 68 *et seq.*) The distinctive feature of the foreban is that its use does not depend upon a bargain to observe a judgment as does the procedure of *Lex Salica* 56. The notion that the defendant's property could be gotten at by judicial action even for contempt of summons was established by *Ed. Chilp.,* c. 8. Doubtless the growth of the foreban owes something to this as well as to the increased power of the court over summons. The notion of eventual confiscation of all the defendant's property however probably derives from the *Lex Salica* 56. It is possible that the word *forisbannitio* comes into use in Chilperich's reign. In *Ed. Chilp.,* c. 8, the expression "rachymburgiis ferrebannitus qui antea andissent causam illam" i.e. who

Unless the indications of available proof are to be flouted the phrase *extra sermonem* must, therefore, be interpreted in terms of procedural function. Quite apart from any weight that may be attached to the evidence of borrowings from Roman law, the passages from the *Lex Salica* themselves yield no positive doctrine of a general king's peace except by the deliberate interpolation of ideas for which no collateral proof can be found. Under the Frankish dynasties there is no general king's peace. There is only the institution of special protections—the *verba regis* just discussed. These are limited in scope and are a manifestation of the royal power to create exceptions from the normal state of affairs. Because the protection is exceptional it lacks the capacity to create a new conception of public order. It expands to embrace certain defined classes of persons and no more.

Although the whole phantasm of a Frankish king's peace vanishes upon sober appraisal of the sources, one must not minimize the crown's direct influence in the maintenance of the law. We have seen how royal authority was used within the folklaw procedural structure modifying the character of the procedure itself without disturbing its premises or purpose. The *verbum regis* is an example of the effect of prerogative in creating the excep-

---

had judged the contempt proceeding antecedent to distraint, suggests that the *ferrebannitus* describes the proceeding. There must certainly have been judgment (i.e. "rachymburgiis sedentes et dicentes") and there is no reason why *ferrebannitus* should not have meant in the sixth century what it later meant. (Opinions *contra* in Behrend, *Lex Salica* 155, note.)

Neither the Burgundian nor the Visigothic law, both greatly influenced by the Roman, had a procedure like the Frankish. The Visigoths supplemented the mulcts for non-appearance with beatings (*Lex Vis.*, II, 1, 19; II, 1, 31; Dahn, *Westgothische Studien,* 249–50). However, the revised law of Wamba (7th cent.) for failure to perform military duty combined exile and confiscation as a punishment on what looks like a theory of contempt. (*Lex Vis.*, IX, 2, 9; 6 Dahn, *Könige der Germanen,* 220.)

The relation of the early ecclesiastical contempt procedure with the Roman is discussed by Steinwenter, *Der Antike Kirchliche Rechtsgang* in 54 Z.R.G.[2] (Kan. Abt.), 65 *et seq.* The question how far this church procedure may have influenced the early Merovingian practice deserves thorough investigation.

tions to the procedural norm. But the most impressive manifestation of the crown's powers, exercised over matters outside the scope of the composition scheme, is yet to be considered. Here it is that changes occur which lead to a modification of old ideas of order and its enforcement.

# CHAPTER II

## FRANKISH CROWN PROCEDURE AND THE
## GROWTH OF PUBLIC ORDER

I F the chroniclers upon whom one must rely for the details of
Frankish history had been less concerned with the impieties
and caprices of princes and more punctual in recording the minutiae of human existence, it would be possible to speak with
some assurance about the problems which the legislation of the
Frankish kings undertook to solve. As the record stands, life in
Neustria and Austrasia seems to have been so constantly unruly
that it is difficult to fix upon this or that as matter for which regulation was thought proper and necessary. Yet it is essential to
view the legislation of Merovingian and Carolingian kings as
efforts to solve problems even if these can only be very generally
stated. We have shown that the lovely fabric of system which
writers have fashioned is woven of a ghostly yarn—the ectoplas-
mic threads of a never-existent peace theory. The rules preserved
in capitularies and formulae are neither numerous nor consistent
enough upon which to construct systems; there is no great and
general pattern to furnish a design. These rules are harsh answers to instant questions: What is to be done about professional
crime? May offenders be executed? Can the fisc take their
property?

There are other reasons why the procedural devices elaborated
in the course of four centuries of Frankish hegemony are better
not viewed as mere undifferentiated phases of a general Frankish law. During this period the royal policy followed in general
two lines. On the one hand, it sought, as we have shown, to direct or modify the process of private prosecution: a policy de-
voted essentially to the amendment of procedural forms. On the
other hand, it struck out into uncultivated fields of regulation,

developing a state initiative in prosecution and punishment: a policy which changed profoundly the underlying premises of law enforcement. These trends should not be confused merely because king's law was at work in both. The stream of composition practice was quite dominated by the ingrown ideology of the folklaw; it was susceptible of restrictions but, because feud was its evil shadow, incapable of expansion on any theory of serving good order. Outside the normal functioning of this process lay the problems of which we have spoken. The answers to these we wish to hold separate. These are distinct problems for they reflect changes in social and political conditions occurring after the settlement of the Franks in Gaul, changes to which the older folklaw could not be responsive. Their treatment was distinct because the postulates of the folklaw were not regarded, and because new standards of order tended to make themselves felt. We shall refer to this new body of law as crown law, for it was initiated as a royal measure and to a certain extent was fostered as something special upon which in one way or another the crown kept its finger.

In its infancy this special crown law is a modest affair consisting of a few procedures instituted to cope with two situations otherwise utterly out of hand: the thief and the professional malefactor. These two problems the state makes its own, and to solve them embarks upon a long series of experiments with administrative and procedural devices. Slowly the scope of its activities widens to encroach somewhat upon matter once the subject of feud or composition. But since this new procedure exists largely by way of supplement it does not grow to sufficient proportions to displace the composition process itself. To be sure the standards of order implicit in the purpose for which the crown procedure was used affected the policy underlying the administration of composition. Yet this influence was not overbearing enough to create a paramount interest of the state in the prose-

cution and punishment of crime. An attempt to lay the foundations for such an interest was, indeed, undertaken by the clumsy
manipulation of the concept of infidelity. But this effort was
premature, and came to nothing. We shall consider the three
main tributaries to the slowly swelling stream of crown law. In
each case it will be necessary to follow the tributary to its source,
to observe its course from the mysterious fastnesses of early society into the comparative sunlight of Carolingian law. We shall
consider, first, the use of state initiative in prosecution, then the
growth of state-inflicted sanctions, and finally the attempt to
assure law observance by invoking sworn allegiance to the king.

It is not to be assumed that among the Franks the victims of a
crime were invariably prepared to act any more than today there
is always a prosecuting witness waiting in the lists. It might be
that their aggressor was unknown to them, and it might be that
feud itself was too dangerous an alternative to dare. Often
amends were simply not collectible either because the offender
could not be caught or because he was insolvent and had no responsible kindred. In the case of the professional malefactor as
he is described in the sources, this situation of complete stale-
mate was clearly posited. The processes of law were equally
frustrated in the case of the secret offender (whether manslayer
or thief) the *bête noire* of law enforcement since the beginning
of time. These types become a social nuisance of major proportions only after the conquest of Gaul, because folklaw procedure
is drawn in terms of known defendants with family connections
and upon the assumption that composition will normally be collectible. In such a scheme of procedure the secret offense will
perforce not be prosecuted. For this, as for the crime committed
by the ranging marauder, there first of all must be police which
act not in family but in public interest. It is at this point that
the first ordinances of the Merovingian kings cut into the
problem.

HABITUAL OFFENDERS AND DISQUALIFICATION THROUGH INFAMY

It is specifically the thief at whom the earliest legislation which bears on the habitual or professional offender is aimed. Included in "theft" were all the variations of interferences with personalty: what we know today as robbery, larceny, burglary, and perhaps what now would be no more than conversion of chattels. The laws in question, moreover, are by no means to be considered as forming part of the steady flow of pronouncements against feud, simply because the state is taking a hand in the prosecution and punishment of the offender. Rather were they a positive entrance by the state upon a field where feud for obvious reasons was not being carried on, and where composition was not obtainable; where, therefore, "private" redress had failed. And this was the understanding at the time. So regarded, the "thief" legislation may be described as the first step in the direction of a public order where initiative in catching and prosecuting the offender devolved upon the state.

Once the Scandinavian sources and their exaggerated interpretation are abandoned as not controlling, the existence of a general police duty in respect to pursuing malefactors is by no means clear. The adherents of the view that a general outlawry ensued upon the commission of a misdeed have found no difficulty in constructing further a duty to pursue, from the presumable fact that an outlaw was the enemy of all.[1] Since the gen-

---

[1] 1 Brunner, *D.R.G.*, 232; 2 *ibid.*, 304, 612. As a matter of doctrinal genealogy it is worth examining the notes in the first reference. They include a reference to the *Capitula Italica* [n.d.] (1 *Cap.*, 217) of the reign of Charlemagne; a citation from *Aethelstan* II, 20, 7; a late Spanish source; a passage from *Decr. Childebert*, c. 4 (596), where a *raptor* is to be *persequatur* as an enemy of God—probably indicating merely no sanctuary; and a late source from the Netherlands. All of this is illuminating on the prevalence of custom, but it is of no help in ascertaining with precision whether or not in early Germanic times of which Brunner is speaking this institution existed. The matter is also discussed in 1 Waitz, *D.V.G.*, 493, and Fehr, *Landfolge und Gerichtsfolge*, in *Festgabe für Sohm* (1914), 389 *et seq.*

eral outlawry theory cannot be proved to have existed among the tribes included in the boundaries of the early Frankish kingdoms, there is double reason to doubt whether such a duty had, in fact, existed time out of mind. The clearest indications of popular police functions may be found in connection with the procedure that ensued when a malefactor was caught red-handed —the handhaving crime. Here, there seems to be no question but that unorganized neighborhood hue was raised.[2] Originally doubtless no more than an alarm and cry for help, the hue became first a normal, then an essential, part of the procedure by which the injured individual—who was privileged to wreak instant vengeance upon a real wrongdoer—achieved the publicity necessary to free his act of revenge from taint of aggression or manslaughter and to make it known in its true character as a wholly lawful reprisal.[3] There are, however, no sure proofs that the hue in the Frankish kingdom was employed for purposes other than neighborhood pursuit of the handhaving offender or that it bears any palpable relation to the procedure made mandatory by the Merovingian legislation other than as a suggestive model present to observation and available for inventive development.[4]

The Merovingian hue procedure proper is introduced in the

[2] 2 Brunner, *D.R.G.*, 628, there related to outlawry as a procedure directed against a peaceless man; and note especially the polemic at *ibid.*, 629 n. 12 of v. Schwerin against Beyerle who, in *Rechtsgang*, 265 *et seq.*, relates the whole question to revenge, the position taken in the text (*infra*, p. 85). On the procedure, Scherer, *Die Klage gegen den Toten Mann* (4 *Deutschrechtliche Beiträge*, [1909]) 66 *et seq.*; Beyerle, *Rechtsgang*, 312.

[3] Beyerle, *Rechtsgang*, 316. Beyerle's most convincing argument relating the handhaving procedure to revenge rather than outlawry is the fact that only the injured party, i.e., the person entitled to feud or plea, can exercise revenge. *Cf. Lex Ribuaria*, 77; *Pactus Alamannorum*, V, 3.

[4] In this connection it should be observed that the motive for the legislation in the *Pactus pro tenore pacis*, which we are about to discuss, is stated therein to be that the night watches which were supposed to prevent thieving were not adequate. This seems to us to point to a much more specialized sort of police than the hue. It is the difference between the watch described in Edward I's *Statute of Winton* for the towns, and the country hue.

*Pactus pro tenore pacis*[5] (511–558), a treaty composed of joint and several declarations by the two Frankish kings, Chlothar I and Childebert I, and executed partly to regulate border troubles. One of the significant features of the treaty is the machinery set up by Chlothar to place the burden of pursuing thieves upon the community at large. A penalty of five shillings is threatened upon anyone who fails to perform.[5a] The hundred (*centena*) is made responsible for the capital sum of the thing stolen.[6] In the joint declaration of the two kings, it is provided that the pursu-

[5] 1 *Cap.* 4. The title of this document taken in connection with its content has led many writers to refer to it as a law for "landpeace" (*Landfriedensgesetz*). This is misleading, since it manufactures a pedigree which relates the later medieval landpeace legislation, emanating from an entirely different set of ideas, to the Merovingian arrangements. The manuscripts have a variety of titles, and no doubt the prevalence of the general peace theory had much to do with the settlement upon this particular designation. The use of the word *pax* in this document is adduced by v. Schwerin in his review of Beyerle's *Rechtsgang* (36 Z.R.G.², 507) as proof that a general peace existed. The *Pactus* might be looked upon as a "landpeace" law if we assume that thefts, the major subject of the legislation, were regarded and spoken of as breaches of the peace. But the concept "breach of the peace" is nowhere expressed or applied directly to a specified misdeed. *Pactus* uses the word peace positively. It does not appear in the individual declarations of the two kings but only in the joint declaration. This is the part of the document that has the definite character of a treaty. "For the keeping of the peace" Chlothar and Childebert institute the system of permitting the pursuing bands of one king to go into the provinces of the other. This is obviously a situation that could lead to trouble if it were not for the permission accorded by the declaration. It is to prevent war and to further international accord that the arrangement is made (and on this problem see Gregory, *Hist. Franc.* IX, 9). It is international and not domestic peace that is meant. The difficulty was similar to that existing between the United States and Mexico in relation to the pursuit of hostile Indians that was regulated by two protocols signed July 29 and September 21, 1882. *Cf.* 1 Malloy, *Treaties, Conventions, etc., of the United States* (1910), 1144, 1145. On the interpretation and especially the date of the *Pactus*, Brunner, *Über das Alter der Lex Salica*, in 29 Z.R.G.², 136.

[5a] *Pactus*, c. 9; c. 17. *Cf.* 2 Brunner, *D.R.G.*, 306 *et seq.*

[6] The question whether or not hundreds were erected by this law or had previously existed is not here involved although the matter bears on the "public" nature of hue. *Cf.* 2 Brunner, *D.R.G.*, 200; 2 Waitz, *D.V.G.*, pt. 1, 399, 405; Sohm, *F.R.G.V.*, 183 *et seq.*

ing force (*trustis*) which the hundred must furnish may follow the thief from one kingdom into the other. The hundredmen who catch the thief may claim part of the composition. These provisions were subsequently strengthened in Austrasia (then including part of Neustria) by the decree of Childebert II (596).[7] The penalty for failure to pursue is stepped up to sixty shillings —the penalty for violating the king's ban—thus indicating clearly that the duty is one of direct concern to the crown. The provision regarding the responsibility of the hundred for the value of the theft is repeated. If the thief is found in another hundred and the latter cannot drive out (*expellere*) or render up the offender, the damage has to be borne by that hundred, and the men of that hundred are required to purge themselves twelve-handed.

One sees the *Pactus* as a venturesome step in the direction of a state control over one troublous problem of wrongdoing. It establishes a new form of liability based not on kinship but upon a mere territorial division.[8] It imposes a public duty of policing on a scale and in a setting theretofore utterly unknown, and with new machinery for enforcement of the duty, if indeed it existed at all as a duty prior to the *Pactus*. It upsets composition theory to the extent of letting members of the posse make claims for amends. Any one of these aspects is a full new deal. Their sum is close to revolution.

No less significant than this regularization and imposition of hue is the bold manner in which the *Pactus* attacks the problem of suspected wrongdoing. An early novel to the *Lex Salica*[9] had

---

[7] C. 9 (1 *Cap.* 17). Sickel, *Zur Geschichte des Bannes*, 12. The rule regarding ban penalty persists: *Cap. Miss. Silvac.* c. 5 (853) 2 *Cap.* 272; *Cap. Carisiac.*, c. 2 (873) 2 *Cap.* 343.

[8] It is true that a form of territorial liability is indicated in a novel to the *Lex Salica*, Cap. I, 9 (Hessels, 73), *de hominem inter duas villas occisum*, discussed *infra* in the text. But this is a restricted liability and does not seem to us to have had the implications of the liability imposed in the *Pactus*.

[9] *Lex Salica*, Cap. I, 9 (Hessels, 73). Behrend, *Lex Salica*, 131, n., and note his references to Brunner's conjectures regarding this legislation.

approached this matter in the "modern" terms of one specific wrong and one specific act. Where homicide is newly discovered the *iudex* or count sounds his horn summoning the vicinage. The neighbors by oath must declare they have not killed and do not know the killer—wholesale compurgation; primitive inquisition.[10] Beyond this the law is powerless, because Salic folklaw procedure is based on various premises of certainty; a certain accuser, a certain offense, a certain offender. The *Pactus,* however, under the influence of a Burgundian model,[11] approaches the matter of suspected crime as a question not of a deed but of a character, not of a particular act but of an individual's reputation. It permits a charge of suspicion as to thieflike behavior in general and here requires ordeal by lot[12]—the judgment of God for slaves.[13] It does not specify how this im-

[10] Sohm, *Process der Lex Salica,* 129, n. 3, relying upon the form of summons, thinks that the count stands here in lieu of the party, i.e., the accuser. Actually he is merely making an inquest.

[11] *Lex Burg.,* Const. Extr. 19, 1. The influence of this on the *Pactus* asserted by Beyerle, *Rechtsgang,* 378, n. 45.

[12] *Pactus,* c. 10 (Chlothar's decree). "Si quis in alterius domum ubi clavis est furtum invenerit, dominus domus de vita componat. Si quis cum furtu capitur antedicte subjaceat legem; [thus far clear handhaving cases]. Et si de suspectionem inculpatur ad sortem veniat et si malam sortem priserit latro. . . ."

In the existing state of procedure the use of *inculpatur* points to a general reputation or an accusation; there seems to be no ground for assuming judgment on the point of suspicion. Bethmann-Hollweg, 4 *Civilprozess,* 511, gets into difficulties since the *Pactus* is in his opinion the work of Chlothar II and Childebert II. The ordeal in Chlothar's decree is the ordeal by lot (2 Brunner, *D.R.G.,* 553), whereas, according to Brunner, in Childebert's *Pactus* the kettle is provided (c. 4). *Contra,* Beyerle in reference cited below.

Note, further, that the *Pactus* represents a transition to an afflictive penalty for theft. For big thefts the penalty is life, which is redeemable with wergeld, and not mere amends for theft. Since no provision is made for petty thefts presumably composition tariffs for theft obtain. *Cf.* on the matter Beyerle, *Über Normtypen und Erweiterungen der Lex Salica,* 44 Z.R.G.[2], 231.

[13] *Pactus,* c. 11, and *cf.* Beyerle (*supra,* note 12) 233. The ordeal theory is that what is hidden from man God will reveal, 4 Bethmann-Hollweg, *op. cit.,* 507. The point is brought out in a letter of Pope Gregory to Boniface (726) the substance of which is in *Corpus Juris Canonici, Decr.,* C. II,

peachment of reputation is formulated, but since the Burgundians furnish the idea, it is possible that their practice of using
witnesses to state suspicion may have been likewise adopted.[14]

The significance of this innovation as a first blow at professional crime is the more profound because the ordinance marks
the introduction into Frankish law of the principle that what is
normally an accused's right of oath purgation may be cut under
by a further and different charge directed at an accused's reputation for lawless behavior. In other words the charge (and evidence) may be such that the usual premise of freeman-capacity
is destroyed. Known rogues and mere suspects are made to stand
on different ground.

This diminution of the suspect's procedural rights is probably
the most drastic interference in the "normal" scheme of law enforcement yet devised.[15] It suggests on its face recourse to the
Roman notion of infamy[16] in the modified form used by the

q. V, c. 5. *Cf.* 1 *München, Das Kanonische Gerichtswerfahren* (2 ed.,
1874), 455–6.

[14] The provision is in *Lex Romana Burg.* XII, ". . . cum tribus ingenuis testibus, ubi suspicionem inveniendi furti habet, ingrediatur." *Cf.*
also *Lex Burg.,* Lib. Const., 16; Const. Extr. 19, apparently the accuser is
to produce the "criminosus quam suspectos." The *Pactus* contemplates
capture in another's house and consequently an accuser.

[15] Childebert's *Pactus,* c. 4 speaks of the freeman "inculpatus" in theft
"et ad ineum (ordeal by kettle) provocatus." It is possible that this passage is a parallel to Chlothar's c. 10 if the claim is correct, that *Lex Salica,*
53 is a Carolingian addition, and that this ordeal is then used only in cases
of suspected persons of ill fame. Krammer, in 39 *Neues Archiv,* 643.

[16] On this, Savigny, *System des Heutigen Römischen Rechts* (1840),
§76; Greenidge, *Infamia* (1894). The essence of the Roman idea was that
for certain acts or because of a mode of life an individual subjected himself to the moral censure of a competent authority in the state, and that
this entailed disqualification for certain rights both in public and private
law (Greenidge, *op. cit.,* 37). In some types of cases *infamia* attached to
the mere making known before a magistrate of acts which would exclude
from public office or honor, whereas in other cases and notably criminal
proceedings the infamy attached upon magisterial sentence. In addition
to these forms of *infamia* to which writers have given the name *infamia
juris* (*ibid.,* 189, viz., the codified infamy of the praetor's edict or subsequent legislation), is the infamy of opinion which the legal texts indicate
was based upon character or standing. This has been called *infamia facti—*
factual infamy (*ibid.*). The essence of this conception was that persistent

church[17] and as it was applied in both the Visigothic[18] and Burgundian[19] law. This was what comes later to be called *infamia*

indulgence in acts morally reprehensible but not themselves entailing infamy of law, would lead to disabilities because such indulgence affects a man's character. The principle of application of factual infamy was the same both in public and private law, and the disabilities such as the exclusion from office or honors, and the lessening of a man's credibility as a witness were in some ways similar to those ensuing upon *infamia juris*. *Cf.* also 2 München, *Das Kanonische Gerichtsverfahren und Strafrecht* (2 ed. 1874), 133; the passage of Callistratus in D. 22, 5, 3, on the point of testimony; the constitution of Constantine, C. 12, 1, 2.

[17] Hinschius, in 5 *Kirchenrecht* (1896), 41, asserts that infamy is practically unknown as a punishment in early times, and becomes important toward the end of the ninth century as a result of the forgeries in Pseudo-Isidore. While this may be correct as to the use of infamy as a distinct punishment, there is no question but that the notion of procedural disqualification because of infamy was adopted in canonical procedure at an early date. The matter apparently builds up about the apostolic doctrine of *testimonium* (I Tim. III, 7) which blossoms into the later *irregularitas ex defectu famae*. Originally the notion of reputation appears as a restriction upon ordination (*cf.* Rickert, *Die Anfänge der Irregularitäten* [1901]). The defect in some cases not removable by penances because of the *notoriety* involved (*ibid.,* 20). The same notion carries over into other aspects of canonical regulation, both in regard to accusation and testimony. The earliest evidence on the latter we find in the Council of Constantinople of 381: 2 Hefele, *Conciliengeschichte* (2 ed. 1875) 24; Canon 21 of the Council of Chalcedon of 451 required inquiry into the reputation of clergy or laymen accusing bishops or laymen: *ibid.,* 524. The doctrine is developed in the African councils, *Conc. Carthage* II (391) c. 6: 3 Mansi, *Concilia,* 694; and *Conc. Carthage* VII (419) c. 2 and 4: 4 Mansi, *Concilia,* 437–8; and *cf. Conc. Carthage* (421) cc. 6, 7: 4 *ibid.,* 449–50. These provisions find their way into early canonical collections, notably the *Dionysus* (on which Maassen, *Geschichte der Quellen und der Literatur des Canonischen Rechts* [1870], 425 *et seq.*); and the so-called *Hispana* (*ibid.,* 671 *et seq.*). There can be no doubt that the Roman judicial practice was influential in the formulation of the canonical theory of testimonial qualification. It cannot be stated, however, when the identification with *infamia* took place. A passage in Isidore, *Etymologiae,* V, 27 generalizes about infamy in a way which suggests the nexus is accomplished in 7th-century Spain. And note also *Conc. Rom.* (826) c. 31: 2 *Concilia* (*M.G.H.*), 580.

[18] *Cf.* Dahn, *Westgothische Studien,* 190; Melicher, *Der Kampf zwischen Gesetzes- und Gewohnheitsrecht im Westgotenreiche,* 172 *et seq.;* Zeumer, *Geschichte der Westgotischen Gesetzgebung,* 24 *Neues Archiv,* 98–9. Zeumer thinks the Visigothic infamy is Germanic but cites no proof.

[19] *Lex Burg.,* Lib. Const., 99, 2. ". . . tres idoneos testes loci illius

*facti,* the infamy which followed immediately from the performance of disreputable acts without the necessity of judicial notation and which resulted chiefly in the loss of accusatory or testimonial capacity.[20]

The absorption of this notion by a legal system which presumed the utter *bona fides* of litigants, but which possessed only
the reinsurance device of gage and pledge and wielded no better than pecuniary sanctions was all but inevitable. For the infamy idea was suited to both social and procedural premises; and
the contact of Frankish law with canon[21] and Roman jurisprudence were constant at the very fountainhead where changes in
official law were effected. In the course of Frankish history, the
repercussion upon secular law of the church's mounting interest
in the infamy doctrine is plainly visible.[22] Indeed, as we shall

est." There are, of course, frequent references to *infamia* in the *Lex Burg.
Romana.*

[20] Zeumer, *supra,* note 18, denies that the effect of infamy in Roman law
was to incapacitate as a witness. See, however, Paul, *Sent.* V, 15, 1. It is a
chief characteristic of the canon law, *cf. supra,* note 17, and of the Visigothic law: *Lex Vis.* III, 5, 3 and *cf.* II, 4. The infamous person went to
the ordeal, VI, 1, 3.

[21] The adoption in France of canonical rules regarding accusation and
testimony is indicated clearly in Gregory, *Hist. Franc.* V, 49. On the early
canonical collections used by the Gallic church, Maassen, *Geschichte des
Canonischen Rechts im Abendland,* 421, 439.

[22] Until the ninth century there is not much trace of this in the express
terms of infamy. A late addition to the *Lex Salica* (13 Add. 2) speaking of
consanguineous marriage says that the progeny "infamia sint notati." This
is supposed to have been derived from *Cod. Theod.,* III, 12, 3, and Zoepfl
says it was enacted *temp.* Childebert II (1 *D.R.G.,* 24, n. 9). On the *Lex
Salica* rule, *cf.* Zeumer, *Leg. Vis.,* 161, n. 1. Note further *Conc. Clichy*
(626), c. 10, regarding incestuous marriage: "neque in palatio habere
militiam neque in forum agendarum causarum licentiam non habebunt"
(1 *Concilia, M.G.H., Leg. Sec.* 3, 198). The texts of the early Gallic councils indicate no use of the word *infamia,* but at Macon in 583 (1 *Concilia,
M.G.H.,* 159, c. 18), the rule already noted about testimonial disqualification is stated. On the reception of this in *Lex Alam.,* 42, 1, *cf.* Beyerle, *Die
Süddeutschen Leges,* in 49 Z.R.G.², 367. Note also *Conc. Clichy,* c. 17, regarding limitations on accusation (1 *Concilia, M.G.H.,* 199); repeated
*Conc. Rheims* (627–30) c. 15 (*ibid.,* 205).

In both Frankish ecclesiastical and Frankish secular law the doctrine of
*bona fama* and *mala fama* are well defined before the final identification of

later see, the infamy notion becomes, for both church and state, basic to their schemes of law enforcement, and eventually to the whole structure of human relationships.[23]

The procedure of the *Pactus* for dealing with theft had the effect of marking out as a matter of law a class of persons, already existing as a result of economic change,[24] who did not fit into the traditional system of remedies. The bait of amends to the thief-catcher created a new category of plaintiffs which the shift in the defendant's procedural rights likewise tended to favor.[25] But the scheme of the *Pactus* was drawn on the assumption that the thief or the suspect was apprehended. It had no weapon against the footloose fellow who lurked in the woods. He is first dealt with in the later Edict of Chilperich discussed in the previous chapter,[26] and then only by a cumbersome system of accusation to neighbors, given legal effect by a foreoath

the latter with *infamia* takes place. *Cf.* as to the church, *Ghaerboldi Epis. Cap.* (802–10) c. 1 (1 *Cap.*, 243); *Cap. Haito Ep. Bal.* (807–23) c. 9 (1 *Cap.* 364); *Conc. Meld.–Paris* (845–6) c. 69 (2 *Cap.*, 415); *Syn. Pontig.* (2 *Cap.* 350). *Cf.* as to secular law *Cap. de Latronibus* c. 4 (1 *Cap.* 181); *Cap. Pip. Italic.* (801–10) cc. 11, 12 (1 *Cap.* 210); *Cap. Miss. Instr.* (829) (in 2 *Cap.* 8). The sources talk in terms of *infamia* after the circulation of the false capitularies of Benedict, the *Cap. Angilrammi* and *Pseudo-Isidore,* where the canonical rules were spoken of in terms of infamy and buttressed by forgeries of papal letters which eventually are used as basic texts in the compilation of Gratian. Contemporary ecclesiastical preoccupation is seen also in glosses on the early canons, Maassen, *Glossen des Canonischen Rechts* (1877), 33, 48; *cf.* also *Conc. Pavia* (829) c. 13 (2 *Concilia, M.G.H.,* 619). The expression is sparingly used in the secular laws *cf.* the fragment 1 *Cap.*, 334; and *Cap. Carisiac.* (873) c. 1 (2 *Cap.* 343, 344).

[23] The relation of loss of capacity and "peacelessness" has an interesting literary history. It is summarized by Naendrup, *Dogmengeschichte der Arten Mittelalterlicher Ehrenminderung,* in *Festgabe für Dahn,* pt. 1, 223. In the eighteenth century the Roman terminology predominated. Largely owing to the work of Marezoll, "peacelessness" was linked with all forms of diminution of rights. This was an achievement in dogmatism without reference to the genetics of doctrine, and it cleared the way for Brunner's sweeping outlawry theory.

[24] Partly as a result of the growth of great estates, *infra,* Chapter III.

[25] *Pactus,* c. 16.

[26] *Supra,* Chapter I, p. 53.

before the doomsmen, with execution contingent upon further eventual accusation before the crown. This was a machinery not likely to be carried through unless the accuser was a man unusually provoked and the *malus homo* a virtual public enemy number one.

But in Austrasia, Childebert II some years later (596), developing the notion of infamy into a tool operative even without proved act, instituted a procedure far more workable because it was geared to local enforcement. His decree[27] provided that in regard to "thieves" and "malefactors," if five or seven men of good fame (*bona fidei*) declared upon oath that such person was a professional criminal (*criminosus*), then since he stole without law he should die without law.[28] To secure the enforcement of this penalty the law goes on to say that if a judge be convicted of releasing a thief once caught, he should lose his own life, suggesting somewhat obscurely that the duty of execution is on the judge. In the succeeding chapter, probably enacted later, it is further stipulated that where the judge may hear (i.e., by the declaration of the seven men) of a *criminosus* he must go to his house and have him secured. Then if the prisoner be a freeman of quality (*Francus*),[29] he must be brought before the king

---

[27] C. 7 (1 *Cap.*, 16).

[28] 2 Brunner, *D.R.G.*, 639, says it is directed against notorious wrongdoers, and that it did not become general, being used only against thieves, sorcerers, and witches in Carolingian times. (*Cap. de Latronibus*, c. 4; 1 *Cap.* 180.) Knapp, *Zum Übersiebnen der Schädlichen Leute* III, in 63 *Archiv für Strafrecht* (1917), 260 says *every* thief or evil doer is meant; and compare Mayer, *Über die Schädlichen Leute* in 64 *ibid.*, 323 *et seq.*; and Mayer, *Geschworenengericht und Inquisitionsprozess* (1916), 195. V. Zallinger, *Das Verfahren gegen die Schädlichen Leute* (1895) 16, agrees with Brunner. The word *criminosus* is used here, we think, in an artful sense, to describe the professional or habitual thief. This is borne out by c. 10 where it speaks of a *criminosus* slave, and makes the master's wergeld liable for refusal to turn up the slave. It seems unlikely that such a heavy penalty would have been inflicted if the word *criminosus* were used to describe a first offender.

[29] Boretius, 1 *Cap.* 17, n. 11, suggests *Francus* = *nobilis,* or *antrustio.* Waitz in 2 *D.V.G.*, pt. 2, 30, renders it Frank. Brunner, 2 *D.R.G.*, 57, says person of higher rank.

(wherein the possible flaw in the procedure gains recognition), but if a lesser person, he must be executed on the spot.[30]

There can be no doubt that Childebert's decree is drawn with reference to the same ideas of disqualification through misconduct as motivated the provisions of the *Pactus* regarding suspicion of thieving. It is closer to the Roman infamy procedure because the oath of the men of good repute, although a mere statement of fact, operates as a notation and takes the place of judgment. It goes further than any previous procedure because, the fact of infamy established, the low-class malefactor has not even the right to an ordeal but the *Francus* gets a sentence at the hands of the crown. The crown cannot be bothered with petty business, but the man of quality, since no offense but only reputation is involved, will have his politics tested.

We have related the provision regarding the pursuit of thieves to those dealing with the proceedings against professional malefactors because all are concerned with state initiative in the matter of arrest and prosecution. Where no man stood forth as an accuser there was, until these legislative steps had been taken, a definite hiatus in the machinery. This lack is now supplied. The institution of supervised and obligatory hue and cry remained seated in the law throughout the Frankish period.[31]

The persistence of the procedure regarding the *criminosus* is

[30] The purpose of the phrase "sine lege moriatur," may be taken as a reaffirmation of the death penalty provided in the *Pactus* or as denying the suspected one a chance even to go to the ordeal, such as the suspected thief had under the rule of the *Pactus*. In the latter law the determination of the suspicion is dismissed by the word *inculpatur*. This may have reference only to a reputation for thievery, and hence, in the absence of an accuser, resort was had to the ordeal. In the *Decretio* the sworn statement of the *bona fidei* men stands in lieu of a certain accuser and the result which the law puts upon their positive findings removes all risks of further proof. This oath has the same effect of producing certainty as the foreoath of the accuser in *Ed. Chilp.*, c. 10. Like Chilperich, Childebert II interposes the severe penalty of death because the case is one where feud will not be waged. This is the purport of words "absque inimicitia interposita."

[31] *Supra*, note 7. Add *Form. Tur.* 30.

less clearly attested.[32] It is overshadowed by the appearance in Charlemagne's reign of a procedure which was even more effective, the accusatory inquest (*Rügeverfahren*).[33]

How this inquest originated is not known. It has been surmised that the method prescribed in the so-called first capitulary[33a] to the *Lex Salica* where a man was found killed may have contributed. The inquest procedure is for the first time clearly indicated in a Carolingian capitulary for Italy,[34] in such form that it appears as an innovation adapted from Frankish sources. It involved a summons by the judge of the most worthy and prominent men of the district. An oath was taken that the men would accuse truly in the case of certain specifically named crimes or would answer questions posited by the judge.[35] In the earliest capitularies these questions appear to have been limited to homicide, theft, adultery and incest, and later laws add to the list misfeasance of ecclesiastical and lay officials,[36] forest viola-

[32] In *Form. Marculfi I*, 8 the count is ordered "latronum et malefactorum scelera a te severissimae repremantur." This indicates persistence of right of execution directed in *Decr. Child. II. Cf. Cap. Haristall.* (779) cc. 9, 11 (1 *Cap.* 48–9).

[33] Brunner, *Entstehung der Schwurgerichte*, 458 *et seq.*; 2 *D.R.G.*, 639 *et seq.*; Mayer, *Geschworenengericht und Inquisitionsprozess*, 158 *et seq.*; 1 *Deutsche und Französische Verfassungsgeschichte* (1899), 233 *et seq.*; Mayer-Homberg, *Die Fränkischen Volkrechte*, 222 *et seq.*; Schröder, *D.R.G.*, 413. Consider also the inquest used for establishment of destroyed title instruments, *Form. And.* 32; *Form. Tur.* 28.

[33a] *Supra*, p. 69.

[34] *Pippini Italiae Reg. Capitulare* (782–786) c. 8 (1 *Cap.* 192).

[35] *Cap. de Missis Instruendis* (829) (2 *Cap.* 8) provides that the accusation or answer is made by virtue of the general oath of fidelity to the crown.

Mayer-Homberg, *loc. cit.*, argues that the duty to answer is at first a general duty, citing *Lex Salica*, Cap. I, 9, although he admits that there is no *inquisitio* since there is no question of a selection of jurors. The judges' demands are addressed to the whole community. Mayer-Homberg thinks it was only a step to select the jurors, since the community in the mass was too bulky to handle, and that the extension of the inquest from a single offense to several and finally all was relatively easy to accomplish. He sees a connection of the procedure in *Lex Salica*, Cap. I, 9 with the later manifestations of inquest because of the form of oath.

[36] *Cap. de Missis Instruendis, supra*, note 35.

tions[37] and sorcery.[38] Moreover, the subject matter in the various capitularies for the itinerant royal *missi* (so like the later English articles of the eyre) is such as to make it probable that the inquisition was used for broader inquiries.

The significance of the inquest is best appraised against the background of the plea for amends as the normal procedure, and the early efforts of the Merovingian kings to deal with suspected or notorious offenders. It is thus seen not as an intentional supplanting of the usual and ancient forms of redress, but as a provision in lieu of private accusation.[39] It supplements originally in the few causes where the crown has attempted an outright change of old law, or where it is bearing the cold fire of morality for the church. It supplements, we say, because once the inquest has pointed the finger of accusation, the victim whose horse has been stolen, or whose kin has been slain, can forthwith step in and carry on the trial as if he had himself initiated proceedings against the wrongdoer.[40] Yet the inquest does more than supplement, for the judge's privilege of questioning and the inquest's duty of answering tended to increase the state's initiative and to strengthen the authority already asserted. This is demonstrated by the lengthening of the list of matter into which inquiry must be made, and by the fact that where jurisdiction has been successfully asserted and maintained—as over the thief—no holder of jurisdictional immunity could refuse to yield up an offender to the crown.[41]

Over and above what the inquest accomplished toward increasing the scope of crown law, the procedure had the effect of

[37] *Cap. Miss.* (802) c. 39 (1 *Cap.* 98).

[38] *Cap. Carisiac.* (873) c. 7 (2 *Cap.* 345).

[39] On the limits of royal policy, 4 Waitz, *D.V.G.*, 507. On other measures to combat robbers *cf. ibid.,* 437 *et seq.; Cap. Aquisgr.* (809) cc. 3, 4 (1 *Cap.* 148) for the thief who is "forebanned." *Cf. Cap. Pap.* (850) c. 3 (2 *Cap.* 86). The penalty for harboring is later stepped up from 15 sol. to that for the thief and the *infidelis. Cap. Silvac.* (853) c. 6 (2 *Cap.* 273).

[40] 2 Brunner, *D.R.G.,* 642.

[41] *Cap. Haristall.* (779) c. 9 (2 *Cap.* 48). *Cap. de Latronibus* (804–813) c. 5 (1 *Cap.* 181).

extending the notion of the unworthy man, the person of disrepute. This followed from the fact that the crown now had an effective means of getting neighborhood opinion or knowledge expressed, and this expression we believe took various forms. Brunner[42] assumed the contrary, and quite without warrant, for he asserted that a defendant was in a position similar to that in which he would have been if a formal complaint had been made: if he denies he must purge himself with oath helpers, but if he is a person of ill fame he goes to the ordeal.

But in view of the judge's right to question, this statement is too general and too inadequate a test of the effect of inquest accusation. Unquestionably an accusatory inquest can answer variously depending upon what is asked. It may say as to act and actor: "we know" or "we suspect." It may say: "we suspect this man of constant malefaction," or "we know this man is a professional." When there is accusation based on certainty or probable suspicion as to a particular wrong, the ordinary rules of proof will be invoked: the freeman not infamous will purge by oath, others by ordeal. But if the inquest merely states the general reputation of a man then the procedural rights are different —no oath proof, only ordeal. This is the burden of the rule in Charlemagne's capitulary about thieves: judgment ensues as to persons and property if good men of good reputation have testified that a man of any class is "reprobate," i.e., notorious. He may go to the ordeal but if he does not go the reprobation is enough, just as the sworn statement of five or seven men in Childebert's day sufficed.[43]

There is, furthermore, some likelihood that group accusation

---

[42] 2 Brunner, *D.R.G.,* 641.

[43] *Cap. de Latronibus* (804–13) c. 4 (1 *Cap.* 180). The procedure in the inquest bears out what we have indicated may have been a probable connection between the rule of the *Pactus,* regarding a freeman suspected of theft and the *decretio* of Childebert II c. 7. The interpretation of the latter as resulting in summary execution upon a declaration of being a *criminosus* indicates a hard rule. It is possible this was relaxed by the two rules *Chlothar II Edictum* (614) c. 22 (1 *Cap.* 23) and *Chlothar II Praeceptio* (584–628) c. 3 (1 *Cap.* 18) forbidding condemnation of a man unheard (*inauditus*). This may have involved the interposition of proof or a

tended to operate as a factual if not a legal disqualification upon suspected persons even where they cleared themselves—not yet the brand of infamy but a taint none the less.[44] This tendency finally takes legal form under Louis the Pious. He orders that a man charged with theft for the first time can clear himself by oath but thereafter if two or three accuse him he can defend only by combat with club and shield, the device then recently introduced where doubt as to credibility existed.[45]

It is convenient at this juncture, and before proceeding to examine the development of final sanctions, to consider certain further extensions of infamy in connection with crown procedure. Up to this point it has appeared as primarily an incident of a particular sort of accusation. It becomes an incident of conviction for the first time in cases of perjury. This is specifically the result of ecclesiastical influence. Since Merovingian days the rule had been settled for Frankish canonical procedure that persons perjured could not be admitted as witnesses. This principle is stated in the seventh-century *Lex Alamannorum,* but it becomes a rule of Frankish secular law by enactment in one of the earliest of Charlemagne's great ordinances, the Capitulary of Haristal (779).[46] It is here provided that the perjurer shall lose his hand. This brutally and automatically excludes him from being a witness, for without his hand he cannot swear.[47]

formal judgment. Note however that "reprobation" *or* ordeal is enough to evoke execution according to *Cap. de Latronibus.*

The rule about ordeal is relaxed in the case of freemen by the capitulary of Quierzy in 873 (*infra*, note 50). We believe this was an innovation (although Brunner treats it as applicable throughout the Carolingian period) and that it was without permanent effect on later law.

[44] Chiefly as a result of the anti-perjury legislation the Carolingian capitularies recognized taint on credibility which falls short of complete disqualification, so in *Cap. Miss. in Theod. Villa II,* c. 11 (1 *Cap.* 124) to avoid perjury witnesses are to be examined before oath: *cf.* on this and related legislation, Brunner, *Zeugen und Inquisitionsbeweis,* in *Forschungen,* 110.

[45] *Cap. Legg. Add.* (818–819) c. 15 (1 *Cap.* 284). Club and shield combat will be discussed in Volume II.

[46] C. 10 (1 *Cap.* 49).

[47] This provision is repeated in 802 and again in 816. *Cap. Miss. Gen.* (802) c. 36 (1 *Cap.* 98); *Cap. cum primis Const.* (808) c. 4 (1 *Cap.* 139);

Shortly thereafter, the canonical principle itself is laid down in the first of the secular-ecclesiastical ordinances, the *Admonitio Generalis* of 789:[48] he who is perjured shall henceforth not be a witness nor be admitted to oath nor swear in his own or another's defense.

The logic which attached to a conviction of perjury the incident of future testimonial disqualification was wanting in the next step by the crown, when infamy was made a consequence of judgment of death. The rule enacted at Aachen in 809[49] stipulated that where a man adjudged to death is pardoned, he can hold and defend property acquired thereafter, but he is not acceptable as a witness nor can he act as a *scabinus* (doomsman). Furthermore, if he is ordered by judgment to swear to anything and if the oath is challenged, he must defend it by combat. As a matter of procedural theory this rule is something essentially different from that in the perjury case because it fixed upon judgment and not upon the execution of the sentence as the determinative point in the trial at which the infamy ensued. This rule was subsequently destined to have a profound effect upon the application of sanctions in the period of feudal government.

It is not necessary here to pursue the accretions to this doctrine further than to note the final drawing together of the threads of development in the Capitulary of Quierzy (873)[50] which incorporates by reference the earlier legislation. It effects also some change. Freemen who are *infames vel clamodici* of robberies, thefts, rapacities, assaults or infidelities, but not handhaving, and whose lives have already been pardoned, are to be

*Cap. Legg. Add.* (816) c. 1 (1 *Cap.* 268); *Cap. Legg. Add.* (818–819) c. 10 (1 *Cap.* 283).

    [48] C. 64 (1 *Cap.* 58). The same rule in purely secular form *Cap. Miss. Spec.* (802) c. 39 (1 *Cap.* 104). Note further that at the Synod of Frankfort (794) it is enacted that *criminosi* cannot accuse their betters or bishops.

    [49] Cc. 1 and 2 (1 *Cap.* 148).

    [50] C. 3 (2 *Cap.* 343). On this *cf.* Mayer, *Geschworenengericht und Inquisitionsprozess*, 197.

dealt with on future complaint as in the capitularies of the ancestor kings (viz., Aachen, 809). Where there is no private accuser, the count summons the *infamis* with distraint as a pressure for appearance. If no accuser appears, the freeman hitherto not infamous or previously convicted can purge himself twelve-handed, but must bind himself by oath never to do in the future the acts with which he has been charged. The *fiscalinus*[51] goes to the ordeal. If an accuser appears, the proceeding is to take the form prescribed in earlier capitularies. The man who does not show up is banned. Here is explicit talk of infamy, reflecting both the wide extension of this notion in Pseudo-Isidore,[52] as well the express labeling of matter in earlier legislation as infamy in Benedict's falsifications.[53] Hereafter these matters remain as aspects of *infamia* in the sense in which the word was employed by canonists.[54] This final technical baptism of long-seated rules about disqualification is more than a mere fixing of terminology.[55] It involved a merging of canonical doctrines and secular rules defining categories of faithful men, the men of good reputation and the men who had forfeited fame. And from this merger come those basic medieval concepts, infamy and legality.

### THE DEVELOPMENT OF AFFLICTIVE SANCTIONS

To a certain extent the perfection of the devices just discussed for catching and prosecuting criminals is connected with the general intervention of the state in the matter of punishment. Here it moves into a field still dominated by the concepts of personal revenge or composition, and its interference is beset with

[51] The half-free, 1 Brunner, *D.R.G.* 375.
[52] 5 Hinschius, *K.R.* 41.
[53] On the use of these by Charles the Bald, 1 Brunner, *D.R.G.* 558.
[54] *Supra* note 22.
[55] The influence of the concept on folklaw procedure indicated in *Cap. Theod. II*, c. 5 (1 *Cap.* 123): breach of a *securitas* punished as perjury. Note also *Form. Sen. Rec.* 16; *Form. Sal. Merk.* 64; *Form. Bitur.* 19; *M.G.H.*, 5 *Epp.*, 126, no. 34.

greater difficulties than where it seeks merely to provide for accusation where there is no accuser, because the underlying reasons for its action rest on a much broader foundation, politically, and economically and perhaps also ethically. Here once more we shall have to consider orthodox theory, and once more recur to early sources to trace the growth of royal legislation.

Since the early nineties the thinking of continental legal historians about sanctions has been dominated by the ingenious theory of Brunner that the afflictive penalties grow up as mitigations or derivations of outlawry.[56] This theory was a result of regarding complete peacelessness or outlawry as the most ancient and the inevitable result of all wrongs. It is a theory which enjoys the advantage of nicely logical formulation, but as stated earlier it rests upon an unacceptable premise and is unprovable in detail. It has only recently been subjected to a suggested modification by Karl von Amira,[57] who conceived that the death penalty in Germanic law was sacral in origin, that it never completely disappeared, and that its reappearance was in the nature of a revival of ancient custom.

Von Amira has distinguished two sources of penal law in pre-Christian Germanic times.[58] One is a purely sacral law in which death is the sole public punishment. The long and persistent emphasis upon ritual in methods of execution, even into the late Middle Ages, serves to establish what he declares were originally acts of cult. The other law, which von Amira envisages as profane, rests upon the idea of outlawry and to this extent he accepts the thesis of Brunner.[59] Apart from the fact that von Amira traversed ruling dogma at various points, his proofs are significant chiefly as social and not as legal data, because they empha-

---

[56] Brunner, *Abspaltungen der Friedlosigkeit,* in *Forschungen* 444.

[57] V. Amira, *Die Germanischen Todesstrafen* in 31 *Abhandlungen der Bayerischen Akademie der Wissenschaften,* Phil.-Hist. Klasse, pt. 3 (1922).

[58] *Ibid.,* 4 *et seq.*

[59] *Cf.* on this the note of v. Schwerin in 2 Brunner, *D.R.G.,* 762, n. 2.

size the method of execution but fail to relate the punishment to the whole procedural structure and to the ends for which this exists. Moreover, v. Amira, like Brunner, was reluctant to admit that matter in the folklaws which seemed to confirm his theories might in many cases not be antique but be a novel manifestation of group action. Both writers emphasize a renaissance of what they believe were institutions that never were completely moribund. This leaves much unaccounted for. Are we to believe that the criminal law of Rome was completely forgotten, despite the large numbers of Romans who were living under a greatly debased imperial law, and despite the fact that Burgundian and Visigothic law are a standing reminder of the power of Roman ideas? Are we also to overlook the effect of the ecclesiastical law exercising its power over sins through a system of penitentials pervaded by notions of punishment exacted by authority, and not of composition?

It is, of course, impossible to view with indifference the possible influence of either the Roman or Canon law. This is particularly true when mutations in any discernible theory of punishment[60] are sought, because the sanctions of the early folklaws are settled in well-marked grooves, and the theory on which they are applied is conditioned by the objectives of the procedure of which they are a final part.

We are concerned here primarily with the rise of sanctions applied by public authority; and this is a procedural problem and must be approached as such. In consequence the sanction has to be treated essentially as final process, without reference to any supposed penal theory. For convenience these sanctions will be separately considered depending upon whether they are bodily afflictive or are taken against the property of an offender.

[60] 1 Günther, *Die Idee der Wiedervergeltung* (1889), 180, asserts that in the early folklaws there is no definite theory set up in respect of the objectives of the law, although he has collected (n. 53) from the various codes statements indicating the existence of isolated objectives, such as prevention, betterment, etc.

Since the procedural development here under consideration relates primarily to causes between freemen, it is not essential to enter upon a discussion either of those phases of family law where the head by virtue of his *mundium* inflicts sanctions on an adulterous wife or unchaste daughter, or of the master's power of discipline over the unfree in the form of death, mutilation or chastisement.[61] Interference by the state in matters of family morals occurs chiefly as a result of ecclesiastical pressure, and is effected by outright legislation framed on Roman-canonical models.[62] This does add to the sum total of the state's powers but it lies outside ordinary procedure and ordinary problems of wrongdoing with which public authority is attempting to cope. So, too, in a somewhat different way, the matter of slave delicts. The law contemplates here the master's liability toward third persons, and when the state intermeddles it is interested only in relief for the master or for third parties. None of its action here is a first step toward a control of the same matter among freemen because the barrier of status stands in the way.

But in the matter of wrongs where the state will develop authority to exact sanctions, its action is conditioned by the fact that the core of early Frankish procedure is built up about feud and composition. There final execution develops from the fact that wrongdoing precipitates revenge, institutionalized as feud, with composition as an alternative. The composition process is one of reconciliation and reparation: the wrongdoer makes reparation for his act on the basis of tariffs scaled on man-values, or the value of the animate or inanimate objects interfered with. He makes reparation to the person and kin he has injured. Public

---

[61] Discussed by Beyerle, *Rechtsgang*, 325, 332 *et seq.* V. Amira, *Die Germanischen Todesstrafen*, 7 *et seq.*, on the power of the sib to punish members, which he bases on the law of the sib; *ibid.*, 15, on what he calls the power to punish by virtue of the law of marriage; *ibid.*, 20, on what he refers to as punishment by the right of revenge which is what we are discussing in the text as the surrender of the wrongdoer to the injured sib. On the punishment of the unfree, *cf.* also Meyer, *Die Gerichtsbarkeit über Unfreie und Hintersassen*, in 2 *Z.R.G.*[2], 89 *et seq.*

[62] So *Lex Salica*, Cap. I, c. 6 (Hessels, 71) *Decr. Child. II*, cc. 2, 4.

authority acts initially as a mere intermediary to promote the process of amends and subsequently to see that the bargain is kept. These are the postulates of purpose from which must be drawn any inferences regarding the earliest instances of afflictive bodily sanctions in cases for which feud can be waged.

In terms of this primitive procedure the use of afflictive sanctions (as a part of procedure) in the case of offenses committed by one free man against another is connected either with feud or with the satisfaction of a bargain to make amends. In the former instance the law which consistently sought to restrict private revenge, temporized with it by recognizing and sanctioning one situation, the case of handhavingness—the thief with the *mainour;* the killer with the bloody knife.

Here summary justice can be inflicted—the offender slain—not, as the dogmatists would have it, because he has made himself outlaw by his crime,[63] but, as Beyerle has demonstrated,[64] because the injured person is allowed his revenge; he is carrying out his privilege of feud instanter. The law recognizes the heat of rage as it still does today.[65] But it insists on no slowing in the tempo of impulse. At the most it concedes that if the red-handed offender escapes from the spot, his victim may pursue if he calls upon his neighbors, may capture and bind the malefactor and present him at a court,[66] where the criminal may say no

[63] 2 Brunner, *D.R.G.,* 629, calls it a procedure against an outlaw or peaceless man. His editor, v. Schwerin, *ibid.,* n. 12, takes the position against Beyerle that the killing of the handhaving thief would be a breach of the peace if the thief were in the peace; since it is not a breach of the peace the thief must be out of the peace. The issue seems to depend upon the question, who could kill? Since the right is given to the injured (i.e., the persons who are competent to wage feud) and not to third parties (Beyerle, *Rechtsgang,* 268) the malefactor can scarcely be regarded as an outlaw whom, according to the usual assumptions, anyone might kill.

[64] Beyerle, *Rechtsgang,* 265 *et seq.*

[65] So the *"furor brevis* of passion," State v. Johnson, 1 *Iredell* (No. Car.) 354, in manslaughter; "the reasonable time for cooling," State v. Mc-Cants, 1 *Spears* (So. Car.) 384.

[66] The capture and binding is a later development; Beyerle, *Rechtsgang,* 310.

word in defense.[67] All this is no guarantee of reasoned procedure; it is mere regulation of a right of self-help. The oath the revenging accuser takes is offered merely to avoid reprisal in the feud which might ensue if he could not show he was not the aggressor.[68] The malefactor is executed as an act of justifiable revenge.

In contrast with the raw character of the handhaving procedure, composition (existing to avert violence) is directed not at revenge but at pecuniary reparation. This limits, of course, the possibilities of applying afflictive sanctions. Indeed, these come into play only indirectly, not as satisfaction for an injury but as satisfaction of a judgment and bargain to settle. The scheme of tariffs in the Salic law contemplates in the case of a personal injury, a normal man value of 200 sol. It expects contribution by kinsmen[69] so that there is a reasonable spread of the incidence of the tariffs. In some cases, notably secret killing, the amends sum rises so far above wergeld that only the affluent would possess enough livestock to make settlement.[70] Specifically in the case of wergeld insolvency, the law abandons the mere pecuniary sanction for bargain breach which rests on a presumption of solvency, and still speaking in the idiom of composition lets the debtor pay with his person.[71] This rule (*de chrenecruda*) is based upon the presumption that proceedings have been entered into,

[67] But the neighbors have to be called to bar the defendant. *Ibid.*, 308, 311.

[68] Beyerle, *Rechtsgang,* 286, 305, 309.

[69] 1 Brunner, *D.R.G.,* 325 *et seq.*

[70] The estimate of values for the period of the *Lex Salica* in 1 Inama-Sternegg, *Deutsche Wirtschaftsgeschichte* (1879) *Beilage* IV. An idea of the later change in values can be deduced from *Cap. de Part. Sax.* (775–790) c. 27 (1 *Cap.* 70) where an ox (fullgrown) equals ten shillings.

[71] *Lex Salica,* 58, and *cf.* Behrend's notes for further references, as well as Schröder, *D.R.G.,* 304, n. 43; Brunner, *Sippe und Wergeld* in 3 *Z.R.G.*[2], 37 *et seq.*; Meyer, *Die Entstehung der Germanischen Todesstrafe* in 89 *Der Gerichtsaal,* 378; *Über Exil überhaupt und Lex Salica,* 58, in 33 *Mitteilungen des Instituts für Österreichische Geschichte,* 607, 617 *et seq.*; v. Amira, *Der Stab in der Germanischen Rechtssymbolik* in 25 *Mitteilungen der K. Bay. Akad. der Wissenschaften,* Phil.-Hist. Klasse (1911) 15.

faith has been pledged, the sum has been assessed. But when all is done and the amount has not been raised by the debtor or his kinsmen, after house, herds and even bodily covering have been tossed into the avid hands of the accusers, he must, says the law, "compose with his life."

How are we to interpret this phrase? That there is a death penalty inflicted by "public" authority is highly unlikely. The suggestion that here is a declaration of outlawry seems equally incredible.[72] What is intended is a surrender of the individual to the injured party either for execution or for enslavement.

The reasons for this interpretation are various. In the first place, it is usual in the folklaws to allow a sib to escape feud by surrendering a wrongdoer to the complainant or his kin. Furthermore, since the law talks of "composing" it may be supposed that it is drafted with reference to composition theory. This is based upon economic reparation, and on a faintly ethical ideal of restricting feud. The fate of the man turned over to his accusers will be determined by these purposes. Just as every lump sum payable as amends represented so many head of cattle, so the individual's life could be reckoned in terms of labor: he is an economic value no less than an ox or an ass. Yet, if the accusing kin desire to waive the economic advantage of servitude, they are privileged to wreak their revenge on the offender, for, by the surrender in legal form, the law has vested the accusers with the execution of the sanction. In either event—servitude or death—the wrongdoer surrenders his life.

The laws which encourage the practice of private execution, and among the Burgundians and Visigoths the tendency is most pronounced, are as we have said pervaded by the idea that this restricts feud.[73] But too much ethics must not be read into this,

[72] Schreuer, *Die Behandlung der Verbrechenskonkurrenz* (*Untersuchungen*, 50 [1896]), 256.

[73] This is the position of Beyerle, *Rechtsgang*, 325 *et seq*. At 328 he deals for instance with *Lex Vis.*, III, 4, 3 *Antiqua* from the standpoint of a special form of *procedure* in contrast to v. Amira who approaches the prob-

or implications that the law seeks to deter or to better or even to retaliate. The feud is a nuisance to be checked only by restricting its scope, and by disturbing party expectation as little as possible. Hence the power of the man who may execute to decide on death is admitted, because it is a deeply rooted corollary of any accusation that *the right of execution was vested in the accuser.*[74] The whole structure of emendation was based upon the precept that satisfaction was made to the party plaintiff: if he does not have this in the form of cattle he may have it in the form of a human life.

The idea that the plaintiff must be satisfied likewise takes another form, conceivably as a result of ecclesiastical pressure, because of its precepts of mercy and the value it sets upon human life. This is the creation of an alternative of redemption where death is stipulated by law. This right of redemption we believe to have been outside the scope of the composition system. In the first place, the use of the word "redeem" in place of "compose" is itself significant, since the transaction stands on an entirely different footing from the composition proceeding.[75] Secondly,

lem of the adulterous wife from the angle of the substantive right of the group (or injured party) to deal with the offender, as the manifestation of what he conceives to be a very ancient right and power of punishment. This does not explain its persistence or the fact that the state resorted to it. Beyerle's insistence that forms of procedure are here involved is borne out by his proof. He concludes that the procedure is fostered by the state because the surrender of a culprit to the injured group is essentially a means of dissolving a state of feud (*ibid.*, 330), and hence is an attempt to restrict feud (*ibid.*, 328). On this see the gloss on *Lex Salica*, 58, *de chrenecruda* (Behrend edition, 123), "Lege quae paganorum tempore observabant deinceps numquam valeat quia ipsam cecidit multorum potestas."

[74] V. Amira, *Die Germanischen Todesstrafen*, 20, 228; Grimm *D.R.A.*, 882. Brunner in 2 *D.R.G.*, 615, treats private execution as an act of private revenge but this does not fully bring out the implication of the laws. That the execution is not *faida* but *compositio* is clear from *Lex. Sal.*, 58. Cf. *Lex. Burg.* II, 1, 7; *Lex Vis.* VII, 3, 3.

[75] Beyerle, *Rechtsgang*, 337 *et seq.*, sees in the *precio redemptionis* a thing *sui generis*, i.e., a purchase price. Cf. 2 Brunner, *D.R.G.*, 798–799. *Lex Salica*, 55, 2, says that the robber of a grave "wargus sit" (i.e., be expelled from the district) but he can be put in the law on the application of the relatives of the deceased whereupon he pays 200 sol. This Schreuer,

the law which allows redemption usually forbids feud and names a penalty. Composition, on the other hand, is posited on the admissibility of feud as an alternative. The right of redemption consequently is essentially a ransom in lieu of surrender for execution. And as a ransom it is unfettered at first by the standard amends tariffs.[76] Like the king's mercy in medieval England for which men make fine and ransom, the amount will be what the traffic will bear.

In the early additions to the *Lex Salica* when king's law first cuts through the structure of composition fact by forsaking tariffs and stipulating death it contemplates surrender for servitude or death and the alternative of redemption, because this is existing practice.[77] Recognition of this practice is of a piece with the state's policy to work with existing procedure already discussed: controlling summons, suspension of hostilities and final concord. Its action is motivated in most cases by a desire to stop feud at the earliest possible point, and in some instances it acts at the instance of the church to set up canonical standards of morality.[78] There is no abstract theory of punishment at work; which explains why public authority is willing to harness up and give legal effect to the injured man's desire for revenge by letting him act as executioner. These early legislative additions represent a transition stage between early complete control of the parties over feud and composition and subsequent exercise by the state of a power itself to execute.[79] This transition is not effected, nor

*op. cit.,* 179, says is a redemption and not amends for the offense, and the sum is divisible between the sib and the authorities. In *Lex Rib.,* 85, 2, the 200 sol. and being *wargus* are alternative.

[76] Brunner, *loc. cit.,* points out that with the passage of time the tendency is for amends and redemption to become indistinguishable. Such a tendency should not obscure the fact that the legal nature of the transaction of redemption differed from a composition payment, since the emendation for the wrong is effected by the surrender of the culprit. It is not wrong and redemption that are related, but execution and redemption.

[77] For example, *Lex Sal.,* Cap. I, c. 5 (Hessels, 70); *Pactus pro tenore pacis,* cc. 1 and 2; *Edict. Chilp.* c. 8; *Decr. Child. II,* cc. 4 and 5.

[78] As in the case of incest, *Decr. Child. II,* c. 2.

[79] Beyerle, *Rechtsgang,* 345–347. A point not raised by Beyerle that

is the basic idea that satisfaction is owed the injured shaken, however, until the notion has gained ground that the state itself has been injured: (1) because the wrong affects the whole community, or (2) because the crown is directly affected, or (3) because no one but public authority is concerned in the wrongful act.

In the narrow field of unemendable wrongs, it is certain that "public" authority in the very earliest times had possessed the power to execute the usual afflictive sanctions.[80] Likewise it must be assumed that infractions of army discipline in so far as they were military offenses were dealt with by the command.[81] So the death penalty for flight or desertion was inflicted by authority.[82] This may be the source of the subsequent royal prerogative in

must have been of consequence is the question whether or not the fisc was able to share in the sum of redemption. In the case of *Lex Salica*, 55, 2, discussed *supra*, note 74, the expulsion is withdrawn upon application by the injured kin to the authorities, so that there is no question of the right to *fredus*. It does not appear that the business of redemption was carried out judicially, consequently there is no reason to believe that a part of the redemption sum went to the state. Schreuer, *Verbrechenskonkurrenz*, 179 *et seq. contra*, but without proof and with no sound reason for his inferences. *Chlothar II, Praec.* c. 6, and *Edict. Chloth. II*, c. 12 look simply to restitution. Brunner, 2 *D.R.G.*, 799 equivocates. No argument can be made from cases like *Cap. Legg. Add.* (818-9) c. 10 (1 *Cap.* 283) when the redemption of the perjuror's hand is treated as an amends. The special legislation suggests rather the contrary to be usual.

[80] Thus the celebrated passage in Tacitus, *Germania*, c. 12.

[81] The earliest evidence on the point is Caesar, *De Bello Gallico*, VI, 23, who states that the leaders chosen for the war have power of life and death. Tacitus, *Germania*, c. 7, says that the power of punishment was lodged in the priests. *Cf.* further Brunner's remarks in 1 *D.R.G.*, 185, and compare v. Amira, *Die Germanischen Todesstrafen*, 227; Baumstark, *Ausführliche Erläuterung*, 364.

[82] 2 Brunner, *D.R.G.*, 83, 775. The obvious connection between the power of punishment in the army and that of the king in civil affairs need hardly be emphasized. On the other hand, it is not to be supposed that even the power of the crown, though arbitrary, was almighty. Thus, *Lex Baiuwariorum*, II, 8, provides that where one kills at the order of the king or duke feud is forbidden against him. *Cf.* also *Form. Marculfi I*, 32, where the king orders that officials who confiscate are to be free of all suits, etc. These are certain indications of the power of the feud-composition ideas and of what difficulties a king's law had encountered.

respect of penalties, a power frequently mentioned in Gregory's history and exercised in what appears to be a thoroughly arbitrary manner.[83] Here, the penalties are either death or exile, the former often expressly connected with the idea of *laesae maiestatis* appropriated from Roman law by the Merovingians.

In one important particular, however, the prerogative of the crown was exercised, not arbitrarily but systematically as a part of its official law—the sanctions taken for misfeasance or nonfeasance in office. Thus, in the *Lex Salica,* the count who refuses to distrain or levies on more than necessary is threatened with loss of life.[84] Similarly in the *Decretio* of Childebert II the *iudex* who releases a thief is so penalized.[85] In the *Lex Salica,* the official is given a right of redemption; in the *Decretio* nothing of the sort is suggested.[86] Now, while one can conceive of a ransom going to the injured distrainee and consequently a correlative right of execution, the *iudex* who releases a thief who has been declared criminous but against whom no certain accuser has appeared is offending only against the crown.[87] In such a case the

[83] For example those listed in 2 Waitz, *D.V.G.*, pt. 1, 194, n. 4; *ibid.*, pt. 2, 32, n. 1.

[84] *Lex Salica,* 51, 2, and 50, 4.

[85] *Decr. Child. II* (596) c. 7 (1 *Cap.* 17).

[86] Behrend in his notes to *Lex Salica,* 50, 4, suggests that there is no death penalty threatened but only the amends of full wergeld and relates this to *Lex Salica,* 51, 2. Brunner, 2 *D.R.G.*, 597 treats the latter as inflicting a death penalty or alternative wergeld. The latter idea apparently comes from a variation in the Herold text of the *Lex Salica,* on which *cf.* Schreuer, *op. cit.*, 180, n. 13. Sohm, *Process der Lex Salica*, 174, says there is a "penalty of life" but nothing about wergeld. With *Lex Salica,* 51, 2, should be compared the threat of *Ed. Chilp.* c. 8 (1 *Cap.* 9).

[87] *Decr. Child. II* (516) c. 7 (1 *Cap.* 17) speaks first of the accusation of the five or seven men that a thief is *criminosus,* and that he must die who steals against the law. It goes on to say that, if any *iudex* is convicted of having released a captured thief, he shall lose his life. We render *comprehensum latronem* as *captured thief* and not *handhaving thief,* because cc. 7, 8 and 10 are all talking about the *criminosus.* There is no indication the thief is in custody when he is declared to be *criminosus.* On the contrary, the *iudex* is to go after him (c. 8); minor officers who fail to help pay 60 sol. ban (c. 9); people who do not present a criminous servant owe wergeld (c. 10). Compare with this passage on the control of the

infliction of the death penalty must certainly have vested in the latter.

The decree of Childebert marks the real beginning of a similar power of execution in respect to persons not officials, who have committed offenses at one time emendable.[88] Here the crown cleaves to the principle set up in the earlier *Pactus* that the *latro* must die, but it abandons the procedure of that law for surrender of the offender to the injured party. Childebert assumes the power to execute because the accusation is made by virtue of crown law in the form of the declaration of five or seven reputable men that the offender is infamous. Since the *criminosus* has no procedural rights because of this declaration, the king's officer can proceed forthwith to apply the final sanction.

It must not be imagined that the assertion of jurisdiction over a particular category of persons meant the establishment of a principle[89]—that the transition to a state-executed penalty was suddenly effected, or that it displaced private execution.[90] In the

*iudex, Pactus pro tenore pacis (Decr. Chloth.)* c. 18 (1 *Cap.* 7). Gregory, *Historia Francorum,* VI, 46, relates of the lesser penalty of blinding as a threat attached to orders addressed by the crown to *iudices. Cf.* also *ibid.,* VIII, 30.

[88] Beyerle, *Über Normtypen . . . der Lex Salica,* 44 Z.R.G.², 231.

[89] The conclusions in the text are based upon the Salic sources. There is no doubt, however, that in the Visigothic kingdom the development was in advance of the law of the Franks. On this *cf.* Dahn, *Westgothische Studien* (1874) 166 *et seq.* At 186 Dahn suggests the use of whipping in cases of offenses by freemen and nobles was due to the arbitrary power of the crown and to the influence of the church. At 189, he attributes to despotism the use of mutilation. In the *Lex Salica* the death penalty is in the first instance the punishment of slaves, except in the case of the insolvent wrongdoer where as we have seen it appears in the form of an ultimate sanction inflicted by the injured party. The arson case in 16, Add. 1, Behrend apparently attributes to a later period. *Cf.* Cap. III, c. 1. The case of the sorcerer who can be burned, *Lex Salica,* 19, 1 (ex Cod. 2) is to be explained on the grounds of the superstition that only by extirpation can the power of magic be destroyed. The use of fire suggests that this passage was composed after the conversion of the Franks to Christianity. *Cf.* 2 Brunner, *D.R.G.,* 874.

[90] Thus even in Charlemagne's time, the convicted conspirators mutilate each other, *Cap. in Theod. Villa II,* c. 10 (1 *Cap.* 124).

period following the *Decretio* the only principle motivating extensions of state power is the notion that a specific interest of the crown is involved and that consequently the crown may punish.[91] Thus the *Lex Ribuaria*[92] seeks to punish by death the impeachment of a royal document and persons who have committed infidelity, adding in the latter case a confiscation of property.[93] So, too, the judges caught accepting bribes are ruled to forfeit their lives.[94] The *Lex Alamannorum,* applying to a more outlying region, threatens with death persons who conspire to kill the duke, but with a right of redemption; and in the case of the somewhat related offense of inviting hostile persons into the province, death or exile, and property confiscations are named.[95] The same alternative exists in case of persons promoting sedition in the army.[96] Similar are the provisions of the *Lex Baiuwariorum* in respect of conspiring the death of the duke.[97] The latter is given the power over the culprit's life and the property goes to the fisc. In the same chapter the law expressly limits capital crimes to the previously mentioned case, the invitation of enemies into the province and conspiracy against the state. The fact that power of life or death is vested in the duke confirms what has been said in respect of public exaction of punishment.

Prior to Charlemagne, thus, the state appears to have wielded exclusive authority to execute in ordinary criminal causes only

[91] Brunner, 2 *D.R.G.,* 616, takes the position that what was originally a right of the injured to punish became a duty so that his act of execution lost the character of a private act and acquired "public" quality. He refers to *Cap. Ital.* (801) c. 4 (1 *Cap.* 205), and he relies upon the prevalence of private execution in later medieval times that we have mentioned. Contrast with this v. Amira, *Die Germanischen Todesstrafen,* 42, where the idea of an unconditional public punishment without exceptions is assumed as the point of departure and such matters as redemption are later exceptions.

[92] *Lex Ribuaria,* 60, 6.
[93] *Ibid.,* 69, 1.
[94] *Ibid.,* 88, 1.
[95] *Lex Alamannorum,* 24, 25.
[96] *Ibid.,* 26.
[97] *Lex Baiuwariorum,* II, 1, 1.

in the case of a particular class of offenders—the *criminosi*. The swing from private to public execution perceptible under the Carolingian kings cannot, therefore, be explained in terms of authority acquired over specific crimes but must be sought in procedural change.

This we believe was chiefly the result of practice not too clearly attested in the sources. By the year 800 death penalty had been stipulated for various wrongs where once feud could be waged or plea made for amends. But in many cases the law was so phrased that execution by the injured sib, while not directly specified, was an expectancy of practice. Furthermore, since there existed an option in the plaintiff to enslave or put to death, defendants were able to forestall the exercise of this choice by entering into voluntary servitude in anticipation of judgment or its execution.[98] This had the effect of vitiating the actual execution of the death penalty threatened by the law. As long as the crown was content with merely checking feud, the chief motive for these enactments, this sort of evasion was of small moment. But under Charlemagne there occurs in the capitularies a sudden invasion of religious zeal for stamping out sin and wickedness,[99] which suggests that some articulate penal theory is being read into existing laws. In any event at least one ordinance directs the infliction of penalty and forbids evasion by self-enslavement.[100]

[98] A formula is *Marculfi II*, 28. On the use to settle composition debts and evade distraint on realty, *infra*, note 100.

[99] For example, *Cap. Miss. Gen.* (802) cc. 25, 33, 37 (1 *Cap.* 96); *Cap. Miss.* (802–13), c. 4 (1 *Cap.* 147); *Cap. a Miss. Dom.* (801–13) 1 *Cap.* 183; and *Missi cuiusdam Admonitio* (801–12) 1 *Cap.* 238 for a generally homiletic instruction. The tendency is to be seen later, e.g. *Cap. Miss. Silvac.* (853) c. 12 (2 *Cap.* 274); *Cap. Carisiac.* (873) c. 7 (2 *Cap.* 345).

[100] *Cap. Aquisg.* (801–13) c. 15 (1 *Cap.* 172). C. 13 directs that no bribes are to be taken from *latrones* adjudged to death and denies right of pardon to local officers. C. 15 uses the word *pro furto* indicating a specific offense. Brunner, 2 *D.R.G.*, 624, regards c. 15 as general, apparently treating *furtum* as a general description of crime much as *latro* is sometimes used to describe offenders of any sort. Brunner's interpretation is too broad. Note, however, *Cap. Theod. II*, c. 15 (1 *Cap.* 125) requiring royal license for a man to enslave himself to an ecclesiastical establishment, and com-

This demand for literal enforcement[101] was an implicit threat at sib execution. Where legislation simply employed expressions like "peril of life" or "capital sentence" and was silent on who was to execute, a rule that the "written law" was to be followed would enable the courts simply to ignore the old practice of sib execution and use their own hangmen. The precise means whereby private execution was thus shouldered aside we believe came about through the exercise of a power of final sentence with which royal judges were vested.

These powers grow up in connection with final judicial acts at the conclusion of a trial. They are based on the mandate power of the royal officer.[102] In certain cases it is possible to distinguish pronouncement of sentence as distinct from the judgment rendered by the doomsmen. This is a development which fits into the picture of the increased authority exercised by the judge over other phases of trial—summons, observance of peace and final concord. The old form of judgment by the doomsmen, medial and contemplating bargain by the parties, was clearly inapposite where an afflictive bodily sanction was involved. For example, in the procedure stipulated by Chilperich whereby a malefactor was to be offered three times for redemption and then surrendered for execution to his adversaries, some form of sentence must have been required. There is language in Chlothar II's Edict of 614[103] which shows clearly enough that the *iudex* con-

pare the later *Edict. Pist.* (864) c. 28 (2 *Cap.* 322) where a king's ban is clapped on. The self-enslavement in lieu of penalty is to be sharply distinguished from the enslavement for debt as e.g. composition debt. On the latter, Lenz, *Zur Geschichte der germanischen Schuldknechtschaft*, 31 *M.I.Ö.G.*, 521. Note finally in the penal case the crown has in any event a desire to see the cause go to judgment since at Aachen in 809 it is for the first time expressly stipulated that in all cases where a man is adjudged to death the fisc gets his property (1 *Cap.* 148).

[101] *Cap. Miss. Gen.* (802) c. 26 (1 *Cap.* 96) judging is to be "secundum scriptam legem."

[102] *Cf.* on this *Form. Sen. Rec.*, 3, 6; "per iussionem comitis." *Form. Sal. Bign.* 9, "recta iudicia terminanda."

[103] *Ed. Chlothar II* (614) c. 4 (1 *Cap.* 21) "nullum iudicum . . . per

demns, and by this must certainly be intended the pronouncement of sentence *ex officio*. This power is unquestionable wherever a ban penalty is inflicted.[104] To some power of this sort the
crown may refer when it says that no one shall judge against a
right judgment (*rectum iudicium*).[105]

The use of final sentence as a legal institution is best attested
in relation to the crown. The king possessed what comes to be
called the right of *definitiva sententia*,[106] broadly an aspect of
the crown's ban power. Such is the *extra sermonem regis* of the
*Lex Salica* (employed because the doomsmen do not have a
power of conclusive judgment, let alone of sentence); the right
reserved by Childebert II to sentence a *criminosus* who is a
*Francus*;[107] the power to pronounce as to high clergy the words
whereby secular penalties are put into effect.[108] This royal sentence is immediate, final and unimpeachable.[109] It approximates

se distringere aut damnare praesumat"; Chloth. II *Praeceptio* (584–628)
c. 3 (1 *Cap.* 18).

[104] *Pactus pro tenore pacis*, c. 17 "15 sol iudice condemnetur; *Decr.
Child. II*, c. 9 "60 sol. omnis modis condempnetur."

[105] *Cap. a Miss. Cog.* (803–813) c. 7 (1 *Cap.* 146). Compare for later
*Cap. Pist.* (869) c. 11 (2 *Cap.* 336) "ut comites et missi ac vassi nostri et
ministeriales regni . . . iuste . . . iudicent."

[106] This is discussed by Seelmann, *Der Rechtszug im älteren deutschen
Recht* (*Untersuchungen* no. 107 [1911]) 43 *et seq.* in relation to appeal
and transfer of causes. The theory of *finire* is too loosely stated (*ibid.*, 12)
with no reference to cases where mere penalty is inflicted. See further Gál,
*Prozessbeilegung*, 4 and 68 *et seq.;* much less didactic. The expression
*definitiva sententia* is derived from certain formulae, e.g. *Marculfi I*, 24;
*Marculfi Add.*, 2; *Cart. Sen.* 28; *Form. Imp.* 32, 41.

[107] *Child. II Decretio*, c. 8. *Cf.* for later *Cap. Pip. Reg.* (754–5) c. 7 (1
*Cap.* 32); *Cap. Aquisg.* (801–13) c. 12 (1 *Cap.* 171). *Cf.* further Conrat,
*Ein Traktat über romanisch-fränkisches Ämterwesen*, 29 Z.R.G.², 249 c. 2,
"Obtimates autem non iudicant ad presentiam regis, sed seorsum et forsan
cum episcopis. et non possunt damnare vel solvere, antequam veniat rex."

[108] 2 *Recueil des Historiens de France*, 621, *Vita S. Leodegarii* (678)
c. 14; 3 Mabillon, *Acta Sanctorum*, 557, *Vita S. Eucherii* (732) c. 8;
M.G.H., 1 *Dipl.* 44, no. 48 (677–8).

[109] The writers have fought over the issue: has the king's court power to
give a judgment with the force of law (*rechtskräftiges Urteil*). The most
convincing case is stated in 2 Brunner, *D.R.G.*, 687. Note also: 1) the existence of a power of equity in the crown is sufficient to explain the occa-

in theory the Roman idea of *condemnatio*[110] in causes criminal and the *condemnatio* of the ecclesiastical law.[111]

This power we think was gradually delegated. The count is given it in small degree[112] but his authority is supposed to be governed by the findings of the doomsmen, a limitation which degenerates into a mere gesture favorable to folklaw judging theory when the doomsmen are made standing officials.[113] The royal judge having a royal commission and using an inquest apparently has it to a rather full extent,[114] and here is precisely

sional revival of judgments; 2) the king can issue charters or precepts which are unimpeachable; 3) the words *finire* and *definitiva sententia* presumably mean what they say.

[110] *Cf.* the treatise on Frankish officialdom (Conrat, *op. cit., supra,* note 107) "damnare aut solvere." This justifies, perhaps, a strict construction of the word *condemnare* in the early capitularies. *Cf. Pactus pro tenore pacis,* cc. 9, 17; *Child. II Decr.,* cc. 2, 9; *supra,* note 104; *Conc. Vernense* (755) c. 9 (1 *Cap.* 35). And compare *Conc. Orleans* IV (541) c. 20 (1 *Concilia, M.G.H.,* 91). On the Roman criminal practice, Geib, *Geschichte des Römisches Kriminalprocess,* 365 *et seq.,* 652 *et seq.* Note further the Roman sources of the Frankish period, *Cod. Theod.,* XI, 30, 2, Interp.; IX, 40, 1.

[111] On the history, 1 Loening, *K.R.,* 260, 286, 293; Nissl, *Gerichtsstand des Klerus im Fränkischen Reich* (1886) 104 *et seq.,* 196 *et seq.* with a *caveat* against the classification of causes there made; *infra,* Chapter III, p. 146. 4 Hinschius, *K.R.,* 757, for Roman; *ibid.,* 842, for Merovingian times.

[112] This is implicit in the *Praeceptio* of Chlothar II cc. 3 and 6 and the *Edictum,* cc. 4, 22. Gregory of Tours twice relates of the condemnation by the count, *Liber in Gloria Confessorum* 99 (*M.G.H., SS.*); *Liber in Gloria Martyrum,* 72. This must probably be restricted to the authority over professional thieves and malefactors (*Form. Marculfi I,* 8). See also the protection, *Form. Marc. Add.,* 2, forbidding *condemnatio,* and *Cart. Sen.* 28, an *iudiculus* to the same effect. This authority is to be distinguished from sentencing by virtue of the limited comital ban power on which Sohm, *F.R.G.V.,* 175 *et seq.;* 2 Brunner, *D.R.G.,* 224–5.

The *iudex* is presumably limited in his sentence by the form of the doomsmen's judgment, *ibid.,* 302, citing *Cap. Omnibus Cognita fac.* (801–14) c. 4 (1 *Cap.* 144) which seems, however, entirely equivocal. See against Brunner on the criminal side, *Form. Sal. Lindbrg.,* 19, "iudicatus est ei ab ipso comite vel ab ipsis scabinis." Compare *Form. Sen. Rec.* 4.

[113] On the institution of these Brunner, *Herkunft der Schöffen, Forschungen,* 248 *et seq.;* Sickel, W., *Entstehung des Schöffengerichts,* 6 *Z.R.G.²,* 1.

[114] This follows from 1) the extensive reservation in Carolingian times

where the power to pronounce sentence will strike most sharply into the prevailing forms of folkjudging, because it will be evoked against men, suspects or already infamous, about whose fate when no accuser appears no one will care. If the law merely stipulates death, the *missus* with a right of final sentence may ignore any expectation of the sib to execute and may order the job done by an official. Indeed, the capitulary which forbids self-enslavement and orders consummation of the penalty indicates certainly the direction that a judge's discretion will take. It is thus, therefore, that the last step is taken to throw into the hands of officials the execution of the afflictive sanctions provided in increasing degree by royal legislation. Private execution is probably not completely set aside; certainly not in the handhaving cases. But a prerogative of constituted authority over penalty is fixed, needing only the single-minded harshness of feudal government to temper it into the hard shape of general rule.

## THE DEVELOPMENT OF ECONOMIC SANCTIONS

The development of economic sanctions imposed by the state for its own benefit is perhaps the most complex aspect of Frankish crown law. Time out of mind men had been accustomed to settle wrongs with tangible values and to relinquish a part of the money settlement to public functionaries for their help. Furthermore the notion that in some circumstances reparation might be owed authority antedates the earliest legal monuments, for these already stipulate mulcts for the infraction of royal precepts.[115] The exactions of these mulcts is governed somewhat by the folk-law theory of a fixed expectancy by the offender. Thus the king's

of the sentencing power of the crown (*cf.* 4 Waitz, *D.V.G.,* 478 *et seq.* and the details there cited); 2) the extension to the *missi* by the crown of the powers to *finire,* i.e., the power *definitiva sententia;* Brunner, *Zeugen und Inquisitionsbeweis, Forschungen,* 203. On the "judging" power of the *missi, Cap. Baiw.* (ca. 810) c. 6 (1 *Cap.* 159) and further the notification *Form. Aug.* B 22. "Tunc predicti missi iudicaverunt e iussione imperatoris." This last is a review of an alleged unjust judgment, and hence may require a different form of judging.

[115] *Supra,* Chapter I, note 117.

ban is set at a maximum of 60 shillings and the count's ban is 15 shillings. This theory is necessarily an obstacle to the inflation of royal claims over an offender's belongings. The crown may project its ban over new matter,[116] may even lay ban penalty on ordinary crimes, but it does not on this theory exact more than a fixed sum.

During the whole of the so-called Frankish period the royal ban with its sixty shillings threat is wielded chiefly as a collateral sanction. In other words it is used to enhance the risks of certain misconduct, to found a specific royal interest in certain causes, but not to exclude private claims. There were, however, other aspects of the king's mandate power whereby the crown establishes for itself a virtually exclusive priority, by sweeping into the till of the fisc all a defendant's attachable values. The various pretexts and the several devices employed to assure and expand this power of confiscation eventually become the core of Carolingian crown law. This development we shall have to trace from the *Lex Salica* through the ninth-century capitularies. But again we shall first have to intone a *salvum me fac* from the reigning hypothesis.

Brunner and his followers have treated confiscation by the Frankish crown as an offshoot or mitigation of the once comprehensive terror of outlawry which is conceived to have involved destruction of property as well as of life. In only one particular, since it was first advanced, has this doctrine been modified. In respect of the destruction of a man's home (a phenomenon that runs through countless laws and customs of the Middle Ages), von Amira, in his study of the Germanic death penalties, has demonstrated with considerable force that this practice is not of itself a legal sanction but is only part of the ceremonials incident to the infliction of death upon a criminal; a superstitious practice or ritual act.[116a] But despite the fact that this explanation disposes of one of the chief props of the outlawry theory in re-

---

[116] *Infra,* Chapter IV, note 38.
[116a] V. Amira, *Die Germanischen Todesstrafen,* 230 *et seq.* Compare

spect of property, the old teachings have not been subjected to any revision.

If we consider again the monotonous refrain of the orthodox outlawry theory, it will be recalled that a general outlawry for the more wicked offenses and a relative outlawry for the emendable offenses is believed to have ensued as the result of the wrongful act. In the former case the misdoer is the enemy of all; in the latter he is the enemy of the injured individual and his kindred. Since the right or duty of retribution is limited in the second instance to the parties in interest, it is quite inconceivable that the group as a whole has any interest that would culminate in destruction of property except in cases of unemendable offenses.[117] On the basis, then, of Brunner's own admissions the practice of confiscation by authority could only have grown out of this presumptive right of destruction in such cases as treason or desertion, where the community and not merely the sib has the right of execution.

Quite apart from the relative plausibility of existing theories there are other reasons to doubt whether there was ever a destruction of property, as legal sanction, in the case of emendable offenses. The earliest evidence of any forms of sanctions taken against property indicate that these were limited to personalty.[118] Consequently, if there was in early times destruction of

Coulin, *Die Wüstung,* in 32 *Zeitschrift für Vergleichende Rechtswissenschaft,* 326, who sees a definite connection with outlawry.

[117] The outlaw advocates are by no means agreed as to the real implications of peacelessness as far as the population at large is concerned. This is clearly brought out in the reference just preceding. If outlawry is merely withdrawal of legal protection, i.e., essentially a negative concept, then it is difficult to construe a general duty to pursue and a right or duty to destroy property. Even under the "shoot-on-sight" theory, there is no rational explanation offered as to why an outlawry of property is involved so that it could be destroyed. The whole theory smells of the briefcase. It is like the juristic conceptualism of prize courts with their doctrine of enemy property "infecting" neutral goods.

[118] 1 Brunner, *D.R.G.,* 409; 2 *ibid.,* 600. Brunner thinks that an execution on realty emanated from the royal power of confiscation. See also his remarks in *Forschungen,* 451. Coulin, *Die Wüstung (supra,* note 116a),

property it must be assumed that this too was limited to personalty. But what the advocates of outlawry lay down about the basis of ownership in earliest times speaks against the likelihood of a legal doctrine of property destruction. Personalty, they aver, was owned in common by the sib or household,[119] and the most primitive forms of inheritance were conceived as accretions to an already vested interest.[120] Destruction of a wrong-doer's chattels would, therefore, involve destruction of an inheritance. There is, however, no sign in early times of a notion of

332 *et seq.*, speaking of property outlawry, says it has two forms, sequestration and ravage. He admits no data exist as to the relative age of the two. He denies that collective ownership excludes sequestration, and asserts that Brunner has no proof of the liability of property before the period of individual ownership. His, *Strafrecht der Friesen*, 177, thinks realty was liable to sequestration before personalty. Viollet, 1 *Etablissements de Saint-Louis* (1881), 106, sides with Brunner but has no definite proof. V. Amira, *Das Altnorwegische Vollstreckungsverfahren*, 108, establishes for the Norwegian law liability only of personalty. Planitz, *Die Vermögensvollstreckung*, 66, sides with Brunner; so also Mayer-Homberg, *Die Fränkischen Volksrechte*, 281; Sohm, *F.R.G.V.*, 117; Schröder, *D.R.G.*, 403.

[119] 1 Brunner, *D.R.G.*, 108, 109; Schröder, *D.R.G.*, 78. Both these writers admit a share went to the dead to be buried with him. See also v. Amira, *Grundriss d.G.R.*, 173. Coulin, *op. cit.*, 330, 331, especially n. 7, insists certain articles were identified with a person, but most of the references are to ethnographic accounts of primitive peoples in modern times. *Cf.* on this Grimm, *D.R.A.*, 451.

[120] Schröder, *D.R.G.*, 77, "ein unentziehbares Anwachsungsrecht." The "heir" in earliest German law really does not get an improved title, but he gets merely an accrual to his interest. It should be added that what we have said refers to the situation in the typical house-community.

Speaking of the subsequent Frankish period, Schröder says (*ibid.*, 356) that the heir did not acquire a new property which had previously belonged to the decedent, but the capacities and powers of the latter passed to the heir. The circle of persons who could be heirs was widened in this period. As Heusler, 2 *Institutionen des Deutschen Privatrechts* (1886) 528, points out, a real idea of heirship or succession develops via the sib. As the house-community idea weakens the principle of relationship and succession becomes operative. *Cf.* also v. Amira, *Erbenfolge und Verwandschaftsgliederung* (1874) 213, on the point in the text and *ibid.*, 1–61, for a discussion of the Frankish law. Note further that the earliest example of special inheritance is the devolution of weapons to the sons for them to carry on feud. 4 Ficker, *Untersuchungen zur Erbenfolge in den Ostgermanischen Rechte* (1898), pt. 1, §1024.

disherison because of a crime. We fail to see, therefore, how the family or sib would have had its interest wiped out except in so far as property may, as *a matter of fact,* have suffered injury or destruction in course of feud—a fortuitous and not a prescribed and legal consequence of the wrong. Indeed the circumstance that when composition proceedings were once initiated a method of set-off prevailed,[121] indicates clearly that all the acts in the course of feud were treated as assessable *facts,* and were not erased from the score as matters justified by law.

There are other aspects of composition practice pointing to the conclusion that property was not subject to destruction as a result of a putative peacelessness, but simply as an incident of feud. In a great many of the folklaws the composition debt was one for which the heirs of the offender were responsible.[122] Since

[121] Beyerle, *Rechtsgang,* 44 *et seq.*

[122] The references in the folklaws deal with the situation after a separate ownership has evolved. The principle, however, is clear. Schröder, *D.R.G.,* 365, 383; v. Amira, *Zweck und Mittel,* 51 *et seq.* A sharp distinction is to be drawn between the case of execution and the case where the offender dies a natural death. In the former case, in many laws, including those of the Franks, the death sentence absorbs amends so that the heirs are not liable for any "penal" sums but for restitution, as in case of theft. Schreuer, *op. cit.,* 151. In the other case the rule that the decedent's estate is liable for delictual obligations is widespread. And the liability is specifically that of the *estate* in the hands of the heir and not of the heir. The liability for the amends in Lombard law is clearly attested. Schreuer, *op. cit.,* 195, n. 38 for references. In the Visigothic law the same rule applies— liability to the extent of the estate (no liability for punishment). Dahn, *Westgothische Studien,* 150, 252. So in the *Lex Burg.,* 65, 1, 2. The *Lex Ribuaria* is clear on the point (67, 1); Mayer-Homberg, *Die Fränkischen Volksrechte,* 362 *et seq.;* Brunner, *Sippe und Wergeld,* 3 Z.R.G.², 46. Mayer-Homberg denies that the same rule applies in the *Lex Salica* (*op. cit.,* 362). He relies on *Lex Sal.,* Cap. II, 1. However, this is a law giving a defense in an *anefang* (pursuit of a stolen object) proceeding (on which *cf.* 2 Brunner, *D.R.G.,* 668). As Schreuer, *op. cit.,* 199, points out, the significance of this law is limited to non-liability for theft amends and is probably a redemption sum. Too broad a conclusion can certainly not be drawn from this.

It should be added that the natural death of an offender does not extinguish the right of feud, and consequently a claim to the full wergeld was legally possible. If we agree with Beyerle's list of "feudable" wrongs, the claims to any part of the wergeld (as amends) likewise outlived the

the policy of these laws was directed at settlement, it seems incredible that the property of the offender ever could have been liable to destruction as a matter of law if there inhered any interest of the sib as co-owners or heirs, for destruction would have defeated settlement by expunging the means of making it.

The almost total absence of matter in the *Lex Salica* pointing to unemendable offenses, let alone peacelessness, and the complete dominance of the composition system leaves small room for conjecture regarding the existence among the Franks of a right to ravage or destroy the personalty of an offender where the act was emendable.[123] On the other hand, in this law there are various passages which refer definitely to an interest of the fisc in the nature of a confiscation. Hitherto, it has been conjectured that these passages are to be related to the so-called outlawry of property of ancient times. It seems more plausible, however, to regard the notion of confiscation as something derived from the Roman law.

In the margin are indicated the outlines of the development of a property confiscation in the Roman law.[124] It was a usual pen-

decease of the offender. As the liability of the kindred to feud was restricted the probability of the survival of a claim to composition decreased. *Cf.* on the point, Brunner, *Sippe und Wergeld,* 44; Schreuer, *op. cit.,* 198, n. 47. On the whole question, Stobbe, *Über das Eintreten der Erben in die obligatorische Verhältnisse des Erblasser,* in 5 *Jahrbuch des Gemeinen Deutschen Rechts,* 297. 2 Heusler, *op. cit.,* 544 *et seq.*

[123] Even *Lex Salica,* 55, 2 (and *cf.* 14, Add. 5) where the penalty for violator of a grave is that he should be *wargus* contemplates nothing like the "full outlawry" of the writers, but on the contrary leaves open a ransom. The passage *Lex Salica,* 19, 1 (ex. Cod. 2) providing for burning of sorcerers is explained *supra,* n. 89. Cases like *Lex Salica,* 51, 2 (the count wrongfully distraining), where death is threatened, while technically not emendable, are included in a loose use of the word, since they provided for ransom. The surrender of the insolvent culprit for punishment contemplated in *Lex Salica,* 58 has reference to a procedure which we have explained and which is based upon a preceding attempt to effect a settlement.

[124] The chief secondary accounts used are Mommsen, *Römisches Strafrecht,* 1005 *et seq.;* Lehmann, W., *Über die Vermögensstrafen des Römischen Rechts* (1904), *passim.* This note is limited to the matter of confiscation, leaving aside the matter of other property penalties. Full or partial

alty, since it was specified for a wide range of crimes. The interests of the heirs were at first not considered, although a certain relaxation on equitable grounds became manifest, culminating in a novel of Justinian which restricted confiscation to cases of *laesae maiestatis*. It was in this form that the Roman law with reference to the matter was embraced in the Edict of Theoderich[125] but it should be noted that the probable date of the composition of the Ostrogothic code renders it unlikely that the *Lex Salica* in its earliest recension was influenced immediately by this source. However the Visigothic law was definitely saturated with the earlier Roman ideas with regard to confisca-

---

confiscation is known in the oldest Roman law. It took the form of *consecratio*. An offender was *sacer*, i.e., belonged to the gods, body and goods. (Lehmann, *op. cit.*, 95.) As late as the last years of the Republic the sequestration of property was effected with sacral forms. (Compare with this v. Amira, *Die Germanischen Todesstrafen,* 230.) The growth of the notion that the administration of criminal law was the duty of the state led to the extension of economic penalties in the interest of the fisc, and the change from *consecratio* to *publicatio*. In the Empire property is taken over as a punishment in a variety of delicts: treason, murder, *peculatus,* heresy, apostasy, killing of Christians by Jews, sexual relations of a guardian and ward, certain misfeasances in office, abduction and implication therein, false coinage. It is also used in connection with certain capital offenses, some of which we have discussed. (*Cf.* Lehmann, *op. cit.,* 24.) The fisc becomes entitled as a result of the judgment (Levy, *Die Römische Kapitalstrafe H.S.B.* [1931], 73).

As far as creditors were concerned the principle was observed that third parties were not to suffer by the transfer to the fisc. The latter steps into the shoes of the condemned man, who is relieved of all obligations.

The children of a convicted person were without right to the confiscated property, although a passage in the Digest indicates that a certain share may be had for reasons of equity (D. 48, 20, 1; 7). *Contra,* where only a partial confiscation. Where a great many children are left, the whole property goes to them (D. 48, 20, 7, 3). The later law made many improvements in the position of the children (C. 9, 49, 10) and the novel (134, 13) mentioned in the text virtually completes the process.

The importance of the Roman rules regarding confiscation in Western Europe, especially the ante-Justinian law, and the apparent absence of the consideration for the heirs which developed in the later Empire hardly need to be emphasized. The main source of transmission is the Breviary of Alarich. Conrat, *Breviarium Alaricianum, Römisches Recht im Fränkischen Reich* (1903), 642 *et seq.*, for the rules on confiscation.

[125] *Ed. Theod.,* 112, 114.

tion.[126] With this law the Franks had direct contact and from it they borrowed.[127]

Brunner's admission that the concept of the fisc was one of the few Roman concepts which the *Lex Salica* received,[128] did not however at all limit his theory as to the origin of confiscation among the Franks.[129] His outlawry theory he maintained largely because certain passages in the *Lex Salica* where confiscation was mentioned were necessary to another favorite theory—king's peace. But on the point here under consideration, all the references to fiscal rights must be considered together.

In the *Lex Salica* and its first novels fiscal rights unconnected with penalty are asserted in respect to inheritance where there are no heirs, and to the interest in the *dos* of a widow.[130] In relation to penalty a right to confiscate is found (1) as a part of the procedure for contumacy; (2) in the dark passage in the novel *Lex Salica* 70 (Cap. I, c. 5) where a free woman marries a slave and is made *aspellis;* and (3) in the treatment of persons who connive in a *raptus* and marriage without parental consent.

[126] Dahn, *Westgothische Studien,* 180 *et seq.* General confiscation was united with exile occasionally, and also with enslavement and the death penalty. On the exceptions in favor of heirs, *ibid.,* 181; *cf.* especially *Lex Vis.* VI, 2, 1; III, 2, 2; VI, 5, 12; VI, 5, 17.

[127] The earliest code, the *Codex Euricianus,* had presumably absorbed the idea of the fisc. Zeumer, *Leges Visigothorum* (*M.G.H.,* 1 *Legum,* Sec. 1, 1902), 28, 31. The Eurician laws date from 469–481. The passages where the fisc appears are not in the Paris fragments but are in the *Lex Baiuwariorum* which Zeumer believes reproduces the Eurician text.

[128] 2 Brunner, *D.R.G.,* 89–90. *Cf.* also 2 Waitz, *D.V.G.,* pt. 1, 89, 105, 181; pt. 2, 290 *et seq.* On the point that Frankish law knows no distinction between private property of the king and public property so that all confiscations go to the king's purse, Sohm, *F.R.G.V.,* 27 *et seq. Cf.* also on the fisc, 1 Dopsch, *Grundlagen der Europäischen Kulturentwicklung* (2 ed. 1924), 225; 1 Meitzen, *Siedelungen und Agrarwesen der Westgermanen* (1895), 590 *et seq.* The economists appear merely to have followed the lead of the legal historians.

[129] On use of *infiscare* and *confiscare, cf.* v. Schwerin, *Zur Textgeschichte der Lex Salica* in 40 *Neues Archiv,* 582. *Cf.* Heyman, *Zur Textkritik der Lex Salica,* in 41 *ibid.,* 449. Note finally the conclusive evidence of the adoption of Roman fiscal practices in Thompson, *Statistical Sources of Frankish History,* 40 *Am. Hist. Rev.,* 627 *et seq.*

[130] *Lex Salica,* 44, 10; 60; Cap. I, 7 (Hessels, 71).

The first of these penalty cases has already been explained as an outright borrowing of Roman fiscal practice as a result of copying the Roman criminal procedure. The origin of the rule about women who marry their own slaves is more difficult since there is no element of contempt involved, and since it cannot be shown that a Salic woman under *mundium* had any property to be confiscated. In view of this inconsistency we believe, with Tamassia, that the Roman doctrine with respect to slave marriages was enacted without reference to the basic facts of ownership among the Franks.[131] The following chapter in the same novel (case 3) punishes with death and confiscation the participation of relatives, as well as principals, in *raptus*. This Brunner has shown was formulated under Roman-Visigothic influence.[132]

The case for a reception of Roman doctrine of confiscation in the *Lex Salica* can be further fortified by reference to the early chronicles[133] in which the preeminence of the fisc as a going concern and as legal reality are patent. Subsequent Merovingian additions to the law are of small help on the question of origin, but they are illuminating on the point so critical to the validity of the outlawry theory, i.e., the union of death penalty and confiscation.

The decree of Childebert II (596), under ecclesiastical influence, introduces confiscation for incest with words that suggest an *extra sermonem regis*.[134] In the chapter dealing with *raptus* which contemplates an official execution of the *raptor* as well as of the consenting woman, the property is apparently saved for

---

[131] Tamassia, *op. cit.*, 21, 25.

[132] Brunner, *Die Fränkisch-Romanische Dos,* in *Sitzungsberichte der Berliner Akad. der Wiss.* (1894), 564; 2 Brunner *D.R.G.*, 862.

[133] Collected in 2 Waitz, *D.V.G.*, pt. 1, 310, n. 1; 316, n. 1; *ibid.*, pt. 2, 292, n. 2; 319 *et seq.*

[134] c. 2 (1 *Cap.* 15). *Cf.* on this legislation, 2 Loening, *K.R.*, 548 *et seq.* The severity of the penalties may be ascribed not merely to the religious scruples regarding consanguinity but to the economic motives of breaking the power of sibs by preventing such marriages and the consequent consolidation of wealth.

the heirs, except for the share to which the fisc is entitled.[135] Similarly the later Edict of Chlothar II which punishes by death *raptus* of women in religious establishments again leaves the property to the heirs.[136] The passages in early Merovingian capitularies dealing with thieves and malefactors contain no indication of confiscation where death is introduced as a penalty.[137]

There is obviously no principle upon which these various rules about property sanction are drawn. The notion that when property is saved for the heirs, an older rule coupling death and confiscation is being relaxed, cannot be supported because there is no proof that such a rule ever existed. There is no relation between confiscation and the right to execute the death penalty, for although the formulae show that there is private execution in the case of *raptus*,[138] in this case the heirs get the property except what the fisc reserves for its share. The fisc apparently takes nothing when public officers execute notorious malefactors.[139]

The most that one is justified in inferring about royal policy in furthering a confiscatory sanction is that it is used whenever a contempt of the crown is involved. This is far from establishing that confiscation is a mitigation of outlawry. Certainly the sort of "outlawry" (i.e., local expulsion) used in folkcourts carried

---

[135] c. 4 (1 *Cap.* 16).

[136] c. 18 (1 *Cap.* 23). 2 Brunner, *D.R.G.*, 862, who treats this rule as directed against *raptus*; Loening, 2 *op. cit.*, 402, regards it as directed against marriage. *Cf. Chloth. II, Praeceptio* (584–628) c. 8 (1 *Cap.* 19).

[137] *Form. Marculfi II*, 16; *Form. Tur.* 16; *Form. Sal. Lindbrg.* 16.

[138] In this connection it should be noted that the absorption of a composition obligation by infliction of death is due to a theory that the death penalty itself is the injured man's satisfaction, because at first privately executed, and that the extinction of an obligation on the heirs to make amends is not due to confiscation. Schreuer, *op. cit.*, 199. This seems to confirm the idea that confiscation is a concurrent penalty and, as we suspect, of later origin. Consequently there is no necessary interrelation of death penalty and confiscation as two phases of an older comprehensive outlawry. Mayer-Homberg, *Die Fränkischen Volksrechte* 126 *et seq.*, discusses death penalty and confiscation as "conceptually" related because he accepts Brunner's thesis of outlawry.

[139] At least the early edicts are silent on the matter. Perhaps such persons are, as *Ed. Chilperich* indicates, notoriously judgment-proof.

with it no such concept.[140] The operative fact in the king's law is not the pronouncement of a peacelessness, but *the contempt of the king's order*. The contempt is why the Romans confiscated property in causes criminal, and it is for the contempt that the Frankish crown suspends the absent defendant's procedural privileges and sequesters his property. This view receives some collateral support from the fact that passages in Gregory's history testify to the use of confiscation in cases of *infidelitas*,[141] the essence of which is a breach of oath to the king, and as *laesae maiestatis* to be classed with the milder offense: contempt of precept. Furthermore, the prerogative spread of the *laesae maiestatis* concept carried with it an increase in the number of confiscations.[142] This is clearly indicated in an early formula.[143]

In the Germanic folklaws which were inscribed subsequent to the *Lex Salica,* in this same period, either older capitulary law

---

[140] Brunner, 2 *D.R.G.,* 608, says that where outlawry was the result of a wrong and not pronounced for contumacy it was a matter of the folk-courts, citing 1 *ibid.,* 240 where a law of Cnut (eleventh century) is referred to; *Lex Sal.* 55, 2 (already disposed of); and *Lex Sal.,* Cap. I, 5 (Hessels 70). He does not indicate that any confiscation ensued as a result of outlawry by a folkcourt. It should be pointed out here that Brunner (*ibid.,* 772) treats the *exilium* of the Franks as "banishment," a "derivative" of outlawry. This he says is pronounced with or without property "outlawry" but he cites the late *Cap. ad Legg. Add.* (818–819) c. 7 (1 *Cap.* 282). Mayer-Homberg, *Die Fränkischen Volksrechte,* 132, obviously under the influence of Brunner's thinking, distinguishes outlawry and exile by suggesting that the former excludes from the "general peace" and the latter does not. He asserts that *Lex Sal.,* Cap. I, c. 5 is practically banishment and confiscation. He thinks that in the Salic law confiscation and exile were necessarily "conceptually" related. For this he relies on Brunner (2 *D.R.G.* 778) who views the death penalty as the operation of the outlawry idea, which punishes by death and loss of property. Brunner cites *Form. Marculfi I,* 32, but this formula deals with rebels and is no evidence of an indissoluble union of death penalty and confiscation in all cases. Note further the fact that the *Lex Ribuaria* does not have the union of exile and confiscation, or death and confiscation (Mayer-Homberg, *op. cit.,* 132).

[141] *Hist. Franc.,* IX, 9, 38. Waitz regards Roman practice as influential in fiscal practice, 2 *D.V.G.,* pt. 2, 290 *et seq.*

[142] 3 Waitz, *D.V.G.,* 307 *et seq.,* for Carolingian precedents.

[143] *Form. Marculfi I,* 32.

is reenacted or the idea of a specific royal interest appears where confiscation is threatened. Thus in the *Leges Ribuaria*,[144] *Alamannorum* and *Baiuwariorum* any form of *infidelitas* or sedition is punished with confiscation; and the same policy declared in the decree of Childebert with respect to incestuous marriages is manifest in the *Lex Alamannorum* and the *Lex Baiuwariorum*.[145] The *Lex Ribuaria* and the *Lex Alamannorum* extend this penalty plus exile in cases of killing blood-kinsmen,[146] and an identical rule is expressed in two Carolingian capitularies.[147] Like the incest legislation, the parricide provision has a definite Roman-ecclesiastical origin. Parricide was punished by death in the Visigothic law, but the heirs' interest was saved.[148] The frequent mention in the ecclesiastical penitentials of this offense with severe penances, and in some cases exile, suggests a source of lay regulation, although Wilda conjectures[149] that parricide and fratricide in the royal families may have contributed to the marking off of this offense from other killings.

The progressive sharpening of individual rights in property[150] during the sixth and seventh centuries undoubtedly affected the scope of fiscal claims. There is, however, no reason to believe that the old restrictions upon execution on immovables were changed. The early sources use the expression *res* (i.e., things) to describe the objects of confiscation and this word implies noth-

[144] Summarized in Brunner, 2 *D.R.G.*, 780. *Cf.* on the *Lex Ribuaria*, Mayer-Homberg, *op. cit.*, 128.

[145] *Lex Alamannorum*, 39; *Lex Baiuwariorum* VIII, 2, 3; *Lex Ribuaria*, 69, 2. The last adds exile.

[146] *Lex Ribuaria*, 69, 2 and exile; *Lex Alamannorum*, 40, and at one time, excommunication.

[147] *Cap. Kar. Mag.* (803–813) c. 3 (1 *Cap.* 143), where the parricide loses the right of inheritance; *Cap. pro leg. hab. Worm.* (829) c. 2 (2 *Cap.* 18) where the fisc gets the killer's share of inheritance.

[148] *Lex Visigothorum* VI, 5, 17. Here is also a loss of the right to inherit from the victim.

[149] Wilda, *op. cit.*, 714 *et seq. Cf.* 2 Brunner, *D.R.G.*, 820, n. 58. Wilda also remarks on the recitals of motives of greed in the laws.

[150] Generally on this Schröder, *D.R.G.* 224.

ing about immovables. Heritable realty reverts to the local community if there is a failure of heirs[151] or if a man has to enslave himself,[152] and this rule does not change during the Merovingian period.[153] The fiscal lands which a man holds by grant from the crown are in principle not heritable, and since the favor of the crown is a condition of tenure,[154] the confiscation of movables is accompanied by a reverter to the fisc of these royal lands.[155]

In the Carolingian period the problem of confiscation as punishment is no longer a thing *sui generis*. It is so definitely a part of the whole structure of economic sanctions that it must be considered in connection with the general methods of distraint: the *forisbannitio,* or qualified outlawry, and the sequestration of property.

It is possible to discern two main purposes in the variety of non-violent measures that can be taken against property in Carolingian times: those that are taken for execution, whether of a private claim or a penalty, and those which are used as an intermediate means of pressure. In the Salic law upon which Carolingian law builds, examples of the former are the provisions regarding extra-judicial or judicial distraint. Examples of

[151] So *Edict. Chilp.* c. 3, and *cf. Decr. Child. II,* c. 1, increasing the scale of heirship. Compare the discussion in 1 Waitz, *D.V.G.,* 135. Note also the fact that the heritage in land is frequently left undivided and is held in common (1 Brunner, *D.R.G.* 282). In these cases the undivided interest cannot be taken by the fisc. This is indicated by the fact that a special procedure for sifting out the offender's interest is not enacted until 816. (*Cap. Legg. Add.* c. 5, in 1 *Cap.* 269.)

[152] Planitz, *Vermögensvollstreckung,* 64 *et seq.*

[153] *Contra,* Planitz, *op. cit.,* 67, citing one document, a forgery (2 Brunner, *D.R.G.,* 600, n. 2).

[154] Köstler, *Huldentzug als Strafe,* in 62 *Kirchenrechtliche Abhandlungen* (1910), 10 *et seq.* Loss of royal grace develops as a punishment out of the disciplinary action against officials, and presently includes persons who have received favors from the crown. Brunner sees in the loss of royal grace a hint of diminished peacelessness; 2 *D.R.G.,* 106.

[155] For instances see 2 Waitz, *D.V.G.,* pt. 1, 317; pt. 2, 291. Waitz attributes the broadening scope of confiscation to the influence of Roman ideas. *Cf.* further, Brunner, *Landschenkungen der Merowinger (Forschungen,* 1, 22).

intermediate modes of pressure are the proceedings for contumacy with the imposition of 15 shilling penalties, and the procedure eventually terminating in *extra sermonem* and confiscation. This procedure may simultaneously serve as a means of final execution.

The *Lex Salica* had always presumed that liability of a man's property rested upon a bargain, except perhaps where a contempt of a royal order was involved. This postulate had been departed from in the Edict of Chilperich (561) which permitted liability to attach when judgment *in contumacia* (viz., where no bargain had yet been made) is pronounced by doomsmen in the court of the count. Levy in the nature of distraint is then made on the goods of the defendant. He is, however, given a right to show cause before the crown. The count and the doomsmen must appear to justify their proceeding; if they cannot, the defendant is given back his property.[156] This procedure stands midway between the rigid bargain insistence of the Frankish folklaw[157] and the summary confiscation for contempt of the crown. From both procedural incidents are adapted. From the earlier folklaw is taken the practice of having the count do the distraining, and at his own risk. From the royal contempt proceeding is taken the idea that the property goes to the fisc to whom the plaintiff must turn for satisfaction of his claim.[158] A new de-

---

[156] It is only the judgment-proof malefactor who is executed, c. 8 (1 *Cap.* 9). On this Planitz, *op. cit.*, 48 *et seq.*; 4 Bethmann-Hollweg, *op. cit.*, 521; Sohm, *Process der Lex Salica*, 199 *et seq.*

[157] The extra-judicial distraint of the *Lex Salica* (50, 2) is based upon a bargain. The plaintiff needs judicial permission before he can resort to it. He does not get title but merely a pledge interest. Sohm, *Die Pfändung durch den Gläubiger* (*Festgabe für Sohm* [1914] 317) treats the proceeding as a form of feud. Planitz, *op. cit.*, 8, says "relative peacelessness." In the case of comital distraint (*Lex Salica*, 50, 3; 51) *fides facta* was also essential. Plaintiff applies to the count pledging his life and fortune. The count takes seven doomsmen (*rachinburgi*), proceeds to the defendant's house and makes a demand. If this is not satisfied or the defendant is absent, the property is seized. The plaintiff gets title to two-thirds and the count to one-third as *fredus*.

[158] Planitz, *op. cit.*, 50. Later additions to the *Lex Salica* (51, 1, 2) de-

parture is that judgment by doomsmen is needed to set in motion the distraint.[159]

There is reason to suspect that Chilperich's edict was a first step toward perfecting the severe types of process used by the Carolingian kings.[160] The earliest form of this new procedure starts with a preliminary or provisional suspension of procedural rights—the *forisbannitio* of the Carolingian law.[161] This is effected by a declaration by the court or royal *missus* following an actual judgment to that effect.[162] The *forbannitus* can be seized by anyone; harboring him or giving him sustenance (*interdictio cibi*) is threatened with a fifteen shilling ban. Moreover, the foreban carries with it a ban upon property, the *missio in bannum* of which we shall speak presently. At what time this provisional suspension of procedural rights came into use is not certain. It is, perhaps, an evolution of the older form of suspension prescribed in the *Lex Salica,* because of the interdict on harboring, the preliminary sequestration and the presumption that a man *extra sermonem regis* could upon appearance have his procedural rights restored.[163] As far as the personal side of the foreban is concerned, it was restricted eventually to criminal causes since in the capitulary of Quierzy (873)[164] thieves, malefactors and *infideles* are named as the ones against whom the foreban is directed. But the liability of property to process sequestration con-

scribe even the earlier comital distraint as confiscation. *Cf.* Behrend *Lex Salica,* 108, note.

[159] In the *extra sermonem* procedure there is simply sentence by the king.

[160] Because there is a judgment *in contumacia,* a confiscation, and because the word *ferrebanitus* is used, *cf.* Chapter I, n. 130.

[161] On this procedure, 2 Brunner, *D.R.G.,* 609; 5 Bethmann-Hollweg, *op. cit.,* 178; Schröder, *D.R.G.* 403, 405; Mayer-Homberg, *op. cit.,* 281 *et seq.* It is not a new procedure when it is first mentioned in 782, Sohm, *F.R.G.V.* 121–2.

[162] *Cap. Aquisg.* (801–813) c. 13 (1 *Cap.* 172); *Cap. Aquisg.* (809) c. 4 (1 *Cap.* 148).

[163] 4 Bethmann-Hollweg, *op. cit.,* 521.

[164] *Cap. Carisiac.* (873) c. 1 (2 *Cap.* 343).

tinues as a general remedy and becomes an important form of procedural pressure.[165]

The chief characteristic of the *missio in bannum,* the expression used in connection with the property phase of the foreban, is the manner of its imposition. In modern idiom it may be described as an official sequestration of a man's land and goods for a year and a day, at the expiration of which period, if it is not redeemed by performance of the obligation hitherto refused, the title of the fisc becomes absolute; in short, the property is confiscated.[166] Originally, the crown determined what disposition was to be made of the *res,*[167] but in the reign of Louis the Pious it was enacted that the claimant was to be satisfied and the balance was to be kept by the fisc.[168]

It will be observed that in this particular device are mingled

[165] 2 Brunner, *D.R.G.,* 600 *et seq.;* Planitz, *op. cit.,* 71 *et seq.,* who points out that once sequestration of property is separated from the personal foreban, the former is a device which, in the sequence of mesne process, may be resorted to before the individual is put in ban (assuming, no doubt, that it is a case where the provisional outlawry is proper). Compare here the roster of intermediate devices used in later English law running from summons through attachment by pledges, habeas corpus, distraint and finally the exigent, 2 Pollock and Maitland, *H.E.L.,* 593. On the general use of *missio in bannum* in all forms of pleas, 5 Bethmann-Hollweg, *op. cit.,* 182.

[166] 2 Brunner, *D.R.G.,* 603; 5 Bethmann-Hollweg, *op. cit.,* 179.

[167] Brunner, *loc. cit.,* n. 22, points out that in two codices of the *Lex Salica* the section 56 is rendered "tunc ipse culpabilis et res suas erunt in fisco aut cui fiscus dare voluerit," indicating to him the early existence of the power of the crown to settle who was to get confiscated goods. This formulation of fiscal practice would permit saving claims of the heirs. *Cap. l. Rib. Add.* (803) c. 6 (1 *Cap.* 118) indicates the crown had the power of decision over the fate of such property after the failure to answer within the year.

[168] *Cap. Legg. Add.* (816) c. 5 (1 *Cap.* 268); which Mayer-Homberg, *op. cit.,* 284, thinks was in reform of the Salic law. He believes further that *Cap. Legg. Add.* (818–819) c. 11 (1 *Cap.* 283) made this into law for the empire. Bethmann-Hollweg, 5 *op. cit.,* 179, thinks the latter capitulary is expressive of previous practice. Important to note in the case of the latter capitulary is the fact that the property taken is limited strictly to that which in fact is owned by the individual, for if an inheritance is undivided,

civil as well as penal elements. Where it is not merely employed as an administrative measure of compulsion it is used in procedure initiated for the settlement of a claim which may arise as well for a delict as for an interference with realty. But when the party summoned does not appear, the *missio in bannum* is resorted to for a contempt, and as a penalty for this the contumacious person is not reseised of the balance of his estate after satisfaction of the claimant.

The effectiveness of these devices for making property liable either as process or as penalty was enhanced by the fact that no longer were merely chattels seized by the Carolingian fisc, but realty as well. This change was not effected before the time of Charlemagne, and is to be explained by the increased mobility of property interests.[169] Land is now more freely alienable because it is more completely the object of individual control. The crown's reversionary rights are more consequent than those of the village community,[170] the concept of heirship is so extended as to have the quality of future claims and not merely present interest.[171] Land can be treated as a means of bringing sanctions

the count can divide it and take only the share of the person proceeded against.

On this whole procedure *cf.* also Schreuer, *op. cit.,* 235 *et seq.* In his analysis Schreuer sees not the outward double penalty of amends plus confiscation, but rather confiscation (as a penalty of contempt) with a claim of the plaintiff reserved, and to be prosecuted against the fisc. From this point of view the *missio in bannum* of property is an important piece of anti-feud legislation, if we can credit Schreuer's statement that no right of feud exists against the individual once the fisc has intervened.

[169] 1 Inama-Sternegg, *Wirtschaftsgeschichte,* 280; Chénon, *Etude sur l'histoire des alleux* (1888), 13. Note also the following capitularies dealing with seizure of lands: *Cap. Miss. Gen.* (802) cc. 32, 36 (1 *Cap.* 97), *hereditatem; Cap. de rebus exerc.* (811) c. 6 (1 *Cap.* 165), *domum; Cap. Legg. Add.* (816) c. 5 (1 *Cap.* 268), *immobiles; Conv. apud Valent.* (853) c. 3 (2 *Cap.* 75) *cum alode; Cap. Carisiac.* (873) c. 1 (2 *Cap.* 343) *alodem.*

See also Mitteis, *Studien zur Geschichte des Versäumnisurteils,* 42 *Z.R.G.*[2], 149–50.

[170] Schröder, *D.R.G.,* 226 *et seq.*

[171] This is to be inferred from the broad extension of heirship to degrees not extant in the *Lex Salica,* Schröder, *op. cit.,* 359 *et seq.*

to bear on the individual because it is his own immediate rights which are being diminished.

But the new rules are chiefly designed to function when plaintiffs are *in extremis,* as a part of the crown's policy of strengthening the judicial function. This is evident from the curtailment of repeated summons[172] and from the fact that the measures just discussed are set in motion only as a severe form of mesne process. The man who will answer summons can defeat fiscal claims by conveying his property to third persons, making his bargain to pay and enslaving himself to his creditor.[173] What the crown will not allow him is to flout its process. It is to this end that the sequestration may with lapse of time ripen into the final sanction of confiscation.

Since confiscation could thus ensue if a man was steadfast in his contempt, one looks for no limitation upon its employment as a part of the final sanctions against crime where the penalty was executed by the state. Actually this was accomplished by the establishment of a general rule laid down in the capitulary of Aachen of the year 809[174] that in those cases where a man is adjudged to death all his property (*res*) falls to the public authority.[175] In other words fiscal claims depend upon judgment—the rule first enacted by Chilperich. It is not the fact of execution but the adjudgment of death which results in confiscation. Thus confiscation, which was previously a collateral consequence, has become an integral part of the death sanction. It is not what some writers have said, "conceptually" a part of the penalty. It ensues from the pronouncement of judgment.

[172] This appears from the later texts *Lex Salica* Cod. 10 and the Emendata; *Cap. Legi. Sal. Add.* c. 1 (819) 1 *Cap.* 292, and *Cap. Legi. Rib. Add.* (803) c. 6 (1 *Cap.* 118).

[173] *Cap. Legi. Rib. Add.,* c. 3; *Cap. Legi. Sal. Add.,* c. 6.

[174] c. 1 (1 *Cap.* 148). The reprieved man is infamous but is given a qualified capacity to acquire and defend property (c. 2). The judgment rule coincides with Roman doctrine, *supra,* note 124.

[175] The importance of judgment already indicated in *Cap. cum primis Const.* c. 2 (808) 1 *Cap.* 139. Note also in this connection the fact that the *missio in bannum* cannot take effect until there is judgment.

The rule of the Aachen capitulary is not to be taken as barring exceptions, for the capitulary *de latronibus*[176] saved the property for the heirs and under Louis the Pious two further reservations are made. Furthermore the Aachen rule is not exclusive; confiscation remains still as an independent sanction.[177] It is used in combination with exile in cases of third offenses against tithe legislation;[178] it is extended to the property of nuns who commit adultery, and in cases of persons excommunicated.[179] It is threatened continuously in the shape of a withdrawal of beneficial holdings.[180]

From small beginnings connected especially with acts in contempt of the crown the power of the latter over the property of misdoers expanded to very considerable proportions during the reign of Charlemagne. Even the few instances where an exception was made to save the interest of the heirs show no very deep-seated desire to hem in the fisc. Unquestionably the growth of a public power of execution had much to do with the elaboration of the idea that the death penalty absorbed all consequences and interests.[181] By roughly shouldering aside both heirs and claimants to composition, the confiscation of property led more certainly to the concept of public order and a public interest in wrongs than any other royal device. To this we make but one possible exception; that was the cultivation of sworn fidelity and the subsequent manipulations of this whereby the Caro-

---

[176] c. 6 (1 *Cap.* 181); *Cap. Legg. Add.* c. 1 (818–19) 1 *Cap.* 281. *Cf.* Mayer-Homberg, *op. cit.,* 129.

[177] So Mayer-Homberg, *op. cit.,* 129.

[178] *Cap. de reb. Eccl.* (787–813) c. 4 (1 *Cap.* 186); *cf.* also *Cap. per se Scrib.* (818–819) c. 5 (1 *Cap.* 288).

[179] In Italy *Memor. Olonn.* (822–823) c. 6 (1 *Cap.* 319). *Cf. Cap. Olonn. Eccl.* (825) c. 1 (1 *Cap.* 326 note h) where probably excommunication was used as a basis of confiscation.

[180] So in *Cap. Haristall.* c. 9 (1 *Cap.* 48); *Conc. et Cap. de clericorum Percuss.* (814–827) c. 6 (1 *Cap.* 362) with possibly a right of redemption contemplated; *Cap. Bonon.* (811) c. 5 (1 *Cap.* 167). *Cf.* also *Cap. Miss. Theod. II,* c. 6 (1 *Cap.* 123).

[181] Schreuer, *op. cit.,* 199 *et seq.*

lingians sought to create a paramount notion of order based upon a direct obligation to the crown and thus increase the effectiveness and the scope of the royal procedures just discussed.

### FIDELITY AND LAW ENFORCEMENT

We have spoken from time to time of the great significance that the pledge of faith had in legal transactions among the Franks.[182] It was fundamental to their system of judicial procedure because it was fundamental to their social system. The antiquity of the idea is attested in various sources which show it to have an ethical foundation quite independent of Christianity.[183] Indeed the notion of honor which underlay it, and which is dramatized in the oldest Germanic epics, was often at odds with the standardized morality of the church. It is not surprising therefore that the rulers of the Franks would attempt to capitalize this feeling for the purpose of government by fostering a direct bond to the crown by the exaction of oaths of fidelity.

There is dispute whether or not the idea of a general oath of fidelity to the crown was adapted from Roman practice, or whether it was a modification of the specific oath that the individuals of a following (*comitatus*) or retinue took to their chief. The relationship between a chief and his following is in some ways analogous to the broader relation between king and subject when the oath of fidelity became usual.[184] The chief-

---

[182] There is a cursory discussion in all the standard texts on legal history but with reference primarily to the legal aspects of fidelity. *Cf.* 2 Brunner, *D.R.G.,* 73 *et seq.* with references to the crown; Schröder, *D.R.G.,* 37, 43, 149, with reference to the *comitatus* and the *trustis; v.* Amira, *Grundriss d.G.R.,* 188 *et seq.;* Gierke, *Die Wurzeln des Dienstvertrags,* in *Festschrift für Brunner* (1914), 40 *et seq.;* 2 Waitz, *D.V.G.,* pt. 1, 206, and 3 *ibid.,* 290 with reference to the crown; Ehrenberg, *Commendation und Huldigung* (1877), 105, 115; Roth, *Geschichte des Benefizialwesens* (1850), 109, 128, 388; Kern, *Gottesgnadentum und Widerstandsrecht* (1914), especially App. XX.

[183] Discussed in 2 Kaufmann, *Deutsche Altertumskunde,* 214.

[184] Schröder, *D.R.G.,* 36.

follower relationship, however, has certain characteristics of mutuality that the relationship of king-subject does not possess. Grounded upon an oath of fidelity, the chief binds himself to protection, sustenance and armament; the man pledges the services that a freeman can give. It is in every way a relationship grounded on mutual fidelity.

The antrustionate of the Frankish kings,[185] the special body-guard and retinue of the crown, is the later offspring of the Germanic following. Due to the fact that it is a royal following it has certain peculiarities: special procedure, higher wergeld and individual privileges which distinguish the *trustis* from other men.[186] Undoubtedly the great lords of the period had similar bodies which performed for them like functions, but barring the privilege of being represented in court these followers had no exceptional procedural rights.[187]

The political significance of the general oath of fidelity exacted by the Merovingian kings lay chiefly in the fact that it was designed to cut through the relationships that existed by virtue of special pledges of faith just discussed. The Merovingian oath of fidelity was directed chiefly to the safety of the king's person and the continuance of his rule,[188] a policy followed because the land was full of pretenders and rebellion was frequent. Its chief legal effect may be described as a gradual marking off of a concept of infidelity. The concept of treason is subsumed under this concept and takes the form of infidelity to the king rather than treason to the country.[189] The form in which this offense ap-

---

[185] 2 Waitz, *D.V.G.*, pt. 1, 336 *et seq.*; Ehrenberg, *op. cit.*, 121 *et seq.*; Brunner, *Zur Geschichte des Gefolgwesens*, in *Forschungen*, 75; Schröder, *D.R.G.*, 149; Grimm, *D.R.A.*, 275.

[186] For the oath taken, *cf. Form. Marculfi I*, 18. For a discussion of the procedural advantages, Brunner, *Zeugen und Inquisitionsbeweis, Forschungen*, 130.

[187] *Cf.* Brunner, *Mithio und Sperantes*, in *Festgabe für Beseler* (1885), 13 *et seq.*, and 2 *D.R.G.*, 351.

[188] Roth, *Benefizialwesen*, 128.

[189] *Ibid.*, 131. It is difficult to be dogmatic on the question of the absorption of treason to the community by the concept of infidelity to the

pears in the folklaws, such as an invitation to hostile persons to enter the land, or conspiracy with enemies, is grounded upon the essential infidelity of such acts. In the same way desertion from the army—the *herisliz* of the capitularies—becomes an act of infidelity. Both treason and desertion existed as unemendable offenses in the time of Tacitus. But with the exaction of a general oath of fidelity, a new element is added. It is the offense against the king. It is, in the language of Frankish sources, *reus maiestatis*. The matter is thus properly justiciable in the king's court,[190] and since it is an offense against the crown, the penalty is death and confiscation.

During the period of Frankish history dominated by the major-domus the general oath of fidelity drops out of sight, or at least there is no evidence of its continued existence.[191] Not until the year 789 is it revived by Charlemagne. The immediate cause of the revival appears to have been a serious conspiracy against the crown.[192] A contemporary capitulary, in ordering the exaction of the oath of fidelity, bases the order on the ground of the conspiracy mentioned and the attempted justification of the offenders that they had taken no such oath.[193] In another capitulary, dated 789, the form of the oath is specified: "that I promise my lords King Karl and his sons that I am faithful and that I shall be so as long as I live, without fraud or evil design."[194] Subsequent instructions to the *missi* at various intervals made a repe-

king. The passage in Gregory, *Historia* (V, 27), where two bishops are deposed because they were *rei maiestatis et patriae proditores* probably does not represent a legal distinction. Certainly as the kingship grows in strength king and country tend to become identified; so desertion from the army is *reus maiestatis* in Charlemagne's time.

[190] Gál, *Der Zweikampf im Fränkischen Prozess,* in 28 Z.R.G.², 236, 243.

[191] 2 Brunner, *D.R.G.,* 75.

[192] Mühlbacher, *Die Treupflicht in den Urkunden Karls des Grossen, M.I.Ö.G., 6 EB.* (1907), 871.

[193] *Cap. Miss.* (792 or 786) c. 1 (1 *Cap.* 66). *Cf.* also 2 Brunner, *D.R.G.,* 76 n. 15. For a discussion of the conspiracy, 3 Waitz, *D.V.G.,* 291 *et seq.*

[194] *Duplex Leg. Edict.* (789) c. 18 (1 *Cap.* 63).

tition of the ceremony obligatory on all persons over twelve years of age. Nor did the crown stop with this, for it became usual to insert in grants a condition of the fidelity of the grantee.[195]

The policy initiated by Charlemagne was continued by his successors, and such oaths were exacted on all manner of occasions. The result was to emasculate the engagement of all political significance. The more men pledged fidelity the less they were disposed to keep faith.[196]

The most significant phase of the general oath of fidelity lay in the attempts that were soon made to fit it to the criminal procedure. The union of the idea of infidelity with that of infamy was an obvious connection to effectuate.[197] The positive function of the oath was extended beyond mere matters of allegiance, to include the performance of religious duties, to abide by the law, to abstain from interferences with fiscal property, and to observe the ban and service in the army.[198]

Fidelity was definitely related for the first time to the problem of crime in a capitulary of the early ninth century when the thief was branded as an *infidelis*.[199] And fifty years later the oath

[195] Mühlbacher, *op. cit.*, 877.

[196] 2 Brunner, *D.R.G.*, 77.

[197] The positive content of the oath of fidelity made this result nearly inevitable. The course of development runs roughly from 802–895. The *fidelis* is by the end of the century a man of good repute. *Cf.* the rule of the Council of Tribur (895): "Nobilis homo vel ingenuus si in sinodo accusatur et negaverit, si eum constiterit fidelem esset cum duodecim ingenuis se expurget; si antea deprehensus fuerit in furto aut periurio aut falso testimonio ad iuramentum non admittatur, sed (sicut qui ingenuus non est) feruenti aqua vel candenti ferro se expurget." *Corpus Juris Canonici, Decr.,* C. II, q. V, c. 15. See also Burchard, *Decreti,* l. xvi, c. 19 (140 Migne, *Patrologia Latina*).

[198] The details are related at length in *Cap. Miss. Gen.* (802) c. 2–9 (1 *Cap.* 92–93).

[199] *Cap. Miss. Cog. Fac.* (803–813) c. 2 (1 *Cap.* 156) "quia qui latro est infidelis est noster et Francorum." Note the interesting identification of fidelity to crown and nation. Brunner, 2 *D.R.G.*, 84 tries to relate the *infidelitas* and outlawry, on the basis of the prohibition of harboring the thief who is also *infidelis*.

of fidelity was made the basis of men's duty to report robbers and thieves and to aid in their pursuit.[200] The duty of answering truly upon inquisition the queries of the judge had long since been made dependent upon the general fidelity men had sworn to their king.[201]

Although the efforts made to attach men to the crown by frequent oath tended to relax the solemnity of the pledge, there nevertheless was built up for the crown greatly enhanced power of arbitrary punishment. This power, being grounded upon a prior definite commitment of the individual, had a legal basis which it had not possessed in Merovingian times, but the mere fact that it was essentially arbitrary defeated any possible design of creating out of fidelity to the crown[202] a broader ethical foundation for law enforcement than was already implicit in existing criminal legislation.[203] Even so, had the successors of

[200] *Cap. Silvac.* (853) c. 4 (2 *Cap.* 272).

[201] Brunner, *Zeugen und Inquisitionsbeweis, Forschungen,* 233–234.

[202] Mitteis, *Lehnrecht und Staatsgewalt* (1932), c. 1, attributes to the infidelity idea a consistent and pervading influence even in post-Carolingian criminal law. This will be discussed in Volume II.

[203] On the procedural side the infidelity concept produced one result—the extension of duel as a form of trial. Literature is cited in Gál, *Der Zweikampf im Fränkischen Prozess,* 28 *Z.R.G.*[2], 236 *et seq.* Battle was originally a procedure of the king's court; Gál, *op. cit.,* 243; Declareuil, *A propos de quelques travaux récents sur le duel-judiciaire,* 33 *N.R.H.,* 81; see also his *Preuves judiciaires dans le droit franc,* 23 *ibid.,* 330. Mayer-Homberg, *Die Fränkischen Volksrechte,* 239, states that the only ordeal for free men in the Ribuarian law is battle. Compare Declareuil, *op. cit.* in 33 *N.R.H.,* 78, "la *lex Salica* et *lex Ribuaria* primitive ignoraient le duel judiciaire." Its existence, although not attested in the *Lex Salica,* is established for the sixth century as a more or less unusual and restricted form of trial: Gregory, *Historia,* VII, 14; X, 10. Brunner, 2 *D.R.G.,* 556, thinks the later use of battle in Salic law may have been a revival of old custom. See also, Baist, *Der Gerichtliche Zweikampf, 5 Romanische Forschungen,* 436, 439 *et seq.* The position of the church on recourse to trial by battle may have been important. The councils held in the eighth and ninth centuries were generally favorable to it. *Cf.* Grelewski, *La réaction contre les ordalies* (1924), 6 for a list of these councils. The rituals for battle are themselves evidence of how far the church was committed. *Cf.* Liebermann, *Gesetze,* 430 and the reference in the late formula in Zeumer, *Formulae,* 719. There is no sound reason for distinguishing between the

Charlemagne been able to maintain a tightly knit political and administrative organization, the royal fidelity concept might have hardened by incessant vigilance into a firm underpinning for the ingenious structure of procedural devices which made up crown law. This condition was not fulfilled. As the West Frankish kingdom slowly disintegrated fidelity to the crown tended to become mere form.

David v. Goliath precedent of battle and the Shadrach, Meshach and Abednego precedent for the ordeal (Zeumer, *op. cit.*, 606). The Holy See, however, from the ninth to the eleventh centuries developed opposition. Grelewski, *op. cit.*, 58. The divorce of Lothar led to a sharp definition of position. *Cf.* Burchard, *Decretum*, lib. 9, 50–53 (and *cf. Corpus Juris Canonici* C. II, q. V, c. 22). *Cf.* also, on the church's position, Pfeffer, *Die Formalitäten des Gottesgerichtlichen Zweikampfs*, in 9 *Zeitschrift für Romanische Philologie*, 8, and 41 *et seq.*, for matter drawn from the French epics.

That a right of trial by battle was originally limited to the royal *trustis*, has been conjectured on the basis of the armament used by the combatants as recounted in the sources, an armament which corresponds to that of the king's retinue. By the time of Charlemagne, however, battle had become usual for infidelity and was no longer restricted to the *trustis*. Due to the considerable expansion of the fidelity concept, battle could be engaged in whenever a breach of this fidelity ensued. At this stage in the development of this procedure, there were two separate methods of initiating an infidelity charge. Either there was a formless complaint, which the defendant would deny, and if no one appeared to make a formal charge, he could then purge himself with oath helpers or by ordeal (Gál, *op. cit.*, 247 *et seq.*). But if a peer (and only a peer) of the defendant made formal complaint, the way was open for proof by battle. (*Ibid.*, 248. Gál relies on an interpretation of a line from Ermoldus Nigellus' *Carmina* [*ibid.*, 242, n. 2] and the passage from Gregory, *Historia*, VII, 14. *Cf.* also Pfeffer, *op. cit.*, 20–21 for evidence from the epics.) This duel is fought with the long-sword—the weapon of the *Ribuaria*, the so-called "household law of the crown." The armament may then be taken as derived of the original body-guard duels, but is more likely to be explained on the ground that the sword is what men swore by when the oath of fidelity is taken. (On this form of oath taking, Grimm, *D.R.A.* 166; Ducange, *Glossarium, s.v. iurare;* 1 Brunner, *D.R.G.*, 258, n. 36; *Lex Rib.* 33, 1; *Form. Tur.*, 30.) In any event this means of waging duel is distinctive for fidelity causes in the law of the empire, i.e., that which rests on crown law, specifically capitulary law. It is not to be confused with the battle form of club and shield introduced by Charlemagne for cases not involving infidelity or a specific oath but involving simply the credibility or reputation of the witnesses, and for this reason a type of ordeal. (*Infra*, Volume II.)

## CHAPTER III

## THE DISPERSAL OF JURISDICTION AND NORMAN RECEPTION OF FRANKISH LAW

WHEN they laid away the earthly remains of Charlemagne in the cathedral at Aachen, thoughtful men may have suspected that the power of the Frankish crown had reached its apogee, but no one could have foretold how swiftly disaster was to overtake the Frankish Empire, and how unhappily the fortunes of the epigones who succeeded Charles were to react upon the whole scheme of justice and its administration. It is true that easy access to courts and maintenance of order and of certain standards in the adjustment of disputes, was professed as the ideal of rulers in the ninth century. The capitularies of those turbulent decades resound with pious and obviously sincere professions of governmental principles,[1] yet their effect upon law

[1] Usually expressed by *pax et justitia*. The word *pax*, alone or in combination, is used in the capitularies of the ninth century in a variety of meanings. There is first of all the use in the sense of peace as a result of a treaty, *cf. Ordinatio Imperii* (817), Preamble (1 *Cap.*, 270); *Pactum Hlud. cum Paschali* (817) (1 *Cap.*, 355); *Conventus apud Marsnam* (847) c. 1, 3 (2 *Cap.*, 69). There is its use as a purely pious expression, *cf. Statuta Rhispacensia* (799–800) c. 3 (1 *Cap.*, 226); *Admon. ad omnes* (823–5) c. 13 (1 *Cap.*, 305); *Cap. Pistensis* (869) c. 12 (2 *Cap.*, 336). There is, thirdly, the use of a "special" peace as discussed *supra* in the first chapter, *cf. Cap. Legg. Add.* (803) c. 3 (1 *Cap.*, 113); *Cap. Ital.* (801) c. 2 (1 *Cap.*, 205) *Cap. Miss. Ital.* (781–810) c. 2 (1 *Cap.*, 206); the so-called *Cap. Francica* (n.d.), c. 6 (1 *Cap.*, 334); *Admon. ad omnes* (823–5) c. 16 (1 *Cap.*, 305). Fourthly there is the use in connection with the procedure for amends, *Cap. Miss. Gen.* (802) c. 32 (1 *Cap.*, 97); *Cap. Miss. Theod. II* (805) c. 5 (1 *Cap.*, 123). Lastly there is its use in what seems to us a loose and untechnical sense of order, *cf. Cap. Miss.* (819) c. 27 (1 *Cap.* 291); *Admon. ad omnes* (823–5) c. 13 (1 *Cap.*, 305); *Cap. post Convent. Confluentinum* (860) c. 7 (2 *Cap.*, 301); *Cap. Tusiac.* (865) c. 14 (2 *Cap.*, 331); *Cap. Carisiac.* (877) c. 18 (2 *Cap.*, 359).
We have examined most of the passages in the capitularies where the word occurs, and the cumulative effect is that *pax* has a technical meaning only in the case of composition procedure and when it is employed to describe church-peace or army-peace. Otherwise it is loosely used and, far

enforcement was no more incisive than a charge to a grand jury. The controls which would have made these a reality were slipping from the hands of the crown. By the close of the century they were lost. The *missus* who had made them a reality for Charlemagne and even for Louis the Pious was no longer the servant, but himself the master. In France and in Germany, the great abbeys, the bishops and the powerful landlords had possessed themselves duly and in good legal form of powers which deflected the administration of justice from a centralized royal supervision, and which gave them at once the profits and the determination of form and procedure. This was the culmination of something long under way. Certain powers of justiciation men with sufficient substance to maintain an establishment had had from the days of Roman rule. The acquisition of additional powers through the grant of a benefice or an immunity had been going on since the early Merovingian times. While centralization was proceeding, the means of its disintegration had been simultaneously contrived. It was the debacle of the late ninth century which completed this process.

From the vantage point of the year 1000 it is easy enough to see how jurisdictional unity had been succeeded by decentralization. The sources for ninth-century history, however, tell two stories. On the one hand, they testify to the continuity of ideas and governmental machinery and sometimes even of development, so that one is tempted to see the "Frankish Empire," to envisage it as a going concern—the momentum acquired in earlier decades unchecked, the institutions marching on to the fate inherent in the logic of their original purpose.[2] On the other

from conveying the notion of king's peace as a general legal doctrine, it seems to have as little technical meaning as our own phrase "peace and order."

[2] This is essentially the position of Brunner in 2 *D.R.G.* He is writing the story of Frankish legal institutions. He pursues his subject matter throughout the so-called Frankish period, and the determinative factor is the Frankishness of the source. No doubt he presumes a knowledge of the political history, but he does not emphasize it sufficiently. For example

hand, the sources tell us of dissolution, of perversions of power, of the reorientation that invasion and starvation make necessary in the orderly pattern of administration, of spasmodic instead of measured governmental action.[3] From these conflicting tales we must draw conclusions as to how the complex system of dealing with wrongdoing fared; what happened to the feud, the composition plea, the inquisition, the public punishment; where was initiative lodged if, indeed, there were those who were disposed to take it? For all the familiar forms are still to be found. The feud persists, but it is something different than the internecine

the capitulary of Quierzy (873) is useful in supplying evidence for the Carolingian policy of repression of professional thieves. Institutionally considered there is a definite thread running back to the capitulary *de latronibus* (803–13) and beyond. But the Quierzy rules are definitely motivated by the peculiar problems which the devastation and depopulation of invaded areas created, and this fact is not sufficiently emphasized.

[3] 1 Flach, *Les origines de l'ancienne France* (1886) 125 *et seq.* approaches the problem from this second angle. Flach possesses a habit in common with certain other French writers, Viollet, Declareuil, and Esmein, to name but a few, who flit about the period variously designated as *"le régime seigneurial," "la société féodale."* Texts from the ninth century compete with charters of the eleventh or excerpts from Beaumanoir in building up a picture of generalities. One gains an impression of tendencies, but on matters of detail one is likely to acquire some strange notions as a result of this contempt for chronology. A typical example is Declareuil, *Histoire générale du droit français* (1925) 332, who, speaking of ecclesiastical jurisdiction in his section *"Le régime seigneurial"* says, "Sa procédure, en grande partie tirée du droit romain, semblait plus rationnelle: elle était écrite, fondée sur enquêtes, admettait les demandes reconventionelles. Pas de duel judiciaire ni même bientôt d'aucune sorte de *judicia Dei*." He cites passages from Gratian's *Decretum,* the eighteenth chapter of the fourth Lateran council, a passage from Beaumanoir and letters of Ivo of Chartres. His statement is misleading since the complete reception of *purgatio vulgaris* by the church was effected in the early "seignorial period," and it is not until the close of the twelfth century and under Innocent III that the great reforms of procedure are put through: 5 Hinschius, *K.R.* (1895) 338 *et seq.*

Many of the French legal historians have slid over the portentous and difficult period from 900–1100, and are content to use the thirteenth and fourteenth-century sources as speaking for this earlier period. But there is some juice to be extracted from the early charters and we prefer conjectures based on contemporary material to fixed generalizations resting on sources too late to be apposite.

brawls of an earlier day. In the course of the tenth century, it becomes the conflict between two lords with men at arms. The professional bad man is only too evident, but he is no longer a man without substance who skulks in the woods, but like as not a *baro* with an adulterine castle for a retreat. Inquisitions there are, but they are taken by others than the king's judges.

Most of the changes which were to occur in France become perceptible in the second half of the ninth century. During the long reign of Louis the Pious, the bonds of royal control are loosened, the machine falters, but catastrophe is still ahead. There are great rebellions, and the first of the terrible invasions by the Northmen occur.[4] These events are but premonitory shadows of what awaits Louis's successor, Charles, in West Francia. It is just before the battle of Fontenoy, in 841, that the initial viking raid up the Seine takes place. Thenceforth there is no peace. Two seasons following the Loire is invaded, and then with dreary monotony the almost annual incursions up the inviting streams of France follow one upon the other. Battles rage in all parts of the kingdom; where tribute is not paid the great ecclesiastical foundations go up in smoke; everything worth pillaging in the way of the vikings is taken. The torch has displaced the sword of justice. From the Channel to the Mediterranean France has become a land of woe. The misery of these years is felt by all alike. In the capitularies are reflected the cares and troubles of the crown; in the chronicles, the unhappy lot of monks and clerics. What awaited the common man is expressed in the poignant prayer; "Summa pia gratia nostra conservando corpora et custodita, de gente fera Normannica nos libera quae nostra vastat, Deus, regna. Senum jugulat et juvenum ac virgi-

---

[4] Generally on the Norman raids of the ninth century, Vogel, *Die Normannen und das Fränkische Reich, Heidelberger Abhandlungen zur mittleren und neueren Geschichte* (1906); Mabille, *Les invasions normandes,* etc., (30 *Bibliothèque de l'Ecole des Chartes,* 149); Dümmler, *Geschichte des Ostfränkischen Reiches* (1 ed. 1862–5), 2 vols.

num puerorum quoque catervam. . . . Dona nobis pacem atque concordiam."[5]

Our chief evidence of the nature and extent of the Norman incursions comes from those most aggrieved and least able to resist—the monks; they had battened upon the land for centuries and had most to lose. They suffered severely; but even where they fled to other regions they kept in many cases their chief commodity, the land.[6] The actual hostilities which resistance to the invaders entailed resembled any other war—assaults upon fortified places and pitched battles in places favorable to the designs of one or the other side. Despite the frequent sackings of rich abbeys or towns, the destruction was cumulative; otherwise the raiders would have had no object in returning so persistently to the same localities, nor could government have been maintained. Moreover, the Normans' greatest strength lay in the mobility of their armies. Here today and gone tomorrow was the secret of their strategy. Except on the occasions when, toward the end, they maintained in France great winter camps and by the fact of occupation subjected the surrounding country to long-drawn-out misery, their forays were thrusts rather than persistent batterings.[7] The economic effects of their presence were consequently conditioned upon the length of their visits to a particular locality.[8]

The curse which the Normans brought upon the West Frank-

---

[5] Delisle, *Littérature latine et histoire du moyen age* (1890), 17.

[6] Or were on occasion given reparations. *Cf.* the charter of Charles the Bald to St. Wandrille (853–4) 8 *H.F.*, 522.

[7] Thus the Seine region was given a six years' respite between 845 and 851, Vogel, *op. cit.*, 115. In other localities like Friesland, the enfeoffment of Rorik and the consequent settlement resulted in temporary safety, *ibid.*, 145.

[8] Vogel prints a map which gives most graphically a picture of the extent of the Norman invasion. He does not, however, seem prepared to take the position that there is heavy overstatement in many of the chronicles, although he brings out the fact that there was a considerable commercial traffic between Normans and Franks, *ibid.*, 233.

ish kingdom did not consist entirely in their own violent presence. Much of it was collateral anathema, the effect of measures taken to repel them, especially in the matter of raising troops. The organization of the army during the reign of Louis had had the effect of professionalizing military service. The old free peasant service had given way to a system based upon the fact that landholders of consequence maintained their own forces or could have recourse to vassals whose tenure depended upon the performance of military duties.[9] When the viking invasions became *de cursu* the brunt of defense fell upon these units. But they were often reluctant to serve. The leaders had their own political plans. If these plans conflicted with royal interests, concessions of power or grants of land had to be made to these chieftains to secure their cooperation. These men, moreover, did not hesitate to take advantage of the program of building castles as bases of operations.[10] The command of these castles was useful for purposes of domestic politics, and during the tenth century it plays its part in the prolific spawning of counts and viscounts and barons. When public authority is decimated by partition the lords who have men at arms and a fortress will get their share.

In other respects, too, the Norman raids affected profoundly the postulates of law administration. The bargains which had to be struck to raise troops to withstand the invaders shifted juris-

[9] On this generally 2 Brunner, *D.R.G.*, 280 *et seq.* Brunner points out that the change in tactics required more costly armament but he believes that the duties upon the seniors was an adequate substitute for the decline of freemen obligated to service. He admits, however, the tendency to professionalization. *Cf.* also Vogel, *op. cit.*, 13: 4 Waitz, *D.V.G.*, 604 *et seq.*

[10] Sackur in 1 *Die Cluniacenser* (1892), 11 maintains that the fortifications were chiefly wooden palisades, and has some support for his views. On the other hand at Pîtres in 864 Charles expressly forbade the building of *castellae* without his permission (*Edict. Pist.* c. 1; 2 *Cap.* 328). The castles must have been strong enough to be a real danger to royal interest. On the Carolingian fortifications 4 Waitz, *D.V.G.*, 627 *et seq.* On the fortified bridges, Vogel, *op. cit.*, 187. On the castles later, *cf.* 1 Flach, *op. cit.*, 445 *et seq.* with references chiefly from the eleventh and twelfth-century documents; Declareuil, *op. cit.*, 193 *et seq.*

dictions as well as lands and so decentralized the administration of law, or tended to remove the controls that had previously existed.[11] This was true of both crown and church. The former would permit a count to exercise and even to pass to his heirs the office of *missus* designed originally to hold the counts in check.[12] The great ecclesiastical immunities were forced to acquire lay protectors who took full advantage of their position.[13] Instead of one directing head, the governmental ideal of Charlemagne, the close of the ninth century saw many; in place of unity of purpose there prevailed a conflict of personal interests.

The same factors which had derailed the machinery of law enforcement supplied it with entirely new problems. These consisted in the creation of two definitely marked classes of lawbreakers. On the one hand were the offenders of family, the men of substance with rebellion in their blood who broke faith, who warred on king or neighbor, and in so doing burned, robbed and killed. This class becomes a major problem in the century following the establishment of the Norman duchy.[14] They are a problem because they frequently are possessed of the dismembered functions of the Carolingian state, and consequently their activities have a quasi-public quality, although

[11] The complaints against the cowardice of the lay lords in the chronicles are frequent. Apparently they were more faithless than timid. There was no rule against forfeiture of benefices for failure to perform military service; for this only the ban penalty was inflicted; 2 Brunner, *D.R.G.*, 343. This may explain why so much new matter had to be conceded by the crown to get reliable troops. On the type of concession mentioned above, *Annales Bertiniani* (*M.G.H.* 1 *SS.* 455) ann. 861, and 866. In this connection *cf.* also Lot and Halphen, *Le règne de Charles le Chauve* (1902), 212, and how power to name bishops was used by the crown.

[12] Thompson, *Decline of the Missi Dominici in Frankish Gaul* (4 Dec. Pub., Univ. of Chicago, 1903), 295.

[13] Senn, *L'Institution des avoueries ecclésiastiques* (1903), 81, 85 *et seq.*

[14] To a certain extent they are a problem in the middle of the ninth century; *cf. Ann. Bertiniani*, 854. See also *Cap. Pap.*, (850) c. 2 (2 *Cap.*, 86) regarding the agreement of Louis II and Lothar. *Edict. Pist.*, (864) c. 6, 7. (2 *Cap.*, 312) *Cap. Vern.*, (884) *prologue*, (2 *Cap.*, 371). Generally on the matter W. Sickel, *Die Privatherrschaften im Fränkischen Reiche* in 15 *Westdeutsche Zeitschrift*, 156–7.

their victims could not draw the fine distinction between an act of private war and a premeditated robbery or murder. It is the behavior of this class which creates the necessity of the peace or truce of God. The other class is that which had long been a problem of Frankish kings—the persons unattached to kin or lord who practice banditry professionally. These persons increase in numbers as a result of the devastations of field and farm by the Northmen. In the middle years of Charles the Bald's reign provisions in the capitularies show that they are considered a serious danger.[15] The state of administration does not appear, moreover, to have been vigorous enough throughout the land to insure effective prosecution. To some extent the solution is found in the absorption of great numbers of vagrants into the establishments of the feudatories.[16] But the prevalence of violence and the general decay of public authority in many regions of France during the ensuing century insures a permanent and unhealthy supply of these malefactors.

These various social effects of the Norman wars are a condition precedent to an understanding of how there came into being the classical phrase of Beaumanoir—*chascuns barons est souverains en se baronnie*. They likewise conditioned the inheritance of Frankish institutions which the Normans appropriated and made their own when they finally became domiciled in France. We do not mean to imply, however, that it is possible to fix on the basis of direct proof the exact source of any single Norman institution, to say that this or that is directly derived from a Carolingian capitulary, or was a governmental device which was suffered to continue unchanged. It is hardly probable that the Frankish stream in Normandy was unpolluted by what had been going on in the adjoining counties of Maine or Vermandois

[15] *Cap. Silvac.*, (853) c. 7 (2 *Cap.*, 273); *Cap. Carisiac.*, (857) c. 1 (2 *Cap.*, 286); *Edict. Pist.*, (864) c. 6 (2 *Cap.*, 313).

[16] Vogel, *op. cit.*, 169 and *cf. Cap. Silvac.*, (853) c. 9. (2 *Cap.*, 273.) On the crown's stern policy of repressing gilds organized for self-protection, 4 Waitz, *D.V.G.*, 434 and 435 n. 1.

or elsewhere in France in the tenth century where the currents of law had been set in motion by the former rulers of Neustria. Our documents are much too rare, the evidence of institutional cosmopolitanism of the tenth and eleventh centuries is much too persuasive, the Norman dukes too steadily embroiled in French politics for us to stake much upon any single theory or conjecture. To make specific the difficulties of the problem: in Burgundy the direct connection of the tenth-century feudal courts with the earlier Frankish institutions has been established.[17] From Burgundy the Abbot William of Dijon proceeds to Normandy to put in order the ecclesiastical establishments of Duke Richard.[18] Can we ignore the possibility that a worldly prelate would not fail to drop hints as to how law is administered in his county? Or are we to prefer the possibility that the Archbishops of Rouen, for generations endowed with vast temporal power exercised upon the models of Frankish local administration, instructed Rollo in the ways of the kings whom he had defeated?

If in general it is difficult to establish the nexus between Frankish and Norman institutions, it is equally so when we attempt to particularize in regard to the fate of the Carolingian system of suppressing and prosecuting wrongdoing. Those portions of this system that depended chiefly upon local organization or ingrained custom, like the feud or handhaving procedure, appear to have had hardy roots. They are the progeny of violence, and violence is the chief preoccupation of men both

[17] Ganshof, *Contribution à l'étude des origines des cours féodales en France*, 7 *R.H.D.F.*, 4 ser. 645; *cf.* also his *Etude sur l'administration de la justice*, etc., 135 *Revue Historique*, 193, for Burgundy. There should be compared with this study the equally interesting study of the Angevin courts, which in some respects show similar development, Halphen, *Les institutions judiciaires de la France au XIe siècle, région angevine*, 77 *Revue Historique* 279.

[18] 2 Sackur, *Die Cluniacenser*, 45 *et seq.*; Steenstrup, *Normandiets Historie under de Syv Første Hertuger, Danske Vidensk. Selsk. Skrifter*, 7 ser. Hist. og. Fil. Afd. V, 1 (1925), 172.

great and mean in the tenth century. On the other hand, devices which are predicated upon political stability, which are motivated by the idea that the preservation of public order is the business of the ruler, or which depend for their performance upon law-enforcing activities by individuals at large as a normal condition, like the inquest, display less capacity to maintain themselves in the face of adverse circumstances. In the process of transition from a centralized monarchy to a congeries of feudal seignories in France, there is no complete succession to the institutional hereditaments of the Carolingians. Some things descend, some are changed and some pass into desuetude. In no province or county will we find the story quite the same. In no place is the process simply the substitution of count or bishop for king. Each seignory is built up as a result of a piecemeal wresting of single privileges. The feudalization of government is the devolution of privileges, franchises and powers, all of them conceived in terms of something definite and precise—the right to hold court, the freedom from toll, the privilege to receive the *fredus*. Some of these are conveyed by grant, some are merely assumed, some pass because a public official becomes more important as a private individual. If a feudatory holds an inquisition he does so not because he deems himself vested with a public purpose, but because somehow he has acquired the power to hold it, and it is advantageous both in point of profit and privilege.

When we see the Carolingian system falling apart into fiscal or administrative privileges bereft of the unifying purpose with which the system had once been endowed, it becomes clear that the objective of public order which was so important a part of the governmental design was bound to disappear or to undergo critical revision. We have observed that the Carolingian system had combined two somewhat antithetical methods of dealing with wrongs—the feud-composition and the public prosecution-punishment procedures. The essential conflict in the basic ideas of these two was subdued as long as the governmental purpose remained undisturbed and centralized control could be maintained. The latter depended, as we have said, upon internal stability in the realm and upon the integrity and continuous functioning of the several devices: watch, inquisition, itinerant justices and the like. The feuds and rebellions of the later ninth and the tenth centuries were no less destructive of this purpose than the incessant partition of single administrative devices among various individuals whereby the institutional fundaments of public order were disintegrated. In a single county, the bishop, the count and a dozen abbots would be exercising the jurisdiction entirely or in part. The very wrongs themselves were subdivided—one individual would have cognizance of arson and robbery, another of homicide and *raptus* in the same district. The objective is no longer peace and order; it is primarily fiscal. The tenth century becomes an administrative bedlam.

One would despair of establishing any continuity between the Carolingian system of law administration and the miserable, fragmentary evidence of judicial activity in northern France at the end of the tenth century but for the fact that there are definite indications that among the several units of the ecclesiastical hierarchy something of the Carolingian tradition was preserved. The objective of the church being to some extent similar to that of the old monarchy, the law-enforcing purpose of many lay institutions which had found their way into the hands of clerics was kept alive.

From the very beginning of Frankish hegemony in Gaul bishops and abbots had moved and ruled in two spheres of authority, the temporal and the spiritual. Under their control are tremendous concentrations of property. Partly because of administrative necessity, partly on account of their activity as public officials and partly as an accessory to their spiritual purpose, there is a steady transfer into their hands of various governmental perquisites, particularly in respect to the justiciation of delicts. Equally with the lay lords do the churchmen participate in the dismemberment of jurisdiction that takes place in the

West Frankish kingdom. But there is one striking difference between the two groups. The layman is mortal: the church is immortal. It is precisely because of the difference in succession, because of the corporate and superhuman faculties of the ecclesiastical unit that a feoffment, gift or grant is more likely to remain in the grantee when it is made to an abbey or bishopric.[19] It is for this reason that the church seems to dominate in the process by which a unified system for maintaining public order degenerates into the widely diffused private or quasi-public jurisdictions of the tenth century. This process we propose to consider in some detail because, as we have already suggested, the atomization of jurisdiction becomes a real obstacle in the way of rehabilitating the sadly battered notion of public order, of making the machinery of justice move once more for the purpose of suppressing wrongdoing and not merely to collect money or effect forfeitures. It is a process that begins with the end of Roman rule in France and reaches its height after the Normans have assumed control of Normandy. Involved is not merely the process of political enfranchisement by authority, but likewise the absorption of ancient social institutions like the authority of a master over his slave and persons in his *mundium,* the vast influence of the social and economic changes induced by the growth of commendation, and the movements of property resulting from the spread of beneficial ownership. All of these are elements that to a greater or less extent become focused against the central authority. For various reasons which will become apparent as the following discussion proceeds, the institution known as the immunity becomes the most potent instrument in the evisceration of the central government. We propose to examine the institution as it was used by the Merovingian kings and to determine how its mutations under the Carolingian kings led to the eventual fractionation of control over wrongs.

[19] *Infra,* p. 161.

### THE MEROVINGIAN IMMUNITY

The immunity[20] is granted by the crown. In its usual and extensive form from the seventh to the eleventh century, the immunity charter conveys varied administrative powers to the grantee (particularly in cases of wrongs) and it exempts the immunist's territories from interference by the ordinary public authorities. From the Romans, the early Merovingian kings acquired both the name and the underlying idea of the immunity.[21] Among the former the word immunity (*immunitas*) meant exemption from taxes and public services, and in the late Empire it was particularly lands of the fisc which were exempted from such burdens. These privileges in a greater or less degree could be and were extended to the possessions of subjects. Lands which the emperor conveyed out of his demesne retained the immunities of fiscal lands.[22]

[20] The literature on the immunities is large. The following have been used: 2 Brunner, *D.R.G.*, 382; Schröder, *D.R.G.*, 213; 2 Dopsch, *Wirtschaftsentwickelung der Karolingerzeit* (1913), 91 *et seq.;* Seeliger, *Die Soziale und Politische Bedeutung der Grundherrschaft im Frühen Mittelalter, Abhandlungen der sächsischen Gesell. der W.* (1903); W. Sickel, *op. cit.;* and *Zum Ursprung des Mittelalterlichen Staates, M.I.Ö.G.,* 2 EB., 198; Stengel, *Grundherrschaft und Immunität,* 25 *Z.R.G.²,* 286; 4 Waitz, *D.V.G.,* 287; Rietschel, *Landleihen, Hofrecht und Immunität,* 27 *M.I.Ö.G.,* 385; Beauchet, *Histoire de l'organisation judiciaire* (1886), 418 *et seq.;* Kroell, *L'Immunité franque* (1901); Senn, *op. cit.* Cam, *Local Government in Francia and England* (1912), 100 has a good brief summary. The studies of the formulae used are in T. Sickel, *Beiträge zur Diplomatik, W.S.B.* (1864), pt. III, and *W.S.B.* (1865), pt. V; 1 Stengel, *Die Immunität in Deutschland* (1910).

[21] Kroell, *op. cit.,* 3 *et seq.,* has the most extensive account. It has not seemed necessary to go into the details of the Roman régime. To be noted, however, is the strong position of the big proprietors, the *potentes, ibid.,* 20 *et seq.;* W. Sickel, *Die Privatherrschaften,* 15 *Westdeutsche Zt.* 119. The latter (*ibid.,* 125) emphasizes the point that the Frank conquerors followed a principle of *uti possidetis* and that the Roman *potentes* are in a sense the core of the Merovingian development.

[22] In this connection should be noted certain police powers exercised by the so-called *assertor pacis,* a Roman peace officer who combines constabulary with judicial duties. Both the title and office are interesting to reflect upon when one considers how the legal historians have insisted

In the earliest extant charter relating to this institution among the Franks the same notion of exemption from taxes and public services is present.[23] Upon the conquest of Gaul the Frankish kings appear to have succeeded to all the rights and interests in the demesne lands of the Roman emperor.[24] From this circumstance and from the indirect testimony of the formulae and charters, the presumption is that the crown lands continued to enjoy the immunities as of Roman times. Furthermore, since these privileges were granted to churches and laymen the increase in the number of individual immunities tended to make this institution important. Such grants were coupled with a conveyance of lands or with the extension of other privileges.[25] Where the grant was made out of crown lands, the immunity may be conceived of as following the lands more or less as of course; but the immunity is certainly assumed to be an independent franchise,[26] and the evidence is overwhelming that it is a personal privilege.[27]

upon the *Germanic* peace idea. On the *assertor,* 6 Dahn, *Könige der Germanen,* 356; Kroell, *op. cit.,* 24. Hirschfeld, *Die Sichersheitspolizei im Römischen Kaiserreich, Sitzungberichte der Pr. Ak. der Wiss.* (1891), 817, 868, shows how the office was copied after the *irenarcha* of the Eastern Empire, but most of his discussion is of the latter.

The *coloni* and tenants on fiscal lands had certain exceptional jurisdictional privileges, *cf.* Brunner, 2 *D.R.G.,* 384.

[23] Of the year 635 (October) in *M.G.H.* 1 *Diplom.,* 16, no. 15; an earlier document of the same year in different form, *ibid.,* 154, said by Pertz to be spurious. *Cf. Form. Marculfi I,* 3. It is assumed from the legislation of Chlothar II that his predecessors had granted immunities, Schröder, *D.R.G.,* 214.

[24] 2 Brunner, *D.R.G.,* 386.

[25] The rule of Frankish law was that church lands and those resident thereon were subject to state taxes and the ordinary courts, 2 Brunner, *D.R.G.,* 387. This explains, of course, the desire for immunities. As Kroell, *op. cit.,* 51, points out, the counts were a rapacious set and self-protection played a great role. Compare especially c. 11 of the Council of Chalons of the mid-seventh century (*M.G.H.,* 1 *Concilia* 210) where bitter complaint is made. The notion of a grant coupled with an immunity is illustrated in two formulae, *Form. Marculfi I,* 14, 16.

[26] Where it is combined with an extension of royal protection as well as with grants of land; 4 Waitz, *D.V.G.,* 288.

[27] T. Sickel, *Beiträge zur Diplomatik, W.S.B.* (1865), pt. V, 334 estab-

Toward the middle of the seventh century an important change in the content of the immunity grant is effected by the addition of a clause prohibiting entries by public officers upon the lands of the immunists for the purpose of hearing causes or making exactions.[28] In the formulae of this period, to which on all major points the charters conform, this prohibition is extended in terms to cover not only the hearing of causes but the collection of *fredus* out of such causes or generally.[29] It will be recalled that the *fredus* was the payment to the state for inter-

lished the point that a general immunity once granted extended to all property wherever situate and to after-acquired lands. It follows from this rule that the privilege is a personal franchise.

[28] Schröder, *D.R.G.*, 214, thinks the prohibition upon special entries probably existed before the time of Chlothar II; *contra*, Kroell, *op. cit.*, 31. The thesis of the latter writer is that the Roman *potentes*, a group which included ecclesiastical proprietors, had, in the sixth century, developed jurisdictions (relying upon the *Formulae Andegavenses*, especially no. 10 and no. 11) which he thinks led to the establishment of the exemption from public official interference. Compare with this the opinion of Waitz, 2 *D.V.G.*, pt. 2, 337, who sees the motive in the collection of fiscal dues.

[29] The interdiction in the immunity charters in reference to the public officers is in various forms, e.g., "nulla iudiciaria potestas presumat ingredere" (*Form. Marculfi I*, 2) and "neque vos neque iuniores neque successores vestri nec nulla publica iudiciaria potestas . . . in villas . . . ingredi non presumatis" (*Form. Marculfi I*, 3). *Cf.* also *Form. Marculfi I*, 14, 17, *absque ullius introitus iudicum*. The substantive matter includes the prohibitions: (1) *ad causas audiendo . . . ad audiendas altercationes ingredire* (*Form. Marculfi I*, 4; 3); (2) *ad aliquid exactandum ibidem non presumat ingredi*, (*M.G.H., Diplom. Merow.* no. 15, p. 16); (3) *ad freta exigendum* (*Form. Marculfi I*, 3); (4) *nec homines de quaslibet causas distringendum* (*Form. Marculfi I*, 4); (5) *nec fideiussoraes tollere* (*Form. Marculfi I*, 3).

The interdiction upon entries did not extend to the exercises of *royal power*. Where there was a special royal order a royal official could enter. 2 Brunner, *D.R.G.*, 392. The exceptions to this interdiction on entries are briefly listed in *ibid.*, 392 n. 49. And note that the count had certain privileges where public duties such as military and watch services were not included in the exception. The *missus* of course as a royal official could enter, Schröder, *D.R.G.*, 216.

Haskins, *Norman Institutions* (1918), 26 remarks that "The Frankish immunity itself . . . did not create exemption from the authority of the count." This is a misleading statement. The authority of the count exercised within an immunity was exceptional. The *absque introitu iudicum* is of the essence of the immunity and all the qualifications of this set forth

vention in a composition plea. The terms of the formulae are such that they are to be interpreted not merely as the state's relinquishment of such payments, but as a positive grant of the fiscal privilege to the immunity holder,[30] since charters containing such provision do not imply an abolition of *fredus,* and one could scarcely imagine an immunist permitting such a privilege to lapse.[31]

The effect of the crown's abandonment of the means of collecting as well as the *fredus* payment itself must have been important in direct ratio to the increase in the number of such privileges granted. It has been established that by the year 840 there was no bishopric and no convent of importance which had not received the privilege.[32] The number of laymen who received it we cannot even guess at.[33] The assumption is that most great proprieties whether lay or ecclesiastical were protected against entry of the local *iudex* or count by the phrase *absque introitu iudicum.* Further, since the charters ordinarily are cast in the restricted terms of *fredus,* this had the probable effect of tending to preserve the old methods of settling wrongs. If we may draw a somewhat dangerous parallel we can compare the situation in an immunity to an English leet jurisdiction. The exempted territory tends to remain a backwater in a stream of progress.[34]

by Dopsch, Seeliger and the other authorities referred to by Haskins are made with this exemption in view.

[30] We are speaking, of course, of the normal "full" immunity. On variations *cf.* Kroell, *op cit.,* 114 *et seq.*

[31] The documents cited by Waitz, 4 *D.V.G.,* 302 n. 2, all Carolingian, tend to establish that the immunist has the power to collect.

[32] Kroell, *op. cit.,* 172 and compare the map at that page.

[33] Kroell, *op. cit.,* 156, has stated that under the Carolingians no laymen were granted immunities, but this has been disproved. (*Cf.* Dopsch, *op. cit.,* 127.) No argument on the matter is admissible from the mere fact that most of our remaining documents are ecclesiastical privileges. A somewhat similar situation prevails in regard to documents relating to legal proceedings, yet no one would dream of suggesting that only clerics were litigants.

[34] *Cf.* the discussion in Goebel, *King's Law and Local Custom* 31 *C.L.R.* 434.

It is one thing, of course, to tell the grantee that the count cannot enter an immunist's jurisdiction to try cases and quite another matter to give the immunist the positive power to try cases himself. In Merovingian times the existence of such a right in the immunist has been the subject of much debate.[35] Some discussion of this matter cannot be entirely avoided since the division of authority over wrongs is regulated by Merovingian legislation, and this regulation more or less determines the growth of extra-public jurisdiction up to the end of the ninth century.

To understand the exact force which the practice of granting immunities had upon the administration of the law and particularly upon holding court, the fact should be emphasized that the immunities had significance not only as franchises of what were essentially public rights, but also as tending to consolidate certain other powers which the grantee already had. Writers have separated these powers according to source or the legal theory upon which these were justified. For the moment we may accept this mode of analysis to determine in what relations an individual, apart from any authority he may have had from an immunity charter, could exercise judicial powers in what may be described as a private capacity.[36]

[35] There is a summary of the conflicting views in Kroell, *op. cit.*, 128 *et seq.* The latter takes the position that the immunity jurisdiction is identical with the special position of the fiscal domains, i.e., grants out of the latter implied an extension of the same privileges which fiscal lands had, and that these privileges were extended to lands which had not been fiscal. *Ibid.*, 133; *cf.* Brunner, 2 *D.R.G.*, 399, who suggests the interdiction of entries did not necessarily import no comital jurisdiction. The answer to this is, of course, that there is no value in a jurisdiction without power of execution. This power of the count the charters certainly restricted. *Cf.* Rietschel 32 *Z.R.G.*[2], 477 and W. Sickel, *Zum Ursprung des mittelalterlichen Staates, M.I.Ö.G.*, 2 *EB.* (1888), 213.

[36] Reluctantly we employ this word "private" since we are conscious how futile is an attempted contrast between public and private in this era. The distinction for the Merovingian period seems to be between groups or individuals exercising powers with a degree of responsibility to the crown and those individuals who, in some relations, are responsible to no

Out of the traditional power of a master of an establishment over various classes of persons of his household, certain judicial powers developed not only in matters concerning the interior discipline of an establishment, but also in matters where third persons outside the establishment were affected. This we have already touched upon in connection with the liability of the master for the wrongs committed by slaves upon third persons.[37] In the passages which deal with this phase of judicial administration one can envisage the master as the connecting link between the public tribunals and the private jurisdiction which he, by virtue of his position as the head of a social unit, may exercise.[38] There is no disposition on the part of the state to destroy this jurisdiction, but simply to provide persons who are in no way connected with it some guarantee for the maintenance of their

one, and only in certain circumstances have to account to the former groups or individuals. The case of the master and his slaves discussed in the text illustrates this distinction.

[37] *Supra,* p. 84. The authority of the *potentes* and the great ecclesiastical establishments in the early Merovingian period to some extent was based upon their legal rights in this relation. On the other hand most of the writers are agreed that even before the Franks conquered Gaul, these magnates had managed to acquire extensive "public" powers which were not surrendered after the conquest. W. Sickel, *Privatherrschaften,* 15 *Westdeutsche Zeitschrift,* 113, 125; Kroell, *op. cit.,* 132; 2 Brunner, *D.R.G.,* 381, who thinks that a sharp distinction must be drawn between the privileges of the establishments which derived powers from Roman times and the normal Germanic-Frankish large propriety. Compare also the passage cited in 2 Waitz, *D.V.G.,* pt. 2, 376, "our fisc remains poor; our riches have been transferred to the churches; no one rules but the bishops; our power has perished and has been transferred to the bishops of the cities."

[38] Schröder, *D.R.G.,* 188–9. 2 Brunner, *D.R.G.,* 369 *et seq.;* Brunner, *Mithio und Sperantes (Festgabe für Beseler,* 1885). 2 Dopsch, *op. cit.,* 91, 99.
The position of the master is different as to slaves, half-free, and free. As to the first, the wrongs committed by one slave against another are entirely in the cognizance of the master who has even power of life and death, Meyer, *Gerichtsbarkeit über Unfreie,* 2 *Z.R.G.*[2], 88. As late as 803–13 in *Cap. de latronibus* c. 9 (1 *Cap.,* 181) this principle is asserted. The half-free have a qualified privilege of appearing in public courts. As to the freemen who are a part of the household, who are in the *mundium* of the landlord or who are domiciled on the land, *cf.* W. Sickel, *Privatherrschaften,* 16 *Westdeutsche Zt.,* 53 *et seq.*

rights.[39] At the same time, it is to be noted that the state has no desire to enlarge the householder-master's powers at the expense of the ordinary system of law administration.[40]

In connection with the ancient master and landlord jurisdiction must be considered the later social phenomena, which has its roots in these times—the institution of vassalage.[41] It is difficult to determine whether, even in the Carolingian period, the relation of vassal and superior included the vesting of judicial powers in a given senior, for there are considerable qualitative variations in the relationship. The *vassi dominici* or crown vassals of Charlemagne's time were something different from their own half-free *vassi;* and even among vassals who preserved their status of freemen, the fact that they did or did not constitute a part of a lord's household made a difference in the extent of the latter's power over them. The freeman owed attendance upon the public court,[42] and it was not the policy of the crown to expunge these public duties. This we may regard as a consideration of primary importance in the question of the judicial subjection of the free vassal.[43] On the other hand, when commendation was coupled with a grant of benefice, as was increasingly the case, certain rights or duties were bound to be attached to services arising out of the grant rather than to the purely personal homage by virtue of commendation.

[39] Thus the *Pactus pro tenore pacis,* c. 5 (1 *Cap.,* 5) makes it a duty of the master to turn up the thieving slave, a principle extended later to other cases where a public punishment is inflicted.

[40] The gradual extension of cases where the master can have the option of surrendering the slave or respond for him in court is in no way a lessening of *public* power.

[41] It is not necessary to enter into the much argued question of the origins of vassalage. The literature is summed up in 2 Brunner, *D.R.G.,* 349 *et seq.* Recently, older theories have been subjected to reexamination. There is a good summary of these in Dopsch, *Benefizialwesen und Feudalität,* 46 *M.I.Ö.G.,* 1, 16 *et seq.*

[42] 2 Brunner, *D.R.G.,* 290, 356.

[43] Brunner states that in general a special jurisdiction of the lord over the vassal did not develop out of this protective relationship; *ibid.,* 356. The notion of representation by the lord develops, as we have stated later

We can observe, moreover, in the regulation of the vassal-senior tie certain factors at work which made this relation subject to the ancient rules which governed the master-servant system of early Frankish law. Thus, the greater degree of power which a lord had over vassals in his household,[44] the practice of holding a lord accountable in the *mallus publicus* for certain acts of the vassal,[45] and the duty of the lord to wage feud[46] represent an adjustment of the law of an older social structure to the problems of a new order where the householder had become a landholder, the master had become a lord, and the old ties of kinship had given way to an alliance grounded upon commendation.[47]

In the time of Charlemagne it is reasonably clear that the rule obtained that the vassal still owed his suit to the ordinary courts, and that causes in which he was involved were there to be judged. Inducing a modification of this general rule was the qualified power of the senior to punish his vassals.[48] This power may be definitely related to the military purpose of vassalage and to the quasi-military discipline which this purpose necessarily entailed. There is some indication that this right of discipline was recognized at the beginning of the ninth century.[49]

in the text, but a special court cannot be said to have existed; 4 Waitz, *D.V.G.*, 462.

[44] 2 Brunner, *D.R.G.*, 375.

[45] 4 Waitz, *D.V.G.*, 269, and note particularly the tendency for the responsibility of the lord to increase as the ninth century wore on, *loc. cit.*, n. 4. The most elaborate account of the whole matter is in Roth, *Feudalität und Unterthanenverband* (1863), 224. The special position of crown vassals may well have affected rules relating to others. *Cf.* also Ganshof, *La jurisdiction du seigneur sur son vassal à l'époque carolingienne*, 27 *Rev. de l'Univ. de Bruxelles*, 566.

[46] Roth, *op. cit.*, 223–4. The capitularies dealing with the matter are for Italy, but two formulae indicate the rule is general.

[47] Hintze, *Wesen und Verbreitung des Feudalismus* (BSB. 1929), 326, who emphasizes that a man who becomes a vassal gives up the protection of the sib. *Cf.* also 4 Waitz, *D.V.G.*, 265 on the senior's duty of protection.

[48] Roth, *op. cit.*, 227. The duty of the senior is either to produce the vassal for punishment (the capitularies here are all after 850) or to punish directly.

[49] *Kar. ad Fulrad* (804–811), 1 *Cap.*, 168, is taken by Roth to import

Certainly in the capitularies of Louis and his successors a recurring emphasis is laid upon this phase of seniorial power.

The attempts to isolate the theoretical constituents of "private" judicial power, useful for the purposes of historical analysis, may not necessarily have an exact correspondence with reality. Powers which are implicit in social arrangements, like these of master and servant, may be separated from those specifically granted or negatively implied, like those exercised by an immunist. Yet if we could take view of what justice a great landholding immunist exercised in respect of servants, vassals and freemen within the territorial limits of his holding at a particular moment, we would likely find that he did things which it would be difficult to attribute to either grant or immemorial right. This must have been especially true of the ecclesiastical units which had the power of ecclesiastical discipline.[50]

As to any type of "private" jurisdiction, an immunity charter was bound to have a certain catalytic effect, for the moment that outside judicial influence was limited or forbidden by grant it is clear that the grantee need not trouble himself greatly over

this power. The capitulary *Admonitio ad omnes* (823–25) c. 17 (1 *Cap.*, 305) gives clear evidence of this power. *Quaere,* if at this period the power was exercisable unless the vassal was actually engaged in a military enterprise. *Cf.* also on this matter Waitz, *Anfänge der Vassalität* in *Gesammelte Abhandlungen* (1896) 196 and 4 *D.V.G.,* 462. Roth is readier to admit a jurisdiction in the ninth century (*op. cit.,* 230). Even if one is not prepared to go this far it is certainly true that the regulations which drove claimants to turn in the first instance to the senior and failing satisfaction to the public courts (2 Dopsch, *Wirtschaftsentwicklung,* 99), tended to set up a barrier between the vassal and the ordinary course of justice. Moreover, the provisions in the capitularies for the protection of the vassal against the senior are recognitions of the *de facto* authority of the senior. *Cf. Cap. Pist.,* (869) *adnuntiatio* c. 2 (2 *Cap.,* 337) ". . . Et si aliquis episcopus, abbas aut abbatissa vel comes ac vassus noster suo homini contra rectum et iustitiam fecerit et se inde ad nos reclamaverit . . ."

[50] Dopsch, in 2 *Wirtschaftsentwicklung,* 119, expresses something of the same notion as that advanced in the text. Speaking of the ecclesiastical holdings which had been consolidated into large units by purchase and exchange he asserts that districts almost entirely separated from comital power came into existence. He proceeds: "Eine Verdichtung der Herrschaftsrechte trat hier ein innerhalb der Immunität, eine Verstärkung, die

the theoretical justification of what he could do on his own land in respect to his own men. Even the patent concern that the crown showed in extending its protection to the free vassal as against the senior would be of very little avail. The man who held a benefice of Roland and lived in his vicinity would probably in future times have found that paladin less than a saint if he had impleaded him before the local count. In Tudor days the copyholders were no less helpless as a practical matter against inclosing lords, despite the fact that they had "rights." The tendency for rules originally devised for one relationship to affect or govern a different relationship must undoubtedly have been at work here, as elsewhere, in giving to rights that originally lay in grant a status independent of any royal charter. In times when physical power is mightier than parchment these metamorphoses are usual. There was no *quo warranto,* and presently no one sufficiently powerful to seal such a writ had it existed. This is why there is such a tremendous increase in prescription and why there is no legal theory to dam it by distinguishing it from grant.

IMMUNITY JURISDICTION OVER WRONGS

Although the negative form in which the privileges of the Merovingian immunist of the seventh century were cast leads one to doubt whether the immunity charter itself conveyed positive rights of justiciation, there can be no doubt that persons who had immunities did exercise judicial powers. The great Gallic landholders of the Roman Empire and the intendants on the Roman imperial domain lands had each possessed such powers although not derived from the immunity.[51] The magnates'

den negativen Immunitätsbegriff der älteren Zeit zu positivem Inhalt weiter entwickelte."

[51] Kroell, *op. cit.,* 132 *et seq.,* and *cf.* also the evidence, *ibid.,* 25 to the effect that in Roman times third persons turned first to the *potens* for relief. 2 Dopsch, *Wirtschaftsentwickelung,* 97, "The immunity did not itself create a new jurisdiction but merely assured the old landlord jurisdiction against incursion by public officials." As to the jurisdiction without the Gallo-Roman region Brunner, in 2 *D.R.G.,* 400, suggests that after the

rights appear to have survived the conquest, and the Frankish fisc when it absorbed the *immunitas* of the imperial domains preserved also something of the administrative arrangements of the Romans.[52] When grants were made by the crown out of fiscal lands it was not unusual for the *immunitas* to be coupled with the conveyance. It has been conjectured, therefore, that the judicial privileges of fiscal lands were continued as a part of the immunity in private hands.[53]

Earlier than any charters are the references in Merovingian capitularies to the immunity. These capitularies, and in particular the Edict of Chlothar II (614),[54] point to something more than a mere immunity from taxes and public services. Not only the description of the purposes of the immunity as *pro pace atque disciplina facienda,* but the specification of certain acts performable by the immunists testify to the existence of a positive power in the matter of preserving order.[55] The Edict, more-

acquisition of an immunity, landlord jurisdiction could expand to limits similar to that of the *potentes.* On the question whether the immunity was granted to extend financial rights or to assure jurisdiction, Seeliger, *op. cit.,* 77.

[52] W. Sickel, *Zum Ursprung des Mittelalterlichen Staates, M.I.Ö.G.,* 2 EB., 215; 2 Brunner, *D.R.G.,* 166.

[53] Kroell, *op. cit.,* 133 lays great emphasis upon the phrase "sicut a fisco nostro fuit possessa" and its variations in the charters.

[54] C. 14. (1 *Cap.,* 22) ". . . emunitate . . . quod ecclesiae aut potentum vel cuicumque visi sunt indulsisse pro pace atque disciplina facienda." On these words *pax et disciplina* in another connection *cf.* the document cited in 2 Waitz, *D.V.G.,* pt. 2, 90 n. 3. They may be rendered by our "peace and order."

[55] *Edict. Chloth. II,* c. 15; "Si homines ecclesiarum aut potentum de causis criminalibus fuerint accusati *agentes* eorum ab agentibus publicis *requisiti* si *ipsos* in audentia pu . . . foris domus ipsorum *ad iustitiam reddenda* praesentare noluerint et distringantur, *quatenus eosdem* debeant praesentare." This seems to point clearly to a police duty. Kroell, *op. cit.,* 135 relates this order-keeping function to the Roman *assertor pacis.* The formula *Form. Marculfi I,* 27 points in the case of a theft to a duty of the bishop to have the offender amend. This formula is discussed in Nissl, *Gerichtsstand des Clerus* (1886) 233.

These texts have been taken to imply more than a mere duty of police, in the sense that they are evidence of the existence of a judicial function. This is discussed in Beauchet, *op. cit.,* 83–84.

over, points to an actual exercise of authority over composition pleas, but it is not certain whether this occurred in regularly constituted courts or by way of arbitration.[56] In any event, this Edict seeks to regulate immunity rights by providing that if the men of churches or lay magnates (*potentes*) should be accused in *causis criminalibus*[57] the offender must be turned over to the public authority. If this is not done the latter is empowered to compel surrender, unless the matter has been settled by composition by the agents of the churches or of the *potentes*.[58]

It is certain from later developments that Chlothar did not remove from the cognizance of the immunists cases of wrongs where composition could be sued. He was not attempting by the expression *causae criminales* to assert a public monopoly over offenses. At the very least he was endeavoring to insure that public interest should not suffer by insisting that cases not settled by amends be turned over to public functionaries, a policy which is of a piece with another section requiring the operation of secular sanctions against clergy.[59] At the most he was insisting upon

[56] But we can surmise that it was in some more or less regular manner. Thus the treatise on Roman-Frankish officialdom defines the intendants of *potentes* as those "qui iudicant causas" in the villa, Conrat, *Ein Traktat über romanisch-fränkisches Ämterwesen*, 29 *Z.R.G.*[2], 254. In *Edict. Chloth. II*, c. 22 it is provided: "Neque ingenuos neque servus qui cum furto non depraehenditur, ad iudicibus aut ad quemcumque interfici non debeat inauditus"; and compare *Chloth. II Praecept.*, (584–28) c. 3. These provisions point to an insistence on regular judicial proceedings.

[57] *Edict. Chloth. II*, c. 15.

[58] The *potentes* are those who have immunities (*ibid.*, c. 14). On the passage which is fragmentary, 2 Waitz, *D.V.G.*, pt. 2, 378; Schröder, *D.R.G.*, 190 n. 87; Beauchet, *op. cit.*, 85. Kroell, *op. cit.*, 144, curiously ignorant of the contemporary procedure, renders the technical phrase "si tamen ad ipsis agentibus antea non fuerit emendatum," "*arranger l'affaire à l'amiable!*"

[59] The provisions of c. 15 were restricted to the *homines* of churches or magnates. C. 4 of the Edict asserts the jurisdiction of the lay courts over clerics in what it describes as criminal "negucia." The purpose of this was to insure the operation of secular sanctions *as against ecclesiastical discipline* in the case of wrongs. The literature on this one section is extensive. *Cf.* esp. Nissl, *op. cit.*, 116 *et seq.*; 2 Loening, *Kirchenrecht*, 526; 4 Hinschius, *K.R.*, 858–61; 2 Brunner, *D.R.G.*, 420.

the operation of the crown procedure described in our previous chapter.[60] This is done in terms of reservation with procedural distinctions implicit.[61] By using the narrow *emendare* the Edict limited the competence of "private" jurisdiction so that it could not extend beyond the older forms of settling wrongs.[62] It does not embrace authority to use crown procedure.

This restriction of the immunity jurisdiction over wrongs expressed in the capitularies received additional fortification from the earliest immunity charters preserved (635) wherein the entry of judicial officers for hearing causes or collecting *fredus* was prohibited.[63] Unless we can suppose that the provisions merely implied a privilege of collection and not of justiciation (a sense-

[60] Brunner, in 2 *D.R.G.*, 401, states that immunity jurisdiction extends only so far as public jurisdiction had financial character; that it covers only cases where *fredus* or ban penalties were paid. "It, therefore, excluded from the sphere of criminal causes, the *causae maiores* where outlawry, or penalties of life and limb were exacted." His references are all to Carolingian sources. Kroell, *op. cit.*, 144 using the same method of proof comes to the same conclusion. Our position is that in the seventh century the concept of public order, or public penalties had not yet pushed out the plea for amends to the point of exclusion even in homicide.

[61] The most comprehensive recent legislation was the *decretio* of Childebert II (596) for Austrasia (1 *Cap.*, 15) where theft, incest, *raptus* and certain homicides were threatened with death. It should be noted here that where the alternative of redemption was offered, as in *Pactus pro tenore pacis* c. 2 (1 *Cap.*, 4) and in various provisions of the *Lex Salica*, the *precio redemptionis* could not be considered as equivalent to the *fredus*. Consequently the immunities could not in this wise acquire a jurisdiction since Chlothar's Edict looks specifically to a composition procedure.

[62] It comprehends, of course, jurisdiction over slaves.

[63] A usual expression is *absque introitu judicum*. The earliest privilege attested by charter is that of Dagobert I (October 635), to the monastery of Rebas (*M.G.H.*, 1 *Dipl.* no. 16, p. 17). T. Sickel, *Beiträge, W.S.B.* (1865), pt. V, 348 states that the use or failure to use the word *fredus* in a document was a matter of scribe's caprice. The *fredus* privilege, however, becomes an essential incident of a grant. Even in the West of Gaul where the crown still exacted of the immunist certain imposts the *fredus* was granted, Kroell, *op. cit.*, 147. For the variations in the types of concession Sickel, *loc. cit.*, 340 *et seq.*, where the whole range of charters to 840 is covered. Kroell, *op. cit.*, 112 *et seq.*, has characterized the Merovingian charters.

less conclusion in the face of the Edict's language)[64] we must regard such franchises as making more or less absolute the judicial control of the immunist in cases where a plea for amends would properly lie. These privileges are at once an abandonment by the state of a fiscal perquisite and of the machinery for exacting it.[65]

Once the interdiction of entries to collect *fredus* becomes a usual franchise, the substance of what the crown was attempting to save in the Edict of 614 becomes more certain. Where the immunist had not been able to settle a wrong by composition procedure, he was required to turn up the offender or the public functionaries would arrest.[66] Since the latter could not under the terms of a charter with an *absque introitu* clause enter to collect *fredus,* it is reasonably clear that their competence was restricted to cases where some other procedure could be taken against the offender. This can have been either that procedure which the crown had devised for cases where composition pleas were not effective, or it may have been more narrowly conceived as that where a death penalty was provided. The expression *causae criminales,* as it is used in the documents of the Merovingian

[64] Kroell, *op. cit.,* 148 n. 1 says it is possible the *fredus* was paid to the immunist but the inhabitants would be subject to the count. A jurisdiction without direct power of process seems unlikely. The statements in 2 Brunner *D.R.G.,* 393, 395, 399 are not entirely consistent. After stating that the prohibition of *districtio* excludes all direct summons, distraint or execution, and admitting that the concession of *fredus* assumes a grant of what the French call *basse justice* over the freemen of the immunity, it is remarked that the interdiction of *introitus* did not exclude comital jurisdiction, a conclusion that needs great qualification. On the point in the text, *cf.* also Seeliger, *op. cit.,* 77; 2 Waitz *D.V.G.,* pt. 2, 345.

[65] It is to be noted that exemption was not accorded from certain public services, especially military service, watch, bridge and road mending. This is not clearly stated until the Carolingian period.

In the case of causes between persons subject only to public jurisdiction and men of a church a mixed court of public judge and the *praepositus* of the church was to judge in public court. *Edict. Chloth. II,* c. 5. *Cf.* 2 Waitz, *D.V.G.,* pt. 2, 378.

[66] We are speaking here of the rights of the immunist. The question of his *duty* is primarily a matter which would be regulated by rules governing contumacy. *Cf. infra,* p. 151, on the later procedure of the capitularies.

period, is significant, therefore, not as a substantive concept,[67] but as expressing a difference in procedure. In an immunity a qualified right of keeping order is confirmed, and where amends are collectible the jurisdiction is exclusive. In cases where the new public procedure is operative the state can step in. As the tendency eventually became pronounced not to allow the composition procedure to interfere with public prosecution and punishment, in a certain defined class of offenses, such offenses became definitely removed from the sphere of the jurisdiction exercised by immunists. Thus, under the Merovingians, the immunity grants definitely added to the powers of individuals and yet preserved for the state the sphere of activity which it was intent upon developing.

[67] As suggested by Kroell, *op. cit.*, 144 relying upon a document 200 years later, the *Constitutio de Hispanis* (815) 1 *Cap.*, 261. One of the most sharply contested points between Seeliger and Stengel was precisely this matter of "criminal" jurisdiction. The major difficulty seems to have arisen out of the fact that *causae criminales = causae maiores* in the Brunner school; that is to say they are so-called outlawry-feud cases (Stengel, *Grundherrschaft und Immunität*, 25 Z.R.G.², 297). Since Beyerle succeeded in prying loose the fictional substructure of outlawry from the early Germanic procedure, this sort of definition does not get us far. Nor does Brunner's suggestion that the money paid in amends merely substitutes for punishment (2 *D.R.G.*, [1 ed.] 538) and that this did not destroy the quality of the offense as *crimen capitalis*. This would only have been true of ransom payments.

Such attempts to fix for *causae criminales* a substantive meaning for this time do not seem useful. In all probability the term was borrowed from ecclesiastical law. It had on various occasions been given partial definition by church councils, but these definitions or specifications are not precise. It alternates with the phrase *crimen capitalis* as an expression for offenses which involve degradation (Nissl, *op. cit.*, 27) or any grievous sins by clerics to which ecclesiastical penalties attach (4 Hinschius, *K.R.*, 807). At Epaon (517) false testimony is *reus capitalis criminis* (*M.G.H.* 1 *Concilia*, 22 c. 13). At Orleans (538) *furtum* is also so designated (*ibid.*, 76, c. 9). But at Macon (583) homicide, theft and sorcery are described as *causae criminales* (*ibid.*, 157, c. 7). Obviously in the face of such variations it is useless to assume that in lay law the expression *causae criminales* has any definite substantive meaning. Compare on the Frankish use of the term, Nissl, *op. cit.*, 10 *et seq.*, and especially for Carolingian usage p. 12 n. 3; Sohm, *F.R.G.V.*, 419; *Geistliche Gerichtsbarkeit im Fränkischen Reich*, 9 *Zeitschrift für Kirchenrecht*, 275.

## THE CAROLINGIAN IMMUNITY

In the Carolingian period the position of the immunity in the Frankish polity undergoes a definite change.[68] The first phase of this change is found in measures whereby the various privileged units are to a certain extent integrated into the general scheme of administration. The second phase beginning under Louis the Pious is characterized by the growth of territorial and political independence, and the destruction of the tissues which connected the immunity with the central organization of the Empire.[69]

Conclusions regarding the exercise of judicial power by immunists under the Merovingian kings are the result of inference, since such power is never conveyed in positive terms. All doubts on this score vanish in the succeeding era.[70] Indeed, the early years of Charlemagne's reign yield two important examples of the direct grant of judicial franchises,[71] which indicate that as a matter of principle[72] there was no obstacle to the extension of the privilege. Once this privilege, moreover, is incor-

[68] The contribution of Kroell lies in the fact that he for the first time distinguished sharply between the Merovingian and Carolingian immunity, and brought into proper focus the measures taken by Charlemagne to make the immunity work for the state.

[69] Rietschel in 32 Z.R.G.², 478. Cf. also the remarks of Dopsch, 2 Wirtschaftsentwickelung, 97; and note his caution (p. 96) that the charters did not put the immunist on a parity with the count.

[70] 2 Brunner, D.R.G. 397; 4 Waitz, D.V.G., 451–2; Kroell, op. cit., 197 et seq.

[71] These are the charters to Trier (772) and Metz (775) in M.G.H., Diplomata Karolin., 95, 131. In the Trier Charter the privilege reads "nec homines eorum per mallobergiis nullus deberet admallare aut per aliqua ingenia presumeret condempnare . . . sed in eorum privatas audientias agentes ipsius ecclesiae unicuique de reputatis condicionibus directum facerent." These charters are discussed in Sickel, Beiträge W.S.B. (1864), pt. III, 225; Kroell, op. cit., 198.

[72] On the other ninth-century charters conveying franchises, similar to Metz and Trier, cf. W. Sickel, Zum Ursprung des Mittelalterlichen Staates, M.I.Ö.G. 2 EB., 212, and 4 Waitz D.V.G., 452 n. 2. While in the text we have been considering what may be called the normal full franchise it must be pointed out that great variations existed. The extent of jurisdic-

porated in the charters, it will require no great stretch of legal theory for the right of justiciation to be regarded as an inseparable incident of a grant of immunity, without reference to any antecedent justification of the exercise of this right. If an immunist holds court it is because he is an immunist and not merely in his capacity as a magnate or an ecclesiast or a master of a big estate.

While the right to hold pleas became the subject of grant, this did not however increase the scope of what was regarded as proper for immunity jurisdiction. A number of Carolingian acts indicate that the distinctions marked in the Edict of 614 by Chlothar II became more sharply defined. In the Capitulary of Haristal (779)[73] it was provided that thieves in an immunity were to be surrendered to the ordinary court held by the count, upon pain of forfeiting benefice and office (*honor*). This rule probably represents a diminution of the privilege of the immunist since it leaves no room for a procedure for amends to ward off the operation of public justice. It is a distinct reaffirmation of the crown's policy to control directly what it regarded as offenses against public order. The crown will not delegate this function.

In 803, there is further regulation.[74] When persons who have elsewhere committed homicide or theft or other such crime (*crimen*) and flee into the immunity, the count is to requisition the offender. The immunist (in terms the bishop, abbot or *vicedomino*) if he refuses to surrender such persons is subject to successive money penalties, with a final right of the count, upon repeated summons, to enter and search for the offender. A similar

tion is measured sometimes in terms of territorial extent, sometimes in terms of personal relations and sometimes the two are combined.

[73] c. 9 (1 *Cap.*, 48) and *cf.* c. 11. Even a privilege as extensive in terms as that cited *supra*, note 71 must probably be understood with reference to the general legislation so that irrespective of grant the state does not relinquish *causae criminales*.

[74] *Cap. Legg. Add.*, c. 2 (1 *Cap.*, 113).

rule is extended in a later capitulary for the apprehension of makers of false coins.[75]

It is possible that the purpose of the mandate of 803 was to prevent an ecclesiastical immunity from having the right of sanctuary that attached to a church[76] and thus from giving any ground for excluding secular officials. It was, more broadly, an implicit denial of the power of jurisdiction over offenses which were committed without the immunity, and seemingly a confirmation of the essentially territorial nature of immunity jurisdiction. Certainly the capitularies of succeeding rulers on the same subject matter render this principle of jurisdiction clear beyond doubt.[77]

In dealing with the general legislation on the rights of immunities it must be borne in mind that a great number of the most important of these franchises were in ecclesiastical hands. Since the tendency in what we may call the penal law was in the direction of afflictive sanctions rather than composition, it was essential to the pursuit of any serious policy of law enforcement that the penalties be executed. This could not be expected of the church. A man might starve to death under a sentence of excommunication, but the church as a matter of policy was reluctant to shed blood.[78] Consequently, whatever its power may have been to effect composition by judicial intervention, its franchises

---

[75] *Ed. Pist.* (864) c. 18 (2 *Cap.*, 317).

[76] 4 Hinschius, *K.R.*, 386, on this, but Hinschius cites c. 3 and not c. 2 of the *Cap. Legg. Add.* of 803. The former chapter is directly on the point; c. 2 is applicable only by inference. In this connection should be noted the decision of Louis the Pious in the matter of the monastery of Aniane (822) where he lays it down that any enclosure was covered, Böhmer-Mühlbacher, *Regesten* no. 751.

[77] *Cap. Carisiac.*, (873) c. 3, (2 *Cap.*, 344). The earlier *Cap. Silvac.*, (853) c. 7 (2 *Cap.*, 273) seems to contemplate a similar rule. The tendency of these capitularies is against jurisdiction on the basis of a personal relationship of man to master in favor of territorial responsibility.

[78] The theory of church penal discipline is set forth in 4 Hinschius, *K.R.*, 691 *et seq.* On the prohibition of any association with the excommunicate, especially feeding him, *ibid.*, 801.

could not include the cases where the death penalty was necessary.[79]

The rule regarding sanctuary thus fits in with the now complete reservation of *causae criminales* to show that the crown was determined to have the afflictive penalties for certain offenses carried out. That its general policy was even more broadly conceived, that the crown would in any event keep control over this class of wrongs may be deduced from a grant in the nature of an immunity to a lay group. This is the grant of powers to the refugees in the so-called Spanish March. In the *Constitutio de Hispanis* (815)[80] what are described as *causae maiores,* to wit, homicide, *raptus,* arson, mayhem, plundering, robbery, theft and invasions of property are reserved for the count.[81] All other matters *inter sese* are left to the judgment of the settlers' own courts.[82] A franchise somewhat similar to that of the Spaniards was granted by Louis the Pious to the fiscal foresters in the Vosges.[83] To these men was given the right of being tried by their own chief foresters but the *causae criminales,* without specification, were expressly reserved.

From what has been said, it may be affirmed with some degree of certainty that from the time of Chlothar's Edict down

---

[79] It is with this in mind that the Bavarian Capitulary (circa 810) c. 1 (1 *Cap.,* 158) must be interpreted "ut habeant aecclesiae earum iustitias, tam in vita illorum qui habitant in ipsis ecclesiis etc." 4 Waitz *D.V.G.,* 455; Kroell, *op. cit.,* 209.

In the bishopric of Chur (Rhaetia) which enjoyed privileges in the nature of an immunity but greater in extent, the *Capitula Remedii* (*M.G.H.* 5 *Leges* 441) make reservation of causes to lay judges where the death penalty was imposed. Here the ecclesiastical authority would execute afflictive penalties such as abscission of members, and retained jurisdiction over the first two homicides by a single killer (c. 2). On this *cf.* 1 Brunner, *D.R.G.,* 522 *et seq.*

[80] c. 2 (1 *Cap.,* 262).

[81] As well as causes of third persons against the Spaniards. *Cf.* also 4 Waitz, *D.V.G.,* 458-9.

[82] In 844, Charles the Bald restricts comital jurisdiction to homicide, *raptus* and arson. *Praecept. pro Hispanis* (844) c. 3 (2 *Cap.,* 259).

[83] *Form. Imp.,* 43 (Zeumer, *Formulae,* 319).

through the reign of Charlemagne and of his successors in the West Frankish kingdom the crown, having marked out by various procedural prerogatives a sphere of activity, endeavored to preserve it. In the immunities, however, were maintained concomitantly the old methods of settling claims arising out of the wrongs. Since these units in many cases survived the shock of the political anarchy in the latter ninth and the tenth century, such powers as they managed to maintain or even to extend were grounded upon what they had legally exercised in less troubled times. But we must distinguish between the legal theory of good times and the practice of disordered days. The limitations upon the immunists' activity in dealing with misdeeds were imposed from above. Where there was no one to gainsay the right to hang, it is unlikely that the culprit would go quit.

### ROYAL PROTECTION AND CONTROL OF IMMUNITIES

To complete the picture of what was acquired by grant or otherwise it is necessary to consider here an important collateral consequence of the quantitative increase in the immunities, to wit, the change in the royal protection. We have seen how by charter a person could obtain the king's protection.[84] This *mundium* is a personal protection. Initially it has no connection with the *immunitas* which, although likewise a personal privilege, is one in respect of public tolls and duties territorial in scope. Even in the early Carolingian times where a monastery is lucky enough to get a royal protection it is a special sort of privilege,[85] and may, indeed, have been limited to churches belonging to the king by grant or commendation (*Eigenkirchen*). After 814, a change in the formulae takes place,[86] and to all churches which have the privilege of immunity the king's protection is ex-

---

[84] *Supra,* Chapter I, p. 47.

[85] Stengel, *Die Immunität* (1910), 570.

[86] Sickel, *Beiträge, W.S.B.* (1864), pt. III, 182. The early charters of protection are sometimes special and sometimes the *mundium* and *immunitas* are combined.

tended.[87] There are occasional grants of special protection in the old form but these tend to disappear. The concept of royal protection has become more general,[88] and we may well surmise less directly efficacious except perhaps in a general procedural sense, i.e., that a right of recourse to the crown is opened.[89] An additional effect is that the protection once extending only to personal activities and injuries becomes a protection *in rem:* it is localized upon lands and objects.

Under strong kings these mutations in the nature and scope of protection would doubtless have been significant. Under the successors of Charlemagne the changes operated only in the direction of consolidating the internal power of the grantees. There is no lack of good will in bolstering up the procedural privileges of the immunists, for the charters are no longer restricted to forbidding entries by public authority, but there are included in their terms interferences by anyone.[90] There are collateral sanctions provided. In 803, a capitulary had set a penalty of 600 solidi upon the wanton infractor of an immunity.[91] This sum, the wergeld of a count,[92] finds its way into the charter formulae and becomes a usual penal sanction embraced in the

[87] Stengel, *Immunität,* 572. And note what he says regarding the tendency in the last half of the ninth century for *defensio, tuitio, mundiburdium* and *immunitas* to stand for one and the same thing.

[88] *Cf.* Waitz 4 *D.V.G.,* 293 regarding the unsuccessful attempt of the clergy to have all church property as such treated as crown property, no doubt because a higher amends lay where king's property was violated; 2 Brunner, *D.R.G.* 57. But see Brunner, *Forschungen,* 183. The whole tendency was in the direction of having immunity property put on a par with fiscal lands.

[89] Stengel, *Immunität,* 573.

[90] *Ibid.,* 441, and note, 448, the rare cases of forbidding entries by *missi.*

[91] *Cap. Legg. Add.,* (803) c. 2 (1 *Cap.,* 113). As early as 779 this sum had been set in a charter (*M.G.H. Dipl. Karol.* no. 123).

[92] It is to be noted that the decision of Louis regarding Aniane, limited the 600 sol. penalty to the enclosed objects. The open fields and woods, however, had a qualified protection as an immunity, breaches to be punished according to local law. Böhmer-Mühlbacher, *Regesten* no. 751; *cf. Form. Imp.* 15, indicating the rule is general if the rubric of this formula is to be trusted.

grant. Moreover, Louis, in 819, had laid it down that the king's ban (60 sol.) was to be inflicted on those who did not observe the regulations embodied in capitulary and charter[93] and the *missi* were instructed throughout the ninth century to punish violators. During the reign of Charles the Bald, when the crown adds the anathema to its threats,[94] it could feel assured that the church would use its own remedy to protect its own rights. In the charters of the West Frankish Carolingians of the tenth century this penalty and the 600 shilling mulct are both present in the grants.[95]

The peculiarly favorable position of the immunity at the end of the ninth century resulting from these efforts at protection has been described as a "special peace"[96] more or less in the sense used in the first chapter. It is to be noted, however, that except for the proceedings incident to the collection of the ban penalty (60 sol.) to which the repeated admonitions to the *missi* in the matter of immunity breach must have had reference, the burden of maintaining the privileges granted lay with the grantees. The 600 sol. penalty was conceived of as an amount due as amends and was collectible upon suit by the injured party, the crown receiving a proportion as *fredus*.[97] In the records of two actions in the public courts, one in 863[98] and one in 933,[99] the complaints set forth the specific terms of the immunity and allege an infraction *"malo ordine contra legem,"* as was the case in any other common wrong.[100] If there were a "special

---

[93] *Cap. Legg. Add.* (818–9) c. 1 (1 *Cap.*, 281).

[94] *Allocutio Missi cuiusdam Divionensis* (857) c. 1 (2 *Cap.* 292).

[95] Lauer, *Recueil des actes de Louis IV* (1914) 29; *cf.* also the 100 lb. gold penalty at 8; Halphen et Lot, *Recueil des actes de Lothaire et de Louis V,* 133; at this time the 100 lb. gold penalty is more usual, *ibid.* 31, 37, 49, 62 etc.

[96] 2 Brunner *D.R.G.,* 395.

[97] *Form. Imp.,* 29.

[98] Thévenin, *Textes relatifs aux institutions privées et publiques mérovingiennes et carolingiennes* (1887) no. 96.

[99] *Ibid.,* no. 128.

[100] *Supra,* p. 40.

peace" it had no special procedural significance; there is no allegation which conveys such an idea as does the insistence of English plaintiffs of a later age that they were in the peace of the king by his hand given.

The hand which gave knew how to restrain. The genius which perceived the administrative value of the *missus* was not likely to be spendthrift of power as appears on the face of the charters of immunity. Some link which would preserve the integrity of royal authority was necessary. This the Carolingian kings discovered in the *advocatus,* an ecclesiastical office which the church had inherited from Roman times.[101] The uses of this office had developed in Merovingian times in cases where churches or ecclesiastical units were represented in litigation. The important innovation of Charlemagne was the establishment of the rule that an *advocatus* must be maintained by the church. This rule was essential because of the efforts of the clerics to avoid personal appearance in the secular courts.[102] A not dissimilar practice of representation was in operation where the interests of the fisc were involved.[103]

Applied to the immunity under Charlemagne the office of *advocatus* was important from two points of view. In the first place the name of the office was used to cover various types of overseers and agents, and the *advocatus'* functions in behalf of the state linked the various forms of enfranchised or private jurisdiction to the central administration. These public functions embraced among other matters the duty of representing the immunity in the public courts when complaints of third parties were not justiciable in the immunity court;[104] of seeing that where military service was due the call to arms was heeded;[105]

---

[101] Senn, *L'Institution des avoueries ecclésiastiques en France* (1903), 3 *et seq.*

[102] *Ibid.,* 9. The crown did not require their appointment but they were apparently numerous. 2 Loening, *Kirchenrecht,* 534 n. 4.

[103] 2 Brunner, *D.R.G.,* 409.

[104] Beauchet, *op. cit.,* 437 *et seq.*; 2 Brunner *D.R.G.,* 411.

[105] *Cap. de Exerc. Promov.,* (808) c. 3 (1 *Cap.,* 137).

and of turning up the criminals over whom the crown claimed jurisdiction.[106] Within the confines of the immunity the *advocatus* acted as *iudex*.[107]

The choice of these officers the crown did not leave to chance. The capitularies set up prerequisites of character which would have satisfied a modern bar association: these officers must above all be *legem scientes et iustitiam diligentes*.[108] In addition, although the bishop or abbot might nominate them, the appointment had to be made before the count or on occasion with his consent.[109] The *advocati* were discharging functions for both king and franchise holder and yet they were not public officers. They were highly privileged[110] intermediaries between the governmental mainland and the islands of immunity.

The increase in number of immunities after 814, and the rule that to property acquired by an immunist after the charter had issued the immunity privileges *ipso facto* attached, led to a constant, and by no means inconsiderable, diminution of comital authority. The *advocatus* displaced other public officers as the representative of royal authority, and consequently as long as this official in fact continued to act for the crown there was not an equivalent decline in royal power.[111] The institution of the *advocatus,* therefore, was the crucial factor in keeping in check the dangerous potentialities of the immunity. It was, however, a very delicately balanced political device, and as is usual where

---

[106] Senn, *op. cit.,* 74; Kroell, *op. cit.,* 277 *et seq.*

[107] Senn, *op. cit.,* 54, 60 *et seq.;* Kroell, *op. cit.,* 272 *et seq.* The jurisdiction of the *advocatus* was equivalent to that of the *centenarius* (on which 2 Brunner *D.R.G.,* 233 *et seq.*), *cf.* 4 Waitz *D.V.G.,* 467.

[108] *Cap. Miss. Gen.,* (802) c. 13 (1 *Cap.,* 93) ". . . legem scientes et iustitiam diligentes pacificosque et mansuetus . . ."; *Cap. Miss. Spec.,* (802) c. 18a (1 *Cap.,* 101).

[109] The *advocatus* is an obligatory office in Carolingian times; Kroell, *op. cit.,* 266; *contra* 2 Dopsch, *Wirtschaftsentwickelung,* 102. On the method of electing these officers, Kroell, *op. cit.,* 267, 2 Dopsch, *op. cit.,* 103.

[110] 4 Waitz, *D.V.G.,* 470.

[111] Kroell, *op. cit.,* 279.

duties are owing to two antithetical groups, not much would have to go awry to upset the *status quo*. We know, of course, that after Louis the Pious died a great deal went wrong, and there was no political genius to set things right. Just where real caution should have been observed in the appointment of the *advocati*, reckless concession was made. About the middle of the ninth century there creeps into the immunity charters the right of free election of the *advocatus* by the immunists.[112] The office is still regarded in the capitularies as on a par with public offices, but there is no doubt that in abandoning the supervision over election,[113] the crown relinquished the chief insurance for the preservation of public interest. The old rule that *centenarius* or count could not serve as *advocatus* was no longer observed,[114] and as a result the nature of the latter office rapidly changed. These were troubled times, and the immunities, the churches and abbeys, where wealth was visibly concentrated, were a constant temptation to Norman raiders and to native freebooters. The function of the *advocatus* ceased to be merely administrative; it became essentially protective.[115] If an immunist elected him it was for his military prowess and not for his learning in the law and his love of justice.

### THE IMMUNITY AND THE FEUDAL POLITY

In the course of the tenth century, the change in the status of the *advocatus* brought about the final disruption of the Carolingian system of coordinating the immunity in the general scheme of administration. Charters creating new immunities still issued from the last Carolingian monarchs in West Francia with the familiar clause, *absque introitu judicum*, with the grants of *fredus* and, as we shall presently see, even more far-

---

[112] Kroell, *op. cit.*, 299. This change is effected by charter.

[113] Free election is the rule in the 10th century, Senn, *op. cit.*, 111.

[114] 4 Waitz, *D.V.G.*, 470 n. 4 and *cf.* also the cases n. 5 where the office becomes hereditary.

[115] Senn, *op. cit.*, 81.

reaching rights. The charters of the tenth century, however, are at best mere surrenders of public powers without the implicit condition of control that existed in Charlemagne's day. Every new franchise of this type added only to the sum total of units which were exercising to a greater or less extent the powers of government which the crown was unable to exercise.

If we regard the feudalism of this period from the angle of the locus of the dismembered functions of the state, it is certain that the immunities composed an important class. It is unnecessary, however, to consider in detail the effect of the institution of the immunity upon the formation of the new type of seignorial polity. Certainly, toward the close of the ninth century, the immunities had become what the German writers describe as public law units.[116] Whatever they managed to retain was the basis of their future political role. It might be that where a count undertook the duties of a protector he exacted a return in the form of cession of privileges,[117] which in the tenth century must have had the legal quality of a feoffment. It might be that the *vidame,* who exercised for an abbot the old functions of the *advocatus,* would become so powerful that he in fact wrested the judicial activities of the immunist into his own hands.[118] In either event the source of the powers was the immunity and no longer the crown.

The significance of the Carolingian immunity in the political arrangements of the tenth and eleventh centuries is not to be deduced entirely from the legal and governmental aspects that have been discussed. To understand how this institution affected

[116] Rietschel, *Landleihen Hofrecht und Immunität,* 27 M.I.Ö.G., 408.
[117] Senn, *op. cit.,* 87 *et seq. Cf.* also two documents in Tardif, *Monuments historiques* (1886) n. 260 and 286, both of the 11th century.
[118] Senn, *op. cit.,* 91 n. 1 and note the cases where a bishop exercises the office of *vidame.* The latter varies greatly as to function. What happens is that the various duties of the *advocatus* are divided among a variety of officers. As Senn proceeds to point out, the story is different in the various parts of France and the variations among the several ecclesiastical establishments are considerable.

the jurisdictional phases of feudalism we must realize the extent of immunity holdings, and consider those factors which made it possible for rights not included in the scope of the charter to be laminated to what was in fact granted. These matters, we believe, bear a direct relation not only to the persistence of Frankish law in Normandy but likewise to the basic changes in jurisdiction over wrongs.

As far as the spread of immunity property is concerned it should be observed that our information is confined to ecclesiastical establishments. It is possible that among the crown vassals there were comparable lay holdings, but as a sense of sin is more potent than gratitude, it was to the curators of men's souls, the monasteries and churches, that the stream of private grants flowed. Some notion of how frequent were these gifts may be gathered from the fact that in the case of Freising we have record of 258 charters between the years 811–835, and that for Fulda, up to the year 900, some 646 grants are known.[119] How far-flung were abbey lands may be seen from the catalogue of the holdings of St. Wandrille prior to its destruction by the Normans.[120] By virtue of the rule that all property of an immunist, even that acquired after enfranchisement, became privileged,[121] the jurisdictional rights, originally peppered over the most widely separated territories, were concentrated by a constant process of exchanging and consolidating properties into contiguous masses.[122] It is hardly necessary to emphasize the political significance of this process of concentration. In the hands of abbot or bishop were the sinews of power.

From the point of view of the state, the churches' accumulation of economic resources was a standing temptation for out-

---

[119] Hauck, *Die Entstehung der bischöflichen Fürstenmacht* (1891) 42–3.

[120] Lot, *Etudes critiques sur l'abbaye de St. Wandrille* (1913), xiii *et seq.*

[121] Stengel, *Immunität,* 578.

[122] 2 Dopsch, *Wirtschaftsentwickelung,* 119.

right or disguised expropriation. The processes by which the state interfered with the control of organized religion over its assets were the direct secularization of property either *in toto* or for limited purposes, and the indirect measures whereby the temporalization of a particular ecclesiastical unit was likely to ensue. The most outstanding example of the former process is the secularization involved in the development of the benefice. As is well known, land was taken from the church and granted beneficially to laymen. This development touches our problem in one important aspect, namely, that property definitely secularized ceased to be immune. We distinguish from this the indirect control of ecclesiastical property, what we have for convenience called the process of temporalization. This was effected chiefly through the consistent pursuit by the crown of the policy of appointing lay abbots to its own abbeys.[123] In such cases immunity

[123] Especially after 840, Voigt, *Die Karolingische Klosterpolitik* (*Kirchenrechtliche Abhandlungen* no. 90, 91 [1917]), 87 *et seq.* Voigt shows how despite prohibitions by synods, this policy was pursued by Charles the Bald because of the necessity of keeping lay lords attached to the crown. In connection with this process of imposing laymen in abbacies must be considered certain economic phases of the matter, especially the division of abbatial and fraternity property, and the measures taken by bishops to insure to chapters and convents property sufficient to sustain themselves and their ecclesiastical purpose. This development has been traced by Pöschl in 1 and 2 *Bischofsgut und Mensa Episcopalis* (1908–9). Pöschl starts out with building up a picture of the Carolingian bishop as a mighty lay officer (1 *op. cit.,* 1 *et seq.,* 154 *et seq.*). To this we shall again have reference. He points out that the military duties imposed by Charlemagne on the bishops (*ibid.,* 155) and the secularization of church property to the use of the count (*ibid.,* 122, 128) with ninths, tithes and census payable to the ecclesiasts, made necessary a division of properties (178, 181). The manner of this division in the 9th century forms the subject matter of Pöschl's second volume. In relation to the immunity it is important to note that there was but one immunity for the whole complex of a single immunist's possessions (II, 38). The privilege is granted without reference to the partition of property. The jurisdiction therefore remained in abbot or bishop. Where property was secularized it was stripped from the privilege (II, 106). The profits of the immunity were usually assigned to the chapter (II, 53, 153). The attempt of the lay lords in Louis the Pious' time to effect a partition whereby only the property necessary for ecclesiastical function was left and the rest expropriated by the state for military pur-

remained although the spiritual purposes of an institution were stultified when its resources could be diverted by the lay heads to carnal uses.[124] Throughout the tenth century this practice was rampant, embracing even bishoprics where the power of election had fallen into the hands of some territorial lord of irreligious disposition.[125] It contributed substantially to the abasement of the church in this period.

Beset by the double threat of outright secularization and temporalization it is not strange that the Frankish prelates[126] should have floated with the stream and participated in the latter process for their own advantage. Damaging as this may have been to the spiritual function of the church, it resulted in many instances in a constant appreciation of the political eminence of the episcopacy.[127] More land might be lost by secularization than was

poses failed (II, 62). Nevertheless there was tremendous secularization of church property and also lay feoffments were made by worldly bishops (II, 75). Measures were taken against secularization or permitting bishops to use chapter property for their temporal services (II, 102) but some of these measures like the consent of the canons probably were useless against a hard-pressed prelate. Pöschl's estimates regarding the extent of bishops' and chapter property are interesting (II, 140 et seq.). The average bishop's holdings in the first half of the ninth century is 2000 *mansi;* in the second half, 1000 *mansi.* The chapter holdings average less than 500.

[124] On the uses of the property, Voigt, *op. cit.,* 173, 235.

[125] 3 Pöschl, *Bischofsgut* (1912), 112.

[126] We are dealing primarily with the episcopal temporal power and are therefore not distinguishing the archbishops or entering into the details of their conflicts with the bishops.

[127] Except for Pöschl's *Bischofsgut* most of the discussions regarding the temporal aspects of episcopal authority in the latter part of the ninth and in the tenth centuries are not particularly informative. Hauck, *Die Entstehung der Bischöflichen Fürstenmacht,* deals chiefly with the bishops in the Empire but at p. 42 *et seq.,* he has some trenchant comments on the Frankish background. Flach, 1 *op. cit.,* 175, has some discussion under the rubric *"Les immunistes ecclésiastiques,"* and 2 *ibid.,* 281 *et seq.,* where he discusses counts and bishops; in 3 *ibid.,* 557 *"Les principautés ecclésiastiques."* But Flach with his theory of jurisdiction at stake, and his scant respect for chronology is of no great use. For the ninth century there is a good summary in Schubert, *Geschichte der Christlichen Kirche im Frühmittelalter* (1921) §§27, 28, 29, 35, 36; Imbart de la Tour, *Les élections épiscopales* (1891), 177 *et seq.;* 195 *et seq.,* has some material on our

gained by the gifts of the penitents. A pious chapter might insist upon a division of episcopal assets so that God might be served. Yet the bishops by devoting incessant attention to their opportunities were in general able to weather economic vicissitudes. These opportunities arose from the fact that Charlemagne had insisted upon the performance of military duties by the bishops and from the fact that for most types of public service they were indispensable.[128] Given the motive of political aggrandizement in the sense of acquiring and perfecting what would today be called territorial sovereignty, it is not difficult to comprehend why at the close of the ninth century the French bishops as a group overshadowed in influence or power all congeries of lay-

question but he is dealing primarily with a special problem in the relations of state and church. In Lesne, *La hiérarchie épiscopale* (1905), esp. 265 *et seq.* there are valuable indications. His work is confined largely to the question of the theory of organization and the relations of the metropolitan to the bishops. 2 Mayer, *Deutsche und Französiche Verfassungs Geschichte* (1899) 260 n. 55 has source material for later jurisdiction. Pöschl, *Entstehung des Geistlichen Benefizium*, 106 *Archiv für Katholisches Kirchenrecht* 1, 363 deals chiefly with the economic aspects of the benefice; *cf.* 385 regarding the prelacies. On the legal side, the material is scattered in 5 Hinschius, *K.R., passim.* On the episcopal power in Germany valuable for comparative purposes is 7 Waitz, *D.V.G.* 183 *et seq.*

It should be pointed out here that the history of prelacies in the tenth century shows a general waning of episcopal power as a whole. *Cf.* the discussion in 3 Pöschl, *Bischofsgut, passim.* For our purposes the factor of significance is that at the moment the Normans occupied Normandy this reaction had not gotten fully under way.

[128] Pöschl's remarks in 1 *Bischofsgut und Mensa Episcopalis* 157 are worth repeating. "The prelates of Charlemagne's time were drawn to other state services (i.e., non-military) and temporal business, to the office of *missus,* to embassies etc. They were expected to attend the king's court. Their temporal position in the state was only little different from that of the lay lords. High churchmen were constantly about the ruler. They were his chief advisers . . ." And at 171, "The constant life at court and in the field, in direct contact with the ruler, activity in the most important and influential offices of state inevitably led the prelates to know and cherish worldly glory and power. The temporal side of the office constantly moves into the foreground. When the office was filled the choice of candidates depended little on the previous capacity to fulfil the spiritual side of the office."

men.[129] Quite apart from the ecclesiastical aspects of their position, in individual instances they had such temporal prerogatives that they were able to compete on terms of equality with the counts, their most serious rivals for the perquisites of the central government.

In order to fix in more detail what relation the general political powers of the bishops bore to their powers as immunity holders and lay lords, it is important to emphasize that in Charles the Bald's reign, the acquisition of public office[130] was esteemed chiefly for the opportunity it offered of integrating the powers of such office with those possessed in other capacities. In this process the possession of an immunity was of prime importance, since it furnished a solid substratum of political and governmental rights upon which to build. The jurisdiction incident thereto, except where property was definitely secularized, continued to be exercised in spite of feoffment or divisions of assets. It was extensible in that it covered new acquisitions. The immunity, then, is the more or less static core of temporal authority. The lands, abbeys and purely fiscal privileges, all things that are susceptible of beneficial grant, are the volatile ingredients of temporal power. Over the latter control waxes or wanes. Sometimes it is lost forever, sometimes a mere fiscal interest is kept, as where property is taken for the use of the count, but sometimes such property is completely recaptured.[131] The grad-

[129] Schubert, op. cit., 405, 412, 435, 558, 573.

[130] The ministeria, 2 Dopsch, Wirtschaftsentwickelung, 88; on the terminology, 3 Waitz D.V.G., 530. Dopsch, Benifizialwesen und Feudalität, 46 M.I.Ö.G. 25, states that it is because of the official position that in late Carolingian times bishops, abbots and counts get regalian rights like market, customs or coinage.

[131] Thus Charles the Bald to St. Nazare, Autun (861) 8 H.F. 566. Clearer is the grant of Charles III to the Church of Langres (887) of "omnia ex iure fisci nostri ad causam comitis pertinentia," because the bishop had built and fortified the town without help of count or iudex in time of danger, Böhmer-Mühlbacher, Regesten (1693), 1740. Looked at from the economic point of view this was a restoration of the bishops'

ual encroachment of the rule of heritability of benefice[132] cuts sharply into the control. But there seems to be something indefeasible about the immunity. The Northmen may come, burn and destroy buildings and crops, but the crown apparently never dreams of utilizing the opportunity of withholding the *immunitas* upon regrant. It is a piece of public right;[133] it is an integral part of administrative machinery. This is why it persists. This is why it can so easily absorb additional public rights apart from the common immunity franchise.

The most important additions to episcopal power susceptible of combination with immunity jurisdiction were no doubt acquired through the office of *missus*. The *missi dominici* had been

property which had been taken for the count's use. Market, toll and coinage as granted in the above charters had been in the hands of bishops in Merovingian times. There are many references to these restorative grants in 1 Pöschl, *Bischofsgut,* 130 *et seq.* For the subsequent development in Germany, 7 Waitz *D.V.G.,* 255, *re* the grant of comital rights. *Cf.* also 1 Viollet, *Histoire des institutions politiques,* 388, for one or two further examples in France.

Prior to Pöschl's work there seems to have been much misunderstanding of what these grants involved. Apparently Waitz's assertion 3 *D.V.G.,* 430, that, under Charlemagne and Louis the Pious it was most exceptional for episcopal and comital power to be united, will have to stand. What we are dealing with is primarily the ebb and flow of specific fiscal rights and lands and not with the change in character of the office. A bishopric may be rich or poor, but it is first and last a bishopric. In the tenth century matters like election, exercise of jurisdiction etc. in various sees probably depended in the final analysis upon how much was concentrated in a particular bishop's hands and what he was able to maintain. Artificial distinctions like public and private rights, or Flach's divisions between seignorial and feudal jurisdiction, are useless. *Cf.* Ganshof, *Note sur la compétence des cours féodales en France* in *Mélanges Pirenne* (1926), 161 n. 1. The measure of what a local ruler can do is the power (economic, ecclesiastical, etc.), of which he is possessed. The power enjoyed by particular units in ninth and tenth century France varies quantitatively so incessantly that generalization seems absurd. If one compares Robert the Pious, who could not even compel attendance on his court (Pfister, *Etudes sur le règne de Robert le Pieux* [1885], 158) with Robert of Normandy the futility of attempting to extract legal theories to explain the crazy-quilt of jurisdiction in France is apparent.

[132] 1 Pöschl, *Bischofsgut,* 151 *et seq.*
[133] Rietschel, *Landleihen Hofrecht und Immunität,* 27 *M.I.Ö.G.,* 408.

intended originally to function as itinerant justices in districts not identified with the private interests of the *missus*.[134] They were agents of the crown who were supposed to keep in check standing officials like the count. During the reign of Louis the Pious the principles of selection were occasionally abandoned, and the incumbents of sees like Tours and Rouen were made *missi* for their own districts.[135] The office tended steadily to become localized and lodged in the hands of count and bishop.[136] The final step in the disintegration was taken at the end of Charles the Bald's reign. At Pavia in 876[137] the Italian bishops succeeded in wresting from the crown the concession of combining as a permanent measure the episcopal office with that of *missus*. In the same year at the synod of Ponthieu the Pavia concessions were confirmed and the West Frankish bishops could lay claim to function as standing *missi*.[138]

As *missi* two governmental devices of major importance were administered by the bishops for the crown: the inquisition procedure, and the king's ban[139] in those manifestations which bore upon judicial administration.

[134] Generally on these officers Krause, *Geschichte des Instituts der Missi Dominici*, 11 *M.I.Ö.G.*, 193; Thompson, *op. cit.*, 5 *et seq.*; 2 Brunner *D.R.G.*, 253; 3 Waitz, *D.V.G.*, 441; 4 *ibid.*, 413 *et seq.*; Beauchet, *op. cit.*, 293.

[135] *Commem. missis data*, (825) in 1 *Cap.*, 308. On the episcopal propaganda for this change *cf.* Lesne, *op. cit.*, 82 and compare the demands of the bishops at the Synod of Meaux-Paris (845–6) that the king by writ and seal give the bishops a full power to call at will on the secular authority, 16 Mansi, *Concilia* 836 c. 71.

[136] Krause, *op. cit.*, 244, discusses how this enables count or bishop to increase his "private" rights.

[137] *Cap. Papiense* (876) c. 12 (2 *Cap.* 103). On which *cf.* 2 Ficker, *Forschungen zur Reichs und Rechtsgeschichte Italiens* 12 *et seq.*; Krause, *op. cit.*, 245. Brunner, 2 *D.R.G.*, 262 n. 45, thinks this measure did not remain in force after Charles' death.

[138] *Synod. Pontig.* (2 *Cap.*, 348). Brunner, *loc. cit.*, *supra*, note 137, doubts whether the confirmation gave the West Frankish bishops missatic powers. *Contra* Krause, *op. cit.*, 246. Not much can be argued from the isolated reference to *missi* after 876 (Thompson, *op. cit.*, 19), or from the terms of the capitulary of Verne (884) c. 9 (2 *Cap.*, 374).

[139] 2 Brunner, *D.R.G.*, 259.

Of all the royal perquisites the ban[140] had the most potential value in building up the territorial independence of any local lord. In some instances the immunities had been granted exemption from *bannus*[141] but it is not certain whether this was more than a fiscal privilege. The most important delegation had been in Charlemagne's time to the counts, who exercised it as royal agents.[142] Perverted later to their own ends, as territorial lords, the ban power becomes an essential part of comital authority in the tenth and eleventh centuries.[143] This is a development that runs parallel to that in episcopacies.

The ease with which the ban powers could be used for a particular prelate's own ends, once he was *missus* in his own district, may be deduced from the fact that the Carolingian crown procedure combined both secular and ecclesiastical sanctions.[144] Where an offender had incurred the king's ban and his goods had been sequestrated, he might likewise be put under the *bannus episcopalis*[145]—excommunication or anathema. He had to

[140] Sohm, *F.R.G.V.*, 103; *cf.* also the discussion in W. Sickel, *Zur Geschichte des Bannes, passim.*

[141] T. Sickel, *Beiträge zur Geschichte der Diplomatik V* 356 *et seq.* Sickel points to a difference in the loose Merovingian use of *bannus* and the strict Carolingian. In the latter period the word, he believes, is restricted to king's ban and he regards this as an exceptional concession. In 4 Waitz *D.V.G.*, 317 n. 3 are listed various charters. Waitz states the ban penalties were a frequent concession of Charlemagne's successors. The sense of *jurisdiction* which the word acquires is a later development. Dopsch, in 2 *Wirtschaftsentwickelung*, 123, suggests that the *advocatus* has the power of levying ban penalties in the king's own ecclesiastical establishments or those in his *mundium*. Seeliger thinks it was general at the end of the ninth century; *op. cit.*, 94. *Cf.* also Stengel in 25 *Z.R.G.*[2], 300. For the later grants Stengel, *Immunität*, 589 *et seq.* For grants of the *inquisitio* to immunities *cf.* Brunner, *Zeugen und Inquisitionsbeweis*, in *Forschungen*, 166 *et seq.*

[142] Sohm, *F.R.G.V.*, 175 *et seq.*

[143] 1 Flach, *Origines*, 325 *et seq.*

[144] The most completely documented account of this mixing of sanctions is in Eichmann, *Acht und Bann in Reichsrecht des Mittelalters* (1909), 5 *et seq.*; See also 3 Hinschius, *K.R.*, 705 *et seq.*; 5 *ibid.*, 373 *et seq.*

[145] The procedure is stated clearly in *Cap. Olonn. I*, (825) c. 1 (1 *Cap.* 326). On the *bannus episcopalis*, Hilling, *Die Bischöfliche Banngewalt* etc. in 80 *A.K.K.R.*, 80, 85 *et seq.*

satisfy both king and bishop. Since there was no incompatibility in combining sanctions, there was certainly no incongruity in having the administration of both in the hands of the cleric. When, in the eleventh century, we see in the north of France bishops exercising blood justice (*bannus sanguinis*)[146] and find no charters, such as there were in the Empire,[147] to explain how this power was acquired, we naturally suspect it is a prescriptive right derived from the days when the bishop was *missus*.[148]

We have dealt with both the economic and legal fundaments of seignorial power at the end of the ninth century, but to grasp their implications it is essential to understand that what twisted the Carolingian cosmos from its axis was the merger of capacities. The *advocatus* ceases to be an intermediary between state and immunity; he becomes the latter's man preserving all his old functions. The count no longer is just local official, landowner and king's agent; he is all three acting for himself. In no case is this merger of capacities more significant than in that of the bishop, because of his dominance in two spheres of authority. As the crown becomes progressively enfeebled, the bishop consolidates in his own interest the rights and functions which he possesses as lay lord, man of God, immunist and king's officer.

The situation is such that the substitution is not difficult. The immunity has long been on a parity with fiscal property.[149] It is

---

[146] We shall have occasion to deal with this more in detail in the next chapter. For the moment *cf.* 2 Mayer, *Deutsche und Französische Verfassungsgeschichte*, 260 n. 55, for instances covering various parts of France.

[147] 7 Waitz *D.V.G.*, 234 *et seq.*; Stengel, *Immunität*, 590 *et seq.*

[148] Pöschl, *Die Regalien der Mittelalterlichen Kirchen* (1928), 13 *et seq.* In this connection it is interesting to note that under Lothar the grant of *bannus* is not unusual; *cf.* Lot and Halphen, *Recueil des actes de Lothaire et de Louis V*, no. 15 (962), no. 26 (966) no. 33, (954–72) no. 56 (979–86). Compare particularly the language of no. 26 (966) a grant of immunity to St. Bavon de Gand ". . . ut nullus episcoporum aut archiepiscoporum, qualicunque causa existente locum ipsum invadere aut bannire ullo modo audeat." In considering the significance of this it must be remembered the monastery was in Flanders.

[149] Brunner, *Zeugen und Inquisitionsbeweis* in *Forschungen*, 183.

organized on the pattern of the Frankish *centena*.[150] The ecclesiastical jurisdiction, itself regal in nature,[151] mirrors in many respects the lay organization with an *inquisitio* for ecclesiastical purposes,[152] episcopal *missi*,[153] and presbyters who act as police.[154] Even the power of corporal punishment that the bishop may exercise in a temporal capacity is applied to spiritual offenses.[155] Under mandate of the crown he can make men accept Christ by flogging.[156] He supports armed forces to maintain himself.[157] In every respect the bishops are endowed with the privi-

[150] Stengel in 25 *Z.R.G.*[2], 296 *et seq.*

[151] Schubert, *op. cit.*, 574, describing the bishop's power, points out that no office was to be set up, filled or ended without his consent; he was the ordinary spiritual judge for lay and clerics alike, and had forced both convents and landlords to recognize his rights. In an immunity like Trier or Metz his power was even greater. Compare with the French bishoprics the picture of episcopal jurisdiction in Worms. (Arnold, *Verfassungsgeschichte der Deutschen Freistädte* [1854], 12 *et seq.*)

[152] 5 Hinschius, *K.R.*, 427 *et seq.*, who states the ecclesiastical procedure is unquestionably based upon the Carolingian accusation and inquisition procedure.

[153] As early as 614, *Edict. Chloth. II*, c. 19 (1 *Cap.*, 23); *cf.* also *Cap. a Missis Dom. ad Comites Directa* (801–13) c. 1 (1 *Cap.*, 184); *Cap. ab Episcop. Proposita*, (825 ?) c. 1 (1 *Cap.*, 358); *Edict. Pist.*, (864) c. 31 (2 *Cap.*, 323); *Edict. Comp. de Tributo* (877) B (2 *Cap.*, 354); *Cap. Vern.* (884) c. 14 (2 *Cap.*, 375).

[154] *Cap. Vern.*, (884) c. 6 (2 *Cap.*, 373).

[155] For the pre-Carolingian practice, 4 Hinschius, *K.R.*, 814. The bishops used whipping for laymen of low status, *Cap. Miss. Suess.* (853), c. 9 (2 *Cap.*, 269). Schubert, *op. cit.*, 628, states that abbots punished monks by blinding and mutilation. He gives no references but there are collected in Nissl, *Gerichtsstand*, 43, n. 1, a great many ninth-century cases. At Rouen, a canon of the ninth century provided beating for nuns who cohabited with clerics, 5 Hinschius, *K.R.*, 78, n. 14. Note also what Brunner, in 2 *D.R.G.*, 790, says about the change in the attitude of the church in favor of afflictive punishments after 779. But Brunner does not discuss the use of corporal punishment by the church itself.

[156] *Cap. Duo Incerta*, c. 2 (1 *Cap.* 257) probably a late ninth-century Frankish capitulary.

[157] On this 1 Pöschl, *Bischofsgut*, 148 *et seq.* He sets the rise of this institution after the capitulary of Haristal. The tendency is toward free vassalage. The relationship is at first terminable at the will of the bishop. Later the position of the vassals is more permanent. The church is able to prevent these vassals from becoming men of the crown.

leges and with the physical might to command and enforce obedience. But most significant of all is the fact that when the Carolingian state goes bankrupt, the ecclesiastical groups are the only ones charged with political power that preserve any unity of purpose and community of interest.[158]

## THE IMMUNITY AND THE NORMAN RECEPTION OF FRANKISH LAW

We have discussed at length the legal and political basis for the fractionation of jurisdiction in France, because it is obvious that when the Normans commenced to settle in and govern their duchy, they received Frankish institutions as they found them and not as they had once existed. In other words, to the extent that later Norman law administration was Frankish, it derives from the days of dispersed power.

This dispersion, however, was so various in degree and extent that the presumption advanced is of little avail unless the means of the continuity can be more precisely delineated. As to this we have a choice. Either the connection between the Carolingian-Frankish and the Norman-Frankish institutions was direct and continuous through the intermediacy of local officials who remained in Normandy, or it was indirect and largely spasmodic through contact with and imitation of law and practice in adjoining territories. As to the first hypothesis we are cast upon the practical difficulty of establishing whether any local officials, counts, bishops, *advocati, centenarii* or what not remained in Norman territory. Our only evidence relates to the bishops and

---

[158] Lot, *Etudes sur le règne de Hugues Capet* (1903), 238, "Le clergé, sa partie éclairée au moins, reste dépositaire des traditions de la royauté carolingienne qui ne diffèrent guère de celles de Bas-Empire."

On the side of the picture not spoken of in the text, i.e., lay control over bishops, especially in treason cases, *cf.* 5 Hinschius, *K.R.,* 409, and the cases in his notes. A full account of the treason of Adalberon of Rheims, Lot, *Les derniers carolingiens,* 155, 195, 201. On the falling off and secularization of episcopal property in tenth-century France, Pöschl, *Kirchengutsveräusserung und das Kirchliche Veräusserungsverbot* in 105 *A.K.K.R.* 33, 45, 61, 87, 368, n. 2, 403, 421, 426, 432, 442, and 3 *Bischofsgut, passim.*

an isolated abbot or two. The bishops are, of course, the most important from a secular viewpoint. As to them, it is essential to determine what basis in fact there may be for accepting the bishop in his capacity as a temporal lord and official as the conduit of Frankish civilization and, more specifically, whether the immunity was of any consequence in the process.

How far the powers of the bishops that we have discussed in general were in fact exercised by the prelates of Neustria and whether this exercise continued in the tenth century is difficult to determine by direct proof on account of the destruction of records. We know, however, that in the reign of Charles the Bald the Archbishop of Rouen is no less important a figure than the other metropolitans. In Louis the Pious' reign he is one of the ecclesiasts made *missus* in his district. Again in 853 he is appointed to this office, and so is the Bishop of Lisieux.[159] The prelates of both these sees and the bishops of Bayeux, Coutances and Sées attend the Synod of Ponthieu[160] where the Pavia concessions regarding the permanent appointment of bishops as *missi* are confirmed. We are badly informed, however, as to the nature of the immunities which these ecclesiasts held. In case of the Archbishop of Rouen we possess a *pancarta* of the year 853[161] wherein Charles the Bald, reciting the destruction of the charters by the Normans, grants a blanket confirmation of antecedent grants. In the margin are indicated the reasons why we believe the *pancarta* was in effect a confirmation of immunities theretofore held.[162] Indeed, with such overwhelming evidence at

[159] Krause, *op. cit.*, 272.

[160] 2 *Cap.*, 348.

[161] 8 *H.F.*, 588 (863). This was after the invasion and plunderings in 857; *cf.* Vogel, *op. cit.*, 154.

[162] Generally on the *pancarta, cf.* Zeumer, *Über den Ersatz verlorener Urkunden* etc. in 1 *Z.R.G.*[2], 89, 100, who points out that the advantage of such a document lay in the rule that a king's charter was not subject to traverse. *Cf.* also Mühlbacher, *Die Urkunden Karls III*, in 92 *WSB.* 331, 453 *et seq.*, Stengel, *Immunität*, 560 *et seq.*

While it may seem curious that so important a privilege as an immunity would not be specifically mentioned in a *pancarta* it is to be ob-

hand regarding the prevalence of episcopal immunities in the rest of the West Frankish kingdom, it is unthinkable that the see of Rouen would have been an exception.

As to the other Norman bishoprics already mentioned we are practically in the dark. At the time of Norman settlement the bishops had ceased to function in Avranches, Séez and Lisieux. The bishop of Coutances was a fugitive in Rouen. Only in the latter see and at Evreux was the succession continuous.[163] For the

served that the form of the latter is so comprehensive, the interdiction by the crown of any attack so precise, that the grantee is really put in the position of enjoying whatever he alleges he once owned, without the trouble of proving it. On the procedure for this proof in the absence of royal charter, *cf.* Zeumer, *op. cit.,* 100 *et seq.*

A case where we know definitely the grantee possessed *immunitas* is the monastery of St. Maur des Fossés. In 864, Charles the Bald issues a *pancarta* very similar in form to that issued to Rouen; Tardif, *Monuments historiques,* no. 193. In a series of antecedent charters this abbey had received immunity, Böhmer-Mühlbacher, *Regesten,* nos. 618, 787, 926, 1090. It is obvious that the *pancarta* in this case comprehended an immunity, for the confirmation is stated in broad enough terms to include it. Subsequently, Charles the Fat, in 886, issued a charter among other things exempting the monastery from military service and confirming the privileges granted by his predecessors by a *videlicet* that the monastery "in nostra tuitione hac mundiburdo permaneat," which is nothing other than a usual phrase for expressing the immunity (*cf.* Mühlbacher, *op. cit.,* 445, 6). On the question whether or not the immunity is understood to be included in the terms of a *pancarta, cf.* Stengel, *Immunität,* 561, n. 9.

How much we can argue from a case like that of St. Maur des Fossés is more or less a question of predilection. But to us the evidence is persuasive. Note, moreover, the fact that in the *pancarta* for Rouen the language of confirmation is even stronger than in the St. Maur charter; after a specification of monasteries, villas, etc.: "omnia videlicet quae praefata Rothomagensis Ecclesia visa fuit quieto ordine possidere quando primum nortmannica vastatione *ipsa* civitas cremata est, vel quae postea ob mercedis nostrae emolumentum eidem Ecclesiae pia collatione restituimus, vel quae a fidelibus sanctae Dei Ecclesiae addita sunt, et ipse honorandus vir Wanilo Archiepiscopus et successores eius perpetuis temporibus Ecclesiastica et pontificali dominatione, *absque testium receptione* integre teneant . . ."

In a charter to the Monastery St. Ouen, in the suburbs of Rouen, 8 *H.F.,* 650 (876), Charles the Bald grants immunity, on the petition of the Archbishop of Rouen himself. It would be curious if an abbey had this privilege and not the archbishopric.

[163] Böhmer, *Kirche und Staat in England und in der Normandie* (1899), 4, n. 3. No bishops in Avranches 862–990, and the bishopric there

great abbeys there are documents attesting the existence of immunities in the ninth century, but these institutions had been in
so many cases destroyed that one is not justified in assuming that
abbatial immunities exerted any formative influence in the early
decades of Norman administration.[164] But with Rouen we are
on a reasonably firm footing. When Rollo's hordes overran the
country the archbishop maintained his post and thereafter was
active in negotiating the peace of Clair-sur-Epte.[165] He is the
only link of which we have any knowledge between the government of the Franks and its successors in Neustria. What governmental arrangements there were in the diocese or what
changes took place we do not know. Nor does Dudo's chronicle,
written about a century after the cession of Normandy, give
light as to how far the leading Christian by birth was able to
guide the newly converted duke into the paths of Gallic civilization. In Richard I's reign (965–996) the bishops are undoubtedly
important, since in a charter for St. Denis restoring to it the abbey of St. Berneval-sur-Mer[166] the signature of the archbishop of
Rouen precedes even that of the duke. We know that in the

appears to have been administered by Rouen. At Séez between 910 and
990, no bishops; and in Lisieux none from 876–990. As to Coutances, 11
*Gallia Christiana, Instrumenta* 217.

[164] It is difficult to know exactly the status of the immunities of ecclesiastical establishments in Neustria before the Norman invasions. For St.
Wandrille the charter of Louis the Pious (815) is preserved, Lot, *Etudes
critiques sur l'Abbaye de St. Wandrille,* 28. For Jumièges, we have a grant
of certain fiscal privileges; *Form. Imp.* 24. The church of Mary in Rouen
is granted certain fiscal lands in 822; *Form. Imp.* 26. The charter for St.
Ouen has been noted *supra,* n. 162; *cf.* the account in 11 *Gallia Christiana*
136. For St. Evroul, in 900, Charles the Simple confirmed the possessions,
Böhmer, *Regesta Carolorum* (1833), 1914; 9 *H.F.,* 489. As to other abbeys
established before the invasions the writer has been unable to find charters.
The eleventh volume of *Gallia Christiana* indicates there are none although this is by no means a certain indication. In this connection should
be noted the references in 2 Sackur, *Die Cluniacenser,* 42, n. 1 as to the
tradition that Rollo after his baptism gave lands to the churches.

[165] On his identity Vogel, *op. cit.,* 392–3; and see the note in 8 *H.F.,*
254 b. *Cf.* also the passage cited by Vogel from Flodoard (392 n. 1) regarding the conversion of the heathen.

[166] 9 *H.F.,* 731.

peace negotiations at that time the ecclesiasts attended the *placitum*.[167] In this connection it is significant that the first reforms of the abbeys and their reconstruction begin at about this period and are pursued with purpose by both Richard I and his successors.[168]

There are other indications that point to temporal activity on the part of the bishops. Chief of these is the change in the character of the men who hold the office.[169] Hugh, a monk from St. Denis[170] who becomes archbishop of Rouen in 942, is married and is reported to have conveyed much church property to his relatives. His successor Robert (989), a son of Richard I, likewise is married, and he is Count of Evreux. Radbod of Séez and Hugh of Bayeux have wives and the latter in particular has the reputation of a stout warrior.[171] Indeed, the episcopacy seems to have fallen into the hands of lusty fellows who were not bothered by the distinction between the things that are Caesar's and the things that are God's. The prelates, however, were in no worse case than their own canons and priests, since the whole church in Normandy was probably in as low an estate as anywhere in Europe.[172] All the tendencies toward temporalization

[167] Lot, *Les derniers carolingiens* (1891), 56. Compare also the *praeceptum* of Lothar for the monastery Mont St. Michel (967) where Hugh of Rouen appears as petitioner. 11 *Gallia Christiana, Instrumenta* 105 (*cf.* Lot, *op. cit.*, 354–5).

[168] 2 Sackur, *op. cit.*, 42. Mont St. Michel is reformed with the archbishop of Rouen abetting (*ibid.*, 43). On the rebuilding of St. Wandrille, Lot, *Etudes . . . sur St. Wandrille*, XLIII. The church at Fécamp is restored in 989, 2 Sackur, *op. cit.*, 44. Apparently Richard I is responsible for restoring the sees at Avranches, Séez, and Lisieux, Böhmer, *Kirche und Staat*, 6. For a table of abbeys at the end of the tenth century listing the persons who possessed them or had the right of presentation, Lot, *Etudes sur le règne de Hugues Capet*, 432.

[169] *Acta Archiepiscope Rotomagensis*, in 147 Migne, *Patrologia*, 277 *et seq*. Cf. also Orderic Vitalis, *Historia Ecclesiastica* (Le Prevost Ed. 1838–55) lib. V c. 9.

[170] Motey, *Origines de la Normandie et du Duché d'Alençon*, (1920), 55. He was the brother of Raoul of Toeny.

[171] Böhmer, *op. cit.*, 11 n. 4.

[172] 2 Sackur, *op. cit.*, 26. Note also what Sackur has to say at p. 26, regarding the feuds of the bishops in France. On the church in Maine at

that we have noted for the preceding century were manifested in an increasingly unspiritual form. A priest's rise to preferment in that turbulent age was not dependent on his ability to say a paternoster. The epics which laud the martial prowess of the bishops reflect the qualities for which men had marked them.[173]

We do not mean to imply that the temporal preoccupations of the Norman bishops necessarily capacitated them to impose the Frankish methods of administration upon the dukes. Yet the mere fact that they were much involved in mundane affairs and participated in the first *placitum* we know anything about seems to point to a continuation of Carolingian tradition in respect of this office. Except for the dukes themselves, it is only the Norman prelates who, as a class and as individuals, loom through the murk of the tenth century from Franco who negotiated the treaty of cession to Robert of Rouen who wages war in 1027 against his suzerain.[174]

The secular institution most clearly related to the well-being and power of the church—the immunity—is the Frankish device, the acceptance of which is earliest attested in Normandy. One is tempted to attribute the adoption of this to the direct influence of the Norman churchmen rather than to imitation of the practice of the feeble French kings who were still issuing charters of this sort, particularly since the purpose of granting a church immunity in Normandy is primarily to guard it from lay interference.[175] But until some effort has been made to gather and

---

this time, Latouche, *Histoire du Comté de Maine* (1910) 78 *et seq.;* in Brittany, 3 La Borderie, *Histoire de Bretagne* (1899), 156 and 168 *et seq.*

[173] Merk, *Anschauungen über die Lehre und das Leben der Kirche im Altfränzösischen Heldenepos* in *Beiheft zur Zeitschrift für Romanische Philologie,* No. 41 (1914), 197, 204 *et seq.* and the passages there cited regarding the martial activities of the bishops. On the abbots and monks as warriors, *ibid.,* 220.

[174] Steenstrup, *Normandiets Historie,* 181. *Cf.* also Haskins, *Norman Institutions,* 267, and what he has to say regarding reaction against the church, all of which seems to point to the very potent influence of the bishops. See on the matter in the text, Pfister, *op. cit.,* 217.

[175] The Norman immunity is discussed further in Chapter V.

collate the earliest Norman charters and to investigate the diplomatics of the duchy there can be no certain conclusions from the language of the documents. In the earliest period of Norman history it seems probable that grants were made orally.[176] But grants there were, for some sort of conveyance William Longsword must have made to Jumièges when he imported monks from Acquitaine and repopulated the abbey.[177] Whether an immunity was included we do not know. It is only in the reign of Richard, William's successor, that there is evidence of abbatial immunities. The earliest charter of this sort, that to St. Denis (964), and one of the few tenth-century Norman grants that have been preserved, is completely in the Frankish tradition and may well have been prepared by the grantees who had enough models to choose from. As the exiled convents slowly returned to Normandy, they no doubt arrived with their proofs of title, for one can suppose that when the fraternity decamped with the reliquaries, their muniments were no less tenderly cared for. At least one chronicle bears witness to this fact.[178]

Not too much can be urged from the form of the early Norman charters, or their accord with the Frankish formularies.[179]

[176] Valin, *Le Duc de Normandie et sa cour* (1909), 145, n. 1, publishes the following excerpt from a charter of Richard II to St. Ouen "Quae omnia noster atavus Rolphus praenominato loco partim restituit, partim et dedit, sed propiis cartulis ad noticiam futurorum minime descripsit. Huic subnectimus cessioni, quae etiam avi nostri Willelmi industria simili modo, absque cartarum notamine concessit." On the decline of the use of written instruments in the tenth century, 1 Bresslau, *Handbuch der Urkundenlehre* (2 ed. 1912), 650 *et seq.*

[177] 1 Sackur, *Die Cluniacenser,* 83. *Cf.* the statement in 1 Stapleton, *Magni Rotuli Scaccarii Normanniae* (1840) clxvi, regarding a grant by the widow of William. Apparently the Abbot of Jumièges was very close to William; Lair, *Etude sur Guillaume Longue-Epée* (1893), 26. *Cf.* also a charter of Richard II to Mont St. Michel in which reference is made to a grant of vills in Avranches by William, 1 Morice, *Mémoires pour servir de preuves à l'histoire de Bretagne* (1742), 351–2.

[178] Lot, *Etudes critiques sur l'Abbaye de St. Wandrille,* XLII; *cf.* Mabille, *op. cit.,* 169, n. 7, quoting from Miracula St. Martin.

[179] *Cf.* on this Tardif, *Etudes sur les sources de l'ancien droit normand* (1911), 7.

Only a monarch with great resources of lands and wealth can grant in blanket form as did Charlemagne and Louis. During the tenth century, especially in the charters of the territorial lords, the conveyances deal with single privileges like woods, fishing, mills, essarts and the like. The general fiscal privilege has become atomized into its component parts.[180] In Normandy, however, there still prevails a good deal of the Frankish formulary tradition.[181] Both Jumièges[182] and Fécamp,[183] in the early eleventh century, are given privileges of the *absque introitu iudicum* type. In other grants the ducal *consuetudines*[184] are

[180] Somewhat differently conceived but more or less to the same effect Kroell, *op. cit.,* 313.

[181] Kroell, *op. cit.,* 306, who sees the Frankish immunity as a thing *sui generis* and part of the Carolingian system insists that the *Frankish* immunity disappears in the tenth century. He points out with some force that when you have no public officers the exclusion of the *iudices publici* has no meaning. The "quicquid fiscus exinde potuerit sperare" comes to mean the so-called regalian rights (*ibid.,* 323). These remarks are generally true, but on the other hand in Normandy where the duke stands as to bishoprics and abbeys *in loco regis,* the grants which employ the old Frankish formulae still have significance. There is early eleventh-century evidence of officials with something like public powers. Thus Fulbert of Chartres complains to Richard of Normandy of the mill-ban which the latter's *ministri* attempted to inflict. Fulbert, *Epistolae* in 141 Migne, *Patrologia,* 210 no. 23 (on the meaning of *ministri* at this time, 5 Waitz *D.V.G.,* 432; Ganshof, *Etude sur les ministériales* [1926], 76). Moreover, the powers of the monasteries over offenses could scarcely have developed in Normandy so extraordinarily if there had been no meaning in the immunity grants. Valin, *op. cit.,* 222–3 is rather cautious but inclines to an interpretation which supports what we have said. Haskins, *op. cit.,* 26–7 does not speak of the Frankish *immunitas* with precision or clarity.

[182] 1 Vernier, *Chartes de l'Abbaye de Jumièges* (1916), n. 11 (1027).

[183] The first charter of Richard I (989–90) grants immunity from archiepiscopal jurisdiction, *cf.* the excerpt in 11 *Gallia Christiana,* 203. The charter of Richard II (1006) in Haskins *op. cit.,* 253 uses a curious formula that seems to imply immunity. The charter of 1025, *Neustria Pia,* 215, uses the same formula as that of Jumièges. *Cf.* also the charter for St. Ouen cited by Valin, *op. cit.,* 222 n. 1, and St. Amand, *ibid.,* 223 n. 2.

[184] Haskins, *op. cit.,* 26, states that the clauses of immunity in the charters are not intended as a general grant of ducal judicial powers as is shown by the practice of granting ducal *consuetudines* in specified places. Except for grants like those to Trier and Metz (and *quaere* even as to these) the Carolingian immunity charter never gave all the grantor's

granted (which may refer only to non-judicial fiscal privileges) and in some the *consuetudines* are combined with *forfacta* (forfeitures), a fact which points toward judicial privilege. All of these early charters have a regal sound.[185] The duke of Nor-

judicial rights, a fact which Haskins does not apparently take into account. The essence of the late Carolingian *immunitas* is the exclusion of public officers and the embodiment of royal *tuitio*. If the formulae extending protection from officers had meaning in the Norman charters, the formulae regarding "Consuetudines que ex ipsa terra pertinebant ad nos," may well be interpreted with the emphasis on last three words, i.e., that the duke grants what he has to grant, the implication being that others already held some *consuetudines* in the place specified. What Haskins says in the succeeding pages furnishes some support for the view, although he does not suggest it. There are charters which show how specific privileges as to certain pieces of property are given, thus Lothar to Sta. Maria de Ripoll (982), Halphen and Lot, *Receuil des actes de Lothaire et de Louis V* (1908), 111, and *Lothar to San Cougat del Valles* (984), *ibid.*, 120, where for example among other confirmations "Ecclesiam Sancte Marie et Sancte Stephani cum decimis et primiciis absque tributo . . . et in castro Olerdula et in eius terminis domos turres terras vineasque cultum vel heremum cum decimis et primicis . . ." and then a clause of immunity prohibiting judicial entries. See also Hugh Capet to Orleans (990) 10 *H.F.*, 556.

The word *consuetudines* offers great difficulties. It is used in the documents of the tenth and eleventh century in two distinct senses, custom as a toll or tax, and custom as a law or jurisdiction (*cf. infra*, c. IV). This confusion is apparent even in Carolingian documents although in the capitularies the word is used to distinguish unwritten law or local observance from written law (3 Waitz, *D.V.G.*, 623, n. 4), and to characterize tolls by custom (4 *ibid.*, 55).

In the Italian immunity charters the word *consuetudines* means tolls (4 *ibid.*, 172 n. 3). In this sense also see the interesting letter of Alcuin to the bishop of Limoges (796–804) (*M.G.H.*, 2 *Epist. Merov. et Kar.*, 457).

In certain charters of Robert the Pious more or less contemporary with the grants of Richard II of Normandy the *consuetudines* granted are by specification clearly jurisdictions. *Cf.* Tardif, *Monuments historiques,* no. 243 (1000), no. 249 (1008) and no. 250 (1008). But see no. 260 (1030) where it refers to the *exactiones*. See also the document in Pfister, *op. cit.*, no. 2 (1002–16): "Omnes consuetudines quae in terris eorum . . . ab antecessoribus nostris constitute sunt ut deinceps non aliquis nostrum sive regnum nostrum inhabitantium audeat ibi accipere latronem neque bannum . . . et quicquid ibi ad nos pertinere videtur . . ." In this relation compare also Robert's charter cited *infra*, note 201.

[185] The practical significance of this was pointed out in the eighteenth century by Brussel in 2 *Nouvel examen de l'usage général des fiefs* (1727),

mandy is the protector of churches and abbeys: the *mundibur-dium* of the Carolingian king has passed into his hands; he stands in *loco regis*. When he threatens a violator of an immunity with 100 pound penalty[186] he is talking the Carolingian idiom.

If the ecclesiastical immunity was continued without substantial interruption in Normandy, if only in the sense of protection from lay rather than public authority, it is persuasive evidence in favor of the hypothesis that the men who remained, the bishops, kept alive latter-day Frankish administrative arrangements and, in particular, the whole concept of diffused jurisdiction over wrongs. When we come to consider the revival of monastic immunities under Richard I and his successors, however, there are phases of the matter which indicate that the alternative hypothesis, the imitation of practice in contiguous territory, can be supported.

In point of form the earliest Norman charters seem relatable to the ninth-century Carolingian grants, but we do not advance far into the eleventh century before it is obvious that as a practical matter the jurisdiction exercised in a Norman immunity is greater than that which obtained as a rule in the ninth century. It is, of course, possible that in the terrible times of Norman forays the hardy clerics who remained in Neustria had, in the absence of organized secular government, already grasped the full control over law and procedure. On the other hand, there

815. Brunner made a comprehensive investigation of unprinted sources in reference to this question. (*Cf.* his *Entstehung der Schwurgerichte* 238 *et seq.*) His conclusions are in favor of the historical continuity with Frankish institutions (*ibid.*, 244). To be noted especially is his statement that by being on a parity with fiscal property churches to whom protection is given by charter are *eo ipso* given the royal right of the *inquisitio*. On the Frankish explicit grants of this right to immunists, Brunner, *Zeugen und Inquisitionsprozess* in *Forschungen,* 166. Brunner in his *Schwurgerichte* characterizes briefly the formulae of Henry II for the protection. For further examples Round, *Calendar of Documents Preserved in France 918–1206* (1899), nos. 609, 759, 820.

[186] Charter of 1035 to Fécamp, Round, *Calendar,* no. 113.

had been certain drastic changes in the basic theory of immunity jurisdiction during the tenth century in territory contiguous to Normandy. Most significant among these changes was the fact that the king's charter of protection no longer protected since the king was too weak to protect, and that the immunity absorbed new incidents of jurisdiction, even those which previously had been denied them. Specifically the division between small causes and "criminal causes" is eradicated; in other words the whole jurisdiction over wrongs can be and is acquired.

Perhaps the best index of changes outside of Normandy is to be found in these royal charters. The latter are in many cases mere repetitions of old forms. There are, however, a number of charters, all to ecclesiastical units, which exclude any and all outside judicial interferences with immunity jurisdiction.[187] This privilege, which had theretofore been exceptional, which probably in those centuries never operated to exclude the royal *missi*, is now granted to relatively unimportant monasteries. It has great significance because there are no *missi* to be excluded.[188] In other words, considering the state of public administration, it is an unqualified grant of complete jurisdiction. Similar in effect are the charters where the crown relinquishes its share of the 600 shilling penalty for immunity breach.[189]

[187] Louis IV to the Chapter of St. Martin de Tours (938), Lauer, *Receuil des actes de Louis IV* (1914), no. 9, *Nec ullas publicas functiones;* Louis IV to Cluny (939), *ibid.,* no. 10; Louis to St. Philibert (941), *ibid.,* no. 16, no count or other lay power "in praefato loco placitum constituere aut tenere"; Louis IV to Cluny (946), *ibid.,* no. 29, "quicquid exinde facere voluerint vel judicare . . ." In Halphen and Lot, *Recueil,* are the following: Lothar to Cluny (955), no. 7, "ab omni extranee potestatis exactione"; the three charters (964–66) nos. 21, 22, 25, to St. Pierre-au-Mont-Blandin; Lothar to St. Vincent de Laon (975), no. 38, "Aliquam judiciariam potestatem exercere"; Louis V to Ste. Croix d'Orleans (979), no. 69, the immunity is granted "remota totius judiciariae potestatis inquietudine."

[188] Despite the disappearance of the old royal *missi,* note the following charters: Charles the Simple to St. Martin (Autun) of the year 900 in 9 *H.F.,* 485 where *missi* are included in the list of officers whose entry is prohibited. *Cf.* also Charles to Tournus (915), 9 *H.F.,* 523.

[189] Thus Charles the Simple to Tournus (915); Louis IV to St. Phili-

In addition to these more generally phrased surrenders of public rights are those specific terms in the charters whereby the century-old distinction between *causae minores* and *causae criminales* is broken down. The first charter that we have found with a specific grant in this new form relates to a monastery in the old Spanish March.[190] There, it will be recalled, Charles the Bald had specifically reserved to the public officials the jurisdiction over homicide, *raptus,* and arson. In 938, Louis IV, in confirming the lands of the Notre Dame de Ripoll, extends immunity and prohibits all counts, prelates (pontifices) and public judges from jurisdiction over causes *"nec homines illorum aliquis distringat nec per homicidium, neque per incendium vel raptum, neque per aliquem negocium. . . ."*

Grants of this sort are not usual, but it is extremely significant that in the region where the preservation of public authority over *causae criminales* is best attested this policy is incontinently abandoned. There are two other charters issued by Louis IV which lead one to assume that the act noted is not an isolated phenomenon. In 944, in a charter to a certain clerk Adalbert, lands in the counties of Bésalu and Girone are given immunity, and entries by all public officers for hearing causes and collecting *fredus,* distraining men *or for taking thieves* are prohibited.[191] In the following year the possessions and privileges of St. Julien

bert (941), Lauer, *Recueil,* no. 16; Lothar to St. Philibert (956), Halphen and Lot, *Recueil,* no. 10. There are numerous other examples.

[190] Lauer, *Recueil,* no. 8. The only royal charter we have found prior to this one which seems to forecast this type of concession is that of Charles the Simple to St. Christopher in Paris (900), 9 *H.F.,* 484 where public authority is forbidden "hominem fugientem expellendi" but this probably is only a fortification of the right of asylum.

With the charter in the text should be compared that of Louis to the Spaniard John (815), Böhmer-Mühlbacher, *Regesten,* no. 567; 6 *H.F.,* 472, that apparently gives a complete jurisdiction, but since it is not specific in respect to *causae criminales* one may suppose the general rule of the capitularies is applied. *Cf.* also the charter of Charles the Simple to Theodosius (898), 9 *H.F.,* 470.

[191] Lauer, *Recueil,* no. 24. The earlier charter of Charles the Simple to Girone (899), 9 *H.F.,* 484 shows no such privilege.

de Tours[192] are confirmed and judicial officers are forbidden *"distringere aut rectum reclamare . . . de ullo forfacto . . . neque de latrocinio neque de sanguine neque de alio magno aut parvo. . . ."*

In the reign of Lothar there are a number of examples of the exemption from *bannus*,[193] and a number of grants which indicate a complete exemption from all external judicial authority.[194] In 977, a grant to St. Quentin en l'Ile[195] contains the following: *"immunis maneat ab omni querela comitis sive regalium ministerialium sed quicquid ea corrigendum sive in latronibus sive in aliis querimoniis fuerit, ex nostra concessione abbas et ministri eius libera utantur facultate."* This same ruler, in 984, grants to San Cugat del Valles,[196] in the march, the jurisdiction of homicide, *raptus,* and arson.

It is a fair inference, as has been indicated, that royal immunity grant during the tenth century was practically tantamount to an exemption from all outside jurisdiction. This inference is strengthened by the fact that in the several charters cited we have direct and convincing proof that the old distinctions had broken down and that *all* jurisdiction over wrongs was exercisable by the grantee. It may well be that in the French charters of the late tenth century the word *bannus* is intended to convey the meaning it has in the Empire, of jurisdiction generally.[197] The evi-

---

[192] Lauer, *Recueil,* no. 25.

[193] A careful search of Louis IV's charters reveals no grant of *bannus.* It is included in the charter of Charles the Simple to Prüm (920), 9 *H.F.,* 548, and in Raoul's charter to St. Laumer de Blois (924) in 9 *H.F.,* 566. Charters of Lothar where it is included are that to St. Bertin (962), Halphen and Lot, *Recueil,* no. 15; to St. Bavon de Gand (966), *ibid.,* no. 26; to Ste. Croix d'Orleans (954–72), *ibid.,* no. 33; Lothar and Louis V to Notre Dame de Paris (979–86), *ibid.,* no. 54. In this connection should be considered also the Le Mans forgeries intended to get full jurisdiction and manufactured in the middle of the ninth century. They are discussed by Kroell, *op. cit.,* 222 *et seq.;* 2 Dopsch, *Wirtschaftsentwickelung,* 98.

[194] *Supra,* note 187.

[195] Halphen and Lot, *Recueil,* no. 42.

[196] *Ibid.,* no. 51.

[197] 7 Waitz, *D.V.G.,* 251. "Wenn dort neben dem Friedensgeld (*fre-*

dence we have offered certainly shows there is no theoretical obstacle in the way of such an interpretation.[198]

How far does any of this bear upon Normandy? To this question we venture to suggest the answer that any practice which became general in ecclesiastical establishments in one part of France was likely to influence the practice in another part. The monks were continually on the move, and from their number

*dus*) auch der sogenannte Bann (die Bannbusse) in Betracht kam, so bezeichnet dies Wort jetzt auch die Gerichtsbarkeit selbst, ja die öffentliche Gewalt überhaupt; und mehr und mehr, namentlich seit Heinrich II, hat man sich des Wortes bedient, um das auszudrücken was den Beamten entzogen, den Inhabern der Immunität übertragen sein sollte."

[198] There is much in the history of the struggle between bishops and territorial lords during the tenth century that explains how complete jurisdiction over wrongs was obtained. The struggles over property, election and other incidents of secular control over the church had in many instances the effect of definitely subjecting a particular see to the local ruler. One phase of the matter was the constant immunity breach. This was a practice forbidden in the ninth-century capitularies, but even then frequently indulged in. 3 Pöschl, *Bischofsgut,* 123. How essential the maintenance of the immunity was to the interests of the church may be gathered from the passages in the Pseudo-Isidorian decretals directed to this end; *cf. ibid.,* 126 where the several passages are listed. Wherever a bishop maintained his position against a local lord it involved complete exclusion of the latter and consequently he must have possessed the full equivalent of secular power (3 Pöschl *Bischofsgut,* 91). Consequently, irrespective of any canonical objections, there was no reason why the bishop, just as any other lord, could not and would not exercise full jurisdiction over wrongs. Furthermore, as to the charters discussed in the text it is fairly to be inferred from the fact that the bishops as a class generally supported the crown (*ibid.,* 156) that the grants of full jurisdiction were attempts to put ecclesiastical establishments in a position of complete authority so that no basis for comital interference would exist. The situation was largely the result of the political incompetence of the crown to maintain the traditional rule of protection. As far as Normandy is concerned we have indicated in the text the possibility of influence from without the duchy. Nevertheless, the parallel between the latter and the situation in France early in the ninth century is very striking. The duke's position in respect to ecclesiastical establishments is essentially that of the Carolingian monarch. He protects, and after the middle of the tenth century there is none of the incessant spoliation of ecclesiastical property that is usual in the adjoining territories. On the contrary the tradition of building up the church is established. It is for this reason that we are so strongly impressed with the continued maintenance of the earlier Frankish tradition.

were recruited the bishops who were politically important. On the instant point it is worth noting that it is only after the old rule against grants of *causae criminales* had been broken down in the Empire[199] that the first charters conveying such franchises appear in France. By the same token it is not improbable that ecclesiastical privileges usual in contiguous territory were of influence in fixing the rights of Norman immunists. The force of such a position is enhanced when one recalls how wide-flung were monastic possessions. When the Count of Rennes grants to the Norman monastery Mont St. Michel *bannus* of homicide, theft and bloodshed in Brittany lands,[200] it is not unlikely that the Norman immunity will be interpreted by the monks to include such jurisdiction, even if before that time the old distinctions may have obtained.[201]

When we sum up the measurable changes in the immunity

[199] Implicit in the grant of *bannus, cf.* the documents cited by Waitz 7 *D.V.G.,* 244 *et seq. Cf.* Konrad I to the Bishop of Freising (912) *M.G.H.* 1 *Dipl. Reg. et Imp.* no. 9 "nullus comes etc. habeat ex illis hominibus ad predicta loca servientibus *quicquid corrigendi vel inquirendi* sed haec sola potestas memorato episcopo sibique subiectis concessa est." Konrad I to Corvei (913), *ibid.,* no. 14, full judicial power to the *advocatus;* Henry I to Corvei (922), *ibid.* no. 3 (p. 41); implicit in the grant of inquisition etc. by Henry I to St. Gall (926), *ibid.,* no. 12 (p. 48); Henry I to Werden (930), *ibid.,* no. 26 (p. 61); Otto I to Werden (936), *ibid.,* no. 5 (p. 93); Otto I to the Bishop of Halberstadt (937), *ibid.,* no. 7 (p. 95); Otto I to St. Maurice in Magdeburg (937), *ibid.,* no. 14 (p. 101). Only those charters are cited where by the formulae a complete jurisdiction is conveyed.

[200] Conan, Count de Rennes to Mont St. Michel (990) in 1 Morice, *Mémoires pour servir de preuves à l'histoire de Bretagne* (1742), 350, "et si aliquis de his habitantibus infra istas villas homicidium fecerit, aut effusionem sanguinis aut latrocinium . . . aut praeterierit hostem aut equitatum sit bannum Principis Michaelis et monachorum suorum." The count keeps homicide by outsiders, *raptus,* arson and other rights. *Cf.* the charter of Alan of Brittany to Marmoutiers saving the various official acts and collections "nec vel ipse bannum." *Ibid.,* 360.

[201] See further the charter of Robert the Pious to Fécamp (1006), in 10 *H.F.,* 587 "nullus officialis habeat in ipsa villa aliquid dominium sive comes, si Vicecomes, vel quilibet improbus exactor; neque in bannis, necque in legibus, necque in fredis aut in aliquo uso indebito, quem Coustumam vulgo nuncupant." The charter of Hugh Capet to St. Columba

concept in the tenth century as shown by the charters it is apparent that the division between public and private jurisdiction is no longer significant. It will take a long time for the line of public authority to rise on the graph of jurisdiction. In the meantime the red line of blood justice, descriptive of the authority of "private" persons or establishments, is in the ascendant. It is not even a solid line, but is made up of a myriad of components, homicide, theft, arson and all the other ancient evils. For in the morcellation of rights and privileges that is characteristic of feudalism, each wrong is itself a jurisdiction susceptible of grant and indisputed exercise as much as a mill, a woods or a stream. One fact of significance stands out: that even where the right to judge in cases of wrongs is dimmed by the mists of prescription, some vestiges of a franchise theory are kept alive. As to jurisdiction exercised time out of mind, there may be no immediate disposition to probe beyond the fact, but when new grants are made the persistence of at least a ghostly franchise theory is obvious. It is this theory combined with the disposition to grant, no less than the incessant wars and forays of these centuries, that makes the reconstitution of public order a problem that has to be attacked *de novo.*[202]

(Sens) of the year 988, has an immunity clause prohibiting "aut bannum seu incendium, aut homicidium vel raptum requirendum," 10 *H.F.*, 553. In a charter of Robert the Pious to St. Denis (1008), Tardif, *Monuments historiques,* no. 250, are granted "quasdam res juris nostri . . . hoc est bannum hominis vulnerati vel interfecti, et infracturam intra vel extra castellum ipsius conoebii et legem duelli quod vulgo dicitur campus . . ." There has been no attempt to collect all examples, but the above convey some notion as to how the substance of matter granted had changed.

[202] As Hintze, *op. cit.,* 328 indicates there has come into existence a new form of polity on a much narrower basis. In this polity the notion of feoffment dominates, and in our opinion probably tended to change the concept of franchise or privilege in the form in which it had previously existed, without, however, destroying the basic idea of delictual jurisdiction as a franchise.

# CHAPTER IV

## CRIMINAL PROCEDURE AND FEUDAL GOVERNMENT

THE immunities and jurisdictions into which the West Frankish kingdom disintegrated, since they had been the depositories of wide administrative powers, are in the tenth and eleventh centuries the sanctuaries of ancient law. But they are sanctuaries in only a very qualified sense. The onslaughts of social and economic change in this period are violent. Except for the devices which, because of their inherent vitality, can be accommodated to the vicissitudes of these brutal decades, much of the jurisprudence of what was then the recent past sinks into oblivion. What remains is often enough a mere degenerate remnant of the old Salic or the Carolingian law.

The fate of Frankish institutions in northern France is intimately joined with the fortunes of myriad political entities, and a history of the law in this early period can be nothing but a reconstruction of what there took place. The only common denominator is the Frankish law, and although the treatment it receives will vary from franchise to franchise, from barony to abbey, such generalizations as can be made must be formulated on the basis of similarities or discrepancies in terms of the persistence or decadence of Frankish law. Using this test, the question of how far one must distinguish between the various law-enforcing units according to the localities that eventually possess their own *coutumes,* seems relatively unimportant.

The difficulties which can arise when the law of the tenth and eleventh centuries are treated as possessing marked provincial characteristics is well illustrated in the results achieved by the application of this method to the law of Normandy. In the period between the cession of Normandy in 911 and the reign of Henry II, Norman law is for the most part still *terra incognita.*

Contemporary Norman sources are sparse and few explorations
have yielded concrete and reliable knowledge.[1] Like the early

[1] The slight information regarding the organization of the invaders is
to the effect that it was democratic. Vogel, *Die Normannen und das
Fränkische Reich,* 40 *et seq. Cf.* also 1 Steenstrup, *Normannerne* (1876),
290 *et seq.* The tales about the institutions of Rollo are difficult to believe.
One may well doubt whether there was much peace or security in his
realm. The surest barometer of the pressure of public authority is the
monasteries. Throughout northern France fear and horror of the Normans prevailed. No exiled convent was likely to return until there existed
real gages in the actuality of ducal protection. Only after the accession of
Richard I (962) is there much monastic repatriation. One may assume
that it is only about this time that a condition of relative law enforcement
exists.

Tardif, *Etude sur les sources de l'ancien droit normand* (1911) has
made the most thorough study of the law before the time of William the
Conqueror. The two chief sources of information are Dudo of St. Quentin, *De Moribus et Actis Primorum Normanniae Ducum* (Lair Ed. in 3
*Men. Soc. Antiq. de Normandie,* 3 ser. 1865) and Wace, *Roman de Rou*
(Andresen Ed. 1877). The first of these was written in the early years of
the 11th century, the second after the middle of the 12th century. In dealing with the so-called laws of Rollo and especially Dudo's very bald and
uninformative remarks about them Tardif has turned to Wace for confirmation. This seems a hazardous method of proof, for some of the
things about which Wace speaks as institutions of Rollo were obviously
achievements of his successors. These details will emerge presently in the
text. We propose, e.g., to establish that the *pax ducis* was the result of the
*pax Dei* introduced in Normandy between 1042–46. But in the *Roman de
Rou* (ll. 1193–1205) this is referred to as an institution of Rollo. On the
other hand, Dudo, where he speaks of peace, uses the word either in the
sense of a treaty of peace (II, 25) or in an untechnical sense of order (II,
32) or in what we have described as a pious ecclesiastical sense. It seems
sensible that if there had been an effective *pax ducis* (paix de duc) in the
year 1000 Dudo would have adverted to it. It was to become eventually
one of the very characteristic things about the Norman criminal law.
Tardif gets into difficulties as an historian because he does not observe the
danger of assuming that what is law in one century may not have been
law two hundred years before.

The evidence regarding Rollo's law is slight. On the one hand is the
tradition of the laws of Frode having been introduced by Rollo. This is
Steenstrup's theory, 1 *Normannerne* (1876), 311 *et seq.,* and *cf.* von Amira,
*Die Anfänge des Normannischen Rechts,* 3 *Historische Zeitschrift* (n.f.),
241, 266 *et seq.,* for a discussion of this view. Of Frode's laws only the
account of Saxo Grammaticus remains. It may well be that the early laws
about which Dudo speaks (II, 31, III, 38, 58) were these. Dudo states
that when Harald came to the rescue of Duke Richard and commanded

new-world cartographers who turned to fantasy when facts failed, historians have delineated strange juristic beasts in this unknown land. The casual appearance of the words *murdrum* and *ullac*[2] have suggested a continuation of Scandinavian customs regarding homicide and outlawry. And for this supposition

the Contentin and Bessin, he ordered the laws of Rollo to remain in force (Dudo, III, 88). This Tardif treats as evidence that Rollo's laws were Scandinavian; a far-fetched conclusion.

Specifically, Dudo speaks of the laws against robbery (II, 31), indicating that it is punished by hanging, and of the protection of the plow. The latter fits with the Scandinavian (Wilda, *Strafrecht der Germanen*, 245). As to robbery, Tardif thinks the death penalty is not Frankish. He cites the practice of redemption from the *Pactus pro tenore pacis*, the Italian capitulary of Pepin (782–6) c. 8, and the *Edict. Pistense* (864) c. 28 (2 *Cap.* 322) which speaks of forbidding enslavement for *theft* (*furtum*). As we know (*supra*, Chapter II), Tardif is mistaken in his statement of Frankish law. His argument that the death penalty is characteristically Scandinavian (*loc. cit.*, 19) is wrong (*supra*, Chapter II). Rollo undoubtedly made laws but beyond these two sketchily documented details in the matter of delicts, it is impossible to conjecture what they were. (*Cf.* 1 Pollock and Maitland, *H.E.L.*, 65.)

As to the persistence of Frankish law, Tardif (*loc cit.*, 61) makes the useful suggestion that by virtue of the principle then in force that laws had a *personal* application, this would be probable. He points also to William I's policy in England. He indicates further acceptance of Frankish institutions in Dudo's reference to commendation (III, 58) and to *bannus* (II, 31); to the use of *placitum commune* (9 H.F., 731), and the use of terms from the Frankish formulae (*loc. cit.*, 7).

In connection with the theory earlier developed in the text it is important to note that Tardif does not believe the ecclesiastics were of importance in the affairs of state until the middle of the tenth century. It is *fait accompli* by 968 when the archbishop of Rouen's signature to a charter for Saint Denis (9 H.F. 731) precedes that of the Duke (*op. cit.*, 26). After 990 when the ducal family dominates in the Norman hierarchy the influence is more pronounced. Tardif regards this as a reestablishment of the Carolingian tradition.

On Dudo *cf.* Waitz, *Ueber die Quellen zur Geschichte der Begründung der Normannischen Herrschaft* in 22 *Nachrichten der Königlichen Gesellschaft Göttingen* (1866), 69 *et seq.*; 1 Freeman, *History of the Norman Conquest* (2 ed. 1870), 234; Lot, *Les derniers Carolingiens* (1891), 346 *et seq.*; Dümmler, *Zur Kritik Dudos von St. Quentin* in 6 *Forschungen z. D.G.*, 361; Prentout, *Etude critique sur Dudon de Saint-Quentin* (1915), esp. 266 *et seq.*

[2] On this word Haskins, *Norman Institutions,* App. D, n. 16; Steenstrup, *Normandiets Historie* (1925), 245 n. 4, n. 6. The passages cited

that Scandinavian law persisted,[3] Saxo Grammaticus' lost laws of Frode have furnished further speculative possibilities. The chronicle of Dudo of St. Quentin has been devoutly ransacked. The *Roman de Rou* (c. 1160) used as a source of early law has supplied a goodly store of anachronisms. For want of contemporary records there has been an irresistible temptation to treat sources of the late twelfth and early thirteenth centuries as reliably depicting the institutions of earlier generations.[4] The risks of relying upon the latter assumption are patent. The sources of one century should never be permitted to speak too boldly for another. The way things happened cannot always be proved by the result.

The barriers of time are thus obstacles that seem to us insurmountable in the employment of records. But the frontiers set up by treaties like that of Clair-sur-Epte are lines that for a time need deter the historian as little as they did the Normans. It is fantastic to think of the Normans in the tenth and the early eleventh century living enclosed within hermetical boundaries engaged in promoting an individual culture. The political flux

from Benoît de Ste. Maure give the word the meaning of pirates or professional robbers.

[3] Steenstrup is the leading protagonist of Scandinavian influence. *Cf.* 1 *Normannerne* §11 *et seq.*; and compare especially v. Amira's criticism of his use of certain passages in Dudo (*ibid.*, 334) in *Die Anfänge des Normannischen Rechts, 39 Hist. Zeitschrift*, 267. Steenstrup's most recent work, *Normandiets Historie*, 204 *et seq.*, 244, 246 adheres in the main to the earlier thesis, although later research of other scholars is referred to.

[4] This was Brunner's method. Without any intent to detract from the remarkable achievements of Brunner in laying the foundation for a scientific study of early Norman law, it should be pointed out here that even some of his most penetrating studies such as *Wort und Form im Altfranzösischen Prozess,* and *Die Zulässigkeit der Anwaltschaft (Forschungen,* 260 and 389) were composed with little regard for chronology, i.e., in a cultural sense. No sooner does one become familiar with the texts upon which a history of Henry II's law can be based than one realizes that Bracton is not for one moment to be taken as a working source for the earlier century. To use again the figure in the text, when historians have two known headlands, they are prone like Charles V's *cartografo mayor* to fill in the gap with hypothetical scallops. This is frequently the best a

was too ceaseless for this. Sharing a common Frankish tradition, cursed with a common passion for warfare, swept by the same natural calamities, the counties of northwestern France may be regarded for the purpose of legal development as a cultural unity.[5] In all of them the factors which molded the ends of law

man can do with his material, but he should never fail to margin his map with caveats. Brunner's own concept of the law as a cultural force made this procedure unnecessary, largely because he seems to believe the law possesses autogenetic power independent of circumstance.

[5] In many ways the period from 900–1060 in French history needs to be marked out from what preceded and what followed it. It needs a term more descriptive than the pallid *"nachfränkische Zeit,"* as certain German writers have dubbed it. It does not fit into the methodological scheme of the French scholars' *"régime seigneuriale."* Since cultural history is conditioned by political history, this period of political bedlam should be marked off from the preceding and following centuries, if for no other reason than as a precaution against the risk of a cultural phenomenon like the law being interpreted in the light of later political arrangements. For example, in the tenth century a man controlling a large territory will seize a fief for a time and be ousted by another fellow from some different county. The significance of this shift is to be measured not in large terms but merely in micrometrics, for most of these sudden transfers of authority are small scale operations. To use a somewhat faulty modern analogy we are dealing in shifts of title rather than of sovereignty, since we now reserve the pompous term for international transactions. Necessarily, the legal development cannot be marked by county frontiers, as long as the political control within a county shifts continually. This is possible only when a central authority with more than local or "feudal" legislative power comes into existence.

The statics of this period are for us the monastic establishments. One need only observe in the cartularies the stubborn tenacity with which the clerics maintained their holdings and jurisdictions to realize that here, if anywhere, the law would have stable ground for orderly growth. At the same time we must take into account the role of the monastery as a source of cultural diffusion, through the control of holdings in widely separated localities. For example, the monasteries of St. Aubin in Angers and St. Vincent du Mans had properties in Normandy; in the hands of Mont St. Michel in Normandy was St. Victeur au Mans. Inevitably there was exchange of administrators and necessarily of the nuances of law enforcement. It is for these practical reasons that we feel justified in relying upon the documents of mother monasteries in regions adjacent to Normandy as a guide in depicting the general trends of the law during this period. In Round, *Calendar,* will be found charters under the names of the non-Norman monasteries that give an idea of the holdings of these establishments in the duchy.

enforcement were substantially identical; in all a similar trend toward new sanctions against wrongdoing existed. This is a period in which we can rarely do more than plot the general tendencies of the law, and here the records of Anjou, Maine or Normandy all point unerringly in the same direction.

The differences that grow up in law and procedure during the bleak era before the conquest of England arise from the fact of extensive dispersion of jurisdiction. There will be haggling over grants of *sanguis*—do they include a thief's chattels as well as his body? There will be dispute whether jurisdiction is personal or territorial. But all these problems are intensely local even if common to all of northern France. They cannot be described in terms as broad or as narrow as Norman, Angevin or Breton. The fate of Frankish law was settled in barony or abbey before duke or count had drawn the strings of political and administrative control. It is for this reason that we consider the question on the basis of evidence in terms of general propinquity rather than in terms of eventual political subdivisions, our reconstruction being made wherever possible from records of the tenth and eleventh centuries.

The task in the present chapter is to ascertain the effect of the diffusion of jurisdiction upon law enforcement, and to observe the extent to which decentralization brought about really basic changes in the treatment of wrongs. We have seen how the long and carefully guarded *causae criminales* were finally captured or granted away, how the pressure for more and more jurisdiction expunged the ancient control over the franchises. These changes laid the basis for new procedures unhampered in their development by the forces which had hitherto kept the law in certain grooves. The controls of this period are different and on the whole negligible. The influence upon the law emanated from social and economic changes acting concurrently with the shift in political control, and to these changes the forms of procedure were made to respond, and take on new functions.

## FEUD AND THE DECAY OF COMPOSITION

To a certain extent the changes through which the Frankish law passed were induced by the very disturbed conditions of affairs which prevailed in northern France for over a century after the cession of Normandy. We have noted below[6] a more or less

[6] 923. War on the French king with mutual invasion: *Flodoard* (Lauer Ed.), 39 *Coll. de textes pour l'étude . . . de l'histoire* (1905), 15–17.

925. An earlier truce is broken, and new invasions: *ibid.*, 31.

926. New conflicts about Arras: *ibid.*, 33.

927. "Peace" restored: *ibid.*, 39–40.

928. William Longsword continues struggles of his father against King Raoul: *ibid.*, 39, and against pagan Normans of Bayeux, Evreux, etc., and against Brittany: William of Jumièges, *Gesta Normannorum Ducum* (Marx Ed., *Société de l'histoire de Normandie* [1914]) 32, and *La chronique de Nantes* (Merlet Ed., in 19 *Coll. de textes pour l'étude . . . de l'histoire* [1896]) 81. In general see Motey, *Origines de la Normandie et du Duché d'Alençon* (1920), *passim*, and Prentout, *op. cit.*, from which Motey borrows heavily.

933–4. Pagan Normans around Evreux rise against William and Christian "French" Normans of Rouen: *Jumièges*, III, 2; but see Dudo, *De Moribus*, II, 41 (Lair Ed., 185) who substitutes a war of William against what he implies are vassal chiefs of Brittany.

939. William, allied with Hugh the Great against Louis IV, pillaged lands of Arnoul of Flanders and is for this excommunicated: *Flodoard*, 71.

ca. 940. According to William of Jumièges, William Longsword welcomes one Heroldus (Harold) with his men and sets them down in the Cotentin to hold the country: *Jumièges*, III, 9.

943. William Longsword assassinated by Balzan (Chamberlain of Arnoul of Flanders) and others, after peace and truce had been made: *Flodoard*, 86.

Revolt of Pagan Normans led by Turmod and Seitric. Hugh the Great and Louis IV, etc., suppress it. Louis retires, leaving Herluin, Count of Montreuil, in military command. He promptly makes war on Arnoul of Flanders and with Norman army defeats and captures Balzan: *Flodoard* 88–9.

944. Division of Normandy arranged: *Flodoard*, 95. But Louis IV after occupying his portion orders Hugh to retire from siege of Bayeux. Latter's troops devastate land in retiring: *Jumièges*, IV, 6.

Normans invade Brittany: *Flodoard*, 94, and 2 Borderie, *Histoire de Bretagne*, 413.

945. Hugh, Bernard (Norman noble) and Harold (independent Norman chief of Cherbourg) seek revenge against Louis—devastate lands of his men: *Jumièges*, IV, 7.

July 13, 945 (date from Lauer, *Louis IV d'Outremer*, 123) Harold

rough calculation of the various wars in which the Normans were embroiled during the first half-century of the duchy's existence. These were the conflicts of sufficient importance to be noted by the chroniclers. One cannot even guess at the number of cases of castle breach, murder, robbery and burnings all supposed to have been more or less usual occurrences in the tenth century.[7] In this age the feud had acquired a new flavor.[8] Owing to the regroupment of society into units whose prime purpose was military activity, the feud was no longer a guerrilla affair between opposing sibs, but rather a form of warfare between military bands.[9] Of course irresponsible individuals conduct in-

ambushes King Louis on way to hold interview with former, and wipes out the king's escort. The king flees to Rouen and there made prisoner by Normans resentful of his treatment of Normandy and Richard: *Flodoard*, 98.

946. Louis, Otto, etc. ravage Norman lands in war on Hugh after latter had freed the king in exchange for Laon and the king had invested Richard with the government of Normandy: *Flodoard*, 103.

961 ff. Coalition against Richard of Normandy consisting of Gerberg (widow of Louis IV), Thibault, Count of Chartres, the Count of Flanders etc., to win back land added to Normandy by Hugh the Great. Evreux besieged and taken, Rouen attacked, Chartres taken and burned. Fighting and pillaging goes on until 965: *Flodoard*, 153.

[7] Orderic Vitalis in his *Historia Ecclesiastica* is relating the events of a later and relatively orderly period, and yet the violent and gruesome episodes that illustrate baronial existence in Normandy are frequent. It is difficult to believe that life in the tenth century could have been much worse.

[8] This was long ago perceived by Wächter, *Beiträge zur Deutschen Geschichte—Das Faust und Fehderecht des Mittelalters* (1845), 39 *et seq.*; 253 *et seq. Cf.* also Huberti, *Studien zur Rechtsgeschichte der Gottesfrieden und Landfrieden* (1892), par. 2.

[9] We say this not so much because of any idea of the recession of family ties in the matter of feud making but because in various chronicles the sorts of feud described are conflicts that only two more or less disciplined bands could have carried on. They do not resemble the mad sporadic affairs related by Gregory of Tours. *Cf.* also the later definitions of requirements for military service in 1 Mayer *Deutsche und Französische Verfassungsgeschichte,* 124 (hereafter cited as *D.F.V.G.*). Declareuil, *H.D.F.*, 215, citing a commentary (thirteenth century) of Sinibald Fliscus on the Decretals takes the position that feud was open to all, rustics as well as gentlefolk. Such a rule was theoretically possible, but it seems im-

cessant forays against the vulnerable ecclesiastical establishments. But the tendency is for the activities that contemporary writers call war to be descriptive of contests between groups that are to be regarded as units in the feudal set-up. This initiative inevitably centered in these groups since the lord to whom a man had commended himself stood in *loco parentis* as far as revenging injuries was concerned.[10]

The charters of the late tenth and early eleventh centuries indicate that the older views regarding the relation of feud and procedure for emendation were not carried on and adapted to the changed character of the former in regions with which we are concerned. The later *coutumes* which concede the right of feud and attempt to apply certain regulations upon its employment likewise disclose that emendation is no longer considered a substitute or a means of ending feud.[11] Not even in the earliest

probable in view of the degree of economic control exercised over the masses that they would have been free to go on feud in their own interest; *cf.* Guilhiermoz, *Essai sur l'origine de la noblesse* (1902), 351, "Seuls aussi les gentilshommes possédaient le droit de 'faide' ou guerre privée."

[10] The rule laid down by Beaumanoir regarding the responsibility of the *capitanus* is clearly a relic of an earlier time. Beaumanoir, *Coutumes de Beauvoisis* (Beugnot Ed. 1842), XXX, 58; XXXIV, 42, 43. *Cf.* Marnier, *Le conseil de Pierre de Fontaines* (1846), XV, 83.

[11] This is evident from the language of Beaumanoir in XXXIV, 42 and 43. No conclusions *contra* can be drawn from the use of the word "amend." Fontaines, in the passage cited above states: "Et par nostre usage, se chevaliers fet force en autrui terre, et meine escuiers et autres gens avecques lui, il seus qui les mena *amende* la force fait: . . ." We propose to demonstrate in the text that *amende* means something different than it did under the Frankish Kings, that it is a payment to the courtholder. For the moment on the thirteenth-century word usage, *cf. Ms. Corone Pledee* (Univ. Camb. Lib.), 21. If an inquest finds an appellee guilty at the king's suit he remains in jail "ieckes a tant ke il eit fet pleinement les amendes vers le pleintif e ensement vers le roy pur le trespas." Since at this time there is no question of composition in England the word *amendes* may be taken to mean satisfaction.

Compare with Beaumanoir the passage from the *Etablissements de St. Louis* (Viollet Ed., 1881), lib. I, 31, 52, and the *Coutume de Touraine-Anjou* (3 Viollet, *op. cit.*), 21, 42. Any judgment regarding the significance of these *coutume* passages must take account of: 1) the effect of *treugae Dei* which were specifically directed at the incidents of feud bearing is there evidence of the existence of a procedure of amends as a solution. The feud of post-Frankish days had become a thing *sui generis*. It resembled war as we are today acquainted with it because in many cases the participants were endowed with the prerogatives now associated with statehood, and for a long time unbridled by a supervening public authority. This character of war it was which largely induced the severance of feud from the alternative of a proceeding for amends. Whether in consequence or in addition, one of the characteristics of feud in tenth- and eleventh-century Europe was that it had the quality of what St. Paul would denominate a calling. This we may attribute to tradition and training as well as to the terrible propinquity of provincial life. Men who have continuously fought an outland enemy for over half a century will not prefer the tedium of essoins to the excitement of blows if they become embroiled with their neighbors. At the same time feud has the terrible power of engendering more feud. The encomium of the motive of revenge in *Raoul de Cambrai,* and in the *Chanson de Roland,* the implicit emphasis upon the idea that only by more blood can shed blood be appeased,[12] furnishes dramatic

earlier peace of God legislation; 2) the development of the doctrine regarding feudal war ensuing upon a proper *diffidatio.* On the latter point see the note in Adams, *Origin of the English Constitution* (1912), 181, n. 30. Clearly the *coutumes* are regulating a different kind of *guerre* than the wholesale warfare of the tenth and eleventh centuries. *Cf.* also 1 Viollet, *op. cit.,* 180, and the text of Louis IX's ordinance regarding feud (1245) in 1 *Ordonnances des rois,* 56.

[12] In the Latin poem *Waltharius,* Grimm and Schmeller, *Lateinische Gedichte des X und XI J.H.* (1838) the motive of bloodfeud is apparent, ll. 691, 926, 951-4. The rapacity of the period is illustrated by the cold-blooded pursuit of the fleeing hero by Gunthari for the treasure he carries; the robbing of the dead of weapons and horses. The candor with which all these details are mentioned and the absence of all moral horror indicates how usual this sort of thing is. The same is true of the first part of *Raoul de Cambrai* (Meyer and Longnon Eds., 1882). The later epics, *Gudrun* and the *Nibelungenlied,* reflect a higher ethical standard in respect of many details of conduct although the basic motive of revenge is still all-powerful.

proof of how ceaseless preoccupation with arms would make composition or ransom the counsel of cowardice.[13]

In both the thirteenth-century Norman compilations, the *Très ancien coutumier* and the *Summa de Legibus*,[14] emendation has in consequence disappeared or receded to a place of minor importance. To be sure the great wave of Angevin reform had swept over Normandy even before the older custumal had been compiled.[15] But there is late eleventh-century evidence to the ef-

[13] While the prevalence of feud contributed to a decay of composition procedure, one may question whether or not the henchman's bloody head was normally a sufficient provocation to send his lord on the warpath. In other words the cleavage between law for the high and law for the low must undoubtedly have existed in the tenth century, even if the subsequent artificial limitations of feud to "gentlemen" expressed in some French *coutumes* had not yet been fixed. Certainly the feud of this era was not something that Jack the Miller could count on setting in motion. If two magnates attack one another, the affair is graced by a few primitive formalities. But when the Norman peasants rebel the occasion is one for contemptuous brutality. *Cf.* William of Jumièges, *Gesta Normannorum Ducum*, V, 2, where Raoul d'Ivry meets the peasants' delegates and cuts off their hands and feet.

[14] The edition of the *Très ancien coutumier* (hereafter cited *T.A.C.*) is that edited by Tardif (1881) in the publications of the *Société de l'histoire de Normandie*. On the date of compilation *cf.* Viollet, *Les coutumiers de Normandie* in 33 *Histoire littéraire de la France* 41. He dates part 1, 1203–4; part 2, 1214–23. The *Summa de Legibus Normannie* (hereafter cited *S.L.N.*) is in the same series as the *T.A.C.* and also edited by Tardif (1896).

[15] The *T.A.C.* treats the liability of a wrongdoer from the angle of penalty rather than composition or restitution. This is clearly demonstrated by the chattel forfeiture and disherison provisions. An examination of the whole custumal fails to reveal any trace of composition payment or procedure. Certainly nothing is to be deduced from the words *emendare*. Thus in c. 2 which preserves the magnates and the duke's entourage from excommunication without the consent of the duke or his justices, it is provided that if any of those persons does something against the church, they are to make amends via the justices or duke. The duke is keeping court for the church. Elsewhere the church acts directly. "Misericordia excommunicati, et emendatio est versus episcopum: catalla, que habet usque ad novem libras preter victum suum et domus sue." The details of this will be discussed in the next chapter. *Cf.* also cc. 14; 16, 3; 31; 41; 55. The chapter 56 [D'Amandes] shows conclusively that the emendation is to the court and is based on a partial or total chattel forfeiture.

The notion of damages in "civil" actions is so well established by the

fect that emendation on a fixed scale of tariffs had been largely
shouldered out of the picture by a new principle of discretionary

13th century that one cannot use the *S.L.N.* for proving what the pecuniary liability of defendants was in the tenth or eleventh century. *Emendare* in this compilation most frequently means a payment to the court like
the English procedural amercements—*cf.* cc. 37, 2; 38, 7; 39, 5; 53, 2, 3;
75, 3; 124, 8.

On the other hand c. 85, 9 provides: "Si vero querelatus de lege quam
vadiavit inciderit, debet maleficium tam leso quam curie emendare: de
percussione palme per v. solidos, de pugni percussione per xij denarios, de
prostratione ad terram, quod cadabulum dicitur, per xviij solidos, de plaga
autem facta cum effusione sanguine per xxxvj solidos. Et he emende inter
simplices personas attenduntur in simplicibus querelis personalibus." This
it will be noted deals with small assaults (except bloodshed) committed
among small people. The next section deals with the punishment of assaults by persons of quality and the penalties are essentially merely dis-
honoring: "De personis autem autenticis, videlicet que tenent francas
serjanterias vel per armorum servicia feoda sua deserviunt, aliter attenden-
dum est de emendis: in querelis hujusmodi debent emende fieri per arma
et hernesia per que feoda sua deserviunt. Si enim fuerit contra militem in
hujusmodi querela convictus, ei debet emendare per plena arma, videlicet
per equum, loricam, scutum, ensem et galeam. Si vero miles non fuerit nec
habens feodum lorice passus injuriam, sed per plena arma feodum suum
deserviat, per roncinum videlicet et gambesum, capellum et lanceam, per
ista debet ei satisfieri de emenda. Et omnino de hujusmodi personis scien-
dum est, que feodum suum per armorum servicia deserviunt, quod eis
emenda in hujusmodi querelis debet exhiberi per arma quibus ad retro-
bannium ducis debent servire vel ad quitationem feodorum." In §11 the
"amends" of the courtholder are limited to 18 s.—a provision that by implication excludes any but the duke/king from the plea of *effusio sanguinis.* §11 goes on: ". . . Solet eciam antiquitus in Normannia usitari
quod major non esset emenda curiam tenentis quam persone injuriam sus-
tinentis."

On its face c. 85 is apparently evidence of the continuation of tariffed
emendation for small causes in the lower brackets of society. Nevertheless
since the *T.A.C.* is completely silent on this form of sanction for wrongdoing one may perhaps regard this as an innovation after the acquisition
of Normandy by the French crown. There is evidence of the survival in
other parts of France of fixed payments for petty assaults or batteries. *Cf.*
*Li livres de jostice et de plet,* (*C.D.I.,* Rapetti Ed. 1850) 279; 2 *Etablissements de St. Louis,* II, c. 24 where 60 sol. go to the court and 15 to the victim plus damages. Viollet in 1 *ibid.,* 246, suggests that this is a continuation of the rule laid down in the *Cap. Leg. Rib.* (808) c. 1 (1 *Cap.* 117).
As to the practice in Burgundy, Valat, *Poursuite privée et composition
pécuniaire dans l'ancienne Bourgogne* (1907), 94 *et seq.*

The section from the *S.L.N.* is discussed by Le Foyer, *Exposé du droit*

mulcts.[16] We shall presently have more to say about this discretionary power. Passing by for a moment the new sanctions that had been devised to cope with the feud (now dissociated from law enforcement), we come upon the fact of paramount significance—that the tariffed composition procedure had been almost if not entirely engulfed in the maelstrom of a warriors' society.[17]

There were other causes besides the running affrays of this period to explain why the emendation of the folklaws disappears even as to the peaceful fellow who is willing to salve his maims with shillings; why a Norman who commits certain wrongs in the latter eleventh century is in mercy of the duke for goods and

*pénal normand* (1931), 199. Le Foyer regards the provisions as a continuation of the ancient system of composition. At p. 247 Le Foyer suggests that the principle that the court is not to get more than the victim is an improvement upon the arbitrary amercement. If he is correct, it would follow that this is not really "antiquitus in Normannia usitari." *Cf.* 2 Pollock and Maitland, *H.E.L.* 459 who see the "preappointed bót in Normandy when we can no longer find it in England." Further on the use of an "amende" to the victim see the curious provision in the *Etablissements de Rouen* (Giry Ed. 1883) c. 15 where a person insulting a man pilloried pays 15 sol. to the town and 5 to the injured party *or* is himself pilloried.

[16] This new principle is clearly present in the Norman Inquest of 1091 (text in Haskins, *Norman Institutions,* 281). Only in respect to chance medley does the inquest use words that suggest a "bót" might have been contemplated. "§3. Et si in exercitu vel in curia vel in via curie vel exercitus mislata evenit que pro precedente ira facta non fuerit, et in ea volneratus vel occisus fuerit aliquis, ille cuius culpa hoc factum est secundum mensuram forisfacti emendavit."

Haskins cautiously says it is not clear that the "secundum mensuram forisfacti emendavit" does not imply the preappointed bot. However, for a nearly contemporary use of this expression where bot is intended *cf. Charta Henrici Coronati* §7 (Liebermann, *Gesetze,* 522).

[17] On the "amende" in thirteenth century Norman law *cf.* Le Foyer, *op. cit.,* 245 *et seq.* ". . . Evidemment cette double amende est à peu de chose près le *fredum* et le *vergeld* germaniques, le *wite* et le *bót* anglo-saxons; mais cependant on peut penser qu'entre le *fredum* et le *wergeld* d'une part, l'amende à justice et celle à partie d'autre part la filiation n'est point absolument rigoureuse, bien que le résultat pratique de l'institution, barbare ou féodale, fut à peu près identique. C'est qu'en effet, le Droit germanique allant s'estompant, à la théorie du *fredum* et du *bannus* du Droit barbare s'était substituée la théorie de l'*amerciamentum* du Droit féodal." The detailed critique of the confused ideas contained in this statement will be found in the text.

body instead of going quit upon paying composition, *fredus,* and perhaps a ban penalty as the Salic Franks before him had done. To account for this change there must have been powerful forces at work. The traditions of centuries are not easily overcome.

It is obvious that among the various Germanic tribes the reckoning of a man's wergeld was based upon certain tacit assumptions as to the normal economic situation of a particular locality or of a group of kinsmen.[18] Under the Merovingians the first breach in the feud-composition system is struck because there are persons without substance with whom this system cannot cope and for whom the state makes special provision and sets up a special procedure.[19] It is probable that the complete decline of the

[18] Brunner in 1 *D.R.G.,* 333, suggests that the differences in wergeld scale of various nationalities were primarily due to considerations of status. He does not offer any reason why the Visigothic wergeld should be set at 300 sol., whereas the Frankish was 200. On the other hand at p. 286 he emphasizes the fact that there is within a status a relation between land holding and the amount of wergeld. No attempt seems ever to have been made to treat the whole problem of wergeld tariffs from the angle of chattel values in various regions. That such a relation existed may be deduced from the fact that payments were normally in terms of cattle, although there are instances of payment with land, *ibid.,* 287. The effect of price movements in relation to the tariffs of the folk laws is interesting. *Cf.* the instance given by Inama-Sternegg 1 *Deutsche Wirtschaftsgeschichte,* 468, of the difference between the horse value 6–12 sol. of the *Lex Alam.,* and the later St. Gall scale 12–20 sol. The tariff remains fixed although the object used to liquidate amends may change in value. The relation of the composition tariffs to the monetary unit has evoked a large literature, *cf.* 2 Brunner *D.R.G.,* 794 *et seq.,* 1 *ibid.,* 322; 2 Dopsch, *Wirtschaftsentwickelung,* 277 *et seq.* The latter attacks Brunner's theory that the "introduction" of a silver solidus resulted in a reduction of the tariff commensurate with the relation of the gold and silver solidus. The problem of a possible inflation and the effect on prices naturally is exceedingly important for the maintenance of the tariffed amends. The man who could pay money would be better off than the man who paid cattle. Dopsch's idea that under the Carolingians there was more precious metal current than is usually admitted (*ibid.,* 308) while useful in considering price variations does not help in deciding the concrete form of the payment by the common man at that time, i.e., whether or not livestock was still the medium. That this presents a problem is readily seen when one considers how little cash the average small farmer even of today ever handles.

[19] *Supra,* Chapter II.

system in the tenth and eleventh centuries was the result of a similar situation, now on a scale of vast proportions, for men in general become at this period literally unable to pay amends according to law, let alone the redemption of afflictive penalties or the king's ban. Consequently some readjustment was inevitable.

It is impossible to follow the details of the Norman invasions, particularly in the north of France, without realizing that the destruction of movable values must have been tremendous.[20] In view of the recurrent nature of the raids especially in the Seine and Loire regions and the later episodes of winter encampments, there can be no doubt that the consumption of farm animals in particular must have been pretty complete. As early as 864, a capitulary[21] speaks of the practice of selling off all land except dwelling places, a practice probably induced as much by the lack of animals for cultivation as by the necessity of raising funds for the tribute paid to the Normans. It is the lack of teams to plow and of cows to milk which explains the failure to repopulate devastated regions, and why the colonization and clearing of lands is not well begun until the middle of the eleventh century.[22] There is moreover an obvious connection between this destruction of livestock and the food shortage in the latter tenth and early eleventh centuries noted in Glaber's chronicle. From

[20] From the angle of the individual the fate of his chattels was by destruction or removal through the Norman raiders, or by transfer for the purpose of tribute; Joransen, *The Danegeld in France* (1923), *passim;* Lot, *Les tributs aux Normands,* 85 *B.E.C.* 58 *et seq.* In either event, the result to him was the same. Since the Norman raids were for a period recurrent there was undoubtedly a considerable *exportation of values.* Joransen, *op. cit.,* c. 18 discusses the Danegeld chiefly in relation to its effect on currency, and its effect in the development of feudal dues. In the years of invasion prior to the establishment of the great encampments of Normans, we are dealing more with a problem of consumption and removal than of mere redistribution of wealth. Thompson, *The Commerce of France in the Ninth Century* (23 *Jour. of Political Econ.,* 857) emphasizes the stimulating influence of tribute on local trade for he believes the Normans spent in France much of what they took. *Cf.* Joransen, *op. cit.,* 212.

[21] *Edict. Pist.* (864) c. 30 (2 *Cap.* 323).

[22] Bloch, *Les caractères originaux de l'histoire rurale française* (1931), 5.

the year 970 to the year 1040 there were in all forty-eight years of famine.[23] Certainly if there were animals left to kill for the satisfaction of hunger pangs, such a steady recurrence of famine would have been remarkable. In our own country the long and tedious recuperation of the South after the four-year Civil War has been laid by one scholar to the lack of draught animals, victims of the struggling armies.[24] The Norman incursions dragged on for over three-quarters of a century, and the destruction was relatively greater both because of the duration of the invasions and because of the more ferocious character of the combat.

Whatever local exceptions there may have been to this general

[23] *Dareste de la Chavannes, Condition matérielle des populations agricoles en France* (37 *Journal des Economistes* 202, 207), *"famines ou epidémies,"* citing no authority. He states that in the tenth century there were ten great famines, and in the eleventh, twenty-six. *Cf.* for detailed references Lamprecht, *Beiträge zur Geschichte des französischen Wirtschaftslebens im 11ten Jahrhundert,* 1 *Staats und Socialwissenschaftliche Forschungen* no. 3 (1878), 118. Lamprecht enters a caveat against assuming these famines were all general in scope. See also 2 Sackur, *Die Cluniacenser,* 272, for other references regarding the eleventh century. Sackur states that famine was worst in "northwest Gaul," Lorraine and Germany.

[24] Sellers, *Economic Incidence of the Civil War in the South,* 14 *Miss. Valley Hist. Rev.,* 179. The individual testimony like that of Lee in January, 1865, to the effect that there was nothing within reach of the army to be impressed is more convincing even than the statistics which Sellers himself states are not satisfactory both because they were fragmentary and because of the fluctuations in the standard of value. On the basis of "corrected" computation the wealth of the South in 1860 exceeded that of 1870 by $1,231,500,000. A great deal of this decline was due to the depreciation of land value. As to livestock, figures of 1866 show a shortage over 1860 as follows: 32 per cent in horses, 30 per cent in mules, 35 per cent in cattle, 20 per cent in sheep and 42 per cent in swine. In 1870 it was estimated for South Carolina on the basis of 1860 supply, a 70 per cent increase in horses, 76 per cent in cattle and 145 per cent in swine would be needed to restore the livestock. In 1860 this state had 23 cows per 100 population. In 1870 only 13. The figures for three other states are similar. Not until 1900 did the figures for livestock ratio approximate those of 1860.

In considering the comparability of the situations in tenth-century France and nineteenth-century America, it must be kept in mind that adjacent to the prostrate South was a congeries of states whose wealth had increased 50 per cent during the war and mounted rapidly thereafter. There was no such stimulus in the case of the regions devastated by the Normans.

economic distress, it is clear that a system of law which looked to settlement by fixed payments in some tangible value could not be maintained as to the general run of human beings. One without chattels, even if he does not lurk in the woods, could not pay the 30 shillings that the *Lex Salica* demanded for laying open a man's head, let alone the 200 for homicide. These sums could not be satisfied out of land which was only exceptionally alienable. The ancient practice of settling through the medium of horses and cattle was continued throughout the Carolingian period as the only practical means open to the ordinary person.[25] In the *Lex Salica* a horse was valued at 12 shillings.[26] In the eleventh century, the average price of a horse in northwest France was 140 shillings.[27] The figures of other chattel values correspond. A wound, perhaps, could be amended, but for serious offenses the wrongdoer has generally not enough to satisfy his creditor in accordance with the legal tariff.

The effect of the wholesale decimation of movable values upon the enforcement of the law along traditional lines must have been profound. Since the initiation of action against wrongdoers had normally rested with the injured individual or his kin, when the expectation of tangible reparation disappeared the zest for prosecution inevitably wilted. No one will trouble to implead a man who is likely to be judgment-proof. And where there are no amends for the plaintiff, there will be no *fredus* for

[25] I Brunner, *D.R.G.*, 314. On the persistence of payments in kind, the whole system of "feudal" dues and exactions is of course the best evidence. On this practice under Charlemagne, *Cap. Bonon.* (811) c. 2 (1 *Cap.*, 166), ordering the army ban to be paid not in lands or villas but in money or chattels. In relation to wrongs a very striking example of the persistence of payment by animals is the charter of Louis VII of 1141 in 1 Teulet, *Layettes du trésor des chartes* (1863), no. 74, confirming certain local usages regarding amends for wrongs in terms of chickens and geese. This charter is interesting not only on the point cited but because it suggests how relative poverty of the individual forced payment in terms of small animals rather than cattle.

[26] I Inama-Sternegg, *op. cit.*, App. IV, 512, for a table of folklaw values.

[27] Lamprecht, *op. cit.*, App. A. 144, 150. The average has been given for the horse in the northwest. In the east the price ranged from 40–200 sol.

the court: at least, no *fredus* exacted in accordance with the law. It is at this point that the immunist, or courtholder, if the wrong-doer has ever so little, will inevitably parley with the tempter. The first signs of surrender are perceptible in the latter half of Charles the Bald's troubled reign, and aberrations then grow apace. Apart from the relaxation of control over officials result-ing from political trouble, the trend of procedure had been con-stantly in the direction of enhancing the power of the courts. The right of free compromise by the parties had been restricted, and the participation of the judge as a party in the *securitas* had tended to give courts a vested interest in the fiscal stake of wrongs and their settlement. Moreover, the ban procedure and its extension had given the courts a sphere of activity where plaintiffs were superfluous. It is not surprising that we have bit-ter complaints against the venality of the judicial system[28] and that some officials even seem to indulge in the unlawful practice of collecting the *fredus* without reference to the injured party.[29]

In the tenth century and after when the authority of the crown had been substantially destroyed so that the ends of justice were determined by hundreds of individual sovereigns, control over local jurisdiction and check upon the rapacity of the court-holder disappeared almost entirely. Men are held to ransom for no reason except for extortion.[30] If a man gives pledges of ap-pearance in court, his property is pillaged as if he were jailed.[31]

---

[28] Hincmar, Letter to Louis (877) c. viii (125 *Patrologia,* 987). Com-pare the *Oratio ad Regem* at the Council held at Fîmes (881) 9 *H.F.* 307.

[29] This is the ingenious suggestion of Mayer in 1 *D.F.V.G.* 193. It is to be noted, however, that Mayer seems to have overlooked the significant effect of the transference of ban power. The frequency of grants of *bannus* in the later charters convinces us that *bannus* was the device whereby the courtkeeper's power was enhanced in northern France rather than by the juggling with wergeld figures.

[30] *Cf.* the text of the *treuga Dei* of Puy-en-Velay (Le Puy) of 993, c. 4, 2 *Gallia Christiana, Inst.* 225 and *cf.* the peace of Warin of Beauvais (1023) in Pfister, *Etudes sur le règne de Robert le Pieux* (1885), LX, no. XII.

[31] Marchegay and Mabille, *Chronique des églises d'Anjou* (1869), 70–71, a document of 1068–78.

Where no certain accuser appears the courtkeeper will assume the role.[32] If a man desires to purge himself the court will illegally challenge his oath.[33] It is wiser, if one is strong enough, to settle with the sword, or by concords on which no judge will put his sign manual and *ipso facto* take his profit. Bargain, the active principle of ransom, succeeds the fixed financial expectation of wrongdoers, if the offender is worth bargaining with, while complete forfeiture awaits the wretch who has little or nothing.

But not all that went on in these times can be laid at the doors of violent men acting without color of law. To a great extent the mutations in local rules, the shifting of the general premises of law enforcement, were induced by outright ordinance and by the bending of what had once been unmalleable rules. In these developments which begin with some foundation of right we can observe the deadly pressure of social change upon the outmoded structure of rights and remedies.

From the nature of the documents that have survived it is clear that one must seek the foundation of right in the incidents of Frankish fiscal privilege. These privileges, in so far as they were connected with profits of litigation, we do not need to recapitulate in detail.[34] It is sufficient if we concentrate upon those that possessed sufficient tensile strength to resist the disruptive effects of war and anarchy.

We have spoken of the *fredus,* the court's share in the amount finally paid over as amends in a judicial proceeding directed to that end.[35] This perquisite had been granted away with lavish hands giving the courtholder in many an immunity the opportunity to use it as a theme on which to compose procedural variations. Adjunct to the *fredus* were the rights in respect of ransoming afflictive penalties, since the price of redemption is be-

---

[32] *Ibid.,* by challenging to battle, the courtkeeper takes the role of accuser.

[33] *Ibid.,* 73 (1080–87). By failing to use the oath of a witness.

[34] *Supra,* Chapters II and III.

[35] Brunner 2 *D.R.G.,* 807 surmises that the *fredus* in the "Frankish" period has the character of a penalty for law-breach.

lieved to have been adjusted in terms of wergeld.[36] Here the powers of the fisc are wider even than in Frankish times. They are no longer of necessity controlled by the claims of complainants. There is implicit a discretion, and that discretion rests in the court. Clearly the device of ransom is something that is going to thrive in a feudal society. And thrive it does to the point of exciting extra-legal use of extortion, and of calling into being special aids by contract in anticipation of such an event.

But aside from these privileges that are so closely associated with the system of composition the Frankish fisc possessed a perquisite more powerful and more dynamic. It is a collocation of devices so nicely attuned to the brutality of the times that one is disposed to find here the source of most of the legal development. This was the king's ban—a term that comprehended at once the power to order, the right to a penalty, and the most drastic of all the Frankish procedural weapons.

### FEUDAL GOVERNMENT AND THE KING'S BAN

The place of the king's ban in the system of law enforcement is most easily traced through its penal aspect. In Charlemagne's time the ban is restricted to eight cases. As to these, the ban penalty is a fiscal prerogative superior to the claims of an injured individual in the sense that the crown has priority, a preferred claim to the assets of the culprit. The penalty exacted runs to the sum of 60 sol. In those ban cases where the wronged individuals recovered amends the crown would have the double stake of *fredus* plus *bannus*. In some cases there can be shown a tendency for the *bannus* to absorb and include the *fredus,* particularly where the latter was less than 60 sol.[37]—in other words the fisc

---

[36] 2 Brunner, *D.R.G.,* 798–9 who believes that the redemption turns eventually into a true composition. This conclusion rests upon certain examples suggested by Schreuer, *Verbrechenskonkurrenz,* 178 *et seq.* See also *ibid.,* 133.

[37] Schreuer, *op. cit.,* 103, 121. In this connection it is well to remember that as the ban power passed into the hands of immunists and nearly independent counts, any royal policy of forbearance, or taking one payment

takes but one payment but takes it by the ban procedure. There are other cases where it is clear that the two payments were kept distinct, and this would be the rule where an immunist could by his charter collect *fredus* alone and the crown had the ban.

The union of *bannus* with certain named wrongs, like homicide, arson or robbery, a not unusual formula of the latter tenth and early eleventh centuries, goes back to the legislation of Charles the Bald. In 857,[38] the ancient eight ban cases were extended to include among other things robbery, housebreaking and wanton killing. If there had been any sharp line dividing the ordinary causes from the objects of special royal protection it no longer existed. The inclusion of bloodshed, theft and other matters as *bannus* in tenth-century documents constantly widened the ban cases.[39]

There can be no doubt, that as the new subject matter was covered by the *bannus* the 60-solidi penalty was carried into the new fields. It is difficult to mark out precisely the limits of this penalty, since its history is various. Under the Franks, in the case

for both *fredus* and ban, was not necessarily followed. This forbearance may be the result of the fact that the composition system had probably led to the ruin of individuals on a large scale: 1 Inama-Sternegg, *op. cit.,* 246. *Cf.* also the conjectures of Ganahl, *Hufe und Wergeld,* 53 Z.R.G.², 227. The large amount of legislation regarding enslavement for amends indicates that this practice was pretty usual: 4 Waitz, *D.V.G.,* 520, for a collection of the texts. Where a man was so poor that enslavement was inevitable it was not entirely academic whether one or both payments were exacted by the state, as the period of servitude was determined by the amount of the debt. These various capitularies necessarily raise some question whether or not the sib was liable for the ban penalty. Apparently this was regarded as an individual debt, because it was essentially a penalty.

[38] *Allocutio Missi Cuiusdam Divionensis* (857) 2 *Cap.* 292,—"De his vero, qui intra patriam residentes rapinas exercent, domos infringunt, homines sine causa occidunt, trustes commovent aut alios dampnant et opprimant, prata defensoria depascunt, fruges aliorum devastant, ex his mandat senior noster: 'ut primum episcopali auctoritate iudicentur et sic postea a comitibus legaliter constringantur et insuper bannum nostrum, id est solidos LX, componant.' "

The earlier extension of the ban in the *Cap. de partibus Sax.* one may look on as an extraordinary measure and not general to the kingdom.

[39] *Supra,* Chapter III, p. 183.

of failure to perform military duty this sum at one time seems to have marked a maximum limit below which a court could act discretely.[40] But in the year 811 a capitulary[41] required the full sum to be paid by offenders who failed to do military service. It is not possible to state whether this policy governing the levy of army ban applied to the ban for non-military cases. The list of these ban offenses was for a long time relatively restricted and there was in regard to these causes more reason for the use of discretion.[42] In certain localities after the break-up of the Frankish kingdom the 60 solidi marks a maximum sum that can be exacted;[43] and one Burgundian document of the early twelfth cen-

---

[40] Ganahl, *op. cit.,* 53 *Z.R.G.²*, 228, n. 1. *Cf.* also *Cap. Miss. Gen.* (802) c. 29 (1 *Cap.,* 96), regarding relief of the very poor from payment.

[41] *Cap. Bonon.* (811) c. 9 (1 *Cap.,* 166).

[42] This was expressly provided by Charles the Bald in the case of the army ban: *cf. Edict. Pist.* (864) c. 27 (2 *Cap.,* 322). On the whole matter Baldamus, *Heerwesen unter den späteren Karolingern* (*Untersuchungen* no. 4) 36.

[43] For example, the *Consuetudines* of La Réole (2 Giraud, *Histoire du droit français,* 510) in 977 has a mulct of 66 sol. for bloodshed (c. 43), and for *raptus* (c. 51). The same penalty exists for violation of the salt ban. Similarly the flat 60 sol. is basic for various offenses in the *Consuetudines* of Chapelaude (Tardif, *Mon. Historiques* no. 290) ban breach, sedition, theft. *Cf.* also no. 291. The *Brevem de Exemptis* in *Cart. Beaulieu,* no. 101 (end of 11th century) fixes the *emendatio* of the *vicarius* who transgresses the *constitutio* at 60 sol. The rules are in other words themselves a ban. In the charter of Guy and Ives for Amiens (1091–5) the maximum *emendatio* is £3: i.e. 60 s.; Thierry, *Rec. doc. inéd. de l'hist. du tiers état,* 22. In Valat, *Poursuite privée et composition pécuniaire dans l'ancienne Bourgogne,* 93 *et seq.* are discussed various Burgundian charters where the ban penalties are usual. *Cf.* also Delattre, *Recherches sur le droit pénal à Cambrai* (1929) charters cited (carrying arms) 110, (bloodshed) 114, (housebreaking) 120, all of which are of relatively late date.

The prevalence of the 60 sol. penalty in the towns was ferreted out by Prou, *Les coutumes de Lorris,* in 8 *N.R.H.* 196 *et seq.,* and its connection with the old king's ban perceived, but he did not appreciate the full implications. Prou cites various royal charters of the 12th and 13th centuries showing a definite policy on the part of the crown to reduce the amount of the mulct.

It is difficult to extract much information from the notifications in the cartularies. A great many of the disputes there recorded are concerned with land, and violent acts are incidental. Wherever a charter had set a

tury speaks of "full justice, by which we mean LX solidi."[44] In other places, it marks a lower limit of justice, a sort of classificatory device, above which are the greater offenses.[45] But this is of a time when economic conditions are improving and distinctions

fixed penalty on violations of a grant, this factor has to be taken into account, for example, *Cart. Marmoutier pour le Dunois,* no. 93 (1111–12) where a £60 penalty is inflicted. Furthermore, the most detailed documents are pacifications which are the result of much bartering. In many instances the delict is wiped out by the individual disseisor's release of all claims to the land, and a sort of *douceur* is handed over by the abbey claiming seisin. In a startling number of cases this sum runs to 60 sol. but the fact may be purely fortuitous.

Some documents have been found in *Cart. Ste. Marie Char.* (3 *Arch. Anj.*) no. 182 (1108), *forisfactis* when amends did not exceed 60 s.; no. 183 (1150). In no. 94 (1085) the right of pardoning 30 s. *de magnis forfactis* suggests computation on a 60 sol. basis. In no. 101 (1115) is a penalty for dodging military service of 15 sol.—the amount of the count's ban. *Cf. Cart. St. Vincent du Mans,* no. 130, but see no. 307 (1080–1100) where 100 s. is exacted for a death. *Cart. Marmoutier pour le Dunois,* no. 53 (1083) has 62 sol. pledge for a forest offense and is one of the cases that hover between damages and forfeit. In the charter to Bec of 1134 (Round, *Calendar,* no. 375) 60 sol. is set as amend for "deliberate assault." Note the scaling down of amends for strikings by monks. In *Cart. Marmoutier pour le Vendômois,* no 32; an amend for theft is 60 sol. (1066–75). In all cases here amend = a payment to the courtkeeper.

The later compilations of local laws offer persuasive proof of the once important role of the 60 sol. penalty. *Cf.* the lists in Prou, *op. cit.,* 198 *et seq.* comprising Beauvaisis, Berry, Champagne, Burgundy, Orleans. *Cf.* also the cases cited in 1 Meyer, *D.F.V.G.,* 141–2. Add also Touraine-Anjou, 2 Viollet, *Établissements de St. Louis,* I, 148, 149, 151, etc.; 1 Beautemps-Beaupré, *Coutumes de l'Anjou et du Maine* (1877), pt. 4 (429) c. 96, 102, 103, 109, etc.; Planiol, *La très ancienne coutume de Bretagne* (1896), 118, 120, 181. It is important to note that in these late compilations we are dealing only with vestiges of a development.

[44] Pérard, *Recueil de plusieurs pièces curieuses servant à l'histoire de Bourgogne* (1664), 210 Charter of Hugh of Burgundy: "In burgo etiam qui claustrum dicitur, concessi ut si latrocinium factum fuisset et clamor ad monachos et ministrales eorum devenerit, ipsi iusticiam planam facerent, quod intelligimus LX sol." (1106).

[45] 1 Morel, *Cartulaire de l'Abbaye de St. Corneille de Compiègne* (1904), no. 125 (1172), a settlement of the respective rights of *avoué* and abbey: "Advocatus non potest hominem potestatis predictarum villarum pro ullo forefacto interficere aut aliquod membrum auferre vel ad duellum ducere nec forefactum illius plus quam ad sexaginta solidos potest ascendere."

in terms of money can again be drawn.[46] Almost invariably when French documents of the eleventh century describe jurisdiction in money terms one is confronted with the ubiquitous 60 sol. It is remarkable that this sum out of all the mulcts in the elaborate tariffs of the ninth century should have been maintained. It was no mean amount in a poverty-stricken society, so we cannot believe it was invariably exacted. Essentially it is a symbol of extensive blood justice.[47]

[46] In certain cases sixty sol. is the basic sum with two and a half, five or seven shillings added. In 1 Mayer, *D.F.V.G.*, 140 *et seq.*, is discussed the nature of the combinations. Mayer is very positive that only two mulcts are owed to public authority. This is a conclusion based on the later *coutumes*. Actually, in the rare cases where a sum due (not horses, cows or lands) is stipulated in a concord it probably is a cumulated amount including the mulcts intermediate in a proceeding. There is no doubt that such intermediate mulcts existed: 1 *Cart. St. Aubin* in 226 (1055–93) "Et pro tali forsfacto wadiaverunt duo villani Sancti Albini, unus nomine Otgerius, quindecim solidos, inter districtum et emendationem . . ." *Cf.* also on the law gage, 1 Viollet, *Établissements de St. Louis*, 245; *Constitutio of St. Vaast* (1020); 1 Marténe, *Amplissima Collectio*, col. 381.

[47] Sixty shillings is the usual mulct for the recreancy involved losing in a trial by battle. The data is collected by Coulin, *Der Gerichtliche Zweikampf im altfranzösischen Prozess*, §52. This penalty is stipulated in the *Summa de Legibus* (60 sol. 1 den.) c. 124, 14. It is carried by the Normans to England, William's *Lad* (1067–77) 2, 2: "Si Francigena victus fuerit persolvat regi LX sol." (Quad.) Liebermann, *Gesetze* 484; *cf.* the variant "si quis victus fuerit" in William's *Articuli* 6, 2, *ibid.* 487. See further *Leges Hen.*, 59, 15, where the rule applies to anyone.
   There are entries in the earliest Norman Exchequer rolls showing the 60 sol. penalty for recreancy: for example, 1 Stapleton, *Rot. Scacc. Norm.* 30, 41, 43.
   That this penalty for *recreantisa* is a descendant of the old ban penalty has been assumed by Mayer, 1 *D.F.V.G.*, 157, citing Beaumanoir. Brunner, *Entstehung der Schwurgerichte*, 180, simply points to the Frankish origin. This latter statement is ambiguous since the sum might represent variations on the older redemption of a hand (i.e., for perjury). *Cf.* 2 Brunner, *D.R.G.*, 805 n. 54. However, note the fact that the Carolingian kings in some cases demanded abscission of the hand plus ban penalty. *Cap. Theod.* II (805) c. 5 (1 *Cap.*, 123). *Cf.* also Sohm, *F.R.G.V.*, 109 on the tendency of the ban to absorb penalties of similar amounts.
   In a cartulary of Poitou this payment is referred to "ex hoc habuit abbas totum bannum suum sc. LX sol." Boutelière, *Cartulaire de l'Abbaye de Talmond* in *Mémoires de la Société de l'Ouest* (1872) no. 161 (1100). A Breton document in Maitre and de Berthou, *Cartulaire de l'Abbaye de*

The content of the term *bannus* as a Frankish crown prerogative had been so vast that there is no reason to interpret the evidence of the persistence of ban penalty restrictively in the sense
that *bannus* had shrunk to a mere right to 60 sol. Except where
some particular incident of *bannus* is transferred it will be exercised in its entirety by those who succeeded to the king's rights.[48]
This is certainly an inescapable conclusion so far as procedural
powers are concerned. Some charters specifically join to *bannus*
the *districtio,* the right of distraint or, more broadly, judicial
compulsion;[49] and *districtio* emerges as an essential incident of

*Ste. Croix de Quimperlé* (1896) dealing with the rights of Alain IV concedes to the latter "dimidium banni quando suus homo cum homine abbatis pugnaret vel Pictavenses sive aliqui alii extranei," no. 74 (1084–96).
This apparently refers to the duel mulct, and confirms the view that the
recreant's penalty, if not derived from, is by now confused with the old
king's ban.

[48] 1 Flach, *Origines,* 323 *et seq.* Flach perceives the importance of the
ban concept but relates it chiefly to the later monopolies, the *banalités.*
On the count's ban Sohm, *F.R.G.V.,* 176 *et seq.*

The grant of *bannus* followed by certain named wrongs without a
videlicet, or mixed with homicide or arson suggests the army ban may
have been meant. (*Infra,* note 68.) Since the term comes to be rather
broadly used, it is not improbable that such a grant might be taken to
mean a general power of *districtio.* Practically, this would give color of
right to the erection and maintenance of monopolies like the mill ban, etc.
These Koehne, 25 *Z.R.G.*², 172, attributes to the vogue of fort building,
but their eventual maintenance as a matter of law may in view of the
association of terms be attributed to the ban power. *Cf.* in general on the
wide use of *bannus* and its relation to the development of regalian rights
1 Mayer, *Deutsche und Französische Verfassungsgeschichte,* 86 *et seq.,*
where a wealth of references is available.

There is valuable comparative material in Pöschl, *Die Regalien der
Mittelalterlichen Kirchen* (1928), Pt. 1. The German charters show a
much richer terminology. Pöschl only deals parenthetically with France,
*ibid.,* 98 and on the later influence of the German development, *ibid.,* 115.

[49] Undoubtedly as a reflection of the charter usage of the Carolingians
(*cf.* Stengel, *Immunität,* 463 for early and later word usage). For example
Lothar's charter to St. Père de Chartres of 985, 1 Guérard, *Cart. de St.
Père de Chartres,* 83; and *ibid.,* §103: "*bannum* et *districtum,* c'est-à-dire
le pouvoir administratif ou la police et le pouvoir coercitif." *Cf.* Tardif,
*Mon. Hist.,* no. 236 of the year 982. In the two charters of King Robert,
*ibid.,* nos. 249, 250, *bannus* is clearly used to mean full judicial power as
specified. *Cf.* also the judgment (1035) in a suit between the abbot of St.

the *vicarius'* power.[50] But the trend of the charters is to leave *districtio* unmentioned, from which can be inferred the fact that when any grant of jurisdiction is made procedural powers attach automatically.[51] In truth it is in the procedural phases of the ban that its power of growth lay, for it is by these procedural devices that the man who had ban could establish for himself a priority in respect of this penalty or, broader still, of complete economic control over the wrongdoer, to the exclusion of even the man wronged.

We have already touched on the early stages of the perversion of these devices, as indicative of a shift in the fiscal interest from participation in composition payments to outright penalty in the cases where the royal fisc was entitled to both the *fredus* and *bannus,* and where the absorption of *fredus* by *bannus* tended to direct action against the offender. Since the ban was an obligation not dependent upon the amount paid as compensation

Germanin d'Auxerre and Waldric of St. Florentin (1 *Cart. Gén. de l'Yonne,* no. 89) "bannum, placitum, justitiam, districtum" as a description of judicial powers.

[50] Lex, *Eudes Comte de Blois,* P.J. no. 13 (1015–23); *Cart. Ste. Marie Char.* (3 *Arch. Anj.*) no. 94 (ante 1080) "vicarius earum distringat forfacientes" etc.; *Cart. St. Vincent du Mans,* no. 312 (1071) "distringens per vicariam II homines"; Marchegay, *Doc. inéd. Anjou,* 126 (1070–75) "neque G. neque vicarius suus eum distringet nisi prius clamorem faciat ad monachos"; *Cart. St. Vincent du Mans,* no. 16 (1099–1100); 1 *Cart. St. Aubin,* no. 221 (1080–1082) "nisi de quo monachi iustitiam facere noluerint forsfacto vicarius de Mosteriolo distringat hominem" etc. In some cases the *districtio* becomes the name of a mulct. *Cart. Ste. Mar. Char.* (3 *Arch. Anj.*) no. 243 (1075) two parts of *districtio* in case of duel. Cf. 1 Mayer, *D.F.V.G.,* 153 on the *districtum* as a mulct. For earlier use in this sense, 4 Waitz, *D.V.G.,* 317, n. 3.

[51] Clearly in Arbois de Jubainville and Prou, *Recueil des actes de Philippe I* (1908) no. 2 (1060) free of "teloneum, bannum, vicariam et omne districtum quod humana lex ab hominibus jubet exsolvi."; no. 52 (1070) more in the Carolingian form; no. 120 (1090) "nullus ibi exerceat ullam judiciariam districtionem, . . ."; *Cart. Marmoutier pour le Vendômois,* no. 122 (before 1064) "non ad alium quemlibet pertineat judicare de his sed qui dominus et possessor est alodii est et per se ipsum districtor et judex forisfacti."

through agreement between the parties, the crown could collect it through administrative measures, distraining the debtor on a theory of contempt.[52] Since this procedure was available it seems unlikely that the crown, where ban penalty was due, would await the event of party agreement. In the ordinary case where no ban was due, the claim of public authority was contingent upon the final concord. The party's plea moved entirely within the framework of the *fides facta*.[53] There had to be party agreement—no court could order the offender to pay. The most it could do was to resort to measures to avoid feud.[54] These measures, a manifestation of the ban power, culminating in confiscation of land and chattels, were essentially ancillary to the party's action. But these sanctions were taken for a contempt, and consequently by sequestering and confiscating the defendant's property the expectation of the plaintiff was destroyed. After 816 the plaintiff was given a right to turn to the fisc for satisfaction,[55]

[52] This was true of the procedure in the case of the army ban—*cf.* Sohm, *F.R.G.V.*, 118. Whether or not the same rule applied equally in the case where the ban was collectible in the case of a wrong is difficult to say. Brunner in 2 *D.R.G.*, 54 says merely that a judicial rather than an administrative procedure was there necessary. In the *Allocutio Missi* of 857 c. 3 where the ban penalty was extended (2 *Cap.*, 292) there seems to be contemplated a separate proceeding for levying the ban. In any event there is not mentioned a proceeding by private accuser. Bethmann-Hollweg in 5 *Civilprozess*, 181 believes that the judicial use of *missio in bannum* which we are presently discussing is derived from the administrative use of the ban. Brunner in 2 *D.R.G.*, 603 n. 26 disagrees, alleging the roots to be in "peacelessness." Apart from what we believe to be the preposterous overextension of Brunner's theory as a reason for rejecting his explanation, the well known tendency of a procedural device to breed similar devices lends color to Bethmann-Hollweg's view. The infinite variety of the English capias is an example of what we have in mind.

[53] Schreuer, *Verbrechenskonkurrenz*, 235.

[54] The court orders the reluctant defendant to appear, constraining by the *missio in bannum*. The confiscation ensues after a year and a day if the defendant remains in contempt.

[55] The plaintiff originally applies to the fisc as a matter of grace. The details of how the rule is changed to give the plaintiff a right first under the *Lex Salica* and later (818) under general law of the Empire are related by Mayer-Homberg, *Die Fränkischen Volksrechte*, 284 *et seq.*

but his claim as a practical matter was subsidiary to the fisc's vested interest in the property taken.[56]

It will be observed that in all cases where the ban power was used the fisc's claim, whether to a penalty for ban breach or for a general contempt, was paramount. The procedure is the fisc's and not the party's to command. Consequently it is not difficult to understand that where the ban power was conveyed, it was tempting to utilize it to exclude all claimants but the court-holder, particularly in those cases where the defendant would be able to satisfy but one claim.

In the Frankish Empire, aside from those cases where ban had been granted to an immunist, its administration was chiefly a matter of comital cognizance.[57] Since the count's income (a third of the property of which the fisc eventually obtained control) was determined on the basis of the net takings of his office, the comital income would be *pro tanto* reduced if he gave a plaintiff satisfaction for his claim. Obviously he would not be averse to preventing a plaintiff from realizing his claims against the fisc. The opportunity of excluding the plaintiff increased as the central control over local officers diminished. By the Edict of Pîtres (864)[58] the rule regarding summons was radically altered

[56] We say "as a practical matter" because the capitulary for the Empire (*Cap. Legg. Add.*, 818-9, c. 11; 1 *Cap.*, 283) leaves to the count or officers (*missi*) the determination of the plaintiff's claim. While the principle is set up: "si nihil super conpositionem remanere potuerit, totum in illam expendatur," the plaintiff needs a royal order to get his claim. And as is pointed out below in the text, the administration of the matter would have made it easy to circumvent a claim despite the principle of the law.

[57] 2 Brunner, *D.R.G.*, 226, 238. Note also the exceptions as to army ban, *ibid.*, 223, and the "reminiscence" as Brunner calls it of the Frankish count's third in the third of the *comes* mentioned in the *Dialogus de Scaccario* I, c. 17; *ibid.*, 226 n. 60.

[58] c. 6 (2 *Cap.*, 313). The change was due to the fact that summons had to be at a man's house. Owing to the devastations of the Normans, the law lets the count send his envoy to the land where a man's house had been and perform symbolic summons. The road is then clear for a judgment of the *scabini* whereby the property of the man summoned can be put in ban and he be forebanned. *Cf.* also the direct procedure of foreban against thieves and malefactors provided for in *Cap. Carisiac.* (873) c. 1

and in effect enhanced the power of the count in wielding the ban. Private accusation still had its uses, but procedure was moving inexorably toward defeating the party's expectation.

When the tenth century opens, the ban as penalty, as a collocation of drastic procedural devices, and as ordinance power, rests in the hands of persons who are using it for their own interests. What happened in the course of that century is shrouded in darkness. The statutes of the La Réole monastery (977), however, if we can take them as typical, give us a fairly illuminating picture of what the trend had been, for several provisions are to be attributed to the possession of ban power. In c. 43 we can observe how this is conceived. There the use of sharp weapons in medleys is forbidden.[59] If a person is injured, damages are due him and 66 sol. are payable to the prior. From the amount of the mulct we are led to assume that here is perpetuated the ban penalty.[60] This conjecture is fortified by the further rule that unless complete (*totum*) satisfaction[61] is made, the wrongdoer forfeits a member, and all his property shall be confiscated by the prior if the victim dies. Such a complete concentration upon the right of the courtholder is explicable only in terms of the *bannus* and, we may add, of its perversion. It is no longer ancillary, a means to fortify individual complaints. It needs no subterfuge of contempt to lead to execution. It has become, to paraphrase Sohm, the *imperium* of the local lord's law.

(2 *Cap.*, 343). The procedure under the Edict of Pîtres is described fully in 1 Brunner, *D.R.G.*, 546 *et seq.*

[59] Giraud, *op. cit.*, 517; *cf.* also c. 48.

[60] The penalty for carrying sharp weapons is 6 sol. The sum of 66 sol. is a cumulation of ban penalty and the 6 sol. for carrying the weapon.

[61] The expression for the redress to the individual injured is "damnum ex integro restituit." It seems unlikely that composition is meant. Certainly in the La Réole document no tariff is suggested. We have rendered the term "satisfaction." Obviously there is implicit here a theory of damages toward which the ecclesiastical law had been working. Definite traces of this particularly in *Pseudo-Isidore*, e.g., *Ep. Eused. II*, c. 13–14 (Hinschius Ed. p. 238). Probably what is intended here is to cast the victim upon his bargain with the culprit, the familiar spectacle of the 11th century.

The nature of the sources with which we are dealing is such
that most of the proof regarding the persistence of *bannus* and
its importance in the molding of seignorial power is collateral.
As one advances into the eleventh century the charters speak of
*bannus* with less frequency. New expressions reflecting the immediate interests of the parties predominate in the formulae. A
lord, secular or spiritual, is intent upon securing as to a specific
territory the maximum financial and general jurisdictional control, because this is the only way that a feudal estate can be successfully managed. This pressure had brought about a constant
widening of the Carolingian formulae, although the transactions involved disparate parties—the grantee and a powerful
royal fisc. When the charters or notifications become remem-
brances of transactions between persons of roughly equal capacity, when there is no royal policy to be guarded, when local interests alone are involved, where the political contact is close and
immediate, the documents are essentially mere bargains with
the warmth of the moment upon them. They are not composed
by a central chancery out of a frozen and sacrosanct formbook.
There is no longer any reason to preserve outmoded terms that
disguise the accretions of prescription, for there is no royal authority with a *quo warranto* against whom grantees feel they
must hold out. These charters reflect realities. They do not talk
in terms of *fredus* when wergeld ceases to exist, for now the
term *fredus* is no longer necessary to conceal an outright mulct
under the guise of a right to a proportionate third of the plaintiff's recovery. They do not promise that there will be no entries
by public officers when there are no public officers to be excluded.
They do not grandiloquently refer to "whatever our fisc can
hope for" because the fisc had been shattered into countless fragments. They pass the sort of jurisdiction that has contemporary
meaning—*consuetudo,* or *vicaria.* They partition financial interest in the exact terms of current usage—a tithe of the viscount's
income, half the ban on specified wrongs. They forbid an *avoué*

to distrain the men of a monastery. In only one point is the policy of long dead kings still etched upon the records—the tendency to reserve to secular control serious wrongs like homicide, arson and robbery. However they vary in detail, the important and significant fact about the new terms of the charters is the clue they yield to the content of seignorial power in this period, and to the drive to make paramount the fiscal rights of a courtkeeper.

Commonest and most pregnant among these terms is the grant of *consuetudo*—custom. This expression was as ambiguous in the tenth century as it is today, and being ambiguous it necessarily led to free interpretation. Then as now it had the double meaning of a payment and a usage. Understood in the first of the two connotations mentioned it was employed to emphasize the financial implications of the jurisdiction conveyed.[62] One need but observe its frequent placement in sentence structure, a generalization succeeded by specifications in terms, or as a final summation of all possible fiscal claims at the end of a grant, to understand what purpose it was intended to serve.[63] In its

---

[62] Most of the documents examined in which the word *consuetudo* embraces tolls, tithes or dues, as well as such matters as homicide or theft, purpose to grant or define jurisdiction. One may account for the implication of usage by looking on the term as a description of a jurisdiction by prescription. On the other hand, as we propose to show in the text, the *consuetudo* of *homicidium* or *latrocinium* is probably thought of in terms of revenue. For a great many charters the rendition would be "we grant the following jurisdictions and/or revenues."

[63] This notwithstanding variations in form. For example: the charter of 1010/1068/1073 to Couture (*Cart. de St. Pierre de la Couture et de St. Pierre de Solesmes,* [1881]) no. 9: ". . . De omnibus autem istis terris omnem dimicit consuetudinem, scilicet vicarie, foreste, venacionis, banni, carri, et ut neque amplius sui vicarii seu forestarii vel brenarii sive canes in his per consuetudinem jaceant terris." The charter to St. Pierre de Bourgueil (Lex, *Eudes Comte de Blois* [1892]) no. 10, of the years 1009-12: ". . . Hunc igitur locum in honore Dei et sancte Marie sanctique Petri dicatum, ea racione vicariam eis trado, ut nullus heres meus, neque parentes mei, neque filius meus, dominacionem nunquam habeat, nec pro furto, nec pro rapto, nec pro sanguine, nec pro homicidio, nec pro incendio, vel aliqua repetundarum legum consuetudine introeundi habeat potes-

other meaning it is obscure, because "usages," as we conceive the expression, do not seem a particularly useful, not to say grantable, right. But the right to *consuetudo* actually conceals a conveyance of legislative power. The grantee gets at once the passive right of receipt and the active power of regulation—the tax and the right to fix the tax or, broader, to control usages. If the terseness of the charters raises doubts as to the correctness of such a view they are set at rest by the evidence of endless wails against *malae consuetudines*.[64] These testify to the fact that changes are made abruptly by persons in power. The acts com-

tatem nullam causam requirendi, qui contrarium eis sit. Igitur . . ." The charter to St. Aubin (1 *Cart. St. Aubin,* no. 4 bis) of 1007–1026: ". . . Et he sunt consuetudines quas integre perdono videlicet: bannum, carraucum, corvatas, forragium et omnem vicariam, cum omni consuetudine, perdono, ita ut nullus vicarius, neque meus, neque alterius, in predictis terris, neque in bosco, neque in plano, neque in aqua, ullam consuetudinem habeat." The charter to St. Julien de Tours (1 Denis, *Chartes de St. Julien de Tours* [1912] no. 18) of 1046–7: ". . . cum sepultura, decimis omnibus, cum terris cultis et incultis, silvis, aquis, molendinis, et cum omnibus rebus ecclesie debitis, cum jam adquisitis vel adquirendis, cum teloneo et mercato, ac aliis consuetudinibus." *Cf.,* finally, the charter to Préaux (c. 1047) in Valin, *Le Duc de Normandie,* 258.

The typical charter of this period, granting *consuetudines* without such specification, is therefore to be interpreted as similarly exhaustive, unless explicitly restricted. For example the following Norman charters: Richard's Charter to Jumièges (*Chartes de Jumièges,* no. 12) of 1027: ". . . Restituit quoque villam que dicitur Goyacus consensu et voluntate Hardradi qui eam eatenus possederat et Walsiardum cum ecclesia et omnibus eorum appendiciis, ex quibus nostro tempore donavit per nostrum consensum Rotbertus archiepiscopus, frater noster, omnes consuetudines quae ad comitatum pertinent, quas ipse ex nostro jure possidebat . . ."; and the charter of 1080, *ibid.,* no. 32. *Cf.* charters to St. Michel du Tréport (Kermaingant, *Cartulaire de St. Michel du Tréport* [1880], nos. 1 and 3) of 1036; the charter to St. Martin de Troarn (Sauvage, *L'Abbaye de St. Martin de Troarn* [1911], Preuves no. 2) of 1068; the charter to Bernai (1 Le Prevost, *Notes sur Eure,* 285) of 1027.

[64] Often enough an "ordinance" of a local lord is called an *exactio,* the term by which something wrong or unlawful is usually meant. The *consuetudines* by fiat were infinitely more numerous than the documents indicate for the reason that they come to light only when considered *malae consuetudines,* and this as often as not in a dispute over jurisdiction between parties laying claim to fiscal perquisites. The situation already suggested in the previous chapter where the *advocatus* or *vicarius* has cut

plained of show that not only exactions but all the procedures incident thereto are regarded as "customs."

More narrow in scope than *consuetudo* are the other jurisdiction-conveying words, *vicaria* and its specific Norman analogue, the *consuetudines comitatus*. Here again the interpretations to which grants were subjected indicates not only the *locus* but also the content of sanctions.

The *vicaria*[65] is an expression considerably narrower than *con-*

away from an ecclesiastical immunist a portion of the latter's rights is typical.

There is evidence as early as the Carolingian capitularies of the efforts of local officers to change existing dues and services—*cf.* the passages cited in 4 Waitz, *D.V.G.*, 13 n. 4. The later documents are numerous; we cite several without attempting a complete list. *Cf.* 3 Bernard and Bruel, *Chartes de l'Abbaye de Cluny,* no. 2406 (997–1007); Espinay, *Les cartulaires angevins* (1864), App. no. 3 (979); Tardif, *Monuments historiques,* no. 286, concord of 1067; Mabille, *Cartulaire de Marmoutier pour le Dunois,* no. 48 (1032–37), no. 173 (1119), no. 180 (1131); Bernard, *Cartulaire de l'Abbaye de Savigny* (C.D.I. 1853) no. 802, a concord of 1070 regarding certain bad customs; 1 Denis, *Chartes de St. Julien de Tours* (1912) no. 5, a conveyance of customs "just and unjust" (1005); 3 Achery, *Specilegium* (1723) 401, a charter of King Henry of 1057 releasing an unjust custom; *ibid.,* 410 a charter of Herbert of Vermandois (1076); Halphen, *Le Comté d'Anjou* (1906) P.J. no. 2, a release of 990–1011; Chartron, *L'Anjou de 1109 à 1151* (1928) 369, a conveyance of 1128.

There are also examples of clauses more or less on the model of the old immunity grants forbidding exactions by judicial officers, attempting to forestall future *malae consuetudines.* 1 *Cartulaire de St. Jean d'Angely* (1901) no. 186 (1039); and compare the royal charter (1174) attempting the same thing, 2 *Cart. St. Père de Chartres,* 651 (no. 43). There is a discussion of the whole matter of the *mala consuetudo* and some further references from Ms. sources in 1 Flach, *Origines,* 413 *et seq.* Flach treats the whole matter of *consuetudo* by fiat as a manifestation of naked power. This is an approach that seems colored by modern prejudice and can be traversed by the fact that wherever the ban power, i.e. in the sense of ordinance making, passed into a lord's hands there is no reason to suppose the *exactio* was necessarily unlawful.

[65] The most complete account is by Lot, *Le vicaria et le vicarius,* in 17 *N.R.H.,* 281 *et seq.* His position is that from the 10th to the 13th century the *vicaria* is "full" justice and above all is what is eventually known as "haute justice." For the functions of the Carolingian *vicarius,* 2 Brunner, *D.R.G.,* 238. There is also a discussion in Espinay, *Les cartulaires angevins,* 58 *et seq.,* covering the Frankish and post-Frankish institution. Espinay cites additional Angevin documents of the 10th century; *cf.* also

*suetudo*. In certain localities and notably in Maine, Anjou, the Vendôme and Ponthieu, the *consuetudines* which had to do with the enforcement of justice were treated as a unit and denominated *vicaria*. The historical reason for this we can assume to have been the fact that in many places the *vicarius*, the Carolingian count's sub-officer, when he blossomed into a baron, had remained in control of his original functions, and that in certain immunities these functions were concentrated in an *avoué* with nearly identical powers.[66] In any event, the *vicaria* toward the

the *Notitia de malis consuetudines* of 979 *ibid.*, 324, and also the concord from the *Codex Niger* no. 44, *ibid.*, 325; *cf.* also Burchard's customs (1025–30) in 1 *Cart. Trinité de Vendôme*, no. 2; *Cart. Ste. Marie de Char.* (3 *Archives d'Anjou*) no. 194 (1115); 2 *Arch. Anjou*, Intro. 11, a charter of Fulk of 1066; *Cart. St. Vincent de Mans*, no. 312 (1071) and no. 16 (1099). There are other 10th century charters of Hugh in 10 *H.F.* 555 where *vicaria* are granted. *Cf.* also the charters of Robert of 997 (Tardif, *Mon. Hist.*, no. 240) and 998 (no. 241). In the *Cartulaire de St. Aubin*, no. 3 of 974 is a grant of *vicaria*, and in no. 4 (1007–26). No. 21 (970) is very explicit: "Concedimus quoque eis ut nulla in eorum terra vicaricia dominetur potestas nisi de homicido aut furto vel incendio . . ." *Cf.* also no. 22 (977).

Lot's conclusions are subject to the qualification that the word *vicaria* in the 11th century charters has a different emphasis depending upon what incident of this full power is claimed. If the matter complained of is fiscal the emphasis will be upon that phase. Thus the charter of Fulk Nerra to Beaulieu in Halphen, *Le Comté d'Anjou* (1007) no. 5 "si aliquis forefactum fecerit infra hos terminos, ex quo vicaria exigere debeat, vel aliquid venderit et vicaria et venda monachis Belliloci sit. . . ." *Cf.* also the *Cartae de Corbaio* (2 Marchegay, *Archives d'Anjou* 11) where one half of the *vicaria* of a territory conveyed are sold. In certain charters the emphasis is upon the power of distraint; *Cart. St. Vincent du Mans*, no. 16 (1098–1100); the *Carta de Vieria Sancti Mauri* of 1066 (1 *Arch. Anjou* 403) where divided control is dealt with in terms of distraint-arrest; the *Carta de Malis Consuet.* (1080–7) in *Chroniques des eglises d'Anjou*, 72; *cf.* also the case in *Cart. Marmoutier Vendôm.*, no. 32 (1066–75) where control of a *vicaria* is claimed by setting up a previous distraint and amends.

It is hardly necessary to add references showing that *vicaria* is regarded as a species of *consuetudo*. *Cf.* however, *Cart. Marmoutier Vendômois*, no. 86 (1066); Depoin, *Cartulaire de St. Martin de Pontoise* (1895), no. 14 (1082) "consuetudinem . . . quae vieria vulgo dicitur"; 1 *Chartes St. Julien de Tours*, no. 17 (1046); Lex, *op. cit.*, App. no. 29 (1035).

[66] Senn, *L'Institution des avoueries ecclésiastiques*, 112 *et seq*. and 117 *et seq*. In this connection *cf.* the order of King Robert restoring to the ab-

close of the tenth century are treated in the charters as a particular collocation of functions, and in the course of the eleventh century this differentiation becomes well marked. The *vicaria* lie in grant, they are sometimes bad in the way customs are bad, and they certainly are regarded as a source of profit.

We must not be misled, however, into assuming that the judicial function is everywhere so clearly delimited as a unit denoted *vicaria*. In many localities the functions connected with justice continue to be referred to as *consuetudines*,[67] and at least one cautious scribe describes a jurisdiction granted as *bannus* and *vicaria* and all *consuetudines*.[68] In Normandy, as we have seen, grants are in terms of *consuetudo,* and rarely are specific. Nevertheless, there is some evidence that the Normans know a form of grant if not identical at least analogous to the *vicaria*. This is the conveyance of *consuetudines comitatus*.[69] The viscount, who is the comital officer, probably exercises a jurisdiction substantially like that of the *vicarius*.[70] Although there are not many documents in which the parallel is recognized, they are sufficient to

bey of Jumièges certain lands near Senlis: "nullius hominis ni se advocationem vel viatoriam (another form of *vicariam,* Lot, *Vicaria,* 300) habentem . . ." 1 *Chartes de Jumièges,* no. 11 (1027).

[67] Thus, *Cart. Marmoutier pour le Dunois,* no. 173 (1119); *Cart. Marmoutier Vend.,* App. no. 12 (1032–1060) "omnes consuetudines et forifacta excepto quod raptus et homicidum domino remanebunt."

[68] *Cart. St. Vincent du Mans,* no. 475 (1075). It is possible, of course, here, that *bannus* has a special meaning, i.e. with reference to army ban; *cf.* 1 *Cart. St. Aubin,* no. 216 (1060–7) ". . . non erat consuetudo quod homines de familia St. Albini ullius banno aut jussu, preter monachorum in hostem pergerent."

[69] 1 *Chartes de Jumièges,* no. 12 (1027) ". . . omnes consuetudines quae ad comitatum pertinent . . ."; Valin, *Le Duc de Normandie,* P.J. no. 2 (Préaux, c. 1047) and the later regrant cited, in Haskins, *op. cit.,* 279, n. 15; *cf.* the charter to Auchy-Aumale cited *ibid.,* 29. Haskins, *ibid.,* 27, regards any grants where the Duke conveys or releases his customs as equivalent to grants of "consuetudines comitatus," no doubt because he regards the viscount as a "public official," *ibid.,* 45. The term is not often used but there is some collateral evidence such as *Cart. St. Michel du Tréport* (1059), no. 1, where a tithe of the money (i.e., income) *de vicecomitatibus* is mentioned.

[70] This was suggested first by Mayer 1 *D.F.V.G.,* 357. On the use of the

raise a presumption that the Normans under another form treated like their neighbors the rights of justice as a unit for purposes of conveyance.[71]

*Consuetudo* and *vicaria,* whatever else they may imply, are words that deal with profits. In the charters they are treated as *res,* in the same way as are tenements, and the reason they are *res* is because they have accountable value. At the same time these are words that express jurisdiction. But it is certain that jurisdiction is regarded as something appurtenant to the fiscal purpose. A baron or an abbot desires *vicaria* not because he wants to carry on experiments in law administration, but because he thinks it will be profitable. And if he wants to make money, he has to have sole power. He, and he alone, must be able to say who is to be hanged and who is to be mulcted. It is this concentration on profits coupled with this procedural exclusiveness that are essential characteristics of the feudal justice of the period. If there were any doubt that this is so, it is resolved by those documents that write finis to some tale of violence and rapine. Apart from specific reparation, such as the return of lands or tithes or tolls, the delictual aspect of a cause is settled with the court and not the litigant. When these documents speak of *emendatio*—the amends—it is something that is made to the court and not the litigant.[72] For the latter there may occasionally be a collateral satisfaction such as an enforced homage or servitude of a wrong-

term *vicaria* in Normandy cf. 1 Stapleton, *Rot. Scacc. Norm.* (1840), lvii, discussing various documents without references. The basis for institutional diffusion exists in the situation presented by a Norman monastery, Mont St. Michel, possessing *vicaria* out of Normandy (*cf.* Brousillon, *Cart. St. Victeur au Mans* [1885], no. 6 [1040]), or the reverse—a monastery with *vicaria* outside Normandy with undefined *consuetudines* in the Duchy.

[71] For example Lot, *Etudes . . . sur St. Wandrille,* no. 57; Orderic, *Historia Ecclesiastica,* l. 5, c. 20: *vicecomitiam, id est viariam.* Compare also the charter of Adela of Blois to St. Martin (*post* 1102) "omnem vicecomitatum et viariam de villa . . ." etc. (1 *Cart. St. Martin des Champs,* no. 98).

[72] In addition to the charters which have been cited to show that the cession or quittance of jurisdiction contemplates fiscal advantage there is

doer. But the amends, the pecuniary mulct that the offender undergoes, is the perquisite of the man who has jurisdiction.

We have dealt at some length with the legal substructure of seignorial power, not only to establish the justification for many things that would otherwise seem to be no more than acts of

much documentary material which shows that the *emendatio* of the eleventh century is definitely conceived as a charge inflicted by the court-keeper either at discretion or in accordance with some multiple of the old ban of 60 sol.

*Cart. St. Aubin,* an Angevin cartulary, has a number of documents that throw light on the subject. We commence with one of the most doubtful (2 *ibid.,* no. 939) of the year 1030. Guy, the son of Geoffrey of Idré, claims the lands of Vaux, and with his relative kills horses of St. Aubin and burns a house. He is taken to Count Geoffrey and turned over to St. Aubin. "Post hec emendavit equas et domos et terram clamavit quietam," and he swears on reliquaries not to make further claim. Here the *emendatio* smacks of compensatory damages. Nothing is said about the wrong. Similarly in a case of 1055–1093 (1 *ibid.,* no. 231) a man who steals ten cows "qui probatus et convictus de furto a predicto monacho, cum, venditis vaccis, non haberet unde illas redderet, [note the idea of reparation] coactus et districtus reddidit pro emendatione earum domum unam et arpennum vinee apud Toartium, quam videlicet domum . . ." In another case (1082–1106) two men who seem not to have had any direct claim to certain lands twice cut trees and carried off the wood, and on the second occasion wounded and killed some men. At the behest of one who was apparently their superior they were made to stand to right. One offender admitted his guilt and gave the abbot of St. Aubin thirty shillings as a gage for the trees cut. Subsequently he petitions for the gage and the abbot taking counsel of his chapter remits all but two *denarii.* Nothing appears regarding the punishment for the wounding or killing. Since it appears from the document that the abbot had all *consuetudo,* the remission may be not a mere scaling of damages but a subtraction of penalty. *Ibid.,* no. 270. There is some evidence of the emergence of a damage concept, *Cart. Ste. Marie de la Charité* (3 *Arch. Anjou,* no. 368) a concord of 1100. Compare also the case in *Cart. Marmoutier Dunois,* no. 53 (1083) where the mulct is a form of pledge.

The St. Aubin cartulary offers evidence that the *emendatio* is the court-keeper's perquisite. In 1080(–82) the seigneur de Montreuil renounces certain bad customs, among them the "sex forsfactorum consuetudinem, que sunt raptum et incendium, sanguis ac furtum, lepus et pedagium, . . ." (1 *ibid.,* no. 221; also Marchegay and Mabille, *Chroniques des églises d'Anjou* 72). In 1087 (1 *Cart. St. Aubin,* no. 222) it appears that more than 500 solidi had been collected on account of these same forfeitures under claim that the persons involved were the seigneur's own men. In *Cart. Ste. Marie de la Charité* (3 *Arch. Anj.,* no. 176) is a docu-

naked power, but also to show how steady was the drive in the direction of penalty. Until this concept is completely embedded in the law and the court's interest in dealings with

ment (1067–8) regarding the seizure of cattle. The culprit "vadiavit forisfactum illud; et de emendatione illa accepit G. C. IV denarios." The judgment in *ibid.*, no. 194 (1115) that a claimant had "nullam vicariam neque potestatem . . . Itaque reddidit quicquid inde acceperat . . ." and he also returns stolen objects previously sequestered to the abbess to whom jurisdiction is adjudged. *Cf.* also no. 243 (1075); *Cart. Marmoutier pour le Dunois,* no. 94 (1114); 1 *Cart. Trinité de Vendôme,* no. 175 (1064); 2 *ibid.,* no. 319 (1084); no. 418 (1108); *Cart. St. Vincent du Mans,* no. 754 (1053).

The term *emendatio* is used consistently in the charters and notifications to describe as well the mulct for a failure to render feudal dues as economic charges. *Cf.* 1 *Cart. St. Aubin,* no. 33 (993): "Si vero de ipso censu tardi aut negligentes extiterint, licentiam habeant legaliter emendandi . . ."; *ibid.,* nos. 40, 282; *Cart. Marmoutier pour le Vendômois,* no. 73 (1064–77); *Cart. Marmoutier pour le Dunois,* no. 6 (991–1000) as the penalty for a wrong. Furthermore, the term *forfactum* or *forisfactum* as a description of the act entailing *emendatio* applies equally to violations of mill ban (*cf.* on this Koehne, *Studien über die Entstehung der Zwangs und Bannrechte,* 25 *Z.R.G.*², 172); for example *cf. Cart. Marmoutier pour le Dunois,* no. 148 (1095) failure to pay toll or dues, and to wrongs like arson or homicide. *Cf.* esp. *Cart. Ste. Marie Char.* (3 *Arch. Anj.*) nos. 93, 94; in no. 243 (1075) *forisfactum* seems equal to forfeiture; *Cart. Marmoutier pour le Vendômois,* p. 292 (no. 12) (1032–60). *Cf.* also 1 *Cart. St. Aubin,* no. 221 (1080–82); *Cart. Marmoutier pour le Vendômois,* no. 52 (1070); *Chart. St. Julien de Tours,* no. 24 (1053) a grant of Norman churches. This intense concentration upon the purely fiscal aspects of wrongdoing necessarily caused the penal *emendatio* to be subsumed in a general category that included any financial sanction. Differentiation or classification in terms of penalty begins only when complete chattel forfeiture or disherison invariably attaches to "criminal" wrongs, as contrasted with sanctions for "economic" offenses, viz., failure to pay *census.* As we shall presently see, this comes as a result of marking out the 60 sol. cases from those entailing trial by battle and eventual forfeiture.

Unquestionably the court-holder has a definite discretion—note especially, *Cart. Ste. Marie Char.,* no. 96 (1085), (3 *Arch. Anj.*), "damus eis licentiam emendi . . . quicquid sibi placuerit"—in fixing mulcts, except as he is restrained by the terms of his grant. This was a practical consequence of those grants in which the profits of justice are divided. For example, a document of 1080, *Cart. Ste. Marie Char.* (3 *Arch. Anj.*) no. 93; *ibid.,* no. 239 of 1050; 1 *Cart. St. Aubin,* no. 4 and no. 4 bis (1007–26). The documents are legion in all northern France. In one notification we have found expressed the principle that later plays so great a role in English law. Ingelbald of Vendôme, releasing in 1060 certain customs, retains

wrongdoers thereby made paramount, the shift from tort to crime cannot take place. But when those Frankish procedures which tend to emphasize the courtkeepers' rights are distributed among countless petty fiscs, generally insulated from external control and endowed with exclusive jurisdictional privileges, the judicial machinery will inevitably grind corn for the court and chaff for the complainant.[73]

four causes "videlicet banno, incendio, rapto et furto et hec mensurate et cum moderantia" (*Cart. Marmoutier pour le Vendômois*, no. 129). The *moderata misericordia* which the Normans bring into England as a discretionary mulct clearly has roots in the 11th century.

As far as Normandy is concerned, it is clear that the same rule obtains regarding amends as the profit of the courtkeeper, as in neighboring provinces. *Cf.* the charter to St. Trinité de Caen (1082) 11 *Gallia Christiana*, Instr. 71; the charter to St. Pierre-sur-Dive (1108), *ibid.*, 155; *cf.* the charter to Préaux cited in Valin, *op. cit.*, P.J. no. 4, a grant of his (Robert of Meulan) "forfeitures which according to human law are collected by ancient custom from homicides, and such others capitally convicted."

[73] In connection with the development of the feudal mulct it is important here to consider the influence of ecclesiastical practice. Without entering into the disputed details of the canonical theory of punishment, it should be pointed out that at the basis of the church's criminal law lay a definite concept of punishment and emendation. (On the theory of punishment, 4 Hinschius, *K.R.*, 747; 5 *ibid.*, 123.) The church was not concerned with healing the breach between the individuals concerned in a wrong but with repairing the relation between the wrongdoer and his God, and as an inseparable incident the injury to the visible church.

The sanctions by which the church sought to enforce its law were primarily spiritual. The core of its system was the penance and the ultimate punishment lay in excommunication (5 Hinschius, *K.R.*, 131, and note especially 136 regarding the use of excommunication as an injunction to prevent offenses). The penitential system was based upon certain acts of abstention and affliction of the individual (Schmitz, *Die Bussbücher und die Bussdisciplin der Kirche* [1883] 11 *et seq.*, 62, for a discussion of theory of penances; Oakley, *English Penitential Discipline* [1923] 43 *et seq.*). Under the influence of the Anglo-Saxon penitentials, which the lay system of composition had affected, the Frankish penitentials received the notion of permitting money commutation (Schmitz, *op. cit.*, 144 *et seq.*). In the ninth century this practice was completely ensconced in the practice of the Frankish church. It is incorporated in the Canons of Regino in the early 10th century, *De Ecclesiasticis Disciplinis*, lib. 2, cc. 444, 445 (132 Migne, *Patrologia*, 369) as well as in the *Decretum* of Burchard, lib. 19, c. 22–3 (140 Migne, *Patrologia*, 983) a hundred years later.

The theory upon which the practice of redemptions was based appears to have been the inability of the penitent to perform the penance. This is

## SANCTIONS IN FEUDAL COURTS

The attrition of ancient procedures involved in the tremendous shift in the purpose of courtholding which the eleventh-century records mark is by no means merely the result of adjustments of old law within each franchise or jurisdiction. It is so general a phenomenon in northern France that the cause must lie in circumstances which affect all jurisdictions alike. Since the control of wrongdoing has become a matter of economics one surmises that the pressure emanates from this direction.

The picture one sees of these regions before the English conquest is of a land-rich and chattel-poor society. What alien invasion and famine had contributed to this condition we know. The

clearly shown by a canon of the Synod of Tribur of 895 (*Cap.* 55, in 2 *Cap.*, 242). Doctrinally the theory is closely related to the church's dogma respecting good works. Both the abstention from enforcing the letter of the penitentials and the teachings regarding alms are manifestations of mercy (*misericordia*). *Cf.* for example Hincmar, *De Cavendis Vitiis*, c. 1, c. 8 (125 Migne, *Patrologia,* 863, 888); the theory is discussed in Lepicier, *History of Indulgences* (trans. 1906), 236 *et seq.* On the commutations, *Poenitentiale Romanum,* Schmitz, *op. cit.,* 473 "Si quis forte non potuerit jejunare, et habuerit, unde dare possit ad redimendum, si dives fuerit, pro septem hebdomadibus det solidos XX; si autem non habuerit tantum unde dare possit, det solidos X; si autem multum pauper fuerit, det solidos III. Neminem vero conturbet, quia jussimus XX solidos dare, aut minus, quia, si dives fuerit, facilius est illi dare solidos XX, quam pauperi solidos III. . . ." *Cf. Poenitentiale Egberti, ibid.,* 587.

While it is not difficult to discover the basis for monetary redemption in the ethical teachings of the church, there can be no doubt that practically the policy of the Frankish hierarchy was affected by secular law: the redemption of afflictive punishment by ransom; the capitularies requiring payments to ecclesiastical establishments for matters like the refusal to pay tithes, the penalties for injuries to churchmen or ecclesiastical property. The church could consequently justify its claim to money satisfaction both on spiritual and secular grounds. A ninth-century document establishes for us the details of this theory. The use of the expression *emendatio* in the canonical literature of this period signifies satisfaction to ecclesiastical authority. It has nothing to do with amends or damages to the individual. As far as the Gallic church is concerned there exists an analogue to the ban penalty—a sum collectible by ecclesiastical authority for breach of law without reference to the claims of injured individuals.

Considering the extensive lay holdings of the church and the political control these possessed, the canonical theory of *emendatio* as a payment

reconstruction of society into two sharply defined classes, the war-wagers and soil-tillers, tended toward economic stagnation, for as the prevalence of feud steadily occupied the former class in destructive works, the number of productive workers was *pro tanto* reduced. The surplus that means movable wealth was not forthcoming, for those who tilled the soil had all they could do to support the warriors from lands which were incessantly subjected to ravage. It is in the measures taken to assure the support of those engaged in the pursuit of arms that we can see how courtkeeping for profit fitted into the economic scheme.

The supply of the warriors was effected through the medium of the most searching sort of direct taxation imaginable.[74] The groundwork for this had been laid at an early period, but it reached its full florescence after the collapse of the Carolingian dynasty. Anything susceptible of a service in kind, any act good or evil, normal or abnormal, upon which dues could be laid was drawn into the scheme of exaction. From birth until death men paid their way through a labyrinth of charges, aids, reliefs, oblates, benedictions, tolls, passages, census, amercements, ransoms, heriots and what not, into the impatient palms of layman or clerk. Since the fisc and its grantees had for centuries been entitled to a share in the money settlement of wrongdoing and to outright penalties, the basis for a practical extension of these claims lay at hand. It was easy for such claims to be lumped with all other types of exaction. It is comprehensible why the victims' expectation of relief had to give way. The lord is entitled to his muid of wine, even when the vines bear no grapes.[75]

to authority could be scarcely less significant than the secular ban theory. Wherever the two powers were wielded by the same hands the pressure in the direction of a payment exclusively to the court-holder must have been nearly irresistible.

[74] These are recapitulated in many texts. One of the most complete listings is in the introduction in 1 Guérard, *Cartulaire de St. Père de Chartres,* §86 *et seq. Cf.* also Deloche, *Cartulaire de l'Abbaye de Beaulieu* (C.D.I., 1859), cxiii *et seq.* There is a discussion of the charges in 1 Clamageran, *Histoire de l'impôt en France* (1867), 196 *et seq.*

[75] The documents often convey the impression that the wrong is treated

The incorporation of the profits of court-keeping into the motley of feudal dues may have met resistance, but the decay of royal or even comital restrictions upon local lord or immunist destroyed any effective recourse. For generations there is no crown procedure competing with or correcting country justice. There is nothing to halt the elaboration of charges except where a claim of old usage is made to prevail, or when the rights of another lord as powerful as the innovator are disturbed. A monastery which has by ancient charter "whatever our fisc can hope for," will itself interpret the aspirations of the treasury. If a baron has *consuetudo* he will make his own customs. The more pontifical the terms of the grant, the easier it is for the wrong to be ranged with other dues.

Profit being the chord into which all the discords of the ancient procedures were resolved, it is understandable why all grants and transfers are subjected to interpretation that will bring forth this sweet sound. But as we have suggested, the seignorial ingenuity does not stop with mere interpretation. If a lord has the full jurisdiction over his tenements he can make ordinances. This ordinance power in the eleventh century is an incident of the *consuetudo* of which the charters are full. The man who has *consuetudo* can make *consuetudines*. Ordinances may be promulgated for single cases or they may on occasion take the form of rather pretentious regulations which are not usually limited to mere matters of toll and tax, but which attack the problem of wrongs, set up procedures, and fix penalties,

as something susceptible to tax like the multiplication of hogs or the crops of the field. This is because the financial sanctions in the 11th century are undifferentiated except in terms of jurisdiction. Whether you fail to pay *census* or you steal cows, you are subject to *emendatio,* although your *census* may be due an abbot and a baron may have *vicaria* over theft. Until the more drastic sanctions like forfeiture become usual the distinction between an economic "offense" and a delict does not exist. There are few documents that distinguish between delicts. *Cf. Cart. Ste. Marie Char.* (3 *Arch. Anj.*), no. 94 "magnis forfactis et de parvis . . ." (1085); no. 419 (1110).

usually fiscal and frequently at variance with the provisions of the earlier folklaws.[76]

The earliest attempts to deal with wrongs by local ordinance that we have found are the statutes compiled in the year 977 for the monastery of La Réole in Acquitaine by the Abbot Richard of St. Benoît-sur-Loire.[77] Before this time special codes existed dealing with the internal regulations of a monastery, particularly with reference to religious duties. A celebrated one is that of Adalhard of the ninth century,[78] and the so-called *consuetudines* of Cluny are well known.[79] We have indicated below other early instances of "feudal" enactments,[80] illustrating innovation

[76] These regulations are the most convincing proof available that the older folklaws did not retain continuous and general validity. At the same time they put in issue any assumption that the so-called *coutumes* of the 13th and 14th century were primarily "Volksrecht." The most recent work on the subject, Le Brun, *La coutume* (1932), 17 *et seq.*, fails to take into account the probable effect of local legislation in the growth of local law. When we regard, for instance, the spread of the old ban penalty of 60 sol. in the 10th and 11th centuries to cover all types of wrong, we are obviously dealing with legislation from above. Consult further, Chénon, *H.D.F.*, (1926), §193 *et seq.*

[77] 2 Giraud, *Histoire du droit français,* 510. The charter reconstituting the monastery is in 9 *H.F.* 733.

[78] 2 Guérard, *Polyptyque de l'Abbé Irminon,* 306. There has been published a 13th century Norman document of this type. *Cf.* Guillorean, *Un fragment de Coutumier de l'Abbaye du Mont S. Michel* in 24 *Revue Catholique de Normandie,* 161, 167.

[79] 1 Achery, *Specilegium,* 641 *et seq. Cf.* also 2 Albers, *Consuetudines Monasticae* (1900). For obvious reasons few of these regulations deal with offenses. But see 5 *ibid.,* 17, *Consuetudines Monasteriorum Germaniae,* c. XVI; 3 *ibid.,* 115, 139, *Capitula Aquisgranensia,* c. LXI.

[80] This type of early feudal legislation has excited little interest. It stands midway between the old folklaw and capitulary jurisprudence, and the later compilations of *coutumes*. In suggesting that there was far more legislation than writers have been willing to admit, we do not wish to imply that much of the old folklaw did not persist as to certain matters, or that new folkways did not come into being. At the same time the subject of wrongs was certainly one where changes in the law were more likely to be by legislation as it was a source of profit.

The habit of legislation was already set in the abbeys as we may deduce from the existence of monastic regulation. The immunity from secular interference favored similar lawmaking for lay tenants. Certainly, in the

respecting procedure and sanctions, and it should be mentioned

early eleventh century, the church itself considered its power within an immunity absolute except as possibly limited by grants. *Cf.* the forms of papal confirmation (1000) Silvester II to Déol "absque omni iugo seu ditione" and no one is "querelam movere, vel calumniam facere vel aliquam potestatem ibidem exercere," and then the later confirmation of Innocent II (1136) to St. Pierre-le-Vif-les-Sens where the prohibition is differently phrased, "ut nulli omnino hominum liceat prefatum monasterium temere perturbare aut eius possessiones auferre vel ablatas retinere minuere seu quislibet molestiis fatigare sed omnia integra conseruentur, eorum pro quorum gubernatione et sustentatione concessa sunt." Wiederhold, *Papsturkunden in Frankreich* (1910) Heft 5, no. 1, and 8; *cf.* also *ibid.,* Heft 6, no. 3 (1112), no. 6; Heft 4, no. 6 (1099).

The ecclesiastical documents are useful in showing the variety of uses to which the word *consuetudo* is put. The monastic *consuetudines,* the charters and papal bulls, all employ this word in its various connotations. In addition to the material already cited, *cf.* Ivo of Chartres, *Epistola CI,* (162 Migne, *Patrologia,* 120), regarding jurisdiction over pseudo-clerics etc. "a nobis distringendi et corrigendi sunt, et ipsi et eorum res nostri sunt juris. Et haec est antiqua et inconcussa consuetudo . . . omnium ecclesiarum." Compare with this the charter of Ivo (1114) in 8 *Gallia Christiana,* Instr. 314, *re* acts of *prévôts.*

Types of out-and-out legislation are the customs for Chapelaude (1073). Tardif, *Mon. Hist.,* no. 290; the regulation of theft at St. Andrew of Vienne (1000) in 3 Achery, *Specilegium,* 382; the *Brevem de Exemplis* of the latter 11th or early 12th century in *Cartulaire de l'Abbaye de Beaulieu* no. 101; the "summa privilegiorum Capituli Remensi" (1068), 10 *Gallia Christiana,* Instr. no. 30, and in more complete form, 1 Varin, *Archives de la Ville de Reims* (C.D.I. 1839) no. 37, is a confirmation of certain jurisdictional and procedural privileges, some of which Varin thinks are of considerable antiquity. Certain provisions are patently "legislation," not usage. In the confirmation of Urban II (1096) 10 *Gallia Christiana,* Instr. no. 29, this collection is called *consuetudines.* Another document in the nature of a concord but which is like a piece of joint legislation (it opens "statutum est") for la Chaise le Vicomte (before 1089) is in Marchegay and Mabille, *Chroniques des l'églises d'Anjou* (1869), 344. In some cases, concords or conveyances contain essentially substantive matter, thus the grant of 1099 to St. Vincent in *Cartulaire St. Vincent du Mans* (1886–1913), no. 16 gives the right of stripping outland thieves; the concords between the Count de Nevers and the Abbé de St. Germain (1121) in 1 Quantin, *Cartulaire Général de l'Yonne,* no. 132 regulates chattel forfeiture and has other penal provisions for economic offenses; the grant of Robert de Meulan to St. Pierre de Préaux (1106) contains a regulation of procedural details, Valin, *Duc de Normandie,* no. 4, p. 258. Other grants where a part of forfeitures or *emendatio* is reserved necessarily involve a recognition of the power to fix the penalty and are a prediction that it will not be small. *Cf.* 2 Marchegay, *Archives d'Anjou,* no.

here that the later charters to cities like that of Louis VI to Lor-

93, 239. There is an interesting document in Trémault, *Cartulaire de Marmoutier pour le Vendômois* of the year 1070, no. 52. One Hilgod had conveyed a *plessis* to the monastery on condition that he be received as a brother twice a year. He turns up and a servant refuses him food. Since no one in authority could be blamed, the prior says "non esse consuetudinem nostram de tali forisfacto facere aliam emendationem nisi tantummodo de famulo sumere corporalem disciplinam." Such a "custom" may have been a folkway but it was the way of the folk in power.

In the many documents examined where a *consuetudo* of murder, arson, theft and the like is conveyed, there is no further specification of what this consists of, and where the grant reads "bannum de homicidio, etc." (*supra,* p. 211) the intent is obviously full jurisdiction which necessarily includes the right to fix penalties.

As far as Normandy is concerned the existence of local legislation of the type discussed rests in some cases upon inference and in some cases on direct proof. There are plenty of grants of *consuetudines* during the 11th century, and when one finds a charter reading "omnes consuetudines . . . ut habeant, teneant et possideant omnia absque ulla inquietudine secularis vel cuiusque judiciariae potestatis" (Robert to Bernai [1072] in 1 Le Prevost, *Notes sur le Départment de l'Eure,* 285), one readily conjectures that, free of interference, an abbot would make his own law. This one may conclude from a writ of Henry I, following an interference by his justice in a homicide and an arson case (Valin, *op. cit.,* no. 5, p. 259)— "precepio et volo quod ammodo teneat predicta abbatia Sancte Trinitatis de Fiscanno omnes dignitates suas et rectitudines et consuetudines tam in placitis . . ." etc. A great many abbeys in Normandy had direct grants of jurisdiction over wrongs, for example, Montivilliers in Harfleur—*sanguinis* (1035) 11 *Gallia Christ.,* App. 326; Préaux (1047)—"dedit consuetudines . . . sc. hainfaram, ullac, rat, incendium" etc.; Henry I to St. Pierre-sur-Dive (1108) conveys "criminal" pleas, has procedural regulation, and in relation to the market peace—"abbas justitiam et rectitudinem faciet et emendatio sua erit," 11 *Gallia Christiana,* Instr. 156–7; *cf.* also the charter of Henry I to St. Evroul, Round, *Calendar,* no. 627.

One should also consider here the possible significance of c. 44 of the Council of Lillebon, Bessin, *Concilia,* 71: "Has consuetudines habeant Episcopi in illis locis, in quibus eas tempore Rodberti Comitis, vel Guillelmi Regis ejus concessione hactenus habuerunt. Quae vero quieta fuerunt, eam quietudinem habeant, quam huc usque solide tenuerunt. In his omnibus justitiis & consuetudinibus Rex sibi retinet quod huc usque habuit." Considering the juxtaposition of "justitiis et consuetudinibus" it is not impossible that this refers to the "legislation" made to perfect the jurisdiction conveyed by charter. In view of the vagueness of the reference to customs in the time of Robert, the chapter is scarcely to be taken as a general confirmation of grants by charter, but of acts done pursuant to such grants.

Of course, the developments in France along these lines have a certain connection with the similar phenomenon in the Empire. The "Hofrecht" (*lex familiae*) of Burchard of Worms (1 *Mon. Ger. Hist. Legum Sect.* IV,

ris,[81] and certain *fueros* of the north of Spain[82] are productions
which have a similar origin and purpose. These *consuetudines*
establish for the places of their redaction the existence of a posi-

639) is one of the most celebrated. The "Hofrecht" and "Dienstrecht"
problem is discussed at length in 1 Maurer, *Geschichte der Fronhöfe*
(1862) 499, 4 *ibid.*, 278 with emphasis on the usage side. There are shrewd
comments on the parallels between "Hofrecht" and "Landrecht," in
Fürth, *Die Ministerialien* (1836), 247 *et seq.* The parallel is familiar to
students of English law in the relation of copyhold tenure and common
law tenure. *Cf.* also on the whole problem 6 Waitz, *D.V.G.*, 409 *et seq.*
On the 11th and 12th century forgeries of "Dienstrecht" *cf.* Brunner-
Heymann, *Grundzüge, D.R.G.*, 122, where literature is cited. Compare
with these the forgery for the Abbey of St. Bernard in Romans in Wiederhold, *Papsturkunden,* Heft 3, no. 1.

For Flanders *cf.* Wauters, *Les libertés communales* (1878) 236 *et seq.*
One of the most interesting and complete of the charters to which Wauters makes reference is that of Henry III to St. Maximin (1056), 1 Beyer,
*Mittelrheinisches Urkundenbuch* (1810), no. 345. In many details the
regulations parallel those in the northwestern French territory.

[81] In relation to the towns the same problem exists—what originates in
legislation, what in usage? For example the Charter of Guy and Ivo to
Amiens (1091–95) in Thierry, *Recueil des documents inédits de l'histoire
du tiers état,* 22, there is a long recital of procedure of which some details
are clearly old usage and some outright legislation. *Cf.* also the "Articles
primitifs" of 1117 (*ibid.*, 39) which allegedly were the result of general
deliberation. A scrutiny of the early royal charters would doubtless reveal
a great deal of local law that had its roots in seignorial decree; for example
the charter of Louis VII to St. Mary and St. Martin (1141), 1 Teulet,
*Layettes,* no. 74, confirms certain *consuetudines:* "De sanguine effuso,
anserem unum." Since the usual penalty where blood was shed was 60 sol.
one can only assume this lower rate was due to ecclesiastical benevolence.
The charter to Lorris is discussed at length by Prou, *Les coutumes de
Lorris,* in 8 *N.R.H.* 139, 267. In connection with this phase of the problem
should be considered the charter of Louis VII to Bourges (1145) 1 *Ordonnances* 9, where a number of *pravas consuetudines* are altered or a previous royal alteration confirmed. It would be hard to explain the matter
changed as mere usage of the burghers. *Cf.* also the charter to St. Riquier
(1126) in 11 *Ordonnances,* 184. These are examples taken at random. The
problem deserves further investigation.

[82] *Cf.* for example, the three *fueros* in 2 *Annuario de Historia del
Derecho Español,* 463 *et seq.*; 5 *ibid.*, 410. Hinojosa, *Das Germanische
Element im Spanischen Rechte* (31 *Z.R.G.*[2], 289), says speaking of the
local *fueros,* "Diese Rechtsdenkmäler sind vorwiegend Zusammenfas-
sungen des Gewohnheitsrechtes." But if one examines for example the
11th century *fuero* of Jaca (5 *Annuario,* cited *supra*) much of the document is patently ordinance.

tive regulative power in respect of wrongs, and one may perhaps assume that the practice of occasionally legislating was fairly general. Even if our observations regarding the poverty of draughtsmen's vocabularies might make us doubtful of the possible implications of the varied contexts of *consuetudo* in conveyance, concord or code, it is difficult to escape the conclusion that a grantee or beneficiary would avail himself of the confusion induced by this ambiguity to hammer out a charge or a right to make ordinances, if it was convenient.

Perhaps even more convincing evidence of the ordinance power than these petty codes emerges from conveyances or concords in which some single detail or procedure is to be regulated. The very casualness with which this is done, the absence of an elaborate recital—that the party is the lord of so-and-so and has *consuetudo,* ban and *vicaria* and therefore—shows that if one has a jurisdiction, the incidents, as Coke would put it, are tacité annexed. An example of this type of ordinance is one that appears in charters from widely separated localities—the division of jurisdiction between two lords over thieves.[83] To the one party will be given jurisdiction of despoiling the culprit to the point of stripping him naked and casting him forth into the arms of the other lord who will then exercise the privilege of hanging. Such regulations put in issue the theory underlying the more drastic feudal sanctions.

[83] For example, *Cart. St. Maur* (1 *Arch. Anjou*) App. no. 63 (1066) the earliest instance we have found of this practice; the charter of Conan of Brittany to Mont St. Michel (1170), Round, *Calendar,* no. 750 seems to recognize this division. *Cart. St. Vincent du Mans*, no. 16 (1099–1100) 1 *Cart. Gen. de l'Yonne*, no. 132 (1121) and *cf.* also 2 *ibid.*, no. 93 (1159).
The distinction may have been based on a real difficulty—the infliction of afflictive penalties by the church as suggested in *Cart. St. Maur*, no. 67 (1174). This may be a later rationalization like the drollery of Henry I in the charter to Bec (Round, *Calendar,* no. 375; 1134) regarding the fitness of clergy to judge rape. In any event a charter of Henry II to Foutervault du Pont de Cé (c. 1177) 2 Delisle-Berger, *Rec. des Actes de Henri II,* no. 503 reserves execution and leaves the profits to the monastery, demonstrating that the distinction was useful in a policy of controlling the execution of malefactors as an incident of maintaining public order.

The procedure of partitioning execution against a single individual is obviously based on a theory of body liability. This theory is nothing new. Enslavement for ban or composition debts had been a usual form of execution among the Franks.[84] To the persistence of the theory there existed no humanitarian objection since the whole structure of society was premised upon various forms of dependent relationship. Sharp lines are scarcely to be drawn between serfdom and other sorts of vassalage,[85] for the rise and fall of an individual's status in the tenth and into the eleventh centuries depended as today on fortune. Charters transferring *milites*[86] as well as serfs are not unusual. For their own sins and even for those of their ancestors free men piously assume the yoke of servitude.[87] The court's power of *districtio* is sufficient to enable it to compel the same thing as a form of execution.[88] What distinguishes the partition of the thief and his

[84] The materials on this are collected in Petot, *L'Hommage servile* in 6 *N.R.H.* 4 ser., 81.

[85] Guérard, *Polyptyque de l'Abbé Irminon,* Prol. 422, "la ligne qui séparait le vassal était souvent bien peu marquée" etc. On the changes later, Bloch, *Les transformations du servage,* in *Mélanges offerts à Lot* (1925), 55 *et seq.* We shall presently examine one critical difference between serfdom and other types of vassalage, not in issue here, the loss of "legalitas" as distinguished from *status* by the process of conviction or enslavement. The effect of changes in status or degree of dependency on the system of juristic thought based upon a relatively static *wergeld* remains to be explored. There is certainly a basic inconsistency between the volatility of *status* in the 10th and 11th centuries and the *wergeld* concept. We may have here further evidence of the destruction of the latter system.

[86] Guilhiermoz, *Essai sur l'origine de la noblesse,* 330, esp. n. 17.

[87] Salmon et Grandmaison, *Le livre des serfs de Marmoutier* (1864) Intro. xiii *et seq.*

[88] The cases indicate action both by the defendant lord and by the court. An example of the former is in 2 Guérard, *Cartulaire de l'Abbaye de St. Père de Chartres,* 297 (1013–1033): "Notum esse volumus tam presentibus quam futuris, ego Arnulfus abbas et omnis sancti Petri Carnotensis cenobii mihi a Deo commissa congregatio, quod Vivianum nostrum collibertum, cum uxore sua, omnemque pecuniam ejus subjugamus servituti Willelmi militis, pro interfectione furtiva cujusdam sui servi, quem ipse et uxor sua latenter interfecerunt, et eo tenore eos dimittimus, ne occidantur pro hoc scelere. . . ." Or the same result is reached by concord where the pressure is extra-judicial. *Cf. Livre des serfs,* no. 105 (1062) ". . . Quos cum in furto rerum nostrarum quas ipsi nobis servare

chattels from the sort of body liability prevalent in Frankish times is, however, that the liability is not for a debt, but for a penalty. The fact that so often there is no whisper of a plaintiff's right shows this to be so. What is laid down in the documents, therefore, is innovation, and innovation that one must again as-

debebant deprehendissemus, et unde nobis redderent quod furati fuerant non haberent, seipsos in perpetuum servos Sancti Martini tradiderunt et nostros . . ."; no. 127 (1097) "Noverint omnes quod Otbertus bergerius combussit quandam grangiam nostram, et cum non haberet unde emendationem ejus nobis persolveret, devenit ideo servus Beati Martini Majoris Monasterii atque noster, una cum Pletrude uxore sua, sicut in alia scriptum est carta . . ." and compare with no. 6 (1064–1084) "Servus quidam de familia nostra, nomine Arnulfus, Gazellus cognomine, fecit quoddam forisfactum Teduino de Rupibus: propter quod, idem servus cum non haberet unde illud posset emendare, traditus est ei loco emendationis, ita ut nichil ad nos ultra pertineret, quicquid de eo faceret Teduinus. Postea cum jam aliquot annis egisset in servicio ejus, interpellavit Teduinun domnus Odo prior, qui fuit prepositus de Chamartio, de servo illo, et precatus est eum, ut redderet Sancto Martino hominem suum. Cujus precibus adquiescens Teduinus, promisit se facere quod petebatur, ita tamen ut servus daret ei non tam pro redemptione quam pre bona voluntate xv solidos. . . ."

Cf. *Cartae de Carboio* (2 Marchegay, *Arch. Anjou* 6) a transfer as a pledge (1050). In *Cart. Marmoutier pour le Dunois,* no. 57 (1084–1100) is a self-enslavement which may be a mere homage. In *Cart. St. Vincent du Mans,* no. 307 (1080–1100), a defendant is ordered to be a *colibertus.* In *Cart. Ste. Marie de la Charité* (3 *Arch. Anjou,* no. 290) is a concord of 1143 where the one party "tanquam famulus, querendo equm suum, abbatissam quocunque vellet ire et eum ducere sequeretur." This may bear some relation to tenure in serjeantry.

As status becomes more sharply defined the practice of body liability assumed less crude forms than enslavement. The persistence of the idea of body liability is evident in the expression "in mercy for his body" that becomes a familiar entry in English plea rolls. As we shall presently see it is the basis of a ransom-bargain with the courtholder.

The *homagium pacis* may likewise be a modification of the practice of enslavement in cases where status had to be reckoned with, or where the man doing homage possessed free land. The *homagium pacis* is discussed by His, *Todschlagsühne und Mannschaft,* in *Festgabe für Güterbock* (1910), 347 and by 1 Mayer, *D.F.V.G.,* 164; Petot, *op. cit.;* Platon, *L'Hommage féodale comme moyen de contracter des obligations privées* in 26 *Revue Générale de Droit* 1, 97, 224, an essay based chiefly on south French material. There is a good summary of the whole matter in Mitteis, *Lehnrecht und Staatsgewalt* (1933), 484.

To His' "viel ältere Zeugnisse liefert Frankreich" (none of which are

sociate with the theory of the *bannus*—a right which gives the court the complete control of the individual wrongdoer, his body and his goods, even to the point of confiscation.

Of the two phases of a courtkeeper's power of execution— against the body and against property—the former is probably of less significance in a system of law governed by economics rather than ethics. It is true that in this period the death penalty is used to an increased extent and this extension, which we may attribute to the ordinance power, is essentially a reflection of the ferocity of the times. It is, furthermore, a development to be expected when one considers the sort of person who is now likely to be the subject of judicial action, and against whom the extant notions of body liability can practically be applied. Robert of Bellesme, ordered by Henry I to stand to right, betakes himself to his castle and prepares for war.[89] It is even less the footloose thief than it is the clodhopper, too poor to own a horse on which

earlier than the 12th century) must be added Petot's Ms. examples and the following *Cart. Marmoutier pour le Vendômois*, no. 47 (1050–1066): ". . . Cunque in capitulum nostrum venisset atque iterum dimisisset calumniam, devenit homo domni abbatis et noster, omnem fidem nobis et nostris promittens. Domnus autem abbas donavit suo homini decem solidos, dimissis illis XXX, et palefredum XX solidorum, pro meliorando scilicet suo servitio . . ."; no. 56 (1063–1084): ". . . Et quod non poterat reddere ea que nobis abstulerat, devenit homo domni Barthol[om]ei abbatis, vice omnium nostrum promisitque se acquietaturum nobis illam terram ab omnibus . . ." 1 *Cart. Trinité de Vendôme*, no. 204 (1070); *Cart. St. Vincent du Mans*, no. 188 (1073–81): ". . . Quapropter suis manibus abbati Raginaldo se commendavit et hec supra memorata forisfacta ab ipso in fevo accepit, . . ."

It should be noted that the earliest evidence of this institution in northern France dates from the middle of the 11th century. Mitteis, *Lehnrecht*, 486, n. 95, 96, has three cases from Ms. Norman sources. The *S.L.N.*, cap. XXVII, 25, regulates the matter, indicating that the homage is *pro pace servanda*. By this time the homage seems to be a mere additional sanction. None of the Norman sources show that the homage is performed with reference to a tariff for amends.

Consider finally *Cart. St. Vincent du Mans*, no. 188, where homage releases excommunication, and Marchegay and Salmon, *Chroniques des Comtes d'Anjou*, 139, where it is a condition precedent to a concord.

[89] The details are in Orderic, *Historia Ecclesiastica*, XI, ch. 3. Mitteis, *Studien zur Geschichte des Versäumnisurteils*, 42 *Z.R.G.*[2], 167 n. 7 treats

to flee, too base to bear feud, upon whom the majesty of the law operates. If such fellows do things sufficiently wicked or are a menace to their locality, they are removed, speedily and profitably. The man who has *bannus* or "all customs" of his lands can perform the prophylactic functions of police against those who are in a state of economic subjection to him without a pretentious theory of infidelity or without taking view of the Carolingian capitularies. He will be called to answer only if and when he oversteps the terms of grant. And pressure will be brought to bear upon him in such case only at the instance of some other immunist upon whose similarly fiscal perquisites he has infringed.

The union of the death penalty with the most drastic of the feudal sanctions, chattel forfeiture and deprivation of realty, is more fortuitous than consequential. The property sanctions are independent, if concomitant, aspects of the exercise of the corrupted ban. Whatever the validity of Brunner's theory that the Carolingian death penalty and confiscation were conceptually one,[89a] the "feudal" ban wielder's death penalty was not a condition precedent to forfeiture since he could impose the ultimate property sanctions for abjuration, exile or flight. Neither in Normandy nor in England is there evidence that these sanctions flow from a concept of civil death, a Roman law idea that revives long after the Anglo-Norman law has taken definitive form. Although the courtkeeper's power to impose the death penalty is in practice established in the course of the tenth and eleventh centuries, so much of the jurisdiction over crimes is controlled by ec-

Henry I's action as an outlawry ("Achturteil"). This expression must be intended as a Germanization of the Norman *forisbannitio* for there is no process in Norman law that has the exact implications of the English outlawry. In any event, Orderic's language "publicum hostium judicavit" probably has a different technical explanation. Some such judgment would be needed to put military action against Robert within the exception of public war permitted by the Norman truce of God, and to permit the requisition of troops. One cannot, however, lay too much weight upon the technical accuracy of Orderic's language.

[89a] *Supra,* Chapter II, pp. 107, 115.

clesiastical immunities that this penalty is to be dormant until the thirteenth century, with the paradoxical result that capital punishment, the central idea of the developed concept of felony, is one of its last accretions.

The sanctions against property that eventually take the form of chattel forfeiture and escheat, are, then, independent penalties. They are probably not lawfully available to the ordinary immunist until toward the end of the tenth century when the *causae criminales* are no longer crown cases. But undoubtedly many a count or bishop had been employing them, since they are rooted in the ban penalty with its attendant *districtio,* whether mesne process or final execution.

### CHATTEL FORFEITURE AND MISERICORDIA

In the Norman law the genetic relation of its forfeitures with the Frankish procedures is most patent in the case of those persons who have left the jurisdiction voluntarily or involuntarily. Just as the Franks coupled with their sentence of foreban against an individual, a *missio in bannum* against his property, so the Normans use a *forisbannitio* against fugitives with a chattel forfeiture attached.[90] This rule is attested in the earlier half of the

---

[90] It is this parity of treatment of the man convicted and the fugitive that makes the fugitive the knotty problem of early medieval law enforcement. Ficker's remarks as to Italy in 1 *Forschungen zur Reichs und Rechtsgeschichte Italiens,* 97 with reference to the two phases of the ban are applicable to the situation in northern France. He says with reference to the ban for contumacy (process) and for exile (punishment): "Beide Fälle des Bannes lassen sich wohl theoretisch auseinanderhalten, erscheinen aber in den Quellen nicht immer scharf geschieden. Insbesondere ist das der Fall, wo es sich um schwere Verbrechen handelt, bei welchen als Regel angenommen wird, dass der schuldbewusste Beklagte sich dem Gerichte nicht stellt. Der Gedanke an Erzwingung eines Gehorsams, der unmittelbar die härtesten Strafen zur Folge haben müsste, tritt dann ganz zurück; der Gesichtspunkt ist mehr der, den Zustand des Bannes so empfindlich zu machen, dass er die verwirkte Strafe, möglichst ersetzt. Dadurch gewinnt dann auch der Ungehorsamsbann den Charakter einer selbständigen Strafe, ist von dem bezüglichen Ausweisungsbanne nicht scharf zu scheiden."

*Très ancien coutumier;*[91] the first exchequer rolls are dotted with forfeitures for flight;[92] a writ of 1154 confirms it;[93] Orderic relates episodes from the reign of Henry I that tally;[94] and the earliest truce of God,[95] in the preceding century, seems to contemplate such a procedure in respect to exiled violators of the peace, the exile being for purposes of forfeiture on a parallel with the forebanned.

In the case of a device like the ban, the perfect procedural counterpart to any claims of jurisdictional plenitude, there seems to be no reason why a substantive justification for the use of forfeiture was necessary even in the case where an individual in fact stood to right. The courtholder was entitled to and could fix the penalty[96] and even a very narrow conception of the right of executing sanctions would justify forfeiture. When the single word *forisfactura* signifies at once the misdeed and the penalty, one does not expect stringent theoretical bounds on a court. The limitations arise simply from the practical difficulty of putting sanctions into effect. In the eleventh century a petty fisc could

[91] *T.A.C.,* cap. XXXVII and note particularly the several summons.

[92] 1 Stapleton, *Rotuli Scaccarii Normanniae* (1840), 11, 16, 29, 33, etc.

[93] Haskins, *op. cit.,* App. H, 4.

[94] Orderic, *Historia Ecclesiastica,* III, 9. In III, 8, Orderic uses the phrase "exulabat." This may be *forisbannitio.* On Norman usage in England, *cf. infra,* Chapter VI, p. 421.

[95] Bessin, *Concilia Rotomagensis Provinciae,* 39, the truce of 1042–7. *Cf.* the discussion *infra,* p. 303. Apart from the question who gets the chattels, it seems clear that the infractor of the truce—who is exiled but has not begun his exile and dies—is treated as one who dies unshriven. The rule in such cases was almost universal that there was a chattel forfeiture. Caillemer, *op. cit.,* 7, 44, 51. *Cf.* also the rule of *S.L.N.* cap. XX, §1. Note also the rule in *T.A.C.* cap. 1 as to the chattels of excommunicates who are legally on a par with the forebanned.

[96] In relation to the general use of chattel forfeiture in Normandy note should be made of the provisions in the Inquest of 1091. The terminology wavers. In §1 the duke "habuit pecuniam suam et corpus eius ad suam justiciam faciendam." If the man proves he offended unintentionally: "per pecuniam fuit in misericordia." In §12 (offenses against pilgrims) "de corpore suo fuit in misericordia." In §13 (coinage) "terram suam et pecuniam forisfecit." Perhaps only in the latter case is a complete forfeiture contemplated.

scarcely inflict a mulct against a lord of equal strength. The great abbeys are powerless against the ordinary knavish baron.[97] Neither in Anjou nor in Normandy is there a public authority strong enough to see its process peacefully executed against the more powerful tenants in chief.[98] Only as to those in a state of substantial subjection politically or economically was the court-holder able to carry through his undoubted powers. Wherever the lord had a right to chattels in the event of a natural death, as in the case of the serf,[99] this right must have been invoked in the case of offenses.[100] As to a person of slightly higher status[101] and attached to the land, where a conviction was had through any procedure entailing infamy, the situation of the guilty was essentially the same as that of a serf, i.e., he was without law and the court could probably dispose of his body. In other words the degradation of the convicted man put his chattels in the situation of a serf's. This was undoubtedly applied in the case of thieves.[102] It seems probable that it is to avert the exercise of this power of forfeiture by foreign tribunals that such constant efforts are made through contract to assure jurisdiction over one's

[97] For example *Cart. St. Vincent du Mans*, nos. 307, 581, 613, all of which seem to be the type of blackmail case already mentioned. *Cf.* also *Cart. Ste. Mar. Char.*, no. 175, 185.

[98] *Supra*, n. 89. Note once more Pfister's remark in *Etudes sur Robert le Pieux*, 158 regarding the process of the French King.

[99] Caillemer, *op. cit.*, 2; Bloch, *Rois et serfs* (1920) 30 *et seq.* Thibault, *La condition des personnes en France*, in 12 *N.R.H.* (4 ser.) 450 *et seq.*

[100] The serf being himself conveyable as a chattel, a distinction between animate and inanimate chattels would scarcely be drawn. *Cf.* Lamprecht, *op. cit.*, 77, Thibault, *op. cit.*, 451.

[101] For example the *colibertus*, Lamprecht, *op. cit.*, 81. His legal state is "fast identisch" with the serf. "Trotzdem macht der Colibertus ungleich mehr Ansprüche." On the *hospites, ibid.*, 95, and note the charters cited *ibid.*, 99 note 12* regarding limitations on emendation to be exacted from them. This class of men were engaged in colonization of overgrown regions and there were specific reasons for particular treatment.

[102] *Supra*, n. 83. *Cf.* also the charter of Henry I to St. Pierre-sur-Dive (1124) in 11 *Gallia Christiana* 158; *Cart. Ste. Marie Char.* no. 194 (3 *Archives Anj.*). Note further the rule in *T.A.C.* cap. XLI regarding baronial jurisdiction over thieves and chattels, and compare the later cap. LXXXII, 11, where the jurisdiction extends only to the point of abjuration.

own men.[103] The later aphorism, *"qui confisque le corps con-fisque les biens,"*[104] has its roots not only in the peculiar associations of man and his chattels but in the forms of execution against men of low degree.

The punishment of free vassals is on a somewhat different basis. As late as the eleventh century there is evidence that there persisted something of the power of discipline that a senior had in Carolingian times, a power that points to the quasi-servile origin of at least some types of vassalage.[105] But when one reaches the higher brackets of the feudal hierarchy, there is nothing of the sort apparent. The nearer an individual approaches the courtholder in economic status, the less one can speak in terms of the vestiges of servility. As to such a person, the rule that mulcts be in accordance with the quality of the crime is a locution for a settlement in which status will be determinative. Punishment is then on the basis of negotiation. It parallels somewhat the bargain procedure of the Franks, except that the major premises are substantially different. The defendant bargains with the courtholder.[106] The courtkeeper possesses

---

[103] For example, Marchegay, *Doc. inéd. Anj.*, 125, no. 10 (1070); Lex, *Eudes Comte de Blois*, P.J. no. 13 (1015-23), a "judgment" which from the subscription assumes the aspect of a contract; *Cart. Marmoutier Vend.* no. 73 (1064-77).

[104] Loysel, *Institutions coutumières*, no. 839.

[105] *Supra,* ch. III n. 44. Note further Mitteis, *Lehnrecht und Staatsgewalt,* 682 *et seq.,* and the material there cited in the notes.

[106] Or as in a case in *Cart. St. Vincent du Mans,* no. 311 (1085-97) the court puts the defendant with his goods in the plaintiff abbot's mercy, obviously to give the plaintiff bargaining power: "Judicaverunt quoque quod si fevum suum amplius de abbate habere vellet, res suas ad voluntatem et misericordiam abbatis anteproferret." *Cf.* also *Cart. Ste. Mar. Char.* (3 *Arch. Anjou*) no. 259 (1110): "Quorum peticionibus domna abbatissa humiliata, pie quesita misericordia, donavit affectu." *Cf.* also *ibid.,* no. 311. Note also the 12th century Norman document (1154-8) in Haskins, *op. cit.,* App. H, no. 3: one Robert restores to Savigny tithes and lands to which the abbot had proved his right "et de chatallis suis misit se in miseratione abbatis et monachorum pro malefactis que ipse et fratres eius fecerant eis."

From these types of *misericordia* presumably some form of concord results. The differences from the Frankish *securitas* would be sharply

the final trump in the play. He can use his position as feudal superior to coerce, through the imponderable sanctions of withdrawal of grace, and what some texts describe as the incurring of indignation.[107] Here is the elusive basis of the *misericordia,* the mercy, which leads the lord to adjust the *forisfactura* in terms of something instead of everything.[108]

The expression *misericordia* first begins to have a technical use in the law of the Frankish Kingdom. It is occasionally used in the capitularies of the ninth century.[109] The scholars who have

marked since there is no bargain in any real sense, but an act of grace by the winning party.

[107] This is the expression in the Empire, 6 Waitz, *D.V.G.,* 461, n. 1. On the use by the papacy, 5 Hinschius, *K.R.,* 34. *Cf.* the Ms. text cited by Mitteis, *Lehnrecht und Staatsgewalt* 683, from Anjou, "nostram vindictam imminere sciat nisi emendaverit." *Cf.* also *Cart. Ste. Mar. Char.* (3 *Arch. Anjou*) no. 125 (1028) where Hamelin has been involved in trying to kidnap the daughter of Fulk Nerra, "cum virilem comitis animositatem (et) promeritam iram nullo alio modo placere posset nisi ad intercessionem confugeret comitisse Hildegardis, cujus benignitas sepe etiam pro malis bona retribuebat, obtulit ei, spontanea voluntate, ecclesiam Cepie perpetuo sibi retinendam aut cui vellet dandam, tantum ut eum seniori suo pacificaret et ei reliquum patris beneficium a comite impetraret."

[108] The earliest case found which illustrates that this process of bargain was carried on is in 1 *Cart. Trinité de Vendôme* no. 16 (1039). One Walter having killed a relative of Count Geoffrey, the count's barons adjudge his whole fief forfeit "Quod Galterius audiens tam per se quam per suos amicos misericordiam apud Goffridum comitem quesivit quam hoc modo consecutus est. Dedit itaque comiti Goffrido in emendacionem forsfacti, duo molendina que ab ipso tenebat apud Vindocinum. . . ."

In this connection should be noted the agreement between the abbot of Mt. St. Michel and Gilbert Paginel (1070–81), Round, *Calendar,* 714, and Haskins, *op. cit.,* 21 where aid is stipulated in case land is forfeited "Auxilium accipiet de terra quam tenet de Sancto Michaele pro sui corporis captione aut pro sua terra, si forisfecerit eam erga regem vel abbatem. . . ."

In both these cases the "forfeiture," actual or contemplated, is of land, but the principle of bargain would in any event be the same. *Cf.* here *Leges Henrici,* c. 71, 1: "Et si (homicida) beneficio legis ad misericordiam vel concordiam protrahatur . . ." etc. and *cf. Hn. Cor.* 8: "non dabit vadium in misericordia pecuniae suae" which indicates the anticipation of bargain.

[109] *Conv. Apud Confluentes* (860) c. 7 (2 *Cap.,* 156); Adn. c. 5 (*ibid.,* 157) *Cap. Carisiac.* (858) c. 3 (*ibid.,* 279).

examined the term[110] have determined that the words are descriptive of the grace of the king, his power of pardon, a certain untrammelled prerogative[111] in respect of his subjects. One has no difficulty in discerning how this power passes on to the Emperors substantially unchanged. In the Empire it is usually described as *gratia regis*,[112] and persons who forfeit this grace do things not otherwise required by law in order to regain it. Of course the basic idea is that an individual who is in a position to make things uncomfortable for persons subservient to him has to be placated. Consequently it was not unnatural that this same notion should be used in the lower rungs of the feudal ladder. Hincmar of Rheims, writing to Ludwig of Germany in 877,[113] uses the figure of the vassal who loses the grace of his senior and does everything in amends to regain favor as a means of persuading the East Frankish ruler to make his peace with God. The placating of superiors must consequently have been a familiar spectacle in the baronial halls as well as in the royal palace.

In ecclesiastical circles, the word *misericordia* has a technical meaning. It is the mercy of God that permits penance to wipe

[110] Brunner in 2 *D.R.G.*, 84 *et seq.*, relates the matter to the enmity of the king and the idea that the *infidelis* is the enemy of the king. The latter has in such cases an arbitrary power of punishment. Köstler, *Huldentzug als Strafe* (*Kirchenrechtliche Abhandlungen*, no. 62 [1910]) has collected a mass of material on the subject. *Cf.* 30 *et seq.*, for the Carolingian practice. He does not emphasize the relation of the *misericordia* to this. But see for the Anglo-Saxon usage *ibid.*, 22 n. 1 where *misericordia* = *gratia*. On this parallel *cf.* also 2 Mayer *D.F.V.G.*, 106 n. 95.

[111] Note particularly on the discretion in the matter of mercy and the idea of the *rationabilis misericordia*, Hincmar, *De Regis Persona et Regio Ministerio* c. 19. "Hoc eo dictum est ut sciamus secundum verbum Dei, secundum rationem dispensendam esse misericordiam debitoribus" (125 Migne, *Patrologia* 846).

The derivation of the *misericordia* in the Frankish capitularies from ecclesiastical sources seems certain. *Cf.* for example the oath of the King in 858 (2 *Cap.*, 296) and the letter of the Synod of Quierzy to Ludwig in the same year c. 12 (2 *Cap.*, 436) and the earlier Council at Verne (844) c. 1 (2 *Cap.*, 383).

[112] *Supra*, n. 107. Köstler, *op. cit.*, 32 *et seq.*

[113] 125 Migne, *Patrologia*, 988.

out sins.[114] And it is mercy which permits the redemption of penances in money.[115] In the dogmatical literature of the ninth and tenth centuries mercy and alms are synonymous,[116] and the monetary commutation of penances is sometimes spoken of as alms.[117] The terminology and the ideas are united almost to the point of ambiguity but the principle at the basis of the system is clear: "without mercy no redemption."[118]

[114] Rabanus Maurus, *De Eccl. Discipl.*, l. 3 (112 Migne, *Patrologia* 1259): "Deus natura misericors est. Paratus est salvare per misericordiam." This is clearly shown in the formulae for the penitentials, Regino, *De Ecclesiasticis Disciplinis*, l. 1, c. 299 (133 Migne, *Patrologia*, 247); Burchard, *Decretum*, l. 19, c. 5 (140 Migne, *Patrologia*, 952): "Ista secundum misericordiam concedimus tibi, non secundum canonum censuram" etc. Note also the absolution in the *Ordo* published by Schmitz, *op. cit.*, 757, "Ab omnibus judiciis que tibi pro peccatis tuis debetur secundum misericordiam suam omnipotens deus te absolvat" etc. *Cf.* also *Poenitentiale Cummeani, Excarpsus,* 1 Schmitz, *op. cit.*, 612. The idea is so completely a part of Christian dogma that it is hardly necessary to cite from the homiletic writings.

Hinschius, 5 *K.R.*, 123, emphasizes that after the 7th century there is no question but that the church intends its punishment as a detriment to the offender. Clearly, as soon as it borrows and canonizes secular sanctions the need for *misericordia* increases. This may account for the wealth of discussion in the period under consideration.

[115] *Concilium Triburiense,* c. 55 (2 *Cap.* 242). This likewise to be concluded from the language of the penitentials. For example, Burchard, *Decretum* l. 19, c. 21 which commutes fasting into a mass where the mercy of God is asked. *Simile,* the "miserere" to be said by those who cannot fast or pay. *Cf.* also the *Poenitentiale Egberti,* c. 13 §11. (Schmitz, *op. cit.,* 585).

[116] Obviously because of the whole doctrine of works. *Cf.* Hincmar, *De Cavendis Vitiis,* c. 4 (125 Migne, *Patrologia,* 888); Rabanus Maurus, *Comment. in Ecclesiasticum,* lib. 1, c. 14 (109 Migne, *Patrologia,* 783); *De Clericorum Institutione,* l. 2, c. 28 (107 Migne, *Patrologia* 340) Regino, *De Eccles. Discipl.* lib. 1, c. 105.

[117] For example, the entry in *Cart. St. Etienne de Caen,* in 15 *Revue Catholique de Normandie,* 40: "Anchetillus hospitalarius Cadomensis habuit 20 solidos Andegav. de misericordia uxoris Radulfi Noereto quoniam habureat infantem de Rogero fratre maritis sui, cui etiam fecit assidare quod penitentiam peteret et susciperet pro hoc peccato a Henrico Bajoccensi episcopo . . ." etc.

[118] *Cf.* the charter of Raoul of Monterevault to St. Florent (1086) in Marchegay, *Doc. inéd. sur Anjou,* 134: "ubi nulla misericordia nulla redemptio."

That the lay use of the term *misericordia* in the course of the tenth and eleventh centuries was unaffected by the ecclesiastical tradition seems very unlikely. To be sure the notion of redeeming afflictive penalties was very old. But the antiquity of the privilege of redemption in any event would not make it any less an act of mercy. Since the courtkeeper had the right to fix the penalty the person convicted might face the complete loss of chattels or even his life. It is an act of grace or discretion if the court lets him have either one, or a part of his chattels. Some such theory must underlie the use of this word *misericordia*. It is posited upon the right of the courtkeeper to his penalty and his execution to the exclusion of other claims; in other words upon the fact that the courtkeeper's fiscal claims are paramount and complete. It contemplates that these claims can or may be relaxed or commuted, for even the ghoulish humor of lawyers will hardly describe the complete confiscation of chattels, or the loss of life and limb, as an act of mercy. This expectation of commutation may, as we have indicated, be historically related to the sovereign prerogative of the Frankish kings, but from the facts of word usage and the greater technical frequency in the ecclesiastical literature there is indubitably a close connection with the exercise oi church discipline. In the practice of the church the expectation in the matter of alms varied considerably, the basic text being the passage from the Gospel of St. Luke dealing with Zacchaeus.[119] In secular practice, the ban drew into the courts' hands all chattels, so that the need of *misericordia* was the greater. That the church's conception of mercy and redemption had some influence upon secular practice may be deduced from various eleventh- and early twelfth-century documents.[120]

[119] Regino, *De Eccles. Discipl.*, lib. 2, c. 445; Burchard, *Decretum*, lib. 19, c. 23 (without reference); *Poenitentiale Egberti*, c. 13, §11; *Poenitentiale Cummeani, Excarpsus* (Schmitz, *op. cit.*, 614).

[120] The most frequent use of the misericordia-alms-redemption idea in the documents is where there is a transfer of property, and the recital is made explaining the conveyance. For example *Cart. Marmoutier Dunois*, no. 77 (1104); *Cart. Ste. Marie Char.* (3 *Arch. Anjou*), no. 114 (1123);

Furthermore, in the class of cases where a redemption was eventually recognized to exist as of right, the rules regarding the assessment of this mercy follow the division of the penitentials be-

no. 170 (1037); *Cart. St. Vincent du Mans,* no. 350 (1097); no. 829; Marchegay, *Doc. inéd. sur Anjou,* 134 (1086); Lex, *op. cit.,* P.J. no. 10 (1009–1012). The charters where the expression *misericordia* itself is used are not very frequent, but the idea is implicit in all grants for the redemption of a soul.

That mercy is sought of men as it is of God is borne out by a number of charters. In 1 *Cart. Trinité de Vendôme,* no. 19 (1038–40) is a petition of Hersende to Geoffrey Martel for aid against the bishop of Mans who has taken her fief: "Precor te, domine mi, ut misericordiam de me habeas, videlicet de mea terra que mei patris fuit, . . ." etc. The commutation of amends at the request of the court, the plaintiff "pie quesita misericordia, donavit affectu. . . ." *Cart. Ste. Mar. Char.* (3 *Arch. d'Anjou*) no. 259 (1112); *cf.* also 311 (1065) where condemnation takes place in the count's court and a gage surrendered to the abbey's *vicarius.* "Quo facto, petiverunt Tetbaudus et filii eius misericordiam ut ipsis miseretur Stabilis" (*vicarius*). In *Cart. Marmoutier Vendômois* no. 116 (1040–60) the victorious plaintiff exercises mercy. *Cart. Marmoutier Dunois,* no. 57 (1084–1100) a local rowdy comes in penitential garb "postulans misericordiam," and as he has no money to satisfy the monks, becomes their man.

In *Cart. St. Vincent du Mans,* no. 206 (*ca.* 1100) we find an excommunicate cattle thief asking *misericordia,* acknowledging his guilt, and conveying his land. This is clearly not a case of penance but the exercise of the sort of mercy that a courtkeeper will exercise. *Cf.* also the stipulation in *Cart. Marmoutier Dunois,* no. 153 (1096): "Unde si rei fuerint et emendatio legalis inde exierit, medietas ejus condonabitur ipsis. De altera vero medietate supplicantes eis et in misericordia ipsorum erunt." The entry in *Cart. St. Étienne de Caen,* 15 *Rev. Cath. de Normandie,* 22, is of the same sort. "Blancardus, in praesentia Rodulfi Constantiensis episcopi et baronum ejus, clamavit quietam totam calumniam quam pater suus, et idem ipse habebat (fol. 51) in ecclesia S. Hilarii de Meltuz, eo quod in ea nihil derationare potuit. Juravit etiam super sancta Evangelia, nullius tamen requisitione ut vicoactus; sed propria voluntate, et episcopi sui concessione, quod nunquam amplius, nec ipse, nec aliis pro se, aliquam calumniam de ipsa ecclesia moveret. Quo facto requisivit abbatem misericorditer ut concederet ei ipsam ecclesiam tenere, quanto duntaxat tempore eidem abbati et monachis placeret. Abbas consentiens concessit pro 100 solidis Rotomagensium unoquoque anno." In the case of the renegade monk in 2 *Cart. Trinité de Vendôme* no. 400 (1100) the *misericordia* of the abbot includes an infamy. No. 418 (1118) sets forth an act of *misericordia* after excommunication and submission without using the term itself.

For *misericordia* apart from penance, see the charter of Peter, bishop of Poitiers, to St. Maur (1105), in *Cart. St. Maur* (1 *Arch. Anjou*), no. 25, where certain churches are confirmed *misericorditer.* Compare also the

tween rich man, middle man and poor man.[121] The passage from the *Très ancien coutumier* setting this standard may have been composed at the end of the twelfth century, but it certainly represents a rule of greater antiquity.[122]

The chattel forfeiture of the eleventh century just discussed is in principle no different from the Frankish concept of confiscation, and the lines which unite the feudal practice to the older *bannus* are consequently perceptible. On the other hand, the final results of adjustments that had to be made when sanctions were taken against realty were so far removed from those at-

letter of Lanfranc to Roger (1 *Opera* 65) "Ab hoc vinculo anathematis absolvere te non possum, nisi misericordiam domini mei regis requiras; sibique et aliis quorum res injuste praedatus es, justitiam facias." In both instances the *misericordia* is like the *gratia* of the Emperor.

[121] *Poenitentiale Romanum* (Schmitz, *op. cit.*, 473 quoted *supra*, note 72). Cf. *Poenitentiale Bedae*, de qualitate hominum (*ibid.*, 563); *Poenitentiale Egberti* c. 13 §11; *Poenitentiale Cummeani* (*ibid.*, 614).

[122] *T.A.C.*, cap. LVI §2. "Si comes, vel baro, vel archiepiscopus, vel episcopus, vel abbas, c. libras dabit; miles vero ad minus dabit xx. vel [nichil]; rusticus, vel alius de populo, v. solidos vel nichil.

"§3. Si pauper miles nequissimus erit inter vicinos, et injuriosus, et in paupertate sua non timens Ducis misericordiam, ponetur in vinculis ferreis in domo burgensis alicujus, et ille per mensem vel per aliquot dies, juxta consuetudinem patrie vel assisie, ibi vivet; [et] est terra vendenda vel invadianda; in thesauro vero Ducis pecunia ponetur illius vendite hereditatis cel invadiate. Et si malefactor ille fuerit de populo, in prisione vili Ducis agat penitenciam.

"§4. Si vero miles fuerit, per milites jurato[s] catalla ejus cognoscantur. Que omnia Dux habebit, preter harnesium suum; arma scilicet, dextrarium, palefridum et roncinum; filii ejus habebunt roncinos; ipse et uxor ejus habebunt sua victualia per annum, et bubulci, et car[r]uca[s], et semen ad terras seminandas. Si burgensis, vel aliquis de populo, similiter habebit victualia sua et car[r]uce sumptus, si car[r]ucam habeat, et arma jurata. Cetera vero omnia [Dux] habebit sacramento militum et burgensium juratorum."

The relation of this section to the penitentials seems probable not merely from the words that the common man "agat penitenciam" in the duke's prison but chiefly from the tripartite division of men. To be remembered in connection with the assessment is the eleventh-century (1060) notification *Cart. Marmoutier Vend.*, no. 129 where the four reserved *consuetudines* are to be assessed "mensurate et cum moderatia." How pervasive the assessment was in the 11th century it is not possible to say.

tained by the Franks that the connection is here by no means obvious. Of course as far as the culprit is concerned, he is deprived of his land; the penal aspect is therefore the same in the eleventh as it was in the ninth century. But the rights of the feudal courtholder work out to be something substantially different from those of the royal fisc. Upon the paramount right of the latter to lands through confiscation there had existed no restrictions. When alodium was taken the vested rights of heirs were carefully sifted out and the benefice, being normally a life estate, could be withdrawn without prejudice.[123] But the diffusion of jurisdictions in the tenth century not only distributed the one-time inherent fiscal prerogative, but likewise created the necessity of adjustment between coordinate or competing claimants. More difficult even than these political obstacles were the barriers which the extensive reorientation in the control and devolution of realty had raised against the swift and irresistible operation of confiscation. The chattel remained more or less intact as the object of outright ownership. It can consequently be confiscated. But realty was so heaped through enfeoffment with a structure of ramified interests that it was only exceptionally something upon which a fisc could lay its hands without impinging upon the rights of innocent claimants.

### DISHERISON AND SANCTIONS AGAINST REALTY

It is certain that legal and not purely factual difficulties forced a reformation of the theories that justified sanctions against re-

[123] *Supra,* Chapter II. The withdrawal of the benefice at a period when heritability is not the norm does not require a theory of confiscation, but is a consequence of the withdrawal of public office. This would seem to follow from the view of Dopsch regarding the nature of the 8th and 9th century benefice. (*Cf. Benefizialwesen und Feudalitat,* in 46 *M.I.Ö.G.,* 1 *et seq.*) There is no question of sparing heirs here, because the law does not contemplate the existence of a claim to succession. *Cf.* also the discussion in Mitteis, *Lehnrecht und Staatsgewalt,* 147, 153 on the use of *missio in bannum* against a benefice, and the possibility of treating the withdrawal of the benefice as a purely contractual sanction rather than a confiscation.

alty. These legal considerations were part of the so-called "feudal law,"[124] the dispositions of which must be examined to appreciate their strength. We employ this expression, however, with the caveat that in the eleventh century "feudal law" in northern France is nothing more formal than the practices of the several polities, that it lacks the system and style of the Lombard jurisprudence, and consequently in relation to the conditions we are considering is a term somewhat pretentious.

The point of departure in French feudalism, as elsewhere, is the contract between the lord and the vassal. Feudal law is largely a regulation of normal expectancy in relation to this contract, and it moves generally in the sphere of bargain psychology. For this reason when it deals with sanctions, these are sanctions for bargain breach and it is misleading to characterize such breaches as "feudal crimes."[125] Of course, the ultimate sanction in a law of this sort is the loss of the land, the consideration for

---

[124] *Lehnrecht, ius feudalis,* is a term of art—the use of which no doubt goes back to the *Libri Feudorum* (*ius feudi* in I, 1, 4). It is occasionally used in Frederick Barbarossa's reign, *cf. Mon. Ger. Hist.* 1 *Const.* 236. See also on the terminology Laspeyres, *Über die Entstehung . . . der Libri Feudorum* (1830) 18 n. 26, 261. The German historians constantly draw distinctions between rules of law according to "Lehnrecht" and according to "Landrecht." The distinction is one between practices or rules that govern transactions between individuals where a lord and man relationship exists, and the folklaw, king's law, or provincial law relating to the same subject matter but without the element of the feudal nexus. The French writers have their "droit féodal," but English legal history has been fortunate in using such terms sparingly. For the purposes of historical analysis, except on the grand scale, the term leads to grave difficulties. It is simpler to deal with the rules governing feudal relations not as a rounded system but as a series of rules applicable to the practices incident to the creation, execution and termination of the feudal contract. In this relation it is well to bear in mind the wise words of v. Gierke, *Erbrecht und Vicinenrecht,* in 12 *Z.R.G.* (o.s.) 430, 461, in relation to the feudal rules of succession: "Denn hier wie überall schöpfte das Lehnrecht mit nichten seinen Stoff aus der Luft, sondern sammelte zahlreiche Bruchstücke älterer unabgeschlossener Bildungen in eine einheitliche Neubildung."

[125] One of Maitland's rare unhappy phrases, used to describe the continental *felonia;* 1 Pollock and Maitland, *H.E.L.* 303. On the point *cf.* Mitteis, *Politische Prozesse des Mittelalters* (XVII *Heidelberger S. B.* [1927]) 70. "Ein eigenes Lehnsstrafrecht gibt es nicht . . ." In his more

the performance of services. Since performance is guaranteed in the first instance by a *fides facta,* the solemn interchange of oath, most comprehensive on the part of the vassal, *the sanctions are taken for the breach of this obligation.* In other words, if a man loses his fief it is for his broken promise, established by his act, desertion in battle or the like. This conduct on the part of the vassal becomes known in the course of the twelfth century as *felonia.*[126]

In respect to our interest in these arrangements there is one further element that enters into the situation. This is the element of the capacity to enter into these bargains, the capacity to take the required oaths. This was a requirement that searched out the worthiness of the individual as a man. But it was a concept that went even further. It asked not only that man measure up to standards of law worthiness and good fame, but it looked also to the class of society into which a man had been born or had been elevated.[127] For the holding of land and the performance of

recent work, *Lehnrecht und Staatsgewalt,* Mitteis (p. 682) suggests that in the middle ages the sanctions of bargain breach were perhaps treated as a punishment. Note further his remarks regarding "true feudal criminal law."

[126] In addition to the discussion of the derivation of the word in 2 Pollock and Maitland, *op. cit.,* 464, *cf.* Diez, *Etymologisches Wörterbuch der Romanischen Sprachen* (4 ed. 1876), *s.v. fello.* The earliest use we have found is the word *fellones* (2 *Cap.,* 440) where it seems applied to bad people generally, perhaps to the *criminosi* or *famosi.* On early French vernacular use of the word *felun cf.* the translation of the Psalm 1, in Bartsch, *Chrestomathie* (1884), 54. It early has the implication of treason: "plus fel que Judas," *Raoul de Cambrai,* l. 1381.

*Cf.* also the use in *chanson* of Leodegard, Voretsch, *Altfranzösisches Lesebuch* (1921), 4. In the earliest recension of the *Libri Feudorum* the term does not appear but it is used in the sections composed after Barbarossa's legislation; Lehmann, *Das Langobardische Lehnrecht* (1896), 79. On the rare use in Norman Sicily *cf.* Niese, *Die Gesetzgebung der Normannischen Dynastie in Sizilien* (1910), 53 n. 6.

[127] That is to say, to hold a certain sort of fief and to do a certain sort of service you had to be the right sort of man—a *rusticus* cannot hold a knight's fee or do knight service. Mitteis, *Lehnrecht und Staatsgewalt,* 464 *et seq.* discusses the problem of capacity but chiefly on the basis of late sources.

service, even in the tenth and eleventh centuries, were dependent upon the status of the individual. In other words capacity was established by two factors, not unrelated: a man's legal character or reputation, and his status. It is manifestly impossible to go into the details of this concept. To some extent, it was an idea that grew up with the feudalization of property, and the multiplication of fiefs tended to propagate the distinctions of status and to mark its limits.[128]

The premises of feudalism as stated are oversimplified, but they are accurate enough to apply to the problem of heritability. As long as the duration of the feudal bargain is restricted to the life of the individual contractants, the successors of an individual are clearly not to be bound as a matter of legal duty by the engagements of the ancestor[129] nor have they any right to succession. When lands are granted for more than a life tenure the heirs take by virtue of a principle outside the bargain concept,

[128] The history of legal capacity in medieval times is yet to be written. There are suggestive remarks in Ehrlich, *Die Rechtsfähigkeit* (1909). On the development of status see esp. 1 Göhrum, *Geschichtliche Darstellung der Lehre von der Ebenbürtigkeit* (1846), 3 *et seq.*, for the Frankish period. For France there is material in Guilhiermoz, *Essai sur l'origine de la noblesse, passim.* Certain aspects of the matter were discussed by the writer in *The Equality of States* (1923), pt. 2, where further references are given.

While for some purposes status and legal capacity are separate concepts it is not possible in the early medieval law entirely to dissociate status from the *ad hoc* legal capacity that can be described as transactional capacity, for the measure of capacity is often enough a man's status. Status as distinct from capacity is illustrated by Guilhiermoz's thesis (*op. cit.*, 478) that in the eleventh century nobility is not a fixed concept. It is no more than a capacity to become a "chevalier." In this situation a man's legal capacity cannot in all respects be affected by status. There are, however, many acts where status is determinative, like the capacity to take an assize in England depending upon the enjoyment of knight status.

[129] We think this is correct despite the documents which show the ancestor taking oath for his heirs. An example of this is in 1 Bernard, *Cartulaire de Savigny* (1853), no. 802 (c. 1070). The cartularies are packed with cases where the ancestor conveys promising no interference by the heirs, or threatening them with penalties if they do. But this does not stop the heirs from proceeding upon the decease of the ancestor.

and then it can be said that the bargain between the lord and the ancestor is struck with reference to anticipated succession. The existence of the relief upon entry is the vestige of an era when this expectation was exceptional.[130] But the homage, the sealing by pledge of faith, is in any event an element that can only be personally performed.[131] Consequently, even if the bargain between the lord and the ancestor contemplates succession, the expectation will be fulfilled only if the heir is capable of making homage.

Although there has never been an intensive exploration of the growth of feudal succession, it is obvious enough that the rules concerning it were fashioned from prevailing folklaw regulations formulated in terms of alodium and chattels, although with certain changes in emphasis made in response to the political or economic requirements of feudalism, as in the case of the doctrines of escheat.[132] The developed Frankish rules of succession, based upon the theory that the father had certain prerogatives in disposing of the property, was not too consistent with the determinative feudal emphasis on the existence of offspring, as heirs capable of taking.[133] In the regions where the Frankish folklaw had prevailed, a difficult adjustment had to be made, in which the principle of voluntary disposition surrendered to the

[130] Guilhiermoz, *op. cit.,* 198.

[131] This was, of course, the relic of the older concept of commendation, the following (*comitatus*) discussed *supra,* Ch. II. The homage problem is simple as long as the man performs personal service to one senior. Subsequently, when the property ramifications become more elaborate and homage is done to the several lords of whom a man may hold fees and when the service is one of supply rather than of actual personal performance, the homage becomes a more formal act. In one respect alone is the older concept preserved with some clarity. This is the *homagium ligium,* the paramount fealty to one lord superior to other homage. For a discussion of this, Zeglin, *Der Homo Ligius und die Französische Ministerialität* (1914); Pohlmann, *Das Ligische Lehnsverhältniss* (1931) 8, 23, 48; Guilhiermoz, *op. cit.,* 180, 438.

[132] 3 Ficker, *Untersuchungen zur Erbenfolge* (1898) 464 *et seq.,* 473, who sees traces of older law from which the feudal rules proceeded.

[133] 3 *ibid.,* 382, 623; *cf.* Schröder, *D.R.G.,* 366.

requirements of a social system. For generations the feoffee's power of alienation was severely restricted, and consequently the rules of succession were unhampered by ancestral dispositions. The facts of birth, legitimacy, primogeniture, and so on, move to the foreground as crucial. It is this change in the basic premises of inheritance that has to be reckoned with in making property liable for the misdeeds of the feoffee.

Before heritability became general in all the ramifications of feudal tenure[134] the rules must have been certain as to what acts were breaches of the bargain relation sufficient to entail loss of fief. The direction that these rules took was marked out to some extent in the early ninth century. As succession spread it is of course not impossible that rules devised for life tenures became equally applicable to heritable fees, and that the sanctions for breach were enforced against the guilty man in possession without taking into account the claims of his descendants or collaterals.[135] There is, however, no evidence that this was so.

It seems more or less inevitable that when the notion of heritability triumphed the interest of the heirs in cases of bargain breach should be attacked from the angle of disherison.[136] In

[134] In the ninth century heritability was the rule in certain upper brackets, but it was by no means general, cf. 2 Brunner, *D.R.G.*, 345. For a long time it was believed that the capitulary of Quierzy (877) 2 *Cap.* 358, had established the rule for all stages of the feudal relation but this theory has been abandoned. *Cf.* Baldamus, *Das Heerwesen unter den späteren Karolingern* (*Untersuchungen* no. 4 [1879]) 90; Declareuil, *H.D.F.* 169, 173, 248; Chénon, *Hist. gén. de droit français public et privé* (1926), 432; Guilhiermoz, *op. cit.,* 198. In the empire heritability was general only toward the middle of the 11th century, 6 Waitz *D.V.G.,* 57 *et seq.* There is a good summary of the whole problem of succession in Frankish feudal law in Mitteis, *Lehnrecht und Staatsgewalt,* 165 *et seq.* For the later period 638 *et seq.*

[135] Thus the loss of benefice threatened in various capitularies, was a rule formulated at a time when a heritable benefice was not usual.

[136] It is important to note that the term "disherison" is chosen to avoid the implication of the word "exheredation." As we shall use disherison we intend to convey the meaning of cutting off a man's heirs from succession as a matter of law so that the property devolves as if there were in fact no heirs. This is the meaning of the term *exheredatio* in the second half

other words when a man committed acts sufficient to terminate
the feudal bargain, to lose his fief, in some way the claim of his
heirs to succession was wiped out.

of the 12th century in England. The *Dialogus de Scaccario* (Hughes et al.
Ed., 1902), II, xvi, uses the term *exheredare:* ". . . aut in omnibus im-
mobilibus, fundis scilicet et redditibus, ut eis exheredetur, quod fit pro
maioribus culpis . . ." At II, xB, Fitz Neale says: ". . . eschaete vulgo
dicuntur que, decedentibus hiis qui de rege tenent in capite cum non extet
ratione sanguinis heres." At II xxiv he says: "Si vero de eschaeta fuerit que
in manu regis deficiente herede, vel aliter, inciderit." This *aliter* may indicate his *exheredatio* is thought of as an escheat. Glanvill, *De Legibus*
(Woodbine Ed., 1932) VII, 12, speaking of the incontinence of female
heirs in wardship says "exheredabuntur," and their share goes to the im-
maculate ones, but if all have sinned the inheritance "ipsis dominis tamquam escaeta remanebit." The *tamquam* indicates a mere analogy. However in c. 17 he says: "Praeterea si quis de felonia convictus fuerit vel
confessus in curia, eo per ius regni exheredato terra sua domino suo
remanet escaeta." The word *exheredatio* is used in a letter of King John
in the sense of "deprive of inheritance." *Cf.* Powicke, *Loss of Normandy*
(1913) 220, 437 n., 479, 480.

The definition of the *exheredatio* as an escheat was perhaps due to the
increasing spread of the Roman law. It was essential that the English law
should have a term which described what English law did, instead of what
Roman law meant by the term. On the Roman law use of the term *exheredare* in the sense of an incapacity which an heir by his own act loaded
upon himself, *cf.* Merkel, *Die Justinianischen Enterbungsgründe (Untersuchungen*, no. 94, 1908), 4 *et seq.*, but here the ancestor must exheredate.
In view of the Roman influence traced by Merkel (24 *et seq.*) in the
French law of the 12th century and later, it is not improbable that the
English use of the word *exheredare* was much affected by the Roman.
But compared with the 12th century French *Brachylogus* (Bocking Ed.
[1829], lib. II tit. 23 *de liberis exheredandis*) it is obvious that Glanvill
is dealing with an utterly different series of concepts. On the Germanic
folklaw use of *exheredare,* in the sense of a disposition of property such
that the heir in fact was deprived of succession, Fipper, *Das Beispruchs-
recht nach altsächsischem Recht* (1879), 54; Merkel, *op. cit.*, 46 *et seq*. The
escheat for a crime, however, is literally a reverter of the property to the
feoffor because of a failure of heirs. Certain contemporary French writers
are not clear on the relation between the Roman theory and the local
practice of *exheredatio* in northern France. *Cf.* Glasson, *Le droit de succession au moyen âge,* 16 *N.R.H.* (1892), 795; Martin, *Histoire de la coutume de la Prevôté et Vicomté de Paris* (1922–1930), uses *désherence* and
*exheredatio* without definition, I, 252, 269, etc.; II, 428, 437.

Caillemer, *Les confiscations,* does not deal with disherison but solely
with confiscation. He expressly leaves out the penal use of property sanctions. Blum, *La commise féodale,* 4 *Tijdschrift voor Rechtsgeschiedenis,* 31

The best evidence that the process whereby the heir was cut off was through disherison is found in the frequent use of the term *exheredatio* in eleventh-century documents.[137] This word had been a term of art in the Roman law used to describe the incapacity of the heir to succeed because of his own act. In the Germanic law, however, it was employed in the sense that a factual disinheritance ensues when the object of inheritance is removed, so that the heir's expectancy is destroyed. It is impossible to give the *exheredatio* of the eleventh century the connotation of Roman law. And while we may regard it as expressing a possible projection of Germanic theory, the disherison of Norman law is a much more subjective idea. This law scrutinizes the heirs. Where they do not exist at all there is an escheat. Where seeming heirs are in being as human entities, it decides whether they are really heirs. If they are not heirs, there is still an escheat as if they had not been in *esse* as sentient beings. Only God can make an heir, but the Norman law can unmake one.

There can be little doubt that there existed certain conditions precedent to heirship which went beyond mere reputation to the roots of capacity. Apart from formal requisites of status the recognition of a stain sufficient to incapacitate could have been accomplished most easily through the extension of the familiar device of infamy.

We have seen that the concept of infamy had made its appearance in Frankish law as early as the first capitularies of the Merovingians, and that during Charlemagne's reign its scope had been extended in the secular law. The notion was seated in ecclesiastical law, but it was chiefly due to the Pseudo-Isidorean De-

does not approach the matter from the disherison angle. His results are not enlightening as far as the Anglo-Norman law is concerned.

[137] For example 1 *Cart. Trinité de Vendôme*, no. 6 (1032), no. 44 (1006–1040) and compare also no. 66 (1046), no. 67 (1000–1047) and no. 130 (1059). On a certain discretion in disinheriting 2 *ibid.*, 399 (1040–45). This is the point on which much of the motive in *Raoul de Cambrai* turns. *Cf.* further the curious language in a charter of William the Conqueror. *Chart. St. Julien de Tours*, no. 29 (1063).

cretals and the false capitularies of Benedict Levita that this device came into great vogue toward the end of the ninth century. Even the most cursory examination of these two collections shows the extensive part that infamy played in the scheme of sanctions developed by the forgers.[138] Since in this age a man to be anyone, let alone to do anything worth doing, had to be capable of oath taking, what canonical and Frankish infamy in fact accomplished was the destruction of a man's legal capacity, so that he was incapable of being a witness, or of bringing actions; so that he must go to the ordeal. Both Pseudo-Isidore and Benedict added to the infamy the punishment of loss of status,[139] a concept that became increasingly important as status became involved in the limitation of transactional capacity.

It was manifestly impossible for a person whose reputation was thus stained to take the oaths coupled with tenure.[140] This principle is stated not in the precise term infamy, but to the same effect, by Fulbert of Chartres, at the opening of the eleventh cen-

[138] Hinschius, *Decretales Pseudo Isidorianae* (1863), Anaclet. c. 20; Calixt. 8, 16; Stephen c. 2; Fabian, c. 5; and in substance Sixtus II c. 8; *cf.* Jul., c. 18; Benedict. Levita, *Capit.* (*Mon. Ger. Hist. Leges II*) II, 97, 361, 383, 410, III, 192, 200, 211, 261, 348. Important to notice is the extension to persons anathematized.

[139] Benedict., *Capit.*, III 235: "Servi si inscio domino confessi vel convicti fuerint violentiam commisse addicti tormentis gravibus puniantur. Si vero iubentibus dominis violentiae crimen admiserint, domini qui inlicita praeceperunt notantur infamiae et nobilitatis vel honoris sui dignitatem tenere non possunt . . ." Compare also Hinschius, *Decr. Pseudo-Isidor.*, 478, *Ep. Liberii,* incorporated in the *Decretum*, C. 24, q. I, c. 32.

[140] This idea is expressed bitingly in the verse of Benoît de Ste. Maure, *Chronique des Ducs de Normandie* (Michel Ed., 1856), ll. 101-3.

> "Que li pere e li fil entre eus
> Sunt si haïnos et si feus [fels]
> Que l'uns ne porte al altre fei."

The capacity to give a plight of troth is the kernel of the medieval concept of legal capacity. A promise on faith—*fidem facere de aliqua re*—is the normal form of contractual transaction, so that if a man pledges his faith he does not offer an additional assurance against which additional sanctions can be taken, but gives the prime guarantee without which no contract is made. Loening, *Der Vertragsbruch*, 518. The dominance of

tury;[141] it is likewise indicated in the first half of the *Libri Feu-dorum*.[142] But to attribute to a man's heirs the infamy of the parent was a step considerably greater than the Roman law had taken except in the case of treason.[143] Up to this time the furthest that the canon law had departed from Roman tenets had been to declare the progeny of incestuous marriages infamous.[144] The purpose of the feudal tie, however, was such that for very practical reasons it was necessary that the person who entered the forfeited fee should be beyond reproach. With this end in view it was essential that if the individual should become unworthy in law his heirs should suffer the like penalty. It would have been

bargain in all forms of transactions, in court and out, necessarily led to the formulation of a concept to describe the man who has the proper legal and/or transactional capacity. This concept is the *legalis homo* of English law. In the *Cartulaire de l'Abbaye de Redon* (Courson Ed., 1863), 220 (892) is a descriptive passage ". . . exinde electi sunt viri idonei, vita et moribus probati, qui nulla iniquitatis mercede seducti falsum testimonium perhiberent." To be a *legalis homo* is a condition *sine qua non*. Cf. also 2 *Cart. Trinité de Vendôme*, no. 333 (1087), for the requisite of legality for waging battle. In the course of the 11th century the *iudicium parium* requirement comes into prominence because of the sharpening of status concepts. On the continent the *iudicium parium* is forced to the fore by the feudal legislation of Conrad II (1037) *Mon. Ger. Hist., 1 Const.*, 90. On this for England cf. Liebermann, *Glossar, s.v. Standesgenossen*. But this requirement of "equality" is in addition to the capacity of "legality."

[141] Fulbert, *Epistolae* (141 Migne, *Patrologia*, 229) no. 58 (1020): "Quod si non fecerit, merito censebitur malefidus: sicut ille, si in eorum praevaricatione vel faciendo vel consentiendo deprehensus fuerit, perfidus et perjurus," incorporated in the *Libri Feudorum* II, 6 (Lehmann, *op. cit.*, 120), and in the *Decretum,* Causa 22, q. V, c. 18.

Fulbert, writing to recalcitrant vassals in 1008 (Epist. 10), threatens excommunication and anathema (i.e., an interdict) and adds, "Postea vero ipsa casamenta quae tenetis aut uni aut pluribus dabo." In other words for contumacy, excommunication, which among other penalties, carries infamy; thereafter, he will take away the fief and regrant it.

[142] *Libri Feudorum*, I, 21, "Quo tempore miles investituram petere debeat" (Lehmann, 106). The *infamia* listed as a reason for postponement is held by the gloss (*Volumen Legum*, Venice, 1583) to apply to the lord. The principle in either case is the same, since the feudal bargain is bilateral.

[143] Greenidge, *Infamia*, 149, app. 209.

[144] In the eleventh century the same device is used in the war upon priests' marriages. Cf. Council of Bourges (1031), c. 8, 19 Mansi, *Concilia*, 504.

absurd to take from the father and allow the son to enter, and thus perchance put at the delinquent's disposal the means of proceeding against the lord.[145]

Beyond such practical consideration, however, lay the more or less basic premise of this civilization that transactional capacity depended upon a man's having and retaining the condition of a *legalis homo*—a legal man. This was essential at once to the maintenance of status, of *locus standi* in the courts, and of both inherited or acquired rights. The concept of the legal man was, however, considerably less complex than the subject of Roman private law. There is no distinction between *aestimatio* eradicated by infamy and the destruction of *caput*. There are none of the gradations of dishonor that the Romans know. In medieval law, the loss, as a result of infamy, of what we would call civil rights imperils the whole structure of what a man is, has and may expect.

A solution of the questions how and why infamy was allowed to operate beyond the limits within which it had long been confined is not to be reached through any tight theory of punishment. The Frankish capitularies were no less pious on the subject of not punishing the innocent than were the canons of the church.[146] Since in relation to loss of fief, disherison was established for bargain breach before it became a sanction of criminal

---

[145] Similarly motivated are the rules regarding harboring of persons banned, and the later rule which gives the Norman duke control of the wife's property during the lifetime of a man forebanned.

[146] The bargain procedure of composition pleas rested on a theory of group as well as individual responsibility. The penalties of composition procedure are specifically bargain sanctions and not punishments. Because the ideas governing the *fides facta* were kept alive in the 10th and 11th centuries, as the concords and pacifications show, it seems sensible to treat the disqualifications and penalties connected with tenure as a development from these ideas rather than as an extension of punishment beyond the individual, particularly since the theory of punishment in the capitularies rests on individual liability.

In this connection must be noted the doctrinal discrepancies in the *Decretum*. In C. I, q. IV, Gratian collected a number of texts relative to the punishment of the innocent, addressed specifically to the question

law, one suspects that some rule regarding succession or family law was involved, some doctrine regarding sanguinity and heirship.

Here there is difficulty in disentangling folklaw from church law. In many primitive legal systems the community of property between parent and child was based upon the mystical notion that the personality of the father was perpetuated in the son.[147] Something of this may lie behind the policy of certain Germanic laws to treat parents and children as a solid bloc.[148] This idea of family solidarity was involved in the rules regarding liability for feud or composition, and in the tenth and eleventh centuries it is still an active principle, if the French *chansons* accurately reflect contemporary thinking.[149]

This way of regarding the family possessed something more than a vague social significance. Active and definite rules of law, based upon sanguinity, gave specific legal content to the idea of the family bloc. Two Frankish rules, in particular, secrete the doctrine of transmitted disability. The first of these lays down the precept that the children of freedmen cannot be admitted to testimony,[150] i.e., the slave's disability to take an oath rests upon

whether parents' sins or crimes were to be attributed to the children; Gratian's position is that they should not be. On the other hand in C. VI, q. I, c. 22 (*si quis cum militibus*) he sets forth the Roman rule from the *lex Julia* regarding the infamy etc. of children whose parents commit treason. Since the passages are apparently irreconcilable, one can only suggest that the general theory was perhaps intended as mitigation of the situation which Ficker in 1 *Untersuchungen zur Italienischen Reichs und Rechtsgeschichte* has shown was general in the 12th century, i.e., of the ban in the cities falling upon the innocent wife and children as well as offender. Gratian's section of treason is then a mere exception to his general principles.

[147] Westrup, *La succession primitive devant l'histoire comparative* (1928), 9, 25 *et seq.*; 1 Mitteis, *Römisches Privatrecht* (1908), 93.

[148] Wasserschleben, *Das Prinzip der Successionsordnung* (1860), 13–14. And *cf.* also 1 Gierke, *Das Deutsche Genossenschaftsrecht* 14 *et seq.*, on the separation of family and sib.

[149] 2 Flach, *Les origines de l'ancienne France*, 446 *et seq.*, and the texts there collected.

[150] This rule is stated by Benedict. Levita, *Capitularia*, II, 352, and was

the second generation. The other excludes the descendants of a freedman from intestate succession until the third generation.[151] The ruling idea behind these regulations is the notion of the identity of the flesh, given theoretical expression by the eleventh-century canonists in their rules to determine consanguinity,[152] and set forth in the later classical dictum of Gratian that father and son are "of one flesh."[153]

The legal vigor of this conception is patent in the Norman custumal where the penalty for a father's accidental homicide of

derived from the *Lex Visigoth*. Brunner in 2 *D.R.G.* 534, surmises, despite the source, that this was a general Frankish rule. For similar rules in other folklaws *cf.* 1 Göhrum, *Ebenbürtigkeit*, 100 *et seq.*

[151] *Cap. Legg. Rib. Add.* (803) c. 9 (1 *Cap.* 118) and *cf.* the discussion in Vormoor, *Beitrag zur Geschichte der Sozialen Gliederung des Volkes im Frankenreich* (1907), 42 *et seq.*

There can be no doubt that some concept of corruption lay at the basis of the Frankish rules which forced the child of unequal marriage to "follow" the lower-born parent. The discussion of this has been chiefly in terms of rules of status with no attempt to determine on what theory if any these distinctions were made. The details are in 1 Göhrum, *op. cit.*, 109 *et seq.*

It should be noted that where a free man was enslaved for the payment of a debt the children, if the mother was free, did not lose their status. *Edict. Pist.* (864) c. 34 (2 *Cap.* 327). Note the inevitable effect when *emendatio* becomes punishment and ceases to be a judgment debt.

The Franks were well on the road to a general classification of persons without law, the so-called "unehrliche Leute" of the later Middle Ages. (Bennecke, *Von Unehrlichen Leuten* [1862].) *Cf.* a Capitulary of uncertain origin: (1 *Cap.* 334 c. 8) ". . . in palatiis nostris ad accusandum et iudicandum et testimonium faciendum non se exhibeant viles personae et infames, histriones scilicet nugatores, manzeres [de scorta nati] scurrae, concubinarii, neque ex turpium feminarum commixtione progeniti aut servi aut criminosi."

[152] Heusler, 2 *Institutionen*, 592, believes the rules to be an expression of an older "national" rule. The canonical rule is first laid down by Burchard in his *Decretum*, lib. VII, 10 (140 Migne, *Patrologia*, 782). *Cf.* also v. Amira, *Erbenfolge*, 46 *et seq.*, and the discussion of Champeaux, *Ius Sanguinis*, in 12 *N.R.H.* 4 ser. (1933), 244 *et seq.*, who draws other conclusions.

[153] C. XXXV, q. II, c. 21. Discussed by Champeaux, *op. cit.*, 266 *et seq.* The problem of consanguinity and degree is only indirectly involved in the present problem, but useful because of the light that the underlying theories of the unity of flesh throw upon the transmission of disabilities of capacity or status.

a son is merely that he do penance: ". . . And because the son has sprung from the blood and flesh of the father, the father is not punished by death for the homicide of the son."[154] Among both the Franks and their successors in France the figure a man was to cut in the world depended in certain instances upon his parent's situation. The first inquiry into whether a man was *probus* and *legalis* involved a scrutiny of antecedents. This was basic in lay law. For the church it had been laid down in the seventh century by Isidore of Seville,[155] starting a tradition that persists certainly until the decretals of Gregory IX. A "defect of birth"[156] due to a forbidden marriage or copulation marked a man no less than what Hincmar of Rheims called an absence of *dignitas natalium*.[157]

It seems very probable that behind these calculations concerning the capacity and status of children lurked both popular and official biblicism. For it is clear that in a Christianized medieval country the crucial moments in family affairs are not only marked by church sacraments but regulated by church law. The pursuit of a man's sins to the third generation is palpably Mosaic. The idea of paternal stain passing to the son, on a theory of family solidarity, is Paulist dogma as interpreted by Augustine.

Early in the eleventh century, when the battle against married clergy was being fought, a synod at Bourges (1031) laid down a canon[158] that the sons of priests, deacons and subdeacons were never to be admitted to holy orders "because they and all others who are not born of legitimate marriage are called the seed of

---

[154] *T.A.C.*, cap. xxxv §1 (De Homicidis) "Et quoniam filius de sanguine et visceribus patris exivit . . ." Of course there may be theological rationalization here.

[155] From the *Etymologia*, lib. 18 c. 15, cited by Greg. IX, *Decr.* lib. 5, tit. 40, c. 10 "Testes autem considerantur conditione, natura et vita." Compare the *Decretum*, C. IV, q. II & III, c. 2–3. "In testibus fides, dignitas mores gravitas moderanda etc."

[156] Génestal, *Histoire de la légitimation des enfants naturels* (1905) 3, *et seq.* (*L'Irregularitas ex defectu natalium*).

[157] Hincmar, *Epistolae* no. 39 (126 Migne, *Patrologia* 259).

[158] 19 Mansi, *Concilia*, 504.

the accursed in the divine scriptures and according to secular law can neither inherit nor be received as witnesses." This canon is illuminating because it definitely relates the infamy of certain persons to the passage in Ps. 37, 28,[159] "and the seed of the wicked shall perish," which an early vernacular translation renders *"la semence des feluns."*[160] But it is the identification of wickedness and accursedness[161] as much as the drawing in of infamy by the prelates at Bourges which leads us into the thinking of time. The provincial synods are attempting to make their sanctions effective, rather than to enforce dogmatic abstractions. In treating the wicked as accursed, the reality of the church procedure has stepped in to nullify the impractical ethics of the sub-

[159] Ps. 36, 28 in the Vulgate.

[160] *Le livre des psaumes* (Michel Ed., C.D.I. 1876), 63. And note also the juxtaposition of the following verse, "Li juste heriterunt la terre . . ."

[161] The commentators on the psalms do not deal with legal implications. *Cf.* Ambrose, *Enarratio in Ps. 36* (14 Migne, *Patrologia,* 1046); Augustine, *Enarratio in Ps. 36* (36 *ibid.,* 389); Bede, in *Ps. Libr. Exegesis* (Dubia et Spuria) 93 Migne, *Patrologia,* 678; Bruno Herbipol., *Expositio Psalmorum* (142 *ibid.,* 159).

Appurtenant to a treatise of Anselm of Canterbury is a curious twelfth century commentary (anonymous) *Declaratio Cuiusdam* in Anselm., *Lib. de Conceptu Virginali* (158 Migne, *Patrologia,* 463) discussing with reference to the doctrine of original sin the whole question of wickedness—accursedness—seed. The following sample should suffice . . . "Juxta quem modum, *semen maledictum est,* id est illi sunt maledicti, qui sunt de semine vel generatione in malitia perseverantium, si ipsi sunt in eodem perseverantes. Non ita est, aiunt. Dicit enim hoc manifeste Augustinus quaerens quomodo est cujuslibet hominis malitia naturalis, et semen maledictum ab initio. Cujuslibet, inquit, hominis malitia naturalis, et semen maledictum ab initio. Sicut enim cujuslibet hominis malitia est naturalis: ita cujuslibet hominis semen maledictum. Dicimus quia non valet hoc zeugma, id est repetitio, a superiori; nec ipse Augustinus eam repetitionem fecit. Quare non cogimur consentire eam facientibus, sed sic dicimus: cujuslibet hominis malitia est naturalis, et ipse est semen maledictum; non ejus semen maledictum, quia in eo non est peccatum. Vel possumus figurative dicere ipsum semen maledictum esse pro eo, quod ex eo erunt qui maledicti erunt; juxta illud: *Maledicta terra in operibus tuis* (Gen. III, 17), id est opera tua in terra. Non enim terra maledicta est, cum ipsa alibi dicatur sancta, licet eam peccatores operentur; ut, *locus in quo stas terra sancta est* (Exod. III, 5), alioquin eadem et maledicta, et sancta esset. Sic *semen maledictum* quia maledicti qui ex semine. . . ."

stantive canons which seek to protect the innocent. We say to nullify, for the final process of the church, the curse of excommunication, while directed at the impenitent individual, inevitably carries to his family a share of the misery that the excommunicate must bear.[162]

The difference between the process of the church as it is formulated and as it is executed shows that in this era the step from ethics to magic is not long. For the anathema is not only the last remedy against the contumacious but it embodies a curse that will either bring him to grace or assure his eternal damnation.[163] It is a curse the gist of which comes from the psalms[164] —the malediction which the church has related to Judas, the man who betrayed his lord. Here is no sparing of the innocent— "when he shall be judged let him be condemned and let his

---

[162] A brief account of the excommunication in 2 Sägmüller, *K.R.* (1914), 355; 2 München, *Das Kanonische Gerichtsverfahren*, 156 *et seq.* The most complete historical account in 5 Hinschius, *K.R.*, 1 *et seq.* 273, 296. And note particularly the remarks regarding the relaxation by Gregory VII in the third quarter of the 11th century as to the immediate family. It is to be observed, however, that the policy of the church after 1200 was to use to a greater extent specific penalties, such as confiscation, infamy of progeny. *Cf.* Innocent III's rules regarding heretics. (*Decr. Greg.* V., vii *de haeret.* c. 10.) *Cf.* also Boniface VIII's rules in *Sext. Decr.* V ix, *de poenis* c. 5. The interdict (5 Hinschius, *op. cit.* 19) which comes into use in this period shows the same contempt of the innocent.
Following Hinschius (*ibid.,* 7 *et seq.*) we are treating the anathema and excommunication as legally equivalent at this time.
[163] The legal writers have dealt so largely with excommunication as process or punishment that this phase has been little regarded. Lea, *Studies in Church History* (1869), 302 *et seq.,* makes the point and sets out with fine malice some of the gaudier maledictions of the period. The importance of the curse is brought out by v. Amira, *Tierstrafen und Tierprozesse* in 12 *M.I.Ö.G.,* 545, 562. On the meaning of anathema, 4 Hinschius, *K.R.,* 702 n. 7. *Cf.* also p. 800. There are numerous examples of the 11th century forms in the volume of Mansi, *Concilia* for this period. A good example is the excommunication of certain invaders of Cluny property (2 Sackur, *Die Cluniacenser* 89) by Benedict VIII in 1012 (19 Mansi, *Concilia* 326) "Sint maledicti stantes & ambulantes, vigilantes & dormientes, ingredientes & egredientes. Sint maledicti manducantes & bibentes. Sit maledictus cibus eorum & potus. Sit maledictus fructus ventris eorum, & fructus terrae eorum. Sustineantque plagas Herodianas, quousque disrumpantur viscera

prayer become sin. Let his days be few and let another take his office. Let his children be fatherless and let his wife be a widow. Let his children be always vagabonds and beg . . . let strangers spoil his labor. Let there be none to extend mercy unto him; neither let there be any to favour his fatherless children. Let his posterity be cut off and in the generation following let their names be blotted out." From the *Acts*[165] comes the injunction, "let his habitation be desolate and let no man dwell therein." In these dark times when superstition[166] crouches in every shadow,

eorum. Et cum Dathan & Abiron de terra viventium perditi, cum diabolo & angelis ejus perpetualiter damnati, maneant in poenis infernalibus sine fine cruciandi. Fiant etiam filii eorum orphani, & uxores eorum viduae. Nutantes transferantur filii eorum, & mendicent. Ejiciantur de habitationibus suis, omnibusque maledictionibus, quae in veteri vel novo testamento contineri videntur, maledicti & anathematizati subjaceant, quousque resipiscant, & nostrae vocationi & monitioni congrue satisfaciant."

Apart from the ideology of the church, as to which there is little doubt, since the damned were destined for Satan (*cf.* C. XI, q. III, c. 32) avowed by Augustine and reproduced by Ivo of Chartres (*Decr.* II, 94), the employment of the curse was in accord with the secular concept of the broken oath as a self-curse (1 Brunner, *D.R.G.* 257). Furthermore, the constant employment in charters of some form of curse in the penal clause points to how usual a phenomenon this was. *Cf.* Studtmann *Die Pönformeln der Mittelalterlichen Urkunden* in 12 *Archiv für Urkundenforschung* 252 *et seq.* Since the formula in general use was derived from the papal formulae (the earliest in the *Liber diurnus*) one consequently will expect considerable ecclesiastical influence in all questions of malediction.

There is some reason to believe that the curse was taken as seriously as the exclusion from the sacraments and other disabilities. Planck in 3 *Geschichte der christlich-Kirchlichen Gesellschafts-Verfassung* (1805) 514, reproduces the charming story of the French bishop who absolved certain excommunicates each night, lest they die while he slept and be eternally damned, and reexcommunicated them in the morning. The tale of la Reine Pédauque, King Robert's queen who, excommunicated, gave birth to a goose-necked son must have indurated a belief in the efficacy of the church's process simply because of the manifestation of the supernatural.

Of course the nature of the ritual for the pronouncement of the church's ban tended to vivify the curse. The provisions are in Burchard, *Decretum,* XI, 3; *cf.* Gratian in C. XI, q. III, c. 106. *Cf.* also the proceedings at Limoges (1031) for the *treuga Dei,* 19 Mansi, *Concilia* 507.

[164] In the Vulgate Ps. 108.

[165] Acts 1, 20; Ps. 68, 2.

[166] Meyer, *Der Aberglaube des Mittelalters* (1884), 148 on the church's miracle cult.

when the fiend himself leads men to burn or kill,[167] there is deep terror in this imprecation from the word of God.

But there are always the hardy. For them the churchman who wields in his immunity his own stout secular arm can make real the curse. The house will be destroyed; the wife will be widowed; the children will be beggared; dishonor will attach to posterity. And all this not as mere collateral detail to excommunication, but as secular penalty. Throughout Europe we can see this happen. In Spain an abbess enters these penalties in her custumal.[168] In episcopal cities like Amiens[169] and Laon,[170] there exists the sacral destruction of malefactors' houses. The rule creeps into general usage.[171] In Normandy the excommunicate's chat-

[167] For example in the ordeal formulae in Zeumer, *Formulae*, 638 *et seq.* Burchard's *Decretum*, XI, 2, is reproduced from an alleged council of Rouen. It sets forth the notion of the offender as a *filius diaboli*, for the devil is indurated in his heart. The influence of these concepts (which at the time had a definite reality) upon the doctrine of corruption of the blood, presently to be discussed, must be kept in mind.

[168] *Fuero de San Pedro de las Dueñas* (1191) in 2 *Annuario de Historia del Derecho Esp.* (1925), 466, . . . "Et si aliquis uassallorum nostrorum contra hoc tam salubre statutum uenerit, uel hoc factum irrumpere uoluerit, pectet nobis dictis dominis centum morabetinos, uel cui nostram uocem dederimus, et destruantur domus eius et amitant hereditates quas hauuerint in dicta uilla sancti petri et in suos terminis et que nos dicti domini possimus intrare omnes hereditates supradictas et dare eas alicuio alio nostro uassallo qui faciat foros per eas et det tributa regi et nobis." . . .

[169] Thierry, *op. cit.*, 41 (charter of 1117, c. 10).

[170] 3 Achery, *Specilegium*, 481 (charter of 1128, c. 2).

[171] Coulin, *Die Wüstung*, 32 *Zeitschrift für Vergleichende Rechtswissenschaft*, 326 *et seq.*, collects a mass of material on the so-called *droit de ravage*, including references to various French *coutumes*. Coulin's conclusions are colored by Brunner's outlawry theory. The most impressive authority against the persistence of a Germanic theory of sacral destruction of dwellings is v. Amira, *Tierstrafen und Tierprozesse*, 12 *M.I.Ö.G.*, 557 n. 5. Coulin (*op. cit.*, 357) endeavours to traverse this but he is not convincing. He reviews various theories without bringing in the influence of Christian ideology. Mayer in 1 *D.F.V.G.*, 208 speaks of a "religious" element without specifying what he means. Gessler, *Notes sur le droit d'arsin ou d'abbatis*, in *Mélanges Paul Fournier* (1929), 293 treats the matter as it appertained to the feudal barons and the towns. Practically all his material is 12th century or later.

Ravage was discussed above (p. 102) as an incident of feud. This the Carolingian Kings had attempted to check. It seems improbable that even

tels go to the duke.[172] In Italy the cities by their ban drive out the wives and children of offenders.[173] In the Empire, the ban formulae repeat the sonorous words of the church's anathema and see to their execution,[174] so that the judgment of the secular law can crush by the added weight of the curse of condemnation which purports to cut off heirs.

In consequence, the criminal law of the twelfth century comes before the problem of land sanctions with the same theory as the feudal law—a theory of disherison. For the justification of this we have no text as clear-cut and as comforting as one from the Empire: *"sicut perjurii infamia sint exleges, ita bonorum omnium fiant exheredes"*;[175] but we have data sufficient for a workable hypothesis. The developed Norman law is stated in a passage from the *Très ancien coutumier*[176] that we believe may be

a constant practice of burning and destroying in the course of private war would alone have normative force. What makes this practice a rule of law is the fact that it gets ecclesiastical sanction. There is no reason why the churchmen in the north of France should have opposed ravage. They were as a group, during a critical period, about as unclerical as one could imagine, and since the practice had scriptural precedent, there is reason to believe that a sacral justification, if there was one, came from this source. With excommunications being hurled forth daily from every corner (*infra*, Chapter V, n. 78), a sense of usualness and propriety sooner or later must attach to this execution of the details of the curse.

[172] *T.A.C.*, cap. I.

[173] 1 Ficker, *Forschungen zur Reichs und Rechtsgeschichte Italiens* (1868) 119 (suggesting the influence of the *crimen laesae maiestatis*), 127 *et seq.*

[174] In Grimm, *Deutsche Rechtsalterthümer,* 40 are late German formulae. Compare also the *Pax Bavarica* (1244) c. 24 in *M.G.H.* 2 *Legum,* Sect. 4, 574. For earlier ones *cf.* 2 Franklin, *Das Reichshofgericht* (1869), 320 *et seq.;* His, *Das Strafrecht des Deutschen Mittelalters,* pt. I, 410 *et seq.,* collects references to other formulae. Obviously in classifying these formulae distinctions must be drawn in terms of regions and nature of immediate political control. To our knowledge this has never been done.

[175] Heda, *Historia Episcoporum Ultraiectensium* (1642), p. 139, a charter of Henry IV of 1077. "Henricus divina favente Clementia Rex Lex est et jus gentium inimicos Regis apertie deprehensos, aperte communem totius regni persecutionem pati; ut sicut perjurii infamia sint exleges, ita bonorum omnium suorum fiant exheredes."

[176] *T.A.C.* cap. XXXVI, §7.

related to legislation of Henry I regarding the truce of God.[177] The law is providing penalties for the man who commits homicide. It says that a man who commits homicide may concord with the duke, but he shall not have his inheritance, neither he nor his heirs, but he shall lose it for his homicide. The land reverts to the lord. To fugitives the same rule applies. Another section, obviously dating from the thirteenth century, connects the penalty with the condemnation for crime.[178]

Apart from the question of date it is certain from the rule stated: 1) that we are not dealing with a confiscation; 2) that this is an escheat. Less obvious is the conclusion that here is an escheat because of a disherison. But a recently published twelfth-century document employs the phrase "exheredatus . . . pro quodam crimine,"[179] and the thirteenth-century rule mentioned above likewise uses the term *exheredatio*. There can be no question but that escheat in the latter twelfth century is understood as a failure of heirs, and that it is used to describe the artificial as well as the natural failure.

Early in the thirteenth century (1204) in an English assize of mort d'ancestor[180] a defendant pleads that the plaintiff's father

---

[177] *Infra,* p. 330.

[178] *T.A.C.* cap LXXXVIII, §1.

[179] Richardson, *A Norman Lawsuit,* in 7 *Speculum,* 383, 389.

[180] *Placitorum Abbreviatio,* 25, rot. 18., Jordan sues Robert for land of which he claims his mother was seised in demesne. Robert defends that Jordan's father "nequam fuit et pro felonia ad assisam de Clarendon perdidit pedem et brachium et ipse genitus est de corpore nequam." 1 *C.R.R.* 180. In 3 *C.R.R.* 42 (same case) is an entry of a day given for judgment in a *placito false mentule.*

In this case this property before the conviction was probably held in a joint seisin in the right of the wife. 2 Pollock and Maitland, *H.E.L.,* 408. The early rule was that if the husband died the seisin of the wife persisted until her death. We may conjecture here that the conviction of the father resulted in the termination of his seisin as if he had died.

The term, plea of a false *membrum virile,* is confounding, and seems to be merely a cynical clerk's description of the corruption of the blood. So far as we know the term is not elsewhere found. In this relation may be considered the picture Ms. of the *Sachsenspiegel,* where the shield ("Heerschild"—symbolic of capacity or status) is lowered or raised to show a

was wicked (*nequam*) and had lost a foot and an arm for felony under the assize of Clarendon and that the plaintiff was "born of the body of an evil person" (*genitus est de corpore nequam*). Here is stated in unmistakable terms the doctrine of the corruption of the blood familiar to English criminal lawyers. The roll entry is a text that lies midway between the scattered materials from which we must reconstruct the theory of the courts.

Our latest source, the *Summa de Legibus*[181] (*ca.* 1270) tells us that the children of the blood of the condemned (*ex sanguine dampnato—ex genere damnatorum*) may retain what "they shall have" before the commission of the parent's crime, but they are barred from succession *iure hereditario*. Next in order of age is the explanation of custom offered to Innocent III, in 1216, after the pope had intervened in behalf of King John, and roughly contemporary with our plea roll.[182] The envoys tell the pope: "It is the custom in the kingdom of France, that when someone is condemned to death, the progeny begotten after the sentence of condemnation (*damnationis*) ought not to succeed; but those born before the sentence ought to succeed." In very similar terms

degradation or improvement of status. *Cf.* the case where it is shown below the waistline, 1 v. Amira, *Die Dresdener Bilderhandschrift des Sachsenspiegels* (1902), Intro. 26, Plate 97 (to illustrate lib. 3 art. 65). 2 *ibid.*, pt. 2, 85, 192, 241, 334. 2 Homeyer, *Des Sachsenspiegels Zweiter Theil—System des Lehnrechts* (1844), pt. 2, 302.

[181] *S.L.N.* cap. XXII, §10. The phrases vary in the Mss. In the *T.A.C.* is a passage (cap. LXXXVIII §2) that shows how the corruption of the blood is strictly a question of parental transmission: "Si plures fratres sint et unus deliquerit, alii innocentes non amittunt hereditatem, neque condempnatur propter factum delinquentis."

[182] 2 Wendover, *Flores Historiarum* (R.S., Hewlett Ed., 1887), 187 and 2 Mathew Paris, *Chronica Majora* (R.S., Luard Ed., 1874), 660: "Consuetudo est in regno Franciae, quod ex quo aliquis est damnatus ad mortem, quod proles suscepta post sententiam damnationis succedere non debet; geniti tamen ante sententiam succedere debent." Note the rule regarding the effect of excommunication stated by Innocent in matters of disherison. There is an excellent discussion of this episode in Mitteis, *Politische Prozesse*, 98 *et seq.*

In a charter of Louis VIII (1225) to Marie of Ponthieu, 1 Marténe, *Amplissima Collectio*, 1198, the progeny of a traitor are apparently "minus legitime nati."

is the curious passage in the so-called *Leges Edwardi Confessoris*[183] (1130–35) to the effect that only children born before the commission of an offense by a man who abjures are not *ex lex* and can inherit, the implication being that afterborn progeny cannot. The important fact that this statement conveys is that the father's infamy is carried over to some of his progeny. For *ex lex* here can mean only infamy or its consequences. It cannot mean outlawry because the English sources yield no evidence that the father's outlawry involves his children except with regard to forfeiture, the very point here in issue. *Ex lex* is the *elos* of the Empire—the man no longer *legalis*.[184] In Flanders near the Norman frontiers this expression is usual. Various Flemish customs draw sharply the line between the *banniti,* the men who have been banned, and the *ex leges,* the men who have been stripped of all law.[185]

These scattered materials establish the existence of a basic con-

---

[183] *Leges Edwardi Confessoris,* 19, 2, Liebermann, *Gesetze,* 645, "Et infantes qui ante malefactum generati fuerint non habebuntur exleges, pro malefacto quod patres eorum fecerunt post generationem nec perdant hereditatem." *Cf.* also §37 regarding usurers. Liebermann says the rule of §19 is not English law in the twelfth century; 1 *Gesetze,* 645, note b. There is a reminiscence of this rule in Bracton, *De Legibus* fol. 130 "Et sicut non valebit donatio post feloniam perpetratam, ita nec valebit generatio quad successionem quantum ad hereditatem paternam et maternam, cum sit progenitus talis de testiculo et sanguine felonis. Si autem ante feloniam generationem fecerit, talis generatio succedet in hereditate patris vel matris a quo non fuerit felonia perpetrata."

[184] 6 Waitz, *D.V.G.,* 493; Schröder, *D.R.G.,* 504; His, *Das Strafrecht des deutschen Mittelalters,* 411, 479; Kraut, *Grundriss zu Vorlesungen über das deutsche Privatrecht* (5 ed. 1872), §49 for a collection of references. That infamy was the basic notion is exceedingly probable. *Cf.* for the eleventh century the *Lex Familiae Wormat.* (1 *Mon. Ger. Hist., Const.,* 640) c. 32 "ut legem sibi innatam propter furtum perditam habeat" etc. *Cf. Innovatio Pacis Franciae Rhen.* (1179) c. 10 (*M.G.H.,* 1 *Const.* 380) "Si vero proscripti in proscriptione Imperatoris per annum et diem fuerint, ex leges erunt et omni iure de cetero carebunt." *Const. Contra Incendiarios* (1186), c. 10 (1 *Mon. Ger. Hist., Const.,* 450) "Si quis autem a proscriptione et excomm. simul infra annum et diem non fuerit absolutus universo iure et honore et legalitate sua privatus habeatur. . . ."

[185] 3 Warnkönig, *Flandrische Staats und Rechtsgeschichte* (1842), 173 *et seq.,* and note esp. the charter of 1180 in 2 *ibid.,* doc. III, where the dis-

ception of corruption of the blood but they are not very illuminating on the reasons for its existence. In the Assises of Jerusalem the explanation why an heir born after the condemnation cannot inherit is that "au jor que son ancestre fu forjugié il estoit en lui, et est de lui descendu après ce que il fu forjugié et por ceste raizon sont les deus une miesme choze et encoru et forjugié ensamble. . . ."[186] One could scarcely venture to suggest that a text expressive of the views of immigrant feudal society should be taken as evidence of what was believed in Normandy. Nevertheless, the parallel between this passage, the canonical doctrine of the identity of the flesh and the Norman passage on the point already cited, is very striking.[187] It seems probable that at the basis of these ideas lie current or earlier physiological misconceptions that find their most fantastic expressions in the scholastics' speculations about the *homunculus*.[188] That the later Nor-

tinction is drawn. Compare Poullet, *Essai sur l'histoire du droit criminel . . . de Liège* (38 *Mem. Acad. Royale de Belgique,* 214) regarding *forjugement de l'honneur,* and the 13th century practice "ilh est hons sains loy, priveis de son honeur et de tous bins etc.," or "atteints de son honeur." *Cf.* also p. 505 for later practice.

[186] 1 Beugnot, *Assises de Jerusalem* (1841), 497 (Livre de Philippe de Navarre c. 24).

[187] In addition to the matter already cited it should be pointed out that the language in which the doctrine of the Trinity is discussed in the 11th century tended to emphasize the identity of father and son. An example is a letter of a Benedictine monk in the year 1060 (3 Achery, *Specilegium,* 401). Of course the sources preoccupied with the problem of evil are more apposite in the question before us. In this connection the writings of Lanfranc possess a particular interest, representing as they do the thinking of a leading cleric-statesman involved in Anglo-Norman affairs. *Cf.* esp. *Elucidarium sive Dialogus* in 2 *Opera Omnia* (Giles Ed., 1844) 200, 235, on the sons of priests: "nec in Ecclesia aliquam praelationem habere, quia ex fornicatione et transgressione sunt procreati. Ex patribus enim venenatis virus veneni transit in filios." Further, *ibid.,* 248–9, on the child suffering for parents' fault: "Quamvis saepe pro peccatis parentum filii in sua injustitia juste deserantur, . . ." *Cf.* also at pp. 252, 253, 254.

[188] The whole theory of reproduction that is held by ecclesiastical writers seems to be grounded upon the notion obvious enough in the Old Testament that it is the male semen from which emerges the progeny. The traditions of the science of medicine were not dissimilar. *Cf.* especially Aristotle, *Historia Animalium,* 7, 6, 7; *De Generatione Animalium,* II, 2, 3. The view of Galen, upon whose work later medieval physiology was

man rule disinherits all the progeny of the condemned is not to
be attributed to an improved knowledge of the facts of life but to

grounded, was that the active agency in reproduction was the sperm.
Haeser, *Grundriss der Geschichte der Medicin* (1884), 66. Patristic writers were in this tradition too; for example Clement of Alexandria, who
asserted that the embryo is formed from the semen mixed with the men-
strua of the woman. The innate powers of the seed works upon the nature
of the blood and produces the formative process. The blood is to him the
substance of the human body. Harnack, *Medicinisches aus der ältester
Kirchengeschichte* (8 Gebhardt and Harnack, *Texte zur Alt Christlichen
Literatur*) 35; note also the theories of Lactantius, *ibid.,* 55. The doctrinal
reasons for emphasis upon the blood are patent.

For the early medieval period in western Europe the writings of Isidore
of Seville were of considerable importance. The following passages from
the *Etymologiae* (Oxford edition, 1911) are significant. Lib. 9, c. 5, §3 *et
seq:* "Pater est a quo nascitur initium generis . . . Crementum enim est
semen masculi, unde animalium et hominum corpora concipiuntur." (*Cf.*
lib. 11, c. 1 §15). In lib. 11, c. 1, §136: "Matrix dicitur, quod fetus in ea
generetur, semen enim receptum confovet, confotum corporat . . ." §139
"Semen est quod iactum sumitur, aut a terra aut ab utero ad gignendum,
vel fructus vel fetus . . . et in utero mulieris susceptus, calore quodam-
modo viscerum et menstruali sanguinis in regatione formatur in corpore."
Lib. 9, c. 6, §4: "Consanguinei vocati, eo quod ex uno sanguine, id est,
ex uno patris semine nati sunt; nam semen viri spuma est sanguinis, ad
instar aquae in scopulos collisae, quae spumam candidam facit, vel sicut
vinum nigrum, quod in calice agitatum spumam albentem reddit."

Isidore's words are repeated and elaborated by Rabanus Maurus, *De
Universo,* lib. 6 c. 1, lib. 7, c. 2 (111 Migne, *Patrologia,* 173, 185) and
Rabanus' school had some influence in their spread. It is important to note
that the concept of the semen as a froth of the blood will explain the constant relation and interrelation of the scriptural passages where blood and
seed alternate as the agencies of carrying on a curse upon an ancestor.
Compare also the passage from the *Summa, supra,* n. 186 and Bracton,
*supra,* n. 183.

Not the least interesting of the medieval treatises on the matter is
Hildegard of Bingen's *Causae et Curae* (Kaiser Ed. 1913) written in the
early twelfth century. "Nam sanguis hominis in ardore et calore libidinis
fervens spumam de se eicit, quod nos semen dicimus . . ." *ibid.,* 33. *Cf.*
also 35, 59–61. "Nunc etiam, postquam semen hominis recte in locum
suum ceciderit, ita quod etiam in formam hominis figurari debet, tunc
etiam de menstruo sanguine mulieris pellicula velut vasculum circa
eandem formam crescit, quae ipsam comprehendit et circumdat, ne hac et
illac moveatur aut cadat, quia ille coagulatus sanguis ibi congregatur, ita
quod eadem forma in medio eius iacet, ut homo in habitaculo domus
suae," *ibid.,* 65–6. Enlightening physiological explanations of the rules
regarding adultery, *ibid.,* 68. *Cf.* also 137, 138.

The tone of the homiletic writings differs scarcely from the physiologi-

the broadening of the scope of infamy that in England led to a complete and absolute escheat.[189]

Even when disherison becomes the means of assuring escheat for failure of the feoffee to perform his bargain, the road is yet to be traversed whereby the same thing can be used as a sanction against crimes. Of course where a courtholder is also the immediate overlord of a malefactor, there would be no practical obstacles in the way of using the sanctions for bargain breach to penalize wrongs. In such cases the affair would have the aspect of an outright confiscation. This is the way it appears in the Statute of La Réole already discussed. But when the courtkeeper is not the lord or where a mesne lord stands between the court and the malefactor a real difficulty exists. The mesne lord may wish to keep his tenant or he may have no objection to the heir's enter-

---

cal. Cf. Anselm, de Conceptu Virginali, c. 23 (158 Migne, Patrologia, 454): "quae sunt ex semine, fuerunt in seminibus ipsis; et nihil fecisse Deum, cum omnia quae procreantur ex semine ipsi fecit prius in seminibus . . . Si enim verum non est ea, quae natura procreat ex seminibus, in illis prius aliquid fuisse, nullo modo exipsis essent." The relation of these physiological ideas to the theories of the identity of the flesh is obvious.

On the *homunculus* idea, which seems no earlier than the 13th century, *Handwörterbuch des deutschen Aberglaubens* (1927—s.v. *homunculus*); Meyer, *Der Aberglaube des Mittelalters*, 53. The superstitions regarding the mandrake are also to be considered here, *ibid.*, 63; Bargheer, *Die Eingeweide im Glauben und Brauch* (1931), 110–12.

[189] In connection with the French rule and that stated in the *Leges Edwardi* should be noted the rule in the archbishopric of Cologne. In the "Dienstrecht" of the diocese it is provided that where a man (*ministerialis*) kills another he is in the mercy of his lord and if he is not received into favor within a year and day to make satisfaction he is put in a chamber "Uxor quoque sua poterit ad eum ingredi et manere cum eo; si tamen prolem de eo intus genuerit proles illa legitima non erit et secularis iuris expers (i.e. expers honoris) manebit," *Iura Ministerialium Coloniensium*, c. 7 in Fürth, *Die Ministerialen* (1836) app. II. And see the discussion *ibid.*, 386. Cf. 1 Stobbe, *Handbuch des deutschen Privatrechts* (1871), 304; *Sachsenspiegel* (Landrecht) art. 37, 38, and the discussion in 2 Homeyer, *Des Sachsenspiegels Zweiter Theil*, 300. For a similar rule in the Scandinavian sources, Wilda, *Von den Unechten Kindern*, 15 *Zeitschrift für deutsches Recht*, 276. He states that in the *Grágás* the children born of a man outlawed cannot inherit. Similarly the rule in the Upland law. But for the territorial spread of the French rule and its existence in Cologne one might suspect the rule of the *Leges Edwardi* was Scandinavian.

ing. The situation is one for which a solution lies in the recognition of a superior law in the sense either that the courtholder's procedure is superior to the rules of feudal bargain, or that the effect of his justiciation is such that even as a matter of feudal law the status or capacity of the parties changes.

As to the first of these alternatives, it is clear that a court-keeper's procedure could not be superior unless his political situation was such that his authority could overbear all objections. This would be true even where, as in Normandy, certain subject matter was definitely the exclusive right of the duke. The jurisdiction can be exclusive without the process having effect beyond the limits of direct control. In other words, the duke can have sole cognizance over coinage offenses,[190] but he may not be able to take away from the maker of false money a fief held of the Bishop of Bayeux, for the reason that the bishop may not like it. Even the overlord has a most limited control over the bargains of mesne tenants with rear tenants. A superior procedure to which all other interests must succumb requires the recognition of a dominant and non-feudal authority. This does not come into existence until the duke takes upon himself the enforcement of the peace of God.

The second alternative, that the courtholder's judgment can for reasons not connected with his political position have a legal effect sufficient to expunge contract or tenurial expectations, supposes a respect for judgments ill in accord with the frequency with which bolstering concords are made after judgment in the eleventh century.[191] The effectiveness of a judgment within a franchise is a different matter. In Frankish law the property sanctions depended upon some form of judgment against the individual. Lands and chattels were not just seized by the fisc.

---

[190] Inquest of 1091, c. 13 Haskins, *op. cit.,* 283.

[191] For example, *Cart. Marmoutier pour le Vendômois,* no. 57 (1064) where after the defendant's repeated refusal to execute a court's sentence, a concord is made between the plaintiff and the defendant, whereby in consideration of the receipt of 40 shillings and a litter of pigs the de-

They were gotten at via the person[192] and by judgment, whether this was the sentence of death, the *forisbannitio* or the *missio in bannum*. For it was by the judgment, which destroyed the capacity of the individuals, that property becomes confiscable.[193] This principle must have survived the violence of the tenth and eleventh centuries: it is clearly stated in the *Summa de Legibus,* which makes the condemnation of death or the *forisbannitio* the point at which the duke's right to property attaches.[194] Unless

fendant promises the plaintiff that he will execute the sentence. *Cf.* also no. 87 (1062); no. 91 (1050–63). In *Cart. St. Maur* (1 Marchegay, *Arch. Anj.* 375) no. 32 (1086–9) no submission nor pacification was exacted. *Cart. St. Vincent du Mans,* nos. 307, 308, 309, 310 (1080–1100), involves a judgment, followed by various contempts and eventual concords. *Cf.* Valin, *op. cit.,* P. J. no. 7 (1129). In this connection may be consulted 1 Beautemps-Beaupré, *Coutumes de l'Anjou et du Maine,* §§5, 6, regarding the power of the court of the count in the 11th century. He apparently assumes the power of a judgment was considerable. Obviously, some of the litigation referred to in the cartularies was mere bedevilment of the monks, a form of blackmail and hence even with a judgment a concord was much desired. See on this phase of 11th century litigation, Lamprecht, *Beiträge zur Geschichte des Französischen Wirthschaftslebens,* 116, n. 33.

[192] Mayer-Homberg, *op. cit.,* 283.

[193] Clearly shown in the disabilities placed on the man condemned to death and then reprieved.

[194] The maintenance of this in Normandy is evidenced by *S.L.N.,* cap. xxii, §3: ". . . nullus sine judicio est damnandus . . ."; §5 as to those forebanned; §8 as to the record of abjuration, the returning abjuror to be treated as if forebanned. The conjecture that it is by the device of infamy that the disherison for crime is achieved is to a certain extent fortified by the fact that the sources tend to emphasize the condemnation as the crucial point when this takes place. Philologically the word is built upon *damnatio.* The term probably comes into secular use among the Franks via the church. In the early Merovingian capitularies it is used to describe a mulct inflicted by authority like a ban penalty, and it is constantly employed in later centuries to describe the process of spiritual authority. While by the 12th century it may have lost some of its quality of a sentence embodying a curse, since the consequences of infamy attach at the moment of condemnation, a good deal of its ancient flavor persists. Procedurally it was, of course, essential to fix a point where the rights of authority to property would attach. Under the older forms of trial, judgment was interlocutory since it was succeeded by proof. Proof acquits or convicts but in the feudal courts, where party bargain is no longer the objective of the procedure, the necessity of a final step at which the fiscal interest attached was obvious.

one is willing to suppose that capitulary law was resurrected in the thirteenth century, the persistence of this basic procedural tenet as a part of ban theory must be posited.

One important type of judgment, at least, probably had a certain extra-judicial force. Wherever a judgment involved infamy, since the pronouncement was intended to destroy a man's legality, such a judgment might affect a man's legal relations with persons not attached in any way to a courtholder. Certainly an infamy resulting from a judgment in the duke's court would not be lightly disregarded by those who were feudally bound to the duke. Stated in modern terms we are dealing with a basic problem of conflict of laws: is a man's law so personal that he can forfeit it as to all the world by any judgment?—is a judgment, dependent on tenure or franchise and hence territorial in scope, recognized beyond a given jurisdiction? On either theory the same result can be obtained. To the extent that the Norman Inquest of 1091 represents a mutual agreement on spheres of jurisdiction we may suggest that there was implicit a recognition of the pervasive authority of an adjudication within a given sphere of right. At the same time there is evidence of a stress upon the personality of law. In a charter of 1074[195] William the Conqueror emphasizes that *jura justicia* a traitor has lost his inheritance. It is not "my court" which has effected this result, but the operation of the law.

The theoretical problems which have been suggested can hardly be solved on the basis of our actual evidence. The Norman documents which show the use of disherison, like the Inquest of 1091, all date from a time after the *treuga Dei* was instituted. And we shall soon see the procedural advantages derived from ducal enforcement of the peace necessarily colored the effectiveness of all sanctions. In other words, a recognition that infamy, incurred as a result of peace breach, or a conviction thereof, operated as a personal disability in all relations, could be

---

[195] 11 *Gallia Christiana,* Instr. 65; also, 1 Anquetil, *Livre rouge de Bayeux* (1911), no. 346.

forced through the machinery by which the duke sought to make the peace effective. A superior authority had come into existence and consequently a superior law.

Perhaps the most convincing picture of the incessant employment of sanctions against realty emerges from the text of Orderic's history. The duke *mancipat*[196] (takes into his hands) property or he *exheridat*[197] (disherisons) someone. We do not expect technical terms, either as to the sanction or the offense. Apparently the escheat is most usually for acts of a seditious sort.[198] The line between treason and breach of feudal obligation is scarcely to be drawn at this time, so one is unable to draw any conclusions as to the extent that the disherisons are for crimes or for mere breach of fealty. The same thing is true regarding the few charters that make reference to lands seized in the duke's hands as a penalty.[199] In the 1074 charter already mentioned the recital speaks of the offender having perjured himself by his breach of fealty. This idea is known to Orderic, for he says, speaking of certain rebels, *"publici hostes et perjuris rei contra regem adjucati sunt."*[200] The Norman churchmen were familiar with the concept of infamy in William's day,[201] and it is hardly to be doubted that the forsworn were regarded as infamous.

[196] Orderic, XII, 37, and then *regrant* to a son not involved in his father's offense.

[197] *Ibid.*, XI, 3. In VIII, 13 abandoned land is taken though the heirs are alive and this action is treated as an exheredation. Note also III, 9, where a man exheredated and banned returns under a safe conduct, but his situation is legally so parlous that when he is poisoned no one dares aid him.

[198] But see Orderic, III, 8 where a man who committed homicide is exiled and is apparently exheredated. In 1 *Cart. Trinité de Vendôme*, no. 16 (1039), where Walter kills Maurice, a relative of Geoffrey Martel of Anjou, the latter's barons adjudge "quod Galterius idem totum ex integro fevum secum forsfecerat quod de Goffridi comitis beneficio tenebat." Walter subsequently concords with a conveyance of two mills.

[199] *Cf.* also, Haskins, *op. cit.*, App. E, 4a (1088–91), certain land restored by Robert Curthose to Fécamp taken by William from the church; *ibid.*, 4c, where the taking appears to have been from a vassel of Fécamp.

[200] Orderic XII, 37.

[201] *Conc. Rouen* (1072) c. 15, 20 Mansi, *Concilia*, 38; *cf.* also the letter

The ambiguity of our earliest Norman sources is helpful on one point—that the penalties against land are by way of escheat. But they do not make clear how the feudal sanction becomes a sanction of criminal law. Certainly it is doubtful whether one can argue from the identity of the penalties in the two cases that it is in either event taken because of a breach of faith. If this hypothesis has any value it should be demonstrated that a crime involved either an actual or a constructive infidelity. Here the early sources do not help. It is true that the *treuga Dei* was buttressed by oath, but as we shall see, its bargain breach is the least significant feature involved in its enforcement. What the law does deal with is the much more workable device of infamy, more workable because it operates without reference to bargains. It is the explicit sanction of all oath procedure, and in the eleventh and early twelfth centuries the Norman trial is built upon oath.[202] A man who fails at battle or at the ordeal is necessarily infamous. Benedict of Ste. Maure is voicing a truism when he writes:

> De ceste laid felonie
> E de l'infame en quei enché
> Par traïson e par pecchié[203]

That these changes have come to pass because of the operation and perpetuation of the ban is implicit in the very nature of the changes. Through all the vicissitudes that have to be weathered courtholders cling to the last shred of advantage afforded by the rich procedural and substantive endowment of the *bannus*. Enough survives the batterings of circumstance for us to recognize the outlines of old prerogative.[204] The parity of treatment

of Lanfranc to Count Roger, 1 *Opera Omnia* 65 ". . . infidelis diceretur et de perjuris vel fraude aliquam infamiam pateretur."

[202] Brunner, *Entstehung der Schwurgerichte*, 175 *et seq.*

[203] 1 *Chronique des Ducs de Normandie*, ll. 14605–14607.

[204] The developed law is set forth in the following passage, *S.L.N.*, cap. xxii—"§1. Ad ducem pertinent omnes forisfacture mobiles. Mobiles autem forisfacture sunt catalla eorum seu mobilia qui per judicium damnati sunt.

"§2. Tripliciter autem in Normannia damnantur homines, prout vite

278 CRIMINAL PROCEDURE

accorded fugitive and convict is explicable only in terms of the ban, the one institution that hovered continually between process and punishment. The continued use of the term *forisbannitio* in this connection is further evidence, and so is the sum of 60 shillings. But conclusive is the constant appearance of the term of the year and the day. Just so long does the duke in Normandy have to wait when his process is used, before his forfeiture of the fugitive's chattels would ensue. Just so long can he retain the lands of the convict and the fugitive, before the persons ultimately entitled enter. It is the ancient term of sequestration of the *missio in bannum*.[205] Only in respect of movables does the ban preserve its integrity as a fiscal weapon. It does not succeed in forcing through a confiscation of realty. Disherison is the defeat that the fisc takes at the hands of society.

The law does not die in the turbulent period of the tenth and eleventh centuries, nor does it lapse into a state of suspended animation: in the face of conditions most unfavorable to or-

merita hoc requirunt: aut per corporis destructionem, ut de suspensis, aut incensis, aut suffossis, cecatis, mancatis, expedicatis et similibus est apparens; vel per forisbannitionem, ut patet de fugitivis, qui aliquo crimine accusati tamdiu ad pacem ducis vocati diffudiunt quod per judicium forisbanniuntur de quibus inferius in sequentibus tractabitur; vel per patrie abjurationem, ut de illis qui aliquo crimine fugitivi, vel vinculis mancipati, vel carceribus detrusi, si forte ad ecclesiam confugerint vel crucem amplexati fuerint, si patriam abjuraverint, que possident forisfaciunt universa."

*S.L.N.*, cap. xxii §9 "Terras autem damnatorum et proventus earum per annum unum princeps habebit Normannorum; elapso autem anno, dominis sunt reddende qui immediate de eis habebant homagium." *Cf. T.A.C.* cap. xxxvi, §7 "Omnis enim homicida, licet pacem Ducis habuerit, hereditatem suam non habebit, nec ipse, nec heredes sui, quam propter homicidium perdiderit; sed eam habebit dominus fundi. Simile est de singulis fugitivis."

[205] That the duke's interest is to be regarded as a remnant of the ancient full power of the fisc upon a *missio in bannum* receives some collateral support from *T.A.C.*, cap. lxxx, §7 "Mulier pro delicto viri non amittit hereditatem; si vero abjuraverit terram, vel forisbannitus fuerit, mulier, vivente illo, non erit in possessione hereditatis sue, nec habebit fructus illius, immo dominus Rex. Mortuo autem marito suo, rehabebit hereditatem suam, nisi ipsa, sicut vir, fuerit condempnata."

derly growth, it proceeds sometimes implacably, but usually with compromise in a direction which can be charted. Politically, the small units where the law was enforced exercised a predominantly anarchic influence. But within immunity and barony were nevertheless evolved along lines of general similarity legal conceptions that were basic in the Norman's law when William crossed the channel. These are ideas which will become central in the English conception of felony. The death penalty, the forfeiture of chattels, the escheat of land, the ducal year-and-day, the *misericordia* have all been worked out during this period, products of the clash and compromise of Frankish law and a ruthless new society. It is a singular monument to the rapacity of the age that it contributes nothing to procedure, and everything to the sanctions of the judgment. What remains to be accomplished in the determination of the common law conception of felony is the centralization of the power to punish crime and the development of trial procedure and of classes of crimes to which to apply this procedure. The Normans are still to make contributions to all three problems, upon which English law then and only then can build.

# CHAPTER V

## GOD'S PEACE AND DUKE'S PEACE

IN Normandy as elsewhere in France the revival of public order was a problem in centralization. The jurisdiction over crime was widely dispersed among feudatories both lay and cleric, each of whom was using his jurisdiction less to preserve order than to administer for his own benefit sanctions against wrongs committed within his fief. These jurisdictions had, moreover, in many cases been exercised by the Norman barons time out of mind, so that not only had they become, in the eyes of their possessors, vested rights, but they had come to be generally regarded as normal incidents of a feoffment. In consequence the problem had from the very first a strong political complexion. The very idea of a general law enforcement was revolutionary in a society whose structure was built primarily to facilitate war. Every constructive step toward peace and order that did not tread lightly on the "customs" of the feudatories, that went beyond mere voluntary cooperation, would arouse resistance, for it would be in derogation of a legal order more fundamental to existing political stability than the state of security it was sought to produce.

In these circumstances the choice of practical expedients was limited. There could be no forthright defeasance of vested jurisdictions: they might at most be brought under control. The close coincidence of Norman and Frankish charter formulae suggests at once the revival of the Frankish franchise theory, as a plausible device for securing this control. But the very term franchise implies an exception to a general norm. In Frankish and late medieval law that norm is a public system of justice of which the immunist is made free. Not until the time when there becomes discernible in Normandy a central power capable of establishing a similar norm to which baronial jurisdiction would be an exception can it be meaningful even to think of the lesser jurisdictions as franchisal. Persuasive of the persistence of an immunity theory the charter formulae might be, if they stood alone, but a currency of such a theory can be established as to either laymen or cleric only if the existence of a concurrent jurisdiction, which is powerful and pervasive enough to control in the absence of affirmative exception, can be proved.[1]

## DUCAL RIGHTS AND FEUDAL PRACTICE

It is well known that in Normandy a franchise theory is demonstrable toward the middle of the twelfth century. Blood justice is then treated as a grant emanating from the duke. But by that time he has enlarged his judicial powers. With this the

---

[1] It is hardly necessary to point out in view of the material hitherto cited that Brussel's assertion in 1 *Nouvel examen de l'usage des fiefs* (1727) 252–3 that the duke had an exclusive right to "haute justice" is incorrect. This was long ago perceived by Stapleton in 1 *Rot. Scacc. Norm.* Intro. xxxiii, and by Brunner, *Entstehung der Schwurgerichte*, 158. Nevertheless in Luchaire, *Manuel des institutions françaises* (1892) 245, and Holtzmann, *Französische Verfassungsgeschichte* (1910) 81, Brussel's statement is repeated. Since Valin, *Le Duc de Normandie et sa cour* (1910) 182, one may expect a final abandonment of Brussel's view.

When a franchise theory of crimes is formulated *temp.* Henry II, the jurisdiction which the duke claims to be vested in him and exercisable only by delegation is described as "pleas of the sword." Discussion of Norman law has been unduly obscured by employing this expression as if it had been current long before its existence can be attested, and this has led to confusion. For example, Powicke, *Loss of Normandy* (1913), 80 *et seq.*, deals with the pleas of the sword as if both phrase and concept had been current in the eleventh century. "The continuity of public justice, if it really existed must be sought in the maintenance by the duke of his authority in special cases or pleas of the sword. In a country so full of franchises [he means jurisdictions] the reservation of these pleas was necessary to the duke's judicial supremacy" (82). He treats the charters to the abbeys as not creating exemption from the authority of the count, and as to the specific terms of the grants states that "later they appear as pleas of the sword." He cites the Inquest of 1091 as the "first list of these pleas." This is an anachronism. The term is not used in 1091: its earliest use in circumstances connected clearly with matters "criminal" (*infra*, p. 333) seems to occur in a statement by an inquest, embodied in the *Très ancien coutumier*, cap. LXX. This is assumed by Valin, *op. cit.*, 181 as taken under Henry I (giving no reason for his view). Tardif, *T.A.C.* (Intro.) lix,

situation even in the last decades of the eleventh century shows but little correspondence. The decrement of baronial jurisdiction has not yet begun. Indeed the first unmistakable traces of a public order for which the duke assumes responsibility do not appear until the year 1080, the date which marks the establishment of clear ducal enforcement of the truce of God. This can be shown to be more than mere coincidence. Haskins has asserted that public order in Normandy does not arise out of the truce of God.[2] We shall prove that the truce of God was the starting point for all public enforcement, and that apart from the evidence relating to the enforcement of the truce there is no satisfactory or convincing proof that either public order or public justice existed.

In dealing with the confusing and scanty evidence of ducal justice in the eleventh century the distinction is often drawn between the powers held by the duke as sovereign and those held by him as feudal suzerain. This sort of analysis is useful simply to describe the trend of institutional development as one of expansion of the sovereign at the expense of the suzerain and the gradual differentiation between these two aspects. One is hardly justified in assuming that men of this period thought in terms of sovereignty *vs.* suzerainty, so complete is the merger of capacities, so dominant is the *person* of the holder of these capacities. The modern analyst who sees ducal protection of the church as a manifestation of sovereignty, the exaction of military service in return for a fief as an exercise of suzerainty, will not fit into either concept so impalpable and yet so real a matter as the withdrawal of grace. It is, of course, tempting, in the face of that long line of hard-bitten Norman rulers, when one is familiar

casually calls it an inquest of Henry II. Perrot, *Les cas royaux* (1910) 306 n. 2 dates it 1150; Haskins, *Norman Institutions* 160, n. 22, suggests *ante* 1171. In view of the facility that writers have exhibited in making later sources speak conclusively for earlier centuries it is not mere pedantry to insist that the expression is not to be used out of its time.

[2] Haskins, *op. cit.,* 38: "Normandy was not one of the countries where the *Landfrieden* sprang from the *Gottesfrieden.*"

with political theories of our recent past, to out-Bodin Bodin. This form of anachronism must, however, be resisted when evaluating the few pieces of evidence regarding early ducal justice.

Historians have not always observed due caution.[3] Either evidence of justice ambiguously feudal or public has been without warrant called public, or a concept of sovereignty belonging to an earlier or a later age has been interpolated, in complete absence of evidence, to produce conclusions about ducal public justice. There is no direct proof until the end of the eleventh century that the duke's court in matters secular was endowed with prerogatives at all different from those enjoyed by his chief tenants.[4]

[3] Mitteis, *Lehnrecht und Staatsgewalt,* 351 "man hat früher meist übertreibend das ganze Gewicht auf die amtsrechtliche Suprematie des Herzogs gelegt," citing Glasson, Flach and Valin. Powicke, *op. cit.,* 52 lays stress upon the fact that the duke owed his supremacy to his feudal position, but at 80 *et seq.* he makes a good deal of the distinction between sovereignty and suzerainty. *Cf.* also Haskins, *op. cit.,* 38 who in general emphasizes the feudal side. It must be remembered that while the Norman duke like the count of Anjou fell heir to royal perquisites once wielded by Frankish kings (Halphen, *Le Comté d'Anjou au XIe siècle,* 112) the whole weight of feudal politics was directed against the translation of these claims into legal prerogatives. They are marks of prestige, but it is doubtful whether they can be treated in the early eleventh century as indices of sovereignty.

[4] Powicke, *op. cit.,* 81, says the direct evidence before 1050 of the duke as the source of justice is scanty. Valin, *op. cit.,* 182 *et seq.* takes the position that the feudatories acquired blood justice at the time of the settlement of Normandy and that the duke only slowly and never completely acquired control over these matters. Both Haskins *op. cit.,* 27, n. 102, and Powicke, *op. cit.,* 80 contest this. Powicke's argument runs as follows. He says that sovereignty implies that the sovereign is the source of justice and that despite exceptions to the duke's authority he was "from the first the source of justice." He asserts his conclusions follow from the fact that the viscounts took the titles of the old counties [*quaere* as to the probative force of this]; that they collected a tax from lands other than the ducal demesnes [these might well be lands allodially held]; that they appear under William not simply as judges in local courts but as judges to whom appeals can be made in certain cases against inaction of local lords [citing nothing earlier than the Lillebon canon of 1080 regarding truce enforcement]. As we have shown *supra* Chapter III, note 184, no reliance can be placed on Haskins' (*op. cit.,* 26–7) faulty analysis of the Frankish immunity and his baseless argument that the Norman immunity did not ex-

Statements and records are equally equivocal.⁵ Indeed, since Ganshof's proof of the ubiquitous metamorphosis of the Frankish *mallus publicus* into a court of vassals,⁶ there is at least a presumption that the concept of "public" as against any other sort of justice had vanished as well in Normandy as elsewhere.⁷ The

clude the count. Nevertheless Powicke accepts Haskins' statement as conclusive. He also evinces a disposition to buttress his arguments by relying on twelfth century evidence (p. 83). The use of late sources to prove an earlier state of politics is misleading. It cannot be denied that there is some evidence of early sovereign powers in the duke; yet the real development does not begin until after 1042 and it moves out of the realm of mere inference only after 1080.

⁵ For example, for the early eleventh century, Valin, *op. cit.,* P.J. 1; *Vita S. Herluini* in 150 Migne, *Patrologia,* 698 B, which Haskins, *op. cit.,* 38, seems to regard as evidence of the duke's power to enforce order. The references in Dudo, Haskins, *ibid.,* are not sufficiently specific to be of any account to a legal historian. Conclusions about rights of public justice cannot be drawn from the ecclesiastical causes in the duke's court, for this jurisdiction is special and exceptional (*infra,* p. 295). *Cf.* for such cases Round, *Calendar,* no. 78 (1080 Holy Trinity, Rouen); no. 114 (1086 Fécamp); no. 165 (1074 St. Wandrille); no. 711 (1061 Mt. St. Michel); no. 712 (n.d. same); nos. 1114–5 (1080 St. Florent in Angers); no. 1170 (*temp.* Wm. I, Marmoutier de Tours); no. 1171 (1063, same); no. 1172 (1060–66, same); no. 1190 (1072–9, same); no. 1212 (1080, same); Davis, *Regesta Regum Anglo-Normannorum* (1913) app. no. 16.

Despotic acts such as the wholesale disherison of certain barons, mentioned by Orderic, lib. III, c. 5 must also be distinguished from judicial acts: they are manifestations of naked power rather than of law. The same thing occurred in Anjou (Halphen, *op. cit.,* 112–3, who explains this by suggesting that the fief was still looked on as a *precarium*).

In two outstanding cases where the duke-king's tenants in chief were made to stand to right, Odo, the Conqueror's brother, and William of Durham, the crown makes no assertion about judging them as "subjects" but as vassals. The evidence in Odo's case (Orderic, lib. VII c. 8) is sketchy compared with the full account in William of Durham's (1 Dugdale, *Monasticon* [1817], 244–50). Additional references to the duke's court in Normandy in Adams, *Council and Courts in Anglo-Norman England* (1926), c. 1, c. 3.

⁶ *Supra,* Chapter III, note 17.

⁷ Haskins, *op. cit.,* 29, n. 109, cites a Ms. grant (1028–79) of the abbot of Fécamp "retenta publica iustitia in consilio nostro," but this phrase is exceptional and can scarcely be said to establish the currency of a concept of public justice. The charter of Robert to Mt. St. Michel in 12 *Mem. Ant. Norm.* 111 uses the expression "publicorum ministrorum inquietudine" in the immunity clause.

collateral evidence of the duke functioning as the head of an autonomous system of justice is no less unconvincing. It is true that the administration of the counties[8] may be regarded as lying outside the normal feudal machinery, and since there was in Normandy a considerable amount of land allodially held,[9] a material reason existed for the duke to step in and fill the jurisdictional gap. This might furnish real ground for supposing that the duke's comital arrangements were not conceived of merely as the administration of his demesne lands. But we do not know whether, in fact, there is any relation between the existence of *alodium* and the county administration. Neither is there anything to show that judicial powers involved in connection with the county organization were *sui generis*. In Richard II's reign there had indeed been a grant of the *consuetudines comitatus* which we have taken to include judicial powers.[10] But apart from establishing that these *consuetudines* were treated as a jurisdiction lying in grant, such a transfer unsupported by other evidence does not mark such incidental judicial rights before the grant as "public." Certainly when William the Conqueror in terms grants blood justice,[11] he conveys these rights in a manner and form undistinguishable from the similar grants of his barons.[12] He shows no intent to designate the jurisdictions as an incident of county administration.[13]

[8] The best account in Haskins, *op. cit.*, 46 *et seq.*

[9] Delisle, *Etudes sur la condition de la classe agricole* etc. (1903) 41.

[10] *Supra,* Chapter IV, note 69.

[11] For example, to Préaux, Valin, *op. cit.*, P.J., no. 2; to Bec and St. Benoît-sur-Loire cited by Haskins, *op. cit.*, 29, n. 109.

[12] The eleventh century grant of Roger of Beaumont to Préaux in 3 Le Prévost, *Notes sur Eure,* 96, grants all *consuetudines,* with a reservation which indicates that blood justice was otherwise conveyed. Delisle, *Des revenus publics en Normandie* in 13 *B.E.C.* 108 n. 3, prints part of a charter of the Count of Mortain conveying blood justice. Note also the phrase from a grant of the Count of Evreux printed in Haskins, *op. cit.*, 29, n. 112. Compare the grant of 1106 of the Count of Meulan, Valin, *op. cit.*, P.J. no. 4; 3 Le Prévost, *op. cit.*, 97.

[13] Haskins, *op. cit.*, 279 treats the grant to Préaux mentioned *supra* note 11 as a conveyance out of the *consuetudines vicecomitatus,* because

Although the sources before 1066 may thus have failed to establish a system of public justice, they will be somewhat more instructive on the possible means of constructing a franchise theory. Here we must distinguish sharply between the redevelopment of such a theory as against the lay baronage and as against the church. In the former case there could be, strictly speaking, franchise only as to a public non-feudal justice; in the case of ecclesiastical establishments it could signify either this or an immunity from feudal or from lay jurisdiction generally, or both. As to the secular lords, their posture toward their own criminal jurisdiction is in general to be deduced from their own vassal grants where blood justice is transferred. These charters, as remarked above, prove to be identical in form with those emanating from the duke. They likewise disclose an identical conception of what is being conveyed, viz., a jurisdiction that lies in grant—which (so far as such a conception applies to those times) approaches "private property." There is not the slightest intimation that the baron-grantor is seeking to divest himself of public powers delegated to him by the hand of the duke, still less, that the powers conveyed are exceptions to a larger and more general system of justice. Not even the most informing extant document concerning the constitution of secular rights of justice, the Inquest of 1091,[14] yields anything to the contrary on this point. It is framed in terms of jurisdiction (property; who owns

they are so styled in a later re-conveyance by the abbot. Whatever the abbot thought he had been given, the ducal description would in any event be determinative for our period, and this phrase is not used in the ducal charter.

[14] In Haskins, *op. cit.*, 281. It is to be noted that in certain matters like protection in going to court, or to the army, the rights of the duke are of a sort generally outside the normal subject matter of feudal grant. They are matters not susceptible of local baronial enforcement. These are, like the coinage, aspects of the duke's power of sovereignty. From cc. 8 and 9 can be inferred the fact that as to certain matters the barons have forfeiture of life and members, and that blood justice is distributed. But there is no intimation of special delegation or franchise. C. 13 indicates certainly that the inquest is only stating what is the *status quo* and that this is to be undisturbed. Of the more general prohibitions like that of castle building etc.

what?), not in terms of franchise (how does he have it?). At most it can be said to be forecasting in some tentative way a later assertion of exclusiveness in ducal jurisdiction and its aspects, and to this extent starting to set a norm from which immunity can later be given or "derived." With regard to those rights of blood justice exercised by the laity, therefore, it is impossible to discover until well into the twelfth century any formulation of a franchise theory divested of tenurial implications. From mere enumeration of single rights in conveyances no argument follows in favor of any autonomous non-feudal franchise theory. Quite apart from the necessary presupposition, already noted, that a general public jurisdiction existed—which it did not—an acid test of such a theory would lie in proof that franchises could be withdrawn by some process other than the normal escheat of feoffments. Such a process does not appear from the record to have existed in the eleventh century.

When one turns to the ecclesiastical establishments there seems to be more reason to believe that a franchise theory existed. *Prima facie,* the continued use of Frankish formulae in the ducal charters would tend both to preserve and to evidence the Frankish immunity tradition.[15] At least one phase of this, the *mundium,* is perpetuated in the right of protection and supervision assumed by the duke in relation to the church.[16] Moreover, in the ducal grants to the abbeys where jurisdictions in general or as to specific offenses are granted, the prohibition upon entries by ducal officers and the fine established for interference reproduces another essential constituent of the Frankish immunity system. The circumstances under which monastic establishments were restored in Normandy with ducal help and encour-

we shall speak later. These are cast in terms of commandments and not of jurisdiction, and are derived from similar provisions in the various *treugae Dei.* Haskins, *op. cit.,* 38, 60, treats these as secular legislation not emanating from that source. *Cf. infra,* note 71.

[15] *Supra,* Chapter III, notes 181 and 185.

[16] Böhmer, *Kirche und Staat in England und der Normandie,* 30 *et seq.;* 2 Brussel, *op. cit.,* 815; Senn, *L'Institution des avoueries,* 95.

agement were such that the greatest guarantees had to be given against secular incursion.[17] And since the bishops in the earlier period conducted themselves like temporal lords, such protection was needed no less against them; consequently many charters contain exemptions from episcopal interference.[18] Hence the abbatial privileges may indeed be deemed immunities—but not immunities specifically from *public* justice, but immunities from any judicial interference whatever.[19] One cannot assume, therefore, because immunities are granted, that any system of public justice may be implied. If the duke's justice intervenes to carry

[17] See the account in 2 Sackur, *Die Cluniacenser,* 41 *et seq.*

[18] For example, Fécamp (980–990), *Neustria Pia* 208; 11 *Gallia Christiana,* Instr. 8 (1006) and Haskins, *op. cit.,* App. B. no. 2 and *cf.* Böhmer, *op. cit.,* 183; Mont St. Michel (*temp.* Rich. II) *Neustria Pia,* 378 and *cf.* on this Haskins, *op. cit.,* 35 n. 137; St. Trinité of Caen (1082) 11 *Gallia Christiana,* Instr. 71; Montvilliers (1035) 11 *ibid.,* 326. *Cf.* also the grants to St. Stephen (1082) 11 *ibid.,* 73; to St. Sauveur (1060) *ibid.,* Instr. 126 and 231 (*temp.* Richard); to Troarn, Sauvage, *L'Abbaye de St. Martin de Troarn* 356 (1101) going back to grant of Odo of Bayeux. The problem of the exemption from episcopal authority has never been studied adequately. In the case of the grants last cited the lands had apparently by prescription become free of episcopal authority. The case of Mont. St. Michel discussed by Haskins, *op. cit.,* 35, indicates that despite charter provisions the bishops claim the right to interfere. Since the bishops exercised both temporal and spiritual authority, the secular grant could conceivably be understood only to affect the former, as the tendency under William the Conqueror to distinguish the jurisdictions became apparent. Finally, should be noted the fact that the charters are witnessed by the bishops, and sometimes there is recited in the body of the instrument the consent of the bishops. The legal significance of this may be more than merely formal, depending upon the degree of control over the episcopacy exercised by the duke, on which *cf.* Böhmer, *op. cit.,* 31.

[19] Implicit in such phrases as "absque ulla inquietudine cujuslibet secularis vel judiciarie potestatis," Jumièges (1027) 1 Vernier, *Chartes de Jumièges,* no. 12; Bernai (1027) 1 Le Prévost, *op. cit.,* 285; St. Ouen (*temp.* Richard II) Valin, *op. cit.,* 222, n. 1. Robert's grants to St. Amand, 6 *Monasticon* pt. 2, 1101 and Mont St. Michel, in 12 *Mem. Antiq. Norm.* 111 are only as to his own justice. It should be observed that in some formulae used by William the Conqueror the implication of immunity is much less clear than in his predecessor's charters, for example St. Trinité of Caen, 11 *Gallia Christ.,* Instr. 59; St. Victor en Caux, *ibid.,* 13, but see the charter to Montebourg, *ibid.,* 229; and note also the confirmation to Jumièges, 1 Vernier, *op. cit.,* no. 32. The charters of Henry I, like that to

out these protective warnings when bishop or baron infringes the charter, his jurisdiction need not be, and probably is not a claim to wider and more general judicial rights over wrong-doing. It is in pursuance of a specific power and duty of protection which may derive from his own private promise, or from his predecessor's.

The most striking aspect of this ducal power and duty of protection over churches appears in connection with vassal grants to such. During the eleventh century a ducal confirmation is included or appended to such a great number of the gifts to monasteries that it is hard to escape the conclusion that this is because a rule of law requires ducal assent.[20] Indeed, after 1066 the practical difficulties of getting the busy monarch of two lands to attend to the matter make it unlikely that anyone would go to the trouble of procuring ducal confirmation if it were not for some reason or other necessary to the validity of the grant. The requirement of ducal confirmation is usually regarded as an example of an alleged rule of feudal law requiring the consent of

St. Pierre-sur-Dive, 11 *Gallia Christiana,* Instr. 156, and to St. Evroul, *ibid.,* 204, show the immunity idea in a pronounced degree.

[20] For example, Kermaingant, *Chart. St. Michel du Tréport,* no. 1; Fontenay, 11 *Gallia Christiana,* Instr. 61; Préaux, *ibid.,* 199; Lessay, *ibid.,* 224; Troarn, Sauvage, *op. cit.,* 302, 352; Jumièges, 1 Vernier, *op. cit.,* 20, 25, 31. *Cf.* also Round, *Calendar,* nos. 73, 74, 449, 920, 1114, 1410. In carefully edited cartularies like Lot, *Etudes sur St. Wandrille* or Vernier, *Chartes de Jumièges,* the accumulation of this evidence is impressive. It should further be observed that frequently where no confirmation is included in the document, it may well have been in a separate instrument like that printed in Lot, *op. cit.,* 71. Génestal, who was one of the most learned and best informed legal historians of Normandy, has stated that this method of confirming was usual in Normandy; *cf.* 6 *N.R.H.* (4 ser. 1927), 158. The mere absence of a confirmation in a document is consequently not at all conclusive. Note should further be made of the blanket and retrospective confirmations, a form due no doubt to the peripatetic habits of the king. For example Round, *Calendar* no. 569 (1130–3) by Henry I of all antecedent grants by certain grantors, and no. 570 by Stephen; *ibid.,* no. 371, Henry "grants" all lands, etc. confirmed by his father and brother (1100–1107) and also no. 373; no. 623; no. 795. In connection with the Norman rule, *cf.* the policy in England under William I, attested in 2 *Domesday Book,* 13, where a royal writ or grant was needed.

the lord for any vassal alienation.[21] But it is evident at first glance that this rule is much too broadly stated: the evidence on which it rests consists almost entirely of these same aforementioned ducal confirmations of vassal grants to churches; charters from layman to layman are rare, for the laity convey to one another by symbolic livery, which dispenses with record of any participation by the lord.[22] Nor can ducal confirmations of these vassal gifts to monasteries be considered as manifestations of a milder rule of feudal law requiring the lord's consent to such vassal grants as work a change in the nature of the services,[23] because there was no demonstrable rule of law in the eleventh century, as there was later,[24] limiting gifts in alms. On the contrary, such grants were encouraged by the suzerain.[25] So many of the charters expressly state that confirmation is sought to preserve the inviolability of the conveyance,[26] that these ducal confirmations of vassal grants to monasteries are explicable only on the narrow ground that the duke's protection, assumed over the acquisitions of ecclesiastical establishments, is generally recognized. It could hardly mean anything else since the grants of *alodium* to monasteries are likewise confirmed.[27]

[21] Mitteis, *Lehnrecht und Staatsgewalt*, 629 *et seq.*; 2 Martin, *Histoire de la coutume . . . de Paris*, 8 *et seq.*; Lamprecht, *Wirtschaftsentwickelung*, 121 is somewhat more cautious.

[22] Génestal in 6 *N.R.H.* (4 ser. 1927), 157. In Round, *Calendar*, are a number of eleventh century cases of livery by twig or dagger, some of which indicate that the livery is a bilateral and not a trilateral transaction, nos. 2, 77, 117, 322, 327, 449, 655.

[23] 1 Pollock and Maitland, *H.E.L.*, 245 citing no authority.

[24] The limitations date certainly from 1157 when the ducal court held that there could be no jurisdiction retained without a ducal charter, 15 *Mem. Ant. Norm.* 197. The rule limiting grants in alms to a third of the freehold is in *T.A.C.*, cap. LXXXIX; *cf.* the exchequer decision of 1210 in Marnier, *Etablissements et coutumes de l'échiquier* (1839) 120; 2 Warnkönig and Stein, *Französische Staats und Rechtsgeschichte* (2 ed.) App. 75.

[25] Böhmer, *op. cit.*, 3, 10, 38; 2 Sackur, *op. cit.* 53.

[26] For example Lot, *St. Wandrille*, no. 20; no. 40; Round, *Calendar*, no. 466 (1079-83); no. 83 (1060); no. 73 (1066); Sauvage, *L'Abbaye de St. Martin de Troarn*, no. 2.

[27] *Cf.* the charters in Lot, *St. Wandrille*, no. 23; 1 Vernier, *Chartes de*

It is in connection with vassal foundation grants by persons who are themselves holders of blood justice that the duke's ecclesiastical prerogatives become directly relevant to the existence of any franchise theory. If the Frankish theory of the *causae criminales* had survived, even in its final and attenuated form that the pleas hitherto reserved to the fisc were exercisable by its license, some sign of this would be forthcoming in the transactions in which vassal holders of blood justice establish and endow monasteries. But no such sign appears in Normandy. From the theory that the founder has a special property in the establishment (the *Eigenkirche*),[28] the rule long obtained[29] that the founder, in the absence of express grant, may be taken to have retained whatever criminal jurisdiction he exercised in the land prior to the alienation. This is made probable by one vassal foundation charter which expressly reserves blood justice,[30] but clinched by a pair of charters where the father's foundation grant is silent on blood justice while the son's subsequent grant takes pains to pass the jurisdiction thereby implicitly withheld.[31]

*Jumièges,* no. 37; Round, *Calendar,* no. 703. There are two other equivocal documents: Denis, *Chartes de St. Julien de Tours,* no. 29 where the donor had been exheredated by the Norman duke; Lot, *op. cit.,* no. 27, where *alodium* is transferred but there is a release of a toll, so the confirmation may be as to the latter. Haskins, *op. cit.,* 6, thinks *alodium* has not always "a very exact technical meaning." *Cf.* however 1 Guérard, *Cart. St. Père de Chartres,* Intro. §13. There is a discussion of the variable meaning of the word in Chénon, *Etude sur l'histoire des alleux en France* (1888), 30 *et seq.* Most of Chénon's charter references are culled from Ducange and Flach. Since the solution of this problem depends on an exhaustive study of conveyances not too much confidence can be placed in Chénon's conclusions.

[28] Not yet adequately studied in Normandy. Some remarks in Böhmer, *Das Eigenkirchentum in England,* in *Festgabe für Liebermann* (1921), 301 *et seq.;* Valin, *op. cit.,* 85 *et seq.; cf.* for further references on the general subject, Thorne, *Assize Utrum and the Canon Law of England,* 33 *C.L.R.* 430, n. 10.

[29] Not limited until the Exchequer decision in 1157 cited *supra,* note 24.

[30] The grant of the Count of Mortain, cited by Delisle in 13 *B.E.C.* 108 n. 3.

[31] The two grants to Préaux in 3 Le Prévost, *Eure,* 96, 97. The father's charter is confirmed by the duke and contains a consent of the heir with a reserve of his own rights for life with the privilege of releasing them at

It is clear, therefore, that in the case of vassal endowments blood justice does not run with the land, although it is grantable, i.e., the theory of property in the founder allows him to treat his existing criminal jurisdiction as his own, not only to grant or withhold as he pleases, but as not granted without explicit reference thereto. This falls far short of meeting the requirements of the developed English franchise theory of the future, which insists that any franchise not appurtenant to land lapses by an attempt at its alienation.[32] To restrict the founder's independence in the matter of blood justice even by some standard milder than that of the later English rule the duke would have to be prepared to face the wider political issues involved in a direct challenge of the particular founder's own title to his original jurisdiction. These charters show that he did not dare to undertake this.[33]

If the duke, then, confirms a foundation grant made by a holder of blood justice, this is not because it is a foundation grant nor because it is made by a holder of blood justice nor because blood justice is conveyed nor because it is withheld, but because it is a grant to a monastery. The duke's confirmation is no different in the cases where blood justice is in some way involved[34] than it is in those where land alone is given. It is in pursuance of his ecclesiastical prerogative that he confirms. It is not because of any theory that blood justice is ultimately the duke's. The Norman immunity theory was therefore limited in all cases to ducal protection and to exemption of the internal administration of a ducal foundation from lay and, on occasion, from epis-

---

any time. The second charter consequently is an execution of this reservation already confirmed by the duke.

[32] *Y.B. 6 & 7 Edw. II* (S.S. 29) 181 (Kent Eyre 1313-4).

[33] There does not appear, moreover, any interference with the right under feudal law for the grantor to define his grant. *Cf.* the *placitum* where the Count of Eu decides the grantees' charter right to big fish in *Cart. St. Michel du Tréport*, no. 5 (1101); Round, *Calendar*, no. 232.

[34] For example wherever a grant of *consuetudines* is made there is as we have seen (Chapter IV) the possible implication of judicial rights. Thus the foundation charter of Fontenay in 6 Dugdale *Monasticon*, 1084, was confirmed by William the Conqueror.

copal interference. No franchise theory had been formulated as to specifically criminal pleas, nor any practice.

The early Norman immunity theory, possessing such decided limitations, could thus furnish no legal support for a broad policy of extending ducal control over criminal pleas. Indeed, there is every reason to believe that in Normandy as in the kingdom of the Franks the exemption from external interference facilitated, instead, the inflation of existing local rights through the operation of prescription. This was a problem in itself. It was perhaps one of the most difficult obstacles in the way of any effective criminal law. For years criminal justice appears only as a local and private problem, dealt with by bargain—and largely for profit—among the barons, without reference to any interest of the suzerain or of a "public." Not until the last years of William the Conqueror's reign does even that duke attempt to check such prescription. And he attempts it not as a condition precedent to the development of ducal justice,[35] but rather as a measure to prevent further diminution of his prerogative.

The first steps taken in this direction are by no means broad in scope—though English experience may have made the ultimate aim broader in conception. These first steps are aimed at only one part of the chain of jurisdictions which had continued to fetter the expansion of ducal power as they did not fetter the power of a conqueror. At the Council of Lillebon in 1080 the bishops are told that they may have the customs of Robert's time and those which the Conqueror had granted.[36] Beyond that the

[35] But it is noteworthy as we shall shortly see that it is the Council of Lillebon which sets up the machinery for a ducal enforcement of the truce of God.

[36] Bessin, *Concilia*, 71, cc. 43, 45. Böhmer, *Kirche*, 32, n. 3 thinks the passage relates to spiritual jurisdiction. Tardif, *Etudes sur les sources*, 42–3, does not specify. It seems probable since the duke takes the position that the rights emanate from him, that claims as to jurisdiction in general are intended. Only the second part of c. 45, where the rights of the laity *vs.* the bishops are spoken of, is there an implication that spiritual jurisdiction is meant. In any event the conception that a stop is to be put on prescription is clear. The first sentence of c. 45 which puts the burden of

duke keeps his rights and in the duke's court will be judged all claims. Almost contemporaneously in England a related policy seems to have been launched, for the confirmation of grants is no longer effected loosely; the tendency is rather to freeze the rights of grantees as they stood the day when King Edward was alive and dead.[37] By fixing a *status quo,* by laying down a dead line beyond which reposes a gap which the duke now asserts he has filled and will fill, a concept of asserted residual sovereignty comes into being. Further a base can be laid and will be laid for asserting that all additional rights are derived only by or through him.

It would be a mistake to regard the disposition of the Council of Lillebon simply as a piece of legislation directed at an ecclesiastical problem. The secular authority wielded by the bishops was considerable, territorially and in degree. Any measure that would enhance the control exercised by the duke over those tenants in chief who were vulnerable from the angle of their dependence upon the spiritual prerogative of the duke, a preroga-

---

proof on the bishops in the duke's court is procedurally important, and shows that a definite step toward a franchise theory has been taken, since the bishops are not to take seisin of the rights until proved. Presumably they remain until then in the duke's hands. Compare with cc. 43 and 45 the rule in the precept of Henry II (1151-2) *re* the bishop of Bayeux in 1 *Antiquus Cart. Eccl. Baiocensis (Livre Noir)* no. 16.

[37] Davis, *Regesta,* Intro. xxxii, states that the charters of William I and II "rarely do more than confirm existing liberties." We believe there is perceptible, however, a tendency to fix rights as of a certain time. Many of the charters simply confirm the liberties as they were in King Edward's time, or as King Edward granted them. In *ibid.,* no. 45 (1066-67), is a notification granting land as fully as Harold had it on the day he was alive and dead; no. 47 (1071), as Harold had a manor the day the king crossed the sea. No. 129 (c. 1080) is a precept confirming customs as of the time of Edward's death. *Cf.* no. 149, no. 155, no. 156 (all of 1082), no. 163 (1070-82). Compare also no. 154 a precept to stop new episcopal customs in Ely (1182), no. 164 (1070-82); no. 214 (1078-85); no. 258 (1067-87), no. 276 (1082-7). There are enough of these forms after 1080 for us to assume a deliberate policy was initiated. In this connection, of course, must be considered the effect of the Domesday survey in checking prescriptive rights.

tive already manifested in his rights to investitures[38] and his power over their judgments,[39] would signify a *pro tanto* increase in what will sometime become his sovereignty at large, his public as against his merely feudal claims.

Yet these prerogatives which enabled William to control ecclesiastical justice were scarcely applicable to his lay vassals. Their exercise of blood justice could be controlled only by the expansion of a ducal, and in so far, a public criminal justice upon which baronial criminal jurisdiction, however acquired, could be made dependent as a matter of accepted legal theory. Nor could their prescriptions be curbed unless there were some ducal machinery that functioned observably with more completeness than the barons' local jurisdiction, something that filled the multiple gaps in enforcement which an uncorrelated congeries of merely baronial courts left open. This was perhaps the only workable way in which the barrier could be raised between jurisdiction as a mere incident of tenure, and jurisdiction exceptional to, but to be derived from, the general and "public" authority. Such a distinction would make of baronial criminal justice a power specifically delegated; it would require delegation, not the mere feudal contract. Control on principles that had nothing to do with tenure or service could then come into being and might be raised into the norm. Actually this would have involved and did involve the creation of a concept of jurisdiction the content of which was substantially different from the ideas which had theretofore been current. It would make of ducal judicial rights something wholly different from merely a slightly enlarged version of the rights exercisable by a vassal over his own men—the constant viewpoint of feudalism. In this way the vested rights of the vassals could be disturbed; but on strict feudal theory there could have been no defeasance.

With every feudatory of importance judging the whole gamut

[38] Böhmer, *op. cit.*, 31.
[39] William of Poitou, *Gesta Willelmi* (Giles Ed. 1845) 114.

of crimes committed within his territories, the sphere within which the duke's justice could readily operate to supplement or even to displace baronial activity was constricted. The principles of territoriality and of feudal semi-independence made local jurisdiction self-sufficient. It is consequently absurd to suppose that by any general *mundium*[40] which the duke may have had over all his subjects, he could extend protection to them as against their own lords, or that by any notion of liege homage[41] the duke possessed rights of interfering in an established jurisdiction. The theory of the duke's peace which poetic fancy attributed to Rollo[42] and which supposedly non-poetic historians have found too convenient an hypothesis cannot be proved to have existed in fact before the reign of William the Conqueror. Probably even at his death the term, still rarely used in Normandy, meant no more than a special protection extending to certain exceptional times and places, such as fairs and festivals, where the lord's process might not run. Clearly, as Valin has cogently remarked,[43] ducal justice could not have been generally significant at a time when various specific truces of God are directed at the very incidents over which one might have expected a strong duke with general powers to be already exercising his authority.

If there is reason to doubt that special judicial rights of the duke were much developed even at the end of the eleventh cen-

[40] Valin, *op. cit.*, 188, "Le Duc avait le droit de prendre certaines mesures de protection dans l'intérêt des individus qui vivaient sur le territoire du Duché," and he cites one of Dudo's stories. Later, on p. 191, he admits the intervention would be exceptional, i.e. if the place were specially protected.

[41] The term is not attested in Normandy until the end of the eleventh century, Mitteis, *Lehnrecht,* 558. From *Leges Henrici* 55, 2 the concept has procedural importance only to fix the court where jurisdiction is. "Si homo de pluribus dominis et honoribus teneat, quantumcunque de aliis habeat, ei plus debet et eius residens per judicium erit cuius homo ligius erit."

[42] *Supra,* Chapter IV, note 1.

[43] Valin, *op. cit.,* 191. Powicke, *op. cit.,* 83 n. 5 finds Valin's reasoning too "juristic." This seems a curious characterization. Where Valin fails in his thesis of the duke's peace is in establishing how a jurisdiction over a

tury, there is no question that among certain groups in the duchy public authority was deemed desirable, that, in short, there was support for any ducal effort to extend it. This was not, indeed, because petty crime had become too much a menace, but because the maintenance of order in a large and quasi-political sense was a real and terrible problem. No baron would demur at hanging a vagrant robber or at using local theft as an excuse for forfeiture. But the traditions of his class and the limits of his force would hardly let him envisage as objects of justice in his court any of his peers who might stage a military raid on his domains. Indeed, the feud once begun gave color of right to acts which if committed under other circumstances—or by others than equals —would have been regarded as crimes. The feud was an interminable antiphony of violence; nor could it well be limited to the immediate parties. The problem was to make the outrages which feud involved into wrongs to which the response was not a reprisal by a coordinate, but judgment and execution by a *higher* power. This solution might ultimately have been reached through the existing scheme of jurisdictions except that the feudatories had demonstrated that singly or in combination they had no presently available talent for order, and a more effective talent was at hand. It became consequently a question for which an answer was found outside the feudal setup—though in terms compatible with the more pious of its intellectualized premises.

### THE TRUCE OF GOD

Inevitably the church, which alone in medieval Europe maintains a sense of general social purpose, takes the lead through the institution of the truce of God. First in southern France; gradu-

protected place could be elaborated into a whole system of public justice and how a theory of delegated franchise could be asserted where direct jurisdiction was not exercised. Neither he nor Powicke appreciated the fact that the *treuga Dei* goes through two phases, the merely precatory phase, and the later transformation when secular procedure is harnessed to it.

ally elsewhere.[44] To Normandy the movement spreads. Here church and duke together formulate rules and slowly secure a desultory observance of them. It is as a result of these measures that the duke's justice begins to lose its prior feudal character and to assume the aspect of a "sovereign"—even public—system.

The truce of God is not an indigenous Norman institution. It has, as we have said, a history elsewhere in France before being imported in the early years of the Conqueror's reign. Contemporary statements regarding this peace or truce of God constantly advert to it as something instituted by God Himself.[45] They convey a pious impression that the idea had been newly and dramatically revealed. Actually the prelates were attempting to apply a doctrine that had long been a part of the canon law. This was the so-called *pax ecclesiae*,[46] a peace which a person forfeited upon commission of sin, but which was restored to him upon penance: a concept closely resembling the theory of that peace and breach of peace that some writers have believed to lie at the base of Germanic law generally.

[44] The literature is considerable; here the following have been consulted: Kluckhohn, *Geschichte des Gottesfriedens* (1857); Sémichon, *La paix et la trêve de Dieu* (2 ed. 1869) 2 vols.; Göcke, *Die Anfänge der Landesfriedensaufrichtungen in Deutschland* (1875); Pfister, *Etudes sur le règne de Robert;* Huberti, *Studien zur Rechtsgeschichte der Gottesfrieden und Landfrieden* (1892); 1 Mayer, *D.F.V.G.*, 161; His, *Strafrecht des deutschen Mittelalters,* §2. Wohlhaupter, *Studien zur Rechtsgeschichte der Gottes- und Landfrieden in Spanien,* 14 *Deutschrechtliche Beiträge* no. 2 (1933), has some general material, so also Schnelbögl, *Die Innere Entwickelung der bayerischen Landfrieden* (13 *ibid.* no. 2). The most recent summary regarding Normandy is Yver, *L'Interdiction de la guerre privée,* in *Travaux de la Semaine d'Histoire du Droit Normand* (1928), 307 *et seq.* For the purposes of our discussion there is no need to go into a discussion of the two expressions *pax Dei* and *treuga Dei.* There is a mass of material collected on this by Huberti, *op. cit.,* 250 *et seq.,* who concludes (266) that the term *treuga* is a particular peace limited in time; *pax* is the permanent peace.

[45] Kluckhohn, *op. cit.,* 43.

[46] 4 Hinschius, *K.R.,* 697, citing passages from Cyprian and Tertullian. The relation to the theory of excommunication should be noted. The first use by Gallic councils of the expression *pax ecclesiae* that we have found is by the fourth council of Orleans in 541 (*M.G.H.* 1 *Concilia*) c. 13.

The practical purpose of *pax Dei* in the outgoing tenth and the eleventh century was the creation of a general sanction against lawlessness. Lamprecht was the first to discern, some fifty years ago, that there was a connection between the sporadic attempts to realize this purpose and the economic distress which had been caused by recurrent crop failures.[47] When these periodic crises occurred it was inevitable that the fatter and relatively well-managed church properties should be threatened by violence at the hands of all sorts of persons who were starving or who were looking for a source of gain.[48] The ordinary means of law enforcement were of no avail. The *pax Dei* was intended to supplement them. Pious it no doubt was, and socially useful, but it was also dictated by churchly self-preservation.

The earliest efforts to establish such a *pax Dei* date from the end of the tenth century.[49] Synods at Charroux (989),[50] Norbonne (990)[51] and Anse (994)[52] announced the idea in the sense of a general protection, particularly of church property, involving enhanced sanctions. Since the decay of the royal authority this protection had existed only in special cases. It depended on charter penalties and local immunity protection—if enforced. Even in the earliest council at Charroux the economic motive appears, clearly enough: this notion of protection is extended to farm products, livestock and peasants. At all three councils violators of the ordinances were commanded either to make satisfaction or to be anathematized.[53]

[47] Lamprecht, *Beiträge zur Geschichte des französischen Wirtschaftslebens in 11ten Jahrhundert*, 27.

[48] Indicated by Sackur in 1 *Die Cluniacenser* 308 et seq.; 2 *ibid.*, 266. Cf. also p. 166, 272.

[49] Lot, *Les derniers carolingiens*, 81, asserts that there was an attempt by the bishop of Puy in 975 to introduce the truce of God. This peace seems to be the one made eighteen years later.

[50] 19 Mansi, *Concilia* 90. Three canons were here enacted.

[51] *Ibid.*, 103.

[52] *Ibid.*, 102.

[53] It is to be observed that the real weakness of the synodal prohibition lay in the sanctions. These did not add anything to what the church al-

At Puy-en-Velay in the year 993[54] there assembled with the clerics for the first time various princes and nobles, and a declaration was drawn up somewhat more comprehensive in scope than what had hitherto been attempted. The most important advance in securing the objectives of the church was made in the device of having the persons present swear to observe the peace at a *placitum Dei.* Whereas the synods previously named were merely laying down certain tenets or canons, the council at Puy-en-Velay sought to insure observance by putting upon the individuals present a burden assumed by oath. In a society which depended so heavily upon obligations fortified by plighted faith, it was natural that some trust should have been put upon this sort of pledge.[55] The difficulty lay, of course, in conflicting promises. What the church sought was to make the pledge to keep the peace a paramount obligation. The use of solemn engagements of pacification in the case of individual disputes was still frequent, as it had been in the previous century.[56] The church by making such pledges general and not dependent upon the event of a specific controversy was in fact endeavoring to increase the scope and to make generally applicable the same sense of obligation that people felt when they swore to cease fighting over their individual quarrels.

It is beyond our purpose to go into the details of the remarkable number of local peace efforts which were thus repeated all

ready wielded. Moreover it is hardly to be doubted that the mulcts would go to the ecclesiastical authorities. This was clearly no way to tempt secular cooperation.

[54] Doniol, *Cartulaire de Sauxillanges* (1864) no. 15. The date given follows the suggestion of Sackur, 1 *op. cit.,* 309.

[55] Here, again, although the possible effectiveness of the institution was increased by the cooperation of the laity, the sanctions were not sharp enough: "Si vero aliquis raptor fuerit, aut maledictus, qui hanc institutionem infregerit, et tenere noluerit, sit ipse excommunicatus et anathemetizatus, et a liminibus sancte ecclesie segregatus, usque ad satisfactionem veniat." Presumably the satisfaction is to the proper ecclesiastical official as a means of raising the excommunication.

[56] *Supra,* Chapter IV, note 191.

over France throughout the eleventh century.[57] It was sought to give protection to special places such as ecclesiastical property. It was sought to safeguard special classes of persons, rustics, women, merchants, clerks. It was sought to sanctify special occasions such as going to church, and special times, at first the long week end, and subsequently certain feast times especially in the spring when the sap rises and wars are often begun. The fact that agreement was reached between both ecclesiastical and lay worthies gave to the conclusions of the councils a quality of law.[58] The basic sanction as we have said was the oath. The man who violated the truce not only broke this oath which by its generality had become law as laid down by the council, but he was also personally forsworn.[59] The peace of God resembled the

[57] The next wave of *treugae Dei* comes in the twenties of the eleventh century. Just as the councils at Anse and Puy-en-Velay were precipitated by the raging epidemic of smallpox (Glaber, *Les cinq livres de ses histoires* [Prou Ed. 1886], lib. II, c. 7) so in the twenties of the eleventh century following the terrible famine (*Miracula S. Adalhardi,* in 10 H.F. 378) another series of truces was instituted. These truces are directed not so much against feud as against brigandage, 2 Sackur, *op. cit.,* 166, a fact which seems to point to emergencies of famine. Again in the thirties there is another acute food shortage, (Glaber, lib. IV, cc. 4, 5) and again the truce is sworn in various localities. Within ten years the situation (Glaber, V, c. 1) is repeated. Kluckhohn, *op. cit.,* 27, 28 notes these facts, but he lays the impetus more to a superstitious general fear of the wrath of God. The same motive, i.e. fear of the millennium, has often been suggested as lying at the basis of the first introduction of the truce. While adhesion by the laity was no doubt rendered easier because of their psychological state, and this was played on as shown by the accounts of witnesses and the great display of reliquaries to reinforce the solemnity of the oath (2 Sackur, *op. cit.,* 167), it is hardly to be doubted that the dominant motive of the church was to protect its property.

[58] To wit, convention plus authority with a sanction in the offing. Note how it is conceived at the end of the eleventh century. Ivo of Chartres writes (*Epis.* 90) that it is not sanctioned "communi lege" but is confirmed by authority "ex placito et pacto civitatis ac patriae" of the bishops etc. for the general good of man (162 Migne, *Patrologia,* 111). In other words it is treated as special legislation.

[59] Clearly indicated already in the early truce at Puy-en-Velay as cited *supra,* n. 57. An elaborate form of oath was that of the Bishop of Beauvais printed in Pfister, *op. cit.,* LX, and Huberti, *op. cit.,* 165.

Frankish king's protection,[60] in so far as particular things or persons were singled out. Like the king's ban which had insured royal protection it was a sanction collateral to the usual methods of law enforcement. Like the Frankish oath of fidelity it sought to create a super-obligation. The penalties by which observance was to be enforced were at first exclusively ecclesiastical.[61] The prime intention was to secure emendation, obviously to the church, and the excommunication or anathema was threatened as a final means of coercion. In this the *pax Dei* takes over the theory of penitential discipline. As the ineffectiveness and impermanence of each succeeding truce become manifest, the ecclesiastical sanctions become progressively more elaborate.[62] Sporadic provisions establishing jurisdiction in the laity appear. But even this did little to insure observance or enforcement: not merely cooperation but a strong centralizing hand was needed.

[60] *Supra,* Chapter I, pp. 48 *et seq.*

[61] Excommunication is the chief sanction in the first four attempts to secure a peace of God. So, too, in the Poitevin peace of the year 1000 (19 Mansi, *Concilia,* 266) it is the final remedy, and again in that of *circa* 1030 (*ibid.,* 495). *Cf.* the Council of Tulujas (*ibid.,* 483) of 1027. At Limoges in 1031 (*ibid.,* 529) the interdict is used. The general Aquitanian peace of c. 1039 (*cf.* 2 Sackur, *op. cit.,* 266) adds exile (19 Mansi, *Concilia,* 591). In 1041 is issued a letter by various bishops to the Italian clergy regarding the truce (*ibid.,* 593) which also speaks of exile as a punishment and adverts to punishment by the lay courts (*cf.* Sackur, *loc. cit.,* and Kluckhohn, *op. cit.,* 38). Whether this had become a general practice in France is doubtful. This was the machinery of the Poitiers peace of 1000, but it is not indicated elsewhere; the records of certain councils are so bare that they furnish no basis for an inference. At St. Gilles (1042), 19 Mansi, *Concilia,* 843, excommunication is the sole sanction, but at Narbonne, 1054 (*ibid.,* 827) a much more complicated machinery is provided. Violators of the truce are to be excommunicated, people who kill in violation of the truce are to be exiled; other injuries to be purged by ordeal or exile as the church authorities decide. Finally forty days are given to settle, by double restitution, 40 shillings to the lord where the violation takes place, and an amends to the bishop by swearing no more can be paid or 40 shillings without such oath. We have accepted Huberti's dating of these councils.

[62] In this connection note the steps taken by the Archbishop of Bourges in 1038 to secure an oath from all persons over 15 and to use force against the violators of the peace, Kluckhohn, *op. cit.,* 35–6.

Such in brief were the characteristics of the peace movement in France up to the time of the Synod of Caen (1042–47)[63] when the *pax Dei* was introduced into Normandy.[64] Shortly after the accession of William the Conqueror there had been a rebellion of serious proportions. The state of lawlessness in the duchy must have been serious, for the people at large are reported to have resisted the introduction of the *treuga Dei* prior to this time.[65] In any event at this synod it is provided that the truce is to begin at sundown Wednesday and end at sunrise the following Monday. Within this period no assaults or wounds or killings are permissible nor attacks upon castles or houses. Violators are threatened that if they do not do thirty years' penance in exile and make amends for what had been done against the peace they shall be excommunicated. Persons giving aid and comfort are to make amends or be similarly punished. The truce, moreover, is extended over lands, beasts and possessions generally, and persons who steal things protected by this peace are to be excommunicated until they have made amends. If they wish to amend, they must first return the stolen property or its value, and

[63] Text in Bessin, *Concilia*, 39; 19 Mansi, *Concilia* 597. The date is discussed by Tardif, *Etudes sur les sources*, 29, as between 1043–46, and in n. 5 he states it was held before 1047. Prentout in 8 *N.R.H.* (4 ser. 1929), 783 is reported as fixing the date at 1047. Haskins, *op. cit.*, 37, n. 147 states that "The latest edition of the Norman Ordinance, that of the *M.G.H.*, 1 *Constitutiones et Acta Publica*, 600, does not pay sufficient attention to Norman Mss. . . . ." This is an error. The text in the *Monumenta* is the *treuga* of the bishopric of Thérouanne (c. 1063) in Flanders first published by Wasserschleben in 12 *Z.R.G.*[2] 112 (1891). Haskins asserts in his text that the Norman peace was introduced in the Flemish form. Warnkönig in 1 *Flandrische Staats und Rechtsgeschichte*, 117, states that at Audenarde in 1030 a *treuga Dei* was instituted. In Weiland's note to the Thérouanne truce is some comment on the relation of the Norman and Flemish truces. *Cf.* also Pirenne, 1 *Histoire de Belgique* (5 ed. 1929), 123.

[64] Böhmer, *op. cit.*, 15 n. 7 points out that the text in Bessin is an address by a bishop to his diocese, but he shows that from other sources it can be established that the peace was for the whole duchy.

[65] Hugo of Flavigny, *Chronicon* (*M.G.H.*, 8 *Scriptores*, 403) lib. II c. 30.

thereafter do penance for seven years. The duke alone is permitted to make war. Merchants and alien travelers are to have the special peace. In the final paragraph of the document it is stated the truce is also to extend from Advent until eight days after Epiphany, from the beginning of Lent to the octave of Easter, and from the beginning of Rogation until eight days after Pentecost. If anyone should allege he had violated the peace unknowingly he must take an oath and go to the ordeal of the hot iron.

Before proceeding to a discussion of the sanctions it will be well to examine the later synodal legislation on the subject of the truce. In 1061 a synod at Caen[66] piously recommended the prosecution and punishment of thieves and other criminals. Three years later at Lisieux[67] the synod declared that the truce should be frequently recalled and firmly kept. It forbade the carriage of arms by clerics and assaults by or on them. In 1071 according to Orderic Vitalis, the duke exhorted an assembly of grandees and prelates from Maine and Normandy to observe the peace and enforce the canons, but there is no further memorial of this meeting.[68] Until the synod at Lillebon (1080) the reports of the councils at which renewal or additions to the first Norman truce of God were made are so fragmentary that it is difficult to determine the specific content of the successive sets of resolutions or the effectiveness of the truce in general, and the collateral evidence is sparse.[69] The original truce at Caen is the only one about which enough is known to serve as a basis of discussion.

[66] Bessin, *Concilia*, 48. *Cf.* Tardif, *Etudes*, 31–2 who treats this as a part of the truce movement. The reports of the council are so brief that it is impossible to do more than conjecture at the import of its resolutions.

[67] Published by Delisle in 1901 *Journal des Savants*, 516. Cap. V deals with the carriage of arms and assaults by clergy. Cap. X states "Ut etiam trevia Dei frequenter recenseatur et firmiter teneatur." This looks very much as if the truce were none too effectively enforced.

[68] Orderic, lib. IV, cap. viii, 237 "Tunc [1071] Normannorum et Cenomannensium majores congregavit et omnes ad pacem et justitiam tenendam regali hortatu corroboravit . . ."

[69] Round, *Calendar*, no. 713 (c. 1066) which involves the slaying of a

The mechanics of truce enforcement established at Caen were clearly not intended either as an interference with or as an addition to individual secular jurisdictions. These were no more disturbed than they were when ecclesiastical discipline was inflicted on a man over whom a lay courtholder exercised his own jurisdiction. Only with respect to the disposition of a deceased infractor's property is the truce at all ambiguous, suggesting lay participation in the eventual profits of enforcement. In all other respects the administration is in the complete control of the church.

At Lillebon,[70] after a general affirmance of the truce, an important innovation was added. If a person violating the truce refuses to submit to the bishop, the latter may address himself to the offender's lord, who is to surrender the offender to the bishop's justice. If the lord refuses (*contempserit*) to do this, the bishop may have recourse to the viscount of the duke who must then act without fail. The substantive effect of all this truce legislation is etched in the bleak and colorless paragraphs of the Inquest of 1091. Tersely and with no reference to the *treuga Dei* the inquest notes that men are forbidden to build castles, to burn or plunder, to venture forth to make feud, to take captives or castles. It announces that women, merchants and pilgrims are protected. So close is the coincidence of these prohibitions with the acts proscribed by the original Caen truce, let alone the identity of the protected persons, that it is fruitless to deny or ignore the almost certain connection of the inquest's findings with the truce legislation.[71] Since there is no convincing proof of ducal

monk and may therefore be a peace case. *Cf.* the document in 143 Migne, *Patrologia*, 1387; also in 3 *B.E.C.* 4 ser., 255, published by Delisle without reference to the antecedent publication by Martène.

[70] Bessin, *Concilia,* 67 (c. 1).

[71] Of these paragraphs which open generally, "Nulli licuit . . .," only c. 7 which forbids ambushes in the duke's forests has the stamp of special ducal legislation. Yver, *L'Interdiction de la guerre privée*, 320, says ". . . ces dispositions sont parallèles à celles de la 'Paix de Dieu.' . . . En face de la 'Paix de Dieu,' elles constituent, exactement dans le même sens, 'la Paix du Duc.' " Yver simply follows Haskins' interpretation. Since he

legislation on these points independent of the councils where rules about the peace of God were laid down one can only conclude that by 1091 what appear as secular rules have their source in the conciliar dispositions.

The events in Normandy in Robert's reign soon demonstrated that these rules were not proof against the still untamed baronage.[72] In the year following the great council of Clermont held in 1095[73] when conditions in Normandy were most unhappy, a synod at Rouen made still further additions to the Norman peace.[74] Certain new periods of peace were added, and a continuous peace was declared for all churches, sacred ground, monks, clerks, holy men, and clerical chattels, women, pilgrims, merchants, and their servants, cattle and horses, men at work. The plow was made a sanctuary, for all men who fled to it were in peace. The third article[75] of these ordinances provided that every male of twelve years and older should swear to maintain

does not concern himself with the details of procedure he does not realize that there is a connection between the two types of peace as a matter of law.

Haskins, *op. cit.,* 278, n. 9, quotes Duchesne, *Historiae Normannorum Scriptores,* "Instituit legem sanctam, scilicet ne aliquis homo aliquem hominem assalliret pro morte alicuius sui parentis, nisi patrem aut filium interfecisset." The *legem sanctam* may have reference to the truce. This is the only instance except for the generalities of Orderic that indicates a particular rule of possible secular origin.

[72] *Cf.* Haskins, *op. cit.,* 62, and note the document set forth (63) where cases of injuries *in pace* are recorded. Haskins does not date the document but it is set forth in a chapter on Robert Curthose and so presumably belongs to this period.

[73] 20 Mansi, *Concilia,* 901. There is a discussion of this council in Huberti, *op. cit.,* 398 *et seq.* It was attended by three Norman prelates. Orderic, lib. IX, c. iii.

[74] Bessin, *Concilia,* 77.

[75] Bessin, *Concilia,* 78, "Hoc audiatis vos N. quod ego amodo inantea hanc constitutionem Treviae Dei, sicut hic determinata est, fideliter custodiam, & contra omnes, qui hanc jurare contempserint, vel hanc constitutionem servare noluerint, Episcopo vel Archidiacono in eo auxilium feram: ita ut, si me monuerint ad eundum super eos, nec diffugiam, nec dissimulabo: sed cum armis meis cum ipso proficiscar, & omnibus quibus potero juvabo adversus illos per fidem, sine malo ingenio, secundum meam conscientiam. Sic Deus me adjuvet, & isti sancti."

the peace and to come with arms to aid the bishop or archdeacon in preserving it.[76] The anathema was threatened against all those who would not take the oath or who violated the truce, against all abettors, purchasers of stolen goods, persons who consorted for brigandage and the lords who harbored such persons in their castles. In the lands of such lords the interdict was to rest.

The features of the Norman legislation concerning the peace of God in the eleventh century resemble definitely the measures taken in other parts of France, a fact which is not remarkable in view of the close relation among the clergy throughout the land. The peace legislation was everywhere directed against two classes of lawbreakers—the great men, because they had shown themselves contemptuous of the ordinary processes of law, and the brigands who were unattached and were hence not easily brought to justice under a system where jurisdiction was at complete loose ends. The elaborate business of oath taking of course did not affect the brigand, but it was at least designed to impress on the magnate a more intense consciousness of law observance and perhaps to sharpen enforcement in his own jurisdiction. However, aside from the romantic value of a constant reiteration of the *pax Dei,* the movement everywhere was cursed with administrative futility as long as it was regarded primarily as a part of ecclesiastical discipline. As late as the year 1100 the Holy See was still assuring the French baronage that the truce was not intended to interfere with existing rights and jurisdictions.[77] Rome was not yet ready to trust the procedural aid of the great feudatories. Instead it clung to ecclesiastical sanctions. Politically this may have been wise but it was scarcely calculated to attain the church's announced objective. The books already bulged with canons providing excommunication for nearly all

[76] Böhmer, *op. cit.,* 143, refers to this measure as the introduction of a parish militia.

[77] *Cf.* the letter of the papal legate in 20 Mansi, *Concilia,* 887, ". . . principibus autem & dominis terrarum jura sua & consuetudines non contradicimus in terris suis."

the matters specified in the various truces. The breach of the truce oath only added further and sometimes thornier penances. The excommunication had become far too common for its use in connection with the peace of God to have assumed particular significance. That great churchman Abbo of Fleury complained[78] at the end of the tenth century that there was hardly a man in the realm who at one time had not been excommunicated. Not only did excommunication serve as a means of distraint, but as a punishment it was the eventual threat against every malefactor. The conveyances tacked it on as a threat against both casual disseisors and recalcitrant heirs.[79] Not a synod met but brandished it in the face of the graceless. So usual was this process that when a particularly wicked fellow was to be forced to right a papal anathema was procured.[80] Clearly much of the ineffectiveness of the excommunication lay in the fact that it was utilized, without distinction, as process and as punishment for all sorts of cases.[81] You cannot expect a man excommunicated for

---

[78] *Apologeticus ad Hugonem* . . . 139 Migne, *Patrologia,* 470. Note also, in connection with the general abuse of excommunication the remarks of Peter Damian, 144 Migne, *Patrologia,* 215.

[79] *Supra,* Chapter IV on the use of excommunication.

[80] For example, the anathema against the violators of Cluny property, 19 Mansi, *Concilia,* 324. Compare the wholesale anathemas *ibid.,* 95, 530, 541.

[81] It should be noted that this dual use of excommunication appears both in the truce at Caen and in the canon of Lillebon. As mesne process the excommunication is the culmination of the spiritual proceeding *in contumacia.* The administration of the excommunication in the pre-Gratian period must have varied in France from diocese to diocese. Indeed, there is little known about it in terms of procedure in the eleventh and early twelfth centuries. There are two attitudes on the source of the procedure: 1) that it was patterned on the Frankish *missio in bannum, cf.* Mitteis, *Studien zur Geschichte des Versäumnisurteils,* 42 Z.R.G.², 212, who sees this influence persisting into the decretals of Gregory IX; 2) that Roman law is dominant,—Fournier, *Les officialités au moyen age* (1880) 252 *et seq. Cf.* further on the twelfth-century procedure, Jacobi, *Der Prozess im Decretum Gratiani,* 34 Z.R.G.² (Kan.) 282. On the use of excommunication for the ban in Italy, 1 Ficker, *Forschungen,* 242. The effect of the Romanic practice in the eleventh century (5 Bethmann-Hollweg, *Civilprozess,* 395, 427) on the later church rules must also be taken into account.

failure to pay his debts to quiver more fearfully when the ban is hurled at him for burning a church. It is because the excommunication alone is not a deterrent in the case of the hardy and impious malefactors, whom the truce is designed to reach, that at certain provincial councils in the middle of the eleventh century a pecuniary mulct is attached,[82] that in this period the interdict emerges as a super-ban,[83] and that in some places the details of the curse take form in literal penalties.

It has already been suggested that some form of procedural cooperation with the temporal jurisdictions was the only way to remedy the inadequacies of the truce machinery. The practical reasons for this are obvious. Although excommunication sets the individual without the society of Christians, interdicts all intercourse and business with him, pronounces him infamous and *infidelis,* the contemporary theories of church discipline do not appear to have contemplated a direct physical interference with his person or property. Emendation, property confiscation and exile are all threatened as independent punishments, to which excommunication is joined as a concurrent penalty or threatened as process to assure execution. Wherever procedural methods resembling the secular ban are used in an episcopal jurisdiction, these must be taken to be local variations due to the combination of temporal and ecclesiastical sovereignty. In the eleventh century the excommunication is a purely spiritual instrument of distraint.

But in Normandy, the ducal prerogative in matters ecclesiastical was so great and so well established by the middle of the eleventh century that there were fewer political difficulties in

[82] For example at Narbonne in 1054 (19 Mansi, *Concilia,* 827). *Cf.* also 5 Hinschius, *K.R.,* 37 *et seq.* and 10 n. 6 where there are collected many references to the relation of excommunication and satisfaction. This is a good illustration of how the process and punishment phases of excommunication were mingled. Professor Karl Llewellyn regards these aspects of sanction as illuminating in relation to certain basic tendencies of primitive law and has promised to develop this theme at some time.

[83] 5 Hinschius, *K.R.,* 14 on the personal interdict; 19 *et seq.* on the local interdict.

the way of a process of secular cooperation than elsewhere in France. Until 1055 no papal legate set foot on Norman territory.[84] The duke had been made immune from episcopal anathema, early in the eleventh century, by the pope,[85] so that he enjoyed a position of substantial independence in respect of his prelacy. Indeed, the control that he maintained over the use of the power of excommunication in his realm suggests that it had in Normandy a quasi-secular force.[86] In these circumstances it is clear that temporal support could be furnished for the enforcement of the truce of God more easily than in provinces where the church maintained a greater degree of independence. Under the Franks such a system of mutual use of lay and ecclesiastical sanctions had existed.[87] The man who fell under the *bannus episcopalis* was subject also to discipline by the king, i.e., he could be "exiled" either in the sense of incarceration or actual banishment. The church apparently favored this method of procedure, and it was reluctant to see it abandoned when the anarchy of the dying ninth century overwhelmed the West. With the ardor and the facility of the times, a forged canon, fabricated some time after the Synod of Tribur (895) was devised to perpetuate the institution.[88] This canon provided that if a person disobeyed the bishop

[84] Böhmer, *op. cit.,* 28.

[85] 1 Pflugk-Harttung, *Acta Pontificum Romanorum* (1881) no. 13 (1016).

[86] The "Iudicium pro St. Leonardo" (c. 1077) in *App. ad Scacc. Norm.,* 15 *Mem. Ant. Norm.,* 196. Here it is claimed the establishment was free of episcopal customs and that neither bishop nor archbishop could excommunicate. The cause is laid before the duke who orders John, Archbishop of Rouen, Roger de Beaumont and other barons to make a judgment. They state among other things "Episcopum injuriam fecisse non solum Comiti Rogerio, verum etiam Regi de quo ipso Ecclesiam tenebat." *Cf.* the letter of Lanfranc to Roger of Hereford, in 1 *Opera,* 65, where the implication is clear that the crown has discretion over excommunication.

[87] *Supra,* Chapter III notes 144 and 145; and 2 Brunner, *D.R.G.,* 428–9.

[88] It should be observed that the position of the Pseudo-Isidorean forgers that the church law was superior to secular law would necessarily lead to the statement of so important a procedure in canonical form. The analysis of the forged canon is in Phillips, *Der Grosse Synod von Tribur* 49 *W.S.B.,* 713, 755; the critical text is in *M.G.H.,* 2 *Cap.,* 360, where note

or was contumacious, he was first to be punished canonically, and if this did not bring him to terms, he was to lose his benefices and have his allodial property put in ban, which would become absolute after the usual year and a day. He himself was to be exiled and remain in constraint until he satisfied the church.

We have suggested that the purpose of this forgery was to perpetuate the Carolingian practice of moving against malefactors with both ban and excommunication at a time when the administrative liaison of church and state had been disrupted. It made law for the church and it was obviously intended to bind temporal authority since it was supposed to have been concurred in by both Gallic and German nobles.[89] The subsequent history of this canon is of importance in estimating the probability of its actual use. It does not appear in the collection of Regino, but it is incorporated in that of Burchard of Worms[90] in the early eleventh century. Burchard's collection was widely used both in Germany and France and for this reason acquaintance with the rule was not limited territorially.[91] Moreover, Ivo of Chartres likewise included this canon in his *Decretum*,[92] and consequently it is current canonical doctrine in the eleventh century.

particularly the remarks of Boretius with reference to the so-called Synod of Diedenhofen (Theodonisvilla) which is supposed to have enacted this rule.

[89] "A primatibus totius Germaniae et Galliae." This recital is important since the canon is also setting forth a secular procedure. On the relation of synodal legislation to the state when Burchard's compilation was made, Barion, *Das Fränkisch-deutsche Synodalrecht des Frühmittelalters* (1931), 307 *et seq.* On *primates, cf.* 4 Waitz, *D.V.G.*, 277.

[90] *Decretum*, lib. VI c. vi in 140 Migne, *Patrologia* 767. The reasons Regino did not include it among his canons was because he was probably present at Tribur (Phillips, *op. cit.*, 714) and knew what had been enacted. The same provisions are in the Munich Ms. printed by Schmitz, *Bussbücher*, 739.

[91] On this *cf.* Fournier, *De quelques collections canoniques* in *Mélanges Paul Fabre* (1902) 189, 214. Fournier et Le Bras, *Histoire des collections canoniques* (1931) 44 *et seq. Cf.* also Brooke, *The English Church and the Papacy*, 34; on Lanfranc's use of Burchard, *ibid.*, 58, 68.

[92] *Decretum*, Pars X, c. 135, 161 Migne, *Patrologia*, 732.

The idea of secular assistance although it had received this canonical sanction was for some time neither universally nor systematically used to effectuate the truce of God, since the forgery, although well authenticated, was drawn not on a current but on a closed account, for the Frankish system was dead. Nevertheless wherever the ban persisted as local process there was always the chance that the canonical theory would be put into practice.[93] This is what happened in Normandy. But until the addition at Lillebon in 1080 ecclesiastical enforcement alone, as stipulated in the first truce, was the rule. The Caen sanctions against the person include exile and satisfaction for the broken peace under threat of excommunication. But exile, until the malefactor leaves the country, is a penalty no more fearsome than excommunication for its incidents seem to be identical. No one can harbor the exile or communicate with him, and if he dies before he enters upon his penance of exile he is denied burial.[94] The sanctions against the property of infractors are limited to one case, ambiguously stated: no one can interfere with the goods of a deceased impenitent infractor.[95]

[93] Generalizations regarding the canons in use in particular dioceses during the eleventh century are dangerous. In any event there is some evidence that the idea of secular cooperation in the enforcement of excommunication is kept alive: cf. Conc. Rheims, 991 (19 Mansi, Concilia, 119); Conc. Poitou, 1000 (ibid., 267); Conc. Narbonne, 1054 (ibid., 832). The heretic problem is on a different basis. The evidence on this is in 5 Hinschius, K.R., 377.

[94] The concurrence of these provisions with the rule respecting the harboring of persons civilly banned is striking. It would be possible that even in 1042 the violator of the truce was forebanned, in other words, this is what the word exilium was intended to express, except for the fact that exile is limited in time. Orderic uses the word exilium in connections which clearly are instances of foreban. Stapleton in 1 Rot. Scacc. Norm., ciii, speaks of a case of exile and forfeiture as a punishment, but the circumstances seem to point to foreban. Note further on the use of the word exilium to describe an obvious case of bannus, Gregory VII's letter to Robert of Flanders (1082) in 20 Mansi, Concilia, 371.

[95] Nothing is said about the fate of the property. Tardif, Etudes sur les sources, 30-1 supposes there is a confiscation, but without saying by whom. Actually the destination of the forfeiture has an important bearing on the development of jurisdiction. There were at least three potential claimants,

The secular arm may well have been ready to use its process to support the truce which it was always urging men to observe, but it is not until the Council of Lillebon that secular participation in the enforcement of the *treuga Dei* is defined. Probably the greatest difficulty standing in the way of effective enforcement of these provisions is the fact that the bishop's temporalities are not physically coextensive with the diocese, and his process as baron is therefore limited territorially. Outside his lands he needs cooperation from the duke or the men who have jurisdiction. Such cooperation will follow traditional procedure and finds expression in the Lillebon provision that when offenders refuse to pay him the bishop turns in the first instance to the local lord and then to the viscount for distraint, a precept identical with the Frankish practice of using the ban when the excommunication is ineffective.[96]

After the forged canon of Tribur, canonical authorization for the use of this sort of ancillary proceeding existed, and as the forgery was cast with the Frankish ban definitely in mind, a reunion of ecclesiastical and secular process was not only feasible but to be anticipated wherever the ban was still an active ingredient of feudal justice. Indeed, it is difficult to imagine any other secular device that could have been intended in 1080. As we have seen the whole theory of eleventh-century distraint and in particular the Norman *forisbannitio* is derived from the Frankish ban. The primary object of the Lillebon Council's change in

the ducal fisc, the man's lord, and the church. In view of the duke's control over matters ecclesiastical it is hard to believe that the church, especially since the malefactors would die unshriven, would be allowed to take the goods (*cf.* Caillemer, *Les confiscations,* 44, 51). While it is not until the reign of Henry II (*supra,* note 24) that the doctrine is stated that all alms were in the hands of the duke, the evidence even in the eleventh century of the duke's control over all gifts in alms is so convincing, that one cannot believe that the church would have been allowed by the duke to take possession of a redemption of this sort.

[96] Eichmann, *Acht und Bann,* 17 *et seq.* was the first to suggest that there was a continuity between the Frankish procedure and that of the twelfth and thirteenth centuries for enforcing excommunication by secular process. He does not, however, go into the *treuga Dei* problem.

procedure is to force infractors of the truce to stand to right; and this can be accomplished only by personal arrest or the indirect sanction of sequestration. Both of these measures are comprehended in the *forisbannitio*. It alone can put into the distraining authority's hands the means of final execution against a contumacious malefactor.

It is testimony to the continued diffusion of justice in Normandy that a council which the duke-king convenes directs the bishops to turn in the first instance to the lord of an offender. But this direction was like the other measures where Norman kings did homage to a political *status quo* and simultaneously contrived its disintegration. No baron's process would run beyond his own demesne. This was certainly one major difficulty anticipated by the rule regarding recourse to the viscount. As we know from one source, he would impose the duke's ban.[97] If his process was not already superior to jurisdictional barriers it was made so by this council.[98] Like the Carolingian rule that permitted a count to take certain criminals even from an immunity the Lillebon canon sanctions an ubiquitous vicontiel process. It harbors the first hint of the later droitural writs—"do right or my sheriff will. . . ."[99] The first stone in the structure of a superior criminal process is thus laid.

[97] 11 *Gallia Christiana* 34; Bessin, *Concilia,* 63. The episode was the violence of the monks of St. Ouen against the Archbishop of Rouen briefly related in 4 Freeman, *Norman Conquest,* 97.

[98] Powicke, *op. cit.,* 95 sees the significance of secular cooperation but he says nothing about the process and does not see the implications. With the Norman situation should be compared the truce in Anjou confirmed at Clermont (1095) and set forth in 20 Mansi, *Concilia,* 912. The fines here all go to the archbishop but the cooperation of secular authority is clearly indicated. The state of order in Anjou is indicated by the fact that the use of armed force against violators is stipulated, as well by the provision that twice a year all barons and comital officials are to assemble at "Castronovo," (Tours?) and remain three days to await complaints for violation.

[99] Neither the idea nor the formula is confined to any one chancery; *cf.* the three precepts of Leo IX (1050) in 1 Pflugk-Harttung, *op. cit.,* 15–16 "Mandamus et precipimus tibi ut rectum facias deo etc. . . . Quod nisi feceris . . . excommunicaberis."

Direct Norman sources for the operation of the secular procedure in aid of the church in the eleventh century are wanting. But there is evidence of enough specific early identities in the law of England and Normandy, so that English material on matters where there is no independent evidence of identity can, with caution, be used as a basis for inference. We know from Eadmer's *Historia* that William put the relations of secular authority with the English church on the same footing as the Norman,[100] and in William's famous ordinance separating the church from temporal courts (1070–76), the canon law of the continent was made binding.[101] It was there further established that in cases of contumacy three summonses were to be made after which excommunication was to be pronounced.[102] The rule goes on *"et si opus ad hoc vindicandum, fortitudo et iustitia regis vel vicecomitis adhibeatur."* The use of royal process is thus available just as it is shortly thereafter in the canon of Lillebon. This principle of secular support is restated also in the *Leges Henrici*.[103] That it takes the form of outlawry seems probable from a canon of the Westminster Council of 1127.[104] The *Leges Edwardi* set out the detailed procedure.[105] It is there provided generally that if any one offend against the bishop, the bishop is to have jurisdiction over him, but if the offender refuses to amend, the king is to be advised, and the king shall constrain the wrongdoer that he amend to the person he has wronged, to the

---

[100] Eadmer, *Historia Novorum* (R.S. Rule Ed.) 9: "Usus ergo atque leges quas patres sui et ipse in Normannia habere solebant in Anglia servare volens de huiusmodi personis episcopos abbates et alios principes per totam terram instituit . . ."

[101] *Episcopales Leges*, c. 2 ". . . non secundum hundret sed secundum canones et episcopales leges etc." Liebermann, *Gesetze*, 485.

[102] *Episcopales Leges*, c. 3, *ibid.*, 485.

[103] cc. 11, 15; 11, 16; 21; *ibid.*, 557, 560.

[104] 1 Wilkins, *Concilia Magnae Britanniae* (1737), 410 c. 1: "laicus vero exlex et excommunicatus habeatur." The collateral evidence shows *exlex* here is more than infamy. On the identity of English outlawry and Norman *forisbannitio, infra,* Chapter VI, p. 421.

[105] cc. 2, 6; 6; 6, 1; Liebermann, *Gesetze*, 629, 631.

bishop and to the crown. In another section the bishop is granted jurisdiction specifically over violators of the church's peace, with the provision that in cases of evasion of sentence or contempt, complaint is to be made to the crown after forty days, whereupon the king's justice is to put the man under gage and pledge until satisfaction. If within thirty-one days the offender has not turned up he is to be outlawed. The concurrence of this procedure with Bracton's details of the later writ *de excommunicato capiendo* in cases of ecclesiastical contumacy is so striking that one cannot escape the conclusion that the writ originated in this time.[106] The matter is so circumstantially described in the *Leges Edwardi* that its authenticity is not open to serious doubt.[107]

[106] Bracton, *De Legibus*, fol. 408, 426b. *Cf.* also the writ in *Registrum Brevium* (1687 ed.) 65. For comparative purposes note the accord in 1 Beautemps-Beaupré, *Coutumes et institutions de l'Anjou et du Maine*, 148 (text B, §134 of the thirteenth century).

[107] While there can be no doubt of the close nexus between church and temporal process in Carolingian times, the revival of the practice of the double ban seems to be connected definitely with the *treuga Dei* movement, *cf.* 5 Hinschius, *K.R.*, 310, 391. At the same time we must also take into consideration the fact that the readjustment of the relations between state and church (through the politics of the papacy in the course of the eleventh century) played a certain role in drawing clear the issue between the limits of secular and ecclesiastical jurisdiction and consequently the complementary use of process. The extent to which a prelate addressing himself to a secular ruler could secure cooperation was a question of politics until the scope of the two jurisdictions over substantive matter was defined. The importance of securing actual protection from lay power was emphasized by Leo IX (1049–54), Wühr, *Studien zu Gregor VII* (1930), 30–31. It is possible that the emphasis upon lay cooperation to enforce the truce of God which marks some of the French conciliar legislation at this time is the practical fruit of this policy. Nicholas II (1059–1061) continues his predecessor's work and is specific on such matters as action against robbers of church property, *ibid.*, 32, n. 125. The idea of the state as an arm of the church is subsequently stated in even more emphatic language by Gregory VII, *ibid.*, 38. At the same time note also the cases collected by Flich in 2 *La réforme grégorienne* (1925), 262, n. 1 where Gregory VII wields his ban as if secular cooperation were not of consequence.

Beyond the general political background lay the practical problem how the secular arm was to be used. Although the canonical collections already mentioned furnish some basis for assumptions regarding cooperation, the

Whether or not the identical procedure was used in Normandy even in the later eleventh century is a matter of conjecture. The *Très ancien coutumier* provides[108] that counts, barons and knights of the duke's household are not to be excommunicated without the consent of the duke or his chief justice who are to compel emendation. Other persons excommunicated who fail within a year and a day to be absolved, are subject to chattel forfeiture by the duke. It is significant that the exception of the baronage of the household goes back to William the Conqueror's time,[109] and since the second provision corresponds both as to the period of sequestration and forfeiture with the Frankish ban in aid of the *bannus episcopalis,* this too may be of equal age. While it is possible, owing to the late compilation of the *Très ancien coutumier* that the law may have been influenced by the Romanism of the canonical *"ordines"*[110] of the later twelfth century, the subsequent history of this procedure

introduction of specific rules was a highly technical matter that would have to account for local procedural variations. In Gregory's time there still existed confusion regarding the *ordo* of applying the church's process as *cf.* the letters in *M.G.H.,* 2 *Libelli de Lite,* 27 *et seq.* where a procedure is sought to be extracted out of the patrists. On this *cf.* Mirbt, *Die Publizistik im Zeitalter Gregors VII* (1894), 205 *et seq.* With the church's own process so uncertain the sharpness of the early twelfth century English procedure in aid of excommunication is remarkable, and leads us to suppose that elsewhere the matter was one of local practice.

[108] *T.A.C.,* cap. II, and note the final paragraph 3 "Misericordia excommunicati, et emendatio, est versus episcopum: catalla que habet, usque ad novem libras, preter victum suum et domus sue. Hereditas excommunicati non vendetur nec invadiabitur pro satisfactione excommunicationis. Militi vero absoluto arma et equi sui, cum predictis victualibus, remanebunt."

[109] Eadmer, *Historia,* 10.

[110] The oldest *ordo* was published by Kunstman, *Über den Ältesten Ordo Iudiciarius,* 2 *Kritische Überschau,* 17. After excommunication, "debebit etiam judex bona sic damnati annotare, et conficere inventorium sive repertorium. Hoc facto reus si infra annum venerit et cautionem dederit iudicio sisti bonorum suorum restitutionem habebit. Sed si per annum silverit ad purgationem etiam perpetuo sed ad bona non restituetur in poenam contumaciae." Eichmann, *op. cit.,* 115 relying on the *Summa* of Bernard of Pavia asserts that this is a reflection of Roman law although Kunstman *op. cit.,* 15, seems to doubt this. The *ordo* indicates that seques-

in France seems to support the theory of a revival of Frankish practice.[111]

tration is effected by the ecclesiastical judge, otherwise it resembles the Norman procedure. This document belongs to the second half of the twelfth century. In this connection note also the *Ordo judiciarius* of the *Codex Bambergensis* described by Schulte in 70 *W.S.B.* 285, which Schulte places 1181–5 and suggests was written by an Englishman (*ibid.,* 288): "et cum in tantum excreverit contumacia, quod per ecclesiam non possit, teneri ad disciplinam per extraneas potestates coercetur . . ." (294).

[111] Eichmann, *op. cit.,* 113, is convinced of the continuity of the Frankish procedure in aid of excommunication in France. To be considered in this connection is the fact that except for Normandy most of the evidence of the use of secular process to supplement excommunication dates from the thirteenth century although the rules may be much older than the compilations. 5 Hinschius, *K.R.,* 391 suggests that the power of the papacy was such at the opening of the thirteenth century that it was in a position to insist that secular ban be used. It is certainly true that most of the French rules postdate the efforts of Innocent III in this direction. *Cf.* the examples cited by Hinschius, 5 *op. cit.,* 396 n. 6; 397 n. 1, 2, 3. Further, on the later French procedure Mitteis, *Beaumanoir und die geistliche Gerichtsbarkeit* 35 *Z.R.G.*[2] (Kan.) 342 *et seq. Cf.* also the *Constitutio Cupientes* of St. Louis (1228) 23 Mansi, *Concilia,* 185, and the procedure detailed in the so-called *Curialis* of Rheims (thirteenth century) 1 Wahrmund, *Quellen zur Geschichte des röm. Kan. Prozess* (1905), pt. 3, c. 11.

It seems probable that the adjustment of the investiture controversy in the beginning of the twelfth century and the consequent marking off of the regalia had something to do with the development of this procedure. In the Empire there are some examples of the use of supplementary secular ban in the tenth and eleventh centuries. *Cf.* the so-called *Mainwenden Sendrecht* published by Dove in 4 *Z.K.R.,* 160–162 and the examples in 5 Hinschius, *K.R.,* 377–8. The matter is put on a firm footing by Frederick Barbarossa. In 1158 (*M.G.H.,* 1 *Const.* 245) he threatens excommunication, confiscation and ravage against those who break the peace. In the *Constitutio Contra Incendiarios* (1186) the Frankish procedure is set forth (*ibid.,* 449 c. 7). The matter is obviously a development that is first perceptible in the eleventh century, and gathers strength partly from the fact that mutual benefit is derived by church and state and partly through the literary development of the canon law.

Note finally in connection with Eichmann's theory of persisting Frankish influence upon the *ordines,* the Lombard procedure for dealing with contumacy based on a combination of Frankish and Roman law sources, 5 Bethmann-Hollweg, *Civilprozess,* 386; the procedure used in Rome and Ravenna, *ibid.,* 427 *et seq.* This may have influenced canonical procedural theories in Italy in the twelfth century. There is to our knowledge no evidence that the Lombard procedure influenced the Anglo-Norman law via Lanfranc who had studied jurisprudence in Italy (Böhmer, *Die Fäl-*

With the reestablishment of a procedure for the use of the temporal ban to enforce excommunication and its application to cases of breach of the truce of God, it becomes clear why secular participation in enforcement does not remain ancillary but tends to become exclusive. It is less the ineffectiveness of the anathema than the reality of vicecomital distraint that leads in this direction. For it is impossible to believe that a distraint which involved secular interference with property would eventuate in forfeitures accruing entirely to the church. In truces like that of Narbonne, of Anjou and elsewhere the episcopal fine is fixed. Some booty has to be held out to the secular arm which does the work of collection. This is how jurisdiction was used in the eleventh century and this is its major reason for existence. Moreover, the provisions of the Council of Rouen, where a general oath was instituted embracing a pledge to enforce the peace by arms, cannot be understood as intended to diminish ducal powers over the truce directly acquired.[112] Not even as ineffective a personage as Robert Curthose was likely to allow the clergy to command an armed posse for the pursuit of criminals. Furthermore, the oath stipulated is general in scope, with no saving of other obligations, so that one is tempted to interpret this measure as an admission of ducal prerogative in keeping the peace. Such a view is indeed implicit in the complaint of Orderic Vitalis that the conclusions of the Rouen Council were fruitless on account

schungen Erzbischof Lanfrancs von Canterbury [1902] 133 et seq.; Tamassio, Lanfranco Arcivescovo di Canterbury in 2 Mélanges Fitting 190).

[112] In Ivo of Chartres' letter no. 90 (162 Migne, Patrologia, 111) the fluid nature of the usual oath is evident. A man can except from his undertaking some enemy, if he so wishes. The truce is regarded as essentially contractual. It is consequently impossible to construe the provisions of the Council of Rouen as an intended interference with existing obligations. Of capital importance in this connection is the letter of the papal legate cited supra, note 74. While this sort of assurance may have been a means of securing adhesion to a particular truce, it was nevertheless inevitable that the process of secular ban to enforce the contumacious excommunicate to stand to right would interfere with individual jurisdictions wherever the requisition was made to the overlord. This was the situation in Normandy after the Council of Lillebon.

of the failure of the "duke's justice."[113] It is hard otherwise to account for this statement, unless it represents the status quo of a few decades later when there is less doubt that the primary responsibility for truce enforcement lay with the secular branch.

It is not until Henry I had gained complete control of the duchy in 1106 and set about with vigor to restore order that one can look for an effective resumption of the earlier efforts to preserve God's peace. In that year a council was held in Lisieux.[114] Certain acts were passed for the repression of robbery and violence and the maintenance of peace enjoined. So poor and incomplete, however, is the record of legislation in this reign, that it is not possible to reconstruct the exact relation of the truce enforcement to the developing ducal justice. This is the more regrettable since there is no doubt from writs, charters and occasional judicial records that the duke's court was now developing as a tribunal with sovereign and not merely feudal powers.[115] Orderic's account of Henry's conversation with Calixtus II[116] is no doubt apocryphal; yet it undoubtedly represents a sympathetic contemporary's summary of the duke's achievements in crushing disorders and in curbing the savage contempt for law that had marked the maladministration of Robert Curthose. There unquestionably was a consistent use of ducal process in aid of the bishop's truce jurisdiction, and simultaneously incessant solicitude for the maintenance of the peace, for the last year of Henry's reign is marked by an ordinance which establishes how definitely the *pax Dei* was by that time connected with the duke's judicial prerogative.

In this ordinance of the year 1135[117] it is provided that where

[118] Orderic, lib. IX, c. iii, 473, "Sed, principali justitia deficiente, ad emolumentum ecclesiasticae tranquillitatis parum proficerunt," may be taken as demonstrating dependence by this time of the truce upon the ducal enforcement machinery.

[114] Bessin, *Concilia*, 79; *cf.* Tardif, *Etudes*, 45 *et seq.*

[115] *Cf.* Haskins, *op. cit.*, 92 *et seq.*

[116] Orderic, lib. XII, c. 24.

[117] *T.A.C.*, c. LXXI. The chapter bears the rubric "De Treuga In-

men in the peace of the church are killed and the truce is broken, if anyone wishes to appeal the killer, the duel is to be held in the duke's court. If the slayer is convicted, the bishop in whose diocese the offense was committed shall get his amends ($£9$) out of the convicted man's chattels, by the hand of the duke's justice. If the guilty party has not sufficient to make up the amount the bishop gets all and the duke receives nothing until this amend is made. If no one challenges the killer to duel he is to go to the ordeal in a church. Where a slayer and infractor flees, the amend shall be the same, but if he makes peace with the duke the bishop's fine is not included in the pacification. The man must render it to the bishop or make his peace with him separately.

The most startling phase of this document is the recognition of two distinct interests—the claims of the duke and those of the church. Since these claims arise out of the same injury it follows that by this time there exists a ducal interest in peace cases legally equivalent to that of the church, subordinate only to the extent of nine pounds where the accused stands to right. Where he flees the two interests are independent. The rise of the duke's interest is explicable only in his control over procedure. This is most incisively shown in the case of the fugitive. The bargaining between him and duke can be made without reference to the bishop's claims, for the reason that the effective sanction against flight, the foreban, is solely the duke's to wield or withhold. It is the nature of the duke's process in such instances which gives him a jurisdictional priority, and the cause is treated as primarily secular, a matter for the application of *misericordia* by bargain in accordance with the theories previously discussed.[118]

fracta." The language of the document is interesting especially in connection with the contemporary *Leges Edwardi* (de fractione pacis ecclesie) ". . . de occisoribus, qui homines in treugis et in pace ecclesie occidunt et treugas infringunt."

[118] *Supra,* Chapter IV, p. 245.

As to the killer who does not flee it is obvious that except for the locus of the ordeal,[119] the offender is the duke's to try. Upon this and upon the fact that trial must be had the ordinance is insistent. It is specific on the accuser who will appeal and deraign by his body, and although it becomes vague on the manner of forcing the offender to the ordeal in the absence of challenge,[120] the very insistence upon trial requires the inference that the appeal is not the only form of accusation contemplated. However, the form of accusation is implicit in the form of proof, the ordeal. In the Frankish law the ordeal was inevitably connected with the factor of common suspicion.[121] A man accused of wrong could normally purge himself by oath unless the accusation was based upon common suspicion rather than upon the mere oath of an individual accuser. Common repute thus had the effect of making denial by oath incredible without the divine testimony of the ordeal. This theory was adopted com-

[119] The rule in Normandy appears to have been that the bishop has control of the ordeal. See the interesting case involving the right of St. Wandrille to the ordeal iron in 1082. Bessin, *Concilia*, 75; revised text in Lot, *Etudes sur St. Wandrille*, no. 39.

[120] The passage refers to the absence of any private accusation and is not to be restricted to private accusation begun but terminated before battle. The verb is "defuerit." Round renders this "default": *Calendar*, no. 290. But default is a technical term, and in the *T.A.C.* as in contemporary England it is expressed by the verb "deficere": *T.A.C.* cap. xlii. Individuals are often amerced "pro defectu duelli," e.g. *P.R. 31 H. I*, 48, which would be absurd if the term referred to the absence of any accuser, for then the amercement could not be localized. In the series of entries concerning Johel (John) de Harlea (Aerlea, Aerlega, Erlega) running from *P.R. 14 H. II*, 83 to *P.R. 32 H. II*, 88, "pro defectu appellationis sue" is twice interchanged with "pro defalta appellationis sue." "Defuere" refers to complete absence.

[121] In the Frankish law of the ninth century the ordeal was employed where the defendant could not get oath-helpers, usually because he was unfree (i.e., not a legal man) or because he was under other disability such as being *criminosus* or where suspicion was raised against him. Occasionally where the plaintiff produced proof not traversable by oath the defendant was forced to the ordeal. The basic idea was the incredibility of the individual. *Cf.* on the whole theory 5 Bethmann-Hollweg, *Civilprozess*, 168; Mayer-Homberg, *Beweis und Wahrscheinlichkeit*, 37, 52 for other interpretations.

pletely by the church, so that in terms of canonical procedure, accusation by individuals could be refuted by *purgatio ecclesiastica,* while accusation supported by common repute as stated by the *synodales testes* of the ecclesiastical inquisition led to the *purgatio vulgaris,* the ordeal.[122] The postulates of procedure that link suspicion and ordeal are fundamental to the legal thinking of the time. Indeed when Henry II institutes the secular inquisition at Clarendon he clings to the basic Frankish-canonical tenets and forces men to clear themselves as did the church.[123]

[122] The church takes over the theory entirely as to laymen and to a limited extent as to clerics, 5 Hinschius, *K.R.,* 337, 342. In connection with the church's procedure the provisions of the synod of Tribur c. 22 (2 *Cap.* 225) are of the greatest importance since these rules are incorporated in subsequent canonical collections either fully or in part. (Regino II c. 302; Burchard, XVI, c. 19; *cf.* Regino II, 43; *Decr.,* C. II, q. V, c. 15.) The canon provided, "Si quis fidelis libertate notabilis aliquo crimine aut infamia deputatur, utatur iure iuramento se excusare. Si vero tanto talique crimine publicatur, ut criminosus a populo suspicetur et propterea superiuretur aut confiteatur et paeniteat, aut episcopo vel suo misso discutiente per ignem candenti ferro caute examinetur." This is discussed by Dove, *Beiträge zur Geschichte des deutschen Kirchenrechts,* 5 *Z.K.R.,* 23, 30, who points out the "superiurare" cuts off the right to purgation by oath and by destroying the suspect's credibility forces him to the ordeal.

The method of directing suspicion spoken of in this canon is the ecclesiastical inquisition, 5 Hinschius, *K.R.* 337, 427. This procedure is recounted in Regino's collection and copied by Burchard. It contemplates a public suspicion voiced by a group of legal men on the basis of which the bishop then takes action *ex officio.* If the defendant confesses or the matter is notorious he is punished. If he denies he can purge himself—by ordeal if he is credible, by ordeal if he is not credible. Biener, *Beiträge zur Geschichte des Inquisitions-processes* (1827) 34. The twelfth-century purgation procedure is detailed in Jacobi, *Prozess im Decretum Gratiani,* 34 *Z.R.G.*[2] (Kan), 320 *et seq.* The church takes the view that the burden of proof is on the defendant—or perhaps as we would say the duty of going forward. It is certainly regarded as the practice of the Gallic Church in 1101. *Cf.* the representations of the French clergy at Valence (20 Mansi, *Concilia,* 1117).

[123] The late Norman secular rules regarding purgation, as they are set forth in the *Très ancien coutumier,* indicate a correspondence with the Frankish practice. In cap. XL it is provided that no one is to answer *super aliquam rem* except there is a supporting witness, in which event he can purge by oath. Cap. LI provides that in all offenses involving infamy the malefactor is to be jailed until some one accuses him, and he shall stay there until he purges himself by ordeal of water. These two provisions are

In view of the rising restriction of the use of the ordeals, and in particular the privilege granted knights,[124] the class most affected by the truce, to use oath rather than ordeal in ordinary cases, the insistence on ordeal in 1135 shows persuasively that the procedure leading to the ordeal must have been an extraordinary procedure such as the inquisition. While there is no direct evidence of the use of the ecclesiastical inquisition in Normandy, it is known that in certain cases proceedings on the basis of ill fame were had.[125] And since in the truces before 1080 the church does the enforcing, a function only gradually taken over

not irreconcilable. The first states the general rule for the so-called trial by *testimonium* (Brunner, *Schwurgerichte,* 195 *et seq.*). The second provision is specifically criminal procedure for the person suspected but not yet accused and embodies the ancient rule that the suspicious person is incredible and must purge by *ordeal.*

[124] At the council of Rheims in 1119 in 21 Mansi, *Concilia,* 237, this was laid down: "Si quis autem appellatus fuerit de infractione huius treviae et ipse negaverit: si miles est, purgabit se sua septima manu, reliqui vero Dei iudicio examinabuntur." This council was attended by Norman clergy and although Henry I warned the pope to mind his business about English matters there is reason to believe from Orderic's account that some dispositions of the council were accepted in Normandy, Orderic, lib. XII, cc. 21, 24.

[125] There has thus far been turned up only one equivocal piece of evidence that ecclesiastical inquisition exists in Normandy: *cf.* Haskins, *op. cit.,* 227. Nevertheless, it is scarcely to be doubted that the Norman church knew the procedure *ex fama mala.* At Lillebon (c. 3) in the provision against clergy keeping women it was provided that when the matter was known (eandem culpam visus fuerit incurrisse) if the accusation was made by the officers of the bishop the defendant should purge himself in the bishop's court. But if any of his parishioners or lords should accuse him, the defendant was given time to parley with the bishop, and if he wished to purge himself he should do so in his parish in the presence of many parishioners before the bishop's officers and by their judgment (praesentibus Parochianis pluribus ante Episcopi ministros, & eorum judicio se purgabit). If he could not purge himself he would irrevocably lose his church. It is possible that what is here intended by complaint of parishioners is the *synodales testes* of the inquisition used by the church. In any event, the question is one of *mala fama* since the purgation has to be in the parish, for an official accusation can be tried in the privacy of the bishop's court. This procedure seems to operate on the same theory as the provision of the London council of 1108, that in cases of concubinage accusation could be by two or three witnesses *vel publica parochianorum fama* (1 Wilkins, *Concilia* 388); whereupon purgation.

by the state, the presumption is that truce matters not subsequently handled by ducal procedure remain, residually, church procedure, and the reference to the ordeal in 1135 thus strongly suggests the church procedure of inquisition.

There being no secular vehicle in Normandy for voicing suspicion yet every reason to suppose the church had such a machinery, there remains the further question of the link between the ecclesiastical agency which formulates suspicion and the secular tribunal which alone is authorized to act on it. The ordinance of 1135 points surely toward the bishop. In every homicide *contra pacem* he stands to gain nine pounds. If he accuses, he lays the basis for this claim, just as did the later informer in a *qui tam* action. In making such accusation, the bishop's status seems essentially that of an administrative accuser who need not account for the way in which the cause came to his ears. In other words, since the truce cases retain a quasi-ecclesiastical flavor even after 1135, the *ex officio* power of charging inherent in the episcopacy[126] is retained for some little time thereafter, and ended only by the well-known Falaise ordinance of Henry II (1159) forbidding accusations by the deacon (the bishop's officer) except on the testimony of legal men of the vicinage.[127]

With possible accusation and administering the hot iron

---

[126] In whatever form the notice of breach comes to the bishop, there can be no doubt of his authority to proceed *ex officio*. This is how the procedure by accusatory inquisition is to be understood, 5 Hinschius, *K.R.*, 349, n. 6; 351, n. 5. In the Frankish period and subsequently *ex officio* proceedings were usual, *ibid.*, 337. In the case of *notorium*, during the eleventh century the citation of the offendor was even dispensed with, *ibid.*, 359, n. 5. The account in Orderic, lib. XII, c. 25 of the high-handed proceeding of Archbishop Geoffrey indicates that outside accusation was not necessary.

[127] The ordinance is in *Continuatio Beccensis* (82 R.S., pt. 4), 327. Haskins, *op. cit.*, 330 et seq., thinks that the ordinance was directed at the same problem as the first chapter of the Constitutions of Clarendon. There is no evidence even up to 1160 that ecclesiastical causes had in Normandy been rigidly separated from the secular as they were by William's English ordinance. The juristic basis for a parallel is therefore wanting. Haskins ignores the procedural situation created by the Ordinance of 1135. It was apparently not unusual for a prelate to act in his ecclesiastical

the bishop's participation ends. His amends are to be obtained
through the lay judges, for the machinery of distraint in execution is definitely secular. This aspect of the ordinance of 1135 is
particularly emphasized when Stephen confirms it two years
later.[128] When the bishop receives his £9, he gets it because the
royal officer has brought pressure to bear on the offender, *justitia
mea cogente,* even in the case where the trial has been by ordeal.
The basis for this had been laid in 1080 in the provision for the
secular distraint of offenders. Since distraint involves measures against property—here unquestionably sequestration and
eventual confiscation by the duke's ban—the claims of the
bishop can only be satisfied by the duke's judges in whose hands
the chattels rest. That the method of mesne distraint forced complete responsibility for the whole proceeding upon the duke's
officers was thus inevitable.

The institution of the duel affords a further reason for the
domination of ducal justice. Whether or not this particular form
of trial was accounted a *judicium Dei* among the Normans, in

capacity as a cog in the ducal administrative machine—*cf.* the writ of
Henry I (Haskins, *op. cit.,* 93, n. 31) "Et nisi feceris, archiepiscopus et
iusticia mea facient." Note further the cooperation of the bishop or his
officer in proceedings against clerk slayers in Henry II's letter to the pope,
Diceto, *Ymagines Historiarum* (68 R.S., pt. 1), 410.

As far as we can ascertain there has been no study of the position of the
archdeacon *vis à vis* the lay courts at this time. The most ample discussion
of his functions is in 2 Hinschius, *K.R.,* 189 *et seq.; cf.* also Gréa, *Essai
historique sur les archidiacres* in 2 *B.E.C.* 3 ser. 215 *et seq.,* using mostly
thirteenth-century material. Under the Franks the archdeacon cooperated
with the Count and held a sort of watching brief in matters which once
concerned the church and were subsequently taken over by the secular
arm. Schroeder, *Entwickelung des Archidiakonats bis zum 11ten Jahrhundert* (1890), 108. This was a situation parallel to the one here under
consideration.

[128] Bessin, *Concilia,* 81. It is also confirmed by Richard I in 1190 in a
charter to the bishops, *ibid.,* 99. In view of the advance of ducal justice
this must be taken as the confirmation of a mere fiscal privilege. So too,
the finding of the jury in 1205 regarding assaults for which the penalty
is loss of life or member, 1 Teulet, *Layettes,* 296, 297 col. 2. On the enforcement of Henry's ordinance, *cf.* a writ of Geoffrey in Haskins, *op. cit.,*
140.

William's time it is already clearly distinguished from ordeal.[129] The jurisdictional importance of the distinction lies to some extent in the fact that since a person certain must appear to deraign the charge by his body the duel supersedes *pro tanto* the episcopal accusation by suspicion, and thus lessens church participation in the initiation of procedure. More directly the duel secularizes truce enforcement by making trial thereof impossible except in secular courts. Although the right to hold duel was a jurisdiction exercised in the courts of some Norman monasteries, it was a privilege by secular grant, an aspect of their temporal power over their lay litigants.[130] It is a license to hold duels, not to engage in them. This is shown by William's interference in a case where a monastery was about to wage battle,[131] and by a canon of Lillebon[132] ordering mulcts to be paid by clerks engaging in duels without special license from the bishop. Duel was not a part of the accepted canonical practice, even if it was tolerated and to some extent abetted as a part of lay procedure.[133] The significance of its introduction as a means of proof

[129] Liebermann, *Glossar, Ordal* 1d, referring to William's *Lad,* 1.

[130] Coulin, *Verfall des officiellen und Entstehung des privaten Gerichtlichen Zweikampfes in Frankreich (Untersuchungen,* no. 99, 1909) 49, n. 1 has a long but by no means complete list of the French monasteries which had right to hold duels. *Cf.* also 1 Vernier, *Chartes de Jumièges,* no. 24 (1048–78). The fiscal importance is indicated by the charter to Quimper by the Counts of Cornouville in 1 Morice, *Mémoires de Bretagne,* 376 (eleventh century), "medietatem de emendatione duelli postquam pugilles ingressi fuerint intra cordam."

[131] Lot, *Etudes sur St. Wandrille,* no. 37; Round, *Calendar,* no. 165.

[132] Bessin, *Concilia,* 69, c. 19.

[133] The occasional outbursts of individual clerics against the practice do not prove a consistent policy, still less a general rule of law. Patetta, *Le Ordalie* (1890), 323 *et seq.,* collects these. Up to the thirteenth century, the question is not to be treated as a matter of general canon law. This is due not merely to local variations in the collections of canons used but likewise to the fact that the theoretical separation of temporal and spiritual authority is not a practical test of what went on in a bishopric, or abbey. For example, Burchard of Worms' *Lex Familiae* uses battle on the temporal side (*M.G.H.* 1 *Const.,* 640, cc. 19, 30, 31) and note the limitation in his *Decretum* lib. IX, c. 51. Before Burchard, Regino incorporates in his canons a Frankish rule regarding duel to settle issues between opposing

in truce violations was therefore a mark of secular control over the truce cases. Particularly with regard to the problem of enforcement against the magnate, the social significance of the change is considerable: the man of parts is now given a decent and honorable means of accusing his neighbor or of defending himself. The distinctions of status in connection with methods of proof had been recognized by Calixtus II's general council at Rheims in 1119.[134] There the knight can purge himself by oath, others must go to the ordeal. Henry I accepts the distinction. But he accepts it by offering a device that can be administered only in a secular court, and he stipulates that the court shall be his own.

Secular procedure and the duke's own justice thus make a reality of the peace of God in Normandy. The emergence of the "duke's peace" alongside of the peace of God becomes inevitable. The *Landfrieden* in Normandy evolved as certainly from the *Gottesfrieden*, as it did in the Empire. And it was this *Landfrieden* which gave to the duke's law a characteristic that no other country in France at the time possessed. It was the concept of an order depending upon law, superior to the claims of anyone entitled to a forfeit.

witnesses, and distinguishes the secular and spiritual causes. *De Eccl. Discipl.* lib. II, c. 334. Note further 5 Hinschius, *K.R.*, 345, n. 2, 3 for the posture on ordeal of Ivo and Gratian. It is possible that Otto I's ordinance (967) regarding duel as a mode of settling land cases even where clerks were involved (*M.G.H.*, 1 *Const.* 27) foreclosed for a time any papal action since the pope was supposed to have consented.

At least one formula of Norman origin for the benedictions necessary to battle exists, Delisle, *Cérémonial d'une épreuve judiciaire*, 18 *B.E.C.*, 253, 255. Compare the formulae in Spelman, *Glossarium Archaiologium* (1664), 436 *et seq.*, and that for blessing the weapons from the *Manuale Eboracense* in 2 Franz, *Die Kirchlichen Benediktionen* (1909), 364. In northern France at this time an ingenious system of oblates was devised for duel cases. Schreiber *Kirchliches Abgabenwesen bei französischen Eigenkirchen*, in 36 *Z.R.G.*[2] (Kan.), 460 *et seq.* Clearly where such a source of profit existed one would expect indulgence of the institution.

[134] *Supra*, note 124.

THE DUKE'S PEACE

The ordinance of 1135 represents a definite stage of transition in the reconstitution of the whole concept of jurisdiction which had been current during the eleventh century. The threat against distributed criminal law enforcement that from the first was implicit in the truce of God was now carried forward one more step by the establishment of a virtual monopoly of homicide cases which reduced competitive judicial rights to a mere fiscal privilege and this privilege limited to the church. A lay baron might still conceivably try a mid-week homicide, but if the victim was a protected person or was killed in the time of peace, the duke now took sole jurisdiction of the case, without saving even the baron's *forisfactura*. Should this monopoly be extended in the same terms to other causes it is clear that baronial jurisdiction would soon be stripped of all its worth. This possibility was, however, not at once exploited. Instead ducal policy developed the procedural advantages which the ordinance offered, strengthening its acquired powers by rules about flight, adding afflictive penalties upon conviction, and finally adding to homicide certain other crimes against the peace.

The chronological sequence of these various steps can be winnowed out of various chapters in *Très ancien coutumier*. The first and most detailed of these is the one which Tardif has headed *des Pès Fuitis*.[135] This chapter is a hodgepodge of old and new. Two sections of it deal with a broad list of crimes, punishable by hanging with compromise affirmatively excluded,[136]

---

[135] *T.A.C.*, cap. XXXVI.

[136] §§2 and 3. The third section excepts from hanging nobles and clerks, and stipulates their retirement to establishments like those of the Templars or Hospitallers where they must serve out their lives. This section is by reason of placement and its language a continuation of section 2. In view of the very broad nature of this exception the two sections may mark the first introduction of the afflictive punishment for the cases listed. These social distinctions are more characteristic of the early twelfth century than of the later period; thus, the purgation procedure of Rheims (1119), the

clearly rules much later than Henry I's ordinance which says nothing about afflictive punishments but is explicit on the matter of concord. The bulk of the chapter[137] is completely inconsistent with these sections, for it is in terms entirely of compromises. This inconsistency is resolved by the fact that although the sections of the chapter which are in terms of hanging without concord deal with a number of crimes in addition to homicide, the rest of the chapter, which contemplates concord, is restricted to the case of homicide. Since homicide is the specific and sole plea over which the duke has jurisdiction in 1135, this portion of the chapter must be regarded as an elaboration of the ordinance of 1135. It provides in the first place that the duke cannot concord with a slayer until the latter has concorded with the friends of the slain but this pacification is of no avail unless the duke's peace is obtained. The two concords are thus made mutually dependent.[138] This effect, however, does not extend to the slayer's inheritance for although he is privileged to concord, the land escheats for the homicide. This punishment is likewise extended to fugitives.[139] In both cases a judgment is implicit.

Behind the details of these rules about homicide, flight and

appeal provision of 1135, and the requirements in *des Pès Fuitis* §§4, 5, 6, for the low man wearing the ducal writ of protection while the noble can keep it locked up.

[137] §§1, 4, 5, 6, 7.

[138] Compare the English thirteenth-century procedure for inlawing, Bracton, *De Legibus,* fol. 131, *et seq.*

[139] "Simile est de singulis fugitivis." This may well be a general rule as to all fugitives, not merely the slayers, for the section opens, "Omnis enim homicida, licet pacem Ducis habuerit," a statement broad enough to include the slayer who flees. Since 1080 a big piece of flight jurisdiction had been taken over, which allows the conjecture that it had become even in 1135 a substantial monopoly apart from homicide. The barons could not cope with fugitives unless they indulged in constant disseisins or had bargains for the surrender of criminals; such bargains exist where there is a divided jurisdiction over the man and his chattels (*supra,* Chapter IV, note 83) but we have seen only extradition agreements for fugitive serfs. Note further in connection with the duke's jurisdiction over fugitives that under Henry I the charters or notifications granting a fair peace except fugitives for theft or murder from the operation of the peace.

pacification lie the assumptions of a system of law enforcement, implicit also in Henry I's ordinance, that anticipate, through the application of ducal *misericordia,* redemption by bargain. Only after the accession of Henry II does the expectation of an afflictive punishment emerge as a competitive principle, but it is clear that its appearance depends very largely upon the final removal of the peace cases as a whole from the hands of the church, which had always preserved at least an academic position against punishments of life and member. The state of the sources makes it impossible to say exactly when this transfer of jurisdiction took place. The charters are helpful on general policy but not on the date or extent of the shift. Already in Henry I's reign the duke has commenced expressly to reserve certain causes when he makes grants of jurisdiction,[140] but this policy is more pronounced under Henry II. The bulk of his charters are confirmations;[141] there are few new foundations. The reservations are either in terms of judgment over life and limb, or specifically as to certain crimes.[142] There is no general accord in the

[140] For example to Bec, Round, *Calendar,* no. 375 saving rape; St. Pierre-sur-Dive, 11 *Gallia Christiana,* Instr. 157, reserving army and coinage.

[141] Delisle, *Recueil des actes de Henri II* (1909) Intro. 152, states that practically all the monastic establishments in Henry's domains received confirmations.

[142] The background of Henry II's policy toward the Norman monasteries is to be found in Böhmer, *op. cit.,* 301 *et seq.,* where it is pointed out that the immense extension of papal influence after the death of Henry I had substantially changed both the character of the individual establishments as well as the relations subsisting between the Norman church and the duke. The necessity for the exchequer ordinance of 1157 (*supra,* note 24) which gives the duke a strict oversight over grants in alms was as much political as administrative. Practically it meant that grants of blood justice to monasteries could not be made unless the duke was willing.

In connection with the reservation of ducal rights note the following charters in 1 Delisle-Berger, *Recueil des actes de Henri II,* 225 (Blanchelande, 1156) reserving murder and rape; *ibid.,* 550 (Conches, 1155–73) in murder and theft the forfeit to the monks but justice is the duke's in the English possessions; 2 *ibid.,* 31 (Bec 1172–4) a general confirmation reserving the life and members, but see 2 *ibid.,* 104 (1172–8) of another property where specifically murder, homicide, blows, mayhem, bloodshed,

lists of these reserved pleas in the charters, so it is not possible to suppose that the list of the Assize of Clarendon served as the ground stone of ducal policy. At the same time it is significant that there should be this unconscious recrudescence of the Frankish notion of *causae criminales,* and it is hard to escape the conclusion that the reservation is motivated by a determined pushing forward of the ducal jurisdiction over crime. One point that emerges from Henry II's charters is a disposition to control the punishment of life and members. Because of this fact the misplaced section in the chapter *des Pès Fuitis* otherwise not to be dated, should be taken as an exposition of procedure in Henry II's reign. It states: "Concerning theft, murder, treason, nocturnal arson of houses, robbery done in the peace, there shall be no settlement with the convicted but taken they shall be hung and neither the duke nor the court may accept money." The direct purpose of this provision, obviously an ordinance since it changes procedure in the duke's court, is to establish the penalty for the five crimes enumerated and to forbid any concord after conviction. Since the prohibition on concord is directed specifically against the duke and his justice the conclusion follows that these causes must be ducal pleas. This conclusion is fortified by a passage in the chapter *De Iurea:*[143] "Default, rape, murder, arson, robbery done in the peace, fugitives for any crime, cannot be held by plea except in the duke's court." The two lists coincide in three causes—murder, arson and robbery. In both, the

---

duel, theft and rape are confirmed. This is a confirmation, and the grant goes back to Henry I; *ibid.,* 103 (Trinité et Ste. Catherine du Mont 1172–8), reservation of life and members; *ibid.,* 159 (Berçai 1172) reservation of murder; *ibid.,* 313 (St. Nicholas de Bayeux, 1172–89) reservation of life and members; *ibid.,* 333 (Cormeilles, 1172–89) reservation of arson, army ban, coinage, and attacks on court-goers. In the case of English holdings of French monasteries note also 1 *ibid.,* 98 (Hospitallers, 1155) reservation of life and members; 2 *ibid.,* 45 (St. Lazare de Jérusalem, 1175) reserving murder and theft; 2 *ibid.,* 113 (Fontrevault 1177–9) reservation of life and members; 2 *ibid.,* 284 (Blancheland, 1172–88) reserving murder and theft; 2 *ibid.,* 401 (Montjou, 1185–9), reserving life and members.

[143] *T.A.C.* cap. LIV.

phrase *per pacem facta* follows robbery. In *De Iurea*, moreover, the reference to "fugitives for any crime" suggests the existence of a distinction along some line which marks a generic relation among the specified crimes: the duke is here being accorded jurisdiction over these crimes *per se*, over any other crimes only when there is flight. This relation is indicated by the phrase *per pacem facta*: these are the crimes over which the duke has now obtained jurisdiction because they are specifically breaches of the peace. Other crimes he tries because like assaults on the way to the army the victim is on the duke's business or because upon flight his alone is the process which can make the property sanctions universally effective. There his jurisdiction exists quite apart from the peace. In Tardif's text the effect of the phrase *per pacem facta* is obscured by commas separating off robbery from the rest of the enumerated specific crimes, allowing the interpretation that it is robbery alone which is a peace case. This reading is indefensible in the face of the fact that robbery was no more or no less a matter involving the peace than was homicide or arson, in every truce of which there is record. They are all matters of the duke's peace because they are all matters of the church's truces.

It is hardly to be doubted that both of the sections quoted are statements of the law in a transitional state—early Henry II. This conclusion follows from the record of an inquest[144] not later than 1174[145] where the ducal pleas are for the first time denominated pleas of the sword,[146] and where the list of causes is so much longer and more comprehensive than any antecedent lists that the development of ducal control was certainly about completed.[147]

[144] *Ibid.*, LXX.
[145] *Supra*, note 1.
[146] But *cf.* the charter to Baudry in 1 Delisle-Berger, *op. cit.*, 349; among other tithes of honor the grantee is "custos famulorum meorum ad justiciam gladii mei pertinentium" (1156–62).
[147] Compare the criminal pleas in the earliest Exchequer Roll (1 Staple-

The jury opens with the forthright statement that "these are the pleas that belong to the duke's sword: homicide whether secret or open (this plea and the justice over it and the profits are the duke's alone or belong to those to whom his ancestors or he himself have granted it); similarly of the hacking off or breaking of members" and it goes on to list all the major crimes and also various other matters already ducal prerogative in 1091. Clearly to the certain knowledge of the twelve magnates and other legal men who sat with them the duke has taken into his hands the whole roster of wrongs. The monopoly sparingly asserted in 1135 has grown to sweep competitors from the field. But not quite. For with the same breath that declares these broad prerogatives of the duke the jury says that others can have these rights if the duke or his predecessors have given them. Thus is the Norman franchise theory averred in the same document which details the basis of the system of public justice.

Politically the announcement of the franchise theory is no less astounding than the statement regarding ducal criminal pleas. It has all the earmarks of the sort of compromise that made Henry II one of the geniuses of his time, for it is basically not as far-reaching as the principles upon which Henry I handled ecclesiastical truce jurisdiction in 1135. Pushed to its logical conclusion, the doctrine of the ordinance of 1135 would have meant the substantial evisceration of baronial justice. The jurisdictions over crime would have been reduced to the mere fiscal right of receiving at the hand of the duke's justices the *forisfactura*. The man who had by grant *quicquid exinde fiscus sperari potuerit* (whatever the fisc can hope for) would have discovered that the phrase meant literally only what it said. This would have been intolerable and unworkable in the land of great and warlike barons. It would have been equally impractical for the duke even with his now powerful administrative machine to assume

ton, *Rot. Scacc. Norm.*) of 1180: murder, homicide, rape, arson, robbery, theft, mayhem, wounds, medley, receiving.

the trial of every malefactor in an age where the bonds of fealty still imported a quasi-paternal power of protection and discipline. In consequence the notion of delegation, while leaving unimpaired the sovereign claims of the duke, nevertheless accorded so sweetly with the whole structure of derived rights which went to make up feudalism, that there could be no fundamental quarrel with the duke's position. Besides, the tremendous incursions into the amount of baronial jurisdiction actually exercised, resultant upon the inflation of the ducal jurisdiction over flight, must have left the private rights over blood justice in such a state of comparative unbalance, that it was not difficult to treat them as both local and exceptional. Whether or no far-seeing men realized that the duke had effectually severed blood justice from the usual incidents of tenure, the fact remains that this was to be the most incisive result of the theory of delegation, the inevitable consequence of the creation of a system of law enforcement lodged in the sovereign's hands.

# CHAPTER VI

## ANGLO-SAXON INSTITUTIONS AND NORMAN JUSTICE

IN 1066 ducal authority in Normandy was still so beset by the prescriptions connected with tenure than an exact reproduction of the Norman scheme of government was probably the last thing Duke William would have contemplated instituting in England. His followers, however, being accustomed to the exercise of jurisdiction even over blood justice were naturally more attached to the existing scheme. Having in many cases hopefully dispossessed themselves of their Norman lands,[1] they certainly would not anticipate that English fiefs received as booty would be stripped of rights hitherto undisputed at home. Balanced against these dreams of aggrandizement nurtured for military purposes[2] were political considerations: William's claim to succession by descent, the necessity of salving the church, the difficulties of controlling a large realm by military rule alone. The crown's immediate necessities consequently favored what develops imperceptibly into a third interest. This was the English *status quo* as to government, land and law, and it derived its vigor in legal theory from postulates which even a conqueror could not entirely ignore—the personality of the law, rights and duties immemorially rooted in the soil, the sanctity of territorial[3] custom, all statics in a society of contract, inexpungeable by con-

---

[1] Lamprecht, *Beiträge zur Geschichte des französischen Wirtschaftslebens,* 120.

[2] William's pre-conquest political maneuvers, in 3 Freeman, *Norman Conquest* (1 ed.), 305 *et seq.*

[3] On the personality of the law, Tardif, *Etude sur les sources,* 6; on the influence of English tradition on the type and extent of land-holdings, Vinogradoff, *English Society in the Eleventh Century* (1908), 3, 55 *et seq.; cf.* further Davis, *Regesta Regum Anglo-Normannorum,* no. 191; no. 221; no. 276.

fiscation and re-grant, and sometimes of such supervening force that no bargain would avail against them.

In the settlement of criminal jurisdiction under the Norman kings these factors are operative from the very start, and to suppose that any one of them is consistently dominant in the first century of Norman rule tends to distortion. Thus the advantages which the seignorial principle may have gained during the early interval of military occupation, through the natural tendency to local consolidation of baronial authority,[4] are offset by the crown's reorganization of the county government[5] and its artful policy of dispersing the individual's several tenures[6]—both real barriers to overexpansion of feudal powers. And concurrently in the earliest inquests native *consuetudo* is treated often as vested beyond disturbance, which indeed it is whenever the crown undertakes to safeguard it.

In view of the premises of law enforcement across the channel it was inevitable that the seating of jurisdiction in post-conquest England would be the most vital issue in this competition. Court-keeping rights are central in the growth of feudalism and in the growth of the law, for they mean control of procedure, definition of duty and exaction of penalty, and so, substantive law. Friction over the issue is so consistently recurrent that some legal doctrine inevitably evolves out of the conflict of views. If jurisdiction can be treated as franchise it will depend upon special

---

[4] If Adams, *Council and Courts in Anglo-Norman England*, 155 *et seq*. in discussing "baronial" jurisdiction is referring throughout to England, he goes much too far in assuming no disturbance of local activity. He asserts (p. 156) the state is "little concerned" with franchisal jurisdiction in the twelfth century. We believe the contrary was true. Note that in the text of the present chapter the words "baron" and "baronial" are not used in any technical sense, but are merely descriptive of feudatories at large unless otherwise indicated.

[5] *Cf.* 1 Stubbs, *Constitutional History* (5 ed.), 290 *et seq.;* Morris, *Medieval English Sheriff* (1927), 41 *et seq.;* Adams, *Origin of the English Constitution*, 72 *et seq*.

[6] 1 Stubbs, *op. cit.*, 295; Ballard, *Domesday Inquest* (1906), 98.

grant. There is yet no such principle in Normandy for the king to import, but his new patrimony includes a much more extensive system of public justice than he has at home, and a chancery policy which will have something to add to Norman ideas of immunity. On the other hand if jurisdiction is to be treated as an incident of tenure it may pass by the act of feoffment, or it may run with the fief as something rooted in the land. Contemporary French feudal theory sees jurisdiction as implicit in tenure, but its source there is so impounded in prescription that one can expect what had become indurated in England on the several estates to be determinative even of baronial claims. Inevitably the English status quo as to this becomes of crucial importance as it colors either royal claims[7] or baronial pretensions. It is for this reason that it is necessary to consider here the legal import of the authority over wrongs that was lodged in private hands in Anglo-Saxon times.[8]

[7] It was pointed out in Chapter V that William the Conqueror's charters or writs generally grant rights either "as they were in King Edward's day" and eventually "as they were on the day that king was alive and dead," or rights "as 'they belong' to the crown." A few show a more relaxed form, Davis, *Regesta,* no. 47, "all other liberties pertaining to the aforesaid manor"; no. 106 (inflated or spurious) all things pertaining to a hundred; no. 272. Much the same tendency exists under William II. But see *ibid.,* no. 361, 402, 418. Under Henry I, the practice of reference to antecedent grants or to an earlier situation continues, *cf.* 1 Farrer, *Early Yorkshire Charters,* nos. 15, 16, 18, 90, 91, 92, 97, 98, 130, 430; but see nos. 132, 168, 169. 1 *Cartularium Monasterii Ramsei.* (R.S.), nos. 158, 159, 160, 162, 172, 174, 175, 179, 180; but see 94, 164, 182. Until the Henry charters have been completely compiled it is scarcely possible to draw any conclusions from these variations beyond what has been said about checking prescription, and allowing the local "custom" to determine the content of the conveyance.

[8] We need not consider here the rights vested in the sib, as, for example, execution in the case of murder, II *Cnut,* 56. The procedure is discussed in Beyerle, *Rechtsgang,* 322 *et seq.,* in connection with exclusion from the sib and the enslavement for wrongs. *Cf.* also Liebermann, *Glossar, Strafvollzug.* It is a distortion to think of these as private rights: they are rather the fundamentals of the whole amends concept. However, royal procedures develop so fast that sib rights in the form of sib procedures now become negligible.

### ANGLO-SAXON PRIVATE JURISDICTION

The word jurisdiction[9] can be used to describe private authority in pre-conquest England, if the term is used generally in the
sense of any governmental function or perquisite. Such functions
are widely distributed and something is known about various
phases of this distribution. The major problem has long been
whether the sum of these several functions adds up to actual
courtkeeping privileges. The sources of information fall into
two categories—the dooms,[10] and the charters and writs—but

---

[9] Maitland, *Domesday Book and Beyond,* 277, on one of the rare occasions when he became pedantic, warns that the right to hold court is
"after all rather a fiscal than a jurisdictional right." One may agree with
this without accepting the argument on which it rests, viz. that the lord's
right is not *ius dicendi,* since the suitors make judgment, but merely to
preside and take profits. This generalization does not correspond with the
facts in eleventh century France since the *districtio* is just as avidly bartered
as the *emendatio* or *forisfactura.* The division in Dunwich of the execution of the thief in one place and the chattels forfeiting elsewhere, 2
*Domesday Book,* 312 (hereafter cited *D.B.*) suggests the importation of
these distinctions. From what we have observed regarding the position of
the continental courtkeeper the control of procedure is as important as the
*ius dicere.*

[10] The citations to the dooms are all from Liebermann, *Die Gesetze der
Angelsachsen* (3 vols.) the text volume hereafter cited *Gesetze;* the glossary, *Glossar;* the vocabulary, *Wörterbuch;* the textual criticism, *Erklärungen.* The abbreviations used by Liebermann are here followed, as are
his forms of Anglo-Saxon words, except *infangtheof* and *sac* and *soc,*
where we use the conventional Anglo-Norman spelling. To avoid an utterly italicized text, "bot" and "wite" are treated as modern English words.
The charters used are chiefly from Kemble, *Codex Diplomaticus Aevi
Saxonici* (1839–48), hereafter cited as Kemble; and Birch, *Cartularium
Saxonicum* (1885–93) hereafter cited Birch. The charters badly need another Liebermann. Intelligent legal study is constantly hampered by the
miserable state of English diplomatics. By some occult process never dis-
closed most scholars test and brand documents as forgeries and the lawyer
has to accept the *ipse dixit.* The precedent of frankness set by Maitland, a
mere lawyer, in stating his grounds of suspicion we shall try to follow.
Our tests, no doubt crude and naïve, should be subjected to criticism. For
example, we believe that exclusionary clauses like the Frankish *absque
introitu* are not used prior to Edward the Confessor and further (relying
on Liebermann's observation in *Glossar, Gerichtsbarkeit*), that *sac and soc*
is not a formula *de cursu* before the reign of Cnut. Moreover, when we
find exotic words like *vasallus* or *graphio* in a ninth-century charter, we

they are not mutually corroborative on the question whether or not the Anglo-Saxons had an immunity where justiciary rights over wrongdoing were exercised and from which public officers were excluded. From the dooms can be constructed a picture of special privileges centered in an individual because he controlled land and men. From charters and writs can be extracted a theory of the immunity. But the dooms do not answer questions regarding the inner constitution of the immunity and least of all do they unriddle the perplexing matter of courtkeeping.

The privileges connected with seniority appear as the element of greatest importance in the constitution of Anglo-Saxon private jurisdiction, for they bulk large and expand steadily. At an early date the Anglo-Saxon magnate who was the chief of a following (*comitatus*) possessed powers of internal discipline as well as responsibility for his men.[11] By the seventh century it is demonstrable that on such a lord rested certain powers of po-

regard these as unusual enough to raise doubts as to the whole document. In some cases we have simply taken Liebermann's characterization of a document, even where he has not set forth his reasons, because his knowledge of diplomatics was so superb that it would be unreasonable to suppose he did not reach his conclusion by a scientific process. There is a useful essay on the dating by Treiter, *Die Urkundendatierung in Angelsächsischer Zeit, 6 Archiv für Urkundenforschung* 53. Stenton, *Supremacy of the Mercian Kings,* 33 *E.H.R.* 433 *et seq.* has done brilliant work on a small group of charters. In general *cf.* Hall, *Studies in English Official Historical Documents* (1908), 163, and the Aethelstan study, at p. 341; but this work is by and large not of scientific use.

[11] Larson, *Die Gefolgschaft bei den Angelsachsen* in 2 Hoops, *Reallexikon* 135, points out the earliest form of *comitatus* decays and is revived at the end of the eighth century. It is subject to regulation in Aelfred's dooms, e.g. no lord can take into his following a man who is not clear of wrongdoing without the risk of fine to the crown, *Aelfred,* 37; 37, 2; nor can he in the succeeding centuries get rid of a man who is impleaded, II *Aethelstan,* 22, 2; II *Cnut,* 28, 1. The lord represents his man at court against complainants, II *Cnut,* 20, 1. He can vouch for him to lighten procedural burdens, I *Aethelred* 1, 2; he pays ransom in case of death penalty, VI *Aethelstan,* 1, 4; 9. The materials on this are collected in Liebermann, *Glossar, Gefolge,* 16, 18, 22; *Bürgschaft,* 3. Larson, s.v. *Gesith* in 2 Hoops, *Reallexikon* 240. *Cf.* also Marquardsen, *Über Haft und Bürgschaft bei den Angelsachsen* (1852) 36, 44, 49. Maurer, *Über angelsächsische Rechtsverhältnisse,* 2 *Kritische Überschau,* 30 *et seq.*

lice,[12] in part attributable to his position as a senior and in part to his tenure of land.[13] These powers are well distributed and defined in the tenth century, for the laws of Aethelstan[14] indicate clearly enough that the crown has come to depend upon these landowners as an arm of the state.[15] The not infrequent references thereafter to the duties, powers and especially the fiscal rights of the *landrica* or *landhlaford*,[16] the class of budding seigneurs, are testimony to the rapid accretion of privilege with jurisdictional color. But whether it is jurisdiction in the sense of a right to hold court is by no means clear.

In general the Anglo-Saxon system of dealing with wrongdoing corresponds with that of the continental folklaws, that is to say, it is based upon emendation substituting for feud, wergeld, specific amends tariffs (*bot*) for personal injuries, value compensation for theft, bargain procedure and a sparing use of afflictive penalty.[17] Since the machinery of enforcement is loosely

---

[12] *Ine*, 50, provides that a man who maintains a *comitatus* (*gesiðcund mon*) concords for his man with king or ealdorman, but the lord gets no share of the mulct because he did not prevent his man's wrong.

[13] Liebermann, *Glossar*, s.v. *Gerichtsbarkeit*, 4 b.

[14] VI *Aethelstan*, 11.

[15] Larson, *The King's Household in England before the Norman Conquest* (1904), 100, suggests that the thegn who performed these duties did not necessarily have land. But *cf.* Reid, *Barony and Thanage*, 35 *E.H.R.*, 171–2.

[16] Maitland, *Domesday Book and Beyond*, 286 suggests *landrica* or *landhlaford* = immunist. Liebermann in *Wörterbuch* gives the meaning *Grundobereigner, Immunitätsbesitzer, Gerichtsherr*. His translation of the passage VI *Aethelstan*, 1, 1, renders *landhlaford* Grundherr, i.e. landlord; in II *Eadgar*, 3, 1 it is rendered Grund [Immunitäts]-herr; so too III *Eadgar*, 7, 1. In IV *Eadgar*, 11, it is rendered Grund [und Gerichts]-herr; so too *landrica* IV *Eg.* 8, 1. In the Northumbrian Priest's law (*Northu.*), 54, 1, he renders *landrica* as Immunitätsherr in reliance apparently on Maitland, *op. cit.*, 288 (*Erklärungen*). For our inquiry the use of any word except landlord here practically begs the question, since we are concerned essentially with the existence of judicial immunity.

[17] It is scarcely necessary to enter into a discussion of the Anglo-Saxon method of dealing with wrongs. The older discussions in 1 Kemble, *Sachsen in England* (1853), 218 *et seq.*; Laughlin, *Anglo-Saxon Legal Procedure* in *Essays in Anglo-Saxon Law* (1876), 183 *et seq.*; Maurer, 3 *op. cit.*, 26 *et seq.* are all subject to considerable revision in the light of Lieber-

put together, single activities in connection with administration distributed at large cannot be used to draw broad inferences. Thus those passages in the dooms which give the *hlaford* one-half the thief's chattels,[18] that allow him to distrain cattle for Peter's pence[19] and keep the distrained surety, or that permit him to retain livestock if title has not been warranted[20] are far too ambiguous to be offered as proof that a lord held court in his own right. They imply that someone held a court, to give him these rights, but they are far from saying that he himself held it. Even if every reference to fiscal privileges be held to imply justiciary rights the dooms offer no sign of insulation of private jurisdiction against external interference, which argues strongly that the supposed courtholder was scarcely in a position to re-mold court procedure and substantive law, as he did in tenth-century France. Although individuals are occasionally put in possession of a whole hundred, the landlord seems to have worked no metamorphosis of the hundred court comparable to the conversion of the Frankish *mallus publicus* into a feudal court in France; neither does it appear that the control and di-rection of procedure is a matter of private command.[21] There is plenty in the laws to show that nearly all free men have some

mann's exhaustive discussion in *Glossar, Rechtsgang, Klage, Beweis, Schiedsgericht*, etc., and Bechert, *Einleitung in den Rechtsgang nach A.S. Recht*, 47 *Z.R.G.*², 1. A different, and we believe truer, picture of Anglo-Saxon procedure results if the assumptions of earlier writers are re-placed by the analysis of Beyerle in *Das Entwickelungsproblem im ger-manischen Rechtsgang*. Beyerle is chiefly concerned with central Euro-pean sources, but he has indicated throughout parallels in Anglo-Saxon law and has here and there relied heavily upon the latter when other mate-rials failed, e.g., at p. 126 *et seq.*; 134 *et seq.*; 267 *et seq.*; 282 *et seq.*; 301 *et seq.*

[18] *Hundredgemot* (1 *Eadgar*) 2, 1, 3. Maitland, *Domesday Book*, 287 suggests the passage means lord of the hundred. Liebermann in *Erklä-rungen*, 132, on *Hu.* 2, 1 denies this and says it is the lord of the thief. So too his comment on III *Aethelred*, 3, 2 in *ibid.*, 159.

[19] *Northu.*, 59.

[20] IV *Eadgar*, 8, 1; IV *Eadgar*, 11. *Cf.* also III *Aethelred*, 5.

[21] Grants of whole hundreds are said to have been not unusual from Eadgar on. *Cf.* Birch, nos. 1135 (forged?: "sac and soc"); 1137 (forged?:

sort of lord over them,[22] but beyond the lord's occasional fiscal interest in derelictions, there is little to suggest that causes were withdrawn from public cognizance.[23] The power of the sib, of

"socharum"; exclusionary clause); 1266, 1267 (forged?: "socna"); 1281 (forged? "sac and soc," exclusionary clause). On the suspect documents in this list, *cf.* the form of a century later, Kemble, no. 840 where a hundred is granted with an exclusionary clause. *Ibid.*, no. 849 grants a hundred with *sac* and *soc*, *infangentheof* and the king's forfeitures. *Cf.* 859, and 897 (post 1066) for the statement of rights regarding Taunton where the entry regarding "iii gemót" suggests hundred courts and is so taken by Mayer, *Hundertschaft und Zehntschaft* (1915), 24, n. 35.

Liebermann, *Glossar, Gerichtsbarkeit,* 30, on the basis of Henry I's London charter thinks the grant of hundred gives no more than the power to appoint the presiding officer and to take the profits; procedure etc. remain the same. This obviously is exceptional and in any event does not apply to pre-conquest practice. Neither does the post-conquest *Instituta Cnuti* III, 58, 1, cited by him—bishops "debent habere constitutionem hundredi (hundraedsétene)"—give any basis for inference as to Anglo-Saxon times. If we keep in mind Ganshof's description of the French feudal courts (*supra* ch. III, n. 17) as a standard of continental practice it is hard to establish the details of a transition from a "popular" hundred court to a court completely in a lord's control. Ganshof's test—the nature of suit—cannot be used inasmuch as the Anglo-Saxon laws do not disclose the exact nature and limits of suit in the hundred court, public or private. Liebermann, *Glossar, hundred,* 31 a. The discussion in Vinogradoff, *op. cit.,* 97 *et seq.* on suit is not relevant to this point. There is no such widespread or long-lasting breakdown of public justice in England as there was in France to force the transition from *mallus publicus* to feudal court. This makes Liebermann's conjecture plausible. We agree with his view although his evidence does not seem to us in point.

In the case of a partial grant of the hundred, the grantee's rights in matters of justice are certainly only a *pro tanto* fiscal perquisite. In some of the laws the hundred gets half the chattels of a thief and half goes to the man's lord. *Hundredgemot* (I *Eadgar*) 2, 1. A partial grant of a hundred would conceivably give a cut into the hundred's share. This is clear for Anglo-Norman times, 2 *D.B.*, 22; *cf.* Round in 1 *Victoria County History of Essex,* 342.

[22] Liebermann, *Glossar, Gefolge,* points out this is the assumption both in Aethelred's and Cnut's laws.

[23] The strongest case for the exercise of judicial powers is presented by the passage in the Northumbrian law (54; 54, 1) regarding the *landrica's* function against heathen asylum. Liebermann thinks that by analogy with this passage, §49 of the law can mean judicial activity for the *landrica*. He does not suggest that where such primitive conditions existed in the eleventh century there is reason to expect a rule essentially different from that applicable in more civilized sections. The case of the guard of

tribal organization, is not yet spent as a factor in law enforcement even in the eleventh century: it has not yet been displaced by the growing artificial bond of vassalage. Since actual lord-over-man control has not yet reached the strength and magnitude which it has in tenth-century France,[24] one cannot be too cautious in inferring a court where the Anglo-Saxon laws speak of rights in fiscal terms.

Nearly everything that writers have asserted about Anglo-Saxon private justiciary rights is derived from the charters and the writs.[25] The charters reach back into the early seventh century; the writs are first current in the eleventh century. The subject matter of the charters or landbooks (apart from the grants or confirmations of realty alone) may be divided into positive privileges conveyed and exemptions by which the books are said to create immunities.[26]

The few charters or precepts in Kemble's great collection which make positive grants of privileges fall into two categories.

cattle mentioned *supra* n. 20 and treated by some writers as evidence of judicial powers can be explained on the ground of convenience, for a lord would normally have a pound. Certain matters, like the right of private execution mentioned *supra*, jurisdiction connected with the ancient housepeace (1 *D.B.* 204 a), the duty of maintaining a guide when stolen cattle are being searched for (Liebermann, *Glossar, Geleitsman*) are matters originally not connected with seignorial jurisdiction and where acquired and exercised by a lord do not singly support the inference of a court. Compare the provision in *Aelfred* 35, 2, regarding amends for jailing. Liebermann, *Glossar*, (*Gerichtsbarkeit*, 10 a), thinks this may indicate private jails, and hence a private preliminary or police right of execution. The case of jurisdiction over unfree is discussed *ibid., Gerichtsbarkeit*, 14. It is worth noting here that where the Anglo-Norman compilers use the Anglo-Saxon sources they occasionally add the "*domini*" when the Saxon sources make no mention of them, *ibid.*, 13 e.

[24] Cf. finally on these questions Adams, *Anglo-Saxon Feudalism*, 7 *A.H.R.*, 11; *Origin of the English Constitution*, 44, note B.

[25] *Infra*, n. 86.

[26] Maitland, *Domesday Book*, 270 *et seq.*; Liebermann's critique in *Glossar, Gerichtsbarkeit*, 16 *et seq.* Jolliffe, *English Bookright*, 50 *E.H.R.*, 19, regards the emphasis upon "immunity" as tending to obscure a proper understanding of the landbooks. His discussion of these is illuminating and incisive.

They deal either with privileges which have a definite connection with the control of single wrongs, or with privileges which imply jurisdiction generally without defining its content. It is not without significance to the controversy over justiciary rights within a so-called immunity, that the charters prior to the eleventh century become specific only as to jurisdiction over thieves. The dooms, indeed, show that general landlord rights of jurisdiction are slowly growing and receiving recognition in the law, but until Cnut's day such rights cannot be said to lie in grant. *Sac and soc,* the term eventually so critical in the picture of private jurisdictional rights, has not yet crystallized as a formula at the end of the tenth century,[27] and its exact import even under the Confessor is to this day debatable.

The formulae of exemptions which are believed to create immunity are present in the great body of charters, but initially and perhaps to the very eve of the conquest these are essentially fiscal exemptions. The grantees, usually ecclesiastical establishments, are in terms exempted from secular burdens,[28] excepting as a rule the *trinoda necessitas,*[29] and the formulae by which this is done vary but slightly over centuries. Indeed, so static is the conventional landbook and so attenuated its content in comparison with the rich and shifting matter in the dooms that doubts as to the creative function of charters on the jurisdictional side are inevitable. The purpose of the Anglo-Saxon *boc* was to endow the parcels of realty described with what will be known as the legal

---

[27] Liebermann, *Glossar, Gerichtsbarkeit,* 1 h.

[28] For example, for numerous early forms, Birch, nos. 116, 178, 192, 194. When the charters state that the grantee is freed from *publicis vectigalibus,* Liebermann, *Glossar, Gerichtsbarkeit,* 16, thinks this must be limited to *hospitarium* or what on the continent is called *census.*

[29] Kemble, no. 1233 (961) is typical of the tenth-century forms "Sit autem praedictum rus omni terrenae servitutis iugo liberum, tribus exceptis, rata videlicet expeditione, pontis arcisve restauratione." This reservation of *trinoda necessitas* is also usual in the Frankish grants, 2 Brunner, *D.R.G.* 392; Kroell, *op. cit.,* 107, 181. *Cf.* further on the *trinoda necessitas* in England, Stevenson, *Trinoda Necessitas,* 29 *E.H.R.,* 689. He knows of only one clear and indisputable charter where it is waived.

quality of *bocland*,[30] viz., to expunge its status as *folcland*, to make it alienable and devisable and tax-free.[31] Hence the formulae of immunity from secular dues or exactions are expressive of a definition of *tenure* rather than of an intent to create a *jurisdictional* immunity. Regarding the landbooks in this light cuts sharply into the assumptions which can be made about the maverick charters which deal with matter other than normal exemptions. In other words if the usual exemptions are mere unconvertible quittances, the supposed words of jurisdiction in exceptional charters are robbed of much of their significance as additions to an extant jurisdictional substratum.

As a preliminary to an examination of the charters which go beyond generalized quittance it is important to emphasize again the fact that these specific additional clauses (prior to those

---

[30] The details of early grants vary. Gradually out of these details the legal generalizations are formulated as to what constitutes *bocland*. On the theory of the *boc* the basic study was by Brunner, *Zur Rechtsgeschichte der Römischen und Germanischen Urkunde* (1880), 149 *et seq.* Brunner's conclusions were subsequently altered as a result of a study of *folcland* by Vinogradoff (8 *E.H.R.*, 1) and the latter's article on the creation of *bocland, Romanistische Einflüsse im Angelsächsischen Recht: Das Buchland,* 2 *Mélanges Fitting* 501. On the case of the king making *bocland* for his own benefit with the usual exemptions *cf.* Vinogradoff, *English Society,* 254; Jolliffe, *English Bookright,* 50 *E.H.R.* 12; Liebermann, *Glossar, Bocland,* discusses the institution at length. *Cf.* also Maitland, *Domesday Book,* 226 *et seq.*

[31] Maitland admitted that clauses freeing from all secular dues etc. made the land tax-free but he sought to extend their implications to immunity (*Domesday Book,* 271–2). Braude, *Die Familiengemeinschaften der Angelsachsen* (1932), 12 *et seq.* returns to the conservative view. He states "Boclandschöpfung ohne Lastenbefreiung ist nur sehr selten nachzuweisen." Where words of exemption are missing he thinks we can presume a mere conveyance of extant *bocland.* Liebermann, *Bocland,* 22 says "sehr haüfig" the land was freed of taxes etc. Stevenson, *Trinoda Necessitas,* 29 *E.H.R.,* 699 discusses the exemptions in connection with the antecedent policy of freeing the church from burdens. *Cf.* also Vinogradoff, *Romanistische Einflüsse,* 517–20. The point involved is one of considerable importance, but a count of the charters in the present state of diplomatic uncertainty would scarcely be determinative. Turner, *Bookland and Folkland* (*Tait Essays*) who attempts a new interpretation of the *bocland* problem does not touch the question here involved.

which copy the writ form, *saec.* xi) have to do with theft in every instance. This is not surprising. The central problem in early Anglo-Saxon law enforcement is the matter of theft, because it is the most prevalent wrong and because cattle-rustling acts as a direct incitement to feud. For the sake of clarity, therefore, we may digress into a brief summary of Anglo-Saxon theft procedure before the tenth century, to spot the several charter formulae prior to that time against this background of prevalent law.

Theft cases fall into two sharply distinguished classes in Anglo-Saxon law. Both procedure and sanctions differ widely depending on whether the thief is caught in the act or accused after the act. Where the thief is caught in the act there is in early law no trial.[32] Every man has the privilege of summary capture and execution of such a thief, conditioned solely on performance of a formal ritual to unload himself of the danger of feud. This ritual is collateral; it is in no sense a trial of the thief.[33] The captor has the option also of turning the thief over to the crown for punishment.[34] In such case the early Kentish law says the king will decide whether the thief is to die, be sold into slavery, or be ransomed.[35] The notion of enslavement or ransom exists also in West Saxon law,[36] and so establishes that these alternatives to summary execution are not merely local. Until the middle of the tenth century there is no definite information in the laws on property sanctions for thieves caught in the act, so that there is no basis for inferring that there is forfeiture then, as later.[37]

[32] Liebermann, *Glossar, handhaft; Diebstahl,* 11.
[33] Discussed in Beyerle, *Rechtsgang,* 267 *et seq. Wihtraed,* 25, shows clearly no trial anticipated. The Wessex procedure to avert feud is in *Ine,* 16, 21, 35.
[34] *Ine* 28. The captor receives 10 shillings.
[35] *Wihtraed,* 26. The Kent law gives the captor a half interest in the thief or 70 s. if he kills him.
[36] *Ine,* 12, 24, 1, 62; *Af. El.* 24.
[37] *Ine,* 57 says that where a married man steals and brings the *res furtiva* to his house and it is found, he loses his share [of the household goods] and his wife if innocent retains a third thereof. The idea seems to be one of contamination. The obstacle in the way of forfeiture is the in-

The case of the thief not caught in the act involves different machinery. He is tried by a definite accusatory procedure; he is permitted the defense of third-party warranty of title.[38] It is clear that he is punished by no corporal punishment,[39] and pecuniary consequences no more severe than a repayment to the owner amounting to the value of the object stolen (*angyld*) and a sixty-shilling wite.[40] The wite, it may be observed, is, in the laws, a penalty which authority exacts from offenders in any emendable crime,[41] roughly similar to the *fredus* of Frankish law. But, unlike the *fredus,* it is not reckoned as an aliquot part[42] of the total composition, nor is it conceived as a payment for the intervention of judicial authority.[43] Being thus independent from the other payments for which the convicted offender was liable, the wite was peculiarly susceptible of grant as a purely fiscal right without implying as well judicial privilege in a system of procedure where private accusation was predominant and extra-court arbitration usual.

Such in brief is the early law with reference to which the mutant charters of the eighth and ninth centuries must be read. For convenience and in terms of correspondence of formulae we divide this dozen or so landbooks into two groups. The first group is characterized by formulae which convey an exemption from wite payments coupled sometimes with a requirement that restitution for theft (*angyld*) be paid to the person injured. The second group deals in a somewhat similar manner with rights in respect of handhaving thieves.

consequential value of individual interest in a period of community property; *cf.* Braude, *Die Familiengemeinschaften der Angelsachsen* (1932), 31.

[38] Liebermann, *Glossar, Anefang.*

[39] Unless he is a recidivist, *Ine,* 37.

[40] *Ine,* 7.

[41] The word "wite" alternates as a term for both penalty and afflictive punishment, Liebermann, *Wörterbuch,* 246. The discussion of wite in Chadwick, *Studies in Anglo-Saxon Institutions* (1905), 127, is misleading.

[42] 1 Brunner, *D.R.G.,* 230; Liebermann, *Glossar, Strafe* esp. 4. An account of the variations in the sum, *ibid., Strafgeldfixum.*

[43] *Infra,* note 47.

The charters of the first group, Mercian and West Saxon,[44] run over a period of a century and a quarter (767–888). Since Kemble's[45] day they have been treated as a surrender of public claims to mulcts for wrongdoing, and since Maitland's Domesday essays[46] as the earliest evidence of "private" courtkeeping in England. A few of these charters in freeing the granted lands from various exactions, services and tributes specifically mention wite or *witereden*—the judicial mulct.[47] There is no doubt that a fiscal privilege is here surrendered by the Crown. The difficulty is with the possible implications—whether, as Maitland urged, in exempting from *wite* the king declared that "he and his officers would neither meddle nor make with offences" committed on the immune lands[48]—in other words, whether the quittance cleared the way for private courtholding. This conclusion was not rested on the *witereden* charters alone, but by reading them in connection with a half-dozen grants where the exemption from wite—or as the phrase runs, "nothing out to wite"[49]—is coupled with another charter formula, the crown's express reservation of *angyld*—the payment in restitution to a man wronged. Matching charter with charter Maitland spelled out of this reser-

---

[44] Conveniently assembled in Maitland, *Domesday Book*, 290 but truncated so that we shall cite by charter number in Kemble or in Birch. Although some of this group are suspect, we shall discuss them as if their authenticity were as settled as Maitland assumed.

[45] Kemble, *C.D.*, Intro., lvii.

[46] *Domesday Book*, 274 *et seq.*

[47] "Libera ab omnibus servitiis secularibus, necnon regalibus tributis majoribus et minoribus sive taxationibus quae nos Witeredden appellamus"; Birch, no. 485. See *ibid.*, no. 483, no. 484. Kemble, no. 275 (spurious?), no. 302 (spurious?), no. 313.

On the use of the word *witereden, Ine,* 71. The definition is standard, *cf.* Liebermann, *Wörterbuch*. The phrase in an *angyld* charter *temp.* Cenwulf of Mercia (799–802) (Kemble, no. 116) "popularium consiliorum vindictis," may be an attempt to express the same thing, freedom from *witereden; cf.* Kemble, *C.D.* Intro. lvii. Cam, *Local Government in Francia and England,* 115, thinks however the phrase suggests freedom from suit of court.

[48] *Domesday Book*, 277.

[49] *noht ut to wite*—Kemble, no. 313. The Latin is *ad poenam nihil foras* or variants.

vation the lord's payment of *angyld* to a complainant and hence a procedure whereby the lord acquired jurisdiction over his own men on whose behalf he had paid *angyld*. Since most of the charters conveying exemptions from wite also contained the reservation of *angyld,* Maitland concluded that notwithstanding the ambiguity of the formula "nothing out to wite" standing alone, the phrase about *angyld* founded the justiciary rights. Finally he argued that the eventual disappearance of the *angyld* formula from the charters at the end of the ninth century was itself evidence that the grantees had acquired a still fuller measure of jurisdiction, a right to try causes without limitation of preliminary *angyld* payment, "the highest criminal jurisdiction alone" excepted.[50]

It is no exaggeration to say that from these *angyld* charters was built a most impressive façade for the whole structure of argument supporting the existence of private jurisdiction on Anglo-Saxon "immunities." Swiftly and deftly the scattered evidence was trimmed and mortised, and a cursory summary fails utterly to transmit the net conviction which Maitland's beguiling phrases convey. But it is no profanation if the journeyman mason sets his level against the artist's creation.

The proof that the lord actually holds court when he reimburses himself after paying *angyld* rests upon a strained conjectural interpretation of two nearly identical charters to the same donee, both charters long suspect.[51] Standing alone, and granting even their genuineness, they are feeble. But they are

[50] *Domesday Book,* 282.

[51] Kemble, no. 214 (Birch, no. 366) of 821 and Kemble no. 236 (Birch, no. 413) of 835. Liebermann, *Glossar, Gefolge* 2h asserts categorically the former charter is a forgery; *s.v. Fremde* 5 f, he states the second probably is a forgery. The clauses on which Maitland relies read: "Si pro aliquo delicto accusatur homo Dei, aecclesiae illae custos solus cum suo iuramento si audeat illum castiget. Sin autem ut recipiat aliam iusticiam huius vicissitudinis conditionem praefatum delictum cum simplo praetio componat." The argument turns on the meaning of *vicissitudo* which Maitland conjectures refers to a "transfer" of a suit, relying on *Leges Henrici* 9, 4, notwithstanding the tremendous chronological gap and the fact that this law-

woven by Maitland into a Protean discussion by analogy, touching now upon *infangtheof,* now upon the Frankish *fredus,* now upon the hypothesis that exemption from wite alone confers jurisdiction. It is unnecessary to examine this argument in detail and we will not do it the injustice of attempting to state it here. It will suffice to point out that the soundness of this admirably subtle and devious structure of inference is vitiated by a fundamental misconception of the nature of the plaintiff's compensation in *angyld*. *Angyld* is restitution, not bot (personal injury tariff) as Maitland thought.[52] By mistakenly treating *angyld* as bot, the lord's right under these charters to exact *angyld* from his man and at the same time obtain wite from him creates in the lord a coincidence of bot and wite which is almost persuasive of courtkeeping rights. For bot and wite make up the familiar essentials of the common characterization of Anglo-Saxon com-

book does not use the word at all. Its more proper meaning in this period is exchange or substitution—*cf.* the charters of the years 803 to 824: Birch, no. 324; Kemble, no. 195 (Birch, no. 332); Kemble, no. 199; Kemble, no. 1032 (Birch, no. 381) dealing with the exchange of land. Rendering *vicissitudo* as transfer of jurisdiction obscures the fact that the word is used in the charters when one value is a *quid pro quo* for another value. The passage may be rendered: If a man of God's church is accused of any offense the *custos* may, if he dare, clear the offender by his oath. However in order that he may receive other punishment on condition (reading *conditione* in lieu of *conditionem*) of this substitution let him amend the aforesaid offense with restitution.

[52] Maitland, *Domesday Book,* 274, cites the glossary in Schmid, *Gesetze der Angelsachsen* (2 ed. 1858) but he relies for his definition on Maurer, *Über Angelsächsische Rechtsverhältnisse,* 2 *Kritische Ueberschau* 32. Schmid gives the primary meaning "das Einfache Ersatzgeld oder Entgelt," and criticises Maurer's view. The latest authority on the word, Liebermann, *Wörterbuch s.v.* confirms Schmid's rendition. Maitland obviously glosses over Schmid's correction with his remark "the *angyld* is the money compensation that the person who has been wronged is entitled to receive, as contrasted with any wite or fine that is payable to the king." This enables him in his detailed exegetical note on the *angyld* charters to make the remark (292) "the abbot may pay the bót, the singulare pretium," and thus (282) to come to the conclusion that *angyld* implies "that the immunist will have jurisdiction over any dispute between two men of the enfranchised territory," a statement which makes *angyld* equivalent to bot.

position procedure.[53] The discussion requires only the reference to the equally familiar cynicism that "no one in the middle ages does justice for nothing" to achieve a picture of simple transplantation of the composition system from the king's court into the lord's, on the ground that the crown will see no point to holding court for a lord who collects bot and wite both.[54] Taking *angyld* as bot thus spins the argument down delusively familiar grooves with the net effect of lessening the critical attention which would otherwise be directed at the weakness of the charter proof itself.[55]

This misconception concerning the nature of the compensation involved in *angyld* has an effect more serious than mere discharge of the burden of persuasion resting upon the proof from the charters. *Angyld* applies chiefly to theft, fair warning that it will not involve bot. Standing outside the scheme of composition tariffs for personal injuries, theft, which makes its own tariff

[53] So characterized by Kemble, *C.D.*, Intro. lvii–lviii; substantially so in 2 Pollock and Maitland, *H.E.L.* 451, 458, 462, and compare Lord Sumner's opinion in Admiralty Commissioners *v.* S.S. Amerika, 1917, *A.C.* 38.

[54] Note here Liebermann's caveat against this assumption: "While the state judicial officer would have no interest in judging cases where he received no mulct still the mulct was not the only revenue. Gifts (bribery) played a role and perhaps the king's courtkeeper had an amend for mistakes of form. It is certain the king's reeve held trials where the church received wite," citing Birch no. 1219, *Glossar, Gerichtsbarkeit*, 17, 18.

[55] *Supra* notes 44, 47, 51. Edward's charter to the Bishop of Winchester (Birch, no. 612) has been treated as conclusive on the matter of jurisdiction, Cam, *Francia and England*, 115; Morris, *Constitutional History of England* (1933), 118. The charter of 904 provides *iudicia* in all secular causes shall be exercised to the use of the bishops in the same manner as that in which *iudicia* are settled (*discutiuntur*) in matters pertaining to the king. Maitland, *Domesday Book*, 276, renders *iudicia* as jurisdiction; Cam, *op. cit.*, uses judgment. From the A.S. paraphrase in the later confirmation (Birch 1220 [spurious?]) *iudicia* = *spraec* = claim, complaint, plea (1 *Ew*. Prol.). The passage is puzzling. The crown's interest is to put the episcopal lands on a parity with the demesne lands. The sharing of revenue in the case of the thief who pays redemption and the phrase *ad usum* suggests strongly a mere fiscal arrangement. Compare with this the Latin confirmation, Birch, 1219 (968) also to Winchester. The recital "omnia enim secularium rerum etc.," Liebermann (*Glossar, Gerichtsbarkeit* 18) regards as an order to the king's reeve to hold the pleas.

(viz., the value of the thing stolen)[56] requires special machinery. This is supplied in the laws, quite apart from charter, by the defendant's lord. The lord is made liable for the payment of the compensation, as ultimate surety for his man.[57] If he pays the plaintiff he may have recourse by way of subrogation against his man. This duty of finding compensation for the plaintiff is not optional. It is an absolute duty, an inherent burden, not an advantage of lordship. Furthermore, since the amount of *angyld* due can only be determined with reference to the value of the thing stolen, there being no predetermined tariff as in the case of a maim, the plaintiff cannot enforce the lord's initial duty to pay *angyld* without making a *prima facie* case in a court which will assess the *angyld*. The locus of this court is then the only point of doubt. But this is resolved in some of the charters by the correct naming of the boundary court as the court involved, a court which is a public court and not a court of the lord. For all practical purposes then the real jurisdiction over the wrong begins and ends with this assessment.[58]

[56] *Supra*, Chapter I, p. 20 (n. 42); compare Chapter II, p. 67.

[57] *Ine*, 22: "If your follower steals and escapes from you, warn his surety to pay the value of what is stolen; if he has no surety, pay it yourself. However, this does not serve as composition for the wrong." This is Wessex law of the end of the seventh century. There is no evidence that it becomes national law before Aelfred's late ninth-century compilation. (On the filiation of Ine's and Aelfred's laws, Liebermann, *Erklärungen,* 35–6, 64; *Die Gesetze Ines von Wessex,* in *Mélanges Bémont* [1912] 21). Nevertheless only excess of caution will dispute its application to the Mercian series of 8th and 9th century *angyld* charters, since 1) there is no competing definition of *angyld* grounded in the laws; 2) there is no change in the Mercian charter forms after the West Saxon conquest of Mercia, nor is there any difference between these and the West Saxon *angyld* charters; 3) since the charters deal with a matter of seignorial duty in English society and alter public responsibility in the universal problem of theft there is reason to suppose the Ine rule is merely a single expression of a general institution.

[58] Kemble, no. 117 uses the expression "nisi specialiter pretium pro pretio ad terminum." *Cf.* the variant in the royal confirmation of Birch, no. 455. Maitland, *Domesday Book* thinks this refers to a boundary court. This is not denied by Liebermann, *Glossar, Gerichtsbarkeit,* 8 but he points out the formulae by no means exclude the idea of trial in public

When a charter insists upon the reservation of *angyld,* it is doing much the same thing as when it insists upon the reservation
of the *trinoda necessitas.*[59] It is saying that whatever exemptions
are granted to a lord, he may not interpret these as authorizing
an avoidance of his absolute, apart-from-charter duty of suretyship, any more than as relieving him from building bridges or
supplying castles. The coupling of the exemption from wite with
the *angyld* is done to give the lord substantial encouragement in
the performance of a duty enjoined upon him by general law
because of his position as *hlaford,* although the crown will see
this waiver of wite as a mere limitation upon the lord's liability.
There is no question of courtkeeping, for the reservation and the
exemption runs as to the land. The core of the recipient's rights
is not attributable to grant but to his position as *hlaford.* This
gives him no right to hold court, and nothing in any of these
charters modifies the normal public arrangements to the extent
of allowing restitution to be collected in a court of the *hlaford's*
own creation.

On the basis then of the peculiar formulae used in this group
of charters the most that can be advanced is that a fiscal and not
a judicial immunity is given; there is merely particularization
as to a certain type of secular burden. The phrases respecting
wites indeed suggest a resemblance to Frankish grants exempting immunities from collection of *fredus* by public officers. But
this is at best a faint resemblance for there is no sign that Anglo-
Saxon immunities were insulated in this matter from public interference, and indeed, until the Confessor's reign, no formulae
are used in charters to give color of right to an immunist's possible conversion of the passive right of receipt into the active
right of trying the cause. The Saxon monarchs unlike the Frank-

courts. Our information about boundary courts is from the late *Leges Henrici.* Here they can be either public or private, says Liebermann, *Glossar,
Grenzgericht.*

[59] This seems to gather emphasis from the charters where *angyld* is coupled with the *trinoda necessitas,* and in particular from those charters

ish kings do not by an *absque introitu* prohibit entries by public officers into immune lands.[60] It was this safeguard against outside interference that made the Frankish immunity a self-contained unit.[61] The absence of this protection in England seems consequently to invalidate Maitland's inference that the crown restrained its officers from interfering with the immunities. Certainly the fact that a first tentative employment of the *absque introitu* occurs in a few precepts of the Confessor[62] is persuasive

where the reservation of *angyld* stands alone with no mention of wite. Kemble, no. 116, no. 227, no. 1068.

[60] Had the cautious Maitland realized the effect of this phrase in Francia he would have been less bold in drawing his parallel between English and Frankish immunities. (*Domesday Book*, 278). Cam, *Local Government in Francia and England*, 119, comments on the absence of the *absque introitu formula*, although at 115 she suggests that a phrase in the charter of Ealdorman Aethelred of Mercia of 883 (Kemble, no. 313; Birch, no. 551) mentioning freedom against ealdorman and gerefa may correspond with the *absque introitu* of the Franks. The expression is in any event too rare to form any sort of precedent. The authentic charters in Birch and Kemble use only the "si quis" clause—the threat against anyone breaking, diminishing, traversing or otherwise acting in defiance of the charter. But this is substantially identical with the similar penal formula in Frankish grants against the diminution or violation of a grant and is independent of the specific formula addressed to crown officers where the things they cannot do are set forth in detail.

[61] *Supra,* Chapter III, pp. 137 *et seq.*

[62] The idea has not yet reached a formulary stage. Out of Edward's fifty-odd writs and 60 or more charters, it is expressed, in varying phrasing, in three only—a Latin writ in Norman form (Kemble, no. 909), an Anglo-Saxon writ (no. 840) with a Latin translation, and a Latin charter (no. 907). Kemble (no. 909) to Christ Church says: "Et nolo ut aliquis hominum se intromittat nisi ipsi et ministri eorum"; no. 840 to Abingdon states: "and swa ðaet nán sċyrgeréfe oððe mótgeréfe ðár habban áeni sócne oððe gemót búton ðes abbudes ágen haese unne." This is undoubtedly a forgery. As far as we can ascertain, neither William nor Rufus gave Abingdon a grant or confirmation with a *ne intromittat* clause nor anything approaching it. The first *ne intromittat* is from Henry I (2 *Chron. Ab.,* 164). The occasion for this Saxon confection was very likely William's charter (*ibid.,* 1) which confirmed customs as of Edward Confessor. Although Abingdon was successful on many points in setting up these customs, the account of the trial (*ib.* 1–2) emphasizes the oral testimony offered. If this purported Confessor's writ was then proffered it must have been rejected. No. 907 "sine aliqua exceptione saecularis vel aecclesiasticae iusticiae," and "ullo modo intromittere." *Cf.* weaker forms,

that the Anglo-Saxon immunity had theretofore embraced no exclusive judicial rights.

If the group of charters just considered offers small footing for a theory that courtkeeping rights were imparted by them, the evidence of such rights is not much more persuasive in the series where thief catching is specially mentioned. These charters belong to the late eighth and to the ninth century, for the grants bearing later date all show marks of forgery.[63] The earliest document, a Mercian book for Worcester Cathedral (780),[64] states that no wite shall be paid on account of thieves, and can consequently be treated as a variant of the contemporary wite charters just discussed, viz., instead of a blanket "nothing out to wite," it gives this privilege only as to theft. This meaning can also be given to the quittances in four ninth-century landbooks which add to the exemption from secular dues, "penal matters in thief catching" (*poenalium rerum furis comprehensione*).[65] In other words any liability which might otherwise attach for the payment of the thief wite is discharged, whether this liability is

also widely variant, intermediate between these and the traditional *se quis* clause, nos. 833, 844, 850, 888.

[63] Kemble, *C.D.,* Intro. xlvii states he knew of only seven *furis comprehensio* charters of which only one was beyond doubt. Kemble, no. 728 (Cnut) is included in his list; here the "captio furum" is reserved. Kemble, no. 672 (Aethelred, 990) is marked by Kemble as forged. Kemble no. 686 (Aethelred, 994) is marked by Treiter as a forgery. Birch no. 1351 (959) we believe a forgery because of the blanket "juris regalis fragmine." Kemble no. 756 is from its whole purport forged. Kemble no. 312 (880) uses "cum furis comprehensione" and is marked by Kemble a forgery. Kemble no. 223 (828) uses "cum furis comprehensione intus et foris, maioris minorisve." The distinction between big and petty theft is first made in the laws in VI *As.* 12, 1 (930–40) which seems to point to the doctoring of this charter. The "cum" clauses tacked onto a quittance seem a curious defiance of grammar.

[64] Birch, no. 240.

[65] Kemble no. 246 (840) "poenalium rerum et furis comprehensione"; no. 253 (842) "poenalium conditionum, furis conprehensione"; Birch no. 451 (847) "poenalium causarum furisque comprehensione"; Kemble no. 281 (858) "penalium rerum principali dominatione furisque comprehensione." The use of "and" in three of these, i.e. penal matters and in thief catching, does not mean as Jolliffe supposes (*Origin of the Hundred in*

conceived of as the lord's responsibility for his men, or as a liability of the land itself for the mulct. There are three other contemporary books where quittance of *furis comprehensio* appears without the explicatory *poenalium rerum;*[66] yet this phrase must be read into the grants for otherwise the charter would do the absurd act of discharging land of the duty of catching thieves[67] while reserving the innocuous duty to build bridges.

It is possible to fix more precisely than we have yet done the exact content of the *furis comprehensio* privilege. The expression "capture" is the usual word when the idea of handhavingness is to be rendered. Since there is no whisper of paying *angyld,* these grants are presumably giving rights in the handhaving case; not rights of trial, of course, because the thief gets a Judge Lynch trial and no franchise is needed for what is a common right. But we have seen that there exists a discretion over punishment where the thief is not strung up but is merely laid by the heels. This discretion rests in the king;[68] this he can grant, and only by grant can a man have it, for it costs wergeld if the individual resorts to acts of unlicensed mercy.[69] It is, then, the crown's prerogative to punish, to exact wite,[70] to ransom or enslave, that passes here. The early Worcester charter makes this clear for it says that the wergeld thief (i.e., the criminal who can redeem his neck) if caught handhaving does not have to be surrendered.[71] Subsequently the king stipulates in the grant of another piece of land to Worcester that if a man is three times caught in open crime, he is on the third occasion to be turned

---

*Kent,* in *Tait Essays,* 162) that there are two separate quittances. The *furis comprehensione* is distinctly explicatory of the *poenalium rerum.*

[66] Birch no. 459 (850); Kemble no. 284 (860); no. 300 (869).

[67] So Jolliffe, *Origin of the Hundred,* 163, assumes that the lord can exclude hue from his lands. In the early tenth century (II *Ew.* 4) the lords are required to maintain guides for hue.

[68] *Supra,* note 36.

[69] The wergeld of the thief, *Ine* 36. The passage *Ine* 28, 1 provides wite in case of escape.

[70] A wite of 60 shillings, *Ine* 7.

[71] Birch no. 240.

over to the king's town.[72] It is not necessary to read into this a power of the grantee to try, for there is no evidence that a special procedure exists in case of redemption. It is merely a matter of private bargain.[73]

*Furis comprehensio,* then, boils down to a mere fiscal quittance. The general effect of the provision, moreover, is to speak against rather than for the existence of private immunity courts. For the addition of a special privilege regarding the commonest crime allows the inference *a silentio* that the usual formula of exemption from secular burdens was not understood to impart courtkeeping rights over wrongs generally. Furthermore none of these quittance formulae can by any rule of construction be taken to have effect beyond the specific parcel of realty which is the subject of the charter. They do not create personal privileges. This is the reason why new bookings to a donee already the possessor of *bocland* must contain words of exemption from tax if the new conveyance is to possess that quality. The donee cannot on the theory of personal privilege extend *bocland* exemptions to his *folcland*. It consequently seems impossible for status privilege—the *hlaford's* rights by doom or custom—to fuse with land privilege and produce for his domain an all-embracing immunity within which he was free to consolidate his authority as the Frankish magnate did.[74] It is this lack of real immunity theory in England which in the tenth century sharpened prescription as the real source of jurisdictional claims during this period—a creeping prescription memorialized and thereby legalized from time to time by progressive additions to the dooms.[75]

---

[72] Birch no. 357. A similar grant to a thegn, Birch no. 364.

[73] Jolliffe, *loc. cit.,* concludes similarly the *furis comprehensio* is a right to the redemption but on other evidence, chiefly the forged Abingdon charter discussed *supra,* note 51.

[74] As pointed out in Chapter III it was the personal nature of the Frankish *immunitas* which facilitated the consolidation of the whole complex of an immunist's holdings and permitted the extension of privilege over after-acquired property.

[75] Instances exclusive of the changes after the Conquest are given in Liebermann, *Glossar, Gerichtsbarkeit,* 3 b and c; 20 a, 21 a, 23 c, 23 d, 23 e.

These incursions of prescriptive right in the tenth century are not at all comparable to the demoralizing decentralization going on across the channel, because the circumstances under which the land-owning magnates were given rights in England were utterly different. The *hlafords* were deliberately worked into the main structure of law enforcement, as this was reconstituted in the course of the tenth century, as a part of the policy of strong kings. But these functions give a new starting point for the acquisition of privilege by adverse possession under weak kings or in time of war. For it is significant that these sweeping changes in the law are for over a century not paralleled by the addition of new matter in the charters or by any other forms of written title. This happens only after the changes in police, procedure and sanctions are long settled. In this interval, then, what can be acquired in addition to doom right will only be by prescription.

The situation under which these prescriptive rights grow will be clarified if we take a brief view of the changes in the law in the tenth century. Noteworthy is the reconstruction of the whole system of thief catching and the radical sharpening of the sanctions taken against thieves. The duty of pursuit is imposed directly upon the hundred and the *hlafords,* and is enforced by rigid penalties.[76] The adult thief now suffers death and forfeiture, irrespective of how he is taken or convicted.[77] The forfeitures are divided by giving half to the hundred, and half to the thief's lord after the plaintiff's compensation has been paid.

[76] II *Ew.* 4; IV *As.* 6, 3; III *Em.* 2; *Hu.* 2 *et seq.*

[77] The growth in the sanction is indicated by II *As.* 1, 3 where the captured thief gets 40 days prison and 120 shillings ransom to the king, recidivists, wergeld or prison. III *As.* 6 and IV *As.* 3 provides for transplantation. The London Association doom of Aethelstan provides for seizure of property (VI *As.* 1, 1). *Ceapgield* goes to the person robbed, then one-third to the wife, one-third to the crown and one-third to the association, but if he has *bocland* or bishop's land one-half of this to the lord and one-half to the association. In Eadgar's law (*Hu.* 2, 1) the property is divided after *ceapgield,* one-half to the thief's lord and one-half to the hundred. Any men the thief has go to the thief's lord. *Ceapgield* means amount in restitution.

Where the thief escapes, the duty of paying *angyld* still falls on the surety.

From the viewpoint of sanctions there is no longer a line to be drawn between handhavingness and non-handhavingness.[78] Nevertheless the procedural structure is not changed. The right of immediate execution is implicit in the rules of hue, but apparently there is a trial in the case of a protracted following of the spoor, for the law allows this tracking of the stolen goods to serve in lieu of plaintiff's foreoath:[79] The defendant's right to call warrantors in cases where the goods alone are grounds of suspicion is preserved.[80]

Matching these measures of police and punishment is the elaboration of the system of suretyship for satisfying judgments and for good behavior[81] (of which we shall speak further in another connection), the formulation of a special procedure for dealing with persons whose ill fame set them apart from other men,[82] the setting up of a sort of crime prevention service by designating in county and city persons whose duty it was to witness transfers of cattle[83] to prevent *bona fide* commercial transactions from being upset by hysterical theft charges.

However efficiently the new law may have been enforced there is no denying that there was here an attempt at integration built about the local unit, the hundred. The landlords were to cooperate for police work and to assure judgment, but later evidence indicates they were too important to remain content with the share allotted them. Since they were responsible at two ends of the process of law enforcement, there was ample room for them to make extortions which could ripen into positive custom. The point where seignorial claims could transgress the lines laid

[78] IV *As.* 6. No distinction is even attempted in *Hu.* 2.
[79] V *As.* 2.
[80] Liebermann, *Glossar, Anefang, passim.*
[81] *Infra*, p. 425.
[82] *Infra*, p. 414.
[83] IV *Eg.* 3, 1–6.

down in the dooms was clearly in the commutation of things done beyond the letter of duty: by turning a hue into a distraint, by the familiar expedient of exacting ransom—the man from the jail, the cattle from the pound—by making a forfeiture upon a handhaving hanging and not surrendering the hundred's share.

### ROYAL PREROGATIVE AND FISCAL PRIVILEGE

The defeasance of public rights at the time of Cnut's accession appears to have proceeded so far[84] that a new remedy was needed to reinvigorate the administration of the law. The time had passed when the landbook could be used for this purpose for it had become preeminently an instrument of property law.[85] The matters which needed regulation were questions of personal duty because the dooms had consistently emphasized this. In consequence if private rights were to be moved out of the murk of prescription, a form of documentation not distinctly a deed was essential. This form was the writ.[86]

Cnut is the first king to employ the writ for the conveyance or remembrance of privilege. The writ uses new and distinctive formulae and passes matter theretofore not the object of grant. It does not displace the landbooks for these continue to be issued

---

[84] On the seizure of rights by lords under Aethelred, Liebermann, *Erklärungen* on II *Cnut* 12. The provision I *Atr.* 1, 14 that the king gets wite from *bocland* owners indicates previous encroachments here.

[85] Once a body of "bocland law" is built up (Jolliffe, *English Bookright*, 50 *E.H.R.* 17 et seq.), this was inevitable.

[86] The writs are mostly in Kemble *C.D.* Nothing authoritative has yet been written on the history of the writ form. The best attempts are in Hall, *op. cit.*, 169, 201; Bresslau, *Internationale Beziehungen im Urkundenwesen des Mittelalters*, 5 *Archiv für Urkundenwesen*, 48 et seq. The earliest writ is one of Aethelred. Stevenson, 27 *E.H.R.*, 5 n. 16 denies its authenticity, *contra* Bresslau, *op. cit.*, 48. We need not discuss it because it is not jurisdictional. The earliest writ dealing with jurisdiction on whose authenticity there is general agreement is the Cnut writ, Earle, *Handbook to the Landcharters*, 233. We shall deal with the writs imparting jurisdiction from Cnut to the end of the Anglo-Saxon period, treating them all as valid except where otherwise specifically indicated. There has, of course, been no diplomatic work done on these documents as a group.

both by Cnut and the Confessor in substantially the old form of mere quittance.[87] But the writ has eventually a direct effect upon charter style, perhaps even in Anglo-Saxon times, for there are a handful of charters of the Confessor, supposed to be genuine,[88] where the new formulae, obviously lifted from the writs, are embedded. It is, therefore, correct to say that the new formulary development is definitely connected with the writ and with writ theory and is not due to any change in the concept of bookland or the function of the *boc*.

The earliest writ whose authenticity is generally admitted has been dated 1020.[89] By an unjustified acceptance of the continental distinction between *carta* and *notitia*[90] the writ has long been treated as evidentiary and not dispositive.[91] This description does not fit the pre-conquest Anglo-Saxon writs which deal with privilege. They use past and present tense.[92] When they speak as of the moment they are no less dispositive than the modern deed.

[87] Cnut's charters exempt from *regali tributo* or *terrenae servitutis* or all things "quae ad ipsa loca pertinere dinoscuntur" or the lands are "libera" saving the usual *trinoda necessitas*. The Confessor's landbooks are much the same.

[88] Kemble, nos. 808, 813, 907, 916. All of these charters bear marks of suspicion. No. 808 leaves out the reservation of bridgework; no. 813 uses *ordel* and *oreste;* (Liebermann, *Glossar, Zweikampf* 5 d); no. 817 contains quittance of shires and hundred in Norman form; no. 907 uses the Norman *ne intromittat;* no. 916 renders toll, *theloneum,* and uses the suspicious phrase "nec juris regalis fragmine."

[89] Earle, *Handbook to the Landcharters* (1888) 232.

[90] Brunner, *Carta und Notitia* in 1 *Abhandlungen* 458; *Die fränkisch romanische Urkunde* in *Forschungen* 596; the former recently criticized, Steinacker, *Die Antiken Grundlagen der Frühmittelalterlichen Privaturkunden* (1927) 11.

[91] Maitland, *Domesday Book,* 262. Hall, *op. cit.,* 203, sees that the writ is sometimes dispositive: "In a majority of cases it must be regarded as a precept confirming or completing the privileges or possessions already conveyed by a former grant. In other cases, however, these are actually granted or conveyed by the writ itself." Hazeltine in his preface to Whitelocke, *Anglo-Saxon Wills* (1930), xxxii, n. 4 states: "Documents in the writ form were usually only of evidential value." Stevenson in 11 *E.H.R.,* 733, n. 2, accepts Brunner's dichotomy.

[92] The Confessor's Anglo-Saxon writs of conveyance in 4 Kemble *C.D.,* show that more writs use the present tense than the past. The form "ic

If they are evidentiary they must refer to a charter or to a symbolic livery of seisin. There is no trustworthy evidence of symbolic livery of seisin until Norman times.[93] On the other hand, the charters (with but the few exceptions noted) contain no clauses or formulae to which the formulae in the writs could correspond.[94] One is therefore driven to the conclusion that when the writs deal with privilege they are themselves the muniments of title.[95]

This change in the form of written title is no less striking than the fact that the new substantive matter is passed as positive privi-

wille" (for example, nos. 832, 838) is as immediate an expression as "ic an." In the form "ic an heom eft swa" (e.g. 846) *eft* does not mean "again" but "moreover"; cf. Liebermann, *Wörterbuch,* who so renders this term as it is used in *Lad* for which chancery formulae are employed.

[93] Turner, *Bookland and Folkland,* 358, makes a lot of livery, citing indiscriminately Britton, early French practice, some charters and late English practice. The argument is very adequately disposed of by Jolliffe, *English Bookright,* 50 E.H.R. Most of the writers who argue for livery of seisin by symbol cite Pollock, *English Land Laws* (3 ed.) 199–200. Two of the charters used by him were marked by Kemble as forgeries. "But," says Pollock, "the like incident must have been found in genuine originals which the forger was copying," an incredibly naïve argument especially since Liebermann (*Glossar, Grundbesetz* 16 f) has characterized all the other Kemble charters but one as manufactured after 1066 when the Norman practice of symbolic livery was doubtless introduced. The one valid charter, Kemble no. 12, is obscure: "Igitur subnixis precibus imploro, ut nullus post obitum meum, de ea cespitis conditione tollere uel auferre quippiam, etc." Pollock's two cases from the Black Book of Peterborough were accepted by Stubbs but not subjected to further test. Jolliffe, *English Bookright,* 50 E.H.R., 3–4 makes the point that transfer of the book is enough and that if livery was needed "it found its own symbolism divorced from that of ancient custom." In connection with the controversy about livery it is worth noting that there is one bit of undisputed Anglo-Saxon evidence regarding the carrying of sods to the altar, the charm for hexed land in Grein, *Bibliothek der A.S. Poesie* (Beowulf etc.) (1883), 312, suggesting the ceremony recited in the charters is concerned with benediction, not livery.

[94] The concurrence would have to be in the exemption clauses. The "free of all earthly service" is the only clause to which the writ formulae could possibly have reference. Apart from the fact that the substance here was not *sac* and *soc* and is never so designated, it seems incredible that a quittance would be notified in terms of positive grant.

[95] In the Domesday inquest writ, seal and messenger (for livery) are

lege—not as mere quittance—and that it is conveyed as a *per-sonal* right. This is a radical departure from the landbook tradition which merely liberated land from all earthly services. Obviously an instrument in the terms of the earliest authentic writ: "I proclaim that I have granted to him [Aethelnoth] that he be worthy of [entitled to] his *sac* and *soc* . . ."[96] by giving a personal privilege has a legal effect different from the older form of land quittance in that the individual is enabled to use his franchise without reference to restrictions implicit as a matter of law in a particular type of tenure.[97] It is true the privilege is connected with landholding because the writs ordinarily limit the rights to the donee's lands.[98] But it has no generic connection

regarded as evidence of identical value. Hall, *op. cit.,* 170. Some entries, for example, 1 *D.B.* 47 b; 60 b; 169 indicate that the writ is regarded as the muniment of title in the Confessor's time.

The fact that the writ is addressed to persons other than the donee does not detract from its dispositive force. Obviously a document which gives privileges must notify the officers whose jurisdiction will be decimated thereby. We know from Domesday Book that the Confessor's writs are sometimes produced by the donees (e.g., 1 *D.B.* 59; 78 b; II, 360 b) a point tending to show that despite the address the donee gets the document because it gives him title. Bresslau, *op. cit.,* 50, n. 4 points out the Frankish *indiculus* went to the donee and thinks the same rule probably applied in England.

[96] "I, Canute, the king, greet all my bishops, and my earls, and my reeves, in each shire, in which Archbishop Aethelnoth and the brotherhood at Christchurch have land, friendly. And I proclaim to you that I have granted him that he be worthy of his Sac and Sócn, and Grithbryce and Hámsócn, and Forsteall, and Infangtheof, and Flymenafirmth, in town and out of town, and over Christchurch, and as many thanes as I have allowed him. And I will not that any man shall take anything therein, save himself and his stewards; seeing that I have granted these rights unto Christ, for the eternal salvation of my soul; and it is my will that no man break this,—on my friendship: (i.e., on pain of losing it)." Earle, *op. cit.,* 233. We have corrected the rendition of certain technical words.

[97] The grants are to persons or to Christ and the saint of a particular church. They give the land "mid sac and mid soc" (Kemble, 842) or the grantee is granted "ðat hi habben ðarto sace and socne" (no. 829) or "hy habben ðaerofer saca 7 socna" (no. 843) or the "abbod . . . beo his sac wrðe and his socna ofer his hagan land" (no. 856). The grant to the saint is still understood as made to a person; this doctrine summarized, Goebel, *Cases and Materials,* 563.

[98] There are cases where the right goes as to the grantee's men, e.g.,

with *bocland* or the *boc,* since the matters granted are given without reference to the type of holding, for these are not matters involved in the job which the book charter does. This is clearly to be inferred from the fact that to abbeys which have long possessed books, writs granting *sac* and *soc* and other privileges are issued.[99]

There is not wanting other proof that the privileges carried by writ are personal. Thus the rights (*gerihta*) over which Cnut in his doom asserted prerogative, like ambush, protection breach and *hamsocn,*[100] are occasionally joined with *sac* and *soc* in the king's precepts. These special prerogative rights the king gives, says the doom, "when he wishes to do further honor to some one." The grant of mere *sac* and *soc* may not be made a particular personal distinction but it is passed by the same dispositive words as the prerogative privileges and so it likewise operates *in personam*. The rule once made is fixed. The normal entry in Domesday for *sac* and *soc* is in some person—living man or saint.[101] In the early twelfth century the *Leges Henrici* tell us

Earle, *op. cit.,* 233; Kemble, nos. 831, 856. Liebermann, *Glossar, Gerichtsbarkeit,* 26, says private jurisdiction is a *"Realgerechtigkeit,"* appurtenant to the land. It may well have become appurtenant in certain cases, following the natural tendency in this direction, but the formulae themselves indicate this is not the chancery's theory.

[99] The relations of the *sac* and *soc* grant to the conveyance of realty is shown by two documents in Kemble, nos. 938, 941. The first a notice of grant by Earl Leofric mentions only the transfer of land, whereas the second, a confirmation by Bishop Lifwig, speaks of the grant as given "cum uictu et cum hominibus, cum saca et cum socne, et cum omnibus in quibus constat mandatum regis; . . ." Obviously the king's "mandate" here referred to is an act collateral to the conveyance itself. If the donor had right of *sac* and *soc* or if this inhered in the land he would not need a mandate to pass these rights.

[100] II *Cnut,* 12 and note Maitland's suggestion regarding regional variations in the number of *rectitudines, Domesday Book,* 82. *Cf.* also *infra* note 104.

[101] Note further that in some counties like Northampton and Suffolk it is rare that a *sac* and *soc* T.R.E. (*tempore regis Edwardi*) is vested in a grantee *nunc* (1086). This seems to indicate that the privilege disappeared with the Saxon holder, and was not reconveyed. Note further on the lapsing of fiscal privilege with the death of the grantee, 1 *D.B.* 280 b.

this is a personal franchise.[102] And at a much later day the judges sitting in *quo warranto* cases still adhere to the traditional principle.[103]

We come at length to consider the substance of the new formulae. To all those connected with crime they will impart at the least fiscal privileges. For reasons to be later explained we believe this minimum is all that the grant accomplishes in Anglo-Saxon times. The immediate problem in any event is the identification and description of the particular perquisite named. In every case, since they are words of grant, of grant by the king, a grant which the king is under no obligation to make and may refuse to make, they stand for something beyond and in addition to what the grantee has by law, and for something the crown has to give. As to the special royal rights, the *gerihta,* there is no doubt. On these Cnut has put a double ticket—royal and for special honor. He will give them, but only to favorites. His dooms, moreover, leave no doubt as to the meaning of the several *gerihta—forsteall* is ambush, *mundbryce* is breach of protection, *hamsocn* is housebreaking, *flymenafyrmthe* is harboring of outlaws. A grant of any one of them will at least mean a right to the £5 wite which is the king's forfeit for infraction of any of his special rights.

But there are other privileges enumerated in writs, *infangtheof, toll* and *team, sac* and *soc*—here named in the inverse order of importance—whose quality as something royal is less blatant, for they do not appear in the list of *gerihta.* This does not indicate that they are not as royal or as prerogative as the rights included in that famous list, for royal rights slip in and out of that roster almost at the whim of the scribe indicating that the listing is a matter of convenient description of franchise-granting policy.[104]

[102] *Hn.* 19, 3 "Nec sequiter socna regis data maneria, sed magis est ex personis."
[103] For the general rule that royal franchises unless appurtenant are extinguished by alienation, Rex *v.* Shirland, *Y.B. 6–7 Ed. II* (S.S. 29) 181.
[104] So the reservation of *fihtwite, fyrdwite, griðbryce* and *hamsocne*

*Infangtheof* is a new legal term. It is not even grammatically a mere vernacular rendition and hence a revival of the *furis comprehensio* formula of a century and more ago,[105] for *infangtheof* is given as a positive right, not as a quittance. It is true that the *"fangen"* (capture) in this composite word shows that the hand-having case is still involved. But what indicates that the legal effect of this franchise is something entirely different from the *furis comprehensio* is the lapse of the system of positive law which gave the older term its meaning.[106] *Infangtheof* has as its background a new and different system of rules for dealing with theft, quite inconsistent with those to which *furis comprehensio* owed its meaning. The only common element in the royal grant is in each instance purely fiscal. The *furis comprehensio* was the grant (in form a quittance) of a royal power to ransom, a prerogative vested in the crown by Ine's law. In consequence, when the dooms in force in Cnut's day are silent on this power even in the crown, prescribing ransomless hanging for all thieves, the central element of the old concept disappears.[107] Further the wergeld, the measure of this ransom, which was under Ine's law the sole economic sanction, has given way to complete chattel forfeiture, half to the thief's lord, half to the hundred, i.e., to

for the Danelaw, II *Cnut,* 15. And note in 1060 (Ms. G) *flymenafyrmðe* is added to the rights in Wessex, II *Cnut,* 12.

[105] Liebermann, *Glossar, infangentheof* relates the two, carrying out the suggestion of Kemble, *C.D.,* Intro. xlvii, and Maitland, *Domesday Book,* 276.

[106] The term does not appear before the 11th century after the great corpus of thief legislation from Aethelstan through Aethelred has been enacted.

[107] Jolliffe, *Origin of the Hundred in Kent,* 162–3 doubts the relation of the earlier and later franchise but he uses the term *infangtheof* as if it were identical with *furis comprehensio.* He overlooks the disappearance of ransom in the dooms, but by treating II *Eadmund* 5 as giving thieves respite from the harsh contemporary penalties, conjectures a form of trial. Jolliffe does not explain why he rejects Liebermann's rendition of the Eadmund passage which points to quite the opposite result. Jolliffe goes on to relate *Hu.* 2, to this law of Eadmund despite Liebermann's suggestion that III *Eadmund* 2 is meant. Liebermann's suggestion accords with the rest of Eadgar's hundred law and Jolliffe's suggestion does not.

the crown. By now the crown's right is therefore the right to half the chattels.[108] It passes this by its new grant of *infangtheof,* and no more than this, for the right to hang is still a common right, now indeed a common duty. No grant is needed for it any more than in Ine's day.

The franchises of *toll* and *team, sac* and *soc* both present a question of a quite different order, for before the gist of the franchises can be examined the language intention must be set-

[108] We treat the hundred's share as accruing to the crown for despite conjecture regarding the "corporateness" of the hundred (Laski, *Early History of the English Corporation,* 30 *H.L.R.,* 561; Liebermann, *Glossar, hundred,* 20) there is no direct proof that the hundred can keep any and all revenues which fall to it by the words of a particular doom. There is a distinct change in the wording of these laws over the tenth century indicating a definite shift in fiscal ideas as the hundred grows in importance as an administrative unit. II *As.* 20, 4 gives the men of a distraining party half, and half to the king, but III *Em.* 2, provides a mulct for failure to perform hue—120 shillings to the king and 30 shillings to the hundred. *Hu.* 2, 1, in dividing forfeited property speaks of the hundred as the recipient of half. Clearly by Eadgar's time it is not correct to say as does Maitland (*op. cit.,* 287) "the men of the hundred," for the privilege is no longer several. (*Cf.* also III *Eg.,* 7, 1.) The sum of the mulct (30 s.) spoken of in III *Em.* 2, as going to the hundred is identical with that mentioned in *Af.* 38, 2 for fighting in a lower court before the king's earl's bailiff, suggesting the mulct of contempt of the hundred may be destined for the hundred bailiff. (*Cf.* also I *Ew.,* 2, 1, where 30 shillings is the first *oferhyrnesse,* i.e., contempt mulct to the king.) However, even if the procedural mulcts go to the hundred as a whole the penalty of forfeiture for theft was clearly too large to be left *in toto* to a unit whose function was chiefly administrative in the public interest. We have assumed throughout chattel forfeiture is intended by the phrase "all he has" (eall ðaet he age) II *As.* 20, 4; III *Eg.* 7, 1 (*Hu.* 2, 1 assumes it). If it is intended to include land, the argument against the hundred being the recipient is stronger, for there are charters which show the king takes this upon forfeiture: Birch no. 951; Kemble no. 692; Kemble, no. 1389, 1310; Birch, no. 595.

It should further be pointed out that although most of our evidence regarding royal interest in local revenues not attached to royal demesne is late, what little proof there is points to the judicial profits of the hundred being included in what the sheriff farms if he is farmer, Morris, *Medieval English Sheriff,* 30–1. In the early eleventh century the hundred court is an important court of first instance, where the many mulcts which the dooms say go to the king (short of *gerihta*) were collected. This suggests that where the hundred is named as in *Hu.* 2, 1, it is intended only as a place of receipt.

tled. The resort to alliteration, a convention of Anglo-Saxon poetry that carries over into even the driest contemporary prose,[109] apart from sustaining the manifest rhythm in the writs,[110] has a direct neological purpose. For although in using alliteration discrete ideas are sometimes casually joined to produce a sound effect without destroying the identity of each word, it sometimes happens that as the separate words approach each other in meaning, a new concept will be produced from the union, obliterating the original meaning of each word.[111]

*Toll* and *team* is an alliteration where the two terms retain their identity for their meanings are so discrete that it is difficult to blur them. Taken separately *toll* is said to be the right to take toll, and *team* the procedure where the defendant accused of having stolen goods in his possession may call warrantors. Under the Anglo-Saxons toll is taken at market and at points of transit.[112] Quittance of tolls on single ships had been granted by charter as early as the eighth century.[113] Market rights which were for a long time tightly controlled were granted if at all only by inference as where a grantee was permitted to keep weights and measures.[114] The new franchise of *toll* which is not at all unusual appears first when the restrictions on markets are

[109] Luick, *Englische Metrik* (2 Paul, *Grundriss der Deutschen Philologie* 995) discusses the use in Aelfric's prose. Compare also the piece *Becwaeð*, Liebermann, *Gesetze*, 400. Alliterative formulae collected generally in Hoffmann, *Reimformeln in Westgermanischen* (1885); Liebermann, *Wörterbuch*, *Alliteration* and *Formel*.

[110] The swing is achieved by the cumulation of formulae like "on wode and on felde," "binnen burh and butan burh," "weorc and ware"; "inne freols and ut of freols"; "be lande and be strande," "swa full and swa forð" etc. On the rhythmic scheme of the formulae, Hoffmann, *op. cit.*, 13.

This aspect of the writ has never been studied. The reason for it is probably mnemonic. The precepts are read in shire and hundred and the suitors may be called on subsequently to bear witness.

[111] Ten Brink in 2 Paul, *Grundriss*, 524; Hoffmann, *op. cit.*, 10.

[112] Liebermann, *Glossar*, *Zollabgabe*. Maitland, *Domesday Book*, 194.

[113] Birch, nos. 149, 150, 152, 171, 173, 177, 188.

[114] On the control of market rights, Liebermann, *Glossar*, *Handel* 8 b, *Markt* 2; Stephenson, *Borough and Town* (1933) 65. The grant of weights and measures made as early as 857, Kemble, no. 280. *Cf.* also no.

relaxed.[115] *Toll* as used in the writs looks like a metonymy for the right to have a market, for this is where toll is properly levied.[116] *Team,* however, certainly does not mean the right to hold the accusatory theft plus warranty procedure. This warranty procedure was the subject of constant general legislation and was hence not regarded as subject to local custom. Moreover, a doom of Aethelred had specifically restricted this to the king's towns, i.e., where a king's reeve was sitting.[117] There is, consequently, every reason why a procedure so preeminently royal would not pass as a minor franchise. For in the writs *toll* and *team* is a minor franchise, less even than *infangtheof.* As such, even if one were justified in separating *team* from its companion *toll* it is to be taken not as giving a right to warranty procedure but as giving only the mulcts of such a proceeding. This is an interpretation for which there is some support in Cnut's law.[118] If one emphasizes the combination of *team* with *toll,* there is reason to suppose the word has some connection with the market privilege, perhaps the right to maintain on an estate the standing witness for sales transactions which had been instituted for hundred

316 (starred, but *semble* elsewhere treated as genuine by Kemble, 2 *Sachsen in England,* 61) where weights and measures are given and the grantee gets *toll* on trade in his court. Kemble no. 1084 and no. 1075 are recognitions of market rights *in hiscis verbis.* After Eadward's restrictions such grants necessarily fall in abeyance.

[115] Definite by II *As.* 12, 13, and supplemented under Eadgar (IV 6, 2) where witnesses to transactions are instituted in the country. II *Cnut* 24 speaks of transactions in the country as well as the city. Salzman, *English Trade in the Middle Ages,* 121, asserts that the restrictions of Aethelstan could not be enforced. It is probable that a distinction must be drawn between cattle trading and market for general commodities as soon as the latter type of trade became important. Stephenson, *op. cit.,* 71 states general trade begins under Aethelred. This supplies the background of the toll franchise.

[116] Toll is taken at transit or terminal points and at market according to IV *Aethelred. Cf.* the typical thirteenth-century perversion: the test of the right to hold market is the right to take toll. Salzman, *Legal Status of Markets,* 2 *Cambridge Historical Journal,* 207.

[117] III *Atr.* 6, 1.

[118] II *Cnut,* 24, 1.

and town, and whose existence was a prime condition of a regulated *team* procedure.[119]

The formula *sac and soc* is an instance where, by the alliterative joinder, a deliberate coinage of new meaning is achieved and the primary meanings of the constituent words effaced. *Sac* means plea or dispute[120] in Aethelred's dooms and *socn* is used in the sense of jurisdiction.[121] One might guess the joinder of the words meant "pleas and jurisdiction" but this cannot be proven.[122] Indeed it is only some fifty-odd years after the formula comes into use that *sac* stands for *socn*[123] and *socn* for the phrase *sac and socn*[124] indicating that there is but one idea involved and that the function of phrase is so well understood that either of the constituent words will carry the full meaning.

The elusiveness of the whole formulary design complicates modern understanding of the function of *sac and soc*. The king is giving something out of his rights and we must suppose that a non-specific formula conveys non-specific rights. By non-specific rights here is intended the complex of fiscal privileges (exclusive of *gerihta* and thief forfeits) collected in the ordinary court, the public hundred—wites, wergelds, *overseunessas, miskennings,* etc., which slide off modern pens as "judicial profits." This is in fact the only resource where general words of grant could subtract from royal right. It is, then, from the plea-profits, exclusive of theft and the *gerihta,* collected in the hundred for the king by the local officer that a *sac and soc* grantee is favored. Three passages in the 1060 version of Cnut's dooms show this to be probable.

[119] IV *Eadgar, 6 et seq.*
[120] V *Atr.* 19—*sacu;* X *Atr. Pro.* 1—*sace.*
[121] III *Atr.* 11.
[122] In the dooms the formula is not used. In the private piece *Becwaeð* 3, 2 the combination *ne sace ne socne* appears but there is no clue as to its meaning. The poetic uses in 2 Grein, *Angelsächsisches Wörterbuch,* s.v. *sacu* and *socen.* Liebermann, *Glossar, Gerichtsbarkeit,* 1 *et seq.,* discusses the formula.
[123] 2 *D.B.* 391 b; 409; 416; *Inq. Eliensis* 4 *D.B.* 502 b.
[124] Liebermann, *Glossar, Gerichtsbarkeit,* 1 i.

These passages deal with perjury, robbery and too early marriage of widows, the mulcts in the first case being the equivalent
of *healsfang,* in the other two of wergeld.[125] In the earliest redaction of the Cnut dooms, king or *landrica* alternate as recipi-
ents of a mulct for perjury; the king alone is the recipient of
wergeld for robbery; the king, or "the person to whom the king
has given it," receives the wergeld for the violations of marriage
law. Now it is a significant reflection of the rise of the new types
of writ-grant when the 1060 scribe finds it necessary in the perjury case to qualify the word *landrica* with the phrase, "who has
his *socne.*" The change in conditions is even more sharply indicated in the robbery case. Here the scribe adds a wergeld recipient alternate to the king. This alternate he describes as "he who
has his *socne.*" In the marriage law the 1060 version describes the
"person to whom the king has given it (wergeld)" as "he who
has *socne.*"[126] In all these cases *socne* stands for *sac and soc* because a grant is implied or expressly mentioned and only the unspecific *sac and soc* formula would convey the unspecific mulcts,
i.e., those not given a particular name. Furthermore the fact that
the 1060 scribe does not touch up or qualify other passages in
Cnut's law dealing with the rights that any *landrica* has as a
matter of general law because he is a *landrica,*[127] points unerringly to the existence of a special class of *"landrica* with *socn."*[128]
Finally, the passage dealing with the violation of marriage law
is phrased in terms that indicate beyond any doubt that a fiscal
privilege alone is intended.[129]

[125] II *Cnut* 37; 63; 73, 1.
[126] "þe his socne ahe"; "oððe wið þone his socne age"; þe he [the
king] his socne geunnen haebbe."
[127] So in the new Cnut rule (II, 48, 1) where the *hlaford* gets *fulwite*
for the wounding of church tax collector; repetition of III *Eg.* 7, 1 in II
*Cnut* 25, 1.
[128] The existence of this new status category fixed in II *Cnut* 71, 3
where a higher relief is exacted from a king's thegn in the Danelaw "ðe
his socne haebbe."
[129] "7 si he his weres scyldig wið þone cingc oððe wið þone, þe he his
socne geunnen haebbe." "hit" [wer] of Ms. B. = "his socne" in Ms. G.

Of course the mulcts just discussed are only ingredients of a *sac and soc* grant. All three of them apparently are innovations of Cnut, and so account for the necessity felt by the 1060 scribe to indicate that they were embraced by such a grant, the normal bulk of which was made up of the more ancient wites, collected in the hundred on the basis of the folklaw tariffs. These, being now definitively the subject of grant and of grant by technical formula, can no longer be prescribed for.[130] Beyond what the dooms allow a lord, neither the possession of land nor the faculties of status alone will hereafter make a man "worthy of his wite," as the phrase went in Aethelred's time[131] because this is now a matter of specific privilege.

[130] Liebermann, *Glossar, Gerichtsbarkeit,* 16 B, remarks that the grant of *sac* and *soc* from Cnut's time on seems rather to fix a known state of affairs than to be the introduction of something new. There is some reason to believe Cnut did something to overhaul the structure of private rights. In II *Cnut,* 79 it is provided that the county must certify that a man had performed his duties to the state if he was to enjoy his tenure and have free disposal of it at death. Since in III *Atr.* 14 undisputed possession is set up as a test of land rights, Cnut's law suggests a traverse of prescription by a primitive *quo warranto*—at least to the extent that a quiet enjoyment depends upon the performance of public duties. Of course, the effect of the assertion of prerogative in II *Cnut* 12 is to cut off any right not properly documented. Liebermann has indicated both as to *forsteall* and *hamsocn* there had been some tendency toward this change (*Glossar, Rechtssperrung, Heimsuchung, Kronprozess*) but until Cnut no definite formulation was made.

[131] The expression is used in I *Atr.* 1, 7 providing for wergeld payment by the surety of a man fleeing the ordeal. Liebermann (*Erklärungen,* 145) thinks the distinction between a mere lord and one "privileged" already exists. Except for the wite charters and *furis comprehensio* there is no evidence this early (980–1015) of general privileges by charter. The expression implies a class of persons entitled and VI *Atr.* 51 points to wites being in the hands of church establishments more or less at large. One must suppose in the absence of contemporary documented title that the rights had been acquired by prescription. II *Cnut* 30, 3 b amends the earlier I *Atr.* 5 which gave wergeld to the lord (without mentioning privilege) of the man who failed at the ordeal by adding ðe his wites wyrðe sy. II *Cnut* 30, 6 repeats substantially I *Atr.* 1, 7 but inserts the king as the alternative recipient. This suggests that by Cnut's time the crown is the source of the wite privilege. Since we know the crown now gives privileges by writ it is fair to infer a connection between the dooms' "entitled to (worthy of) wite" and the privilege by writ.

None of the passages which help to build up a picture of the
new franchises are cast in terms which imply judicial powers in
the grantees. Further there is no hint in Cnut's laws regarding
the existence of private courts;[132] neither is there anything to
show a general policy of excluding public officers from the
grantee's lands. As we have already said the tentative use in one
or two writs of a formula directed to this end allows the inference that this was very exceptional. If there were any evidence
that *landrica* or franchisemen could implead a malefactor there
might be some support for a conversion of the grantee's fiscal
privileges into justiciary powers.[133] But there is no sign that indi-

---

[132] Hundred court and county court are the courts with which II *Cnut*,
17, 1; 19; 27, deal.

If one takes the passages in Aethelstan's, Eadgar's and Aethelred's laws
where *hlaford, landhlaford* or *landrica* are used (e.g., II *As.* 10; VI *As.* 1,
1; II *Eg.* 3, 1; III *Eg.* 7, 1; IV *Eg.* 8, 1; IV *Eg.* 11; III *Atr.* 3, 2 *et seq.*)
there is not a rule which is not explicable on the grounds that the personage referred to is landowner, lord, or supposed to aid in a public function.
Liebermann's frequent rendition "Immunitätsherr," seems to beg the issue, because there is nothing whatever to show that any of the rights or
duties stipulated are connected with immunity. That general jurisdictional rights either by prescription or by charter with words of immunity
can scarcely be presumed for the *hlaford* is indicated by the pieces *Rectitudines* and *Gerefa* (960–1060) the tracts on an estate economy. There is
nothing here about judicial rights or functions. *Rectitudines* opens with
the statement of the right and duties of the thegn (i.e. the lord of the estate) which include the *trinoda necessitas* and other matters directed by
the king of which examples are given. The statement that there "arise on
many estates further charges on the land (*landriht*) by king's ban," indicates "public" rather than immunity control. In *Gerefa*, 1, it is stated that
the wise bailiff must know "ge hlafordes landriht ge folces gerihtu." Liebermann (*Gesetze*, 453) renders the *hlafordes landriht*, "Gutsrecht," but
this term does not imply lord's legislation since it must be a reference to
the *landriht* in *Rectitudines*, 1. One charter that points to the lack of legislative power of the lord is Kemble, no. 640 of Aethelred (983) where
violators of the donees' fishing rights are by charter expressly to be held as
*furti criminis obnoxius.*

[133] On the complaint in Anglo-Saxon procedure, Bechert, *Einleitung
des Rechtsgangs nach Angelsächsischem Recht*, 47 Z.R.G.[2], 3, 7. On the
cultivation of approvers, 113. The accusation by the lord comes in with
the Normans: *Leges Henrici*, 63, 1 f; 67, 2; 44, 2. The document, Kemble,
no. 918, is a precept of the Confessor's relict to a hundred in her possession
regarding a plea but it hardly throws any light on the point in the text.

viduals could in any way be deterred from prosecuting their claims in public courts. The most complete procedural document we possess[134] for this period shows that the exaction of the wite mulct in causes of wrongdoing was a part of the whole process of final settlement *inter partes* of a plaint begun by a private accusation. Yet the recipient of the wite is by no means in the position of the fisc in the developed Frankish *securitas* procedure which is essentially a tripartite concord by plaintiff, defendant and *iudex*.[135] In the Anglo-Saxon document mentioned, which deals with the settlement of wergeld payment in homicide cases, the king's *mund* is first proclaimed over the agreeing parties, as an assurance against feud. Then the sums due are paid at stated intervals to the several creditors. The passage indicates that not the arbitrers who bring about the composition but someone else is the recipient of the *fihtwite*.[136] The person entitled appears simply as another creditor, suggesting in consequence that franchises of such wites are mere fiscal rights.[137]

There is no reason to believe that a grant of the royal *gerihta* involved justiciary rights any more than did grant of the unreserved wites. In the passages dealing with the prerogatives it is the fiscal aspect which is emphasized and nothing is said about procedure.[138] The right of the king to bestow the *gerihta* is not

---

[134] The piece designated by Liebermann, "Wergeldzahlung" (*Wer.*) *Gesetze*, 392 (c. 944–1060). The provisions relate to *twelfhynde* and *twyhynde* men. Liebermann (*Erklärungen*, 321) thinks it originates in Wessex.

[135] *Supra,* Chapter I, p. 38 n. 82. By III *Atr.* 13, 3 concord by private contract and by judicial proceeding are of equal effect.

[136] *Wer.* 6.

[137] The passages in II *Eadmund* 7–7, 3 (994–5) to which *Wer.* is related speak of *witan,* i.e., *sapientes,* as intermediaries and the paragraphs are so turned that one sees the law regulating intervention as the performance of an official duty. Like the chasing of thieves this is a public legal obligation and not an immunity right. If there were anything to show that the king's *mund* could be proclaimed by an immunist in any capacity, there might be some ground for supposing an occasional identity of arbitror and *fihtwite* creditor. There is no such evidence.

[138] II *Cnut* 12; 15 (the *gerihta*) must be read in connection with 13, 2 (outlawry) 58 (*borhbryce*) 61 (*griðbryce*), 62 (*hamsocn*).

subject to any express limitation. But it seems most unlikely that grants ran to full cognizance of the offenses (for which £5 were exacted) not only because this would have been incompatible with Cnut's policy of stricter law enforcement,[139] but because the dooms themselves are constantly emphasizing the crown's discretion of final punishment.[140] There is not even an exception made in favor of Cnut's protégé, the church, for the evidence shows that where the church shares the wites it does not have the actual jurisdiction.[141] Here one would expect evidence

[139] Larson, *Canute the Great* (1912), 281.

[140] Cnut apparently extends powers hitherto restricted to a few offenses. The royal discretion respecting death penalty exists as early as *Ine* 6 in cases of brawls in the king's house. In II *Eadmund*, 6, this discretion is repeated as to *mundbryce* and *hamsocn*. *Cf.* as to thieves, VI *Aethelstan*, 1, 4; III *Eadgar* 7, 3; false coiners III *Aethelred* 16; IV *ibid.*, 7, 3; violators of church peace, VIII *ibid.*, 1, 1. The scope of discretion in Cnut's law is best understood in the light of the penalties for major offenses. As of old, brawls in the king's court are punished by death with discretion in the crown, II *Cnut*, 59. *Husbryce* and arson, open theft, *murdrum*, and treason are botless, *ibid.*, 64. The false coiner loses his hand and has no right of money redemption, *ibid.*, 8, 1. The same punishment is set for wounding collectors of church dues but with a right of redemption, *ibid.*, 48. Perjury—a hand or half wergeld, *ibid.*, 36; *murdrum*—surrender to the injured kindred, *ibid.*, 56. Robbery—wergeld to the king, as redemption. *Griðbryce* in the army is punishable by death, II *ibid.*, 61. But *hamsocn* has only the £5 penalty. *Griðbryce* is punishable by loss of life and property with discretion in the king to pardon, I *Cnut*, 2, 2. The mutilations are explained in II *ibid.*, 2, 1 as a mitigation of death for the preservation of God's handiwork. The existence of occasional redemption to the king, or pardon, indicates a wider discretion than claimed theretofore. The theory is stated most broadly in II *Cnut*, 13 "se ðe útlages weorc gewyrce, wealde se cingc þaes friþes." The *Quadripartitus* renders *útlages weorc— opus utlagii* and it may mean generally any act entailing outlawry, *cf.* also Liebermann, *Wörterbuch, utlah.*

[141] Liebermann, *Glossar, Gerichtsbarkeit,* "It is certain the king's reeve held court in trials where the mulct flowed to the church. . . . The countless cases where church and state shared mulcts are all cases of trial before secular courts." As to perjury, II *Cnut,* 36; wounding of tithe collector, II *Cnut* 48; adultery, II *Cnut* 53, 1, where the trial is certainly secular, the bishop however fixing the penalty. Compare the 9th century grant of Aethelred the Ealdorman, Kemble no. 1075, dividing only the fiscal incidents.

　　In this connection consider also the letter of Aelfric to Wulfstan (1003-4) in Fehr, *Die Hirtenbriefe Aelfrics* (1914) 226 "Non est episco-

the other way if the right to a wite was also a right to hold court, for the church courts are already a going concern. This being the case in matters of ecclesiastical color like perjury, tithes, adultery, etc., there is little reason why a grant of *forsteall* or *hamsocn* would be intended to convey more than the right to receipt of profits.

When one compares the Frankish chartered immunity with the Anglo-Saxon it is difficult to escape the conclusion that whatever jurisdictional rights were exercised on the Island the privileges given by the charter had nothing much to do with powers of courtholding. In England before the appearance of the writ, private jurisdiction which piles up through prescription is connected essentially with status and with ownership of land and is officially recognized as a part of public duty in those laws that expect thegn or *hlaford* to perform public functions of police. The rights correlative to the duties are destructible through the loss of thegnship by the loss of status.[142] There is no wall of immunity raised about them. Nor does the writ do this when the magnate is given broad personal rights exercisable in all his lands. The one situation most favorable to private court-keeping is the possession of a hundred, yet no clear proof bolsters the conjecture that the transfer of the territorial unit facilitates a welding of feudal with public rights.[143] But admitting even the validity of this supposition, it is not to be conceded that when the Confessor breathed his last, private jurisdiction in England approached in nature or extent that exercised in the great Norman abbeys of Jumièges or Mont St. Michel and in the fiefs of his kinsman's chief tenants.

One phase of the Anglo-Saxon immunity remains to be con-

pus constitutus ad hoc ut sit iudex furem et latronum . . ." This may be addressed only to exercise of *any* secular functions by the bishops, but the fact that such a question is mooted as late as the 11th century indicates the bishops have a very different temporal background than their colleagues in France.

[142] *Cf.* III *Eadgar* 3; II *Cnut*, 15, 1.
[143] Compare here Maitland, *Domesday Book*, 289.

sidered. This is the quality it maintained to the very end, of something emanating in the first instance from the crown.[144] This stands out particularly in the case of the major wites which are rights not appurtenant to the land but royal privileges specially delegated. Whatever control over wrongs a single unit may have absorbed, it is not to be doubted that after Cnut had marked out the *gerihta* of the crown, these particular rights were thereafter not exercisable except by a special grant from the king, and they certainly could not be prescribed for. This is obvious from the positive grants of *fihtwite, mundbryce,* etc., but still more so from a laconic writ of the Confessor where a grant of *soc* is followed by the warning: "I am not aware that I granted thence to any man *hamsocn* or *grithbryce* or *forsteall* . . . or any of the rights which rightly belong there . . ."[145]

The question whether or not the *gerihta* were actually more than fiscal—were in fact justiciary rights—is not in issue on the point that after Cnut these major franchises were regarded as an independent *res* delegable only by the crown. In this respect the Anglo-Saxon franchises of a king's right were something more "public" and less "feudal" than the correlative right of blood justice in Normandy. If the Norman kings had forgotten or had never heard of the Carolingian theory of *causae criminales,* the practice of the Saxon kings was alternatively a sharp reminder or an inspiration for a policy still barred by circumstance in Normandy. Whatever the immigrant baron may have thought about or done with his grant of *sac* and *soc,* his *infangtheof* or his particular wites, the fact remains that the source of his rights over wrongs was constitutionally something less vague than it was at home.

[144] Cam, *Local Government in Francia and England,* 118, who makes the point that while magnates make grants, the documents are regrants of privileges from the crown and the consent of the king is sometimes referred to in the charter. *Cf.* also the writ in Kemble, no. 882, where the crown confirms.

[145] Kemble, no. 883.

KING AND FEUDATORY AFTER THE CONQUEST

The preservation of certain Anglo-Saxon words of art in the Conqueror's writs and charters links his policy toward franchise and immunity with that of his predecessor at least to the extent of furnishing a presumption of continuity.[146] This is, however, a presumption only as to the saving of royal rights implicit in the formulae. It cannot aid in defining jurisdictional matter granted after the Conquest, for changes in tenure, importation of foreign status concepts and current feudal ideas of courtkeeping shifted the whole societal structure which underlay documented privilege. The substance of matter granted therefore, even though expressed by so old a term as *sac and soc,* must be measured with reference to these changes. The most cursory view of Anglo-Norman sources shows this to be so. Domesday Book uses the Anglo-Saxon terms but it also has circumlocutions for *sac* and *soc* in sense of a right to penal mulcts,[147] or suit of court,[148] or jurisdiction generally, and the word is Latinized as *placitum*[149] or *consuetudo.*[150] In the translations of Cnut's dooms, *soc* ap-

---

[146] Liebermann, *Glossar, Urkunde* 2 a, citing Larson (*King's Household,* 199) states the Normans adopted the Saxon writ. *Cf.* also Haskins, *Norman Institutions,* 53–4. There is a possibility the Normans may have inherited vestiges of the Frankish *indiculi* (on which Brunner, *Schwurgerichte,* 76). Bresslau, *op. cit.,* 48 sees a similarity between these and the Anglo-Saxon writs. On the possibility that the Anglo-Saxon writ is due to foreigners, Lotharingian or Norman, in the Chancery, Davis, *Regesta,* Intro. xii. For comparison of the Anglo-Saxon *habenda* with Lotharingian documents, 1 Beyer, *Mittelrheinisches Urkundenbuch,* nos. 182, 189, 238, 274, 278, 293, 294. There are no Norman pre-conquest writs known.

[147] Maitland, *Domesday Book,* 99.

[148] *Ibid.,* 84 *et seq.*

[149] This is the apparent purport of entries like 1 *D.B.* 58 "placitis terrae," 1 *ibid.,* 175 "placitis francorum hominum," *Exon. Domesday,* 198 "consuetudines placitorum." In this connection it should be pointed out that Liebermann, *Glossar, Gerichtsbarkeit,* 16 suggests the *iura regalia placitorum* in Kemble, no. 915 is a 1050 rendition of *soc.* This document is apparently related to the Confessor's writ, no. 883, which is obscurely phrased "half nigende hundred socne" and suggests that no. 915 was a fabrication in aid of the presumably authentic no. 883.

[150] 1 *D.B.* 52; 2 *D.B.* 208; *Exon. Domesday,* 198, *consuetudines placi-*

pears as *consuetudo* or *privilegium,* wite as *forisfactura, mund-bryce* as *monte fractura* (breach of writ).[151] The *Leis Willelme* with its free use of French legal jargon suggests a wholesale effacement of ancient meanings.[152]

It is only their formal certainty which makes writ or charter a convenient point of departure for an inquiry into the distribution of jurisdiction after the conquest. The eventual definition of the elusive content of the form arises, as we have said, from the rivalry of royal policy and baronial pretension, with English status quo usually a pawn but occasionally a more mobile piece.

*torum.* In some cases *omnes consuetudines* follows *sac* and *soc,* e.g., 2 *D.B.* 330 b, 356 b. On the other hand in 1 *ibid.,* 280 b (Nottinghamshire) *sac* and *soc* appears as distinct from *consuetudo regis.* Again 2 *D.B.* 349 (Suffolk) *soc* can clearly not be as high as the king's forfeits. *Cf.* also *Exon. Domesday,* 162, where *consuetudo* embraces the latter. The conclusion seems to follow in such cases that *sac* and *soc* = *omnes consuetudines,* unless to *consuetudo* is added the modifying *regis.* Note further the rendition *wite* and *gerihta* of the king in Domesday: 1 *D.B.* 179; *ibid.,* 238 b; 2 *ibid.,* 244; 373; 413 b. On the difficulties of generalization out of Domesday, *cf.* the discussion, Vinogradoff, *English Society,* 116.

[151] The rendition of terms in books like the *Instituta Cnuti,* the *Consilatio Cnuti,* and the *Quadripartitus,* all of which are largely mere translations of earlier Anglo-Saxon dooms, shows the mechanics of legal transfiguration. Thus in the important passage II *Cnut* 12, the word *gerihta* is rendered by *Q., iura;* by *Inst. Cn., consuetudines;* by *Cons. Cn., rectitudines. Utlagas weorc* in II *Cnut* 13, *Q.* renders *opus útlagii; Inst. Cn., opus expulsi; Cons. Cn., exlegis factum. Flyman* (outlaw) in II *Cnut* 13, 2, *Q.,* renders *forisbannitum; Inst. Cn., exulem; Cons. Cn., exlegem.* The rendition of *socne* in a passage which speaks of a wergeld payment to the king or to one to whom the king has given *his socne* (II *Cnut* 73, 1, ms. G.) in *Q.* is "cui rex concesserit," so also *Inst. Cn.,* but *Cons. Cn.* is more explicit: "cui rex concessit sc. dominum qui privilegium habet in forefacturis suorum." This passage is dealing with a special wite. The passage 71, 3 uses *socne* in a general sense, i.e. it is speaking of a king's thegn with *soc* and is rendered by *Cons. Cn., privilegium,* but *Q.* is pavid and uses *socnam.* The implications of these renderings on the whole problem of reception is a matter that requires a great deal more study than has yet been given it. Liebermann is motivated chiefly and necessarily by the persistence of Anglo-Saxon institutions.

[152] For example, *curt—Leis Willelme* 5, 2; 6, 1; 24; 42, 1; *franchise—ibid.,* 2, 3; 39, 1; *seinur—ibid.,* 2, 4; 7; 12; 20, 2; 27; 27, 1 etc. Liebermann, *Ueber die Leis Willelme,* 106 *Archiv für das Studium der Neueren Sprachen,* 129 gives a list of the English words.

The set-up can be diagrammed from the *Leges Henrici,* compiled in the early twelfth century by a king's officer. This lawbook assumes seignorial courtkeeping as usual[153] and extensive. It is articulate about royal policy and royal power. And it contains so much of Anglo-Saxon law that one sees this as an active if not wholly independent factor. But the book *Leges Henrici* registers achievement, it does not recount history. It does not say how much seignorial courtkeeping has owed to the continental view which united this function with tenure, how much it has resulted from native law, how far it has been affected by the English tradition that *sac* and *soc* lay in grant.[154] It is voluble on *soc,* what sorts there are, who has it, how it is gained, and how it is lost and because of this descriptive matter some explanation of contemporary charters can be attempted, for it gives an insight into feudal organization and how the crown tries to control it.

The relations of crown and feudatories on the matter of jurisdiction are best understood against the background of certain institutional changes which began with the Conquest and were going on in the country at large. In the first place a certain undermining of the system of fixed tariffs, bots, was inevitable.[155] The Norman's idea of *emendatio* was a payment to the courtholder. He was used to arbitrary mulcts, to forfeitures, and to disherison.

---

[153] Note also the assumptions regarding seignorial jurisdiction in Henry I's precept regarding the county courts, 3, 1—3, 3 (Liebermann, *Gesetze,* 524) and compare the discussion in Adams, *Origin of the English Constitution,* 380 (App. II); Davis, *England under the Normans and Angevins,* 522 (App. II). On the meaning of *vavassor* in Henry's precept, Stenton, *English Feudalism,* 21.

[154] No better indications of the early confusion felt by the Normans than the report of the Pennenden Heath case, Bigelow, *Placita Anglo Normannica,* 4; Wilkins, 1 *Concilia,* 323–4, gives the text from *Textus Roffensis* compiled *circa* 1125. The phrases, "verba de consuetudinibus legum," "cum omnibus consuetudinibus et rebus quae ad easdem terras pertinebant," "omnes libertates ecclesiae suae et omnes consuetudines suas . . . diratiocinavit, soca, saca etc." show three distinct concepts. Note also the variants in the Canterbury text, Levison, *A Report on the Pennenden Trial,* 27 *E.H.R.,* 717. The various texts discussed by Douglas, *Odo, Lanfranc and the Domesday Survey* (*Tait Essays*), 47 *et seq.*

[155] This is discussed by Pollock and Maitland (2 *H.E.L.,* 459 *et seq.*)

Assuming even an attenuated franchise, his expectancy in terms of Saxon law would include *manbot* (the lord's compensation for a slain man) or the *despectus,* a possible redemption by full wergeld of an afflictive penalty, and wites as and where granted.[156] All of these incidents could be treated as Norman *emendatio.* Except possibly for the case of mere blows, the Normans, it will be recalled, had no system of tariffed amends for injuries.[157] If a jurisdiction entailed any wite not marked as

who point out among other things the change in the monetary system and its effect upon increasing the amount of wite.

The eleventh-century Anglo-Saxon classification of botworthy and botless offenses is replaced in the *Leges Henrici* by another classification, between *causa capitalis* or *criminalis* and *causa communis, causa exactionalis* or *quae ad witam vel weram pertinent.* For the botworthy wrongs the official acts like *Hn. Cor.* (8) use the concept, *forisfacta emendabilia;* the London charter (7) speaks, "de placito quod ad pecuniam." In passages of the *Leges Henrici* which incorporate old sources, there is of course strong evidence of the old classification, e.g. *Hn.* 11, 1 a; 11, 17; 12, 1; 79, 5. Against Pollock and Maitland's certainty on the disappearance of composition may be cited the frequency of reference to wer in the *Leg. Hen.* Sec. 70, 1, states the *were* of *villani* at £4 and of thegns at £25; *cf.* 74, 1 a; 76, 4; 6 a. Henry I's London charter (7) fixes the wer at 100 sol.; so the *Leis Will.* 8; 8, 1: "la were del thein xx lib. en Merchenelahe xxv lib. en Westsexenelahe. La were del vilain c. sol en Merchenlahe e ensement en Westsexene." The possibility of anachronism makes any positive conclusions dangerous. Still, in the passages in *Leg. Hen.*, the wergeld figures are preceded by sec. 69, *De occisione Anglici,* and there are two significant interpolations "Anglicus sine merito suo" and "loci consuetudinem" by the compiler into a passage taken from the Anglo-Saxon *Wer.*, 2; then another passage original with the compiler "et wita et manbota dominis sicut iustum est ad modum ipsius were." While Liebermann in *Erklärungen,* 314 (9) warns that the writer is not aware that the growth of a public criminal law is pushing out bot, and punishment is taking its place, the passages cited above with the limitations to Englishmen and the reference to local custom suggests the utter abandonment of the bot system had by no means yet taken place. Moreover *Leges Henrici* lays down new rules, i.e. there are no earlier Anglo-Saxon precedents. So, the rule that no wer is paid where two persons of the same rank kill each other, *Hn.*, 70, 8, 9 a; the requirement that the wergeld claimant must prove his relation to the slain, *Hn.*, 92, 13; the provision for mere symbolic payment, *Hn.*, 78, 5; the sharp incursions of the concept of intent on which *cf.* Liebermann, *Glossar, Absicht,* 5, 6.

[156] *Cf.* Liebermann, *Glossar, Schutz,* 7 d. On the variety of payments recognized in *Hn.*, *cf.,* for example, 70, 4; 78, 5.

[157] *Supra,* Chapter IV, p. 199.

royal,[158] the Norman courtkeeper would see it as a mulct dissociated from the monetary claims of the injured accuser.[159] The
Anglo-Saxon law had generally given wite payments a priority
over bot.[160] This rule favored the Norman courtkeeper and the
tendency was for nothing but wite to be collected because the
native population had suffered from the shift in wealth through
the destruction or seizure of values.[161] When the lord had to be

[158] Thus the *blodwite* of the *socmanni* of Ramsey, I *D.B.* 204 a; the
Wallingford householder's "sanguinem," I *D.B.* 56 b. In *Hn.*, 23, 1 and
81, 3, *blodwite*, *fihtwite* and *legerwite* are treated as *minora forisfactura*.
Jurisdiction over these clearly does not depend on specific grant of *fihtwite* or *blodwite* for the case goes to the soc lord of the offender if he is not
caught or impleaded at the locus of the offense (*infra*, note 204). *Cf.* 70, 4,
and Liebermann, *Gesetze*, 588, note h. Note further *Hn.* 80, 6, where the
right to *fihtwite* in a homicide case depends on possession of *sac* and *soc*
if the man is put under pledge and accusation. Homicide is not a *causa
capitalis* in *Leges Henrici*, except when aggravated, viz., murder or in
breach of special protection.

[159] The increased dominance of the courtkeeper is patent in various relations. Thus in Henry I's time the private complaint is subject to various
artificial restrictions based upon a theory of priority in terms of graded interest. For example, *Hn.* 7, 3 where in the county court ecclesiastical claims
precede royal. In *Hn.* 43, 1 the crown's priority is again asserted and limited only if the defendant is *debitor domini sui* which may refer to a priority in execution. *Cf.* 61, 6 b as to the priority of the liege lord. These passages are significant in connection with the destruction of the kindred's
initiative in prosecution. Furthermore the lord can accuse without witnesses or *cogentibus circumstantiis*, *Hn.* 63, 2. This book apparently does
not consider such accusations are to be made in a higher court for *Hn.*
32, 3, allows a lord impleading his man to set up his own doomsmen. *Hn.*
24, 1, provides a higher instance only for offenses against the lord's person.
The provision in *Hn.* 36, 1, says that no one can have his own *overseunessa*
but the lord over him gets it. This can mean simply a division of mulcts
and is not even an implicit denial of the lord's right to try the case where
he himself accuses.

[160] Liebermann, *Glossar, Priorität*. In *Wer.*, 5, the *healsfang* (the blood
money that goes to direct family) is first; then *manbot* (*ibid.*, 6); then
wite; then the kins' wergeld share. These provisions recapitulated in *Hn.*
76, 1 c *et seq. Cf. Leis Will.* 9. To be distinguished are the special rules for
cases lying outside the bot and wite system, e.g. *anefang* (*Will. Art.* 5);
restitution of value (*ceapgield*) to claimants before forfeiture where a
*tihtbysig* person is involved, VI *Aethelstan*, 1, 1; II *Cnut*, 25, 1. In *Will.
Art.* 8, the rule is more generally put and rests on a theory of contempt.

[161] The description of the Conqueror's court at Fécamp in Will. Pict.,
*Gesta* (Giles Ed.) 156, indicates something of the looting that had oc-

satisfied first, there would be little left for plaintiffs and their kindred. The displacement of the Anglo-Saxon fixed tariff by the Norman arbitrary mulct was under way before the coronation charter of Henry I where he promised to restore the ancient scheme.[162] But this assurance did not stay the gradual disintegration of the old system.[163] Even if there was locally a disposition to preserve native forms for Saxon tenants, the pressure of the barons' continental experience was toward their destruction. Acts by which this pressure was exerted were made colorable because at the beginning of William's reign the Normans were given certain Norman procedural rights,[164] a factor of more practical consequence in a feudal ménage than royal promises. With a mixed tenantry, or where there was a preponderant number of Norman suitors in a court, the law would be molded by imported procedure.[165] This accounts for the completeness

curred. The tales in *Anglo-Saxon Chronicle* (23 R.S. pt. 2) while undoubtedly exaggerated fit in. *Cf.* especially at 170, 173, 174, 176, 184, 185. A check on these statements exists in the accounts of pestilence and famine, *ibid.* 184, 187, 201, 202, 203, 206. *Cf.* also Baring, *The Conqueror's Footsteps in Domesday,* 13 E.H.R. 17, and *Oxfordshire Traces of the Northern Insurgents, ibid.,* 295 on the waste incident upon the marches of the Conqueror's army.

[162] *Hn. Cor.,* 8.

[163] In *Quadripartitus,* Dedicatio 4 (the date of which Liebermann has fixed at 1114) are remarks about the changes in the criminal law which may be a reference to the sharpening of the extant system.

[164] *Willelmes Lad,* 1, 1 *secundum legem Normannie.* This law regulates the proof between Normans and English, not as between Norman, but the recognition of the personality of law would cover the situation. The reference in *Dial. de Scaccario* i, 16 a, "Rex Willelmus . . . legibus anglicanis . . . transmarinas Neustrie leges adiecit," may indicate more than what is in the *Lad.* Note also *Hn.* 18; 64, 3 a, regarding the advantages in oath-taking of the Norman.

[165] Entries in the *Anglo-Saxon Chronicle* (23 R.S. pt. 2, e.g. 187) point to the abandonment of the fixed wite system on the fiefs, in favor of mulcts. "And he [the Conqueror] recked not how very sinfully the reeves got it from poor men or how many illegalities (unlaga) they did; but the more that was said about right law the more illegalities were done. They levied unjust tolls and many other unjust things they did." *Cf.* 189–90, and vague references to unjust imposts or exactions, *ibid.,* 203, 207, 208, 213, 214, 215. For 1124 the Chronicle ends "the man who had any goods was

with which procedure in seignorial courts is described by the *Leges Henrici*. In contrast, the materials on ancient English procedure are but pale shades.

## THE GROWTH OF A FRANCHISE THEORY

The substitution of Norman for native law on the fiefs is not an entirely spontaneous and free development. The crown endeavored from the first to keep its fingers on local justice. In view of the traditions of Norman feudalism a franchise theory was probably the best compromise available, and a franchise theory did in fact evolve in England decades before it appeared in Normandy. Since tenure and jurisdiction were matters not readily separated by a Norman in the eleventh century, crown policy centers at first upon the control of land. Ready at hand is the sweeping theory that the land of England was conquered and hence vested in the king-conqueror.[166] This severs each chain of title; land ceases to be *hereditas* unless this quality is restored to it.[167] Privileges die unless revived by confirmation.[168]

bereft of them by violent exactions and violent courts; those who had none died of hunger."

[166] Adams, *Political History of England,* 12–13, conjectures the Conqueror did not regard the lands as forfeit, denied by Ballard, *Domesday Inquest* (1906) 5. The Frankish theory of conquest was that the conquered lands fell to the crown. *Cf.* 2 Brunner, *D.R.G.,* 103; on the practice followed by Charlemagne, 3 Waitz, *D.V.G.,* 151. It is of course impossible to establish that this theory was consciously carried on in France during the tenth and eleventh centuries. On the continuation in the Empire 8 Waitz, *D.V.G.,* 254–5. Note further the fact that as to England the Conqueror's claim to succession obfuscates the legal theory of conquest, *cf. Leg. Edw. Con. Prol.* and Liebermann's comment in *Über die Leges Edwardi,* 39. Compare *Willelmi Art. Inscr.* and the *Leis Willelme Pro.— cunquest* in French, *adquisicionem* in the Latin version. Finally, *cf.* Adams' latest theory in *Origin of the English Constitution,* 14–15, which accords on the whole with statement in the text, and Stenton's sensible summary of the facts, *William the Conqueror* (1908) 232 *et seq.*

[167] William's *London Charter,* 3. Liebermann, in *Glossar, Erbgang,* regards this provision that every child should be his father's heir as a relinquishment of rights of conquest, the result of the Londoners' resistance.

[168] Stubbs, in 1 *Constitutional History* (5 ed.) 281, doubting this, draws a curious and it would seem legally useless distinction between the "feudal

Domesday statistics convince that under the Conqueror this theory was consistently applied to native landholders.[169] William Rufus, however, incautiously stretched it to the new feudatories, affecting to treat his vassals' holdings as *precaria* to extort new revenues.[170] Had he been less greedy the more limited claim to order jurisdictions alone might have succeeded on the same theory. By demanding too much he aroused an opposition which triumphed when Henry I in his coronation charter had to abjure these extraordinary claims.[171] From this time on the theory falls into political abeyance,[172] although it is obvious that Henry's subsequent interference with "ideal" feudalism[173] can only be explained as manipulations of ultimate land title, so disparate are the rules in his continental duchy.

Apart from its broader claims, the crown through its possession of a huge demesne in England was in a position to formulate a franchise policy which it did not have the means or the power to execute in Normandy, where lands complete with prescriptive jurisdictions had been in private hands for generations before the duke became a factor of political importance. Technically, indeed, no distinction is to be drawn between forms and policies in granting out of the ducal or the royal demesnes.[174]

lawyer's" view and the plundered proprietors'. Vinogradoff, *English Society*, 219 asserts the rule of new title.

[169] Ballard, *op. cit.*, 6 points out that not more than 1 per cent of the land in England was in 1086 held of the king by those who held it in Edward's time or by their heirs or widows. *Cf.* also, *ibid.*, 85 *et seq.* on the sharp increase in *terrae regis*.

[170] Davis, *England under the Normans and Angevins*, 79; 1 Freeman, *Reign of William Rufus* (1882) 337; Round, *Feudal England* (1895) 309 *et seq.*, on the reliefs.

[171] *Hn. Cor.*, 2; 6.

[172] The subsequent medieval theory of domains by conquest is one phase of the vitality of the doctrine. *Cf.* 30 *Columbia Law Rev.* 273, and 31 *ibid.*, 417 note 5, where additional references are cited.

[173] So the disposition of suits between men of different lords in *Hn. Com.* 3, 2. The land title theory seems for the period a more suitable explanation of this legislation than ideas of sovereignty. The forum otherwise is the lord's for *causae communes*, *Hn.* 25, 2. *Cf.* also *Hn.* 57 *et seq.* for rules regarding venue.

[174] *Supra*, Chapter V, regarding Normandy.

The Conqueror and his sons conveyed some privileges and withheld others. But there is a most decided political difference in the degree to which pretensions could be asserted as duke or as king over matter granted. There is no doubt that conveyances of privilege were completely welded with lay tenure in Normandy.[175] In England, however, the royal grantor kept some bonds of authority. This authority which the crown wedged between tenure and its incidents it was able to assert less because of its theoretical rights arising out of conquest than because it clung to the royal prerogatives of its Anglo-Saxon predecessors, and because it retained the set-up of local public justice. These were two pieces of jurisdictional reality which every conveyance of land had to take into account. Consequently the process of feoffment from the first appears as a process of adjustment of particular grants to these factors extraneous to baronial reckonings.

These advantages of the Norman kings can hardly have failed of immediate recognition, for the period immediately after the Conquest was uniquely distinguished by a widespread concern about this very question of the source and scope of the rights and privileges which constitute jurisdiction. The occasion was the investiture struggle in which England like the rest of western Europe was involved.[176] In attempting to find a *modus vivendi* between church and state the whole complex of temporal rights was subjected to analysis and classification, by several generations of polemicists and diplomats.[177] Even in England this ran much beyond the conventional separation of *spiritualia* and

[175] This must be inferred from the flatfooted assertions regarding baronial blood justice in the Inquest of 1091, cc. 9 and 10.

[176] The controversy between Pope and Emperor runs on until the concordat of Worms of 1122, 2 Hinschius, *K.R.*, 541; on the details of the separate English concordat of 1106, Schmitz, *Der Englische Investiturstreit* (1884); Böhmer, *Kirche und Staat,* 147, 258, 288, 301; Rule's introduction to Eadmer, *Historia* (R.S.) xliv *et seq.;* Liebermann, *Anselm von Canterbury and Hugo von Lyon (Historische Aufsätze dem Andenken an Waitz Gewidmet),* 156.

[177] The tracts are collected in *M.G.H., Libelli de Lite.* Discussion of the legal as distinguished from political theory in Pöschl, *Die Regalien der Mittelalterlichen Kirchen* (1928).

*temporalia*[178] of which the Conqueror's "Episcopal laws" seems an obvious practical recognition,[179] for there are in England obvious repercussions of the sharply defined continental concept of *regalia,* i.e., rights apart from land had from the crown alone,[180] for which homage had in any event to be done, held separate from *possessiones,* title to which might have some other origin.[181]

So much in this contemporary thinking provoked by the problem of investiture fits into the grooves of early Anglo-Norman theory and practice of treating land and jurisdiction as separable that it is tempting to believe there was here a real source of legal innovation.[182] In the present state of learning on the matter,

[178] That the English crown retained the temporalities is as far as historians generally have described the matters reserved by the crown. Davis, *England under the Normans and Angevins,* 132; 1 Norgate, *England under the Angevins,* 18; Morris, *Constitutional History of England,* 251: "they [the prelates] were required to become his vassals." The contemporary statements, William of Malmesbury in 179 Migne, *Patrologia,* 417; Eadmer, *Historia* 186.

[179] Reflected also in the measures taken at Lillebon (1080) to separate ducal from episcopal rights. *Supra,* Chapter V.

[180] Listed by Paschal II in his first promise of 1111 (*M.G.H.* 1 *Const.,* 138): ". . . id est civitates, ducatus, marchias, comitatus, monetas, teloneum, mercatum, advocatias regni, iura centurionum et curtes quae [manifeste] regni erant, cum pertinentiis suis, militiam et castra [regni]." On the various terms, 7 Waitz, *D.V.G.,* 255, 332, 8 *ibid.,* 2. The concept is fixed by the Pope; the content expanded by Barbarossa at Roncaglia (1158) *M.G.H.,* 1 *Const.,* 244. The French follow the imperial usage: Phillips, *Ursprung des Regalienrechts in Frankreich* (1870), 23; Pöschl, *op. cit.,* 105, 115.

[181] Distinguished by the pope in his *privilegium* (*M.G.H.,* 1 *Const.,* 141). The pamphleteers discussed Pöschl, *op. cit.,* 35 *et seq.* Note especially Gerhoh of Reichersberg's list in 3 *Libelli de Lite,* 154. See also 8 Waitz, *D.V.G.,* 455; and 4 Carlyle, *Medieval Political Theory,* 342 *et seq.*

[182] The place where these theories could best be tested is in relation to the treatment of lands and franchises during episcopal and abbatial vacancy. About this almost nothing precise is known. A solution depends on: 1) a study of the division of episcopal and abbatial property from that of chapter or convent; 2) a study of the charters showing how far the crown actually took over the whole concern, especially grants from hands other than the crown; 3) a study of the franchises whether they ceased to be entirely personal and were treated as "corporate" property. Such studies fall outside the scope of what is here being undertaken. Heretofore the emphasis has been entirely on the "feudal" vs. spiritual position of the prel-

however, the most that is clear is the extreme currency of radical theories separating land and jurisdiction along the line taken by the Anglo-Norman kings. The accord of such theories with the antecedent Anglo-Saxon policy of treating franchise grants as personal, quite apart from such political realities as the consequences of conquest and the existence of a system of public courts, was sufficient to make possible a concept of franchise such as that developed by the author of *Leges Henrici*. Familiar as he was with the legal theory of the investiture controversy,[183] he had only to look abroad at foreign monarchs' failure to capitalize the anti-feudal implications of the theory[184] to realize that in the uniquely favorable position of the English king lay opportunity for success.

The story of what happens in England is not to be told however from the bitter exchanges over king's right and pope's right but from analysis of the documented conveyances. Land may be commonly transferred by livery alone,[185] yet we do not know whether by livery more than seisin of the land could pass. There

ates. While it is necessary to have clear the general feudal relation of crown and prelates (*cf.* Round, *Feudal England* 311), the relation of franchise and land can only be determined by less general studies than for example Freeman's on Rufus (2 *William Rufus*, 264) and Böhmer's on Henry I (*op. cit.*, 288, 301). The episode related in 1 Madox, *History of the Exchequer*, 109 (*temp.* Hy. I) indicates the monks had a lively appreciation of convent as against abbot's rights. Henry I's writ for Bury (24 *E.H.R.*, 425, no. 7), and his subsequent alleged disregard of it shows the matter was the subject of real controversy. On the matter specifically here at issue the treatment of the lands by the crown must be supplemented by an examination of the administration of the franchise during vacancy (e.g., *Chron. Mon. de Bello*, 48) and by a study of the verbiage of the writs issued to new incumbents. In Henry I's reign the franchise right was clearly still regarded as personal, *cf.* the writ, 2 *Chron. Abingdon*, 162.

[183] Liebermann, *Quadripartitus* (1892). He was associated with Gerard, Archbishop of York (§57) who had stood by the crown in the investiture controversy. *Ibid.*, §§78, 79. On the identity of the author of *Quadripartitus* and *Leges Henrici*, Liebermann, *Über die Leges Henrici* (1901) 3.

[184] Mitteis, *Lehnrecht und Staatsgewalt*, 426.

[185] Wissmann, *Förmlichkeiten bei den Landübertragungen in England*

are enough entries in Domesday to suggest the existence of a policy that where there is no writing, there may be no privilege,[186] so that the rule in *Leges Henrici* regarding franchises connected with status[187] may be an exception both to the requirement of record, and to the normal effect of livery.

The grants attested by extant writs or charters fall into two classes—those which deal with mere transfers of land and those to which specific privileges are added. The first of these can be dismissed with the caveat that, depending upon the status of the grantee, some privileges might automatically attach. The documents which recite privileges are either confirmations or new

. . ., 3 *Archiv für Urkundenforschung,* 251, 256, where there is some discussion of symbolic livery. Wissmann has collected cases of transfer in hundred, county or halmote. The significance of this for purposes of record is obvious. But it is by no means clear whether a hundred could testify beyond the mere fact of livery; *cf.* the case in 2 *D.B.,* 172 b, and, for later, the writ of Stephen in Voss, *Heinrich von Winchester,* app. 155. In Wulfstan's case (Bigelow, *Placita Anglo-Norm.* 17) the bishop claimed the right to call witnesses who "hoc viderant et predicta servitia ad opus episcopi susceperant." This was *circa* 1077. The use of oral proof regarding even franchises is affirmed as early as the Pennenden Heath trial (and frequently thereafter), c. 1071 (*ibid.,* 4). This resembles also the practice in Normandy, Round, *Calendar,* no. 1190. Such a practice was clearly admitted for questions which ran to rights under the Confessor, as the procedure in Domesday best attests. The Confessor's charters were treated as proof by the Normans, Vinogradoff, *English Society,* 222–3. A writ of the Conqueror (c. 1071), Davis, *Regesta,* no. 49, apparently initiates the demand for written proof. The superiority of written title over inquest testimony of seisin *T.R.E.* is clear from the writ of 1082, Bigelow, *op. cit.,* 24; Davis, *Regesta,* no. 155. As the crown's franchise theory takes form, the insistence upon this will necessarily increase. In connection with the competence and completeness of hundred testimony note also the fact that it is at the county court where writs are read, Morris, *Medieval English Sheriff,* 61. Clearly even with a charter the hundred is unlikely to know the details of franchise. This may explain the frequent "nesciunt quo warranto" in the 1274 hundred inquest.

[186] 1 *D.B.* 178; 373 b; 2 *D.B.,* 195; 208; 360 b. There is every reason to believe the rule of a writing was effective beyond merely king and tenants in chief. Stenton, *English Feudalism,* ch. II gives various examples of precepts by magnates which show clearly enough that the use of writings was by no means confined to crown business. Note also the precepts *ibid.,* 104, 106, 107, where franchises are conveyed.

[187] *Hn.* 20, 2.

grants out of demesne. The same principles govern in either case, for even in those confirmations of estates where rights may have adhered to the land as indisseverable custom, the title itself is new by virtue of the theory discussed above.

The privileges issued by the Conqueror run from *sac* and *soc* alone to the rarer extension of the royal prerogative *forisfactura*. Intermediate are grants of *toll, team,* and *infangtheof.* The tradition is essentially that of William's Anglo-Saxon predecessors. He was not doing a meaningless act in using these terms, for none of the rights they stand for went as a matter of course with the land.[188] Hence even if they are no more than well-marked fiscal privileges, mentioning them as special matter in a grant indicates that they have a normal situs from which they are thereby transferred. Since the grant emanates from public authority this situs is necessarily something within its control— hundred, county, sheriff, the crown itself.[189] It is into the func-

---

[188] *Hn.* 19, 2: "in all lands which the king has in demesne the king has soc as well. In some of his lands he gives the manor and at the same time soc of sole [i.e. capital] and/or common causes [i.e. amends]; of some he gives the manor but retains the soc himself." Without prejudice to the question of the identity of the content of the grant of *sac* and *soc* in Anglo-Saxon and Anglo-Norman times, it must be noticed that this theoretical statement of the separability of franchise and land continues the policy initiated by Cnut, wherein franchise grants, being personal, are sharply distinguished from land, with which they might or might not be conveyed. *Supra,* p. 364. For identity of practice: *T.R.E.* grant of *sac and soc* in consideration of ship service 1 *D.B.* 1 a; *temp.* Hy. I, money payments for grants of *sac and soc, P.R. 31 Hy. I,* 36, 98.

[189] The Domesday entries raise many insoluble questions concerning the distinction, if any, between the rights of the crown itself and those of other authority which is not vested in private hands. There are plenty of instances where there is no entry whatever concerning the *soc* over a particular hundred: here probably, the hundred court is still competent. The entries to the effect that the *soc* is the king's may be simply a circumlocution to the same effect, or it may indicate that the local court revenues have become attached to a royal manor. *Cf.* Vinogradoff, *op. cit.,* 123. Since the profits of pleas usually split two-thirds to the king and one-third to the earl or sheriff (*ibid.,* 105) royal manorial *soc* over a hundred has significance only as absorbing the earl's penny. It does not help in specifying jurisdiction as between sheriff and crown, for even where a county is farmed the farm is composed of the pleas of the county and the farm of

tions or rights of these that a conveyance of privilege cuts. It is rare that the franchise will run to matters of county court jurisdiction.[190] Owing to the wide distribution of small holdings to make up even the greatest fiefs, it is the functions of the territorially small and judicially less important unit of public justice, the hundred,[191] that are most freely distributed and are made immune—suit is shifted, court business reduced and judicial revenues decimated.[192]

That a transfer of public rights is involved in these grants is a

king's demesne (Morris, *Med. Eng. Sheriff*, 63). This indicates that for Domesday's exchequer purposes the distinction between royal revenue and "public" revenue is of no consequence and hence any grants out of either are on the same footing.

[190] The major *forisfactura*, like *hamsocn, forsteall,* which were probably justiciable by the county court (Liebermann, *Glossar, Kronprozess,* 18, *Grafschaftsgericht,* 13 c; *Hn.* 60, 3; 66, 9) were rarely granted. On defeasance of shrieval jurisdiction through the *ne intromittat* clause, *cf.* note 193.

[191] The hundred is the ordinary criminal court. Morris, *Frankpledge System,* 113; Cam, *Hundred and the Hundred Rolls* (1930), 17. There is no doubt that any criminal cause can be tried in it in Anglo-Saxon times, Liebermann, *Glossar, hundred,* 35, 36. It is by no means clear whether its competence was equally great under the first Norman kings. Passages like *Hn.* 9, 4; *Leg. Edw. Conf.* 22, 5; 23, 4 are equivocal, while *Leg. Edw. Conf.* 9, 3 suggests strongly no limitation on the jurisdiction. From Vinogradoff's conjecture of the non-attendance of lords at hundred court (*English Society,* 98, n. 3), if true, follows the inference that the jurisdiction diminishes in Anglo-Norman times rather than holds its own. In Cnut's law (II *Cnut* 19) it is the court of first resort (*cf.* also II *Cnut* 22, 1; 30; 31 a).

[192] *Leges Henrici* shows in several places the process of adjustment necessitated by the intrusion of the enfranchised lord; *Hn.* 7, 7; 7a, the baron or his steward may discharge county suit duties resting on his whole land, in the stead of the normal representatives. *Hn.* 7, 8 a similar provision for hundred suit *de causis singulorum* (i.e., sole royal cases, viz., *infangtheof: supra,* note 188), which is a provision to take care of the franchise which grants only *sac* and *soc,* so that part of the hundredal jurisdiction over land remains communal, for which suit is still due from the enfranchised land. *Hn.* 92, 17, for the procedure for asserting a quittance of *murdrum* on enfranchised territory, lifting it out of the hundred's ordinary liability. *Hn.,* 57, 1 a: where litigants have the same lord and he has *soc,* the lord's court is competent, otherwise the hundred. The condition precedent of *soc* here indicates the equivalence of privileged lord's court and hundred.

conclusion most strongly emphasized by those charters where in the continental tradition a *ne intromittat* is added,[193] particularly where the exclusionary clause is explicitly directed at the sheriff or his bailiff. The public servant has to be warned out of places where he would normally go to attend to public business because this business is no longer included in the scope of his duties. The *ne intromittat* is of course not an essential to the transfer of public rights to private hands. It is a mere safeguard. But because of the nature of the shrieval office, it is important enough to evoke frequent forgery, and in Henry I's time becomes a matter of course.

In addition to the light which the use of the *ne intromittat* formula throws upon the Anglo-Norman grants as transfers from public to private authority, their regularization and multiplication help in ascertaining what sort of jurisdiction was conveyed. As long as a grant was merely a right to judicial revenues an exclusionary clause had no real purpose. But no sooner do Norman feudatories, lay or ecclesiastical, put into practice their notions that jurisdiction means the right to hold court than it be-

[193] Davis, *Regesta,* no. 52 (questionable); also p. 120; no. 106; App. no. 162. No. 186 is a variant if the reading given by Davis, p. 51, is correct, but the full text on p. 125 intends no exclusion. *Cf.* nos. 233(\*), 234(\*), App. 235, 252; 275(?). Under William Rufus the formula continues, *ibid.,* 294, 306, 311, 344, 408, 421, 453. The calendar does not always note the *ne intromittat* clause, so that there may be additional examples. Some shrieval exclusions, *temp.* Henry I, collected in Morris, *Sheriff,* 91, note 143. In the absence of any adequate diplomatic guide for Anglo-Norman documents, the legal historian has to work by constant analogy, and comparison with continental material where Sickel, Stengel, Bresslau and others have supplied the lawyers with sharp tools.

On the continent the *absque introitu* is the most general and effective clause in constructing immunity, *supra,* ch. III. The intent of the English *ne intromittat* seems to be the same, going beyond clauses of slighter scope which also reduce *pro tanto* the powers of normal public authority, e.g. writs regarding suit, making the king's court the sole forum, quitting of shires and hundreds. The *ne intromittat* attached to a limited positive grant—*sac, soc, toll, team, infangtheof* (e.g. Davis, *Regesta,* nos. 106 or 275)—is of course a qualified protection limited by the specific matter granted. The parallel with the Frankish *absque introitu* where *fredus* alone is specified and where *bannus* is omitted is worth noting.

comes useful to have specific insulation against the officers who would otherwise be keeping court. The *ne intromittat* becomes usual under Henry I because baronial courtholding under the franchises is usual.

That a theory about franchise is in full and conscious operation during the early twelfth century is attested by the *Leges Henrici*.[194] This book divides causes into those capital-criminal,[195] and those which are common,[196] a distinction basic to its treatment of the whole problem of jurisdiction. The capital cause is one involving royal procedure or royal penalty. The common cause is one not otherwise distinguished or earmarked with royal fine or *misericordia* but emendable by lesser mulct. *Soc* of the capital cause lies in the crown but it is susceptible of grant.[197] The *soc* of the common cause likewise lies in grant,[198] a rule subject to the notable exception that on lands held *virtute officii,* magnates such as bishops and counts have *sac, soc, toll, team* and *infangtheof* even without grant, and on lands acquired by exchange or otherwise, these notables have automatically *sac* and *soc* alone.[199] Barring this exception due to status, *sac* and *soc* is acquired only by special grant and not every lord

---

[194] Maitland, *Domesday Book,* 81, offers an interpretation of the *Leges Henrici* theory which varies from the position here taken. In particular, Maitland's importation of the anachronistic "high justice" and "low justice" confuses issues unnecessarily. Liebermann's subsequent work on the *Leges Henrici* and on the *Leg. Edw. Conf.* makes it possible to state certain points with greater assurance than Maitland seems to have felt.

[195] The expression varies but the basic idea is that this is a matter primarily royal. *Hn.* 9, 5, "que solum pertinent ad ius regium;" *Hn.* 9, 11, "soca . . . ad fiscum regium et singulariter"; *Hn.* 19, 2, "soknam simul singularem"; *Hn.* 11, 16 a. The passages regarding the *causa capitalis: Hn.* 9, 5; 20, 3; 26, 2; 34, 1 b; 47; 60, 3; 61, 18; 64, 2 a.

[196] *Causa communis, Hn.* 20, 2; 25, 1; 35, 1; 49, 6; 64, 2. It is also called *emendabilis, Hn.* 59, 2; 61, 4; *pecunialis, Hn.* 9, 5; 34, 1 b; *exactionalis, Hn.* 61, 19. Generally on the identity of these terms, Liebermann, *Glossar, Kapitalverbrechen,* 1a.

[197] *Hn.* 9, 11; 19, 2.

[198] *Hn.* 9, 11; 19, 2; 20.

[199] *Hn.* 20, 2. *Cf. Inst. Cnuti* III, 58, 1: "In multis tamen locis secundum justiciam in sua [i.e. episcopi] propria terra et in suis villis debent habere constitutionem hundredi" etc.

has it.²⁰⁰ The common cause is regarded as practically synonymous with *sac* and *soc*.²⁰¹ It results moreover from the compiler's
careful elimination of the capital cause, the distinction of *infangtheof* as a matter of capital character,²⁰² the recognition of *team*
as a special franchise,²⁰³ the setting apart of feudal causes justiciable because of commendation²⁰⁴ and the distinction of land

²⁰⁰ *Hn.* 25, 1; 57, 1 a; 57, 8; 59, 19. Compare *Leg. Edw. Conf.* 21, 1; 22,
5; 24, 3, 4. In the *Leis Wil.*, 2, 4, in the Danelaw a man's *seinur* has certain fiscal claims; see also 27. *Cf.* the famous entry for Wye, 1 *D.B.*, 11 b.

²⁰¹ *Hn.* 25, 1: "Si exurgat placitum inter homines alicuius baronum socnam suam habentium, tractetur placitum in curia domini sui de causa
communi"; *Hn.* 25, 2: "Si est inter homines duorum dominorum socnam
habencium, respondeat accusatus in curia domini sui de causa communi."

²⁰² *Hn.* 20, 2; 26–26, 4; *Cf. Leg. Edw. Conf.* 22, 4. The *Hn.* 26–26, 4, passages are in terms of *furtum*, but from *Hn.*, 10, 1; 13, 1; 24, 2; the "capital"
character is clearly obvious. *Cf.* also *Inst. Cn.*, III, 55; 58.

²⁰³ *Hn.* 20, 2.

²⁰⁴ *Hn.* 23 looks like a blurring of the distinction between franchise
jurisdiction over crime and the feudal jurisdiction, for it states that "if
anyone incurs [*forisfaciat*] *blodwite, fihtwite, lecherwite* and the like, and
evades arrest or, being pledged to answer accusation [*divadiatio* or *calum-
nia*], the plea belongs to his lord. But "his lord" does not mean the lord to
whom the offender is commended because there is no criminal jurisdiction independent of *sac* and *soc* exercised by virtue of commendation,
for mere commendation is excluded here by 59, 17 "et omnis tihla vel com-
pellacio sit eius qui *socam et sacam* suam [plene] habet [et] de suis
hominibus et in suo." *Tihla* (Liebermann, *Wörterbuch, tihla*) means procedure by accusation, cases of *divadiatio, calumpnia, compellatio, cravatio,
inculpatio* (the terms are interchangeable, Liebermann, *Glossar, Anklage-
zustand; Hn.* 9, 6) which of course includes the non-handhaving case just
described in *Hn.* 23. For this, possession of *sac* and *soc* is a condition *sine
qua non.* 1 *D.B.*, 1 a, states a rule similar to that of *Hn.* 23: if a man accused of *grithbreche* evades [*non calumpniatus*] the king's reeve he is quit
as regards the king, but not as regards his lord. It is to be interpreted precisely as we have just read *Hn.* 23, for 1 *D.B.* 32 a (Southwark) states the
same rule but instead of the lord it is the man who has *sac* and *soc* "Si
quis forisfaciens ibi calumpniatus fuisset regi emendabat; si vero non
calumpniatus abisset sub eo qui sacam et socam habuisset, ille emendam
de reo haberet." *Cf.* 1 *D.B.* 30 a. Thus, when "lord" is mentioned in criminal cases, it is always to be taken as "lord with *soc.*" This accords fully
with the basic distinction in Domesday between *soc* and the freedom or restriction of commendation (Round, *Feudal England, 30 et seq.;* Ballard,
*Domesday Inquest,* 113 *et seq.;* Maitland, *Domesday Book,* 67 *et seq.;*
Stenton, *Types of Manorial Structure* [1910] on the meaning of soke-
land). For example, A is commended to B but is in the *soc* of C. A com-

cases.[205] This forces an identification of *sac and soc* with the *causa communis,* the delicts punishable by mulct, i.e., by the exaction of *blodwite, fihtwite, legerwite* or the like.[206] Its character

mits a battery in the land of D who has *sac* and *soc* there. If he is caught there, D will try him. If he escapes, it is C, not B, who can try him. This is the only way that the passages in *Leges Henrici* can make sense. The consonance of this interpretation with charters and *D.B.* (especially the case II, 401 b) is what makes *Leges Henrici* franchise theory more than wishful thinking.

Far from having jurisdiction over his man, the lord by commendation owes his man a duty of defense in criminal litigation in *sac* and *soc* causes. The man impleaded may have a continuance to call the lord "whether or not he has *sac* and *soc,*" unless in a capital cause: *Hn.* 57, 8; 61, 14, 16, 17.

*Hn.* 55, "*De Privilegio domini super hominem suum.* Omni domino licet submonere hominem suum ut ei sit ad rectum in curia sua" is under no circumstances to be read as implying criminal jurisdiction through lordship. In the first place it probably applies to honor courts alone. Liebermann, *Glossar, Honor;* Stenton, *English Feudalism,* 41; Maitland, *Domesday Book,* 81. Taken most broadly it applies to the lord with vassals (e.g., *Hn.* 41, 3; 43, 4) in feudal causes alone.

[205] The *causa communis* can hardly embrace the plea of land since the rules of jurisdiction and venue laid down in *Hn.* 25, 2 for the *causa communis* are opposed to the rule in Henry I's county court precept (*Hn. Com.* 3, 2) for land cases. Again, the special rules regarding fee farm in *Hn.* 56, 2, and the complaints against baliffs, 56, 4; 5, are not at all like the rules for *sac* and *soc* causes.

[206] The identity of *causa communis* (*causa emendabilis—minora forisfacto*) and *sac* and *soc* is further indicated by: *Hn.* 80, 6—*fihtwite* to the lord who has *sac* and *soc* where homicide is done on his land if the offender is arrested or put under pledge to answer accusation; *Hn.* 80, 12—wite for medleys in the house if the householder has *quaestio* (= *soc,* Liebermann, *Gesetze* 597 note o). *Cf.* also *Hn.* 37, 1; 39; 70, 4; 80, 6 a; 81, 3; 94.

On the confusion in the last passage, Liebermann, *Glossar, blutig fechten* 1 g–i; 11; 14. In *Erklärungen,* 329, Liebermann points out that *overseunessa* is sometimes used as equivalent of wite. Some of the difficulties are resolved if one takes as the compiler's premise the franchise of *sac* and *soc* as prerequisite of the receipt of wite. This is certainly the case in *Hn.* 94, 1 a. If two men of one lord fight, there is *overseunessa* to the lord. If one participant is the man of another lord and is caught and accused, the lord of the place gets *overseunessa,* and *fihtwite* goes to him who is privileged. *Manbot* does not depend on franchise (Liebermann, *Glossar, Manbusse* 5) and the *overseunessa* is conceptually different from the wite. (Liebermann, *Glossar, Schutz* 4). It is conceivable that the *overseunessa* is the insurance for proper manorial police where no franchise is granted and hence no right to wite, and is in a sense a device for preventing collisions between the enfranchised lord and the lord who has no

as franchise follows from the fact that the forum for the *minora forisfactura* is in the public hundred[207] in the absence of specific grant. The hundred, then, is the one constant in the change which the Normans worked in the Anglo-Saxon concept of *sac* and *soc*. Under the Norman kings *sac* and *soc* is no longer merely the receipt of hundredal mulcts; it has ripened into jurisdiction over the causes normally handled by the hundred court. Whatever violence was done to the royal scheme then and later by barons not to be kept in hand, eviscerated public hundred courts with nothing but the ungranted thief jurisdiction[208] remain in after years mute witnesses to the truth of what in crabbed Latin the *Leges* tell us about *sac* and *soc*.

While the *Leges* throw no light upon the question of delegation which later becomes crucial,[209] it leaves no doubt that the

franchise but who has duties of protecting and representing his men. Finally, it is important to note that the discussion in *Hn.* 94 *et seq.* is in terms of lords, not hundreds, receiving mulcts. This accords with *Hn.* 27 where it is said that vavassors who have free lands—*liberas terras* (Liebermann, *Gesetze*, 582, note *k*, "privileged with jurisdiction")—have pleas of *wite* and *wer*. Liebermann's reading of *liberas terras* is necessarily controlled by 20, 2, i.e. the *comes*, not the vavassor, has *sac* and *soc* because of status.

[207] *Supra*, note 191.

[208] Jolliffe, *Origin of the Hundred in Kent (Tait Essays)*, 161, "The hundred seems to be a court for a very narrow range of causes, perhaps, with a single exception for none but the petty torts and transgressions which are of common feudal right. Again and again, charters, inquisitions and plea rolls present us with hundreds which are courts for one plea only, infangthef, or the trial of thieves *cum manuopere capti*." The factor most persuasive in Jolliffe's proof is the lateness of the evidence used. His argument both here and in *Northumbrian Institutions* (41 *E.H.R.* 32) is directed toward matters of local history, but it has general significance in the fact that *sac* and *soc* is the minimal and most common franchise. *Infangtheof* is less often granted and being an independent franchise its subsequent lingering in the public hundred supplies excellent factual proof for the correctness of the present interpretation of *sac* and *soc*. *Cf.* further on the relation of *sac* and *soc* with the jurisdiction of the hundred, Douglas, *The Social Structure of Medieval East Anglia* (1927), 189 *et seq.* Compare, finally, the Quarre Charter (ca. 1142) ". . . ut ad nullam hundredum eant nisi ad hundredum de latrocinii." Galbraith, *Monastic Foundation Charters*, 4 *Cambridge Historical Journal*, 297.

[209] Franchises are delegated: *cf.* the charter in Stenton, *Types of Mano-*

basic principle of franchise is settled, for it states rules for royal supervision over franchise courts,[210] the crown's authority to punish for failure of justice,[211] its power of actual supervision and interference where franchises are exceeded,[212] the requirement that royal officers attend punishment of thieves.[213] In contrast with the book's brevity on the feudal lord's jurisdiction over his men *ratione privilegii domini*[214] and its disinterested vagueness on jurisdiction appurtenant to the economy of an estate,[215]

*rial Structure,* Appendix; the charter of feoffment in 42 *E.H.R.* 247, where the big franchises are reserved; *sac and soc* goes to the feoffee because the land is *libera* (*cf.* Liebermann's comment on *Hn.* 27) but reserved by the feoffor over Frenchmen. *Cf.* also 6 *Monasticon* 221, 251.

[210] *Hn.* 24, 3: "Nullus enim socnam habet impune peccandi," the basic idea. *Hn.* 24, 4: if a king's officer first learns of an offense in the territory of one having *soc* he does not take the case unless the *soc* is exceeded. *Hn.* 24, 1: "Super barones socnam suam habentes, habet iudex fiscalis iusticie legis observancium, et quicquid peccabitur in eorum personam . . ." Liebermann, *Glossar, Gerichtsbarkeit* 34 treats "legis observancium" as jurisdiction over them as defendants. The expression is general enough to suggest supervision of the *soc,* made specific in *Hn.* 24, 3, above. Henry I's judges were present in the court of the Bishop of Exeter, Haskins, *Bernard the King's Scribe* in 14 *E.H.R.* 421, doc. no. 15. The case in 1 *Cart. Mon. Ramsei.* (R.S.) 239, may be evidence of the same rule. *Leg. Edw. Conf.* 9, 2: a king's justice must be present when a man of another baron is involved. Liebermann, *Über die Leges Edwardi,* 89, limits this, without sufficient warrant, to cases where ordeal is to be used.

[211] *Hn.* 10, 1; 22, 1; 33, 1 a. And *cf.* also *Hn.* 57, 5; 59, 14; *Leg. Edw. Conf.* 9, 1.

[212] *Hn.* 22, 1 *et seq.*

[213] *Hn.* 26–26, 4.

[214] *Hn.* 55.

[215] The *Leges Henrici* mention this jurisdiction in the most indirect way. Although domanial jurisdiction is often described as halmote by modern writers (e.g., Ault, *Private Jurisdiction in England* [1923], 8) the *Leges* do not treat halmote as an independent type of *soc.* In passages like *Hn.* 9, 4, "vel halimoto socam habentium"; 20, 1 a, "sub prepositis maneriorum in iis adiacentibus halimotis," 57; 8; 78, 2, the compiler is talking in terms of courts, not their jurisdiction. The halmote obviously means here only the court of a lord, as against a county or hundred court. The one passage which suggests definite franchised content for the halmote is 20, 2, mentioning the lands of magnates who for reason of status "socam et sacam habent in causis communibus et halimotis pertinentibus." This suggests that the so-called halmote jurisdiction is franchisal. Liebermann, *Glossar. Hallengericht* and *Gericht* 11 c, thinks that expressions like *in ipso manerio*

it is prolix on *soc* derived from the crown. It is for this reason that it sees private jurisdiction as preeminently franchisal.

### CROWN PLEAS UNDER THE NORMAN KINGS

The growth of royal franchise doctrine has been considered here in its relation to the implications of tenure and from the angle of what was granted by the crown. This approach, while essential to an understanding of how the problem of local enforcement in "private" hands was managed, does little justice to the even more significant question: how did the crown promote its own direct jurisdiction over wrongdoing? This is the familiar problem of the so-called crown plea, the cornerstone of modern criminal procedure.

It is commonly averred that the crown plea was something well recognized in Henry I's day and that even by this time the Norman kings had marked out a prerogative, distinct from their ordinary public authority. These prerogatives are supposed to have extended to specific subject matter, to have been maintained and expanded until the principle of royal monopoly over major crime was established. In this tale there is much askew. Through it has run the murmur of innuendo that thirteenth-century legal distinctions were already known in the opening decades of the twelfth century. It has been embellished like a medieval miracle book with theoretical fantasies. We propose to consider the development of the crown plea on the basis of such scattered facts as survive regarding exchequer, chancery and judicial procedure, and to determine how far accepted doctrine is acceptable.

*Hn.* 56, 4, and sometimes *curia domini,* are used in the sense of a domanial court. Except for *Hn.* 78, 2, dealing with self-enslavement, and section 56 on farms, the *Leges* have practically nothing to say about economic questions. Stenton, *English Feudalism,* 43, speaks of these courts as "local courts mainly concerned with the affairs of peasants." Maitland, *Domesday Book,* 82, thinks every lord can hold a court for his villains. The most that can be said is that if *maneria* in the *Leges* occasionally means domanial court, the right is not part of *sac* and *soc,* since in *Hn.* 19, 2, the grant of a manor is clearly distinguished therefrom.

It is important to note at the outset that under the Norman kings it is not exchequer practice to treat royal-public rights as an indivisible fiscal entity. This is clear enough in Domesday.[216] To a certain extent it can be deduced from variations in the dispositions of charters. Royal grants carrying the lesser franchises will cut into royal or shrieval income, depending upon whether or not the *soc* is farmed.[217] If the charter runs to *hamsocn, forsteall* and the like, the king alone loses.[218] Obviously the distinction between revenue farmed and revenue directly taken, like the distinction between public function permanently delegated to public officers and that reserved for direct action by the crown, is one favorable to the formulation of prerogative rights. This is far from saying that there already existed standards of separability based upon some political principle. We believe it unlikely

[216] Most clearly shown where the book deals with the rights of *ministri regis* as against the sheriff or his *ministri*. For example, as to the former, 1 *D.B.*, 157 b; 162; 2 *ib.*, 287 b; as to the vicecomital *ministri*, 1 *D.B.*, 69. Cf. *Hn.*, 9, 11, for the distinction between sheriff and *ministri regis; Hn.* 10, 4 and *Hn.* 19, 1, for the recognition of *ministri vicecomitis*. Morris, *Medieval English Sheriff*, 54, makes too sweeping a conclusion regarding the sheriff's control of these king's officers. His references do not support his premise. Note further for references to the king's ferm, 1 *D.B.* 50; 60 b; 86 b; 184 b, which may indicate an accounting distinct from the sheriff's ferm. Besides the division as between sheriff and king, the separation of lay and ecclesiastical jurisdiction by William leads to another type of partition of public rights as between king and church, as evidenced later in *Hn.* 11–11, 17.

[217] Generally on the sheriff's ferm of king's demesne, Ballard, *Domesday Inquest*, 74, Morris, *Medieval English Sheriff*, 65. Note also in this relation the references in the preceding note to the king's ferm. The mechanics of a charter grant cutting into a ferm appear with clarity in a charter of the Earl of Chester (1119) in 1 *Chartulary of Chester Abbey*, no. 6. Two entries in *P.R. 31 Hy. I* (7, 109), suggest accountings for a grant which has subtracted from a ferm; see Round, *Commune of London* (1899) 73. For later, Parow, *Compotus Vicecomitis* 32.

[218] The king's *forisfacturae* are *extra firmas*. For example, Kent—1 *D.B.* 2; Worcestershire—*ibid.*, 172; Yorkshire—*ibid.*, 336; Oxford—*ibid.*, 154 b; Berkshire—*ibid.*, 56 b; Salford—*ibid.*, 270. The variations of the sum due the crown are discussed in Liebermann, *Glossar, Strafgeldfixum*. Note further 1 *D.B.*, 252 (Shropshire), where it is stated, *grithbryce, forsteall* and *hamsocn (Heinfar)* were *extra firmas T.R.E.* throughout England.

that there was in Henry I's day a *legal theory* which clearly divided prerogative and ordinary public authority.[219] The several bits of evidence for the factual existence of this division do not support a conclusion that governmental practice as yet yielded legal generalization. This is a caveat of particular consequence in matters of criminal justice. To illustrate: a plea like *grithbryce* (protection breach) can involve a special forfeit; it can be separately accounted for in the exchequer; it can be tried only in a certain court in a certain way; it can lie in grant. But over the peace or protection given directly by the king himself, the plea is never specifically granted; the offender is in the king's mercy, he may even be triable only by the king himself. In both cases the different incidents may exist by virtue of a royal prerogative, yet clearly the implications of one plea cannot be carried over to other pleas. Whatever may have been departmental trends, there is no class of *placita coronae* by any combined office test in Henry I's day.[220] There is king's *soc,* sheriff's *soc* and baron's

[219] Adams, *Origin of the English Constitution,* 88, seems to imply there was. It is true the distinction between protection by the hand of the crown and that via the sheriff, and the rules of regional peace where the king is, tend toward a separation of prerogative from other public rights. On the other hand, the *Leges Henrici* show clearly that the contrast which is of weight in the law is as between royal-public rights and baronial as, for example, the privilege of the *iudex fiscalis* (*Hn.* 63, 1) to accuse without witnesses which is paralleled by a similar but more limited right of the *dominus* (*Hn.* 63, 2; 44, 2): the rule that until the king is answered no one can implead a defendant (*Hn.* 43, 1).

[220] The term appears in *Hn. Lond.* c. 1 (Lierbermann, *Gesetze,* 525), but in no other scientifically tested Henry I charter which has come to our notice. It is no more a word of art than the phrases "regalia placita" in a chronicle account of a trial *temp.* Wm. II (Bigelow, *Placita Anglo-Normannica* 69), or "placita que corone regis pertinent," *P.R. 31 H.I.* 91, or placitis et forisfactis que pertinuerint ad coronam meam" in a charter of the Empress (Round, *Geoffrey de Mandeville* [1892], 92, and *cf.* 1 Dugdale, *Baronage,* 202). It is not used in *Leges Henrici,* the one purported legalistic exposition of royal rights over crime; instead, *cf.* half a dozen circumlocutions, collected in Liebermann, *Glossar, Kronprozess,* 1c–d. To treat *placita coronae* as a concept of unique and specific meaning *temp.* Hy. I (*ib.,* 15b; Morris, *English Const. Hist.,* 172–3) is misleading. Not until fifty years later is it so identified.

*soc.*[221] In all of them the element of king's prerogative is greater or less depending upon the specific jurisdiction exercised.

It is, of course, impossible to advance an hypothesis regarding the standard of separability already mentioned, particularly as this involved royal authority in matters criminal under the Norman kings, without examining the supposed liaison of prerogative and *placita coronae* set forth in the *Leges Henrici*. The orthodox gambit has been from II *Cnut,* 12, to *Leges Henrici,* 10: from the *gerihta* of the Dane in Wessex to the rights of the Norman "over all men." The modest enumeration of Cnut's doom— *mundbryce, hamsocn, forsteall, fyrdwite* [*flymenafyrmthe*]—is supposed in some mystical way to have expanded over the ensuing century and to have acquired the generic name *placita coronae*[222]—judicial prerogative over certain specific offenses.

The compiler comes to this list of Henry's rights just after he has finished explaining the *soc* of mulcts/pleas.[223] Some he has

---

[221] *Hn.* 9, 11.

[222] Maitland, *Constitutional History of England* (1920) 107 *et seq.;* 2 Pollock and Maitland, *H.E.L.,* 453 *et seq.* Holdsworth's version, 2 *History of English Law,* 47 *et seq.,* varies, with greater emphasis on the king's peace. The Maitland theory is adopted by the modern treatises on English constitutional history, e.g. *cf.* Stubbs, *Lectures on Early English History,* 154–5; Adams, *Constitutional History of England* (1921), 84; Morris, *Constitutional History,* 171, 231. The materials and notes in Goebel, *Cases and Materials on the Development of Legal Institutions* (1931) were compiled before the research on the present volume was begun and the editor desires at this point to repudiate any underwriting of the orthodox theories of *placita coronae* and king's peace.

[223] *Hn.* 9, 11. The fractioned form is used in the text because *placitum* is an expression which is as often to be rendered "mulct" as "plea." In the pipe rolls of Henry II it is constantly used as mulct, *cf.* 1 Ramsay, *Revenue of the Kings of England* (1925) 45, 49. Liebermann, in *Wörterbuch* 173, gives the two chief meanings from the Anglo-Norman sources as *court, cause (Prozess),* although he renders the *placita* of *Hn. Cor.,* 6, as "gerichtlicher Anspruch," i.e. judicial claim; *plait,* however, he renders "Prozessabhandlung samt Sporteln." For the contemporary use in the sense of mulct, *cf.* the letter of Herbert of Losinga to Roger of Salisbury (*Epistolae Herberti Losingae* [1846] no. 26) "In terris meis exiguntur quinquaginta librae pro placitis, cum earumdem terrarum mei homines nec in responsionem nec in facto peccaverint." Note also Round, *Geoffrey de Mandeville,* 105.

said belong to the fisc of the king solely, and some it shares; others belong to sheriffs and king's officers in their ferm; and some belong to barons who have *sac* and *soc*. Then follows the famous section 10—*De iure regis:* "These are the rights which the King of England alone has in his lands over all men"[224]— followed by the long and "disorderly" enumeration. The law-book goes on: all royal roads (*herestrete*) are the king's entirely, all places of execution are entirely in the king's *soc*. And all persons ordained, aliens, the poor and abject are in the king's guard if they have no one else. "These are the demesne pleas of the king; nor do they belong in the ferm of viscounts or of their bailiffs or officers unless by specific agreement."[225] There follow eight rubrics dealing with the pleas of the church belonging to the king, the list of emendable pleas, the pleas that put a man in the king's mercy, reliefs, danegeld, peace of the king's court, forests, proof.

If some regard is had for the structure of the book the section *De iure regis* is to be taken as the elaboration[226] of the first class of *"soc* of pleas," i.e., the sole rights of the royal fisc; and the last statement quoted above is simply a characterization of the whole list, a final warning that the sheriff cannot incorporate these matters in his ferm. The *De iure regis,* then, is properly regarded as a statement of fiscal fact.[227] The list of matter ceases thus to be disorderly because it is not intended as a description of judicial activity, any more than a statement of United States Treasury

---

[224] "Hec sunt iura que rex Anglie solus et super omnis hominis habet in terra sua."

[225] *Hn.* 10, 4.

[226] This is typical. In the structure of sections 10–19, for instance, §13 on *misericordia,* §14 on reliefs, §15 on danegeld, §16 on the peace of the king, §17 on forests, are all specifications of §10, 1 a, series of involuted glosses on items from the main passage, §10, 1.

[227] Liebermann, *Über die Leges Henrici* §36 thinks the compiler not specially involved in exchequer practice. Morris, *The Sheriff and the Justices,* 7 *California Law Review,* 237, remarks that the author of the *Leges Henrici* had made a study of the king's ferm, but in the *Constitutional History,* 166, 168, 231, he merely states the orthodox interpretation of *Hn.* 10, 1.

receipts is a description of the jurisdiction of United States District Courts. The clinching proof of this lies in the close correspondence between the items of the list in *De iure regis* and the accounts *extra firmas* in the surviving exchequer account from the reign of Henry I.[228]

It is probable that the significance of section 10 would not have been obscured for so long had the compiler of *Leges Henrici* made its setting more obvious by developing in equal detail and

---

[228] In testing against the entries in *P.R. 31 Hy. I* the items in the list of *Hn.* 10, 1, it is proper to note at the outset that none of the matters listed relating to foreign war or rebellion (castles, treason and infidelity, peace breach in the army, *fyrdinga* or flight in battle) are entered nor would they be likely to appear since the year for which accounting was made and the years immediately preceding were peaceful. The items of danegeld, forests and reliefs appear with constancy in practically every county. Specifically criminal matter is accounted for as follows: *infraccio pacis regis, P.R. 31 Hy. I*, 11, 15, 45, 46, etc. (a great many entries as is to be expected from the many protections issued by Henry I); killing or injuring the king's servants, 100; *utlagaria*, an accounting *ne disfaciant utlagos*, 37, *de terris utlagorum qui aufugerunt*, 143; *furtum* punished with death, an entry *propter duellum latronum*, 103, for the sanction in criminal duel cases is death; murder, *passim* (*cf.* entries on homicide, e.g. 66, 75, 90, 149, 156, 159); moneyers, 9, 35, 42, 112, etc.; *hamsocn* (*heimfar*), 112; *flemenafyrmthe*, possibly *pro latrone quam celavit*, 73; assault, *propter assaltu navium et domorum Lond.*, 146, which may, however, be taken as another form of entry for *hamsocn*; *stretebreche, pro una calceda quam fecit in via regis*, 117; rape and/or *raptus*, 90, 111. There are no identifiable entries for the offenses *forsteall, incendium* (common *temp.* H. II), robbery (common *temp.* H. II), fighting in the king's house, or harboring excommunicates (*cf. P.R. 22 Hy. II* [1176] 57 pro recpt. excomm. 40 s.). On miscellaneous rights: treasure trove, *P.R. 31 H. I*, 68, 91 etc.; *maris laganum*, no entries; wreck, 116, 121; unjust judgments or failure of judgment, 85, 115, 120; contempt of writs, no entries; *despectus* or *maliloquium*, 136—*pro falso clamore* (which is a form of *despectus: Hn.* 59, 14); *trinoda necessitas, P.R. 31 Hy. I*, 141. There are no clear entries for *presumptio terrae vel pecunie regis*, but the entries *ibid.*, 2, *propter nemoribus regis que adeo destructa sunt quod nullus vicecomes potest inde reddere firmam* (i.e., a fiscal, not a forest, offense), and the large sum *quas injuste abstulit villanis et burgibus de propriis maneris Regis* look like purprestures. The meaning of *prevaricacio legis regie* is doubtful (*cf.* Stubbs, *Lectures in Early English History*, 155), and we notice no entries which seem to illustrate it. There are no entries for *borgbreche,* but the sums paid, *ibid.*, 91, 113, for flights and escapes may be for quittances from the liabilities of pledges.

in immediate sequence, both the other types of *soc,* vicecomital and baronial, of his tripartite division. The latter he considers at length[229] in a running commentary throughout the book, but the sheriff's ferm defies cataloging because it is a matter of contract, although a head of jurisdiction. In two separate places[230] occurs the remark that the sheriff's ferm is contractual, as a caveat in regard to royal rights and as an excuse for not elaborating upon the ferm. Of course, the nucleus about which the bargaining of king and sheriff will revolve can be gathered from other passages in *Leges Henrici,* as, for example, the omission of the "common causes" from the list of royal rights, and from the scattered statements about summons and other references to shrieval courtkeeping.[231] It is this fact of courtkeeping, which is the legal foundation for the real inducement of the bargain, the opportunity of extortion, the precedents for which stretch back into the manipulations of *consuetudo* by the French feudatories.[232]

There are other reasons for believing that the section *De jure regis* is not cast in terms of *placita coronae* as the expression is later used. It is about king's rights, not as sovereign of the realm but in *terra sua*[233]—in the king's land, demesne land, land the

[229] *Supra,* pp. 394 *et seq.*

[230] *Hn.* 10, 4; 19, 1.

[231] The passage *Hn.* 7—7, 7, *De generalibus placitis comitatum* . . . has only general information. The *communis causa,* (*supra,* and see especially 9, 4) falls within shrieval jurisdiction in the hundred or county court, unless it is granted as a franchise of *sac* and *soc.* Other substantive shrieval jurisdiction arises out of control over roads and waters not royal. *Leg. Edw. Conf.* 12, 9; duties in connection with process, e.g., summons, *Hn.* 41, 5; 60, 3; *capias excommunicatum, Episc. Leges* 3, 1; distraint, *Hn.* 51, 4, 6. To be sharply distinguished are passages like *Hn.* 66, 9, where the sheriff or royal justice can implead for major crimes, for these matters clearly form no part of the ferm.

[232] The later hundred rolls, compiled in a period of great expansion of royal authority, give the classic picture of the opportunities and how they were improved. *A fortiori* the extortions of sheriffs must have been a pretty thing in the earlier period. Some remarks in Morris, *Medieval Sheriff,* 99, *et seq.*

[233] The mention of *terra sua* in the *De iure regis* must be read with *Hn.*

king has not made immune or otherwise discharged, although in
such cases these rights where granted are an act of royal indulgence. Even where the discussion moves to the highways and
places of execution, these are stated to be in the king's *soc,* i.e.,
they are not treated as a vague prerogative at large but as property.[234] He uses *regnum*[235] when he means the realm, and *terra*
when he has in mind the rights which men of his age are still
unable to disassociate from the soil and its tenure.[236] His distinctions are expressed as between things owned and possessed
as against things owned but hired out to possession. The matters
listed in the *De iure regis* are *dominica placita*[237]—the *demesne
soc;* they are something the king himself possesses as against

19, 1, the summary phrase following nine sections of detailed exposition
of the royal rights: "these [the preceding matters] with their appurte-
nances are reckoned (*censentur:* the word seems to be used in a technical
fiscal sense) matters for the justice or indulgence of the king and for his
own fisc . . . wherever, by whom or in whom they be, whether the
demesne and *soc* be with the king or it is one of the two"—i.e., he has one
or the other. The writer goes on to explain why *soc* is inherent in king's
land and how he grants it. The main point of the passage is that, whether
the crown has retained both title and *soc* or has conveyed either one, the
rights enumerated are accounted for to the fisc. In this connection compare the writ of Henry I (21 *E.H.R.* 506) regarding the taking of oath for
the impending hostilities with Robert. The sheriff is to attend to it for the
King's men (dominicis hominibus) while the barons are to arrange for the
same matter as to their men. The crown wishes to be assured by oath
"terra*m* mea[m] Anglie ad tenendum et ad defendendum contra omnes
homines. . . ." In other words, the king is requesting a reaffirmation of
a *feudal* duty respecting the tenements of which he is suzerain. The manner in which the affair is to be executed indicates clearly the precept is
drawn in the idiom of feudal law. This precept is worth considering in
relation to the Salisbury oath saga, on which see 19 *History* (1934–5), 248.
    [234] The poor and abject are said to be merely in the King's sib and pro-
tection or representation without use of jurisdictional words.
    [235] E.g., *Hn.* 6; 9, 10; *cf. Quadripartitus,* Arg. 2.
    [236] *Hn.* 20, 2; 27; 41, 1 etc., see also Liebermann, *Glossar, Lehnwesen.*
Between this feudalist's use of *terra* in the early twelfth century and the
later *lex terrae* in Glanvill there has occurred some blurring of terms: *cf.*
Radin, *Glanvill: Lex Terrae and Ius Regni,* 82 *Pennsylvania Law Rev.*
26 *et seq.* In *Leges Henrici* the expression *lex terrae* does not occur: Glanvill's idea is expressed by *ius publicum,* 45, 1–63, 3. *Lex Patrie* 11, 17 is
Anglo-Saxon law.
    [237] *Hn.* 10, 4.

what he has let out or enfeoffed,[238] just as the king's court is
*dominice curie,*[239] and the *dominica necessaria*[240] are matters not
let to ferm. These feudal concepts and distinctions are basic in
the crown's theories and they persist in the face of its growing
sovereignty. Two reigns later escheated fiefs are not assimilated
to the demesne royal any more than they were in Domesday,[241]
but are separately accounted for and administered, and upon
refeoffment are held *ut de honore.*[242]

It is evident that once one discards modern theories of sovereignty and regards the *Leges* as the product of a mind steeped
in feudal lore,[243] the section 10, *De iure regis,* with its satellites
11–20, can be regarded as nothing more pretentious than a curt
and unbalanced *tractatus de scaccario,* the first few lines of such
a treatise as the chief of the Domesday commissioners could
have written had he sought to synthesize his reports. This view
necessarily forces an abandonment of the unhappy liaison so
long supposed to have existed between the *De iure regis* and the
*placita coronae* as they later evolved.[244] The crown is not concerned with grasping and cherishing a monopoly of any single

[238] Compare *dominica captalia, Hn.* 13, 5; 91, 3, a manor *de dominio
et firma regis* and *Hn.* 19, 1 lands *quas rex in dominio suo habet.* The same
distinction of course carried out as to the barons, *Hn.* 7, 7; 56, 3.

[239] *Hn.* 49, 4.

[240] *Hn. Com.* 2, 2; and *ibid.,* 3, the *dominicos barones. Cf.* also *P.R. 31
Hy. I,* 131, where money is liberated to two men "dum fuerunt ad necessaria regis facienda in episcopatu."

[241] The Domesday rule is that land escheated to the crown remains
geldable. Eyton, *A Key to Domesday* (1878), 102. The royal manors were
held exempt "in principle" from the payment of geld, Vinogradoff, *English Society,* 182.

[242] *Dialogus de Scaccario* II, 24, 27; 1 Stubbs, *Constitutional History,*
433. Mitteis, *Lehnrecht und Staatsgewalt,* 688 misunderstands the situation. *Cf.* also *In re Halliday* [1922] 2 Ch. Div., 698.

[243] "Er ist überhaupt der feudalste unter Englands juristischen Schrift-
stellern," Liebermann, *Über die Leges Henrici,* 48.

[244] The words "commoda pacis ac securitatis institutione retenta,"
which immediately precede the list itself, no doubt have colored interpretation due to the currency among writers of the "peace" theory of jurisdiction. *Cf.* Stubbs, *Lectures,* 154. The words are no more than the senten-
tious preamble which garnishes so much legislation old and new.

wrong at large whenever and by whomever perpetrated. Its judicial activity is still too much a matter of supervision rather than direct jurisdiction.

By far the most interesting illustration of this is *grithbryce-mundbryce*. This term had appeared in Cnut's list of fiscal rights, is still granted by Henry I, yet it is strikingly absent from the list in *De iure regis*. This attests with conclusiveness the fact that the *De iure regis* is a statement of exchequer practice, not even of exchequer theory and much less of a franchise theory of pleas of the crown. For the exchequer has ceased to regard *grith-bryce-mundbryce* as something special. The plea carries as penalty only the traditional 100-shilling royal mulct,[245] while breach of the writgiven or handgiven peace is enforceable by the more flexible and profitable Norman *misericordia*. The feudatory is thus allowed to pick at the leavings while the crown satiates itself with fresh kills. Out of the big list of criminal matter in section 10 only *hamsocn, forsteall, fihtwite, latrocinium, infang-theof* and *flymenafyrmthe* are ever granted in terms by the Conqueror and his sons, and this fairly sparingly. Under Henry I the heads of grant are extended once to include moneyers,[246] and twice to include wreck.[247] The crown allows only ancient traditional matter to become franchisal. *Sac* and *soc* is freely carved out of shrieval perquisites. But matters like contempt of writ, king's protection, duel, or outlawry are never specifically turned over to the barons to run the risk of feudal manipulation. How-

---

[245] *Grithbryce,* although the subject of grant, is not in *Hn.* 10, but is listed in *Hn.* 12, 2 as a matter for which 100 sol. is the penalty.

[246] To the Archbishop of York 1102, 1 Farrer, *Early Yorkshire Charters*, no. 14, "et nova statuta mea de judiciis sive de placitis latronum et falsorum monetariorum exequatur et faciat per suam propriam justitiam in curia sua." This is to be distinguished from grants of the right of minting, e.g., William II to Bury St. Edmunds, Davis, *Regesta*, App. no. 63, for there is no indication that the grant of minting gives this criminal jurisdiction. The Hereford moneyers have *sac* and *soc*, 1 *D.B.*, 179, but this certainly does not include judgment of life and limb.

[247] *Chronicon de Bello*, 49 and cf. 66; *Chron. Abb. Ramsei.*, 281. It is possible there are other grants. We believe we have examined all these in print.

ever a feudatory may have viewed a grant of *plena curia,* quittance of shires and hundreds, all royal liberties and customs, the crown did not estop itself by specification beyond the *forisfactura* with which great men had been honored since Cnut.[248]

The reservations while directly probative only of reserved fiscal rights suggest, however, the existence of a body of jurisdictional matter, a king's *soc,* not decimated by conveyance. This inference is buttressed, moreover, by considerable evidence in the legal sources of procedural matter related to, or indeed an infinite part of this *soc.* In short, the crown in Henry I's time has a law which is not feudal, and the content of this law we believe was built up by the Conqueror and his sons by ordinance and by the maintenance of a monopoly over criminal procedure to the sole use of the crown.

### ROYAL CONTROL OF PROCEDURE AND SANCTIONS

For a leader coming in with an invading army, criminal law is not a minor administrative detail to be attended to at leisure. There are contemporary and vestigial evidences of the initial stage of martial law in post-conquest England[249] but drumhead jurisprudence even in a conquered country leads to too much racial friction to suit a conqueror who not only proposes to settle his men there permanently and if possible peacefully, but who advances his claim on a theory of legitimate succession. A factor which must have led the Conqueror to project a national criminal law was the danger of headstrong application of sanctions by his followers, and he had ready to hand in the royal prerogatives inherited from Cnut the core of right to claim control over major crime. The first of William's ordinances of which there

[248] II *Cnut,* 12; *Hn.* 20, 3.
[249] So the penitential composed for the invading army contemplates all variety of brutality. Bessin, *Concilia,* 50; 1 Wilkins, *Concilia,* 366. That the provisions for murder fine are initially a measure of martial law is made clear by the fact that Normans, domiciled ante-conquest, are not included, *Wl. Art.,* 4.

is any record is therefore the *Lad,* regulating proof in causes between English and French.[250]

On its face the *Lad* abounds in inconsistencies, and its parts are so badly correlated that it seems to be made up of fragments. Opening like a writ it has the inconclusive ending of an incompleted draft.[251] This indeed it may well be, although it has as well the appearance of sections in the *Très Ancien Coutumier* where separate decisions are sometimes loosely strung together under a single rubric. To iron out its inconsistencies it must be broken up into its constituent parts.

The *Lad* is cast in procedural terms, and consequently every technical word is to be construed strictly in terms of contemporary procedure. So taken the document divides into three parts: 1) the general rule changing English law; 2) the detailed rules regarding battle in cases less than *utlagaria;* 3) the detailed rules for major crimes.

The first section lays down the rule basic for the whole act, a change in the personal law of Englishmen—they may use battle not only in theft or homicide cases but "in any other case where battle or ordeal is proper." By this broad language must be understood the trial as well of land actions as of crimes, to avoid inconsistency with the section immediately following, which announces that where no offer of duel is made the French defendant can defend "by oath with witnesses,"[252] a procedure which in contemporary Norman sources is used only in land cases,[253] never in criminal cases, although in later Norman law it appears in cases of assaults.[254] The same right to resort to "testi-

---

[250] *Willelmes Lad* (c. 1066–77) *Gesetze,* 483. Davis, *Regesta,* 238, regards it as spurious, a canard disposed of by Liebermann, *Erklärungen,* 272.

[251] Liebermann, *loc. cit.* argues for a lost original.

[252] Generally on this Brunner, *Schwurgerichte,* 195 *et seq.*

[253] *Ibid.,* 196 *et seq.,* for contemporary Ms. charter references; Round *Calendar,* 1114, 1190. No. 116 is also in point, the form of attestation indicating procedure by witnesses: Brunner, *loc. cit.; Chart. Mon. St. Trinité (C.D.I.)* no. 82.

[254] This is our reading of the Latin version of *T.A.C.,* cap. XV, 3. The French version (Marnier, *op. cit.,* 15) is completely inconsistent.

mony" is given to Englishmen,[255] a rule which must be taken not as confirming extant English law of purgation by oath but as introducing testimonial proof as it was employed in Normandy, for it is clearly distinguished from the subsequent use in the ordinance of the technical word for law wager (*plano iuramento*). Another rule consistent only with civil procedure allows a "defensor," a champion to the defendant Englishman who is incapable or even merely undesirous of fighting, for in criminal cases of later English law the defendant may not escape battle except on a ground of physical disqualification, and even then his option is not a champion but the ordeal.[256] Finally, the rule that the defeated Frenchman pays 60 shillings is sensible only if taken as the usual Norman penalty for the loss of a land action:[257] it would be absurd as a statement of the economic sanction for conviction of crime,[258] for here the closely contemporary Domesday puts the offender in mercy for life, limb or chattels.[259]

At this point the *Lad* turns to the specific consideration of criminal causes and states for Englishmen accused of crimes in-

[255] *Lad,* 2, 3, "bellum" and "testimonium" are equated. Ordeal is a third alternative if the first two are distasteful. On the use of witnesses in English civil cases, Wulfstan v. Walter (c. 1077), *Plac. Anglo-Norm.*, 16. Offers to prove "omni modo" in Domesday may fairly be taken to include "testimonium." 2 *D.B.* 285 b.; 2 *D.B.* 371 (*omnibus legibus*); 2 *D.B.* 338 b; compare *Hn.* 48, 12 "Et in diraciocinacione feudi precedere debet feudatus testem suum ad bellum vel aliam legem."

[256] Glanvill, XIV, 1, states the rule for criminal cases. *Cf.* for civil cases II, 3.

[257] Coulin, *Gerichtlicher Zweikampf,* 153; clearly implied in *T.A.C.,* cap. XLI.

[258] Liebermann suggests that it is the penalty on a defeated plaintiff. *Gesetze,* 484 col. 3. Liebermann's interpretation of the whole document is colored by an assumption for which there is no proof whatever, i.e., that there existed official prosecution under the Conqueror. Consequently he treats *Lad,* 1, 1, as applying to appeals by a private party and *Lad,* 3—3, 2, as official prosecution. This ingenious suggestion does not take into account the use of varying technical expressions in the several sections; it fails to explain the obvious inconsistency between 2, 3, 3 and 3, 1; it incorrectly accounts for *furtum* and *homicidium* as something different from *utlagaria* when we know outlawry is used as process for these crimes.

[259] 1 *D.B.*, 154 b 2; 262 b 1.

volving outlawry[260] (i.e., major crimes where outlawry is process) the harsh principle, long operative in the Norman *treuga Dei* procedure, of purgation by ordeal. He still has, as plaintiff, an option, for if he appeals a Frenchman of such an offense and offers to deraign by his body, the Frenchman must accept the challenge to battle. If the Englishman does not dare to fight, the Frenchman can purge by simple oath.

The care with which the word "complain" (*compellare*) is employed throughout the early sections of the *Lad* serves as a caveat that minor causes are likely to be involved, for it is only when speaking of *utlagaria* that the technical "appeal" (*appellare*) is used.

The radical change in English procedure effected by these measures has implications beyond the mere matter of pleading and proof. By undertaking to regulate the method of trying the major crime the crown here begins the process of absorbing full cognizance; and, further, by the very method of regulation implicitly establishes in England the inevitable concomitants—the Norman judgment and that part of the Norman sanctions connected therewith. We say implicitly, for such a judgment would be a tacit incident of the Norman form of proof, and there is no direct evidence of special legislation on punishment. It is true a London council of 1075 forbids participation of clerics in pronouncing sentences of death or mutilation[261] and the *Willelmi*

---

[260] *Utlagaria—utlaga þingan, Lad,* 3; 3, 1. Holdsworth, 2 *H.E.L.,* 150, and Robertson, *Laws of Kings of England* (1925), 233, translate "charges involving outlawry." This is misleading. Liebermann considers it merely classificatory (*Wörterbuch,* 231; *Glossar, friedlos,* 10; *Verbrechen,* 2a; *Die Friedlosigkeit bei den Angelsachsen,* in *Festschrift für Brunner,* 17). Liebermann's interpretation is probable for 1) the passage is a rule about trial, whereas there is no trial—in fact, no accusation of outlawry, outlaws are to be killed on sight (1 *D.B.,* 154 b); 2) *Willelmi Articuli,* 6 renders the same statute by specification, substituting for *utlaga þingan* or *utlagaria* the enumeration of the specific crimes of perjury, murder, theft, homicide and robbery [*ran, apertam rapinam*], as subjects of the appeal.

[261] 1 Wilkins, *Concilia,* 365: "Iterum, ut nullus episcopus, vel abbas, seu quilibet ex clero hominem occidendum, vel membris truncandum judicet, vel judicantibus suae auctoritatis favorem commodet. Hoc sancitum atque

*Articuli* (1090–1120) notes a change in the law from hanging to mutilation.[262] Both of these documents make it clear that afflictive punishment has been made general, but neither allows the inference that this was done by any formal act, although this seems probable because the Norman Kings would never have been satisfied with the Anglo-Saxon rules for failure at ordeal.[263]

As the final sanction was used in Normandy, at least the execution against land required no greater specificity than failure of proof. For failure at battle or ordeal entailed infamy, and the effect of infamy was disherison. In Normandy this was a consequence collateral or in addition to the punishment laid on the crime itself,[264] and this distinction between the consequence for failure of proof—disherison—and specific punishment is introduced into England. The rule of escheat in *Leges Henrici*[265] for defeat in battle or failure at the ordeal is embedded in a passage

confirmatum est coram duobus archiepiscopis, et xii episcopis, et Aschetillo, archidiacono Dorobernensis ecclesiae, et xxi abbatibus de archipraesulatu Cantuariensi."

[262] *Wl. Art.,* 10.

[263] Liebermann, *Erklärungen,* 273, for *Lad,* 2, 2, states only that the false complaint of the Englishman is punished by Anglo-Saxon law—*cf.* II *Cnut,* 16 (from III *Eg.* 4) tongue or wergeld. II *Cnut,* 30, 3 b—5, states the punishment for failure at the ordeal: for the first, payment of double amends and wergeld to the *hlaford* entitled to wite payment; at the second failure hands or feet are cut off according to the deed; and if the convicted party has committed "greater offenses," eyes are torn out, nose, ears, upper lip are cut off or he is scalped. The rule in 1 *Aethelred,* 1, 6 is decapitation. Liebermann, *Glossar, Rückfall,* treats the separate punishments in II *Cnut* as for repeated offenses. Where the ordeal is triple as for persons of ill fame, the iron weighs more (*ibid., Eisenordal,* 8) or the hand goes deeper into the kettle, *ibid., Kesselfang,* 9 b.

[264] *Supra,* Chapter IV.

[265] *Hn.* 43, 7: "Qui furtum fecerit, qui proditor domini sui fuerit, quicunque ab eo in obviacione hostili vel bello campali fugerit, vel victus erit vel feloniam fecerit terram suam forisfecerit." Liebermann, *Gesetze,* 569 amends the *victus* with *bello iudiciali.* There seems no particular reason why this emendation should be made, for it implies a distinction between trials by ordeal and battle inconsistent with the theory of the *Lad* and Norman procedure generally. In the *Instituta Cnuti, victus* is used in rendering II *Cnut* 37 (*oferstaeled*). *Quadripartitus* uses *probatus; Consilatio Cnuti* uses *convictus.*

dealing with land "forfeiture" and enumerating theft, treason, flight in battle and feudal felony, indicating that escheat upon conviction is what the compiler has in mind. This is innovation, for the Anglo-Saxons although familiar with infamy[266] did not treat forfeitures as a general consequence of infamy but specified it from time to time as punishment for this or that particular offense,[267] and certainly had not pushed the effects of infamy beyond procedural disqualifications.[268] On the continent, however, judicial combat, infamy and exheredation had nested together so long in post-Frankish procedure that once the form of proof was introduced in England, the incidents of conviction followed as of course.

The case was otherwise with *misericordia* as punishment. Norman law, as we know from the Inquest of 1091, links this punishment to a specific offense. It is not because a defendant fails at a particular sort of proof, but because he has failed to prove that he did not make false money or did not waylay a man

---

[266] Aethelstan's dooms (II *As.* 7, VI *As.* 1, 4) are familiar with the notion of the person often accused or often convicted *pro tanto* under procedural disadvantages. The dates (925–40) are late enough for *Pseudo-Isidore* to have been at work, Böhmer, *Kirche und Staat*, 46. But *Pseudo-Isidore* had not been "received" and there seems to be only a "trace" of its use at the opening of the eleventh century; Fehr, *Die Hirtenbriefe Aelfrics*, cx *et seq*. Of course the infamy idea may have come from Frankish temporal sources. But the clumsy way in which the law in II *As.* 20, 4 is trying to formulate the concept "criminous" seems to exclude this. The word *tihtbysig* by which the state of reputation is expressed appears first in III *Eg.* 7 (959–962). In III *Eadmund*, 7, 1, of which only *Quadripartitus* text survives, rules regarding the *infamati* are laid down indicating that the Latin synonym for the term *tihtbysig* may be earlier than Eadgar. *Tihtbysig* is used both in Aethelred's (e.g. I *Atr.* 1, 1, III *Atr.* 3, 4) and Cnut's dooms (II *Cnut* 22, 25 etc.) rephrased, *getreowa* = not *tihtbysig*, and *ungetreowan* = *tihtbysig*. The words are rendered in II *Cnut*, 22, 1, by the Anglo-Norman scribes *incredibilis* or *infidelis*, whereas in II *Cnut*, 25, *tihtbysig* is *infamatus* while *ungetreowe* is *incredibilis* in *Quadripartitus'* text.

[267] On this Liebermann, *Glossar, Vermögenseinziehung*, 10 *et seq*.

[268] This seems clear from III *Eg.* 7, 1 and II *Cnut*, 25 a—25, 1 (which repeats the Eadgar rule) for if the *tihtbysig* man cannot find pledges he is taken alive or dead, and deprived of all he has. The complainant gets

going to court that he is in the duke's mercy.[269] This same specificity as to crimes rules in the list of matters for which the
*Leges Henrici* stipulate *misericordia*.[270] The book generalizes
here only as to *utlagaria* by which it intends serious offenses,
what it elsewhere calls *graviora placita*.[271] The expression *utlagaria* links the rules of punishment in Henry's time to William's
*Lad* where the word is used in connection with proof. Although
this alone is no warrant for assuming that a broad rule of *misericordia* was imported simultaneously with duel, in Henry I's time
the causes where death or mutilation is threatened (treason in
various forms, murder, theft, arson, robbery, housebreach, homicide in church or where a man has a king's protection, perjury,
false coinage and rape)[272] are the capital causes and for the capital cause the form of trial stipulated is battle.[273] That ordeal may
also be used is to be deduced from the rule about foreoaths.[274]
The two currents of proof—as to punishment and as to manner
of trial—intermingle so persistently in the early twelfth century
that there is some logic in supposing the nexus existed from the
early years of Norman occupation, particularly as Henry's coro-

*ceapgyld* and the offender's lord and the hundred divide equally the re-
mainder. Obviously the state of being *tihtbysig* does not disqualify a man
from capacity to own property.

[269] Inquest of 1091, cap. 13 and cap. 1, i.e., offenses against the duke.

[270] *Hn.* 13.

[271] *Supra,* note, *Hn.* 11, 16 a: ". . . ut graviora placita magisque puni-
enda soli iusticie vel misericordie principis addicantur."

[272] *Hn.* 11, 6; 12, 1 a; 13, 12; 26, 3; 47; 59, 3, 18; 61, 9 a, 17; 64, 2; 66, 8;
82, 3. *Leis Wil.* 18—18, 2.

[273] *Hn.* 59, 16 a. *Cf.* also *Hn.* 49, 6; 92, 14.

[274] *Hn.* 64, 1 e, *Hn.* 64, 2. The fractionated oath (*sacramentum frac-
tum*), as *Hn.* 64, 1 f, indicates, is so dangerous for reasons of form that
ordeal is preferable. The rule in *Hn.* 64, 2 is for Wessex and the purpose of
a fractionated oath in theft, murder, treason, arson, *husbreche* and causes
for mutilation is obviously to force to the ordeal since no foreoath is needed
to force to battle (*Hn.* 92, 14); the offer to deraign subrogates therefor.
Liebermann, in *Glossar, Stabeid* 5, treats *Hn.* 64, 2, as referring to purgation by oath. This runs counter to so much in *Leges Henrici* that it is
necessary to regard the passage as referring to foreoaths, especially since
*Hn.* 64 is in general concerned with this specific question.

nation charter discloses that Norman "mercy" may have been for some time at work.[275]

The Conqueror's ordinance on proof is remarkable because it is a departure from the principle that law is personal, and because it is an assumption of a prerogative which in Normandy the duke did not as yet possess.[276] The duel procedure is not allowed to creep in with Norman rules of tenure, but with the need of enforcing specifically the criminal law, it is introduced through an exercise of sovereign power[277] as a change in the law at large. The whole combination of circumstances and motives resulted thus in moving forward the conception of public order to a point beyond its progress in Normandy and certainly in advance of pre-conquest English law. It is also too early to characterize the ordinance as defining what *Leges Henrici* call *ius regium*[278] for its immediate effect on crown rights was probably no more than to outline a field of authority where regulation might be developed. But events in Normandy have shown that this particular line of kings never slumbered on their rights.

[275] *Hn. Cor.*, 8.

[276] Brunner, *Schwurgerichte*, 159. Duel is regarded as the Norman "law of the land" by a contemporary—William of Poitou, *Gesta Willelmi*, 130, who recounts the challenge to Harold: "Praesto ego sum ad agendum causam contra illum in iudicio sive placet illi juxta jus Normannorum, sive potius Anglorum."

As shown in the previous chapter the distinction between modes of proof connected with blood justice and with tenurial matters cannot be drawn for Normandy at this time. The Norman decision of 1155 in *Chron. Robert of Torigni* (R.S.) App. 333 is less on the seignorial right to try by battle than on the venue at the *capitalis mansio*. The rules in *T.A.C.* are clearly the result of developing the pleas of the sword. Compare also the much later passage from 1 *Les Olim, C.D.I.* 334 (1270) "retulit curie quod ipsa domina habet ibidem justiciam de fundo terre usque ad duellum et congniciones mesleiarum, sine sanguine et sine discrevra." *Quaere* finally, how far the procedure fixed in the Empire for land cases by Otto (967), *M.G.H.*, 1 *Const.* 27 affected French feudal rules.

[277] This is obvious from the opening of the *Lad*, "mando et precipio," and Williams's other great innovation, the *Episcopales Leges*, 2, "mando et regia auctoritate precipio. . . ." These expressions became common writ form. Liebermann (*Wörterbuch* s.v. *cyðan*) indicates that not until the conquest does *cyð = precipio*.

[278] *Hn.* 9; 9, 5; and compare 9, 10 a.

Until the reign of Henry I there is no proof that duel was a procedure used only with royal license. The litigants who in Domesday offer to deraign by battle or ordeal make this to royal officers.[279] The two recorded cases in Rufus' reign are both for treason.[280] The practice in baronial courts is not known. That the propriety of combat there was an issue, however, is certainly to be inferred from the fact that in his county court ordinance Henry I provides battle for the trial of land cases in seignorial courts.[281] In the ordinary *causa communis* of which the lord with *sac* and *soc* will have cognizance, the *Leges Henrici* tell us that compurgation or ordeal is the rule,[282] and since ordeal is the only form used in seignorial courts about which the *Leges Edwardi* speak,[283] the sources seem reasonably conclusive on the restrictive use of battle. Such a restriction can mean only a fairly tight control by the crown, for a royal ordinance is needed to make legal its use in land cases tried by the baron. Furthermore, the *Leges Henrici* vouchsafe one additional piece of evidence on the same point, the limitation of battle to cases involving more than ten shillings (clearly land cases since the *causa communis* is not so triable) saving theft, breaches of the king's "peace" or matters punished afflictively, i.e., the capital cases, over which

[279] The cases are conveniently assembled in Bigelow, *Placita Anglo-Normannica*, 38, 40, 41, 42, 43, 44, 60, 61. Note also that the case of Wulfstan *v.* Walter, *ibid.*, 16 where duel is offered is also before a royal justice.

[280] 2 Freeman, *William Rufus*, 65, 615.

[281] *Hn. Com.* 3, 3.

[282] *Hn.* 49, 6 "in causis vero communibus tractande simul et finiende sunt querele de pluribus, que lege sacramentali vel iudicio promoventur."

[283] *Leg. Edw. Conf.*, 9, 3: "Et si barones [i.e., with own courts, *ibid.*, 9, 1] sunt qui iudicia [ordeal] non habeant in hundredo ubi placitum habitum fuerit, ad propinquiorem ecclesiam, ubi iudicium [ordeal] regis erit determinandum est, saluis rectitudinibus baron ipsorum." The rubric for section g reads *"De hiis qui ad iudicium aque vel ferri iudicati sunt a iusticia regis."* The *Episcopales Leges*, 4, 2 indicate control of ordeal by bishops and their power to license. *Cf.* also *Inst. Cnuti*, III, 59. The control over the ecclesiastical ritual for duel is apparently not comprehended in the grants respecting "ordeal." A royal charter for monopoly mentioning duel is needed, *cf.* Stephen's charter to York Minster confirming one of Henry I (3 Raine, *Historians of York* [R.S.], 36), but not embodied in Stephen's second charter, 1 Farrer, *Early Yorkshire Charters*, 121.

the crown claims jurisdiction.[284] All these rules tend to establish the continuity of royal control over duel. The not infrequent entry of fines *pro duello* in the *Pipe Roll 31 Henry I*[285] are to the same point even if it is too hazardous to take them as standing invariably for the licensing of duels not otherwise to be held in seignorial courts.[286] The proof of royal control, however, does not support the proposition of exclusive use in royal courts in an era when almost anything can be bought and enforced by writ or ordinance. Moreover the stipulation of battle in theft cases suggests the possibility of this procedure running with the frequent franchise over theft. In later times *infangtheof* franchise clearly does not comprehend battle; and the rule of *Leges Henrici* that summons, final judgment and execution in a vavassor's court must all take place in the presence of a king's officer leaves no loophole here for unauthorized trials by battle.[287]

That the Norman Kings cut into the whole problem of public order in England via the control of procedure[288] is further evidenced by their handling of process. Outlawry, as we know, is

---

[284] *Hn.* 59, 16a.

[285] *P.R. 31 Hy. I*, 11, 42, 48, 55, 89, 97, 103, 104, 112, 130, 132, 135, 155. The sums accounted for range from 105 m. to 5 m. These entries do not stand for *defectus duelli* for there are two specific entries on this, *ibid.*, 48, 119, for smaller sums, 2 m. and 1 m. respectively. At 42 is an entry of 40 s. "ut duellum remaneat inter J & R, fratrem suum." At *ibid.*, 19, is an entry of 2 oz. gold "ut posset dirrationare terram suam per corpus suum." At *ibid.*, 4, M. de V. owes 100 muid of wine for concord of a duel. The specificity in these cases strongly suggests that the *pro placito duelli* is for the license to fight either where the cause is not normally a duel cause or where the court is without power to hold duel. In either event the significant fact is that the crown gets a payment, indicating it possesses some extraordinary authority over the subject of duel.

[286] The evidence of a much later date on the seignorial right to duel in criminal cases is at best equivocal, e.g. *P.R. 16 Hy. II* 148, 10 m.: "pro duello concordato et iudicato in curia sua de latrocinio [vacce]" (*P.R. 17 Hy. II* 105). The mulct may be either for the unlicensed concord or holding duel. *Select Civil Pleas* no. 104 (1201) must be taken to mean all procedure in the abbots' court *except* that which is in the hundred.

[287] *Hn.* 26—26, 4.

[288] It should here be pointed out that apart from duel, *P.R. 31 Hy. I* shows persuasively that a general power over procedure was resident in

sharpened into an edged weapon for those too pavid to stand to right. When the Normans come into England the Saxon out-lawry procedure while it resembles *forisbannitio* is apparently a much less artful device.[289] Outlawry is claimed by the crown un-

the crown. For example, at p. 35 a fine for the right to purge by oath in-stead of ordeal; at p. 97 a fine for false testimony; at p. 136 for fine to "hear" if an appellor was *legalis*. This prerogative parallels that over pun-ishment as *ibid.*, p. 42, £20 for not being mutilated, and *ibid.*, p. 124.

[289] The best account of outlawry in the Anglo-Saxon period is Lieber-mann, *Die Friedlosigkeit bei den Angelsachsen*, in *Festschrift fur Brun-ner*, 17 *et seq.*, and *Glossar, friedlos*. Liebermann's interpretation is to some extent influenced by the theories of Brunner about outlawry, dis-cussed *supra*, Chapter I. He states, *Glossar, friedlos*, 10 c, "Jeder entflieh-ende schwere Verbrecher ward friedlos, doch ist in den Quellen weder dieser Satz allgemein hingestellt noch auch die Gruppe der mit Todestrafe oder Verstümmelung oder Verknechtung oder Vermögenseinziehung oder Auslösung durch Wergeld belegten oder busslos genannten Ver-brechen unter Friedlosigkeit eingeordnet, *wenn sie auch im Sinne heutiger Germanistische Rechtsgeschichte hierher gehört*" (italics ours). Since this latter view is here rejected it is essential to distinguish carefully words merely descriptive of flight, words imposing death sentence, words imply-ing loss of royal favor, and words where some sort of process or judicial sentence (i.e. exile) is indicated.

We have already pointed out that the early Anglo-Saxon law uses the expression *fliema = profugus*, i.e. person in flight. The word *utlah* with which it is later equated is a Scandinavian word not used in England earlier than 922. In the earliest Anglo-Saxon sources, the state of "peace-lessness" is only as to the person injured or his sib, that is to say, it is simply a state of hostility in fact; Liebermann, *Glossar, friedlos*, 2 b. This is the situation depicted in the piece known as "The Wife's Lament," Grein, *Bibliothek Angelsächsischer Poesie (Beowulf*, etc.) 302. The earli-est use of outlawry as judicial process is *Aelfred* 1, 7. Apart from excom-munication there is no indication of the formalities. For comparative pur-poses note here the Danish practice in the *Witherslag* which shows how rudimentary process could be. The outlaw is free to escape by woods or water and is given a head-start before hue commences, Lehmann, *Königs-frieden der Nordgermanen*, 140. Outlawry in Anglo-Saxon law is used only in cases of flight. *Cf. Af.* 1, 7; II *As.* 2, 1; 20, 8; 1 *Atr.* 1, 9 a; 1, 13 (re-peated II *Cnut* 30, 9; 31, 2). Even *E.Gu.* 6, 6, phrased in terms of out-lawry as penalty for killing collectors of church dues, is predicated on flight alone, for it sets up a provision for hue and cry. Liebermann conjec-tures (*Brunner Festschrift* 32) that outlawry is used generally upon flight after acts unemendable or punishable by death, although the dooms never explicitly say so. He likewise gives a full list (*ibid.*, 30–2) of cases where he believes outlawry is explicitly provided. Excluding the vague chronicle

der Cnut as a prerogative right and is indeed proclaimed by the king himself, although it can also be proclaimed both by the county and by the hundred.[290] In an earlier period outlawry as process and not as a mere description of flight was a district or local measure,[291] for legislation is necessary to make it operative

references, Domesday and other Anglo-Norman sources, the doom references show three distinct legal concepts which cannot be lumped together as manifestations of outlawry: 1) the process upon flight (the instances cited *supra*); 2) exile, i.e., not process, since flight is not involved but punishment (*Hu.* 3, 1 for failure to perform hue duties; II *Cnut* 39 for killing priests and perhaps II *Cnut* 41, 2 for failure to go on expiatory pilgrimage); 3) loss of the king's grace (II *Ew.* 5, 1; II *As.* 20, 7; 25, 2; II *Em.* 1, 3; 2; IV *Eg.* 1, 5). The punishment for *mord* is death (2 *As.* 6, *Blaseras* 3) or surrender to the sib (II *Cnut* 56). These last passages Liebermann obviously includes because of Brunner's "peacelessness" theory. The passage III *Atr.* 15 seemingly supports this theory by providing that in open robbery if the matter is proclaimed in three towns, the robber *paet he ne beo nanes fryðes weorðe*. This seems to us either directed at hue or, as Liebermann suggests (*Glossar, Tag*), bars the robber's right of purgation.

The passages threatening loss of king's friendship or being an enemy of the king are strikingly like the penalty of loss of grace used in Francia. So "friendship" is lost, II *Ew.* 5, 1, and harboring is put on a parallel with outlaw harboring. See also II *As.* 25, 2; IV *Eg.* 1, 5. A man who wrongfully seeks revenge is *fah wið ðom cyng,*II *As.* 20, 7; II *Em.* 1, 3; 2 (*gefah*). 1 Grein, *Angelsächsisches Wörterbuch*, 266, gives for *gefah* the meaning *proscriptus* or *inimicus*. It is worth noting that the Anglo-Norman translators who render *utlah* as *forisbannitio* or *exlex*, use in II *As.* 20, 7, *inimicus;* in VI *As.* 1, 5 *vita forisfactus sit—nisi rex ei velit misereri;* in II *As.* 25, 2 *perdat amicitiam*. On the other hand *Aelfred* 1, 7 *afliema* = *forsbannitus;* E.Gu. 6, 6 *utlah* = *utlaga vel exlex;* so too *Hu.* 3, 1 *exul vel exlex;* 1 *Atr.* I, 9 a, *utlah* = *utlagatus,* but in 1 *Atr.* 1, 13, = *forisbannitus;* II *Cnut* 39, *utlah* = *utlaga* in *Quadr.;* = *exul* in *Inst. Cn.* = *exlex* in *Cons. Cn.* II *Cn.,* 41, 2 *utlah* = *extra legem* in *Quadr.;* = *expellatur a terra et exul* in *Inst. Cn.;* = *exlex* in *Cons. Cn.* These renditions are of no retrospective value but they indicate clearly that the Normans saw a sharp distinction between outlawry and the basis of *misericordia*.

It is by no means clear that property sanctions were taken as a result of outlawry. In the "loss of grace" and exile cases the loss of land appears as a separate sanction, II *Ew.* 5, 1; II *As.* 25, 2; II *Ew.* 1, 3; *Hu.* 3, 1; IV *Eg.* 1, 5; II *Cnut* 39. There is no proof that the process of outlawry embraced a land sanction. II *Cnut, 13,* 1, is merely a statement of the king's right to *bocland* if a man does *utlages weorc* but this expression = misdeed.

[290] *Anglo-Saxon Chronicle* (pt. 2) 148. *Cf.* also for later *Leg. Edw. Conf.* 6, 1 for the outlawry by the king. For outlawry by the hundred, *Hu.* 3, 1. See also *Af.* 1, 7; II *As.* 2, 1, no forum indicated.
[291] Liebermann, *Die Friedlosigkeit bei den Angelsachsen*, 26.

throughout the land.[292] Its acquired character as a royal process is fixed in Cnut's day when the procedural prerogative is assured by the king's fine of £5[293] which harborers of outlaws must pay. Its connection with wrongs is indicated by the fact that *utlagaria*[294] is employed in William's *Lad* as a generalization for the worst offenses.

It is clear from Domesday Book that the Norman kings treated outlawry as a particular right of the crown[294a] but it does not appear that either the Conqueror or his sons attempted any innovations in the outlawry procedure beyond making automatic the property sanction.[295] As we have said, the Anglo-Saxon device resembled the Norman *forisbannitio* in many particulars and indeed the Anglo-Norman writers use *utlaga* and *forisban-*

[292] III *Atr.* 10, "And every outlaw shall be outlawed in every place who is outlaw in one."

[293] II *Cnut*, 13, provides that whoever does a misdeed (*utlages weorc*), the king shall determine about the peace. The *Quadripartitus* rendition is interesting: "Et qui opus utlagii fecerit eius revocatio sit in misericordia regis (pacis emendatio in solius regis consistat imperio)."

[294] Liebermann, *Die Friedlosigkeit bei den Angelsachsen*, 28–29. And note further his suggestion that in the procedural development of the tenth century none of the French canonical writings were of as much influence as the contact with Danish institutions. Liebermann seems to imply *ibid.*, 29 that the meaning of *utlagaria* in Cnut's day is substantially a prerogative over cases where outlawry will be used. This seems inconsistent with the enumeration of his *gerihta*, and in view of the recent legislation of Aethelred (III *Atr.* 10) it appears more justifiable to treat this simply as a claim to procedure and the forfeiture of *bocland*.

[294a] Certainly to be inferred from the power of inlawing: 1 *D.B.*, 262 b; 298 b; 336 b.

[295] Ballard, *Domesday Inquest*, 4, states that the Conqueror regarded all persons in arms against him as *ipso facto* outlawed and their lands forfeit. We have seen nothing which refers to a specific legal procedure to this effect, and it may be remarked that proof of such a procedure would go far to diminish the broader claims of the crown to title by conquest. There are some Domesday entries which relate to outlawry and although some are statements as of *T.R.E.*, the procedure may actually be of later date. Thus, 1 *D.B.*, 172 a, breach of the king's handgiven peace—*utlaghe iudicatur; semble*, 1 *D.B.*, 252. In form these two entries suggest outlawry as punishment not process, although Liebermann thinks the Normans did not use outlawry except for flight. 1 *D.B.*, 262 b, says that killing a man with a king's protection in his house results in forfeiture of lands and chattels and the offender is outlawed. 1 *D.B.* 298 b uses *exul* which shows Norman in-

*nitus* interchangeably.[296] Both in the *Leis Willelmi*[297] and the *Leges Henrici*,[298] outlawry is a device that is used upon flight. The man judicially summoned who sits contemptuously at home is distrained and mulcted, and even has judgment found against him.[299] But he does not seem to have been outlawed. It is only the offender who takes to his heels against whom this rigorous procedure is set in motion. It is this confinement of flight in causes criminal and of these the most serious, the crown cases, that makes significant the royal monopoly over outlawry.

In Henry I's day it is still the king's privilege to proclaim outlawry,[300] but the usual place is in the county court which eventu-

fluence, and, *ibid.*, 154 b, uses the same term, with a clear *misericordia* if the individual is captured.

The rule of automatic property sanction is implicit in *Hn.* 13, 1 which includes *utlagaria* in cases where a man is in king's mercy. There is one entry *P.R. 31 Hy. I*, 143, for *terris utlagorum*.

[296] *Supra,* note 151.

[297] *Leis Wl.* 52, 2.

[298] *Hn.* 41, 10; 53, 1 e.

[299] The *Articuli* of William, 8, 2 *et seq.* provides that when a man is summoned to the hundred and/or county and does not appear he shall be summoned a second time, and a single ox is taken. A third contempt is punished by a second distraint of an ox. On contempt of the fourth summons, the case is handled by the rendition of *ceapgield*, i.e. restitution to the complainant, and then the *forisfactura regis*. The rules as stated (*Hn.* 53 *et seq.*) provide for contempt of summons "a iusticia regis ad comitatum" and for this reason perhaps are sharper. A first contempt costs king's *overseunessa* of 20 marks in Wessex. If the cause is a plea certain (*nominata placita*) the defendant loses the cause plus the mulct. Refusal to carry out the judgment is followed by a capias and putting the prisoner under pledge. This, if unsuccessful, results in a distraint of all property and another capias unless pledges are found. The man who still held out could be killed. The final passage is taken from Aethelstan's law (II *As.* 20 *et seq.*) to which the contempt passages in *Hn.* bear a resemblance.

The *Leges Henrici* provide in the hundred courts a mulct of 30 d. for first and second contempt and full wite for the third contempt. The hundred has the right to distrain and the defendant is put under pledge until his day. He is reseised when he pleads. *Hn.* 29, 2; 2 a; 53, 5. The proceeding in the county (i.e. without king's justice) involves 20 marks in Wessex for contempt of a second summons. This is the limit of liability if the plea is not specified. But if it is a named plea, if the defendant has not a lawful essoin he will be adjudged for what he is impleaded.

[300] *Leg. Edw. Conf.* 6, 1.

ally becomes the only competent forum. Not only is the regional outlawry quickly eradicated under the Normans[301] but there is no hint that a franchise holder can use outlawry.[302] Indeed its connection with the very causes which the king claims would preclude this, and what the *Leges Henrici* have to say about process in feudal courts leads one to conclude that seignorial process did not go beyond the sequestration of the delinquent's property.[303]

### THE KING'S PEACE

The fiscal and procedural rights controlled by the crown in Henry I's time were in combination with existing administrative machinery sufficient to form a solid foundation for royal prerogative in matters criminal. It is impossible, however, to proffer such a matter-of-fact explanation of the beginnings of English criminal law without reckoning with the long-seated theory of the king's peace as the point of departure for the great expansion of crown law. We have scrutinized the possible heritage of the Normans. It remains to examine what the conquerors fell heir to in England.

In the Anglo-Saxon dooms the word peace (*frith*)[304] is used generally in an unartful sense of public order or general secu-

---

[301] There is some trace of this in the Anglo-Norman *Instituta Cnuti,* II, 15 a which provides for a *despectus* for harboring of outlaws, running to the person who does the outlawing; *cf. II Inst. Cn.* 66, and compare for Yorkshire 1 *D.B.* 298 b.

[302] *Hn.* 50, 1 provides that if a man is impleaded by his lord or superior of a named plea and does not appear at the day fixed, he is liable to the amends for all named pleas of which he is impleaded, unless he get a continuance. It is otherwise if he is merely summoned to be present on this or that day and has no notice of the nature of the plea, for in this case he pays the *overseunessa* of the place, if he has no legal essoin, and is then given a day where he can plead or amend. This passage which resembles the rules about summons in hundred and county has no Anglo-Saxon precursor and leads one to believe that all the summons rules in *Hn.* are living law.

[303] *Hn.* 43, 4.

[304] On this word *cf.* Liebermann, *Glossar, Frieden.* 1 Grein, *Angelsächsisches Wörterbuch,* 347 s.v. *friđ* where note especially passages from Biblical literature.

rity,[305] and once or twice in the sense of international peace.[306] On two occasions the specific problems of feud and thieves[307] are before the legislators when they resort to this term or its equivalent; and once the admonition to "earnest concern" about the peace is combined with money reform.[308] *Frith* is nowhere a technical term, and only a rosy imagination can read into passages where it appears a concept of folk peace,[309] let alone a notion that peace and law are synonymous. The passages do no more than express the objective of good government about which all persons in authority are supposed to be anxious.[310] Only once does the peace idea come into sharper form. Under Eadward I the crown assumed, as Liebermann believed,[311] a more direct stewardship over the peace, for there is direct reference to some sort of oath of fidelity which is henceforward to comprehend the duty of obeying the rules for public security,[312] and the failure to take the oath is threatened with loss of royal grace and confiscation. But this oath does not seem to have made more palpable the references to peace, to have lent to the word any legal substance. Even when the passages dealing with public

[305] E.g. II *Ew.* 1; V *As. Prologus;* IV *Eg.* 2; I *Atr. Prologus;* III *Atr. Prologus;* V *Atr.* 26, 1.

[306] *A. Gu. Prologus; E. Gu. Prologus;* II *Atr.* 1; *Cf.* 1 *Anglo-Saxon Chronicle,* 258, 261, 264 where *fri∂* and *gri∂* are used interchangeably.

[307] II *Em. Prol.* 1, 2, where feud is mentioned; VI *Atr.* 32 points at theft as the motive. *Cf.* also IV *Eg.* 2, 2; 12, 1.

[308] V *Atr.* 26, 1 where the *trinoda necessitas* is also mentioned; again VI *Atr.* 31 where peace and money alone are mentioned. II *Cn.* 8 repeats this admonition combined with VI *Atr.* 32 as to thieves.

[309] IV *Eg.* 12, 1 refers to his ordinance regarding sales and warranty as made "to gebeorge, 7 to fri∂e eallum leodscipe." *Fri∂* has here no technical significance. *Cf.* also on this point Liebermann, *Glossar, Frieden* 3, who states that originally "peace proceeds from the people." Note further that in some passages adduced by writers in support of a folk or king's peace are used the expressions, *gesibsumnesse* (II *Em. Prol.* 1) and *Sib* 7 *som* (VI *Atr.* 25, 1), both of which are essentially untechnical, not to say homiletic.

[310] V *As. Prologus.*

[311] Liebermann, *Glossar, Frieden* 4.

[312] II *Ew.* 5.

security are buttressed by those which refer to outlawry in terms of "unworthy of peace,"[313] it is difficult to attribute to them more than descriptive force, tinged with the homiletic color so clear in the parallel pieties of the coronation oath.[314] They cannot be said to create a legal order because there are no sanctions which did not exist before. Nor can such sanctions be supplied by a possible union of the idea of public order with suretyship (*borh*) and tithing. The scheme of *borh* which is systematized by Eadward's successor Aethelstan[315] is in no sense intended as a suretyship for keeping the peace. It is initially a sharpening of kinship responsibility, or a surrogate in the form of seignorial responsibility to secure the fulfilment of judgments. The only man who needs more than surety is the person of ill repute.[316] Furthermore this institution of *borh* was neither used throughout the kingdom nor was it under Aethelred and Cnut a permanent obligation.[317] The system was intended to aid in the enforcement of the law but it was not a system of police for the maintenance of the peace. On the other hand, the tithing which in Eadgar's time appears to have spread from London to the rest of Wessex[318] has

[313] III *Atr.* 15: the man who steals in daylight and is complained of in three localities is not *fryðes weorðe;* II *Cn.*, 15 a, speaks of the *friðleasan* man who is harbored.

[314] *Sacr. Cor.* 1, 1; Liebermann, *Gesetze* 216–7.

[315] Morris, *Frankpledge System*, 15 *et seq.;* Marquardsen, *Über Haft und Bürgschaft bei den Angelsachsen;* Liebermann, *Glossar, Zehnerschaft.* The doom of Eadward which refers to the oath of peace-observance looks to a *borh* outside the sib in cases of theft, but does not set up permanent suretyship, II *Ew.* 3; 3, 1. The noteworthy thing about Aethelstan's legislation is the extension and systematization of the ancient *borh* institution, a process reaching its culmination under Eadgar.

[316] So II *As.* 20, 5; III *Eg.* 7; 7, 1; 1 *Atr.* 1, 5; 4; II *Cn.* 33.

[317] Morris, *Frankpledge System*, 26, 27.

[318] The gild in London for which regulations are contained in VI *As.*, is organized for police purposes. *Cf.* Liebermann, *Erklärungen* 116 and further the discussion *Glossar, Genossenschaft, 9 et seq.* Morris, *Frankpledge*, 10, emphasizes the peculiar character of this and adopts Waitz's view that it is an association for insurance against cattle theft. Liebermann *Einleitung zum Statut der Londoner Friedensgilde unter Aethelstan* in 2 *Mélanges Fitting,* 77, §11, discussing the function of the gild states that

the functions of thief catching,[319] but it is not connected with the suretyship or the peace. In Cnut's reign men have to be both in tithing and *borh*, but the most determined efforts have not established sure proof of the conjectured merger of the two institutions in Anglo-Saxon times,[320] nor does proof exist that a "peace association" was intended by the Danish king.[321]

Although the crown's responsibility for public security appears in the dooms primarily as a political generalization there is on the other hand evidence of a more concrete king's "peace" in the form of heavy mulcts for acts done in the king's household, and for violations of protection emanating from him.[322] The idea of special sanctity attaching to the royal person has been discussed in connection with Frankish institutions[323] and it may here be added that the notion is more fully developed in the Anglo-Saxon dooms. Not only has the king the highest wergeld,[324] but when his property is stolen ninefold restitution is exacted.[325] A permanent protection surrounds his residence and wherever he may happen to be.[326] This *mund* or protection is also extensible under circumstances unconnected with the king's

the name is a composite found nowhere else and that *fri∂* is a technical word for political order and safety.

[319] Liebermann, *Glossar, Zehnerschaft* 7a. The functions also include a supervision over the provision of cattle and collection of alms.

[320] Discussed in Liebermann, *Über die Leges Edwardi*, 81 who says sometime before 1087 the union takes place. In his article on *Zehnerschaft* 11c he thinks the tithing and *borh* were merged under Cnut. This latter view was expressed obviously as a result of Morris' conjecture, *Frankpledge*, 27–8, which is inconsistent with his assertion that *borh* is not a permanent obligation under Cnut.

[321] In the sense of the *Friedensverband* so beloved of the peace advocates. The objectives of the *borh* and tithing are for one thing too narrow, and further the oath which must be taken, II *Cnut*, 21, is simply not to be a thief or an abettor of thieves.

[322] Discussed by Liebermann in *Glossar, Königsfrieden*.

[323] *Supra*, Chapter I.

[324] Liebermann, *Glossar, Wergeld* 11.

[325] In *Aethelberht*, 4 (601–4) but apparently no trace between then and *Gri∂*, 7 (1028–70) which may have used the early Kent law. *Cf. Inst. Cnuti*, III, 56, 1 from *Gri∂*.

[326] *Aethelberht*, 3; 5.

presence, as in the compromise procedure for wergeld settle-ment,[327] to persons who have found asylum[328] and perhaps also during ordinary session of the courts.[329] These manifestations of the king's peace bear some relation to the institution known as *grith,* the handgiven peace, i.e., the protection which orally, by hand or by writ and seal the crown uses to take in its guard par-ticular persons.[330] The *grith* is alien; whether Frankish or Scan-dinavian is immaterial.[331] It comes into use in the Danelaw[332] at a time when Saxon kings needed extra insurance for messengers, officials or prelates who ventured among the newly settled in-vaders. This protection is marked by punishments of life and confiscation and by mulcts of extraordinary severity[333] in con-trast with the ancient £5 wite for *mundbryce.* The difference in

[327] *Wer.,* 4.

[328] *Grið,* 4. In §2 this collection speaks of the *handgrið* of the king (from I *Cn.* 2, 2) for the church so that the peace of the asylum may be regarded as a handgiven peace, but in §6 where the Kent law is described breach is called *mundbryce.*

[329] II *As.* 20, 3 and compare III *Atr.* 1, 1 regarding the *grið* which the ealdorman or king's reeve proclaims in certain courts. The protection of persons summoned by the crown is in the earliest Kent law, *Aethelberht,* 2, *cf.* also II *Cn.* 82.

[330] Generally, Liebermann in *Glossar, Handfrieden.*

[331] Liebermann, *loc. cit.,* following 2 Steenstrup, *Normannerne,* 362 (where the proof of Scandinavian origin seems tenuous) suggests that the *grið,* viz. handgiven peace, comes in with the Northmen. The institution of protection by writ is also certainly Frankish and may originate in Merovingian times, *cf.* 2 Brunner *D.R.G.* 66 *et seq.* and 67 n. 24 for Frank-ish *formulae.*

[332] Liebermann, *Glossar, Handfrieden* 2.

[333] In connection with the church, penalties of life and property, I *Cnut,* 2, 2. *Grið* mentions life as the penalty for breach of king's *grið* in the law of the south English, and contemplates (§6) a mulct for Kent. *Quaere* whether Liebermann correctly reads a death penalty in *Grið* 2. The later sources (*Hn.* 13, 1; 79, 2) give *misericordia* as punishment; *Leges Edw. Conf.* 12, 3, gives for the Danelaw £144 and life, but *lege Anglorum* only wergeld, although in chapter 33 this book gives £84 as the sum for "Saxonia" and East Anglia. *Leis Wil.* 2, 2 gives £144 for those who break "la pais le roi." *Cf.* further 1 *D.B.* 154 b; 172 a; 252. In Yorkshire it is £96, 1 *D.B.* 298 b. Liebermann thinks that a *mundbryce* heavier than the old £5 mulct may have developed in connection with *griðbryce* and this may explain the discrepancies in figures.

the degree of punishment can hardly account for a distinction between *mund* and handgiven protection in terms of different origins. The *mund* is general in scope like the ban which protected orphans, widows, etc., in Francia. The protection (*grith*) is specific for it goes to an individual and having been pronounced with the royal voice or carrying the royal seal it is decidedly an emanation of the royal person. This is why breach is treated as if the crown itself were subjected to bodily injury.

The consistent use of the terms *frith* and *grith* is no justification for treating all the situations where these terms are employed in the Anglo-Saxon law as related or even as several manifestations of the same basic idea. The most that can be conceded in this direction is that the forms of king's protection are related. *Frith,* as public order, is a political rather than a legal concept and thus lies in an entirely different stratum from the protection which is procedurally guaranteed. There is nothing to show that even in the Confessor's day the lines of separation blur and a general merger of ideas ensues. Least of all can proof be adduced for the notion that every man has a peace and that the king has a peace which devours all others.[334] Such a thing for all its folktale charm would have baffled the Conqueror, to say noth-

[334] The peace theory is so phrased in Maitland, *Constitutional History* (1920 ed.), 108; re-phrased in 2 Pollock and Maitland *H.E.L.,* 453. After pointing out that church, sheriff, lord with *soc,* and householders each "has his peace" (with no attempt to distinguish or qualify, citing VIII *Atr.* 5, I *Cnut,* 3, as to the church; *Ine* 6, *Alfr.* 39, *Hn.* 81, 3, 4, all on housepeace, as to the rest) the *H.E.L.* says: "The time has not yet come when the king's peace will be eternal and cover the whole land. Still we have here an elastic notion:—if the king can bestow his peace on a privileged person by his writ of protection can he not put all men under his peace by proclamation?" Holdsworth, 2 *H.E.L.* 48 remarks, "In this period the king's peace has many competitors. Its extent can be accurately measured. It is only on certain occasions at certain times or if specially conferred that a wrong will be a breach of the king's peace. Until a much later period it will die with the king" (here citing the *Anglo-Saxon Chron. ad ann.* 1135 where the statement regarding Henry's death is followed by a remark that soon there was trouble and people began to rob!). At the basis of all this is Pollock, *The King's Peace* (*Oxford Lectures,* 65) a lecture deliv-

ing of bewildering the Domesday commissioners in their dry and matter-of-fact inventory of estate bookkeeping. The Normans could understand general protection and special protection, not only because they used similar devices[335] but because these were both matters that could be translated in terms of judicial practice and could be measured in *forisfactura* and *misericordia*. But to men who had lived with a *treuga Dei* spelled out as no fighting on certain days, as covenants against feud, as ordeal for breach, as excommunication and forfeiture for offenders, a "peace" to be of institutional utility could not be devoid of procedural implications, must be assessable, must have conveyable substance. The *frith* of the doom prologues had none of these characteristics, any more than the "peace" of the nineteenth-century romantics.

The evidence of Domesday shows that after the Conquest the distinction between the general protection and the special protection was preserved.[336] The former is in the cure of the sheriff, because the king uses him as an intermediary to proclaim it or to pass it on and it is sanctioned by mulct.[337] But the special protection which comes directly from the King is guarded by *miseri-*

ered in 1884. Due to Pollock's faulty reading of the texts, the peace of the dwelling is carried over by him to the individual. "Every man was entitled to peace in his own house. The brawler or trespasser in another's homestead broke the owner's peace and owed him special amends" (*ibid.*, 70); the summary (*ibid.*, 73) "Thus far then every man has his own peace of which the breach is a special offense," indicates clearly enough that Pollock does not see the fine but absolutely basic distinction that the peace is associated first and last with the house, so conclusively shown by the early doom *Hlothaere & Eadric,* 11 (685–6). Pollock's essay probably accounts for the spread of the idea that every man had "a peace." The *overseunessa* mulct has been treated as inflicted for breach of the peace whereas it is perfectly obvious that the dooms treat this fine as levied essentially for contempt of a superior's protection.

[335] The special protection discussed *supra* chap. V. On the general protection, note again the Inquest of 1091 (Haskins, *Norman Institutions,* App. D) c. 1 persons going to court; c. 2, 3 persons going to the army; c. 11 merchants; c. 12 pilgrims.

[336] *Supra,* note 219; to be further discussed in volume 2.

[337] 1 *D.B.* 172 a; 252 a; 298 a. III *Inst. Cn.* 50.

*cordia* and threatened with outlawry.[338] There are a respectable number of these handgiven protections still extant.[339] They constitute no particular problem because their scope and the machinery of enforcement are well defined.[340] The spread of general protection is, however, less clearly marked. The Conqueror

[338] 1 *D.B.* 154 b; 172 a; 252 a; 262 b; 298 a; *Hn.* 13, 1. It is separately accounted for, *Hn.* 10, 1, and *supra,* note 198, instances from *P.R. 31 Hy. I* are given. *Leg. Edw. Conf.,* 27, says the cause is tried in the shire where the breach occurs. On the sheriff's third penny, *ibid.,* 27, 2; 1 *D.B.* 336 b.

[339] For example Davis, *Regesta,* nos. 9, 14, 25, 36, 104, 189, 240, 253 (from the size of the forfeit), 298, 311, 377, 396. Nos. 329–332 taken together form an exceptional and explicit protection. And compare Lanfranc's letter, 1 *Opera* (Giles Ed.) no. 46. In 1 *Chart. Chester Abbey,* 21, is a suspicious document of 1093 regarding protection of thieves at a fair. For Henry I's reign the following examples of protections: 1 *Cart. St. Frideswide* 12 (1122); *ibid.,* 15 (1131); 1 *Cart. Mon. Ramsei.,* 240 (1110); 2 *ibid.,* 101 (1110); 1 *Regist. Malmesbury,* 332, 333, 335; *Hist. Mon. Augustine Canterbury* (R.S.), 358, 365; 1 Farrer, *Early Yorkshire Charters,* no. 44 (1121–2), no. 167 (1119–33), 168 (1120–33), 169 (1123–33), 205, 477 (1115–28). Compare also 1 *Chart. Chester Abbey* 47 (1121–9) and 69 (1139–53); 2 *Chron. Mon. Abingdon.,* 78, 80, 89.

[340] Round, in 29 *E.H.R.* 349, discussing the writ of Rufus (Davis, *Regesta,* no. 396): ". . . et si aliquis eos desaisierit aut aliquam iniuriam eis amodo fecerit, volo sciatis quod pacem meam super eos infregerit . . ." remarks that "The principle that disseisin was a breach of the king's peace and rendered the culprit liable to an amercement is well brought out in the . . . extract." The writ, of course, sets up no such "principle." The crown is not talking about a general "peace" but it has ordered a reseisin and in extending protection is warning against a contempt of the order or is simply indicating that a breach will be treated thereafter as a breach of protection. In the earlier correspondence between William of Durham and the crown there seems to us no hint that the disseisins by the crown were regarded as a breach of peace. On the contrary, the bishop puts his case squarely on established procedural rules by asserting that he has never been appealed of any offense, and insisting that the crown's course is to appeal him and he will give security of appearance, otherwise the disseisin is unjust. (Symeon of Durham, 1 *Historia Eccl. Dur.* [R.S.] 171–2.) The rule the bishop has in mind is in *Hn.* 61, 21 "et nemo placebit dissaisiatus." But note in *Hn.* 53, 5 this does not apply if a disseisin is in issue. The rule against pleading when disseised is old. It is thoroughly discussed at the Council of Rheims (991), 19 Mansi, *Concilia,* 122–3: "Nec seculi quoque leges haec secularibus fieri permittunt: sed prius ejectos vel oppressos aut expoliatos, cum suis omnibus restitui iubent: & postea suo tempore (sicut lex eorum continet) ad placita venire praecipiunt."

puts his followers *"in pace mea,"*[341] a peace which is real because it is linked by the device of murder fine to a system for making men careful about violating this peace.[342] He takes the bishops and gives them a conditional protection both against his own officers and laymen generally.[343] He claps on to the charters of the ecclesiastical houses, words of protection identical with those used by him in Normandy.[344] The king's rights over the highway are sharpened[345] and some time before the middle of Henry I's reign the poor and abject are added to the alien and ordained persons as objects of the crown's *mund*.[346] These cases are posted with "my forfeiture."

No one of these measures is an expression of a single theory; each has its own rationale: the *murdrum* is a quasi-military defensive; the protection of bishops and monasteries is connected with ecclesiastical prerogative. Royal rights on the highways are emphasized for reasons of trade and moving troops. The poor and abject are protected for reasons of Christian charity. Compared with the gestures at coronation by the Conqueror,[347] and

---

[341] *Wl. Art.* 3, and note especially Liebermann's comment, *Erklärungen*, 280 to the effect that a written ordinance was before the compiler and that the matter was so cast as to make it appear to the Saxons as a species of their king's peace, i.e. *mund*.

[342] *Wl. Art.* 3, 1–4; *Leis Wil.* 22. *Cf.* further Liebermann, *Glossar, Murdrum*. The most thorough discussion is by Yntema, *Lex Murdrorum*, 36 *H.L.R.* 146.

[343] *Episcopales Leges* 4.

[344] *Supra*, note 339; add Davis, *Regesta*, nos. 58, 186, 395, 429, 465—the last three of William II.

[345] Liebermann in *Glossar, Strasse*, 8, thinks with reference to IV *Atr.* 4 (only the *Quadripartitus* text extant) that at the end of the tenth century the kings may have had a highway prerogative. Most of the evidence, beginning with the Pennenden Heath case, is post-conquest. *Cf.* 1 *D.B.* 1; 2; 280; 298 b. Compare Ballard, *An Eleventh Century Inquisition* at fo. 22, and fo. 27 at end. *Hn.* 10, 2; 12, 2; 35, 2; 80, 5 a. *Cf. Leis Wil.* 26 and *Leg. Edw. Conf.* 12; 12, 8.

[346] *Hn.* 10, 3. The protection of clerks and aliens goes back to *E.Gu.* 12 (921–38); in somewhat different form VIII *Atr.* 33; II *Cnut*, 40. See also *Leg. Edw. Conf.* 15, 7 on aliens.

[347] So 1 Florence of Worcester, *Chronicon* (Thorpe Ed. 1848), 229.

by his son Henry's promises in support of general peace,[348] that
can be taken as no more than an earnest of their good intentions,
these objectives had legal immediacy and fiscal measurability.[349]
The protections were one of many devices for attaining general
public security but they cannot be taken to be the first extensions
of an elastic theory of manifold peace.[350] On the contrary, the
king's *mund* is something which cannot be lightly asserted.[351] In
Henry's time if allegations of breach are made they have to be

[348] *Hn. Cor.* 12 "Pacem firmam in toto regno meo pono et teneri amodo
praecipio." Note further *Hn. Com.* 4 the rule that for no "pacem meam
vel quietudinem" are men to be relieved of suit of court. Morris, *Frankpledge*, 114 has misinterpreted this passage. The two passages cited show
sharply the contrast between the merely political peace and the legal peace-
protection. It should here be observed that Liebermann, *Glossar, Frieden,*
8 d; suggests that *Hn. Cor.* 14 (where a person who had taken values in
the interregnum is threatened), indicates a notion of the king's peace
(*Landesfrieden*) expiring with the demise of the king. But Henry says
"si quis aliquid de meo vel de rebus alicuius post obitum regis Willelmi
. . ." etc. with no reference to peace.

[349] Even the abject were sometimes worth money: *P.R. 31 Hy. I,* 149.

[350] The case of William of Durham shows clearly that whatever stock
the small man may have taken in a general king's peace, the only assurance of value was a protection. The Bishop of Durham first seeks a protection from the sheriff of Yorkshire. This is refused and he then requests one
from the crown. Since the Bishop was himself no small baron, but a person of great power, his insistence upon a special protection, even shrieval,
seems to us to indicate the protections were the only "peace" of any account at the end of the eleventh century. 1 Simeon of Durham, *Hist. Eccl.
Dun.,* 172 *et seq.* In his letter William of Durham states: "Vobis vero vice
illa non placuit mea mihi reddere, sicut ego requirebam et justum mihi
videbatur, sed per breve vestrum pacem mihi dedistis ad vos secure veni-
endi, et vobiscum morandi, et a vobis redeundi, et in eodem brevi fidelibus
vestris per totam Angliam praecepistis, ut omnia mea in pace essent donec
sciretis si vobiscum remanerem. Quod breve cum misissem Radulpho
Paganello, non solum mihi pacem negavit, sed et de parte vestra me diffi-
davit, et in crastinum terras ecclesiae nostrae rapina invasit, praedicta dis-
tribuit, hominum vero quosdam vendidit, quosdam redimi permisit;
monachum autem portantem breve pacis vestrae homines Paganelli in captione miserunt, et equum suum ei occiderunt. Super haec omnia dictum
est mihi vos dedisse partem terrarum mearum; et cum ad vos pro his omnibus mittere vellem, defendit Paganellus legatis meis transitum per terram
vestram."

[351] *Hn.* 22; 24, 2; 59, 27.

proved—and not to the other party but to the judge.³⁵² In other words, the sphere of protection at large is governed by conservative considerations.

Neither in the *Leges Henrici* nor the *Leges Edwardi* is it possible to track down a king's peace except as related to the two sorts of protection discussed. The *Leges Edwardi* describe the king's peace as manifold,³⁵³ but this turns out to be the peace by hand or seal, the eight days after coronation, after Christmas, Easter and Pentecost, the protection of the four great roads and the great rivers. The earlier *Leges Henrici,* coming from the hand of a lawyer, are more terse. The old *mundbryce* is no longer included in the matters in king's *soc* although elsewhere we are told *grithbryce* involves a fine of 100 shillings. The hand-given peace, however, if broken, puts a man in the king's mercy. Otherwise the *mund* of the king is in this book simply a factor in aggravation of an offense:³⁵⁴ thus, if homicide is done in churches, royal residence, army or household, cities and such places where a perpetual peace reigns, or on feast days, if the king is at war or if he happens to be in a particular county,³⁵⁵ if the persons killed are king's sergeants, or a lord's officers who have protection by writ or otherwise.³⁵⁶ The procedural or fiscal implications of these incidents are all attested in the *Leges Henrici*³⁵⁷ and because of these incidents they possess legal

³⁵² *Hn.* 59, 28.
³⁵³ *Leg. Edw. Conf.* 12 *et seq.;* 27.
³⁵⁴ *Hn.* 68, 2.
³⁵⁵ An extension of the idea of the verge.
³⁵⁶ This treatment in *Leges Henrici* of the *mund* idea, i.e., the general protection, shows conclusively to what its procedural implications had reduced—mere aggravation. If it had possessed in Henry's reign any potentialities for expansion, the jurists obviously did not use it beyond the purpose stated.
³⁵⁷ *Hn.* 13, 1 *misericordia* for breach of handgiven peace, for injury to royal servants; *Hn.* 13, 7, life for fighting in the king's residence, *cf.* also *Hn.* 80; 80, 7 a; *Hn.* 13, 8, life or wer for breaking peace in the army; *Hn.* 11, 1 a, homicide in churches; *Hn.* 62, the feast days are a judicial holiday. On the antiquity of this, Liebermann, *Glossar, Gerichtsferien.* The rule

reality, in contrast with the merely literary or political use of the word peace when the compiler remarks that the demesne revenue of the crown is for reasons of peace,[358] or that for reasons of peace the big crimes are more severely punished,[359] just as *Leges Edwardi* describe the frankpledge as *pax maxima*.[360]

So far as an extant system of law and procedure can be constructed out of these two books with the aid of charters, writs and pipe roll, a jurisdictional balance can be discerned that leaves small room for an antic theory of king's peace. Even if the realism of the law books be suspect, as theory alone they are a standing challenge to undocumented intrusion. Specifically what they lay down about franchise, in the hands of feudatories, together with the rules of law devised for the safeguard of both private and public interest,[361] to some extent verified by writs, establish just that balance of which we have spoken. Until 1135 the crown was here neither reckless nor ruthless. What was granted was to be used, and far from showing the contracting effects of a king's peace the charters exhibit a constant accretion of liberties which tended to strengthen rather than diminish the

in 1 *D.B.* 1 a, regarding the feast day *treuva regis* in Dover, takes its origin from this. *Cf.* also Chester, 1 *D.B.* 262 b, on the week-end peace.

[358] *Hn.* 10, 1.

[359] *Hn.* 11, 16a.

[360] *Leg. Edw. Conf.* 20 "Alia est maxima pax per quam omnes firmiori statu sustentatur" etc.

[361] The following examples will suffice to illustrate: For the crown: *Hn.* 24, 1, general supervision; 24, 3, *soc* gives no license to do wrong; 24, 4, the watching brief of the king's bailiff; 26, 4, the supervision of execution; 22, the rules regarding removal for exceeding jurisdiction and *cf.* 80, 9b; *Episc. Leg.* 4, control of ordeal and *cf.* also *Leg. Edw. Conf.* 9, 3; *Hn.* 43, the king's priority. For the seigneurial jurisdiction: *Hn.* 27, the rights of cases of wite and wer and personal jurisdiction; 25, rules of venue; 55, the feudal jurisdiction; 24, 4, the privilege of proceeding once jurisdiction is taken; 59, 11, priorities; *Leg. Edw. Conf.* 9, 3, right to profits where ordeal is taken out of lord's court. It may here be remarked that the system of checks and balances can be proved by dozens of other passages. Some such adjustment was inevitable in view of the conflicts of law: 1) king's law; 2) the tripartite regional law; 3) the more local custom. Or again king's law *vs. lex terrae;* or *lex terrae vs. lex patriae.*

substantive rights conveyed. It is true that as to the public rights controlled or conducted by the sheriffs the position of the sovereign was on a less stable footing. The theory of *Leges Henrici* is that the matter is one of contract, and the bargaining position of the crown is indicated by the list of demesne revenues. This theory and the recognized practice of separate accounting permit the inference that if the crown wished to withdraw matter from the ferm at the expiration of the bargain it could do so. That it did not always wait is shown by the statute of moneyers.[362] Certainly when land plus jurisdiction was withdrawn during the term the sheriff was compensated.[363] Outside the contract the sheriffs, being public officers, are subject to royal order as the variety of writs in Henry I's reign shows.[364] The use of a

[362] Liebermann, *Gesetze*, 523; *cf.* also 2 Florence of Worcester, *Chronicon*, 57. The writ is dated December 25th, and if the principal audit of the year was already at Michaelmas as it was 1113 (Morris, *Med. Eng. Sheriff*, 95) the statute must have cut into extant forms since it asserts a new prerogative and *Leges Henrici* 10, 1 list the pleas of false money as a matter separately accounted for.

[363] *Supra*, note 217. In connection with the adjustment made in the sheriff's favor compare the king's writ in 1 *Early Yorkshire Charters*, no. 428 (1100–15) ordering the saving of chapels and tithes to certain churches despite "socas quas inde dedi quibusdam baronibus meis."

[364] Writs on reseisin already under William Rufus, Davis, *Regesta*, no. 351, 396, 413. Writs of Henry I in *Cart. Gloucester*, 264; 2 *Chron. Mon. Abingdon.*, 73; Galbraith, *Royal Charters to Winchester*, 35 *E.H.R.* 382 no. 33; Stenton, *Facsimiles of Early Charters*, no. 3 a, and compare the writ of Stephen of Mortain in Stenton, *English Feudalism*, App. no. 13, and no. 20 of William of Warenne. Other types under Henry I of writs in the nature of a *praecipe*: 1 *Cart. Ramsei.*, 247; *Chron. Ramsei.*, 280; Galbraith, *op. cit.* no. 23; writs quitting of geld 1 *Early Yorkshire Charters* no. 91, 2 *Chron. Mon. Abingdon.*, 70; a writ relieving of castlework and *expeditio*, 1 *Early Yorkshire Charters*, no. 130; a writ regarding forest rights, *ibid.*, no. 352; tithes in New Forest, 1 *Reg. St. Osmund* 206; precursors of the writ of right 2 *Chron. Mon. Abingdon.*, 77, 85, 86, 92; a writ ordering a hundred session to do right, Galbraith, *op. cit.*, no. 27; a precursor of *de nativo habendo*, 2 *Chron. Mon. Abingdon.*, 81; a writ to divert a road, Foster, *Registrum Ant. Linc*, no. 46. In addition to the fines already noted from *P.R. 31 Hy. I* are the following entries which point to writs: 66, *ne placitet contra F de F. nisi secundum cartas ecclesiae sue*; 114, *ut habeant consuetudines suas sicut rex precipit per breve sua*; 134, *ut homines sui de P. faciant*

king's peace theory presumes, however, an opportunity for prescription in the shrieval office, i.e., the chance to increase jurisdiction which the king later must recapture. For this the *Leges*
theory leaves no loophole. Extortions could acquire prescriptive
force, but only as to the king's subjects.[365] When the crown lays
claim to the *causa capitalis,* and the procedures connected therewith, when it sets up *custodes* and royal justices who can take
cognizance of these matters,[366] it seems farfetched to assert that
it resorted to so unartful a dodge as a fictive peace.

If the galaxy of procedures at the crown's command without
a theory of king's peace were adequate to promote a steady
growth of criminal jurisdiction, there was hardly any necessity
to resort to the truce of God, particularly as feud was non-
existent. None of the obstacles, particularly the prescriptions
which eventually induced the dukes in Normandy to harness
their processes to the enforcement of the truce, impeded their
policies in England. Under the Anglo-Saxon kings, there had
existed a remarkable merger of ecclesiastical and secular powers
and functions in many ways reminiscent of the Frankish régime
under Charlemagne.[367] Especially in the reign of Aethelred and
then of Cnut, was royal protection of the church developed in

*ei consuetudines suas sicut fecerunt patri suo.* The development of the writ
lies outside our problem. The subject has not even been scratched.

[365] 2 *Chron. Mon. Abingdon.,* 230. The abbot pays 100 s. annually to the
sheriff of Berkshire, "ut abbatiae homines lenius tractaret, et eos in placitis et hundredis, si quid necesse haberent, adjuvaret. Quod postquam pro-
cessu temporis in consuetudinem versum est. . . ."

[366] The best account in Morris, *Medieval English Sheriff,* 100 *et seq.;*
compare also Adams, *Council and Courts,* 148 *et seq.* The relation we
have here in mind is well brought out by a writ in 2 *Chron. Mon. Abingdon.,* 85. Keeping in mind first the exchequer distinction between demesne
revenue and ferm, second the free use of writs for the crown's interest, the
significance of an order to a baron with a "nisi . . . feceris praecipio quod
*W.G.* faciat et si ipse non fecerit Hugo de B. [the sheriff] faciat" is apparent, viz., the crown has two strings to its bow. Compare also *ibid.,* 77 to
W. de M., and the writ in 1 *Cart. Ramsei.,* 247–8 directed to the king's
chamberlain with the sheriff as final resort.

[367] The best discussion is in Boehmer, *Kirche und Staat,* 42 *et seq.; cf.*
also 1 Stubbs, *Const. Hist.* (5 ed.) c. 8 esp. §88.

legislation to a degree that made superfluous the use of sworn truces for the safeguard of ecclesiastical properties.[368] This legislation was essentially a projection or strengthening of the idea of a special church peace such as appears in the earlier continental folklaws.[369] It emphasized the sanctity of holy ground, of the immunity of immediate property.[370] It fostered as a result, the asylum,[371] the feast day,[372] and it guarded the persons of the ministers of God.[373] Procedurally this policy was made effective by special mulcts and special punishments which not only the crown but the prelates required for breach,[374] just as in France a ban penalty and the huge immunity mulct had been the accustomed sanctions. The executions of these penalties presupposed strong kings. Yet independent of this, one can attribute to the laws some administrative reality, because they were articulated to the existing scheme of bots and wites. The wergeld system provided willing complainants, and it is this fact, plus the wide distribution of the profits of a suit, that insured some regard for enforcement. The special mulct for infraction of church

---

[368] V *Atr.* 10, 1; VI *Atr.* 13; 14; 42, 3; VIII *Atr.* 1–5, 2; I *Cnut*, 2–4, partly repeating from Aethelred and to some extent new. The rules are old but in the earlier dooms not as fully developed. On the whole matter, Liebermann, *Glossar, Kirchenfrieden*. On Cnut's policy, Larsen, *Canute the Great*, 162 *et seq*. It will be recalled that when Cnut made his pilgrimage to Rome, 1027, the *treuga Dei* movement was in full swing on the continent. Cnut in his proclamation of 1020 had already remarked on the pope's injunction regarding the peace (§3) that may have been directed only to the church peace. The passages in Cnut's dooms (*post* 1027) are so complete that one can with justice regard them as an attempt to realize by command the same objective which on the continent was being sought by voluntary covenant.

[369] *Supra*, Chapter I.

[370] The following passages in the later dooms are particularly germane: *Griđ* 2, 19, 25; *Northu.* 19; VI *Atr.* 14; VIII *Atr.* 4–5; I *Cnut* 2, 2; 3–3, 1. Cf. also *Af.* 5; *Ine* 5; *E.Gu.* 1 and *Norđhymbra Cynicgriđ*.

[371] II *Em.* 2 in connection with 1, 3; VIII *Atr.* 1; 5, 1; I *Cnut* 3, 2.

[372] *E.Gu.* 7–7, 2; V *Atr.* 19–20; VIII *Atr.* 16, I *Cn.* 14, 1, 2. On the rules of stay of procedure, II *Cn.* 38, 45.

[373] VI *Atr.* 45; feebler in I *Cn.* 4; *Griđ* 19, 24; and *in extenso* in *Hadbot*, 1 *et seq.* (1030–50).

[374] *Griđ* 5; 6; 7; 9.

peace was simply a tax[375] in addition to lord's share, defendant's share, family's share and king's share. In France the narrowing of fiscal interest had made the older forms of church protection meaningless, and had forced a complete reconstruction of sanction. This situation did not exist in England.

Apart from the special protection used for ecclesiastical establishments the measures taken by the Norman kings to safeguard the church in general start from the Conqueror's decree separating law and spiritual jurisdiction, and the extension of direct royal protection over the bishops.[376] This change was accompanied by the order that secular process could be resorted to in aid of the ecclesiastical.[377] The result on the problem of church peace appears to have been that Cnut's assertion of prerogative is retained but is assured by a different procedure. We say this because the *Leges Henrici*[378] describe the king's authority over matters spiritual in the language of Cnut's dooms until they reach the question of process when they remark that secular distraint is used to compel observance of the church's law. The question of original jurisdiction, however, is answered in the *Leges Edwardi*[379] which relate that when the peace of the church is broken, justice is the bishop's. If recourse has to be had to royal process the king will put the man by gage and pledge and thereafter the bishop is first satisfied and then the king. Outlawry is the final process. This corresponds, as we have seen, with the process that is coupled with truce enforcement at the

[375] This is very clear from the eleventh-century *Hadbot*. For example for the homicide of a cleric (§2) "to the legal wergeld" (*rihtwere*) is added the bot of £1 for "clergy bot." So phrased also in the other sections.
[376] *Episc. Leges*, 4.
[377] *Ibid.*, 3.
[378] *Hn.*, 11–11, 15 substantially all on the basis of I *Cnut* and II *Cnut*. Two passages from *E. Gu.* are used. In *Hn.* 16, Liebermann detects the use of *E. Gu. Prologus,* 2, but the presence of the continental *districtio* indicates that the process of the crown as stipulated by William is what the compiler has in mind. *Cf.* also *supra,* Chapter V.
[379] *Leg. Edw. Conf.*, 2, 9; 6. Compare Stephen's Charter.

Norman Council of Lillebon.[380] But it is very doubtful whether the "peace of the holy church" in England has implications beyond immunity and asylum. The *Leges Edwardi* reproducing a continental codex[381] state that all clerics and scholars and their possessions have the peace of God and the holy church. It adds a number of holiday periods throughout the realm and the sabbath week end, at which time persons going to and coming from church are to be unmolested.[382] There is no convincing collateral evidence that this peace of God was English.[383] Indeed, the feast days are clearly sanctified because of royal protection. When we read in *Leges Henrici* that a *pax Dei*[384] protects the places where men gather to drink, we realize that this notion is something outside the scope of legal procedure.

Applying the Norman's own infallible test, translation in terms of procedure, the king's peace, which is supposed to have been Henry I's great contribution to criminal law administration, shrinks to what it had ever been in England, a scheme of special protection. The lost peace bemoaned by men in the dark days after the Beauclerc's death was none other than the sense of security which proceeded from the enforcement of the king's

[380] *Supra*, Chapter V.

[381] Liebermann, *Über die Leges Edwardi,* 59; *Leg. Edw. Conf.,* 1, 1–2, 8 a.

[382] The text can be read so that the periods of peace are intended to cover the churchgoers (*Leg. Edw. Conf.,* 2, 7–8). Liebermann, *Über die Leges Edwardi,* 61 treats this as a "peace" additional to the periods named —comprehending over half a year. Since the compiler does not otherwise state the implications of his *pax Dei,* which is stipulated in the Norman truces and in the Flemish, it seems reasonable to suppose he intends to protect specifically churchgoers.

[383] Note further in this connection the statement in *Brevis Relatio* (Giles, Ed.) 10, regarding the transfer of the truce of God to England by William, a statement not otherwise evidenced. The remarks in *Dialogus de Scaccario,* I, xvi A, regarding the introduction of Norman law for the peace, can hardly be a reference to a *treuga Dei,* but refers rather to matters like proof and punishment imported from Normandy.

[384] *Hn.,* 81, 1. The *pax domini* of the householder is a housepeace which gives him rights of jurisdiction and mulct.

law. This the Norman dynasty had promoted in England in much the same spirit and with the same sense of procedural resourcefulness which characterized their administration in Normandy. But in England they succeeded to a degree which transcended their accomplishment across the channel leaving a foundation which even the anarchy of protracted civil war could not destroy and on which the achievements of the Angevins were to rest.

# INDEX